Corel *PHOTO-PAINT*™
Unleashed

Corel

Core

Corel *PHOTO-PAINT*™
Unleashed

David Huss

SAMS
PUBLISHING

201 West 103rd Street
Indianapolis, Indiana 46290

This book is dedicated to God.

PUBLISHER

Richard K. Swadley

ACQUISITIONS MANAGER

Greg Wiegand

MANAGING EDITOR

Cindy Morrow

ACQUISITIONS EDITOR

Christopher Denny

DEVELOPMENT EDITOR

Dean Miller

SOFTWARE DEVELOPMENT SPECIALIST

Wayne Blankenbeckler

PRODUCTION EDITORS

Matthew Usher

EDITOR

Joe Williams

EDITORIAL COORDINATOR

Bill Whitmer

EDITORIAL ASSISTANTS

Carol Ackerman
Sharon Cox
Lynette Quinn

TECHNICAL REVIEWER

Daniel Semon

MARKETING MANAGER

Gregg Bushyeager

COVER DESIGNER

Tim Amrhein

BOOK DESIGNER

Alyssa Yesh

DIRECTOR OF PRODUCTION AND MANUFACTURING

Jeff Valler

PRODUCTION MANAGER

Kelly Dobbs

MANUFACTURING COORDINATOR

Paul Gilchrist

PRODUCTION ANALYSTS

Angela D. Bannan
Dennis Clay Hager
Mary Beth Wakefield

GRAPHICS IMAGE SPECIALISTS

Brad Dixon
Clint Lahnen
Mike Reynolds
Dennis Sheehan
Craig Small
Jeff Yesh

PRODUCTION

Troy Barnes
Don Brown
Michael Brummit
Jama Carter
Mary Ann Cosby
Judy Everly
Donna Haigerty
Mike Henry
Louisa Kluznik
Ayanna Lacey
Cheryl Moore
Casey Price
Brian-Kent Proffitt
Erich J. Richter
SA Springer
Tina Trettin
Jill Tompkins
Holly Wittenberg
Michelle Worthington

INDEXER

Bront Davis

Overview

Contents

IX

Acknowledgments

I know where Jimmy Hoffa is buried! Not really, but I thought it might get your attention since people rarely read this section. I like credits in a movie. To me this acknowledgment section is just like the movie credits except it is in the beginning. Writing a book about a product that had almost no documentation is much like being put in a pitch-black room with instructions to make an inventory of everything. What you hold in your hand took a year to create and is the result of the efforts of many people, some of whom were not even aware that I was writing the book. Thought I would break the kudos up into sections. First the Corel folk.

The PAINT team:

This band of 4 (now much larger as they are working on PAINT 6) lead by Lucian Mustatea worked long and hard to produce both versions of PHOTO-PAINT 5. Their pictures are in the color plate section. Considering the diverse nationalities in the group it was like being in a little United Nations up there in Ottawa. Lucian (he is Romanian which explains why he gave me weird looks when I would try to speak to him in French) is greatly appreciated for the time he took out of his busy schedule to explain some of the subtle features of PAINT to me early on in the book. Alan Yeung had to endure me the most since he was in charge of filters. It was Alan who gave me the first clue as to how PAINT 5 worked. For this I will always be grateful. Rob Wineck seemed to enjoy the program as much as I did, and came up with some excellent work. I regret it didn't make it into this book, but it will be in the PAINT 6 book for sure. Dan Leroux and Steve Shaw were always there to answer questions as well. Actually that's only partially true. Often Dan seemed to be out of town whenever I blew into Ottawa, which makes him smarter than the average bear. There are others that devoted time and effort to make PAINT the outstanding product that it is and I thank all of them.

Acknowledgments of the Ottawa crew would not be complete if my hat wasn't tipped to Eid Eid who has done such an incredible job having taken over the reins from his predecessor, Susan Wimmer. Of course, many thanks to buds and friends Arlen Bartch, Julie Galla, and Fionia Rochester whose assistance made the work on the book a little easier.

Local help:

Most of the help I received in Austin, Texas, came from non-technical people. They range from my personal banker at First State Bank, Jana Emmons; all of my technical friends at AES Computers (finest collection of technical knowledge in the state) to all the gang at Bob's Barber Shop. I would also be remiss if I did not include our my family's dear friends Lane and Sandra McShannon, and our neighbors Larry and Francis Garner. (This is really beginning to sound like the Academy Awards.)

Top awards in the Austin department go to my own family, who got to see more of the back of my head than they ever thought they would.

Scott Hamlin's contribution of several chapters in the book is appreciated. Scott is a Photoshop veteran and gave the book some unique perspectives on PAINT.

And for the toughest job of all...

The crew at Sams Publishing. This was my first major work and I believe I was able to make every single major author's mistake possible. I am sure I didn't miss a one of them. Yet, when you look through this book, it's laid out in an orderly fashion and the screen shots are in the right place. All thanks to the talents and efforts of Dean Miller. Matthew Usher had the unenviable task of trying to take what I said and change it into what I meant. Wayne Blankenbeckler (how's that for a handle?) found all of the neat stuff that ended up in the CD-ROM. Mucho thanks. And the winner is... Chris Denny, who stuck through this project from the beginning, which is no small feat. My special thanks to him for hanging in there.

So, where is Jimmy Hoffa buried? On the grassy knoll, of course. Who killed him? I'll tell you that in the acknowledgment section of *Corel PHOTO-PAINT 6 Unleashed.*

About the Author

David Huss was born in a log cabin and had to walk ten miles to school in the snow everyday (uphill both ways). Sorry...

David has been using CorelDRAW since the heady days of 1.2. A former member of the Corel Advisory Council, David was contracted by Corel to write the user manual for PHOTO-PAINT 5 Plus while writing this book. He has served as a graphics/DTP consultant for several Fortune 100 companies. He is a popular speaker at Corel seminars and when he is not writing or speaking, he can be found in Austin, Texas, where he resides with his first and only wife of 21 years (that's 21 years of marriage, he's not allowed to reveal her age), two terrific children, two small dogs, and a bird.

Introduction

Conventions Used in This Book

- Placeholders in syntax descriptions appear in an *italic computer* typeface. Replace the placeholder with the actual filename, parameter, or whatever element it represents.

- *Italics* highlight technical terms when they first appear in the text, and are sometimes used to emphasize important points.

Within each chapter you will encounter several icons that help you pinpoint the current topic's direction. Their meaning should be clear when you see them used in the context of the book.

1

An Introduction to Corel PHOTO-PAINT 5

The Journey Begins

You are about to begin an incredible journey into the world of digital imagery. This world was once the exclusive domain of multimillion dollar computer systems and dedicated graphic artists. With Corel PHOTO-PAINT 5, you will quickly produce images that can make your projects dazzle.

Photo-editing programs have traditionally been labor-intensive. They required many hours of tedious effort in order to manipulate images (removing trees, adding people, changing sky color, etc.). With PHOTO-PAINT 5, you will be creating images that you never thought possible, and with relative ease. Just as CorelDRAW enables you to achieve professional computer-graphic effects with little effort, Corel PHOTO-PAINT will allow you to reach that same professional level in the manipulation of photographs, paintings, and other bitmap images.

PHOTO-PAINT History

Corel PHOTO-PAINT began its life as a software product called Photofinish, created by Z-Soft. It was introduced as Corel PHOTO-PAINT 3 in May 1992. It was then an interesting bitmap editing package of limited usefulness.

There are many unfounded rumors that float around the computer industry, and one of these rumors is that Corel PHOTO-PAINT 5 is still made by Z-Soft and is actually their current product, Photofinish 3. This is not true. When Corel PHOTO-PAINT 4 was released in May 1993, there were many improvements, and only a small amount of the original Z-Soft Photofinish program remained in it. PHOTO-PAINT 4 still had limitations in the size of the image files it could handle, and the absence of several other key features prevented it from being a first-class product. But the newly-released Corel PHOTO-PAINT 5 is emerging as a serious photo-editing program in its own right.

Corel *NOTE!*

When Corel introduced PHOTO-PAINT 5 in May of 1994 it was a product in motion. There were many changes in progress when the final bell sounded. As a result, when the maintenance release appeared in September (also referred to as the E2 release), PHOTO-PAINT 5 had substantially changed. Keyboard assignments, drop-down lists and dialog boxes had all been modified to improve the product. Because the E2 release was provided free of charge to all registered users of CorelDRAW 5, I have not included information about the original release in this book. All references to PHOTO-PAINT 5 are to the E2 release. At the time I am writing this there is talk about an E3 release for PAINT. If the E3 release materializes it will not affect the User Interface (UI) but instead correct some technical issues (notice I didn't say bugs).

Alice in PHOTO-Land

One of the things that makes Corel PHOTO-PAINT such a powerful package is that there are so many combinations of tools and functions available. One of the things that makes Corel PHOTO-PAINT so confusing to the new user is that there are so many combinations of tools and functions available. (Do I sound like the Cheshire cat in Wonderland?) If you are new to photo-editing programs, we have included a complete graphic-arts reference section in this book to help you understand the world of bitmap images. And if you are an experienced Photoshop user, you really need this book more than you realize. I have found over the past year that the users who have the greatest difficulty with PHOTO-PAINT are those with experience in Adobe Photoshop. Why? Because these users try to do things in PHOTO-PAINT the same way they do it in Photoshop. The result is like flying from Dallas to New York via Hawaii—you still get there, but what a detour! For example, to make a drop shadow under text in Photoshop requires from six to 14 steps (depending on how you do it). In PHOTO-PAINT it take two steps.

Figure 1.1.
This doesn't look like much, but consider that the girl on the right wasn't in the original photo. It took just a few minutes work to place her in the image with the Clone tools.

If you have worked with Corel PHOTO-PAINT 3 or 4, you will be impressed with the changes that have been made for release 5. The interface has been changed somewhat, but essentially it has the same appearance as Corel PHOTO-PAINT 4. The exciting news is in the program itself. But we are getting ahead of ourselves. First let me formally introduce to you Corel PHOTO-PAINT 5.

The Envelope, Please...

Corel PHOTO-PAINT 5 is foremost a photo or image-editing program. It is in the same league as Adobe Photoshop, but it costs hundreds of dollars less. As a photo-editing program, it offers all of the features one should expect from a professional photo-editing package, and in several areas you will able to do more with Corel PHOTO-PAINT 5 than with the aforementioned products.

Figure 1.2.
Tiger in the tank? How about a tiger in the box using Transformation filters?

One of the more useful tasks you can perform with this application is to take a poorly composed, overexposed, scratchy photograph and make it look as if the photographer did a great job. Only you and Corel PHOTO-PAINT 5 will know the truth. People today tend to get excited about all of the breath-taking sur-realistic effects that they can achieve with photo-editing packages such as PHOTO-PAINT 5. And in truth, I get excited, too. But it is the everyday work of making the images in our documents look as professional as possible, with the least amount of effort, that makes Corel PHOTO-PAINT 5 such an important addition to your desktop-publishing library.

Changing Reality (Virtually)

With Corel PHOTO-PAINT 5 and this book, you will learn how easy it is to add people or objects to existing images. More importantly, you will find it even easier to remove unwanted objects. You can change a photo background that is drab and cloudy into a beautiful, sunny sky. You will even be able to change the way people look. I recently did a brochure for our church. The photo of one of the pastors had been taken several months and 20 pounds ago. No problem with PHOTO-PAINT. I took off those excess pounds in less than an hour—which is more than the pastor or the diet industry can say.

*Figure 1.3.
When you need to
show the home planet,
don't search through
clip art—make it
yourself. We'll show
you how to make it
with the Map To
Sphere filter and a few
clever tricks.*

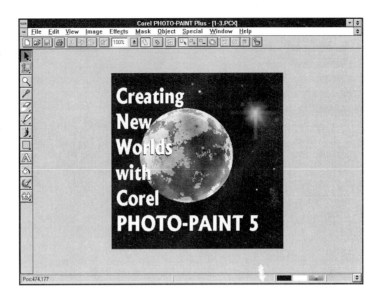

*Figure 1.4.
Beauty and Art. Many
times we take photo-
graphic perfection (left)
and make it look like
art (right). Did I make
her look worse? Think
what Picasso would
have done to her.*

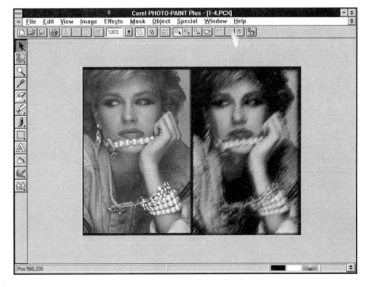

Altering people's appearance (removing blemishes, changing hair color, etc.)
has been done by professionals for a long time. I knew a guy who was one of
the kings of the airbrush (back in the pre-digital days), who was greatly appreciated by more than one playmate-of-the-month. Now, like my friend you will be
able to change the way people look. The only difference is that PHOTO-PAINT 5
doesn't require an airbrush, long hours, or years of experience.

What else can you do with Corel PHOTO-PAINT 5? We have been talking up until now about changing existing images, but you can also create original images. If you're not an artist, do not feel excluded from this discussion. Just as you are able to take clip art and assemble it to make exciting images with CorelDRAW, you can do the same with Corel PHOTO-PAINT 5. Using the PHOTO-PAINT filters and its powerful editing tools, you will quickly learn to create all kinds of original images, logos, and what-have-yous (and still maintain your not-an-artist standing).

Figure 1.5.
This is the underside of
a stained-glass project
you will learn how to
make. I included it to
show how you can take
a CorelDRAW image
and make it look like
pewter.

The following is a list of the important features incorporated in Corel PHOTO-PAINT 5.

- **Support for plug-in filters:** Commercially available plug-in filters can be your gateway to a world of incredible digital effects. The plug-in filter concept was introduced by Adobe with Photoshop. Today, many third-party developers make products that can tap directly into the powerful Corel PHOTO-PAINT program to produce effects such as making a photograph look like an oil painting. Filters can take a picture of a stationary bus sitting in a parking lot and make it look like it is rocketing down the road at warp-factor four. PHOTO-PAINT already comes with an impressive set of built-in filters, while support of the plug-in standard means that you can purchase third-party filters such as Aldus Gallery Effects, Andromeda Series, or Kai Power Tools and achieve even greater graphic effects.

- **Creation of objects and layers:** You might have to log some serious hours on another photo-editing program to appreciate this feature. In Corel PHOTO-PAINT 4, as with other professional photo-editing programs, when you placed something on the base image (the underlying image area), it became part of the picture and was there to stay. This has always been one of the challenges of photo-editing. With Corel PHOTO-PAINT 5, you can select and remove a tree from one photo and place it in your working image as an object. Then if your boss says "I don't like the tree," you simply smile, select the tree object, press the Delete key, and make it go away. This is a great time-saver.

*Figure 1.6.
This is the finished
stained glass. All of the
effects were done with
Corel PHOTO-PAINT 5
without using any
third-party filters.*

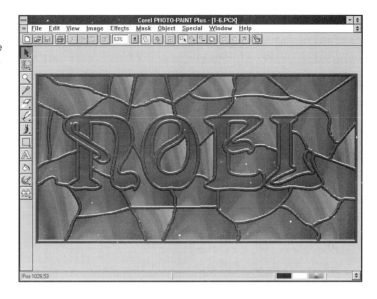

*Figure 1.7.
Playing around with
Bitmap Texture fills
and Mapping filters.*

■ **Larger image-file capacity:** The previous releases of Corel PHOTO-PAINT 3 and 4 were restricted in the size of the image files that could be loaded. When you begin talking about 24-bit color images, you are talking about files that can be 4 to 80MB in size, or even larger. PHOTO-PAINT 5 has a greatly increased image file-handling capacity. For files that are too large for your system memory, PHOTO-PAINT now provides a way to load partial areas of the image so they can be edited and then combined into a single image file.

Figure 1.8.
Although PHOTO-
PAINT 5 is not a
natural-media program,
you can use it to create
very "natural"-looking
images with the cus-
tom brushes and a little
know-how.

- **Ability to convert to and save in 32-bit CMYK format:** If that doesn't mean anything to you, it means you probably do not do a lot of work in the digital pre-press world. For those who work daily in this profession, this feature will prove very handy.

- **Improved masking:** The most time-consuming part of digital photo-editing is the creation of masks. Masks are required to isolate the part of the image you are working on from the rest of the picture. New, powerful masking features in PHOTO-PAINT 5 will save you hours and hours of tedious work when trying to apply effects to limited areas of images. Now you will be able to create extremely complex masks with little or no effort.

- **Mesh warp capability:** This feature enables you to make two-dimensional objects appear three-dimensional.

This is only a partial list of the improvements that have been made to Corel PHOTO-PAINT 5. I hope you are excited about some of the things that you will be able to do with this program. But before we run, we must learn to walk. This the next chapter begins with a quick tour of PHOTO-PAINT 5 basics.

Figure 1.9.
Using some of the
features in PHOTO-
PAINT Plus, I was
able to create quickly
the rock concert sign
shown here.

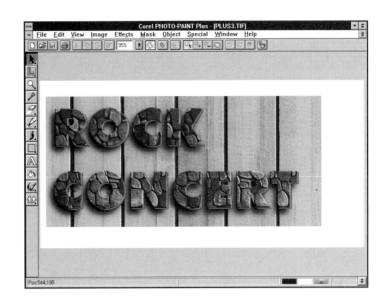

A Quick Tour of PHOTO-PAINT 5

I know you want to get going as soon as possible, and many of us (including me) tend to skip the introduction and the really basic chapters of a book such as this one. However, there is a lot of useful information in this chapter, so I urge you to look through it.

Elements of the PHOTO-PAINT Screen

Figure 2.1.
The Corel PHOTO-
PAINT 5 main screen
shown with two of the
sample files loaded.

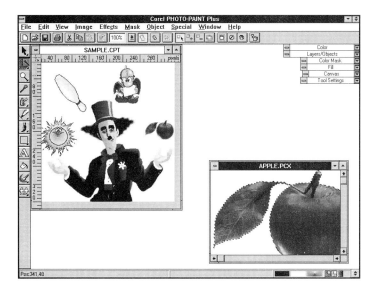

The following are the elements that compose the PHOTO-PAINT screen. (See Figure 2.1.) Following this list, some of the key elements will be described in more detail.

- **Control menu boxes:** These standard Windows control menus are found in the application and image area. They provide commands to move, resize, minimize, maximize, and close windows. Each of the PHOTO-PAINT roll-ups has control menus with their own commands. The control menu boxes provide a short-cut to information about roll-ups. By selecting the Help option in the control menu, the online help information about the selected roll-up appears.

- **Menu bar:** Press any menu heading in this bar in order to access dialog boxes, submenus, and commands. Access is also available by depressing the Alt key followed by the highlighted or underlined letter in the command.

- **Title bar:** Displays the image title. The title-bar background is grayed out when the image window is not selected.

- **Minimize button:** Click the application's Minimize button to shrink PHOTO-PAINT to an icon. Click the image window's Minimize button to shrink the active image to an icon. (Note: Shrinking the image area to an icon does not reduce the amount of system memory that is consumed by the image. The advantage of reducing the image is that it speeds up image redrawing on the screen, which is very handy if you have a sluggish graphics card.)

- **Maximize button:** Click the application's Maximize button to enlarge the PHOTO-PAINT window. Click the image window's Maximize button to enlarge the image window. When a window is at maximum size, the Maximum button becomes a Restore button with up and down arrows. Click the Restore button to restore a window to its previous size.

- **Roll-ups:** PHOTO-PAINT's roll-ups are used to streamline operations using commands that are repetitively accessed. Roll-ups are opened through commands on the menu bar or through keyboard combinations. A roll-up provides access to controls for choosing and applying fills, outlines, text attributes, and other options. Roll-up windows contain many of the controls found in dialog boxes: command buttons, text boxes, drop-down list boxes, and so on. But unlike most dialog boxes, the window stays open after you apply the selected options. This lets you make adjustments and experiment with different options without having to continually reopen a dialog box. When you are not using a roll-up, you can roll it up through its control menu, leaving just the title bar visible. When you begin to accumulate a lot of roll-ups all over your screen, you can select Arrange All from the control menu, and they will all roll-up and go into the corner nice and tidy.

- **Rulers:** Select Rulers from the View command in the menu bar. The position of the cursor in the image window is indicated by dashed lines on the rulers. The rulers' units of measure are selected using the Preferences command in the Special menu. (Note: The rulers in PHOTO-PAINT are a little rude. When they are selected, the image window does not increase to accommodate them. As a result, if the image fills the entire window, the rulers cover part of your image. Quick solution: Click on a corner of the image window and drag it to make it a little larger.)

- **Image window:** This is the image-display window. The zoom factor of each image window is controlled independently by the Zoom command in View or by the Zoom control in the ribbon bar. The default setting of Zoom is set in the Preferences section of the Special menu. The default setting is 100 percent. If you have a good graphics board in your system, choose Best Fit.

- **Toolbox:** Contains all of the tools used for image editing. Many of the buttons in the Toolbox have flyouts to allow access to additional related tools. (See Figure 2.2.)

- **Ribbon bar:** Buttons on the ribbon bar provide quick access to commonly used commands. The appearance of the ribbon bar and the number of buttons is dependent upon tool selection.

- **Status bar:** The status bar contains a wealth of information. Unfortunately it is either confusing or located in such a distant location that it is sometimes difficult to remember to look at it. The information is located on both the left and right side.

The *left* side displays the cursor position (using units of measure selected in Preferences) when the cursor is in an image window. When it is over the Toolbox or ribbon bar, it provides a brief description of the tool or command. When it is over any other area, it retains the last information displayed. If a tool is selected, then it displays information that is relevant to the tool. For example, when the Rotate function is selected, it shows degree of rotation as the object is being rotated. The trick to using it is to actually find the information in what looks like a Wall Street ticker-tape of data.

The *right* side contains three rectangles, which display the currently selected foreground (called Paint) color, background (called Paper) color, and fill colors, respectively. The fill-color rectangle also shows a representation of the type of fill that is selected (e.g., Fountain, Uniform, etc.). The area to the right of the color display is used for the Mask, Color Mask, and Transparency Mask icons.

- **Window border, Window corner:** Click and drag a horizontal or vertical border or corner to resize the window.

- **Scroll arrow:** When the image is larger than the current window size, the scroll arrows appear. Clicking the up or down arrows provides movement (panning) of the image in the window. The Hand tool in the Toolbox provides a much quicker way to perform the function of the scroll arrows.

Toolbox Basics

The Toolbox comes in a variety of shapes and sizes. Don't worry yet about what the tools do; let's first learn how to configure the Toolbox. Figure 2.2. shows the Toolbox *grouped* (default). When it is grouped, depressing any of those tool buttons with a small triangle in the lower right corner for more than half a second causes a *flyout* menu to appear, such the one shown in Figure 2.3. The flyout displays additional related tools. Clicking on any tool in the flyout places the selected tool button at the head of the flyout. To see all the tools at once, you must *ungroup* the Toolbox, as shown in Figure 2.4. (After you have seen what the tools look like ungrouped, you might understand why Corel left them grouped.)

Figure 2.2.
The Toolbox shown grouped (default).

Figure 2.3.
The Toolbox with one
of its many flyouts
shown open.

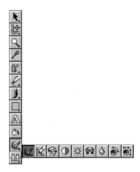

Figure 2.4.
The Toolbox
ungrouped.

You can place the Toolbox anywhere you want in the PAINT work area. You can move (float) the Toolbox to any location on the screen by clicking on the Toolbox while holding down the Shift key. This allows you to place the Toolbox on the screen where it feels most comfortable while you are working. To return the Toolbox to its default position, non-floating, click the Toolbox control menu and deselect floating.

Figure 2.5.
Toolbox control menu
gives quick access to
configuration controls.

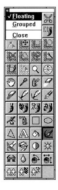

Corel *TIP!*

Once you find a position and location for the Toolbox that is comfortable for you, keep it that way. Constantly changing the Toolbox location and configuration slows you down when working on a project.

The Toolbox arrangement can be changed when the Toolbox is ungrouped. Use the mouse and drag one of the sides of the Toolbox. You will notice that the cursor becomes a double-ended arrow as it comes in contact with one of the sides. Clicking and dragging the sides of the Toolbox changes the row and column arrangement.

To make the Toolbox invisible, depress Ctrl+T. The Toolbox can also be made invisible by selecting Toolbox, and clicking Visible in the View command on the menu bar. The Visible command is a toggle. Each time it is selected the Toolbox changes from invisible to visible.

The Ribbon Bar

The ribbon bar (Figure 2.6) is new to PHOTO-PAINT 5 and is similar to the ribbon bar found in many other Windows applications. The ribbon bar contains buttons that provide quick access to many commands and modes. The overall appearance of the ribbon bar and the number of buttons it contains is determined by the tool selected and the mode PHOTO-PAINT is in. The ribbon bar is controlled by a Preference checkbox labeled Show Ribbon Bar. Unchecking this box deactivates the ribbon bar and makes it invisible. Preferences is accessed under the Special command in the menu bar.

Figure 2.6.
Ribbon bar shown
with first seven
buttons active.

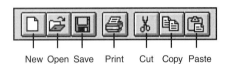

The first seven button are common Windows functions and are very handy.

New	The New command activates the Create A New Image dialog box for creating new image files.
Open	The Open command activates the Open An Image dialog box to open existing files.
Save	The Save command saves the currently selected image. This button is grayed-out (unavailable) until the selected image has been modified.
Print	Open the Print dialog box to allow printing of selected image.
Cut	The Cut command cuts (removes) the defined (masked) area and copies it to the clipboard.
Copy	The Copy command copies a defined (masked) area to the clipboard.

Paste	The Paste command button pastes (copies) the image in the clipboard into the selected image as an object. (Note: Unlike the Paste *command*, which gives you a choice of pasting as an object or as a new document, the Paste *button* does not give you a choice.)

Roll-Ups

Roll-ups are a special type of window with controls for choosing and applying fills, outlines, text attributes, and other options. Roll-up windows contain many of the controls found in dialog boxes: command buttons, text boxes, drop-down list boxes, and so on. But unlike most dialog boxes, the window stays open after you apply the selected options. This lets you make adjustments and experiment with different options without having to continually reopen a dialog box. When you are not using a roll-up, you can roll it up, leaving just the title bar visible.

Corel *TIP!*

> Roll-ups are wonderful, but they have a negative side. Each roll-up that is open consumes system resources. System resources, when they get too low, can cause system crashes or abnormal program behavior. Get in the habit of closing (not just rolling up) roll-ups when you are finished with them.

Roll-ups can be opened through menu-bar commands or keyboard combinations.

Roll-ups can be closed (removed from the screen) or arranged (rolled-up) individually or as a group (all of them) through the roll-up control menu. (See Figure 2.7.)

Figure 2.7.
Roll-up control menu
provides a quick way to
get online information
about the roll-up.

Each roll-up can be rolled-up individually through the arrow button to the right of the title bar. The roll-up can be moved anywhere in the work area by clicking and dragging the title bar.

Next we'll move on to to image-file management. If you are an experienced PHOTO-PAINT 4, Photoshop, or Picture Publisher user, you can just skim this chapter. If not, invest the time to learn all of the things that can be done when opening an existing image and some hints on creating a new image.

Image File Management

Hey! Where's the Page?

The first thing you notice when you launch
PHOTO-PAINT 5 is that there isn't a rectangle
indicating where the page is located. There is
only an empty workspace. If you have ever
tried to do something in that empty space, you
quickly found out that nothing worked. To
begin work in PHOTO-PAINT 5 (or any bitmap
application), you must either open an existing
image file or create a new one. Creating an
image file with vector-based programs such as
CorelDRAW involves very few decisions. You
are asked to select paper size (letter or legal)
and orientation (portrait or landscape), and
little else. With PHOTO-PAINT, there are many
options available when you create a new file.
That is why I have dedicated an entire chapter
to this subject.

While there is nothing that is more exciting than jumping right into the middle of a new program and producing fantastic results, it only happens in the training videos. Invest some time in this chapter, learning the basics, and you will save yourself hours of wasted effort later. In this chapter, you will learn how to launch PHOTO-PAINT, create a new image, open an existing image, manipulate the image, save the image, and exit PHOTO-PAINT.

To Start PHOTO-PAINT

1. Double-click the PHOTO-PAINT icon in the Corel group folder in Windows Program Manager. If you have PHOTO-PAINT 5 Plus, the icon may be located in another folder.

To Create a New Image

1. Click the New File button on the ribbon bar or choose New from the File menu. (See Figure 3.1.) The Create a New Image dialog box opens. (See Figure 3.2.)

Figure 3.1.
Open a New File from
the File menu.

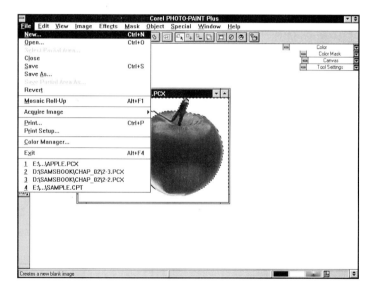

2. Select the Color Mode for the new image. A drop-down list of the available selections can be accessed by clicking the down arrow. The choices available are as follows: black-and-white, grayscale, 16 color (4-bit), 256 color (8-bit), 24-bit color (sometimes referred to as 16.7 million color or true color), and 32-bit color (CMYK).

Figure 3.2.
The Create a New
Image dialog box opens
when New Image is
selected in the File
menu.

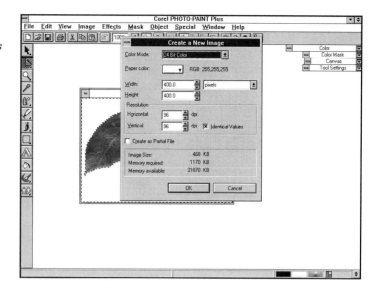

Corel *TIP!*

Choose a color mode that matches your requirements. For example, selecting 32-bit color when the final output only supports grayscale results in a file that is very large, difficult to manage (larger files slow down program operation), and a nightmare to transport to another system (at a service bureau) for output. It is like a man building a boat in his basement and then finding there is no way to get it out.

3. Choose Paper Color. The currently selected color is displayed in the small preview area. Clicking the preview area opens a color palette, allowing additional color selections. The colors that are available are dependent on the Color Mode that is selected. Displayed to the right of the preview window is the numerical value of the selected color. The numerical system that is used is dependent on the Color Mode selection. For critical applications, you may specify a color model and the numerical equivalent by clicking on the color preview window and choosing the More button at the bottom of the palette. This action opens the Select Color dialog box, which is discussed in Chapter 7,"Flood Fill Tools."

Corel *TIP!*

> The color palette that appears will always be the same, regardless of the color mode selected. This can be confusing if you pick Grayscale and are presented with a color palette when the preview button is clicked. The color mode is correct even though the palette does not always correctly reflect it. As in the example of Grayscale, clicking on one of the colors returns a gray value in the preview and is displayed numerically. Clicking on the More button opens a Select Color dialog box set to Grayscale. While this is inconvenient, it happens because Corel PHOTO-PAINT shares many modules with other Corel Applications and technically it wasn't a good method to bring up a grayscale palette. Maybe this will change in PHOTO-PAINT 6.

A rose by any other name: What PHOTO-PAINT calls Paper color is referred to as Background color by everyone else on the planet. I understand the paper analogy, and it is appropriate; however, it is difficult to change common industry names this late in the game. Remember the following:

Paper color = Background color. Paint color = Foreground color.

4. Enter values for Width and Height. Values can be entered by typing or by clicking on the up/down arrows. Units of measure can be selected from a drop-down list that appears when the down arrow is clicked. If PAINT is set to defaults, the units of measure that appear first are Pixels. (If you think pixels are little mythical creatures with wings, I recommend that you spend some time in Chapter 21, "Color and Digital Image Basics.") When choosing values for image size, be aware that the larger the image, the larger the resulting file size. As you change the Width and Height values, the Image Size and Memory Required values at the bottom of the dialog box change, reflecting any changes in file size.

Corel *TIP!*

> Keep the size of your image small when you are experimenting with filters or effects. Everything operates faster, and when you are satisfied with the result, you can make the image the desired size and then apply the effects.

5. Enter values for Resolution. If the Identical Values checkbox is checked, any value entered in one field will be automatically reflected in the other. Here are some general guidelines about setting Resolution:

■ Keep the Identical Values checkbox checked unless you have a specific requirement for non-identical resolutions.

- For 24- or 32-bit color: Keep your resolution below 200 dpi.
- For black-and-white (but not grayscale): Use a resolution that is equal to that of the final output device.
- For grayscale: Keep the resolution at or below 150 dpi if the final output device is a laser printer (even a 600 dpi printer).

  If the values entered in steps 4 or 5 cause the projected Image Size to exceed the Memory Available displayed in the lower part of the dialog box, PHOTO-PAINT will display a box advising that the file will be created as a partial file, as seen in Figure 3.3. This feature enables you to create files in partial segments that would normally be too large for your system. (This feature is discussed in greater detail in the section of this chapter on "Opening an Existing Image.")

Figure 3.3.
When system resources are smaller than the image size, PHOTO-PAINT displays this message advising the user that it will be a partial file load.

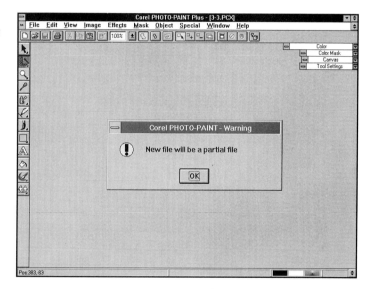

Corel *TIP!*

If the new image will be larger than 16MB, PHOTO-PAINT will automatically load it as a partial file.

As the image is being specified, the projected Image Size, Memory Required, and the amount of Memory Available is continually updated and displayed at the bottom section of the dialog box. This provides an interactive method to see what effect the changes made to the image values have on the final size of the new image.

6. Click OK or press Enter. A new image window will appear . All new images are automatically named by PHOTO-PAINT with the title "NEW-*x*.CPT", where *x* is a number assigned by PAINT. For example, the first new image you create after opening PHOTO-PAINT will be NEW-1.CPT, the second NEW-2.CPT, etc. This internal image counter resets each time that PHOTO-PAINT is closed, so that the first New File when PHOTO-PAINT is reopened will always be NEW-1.CPT.

In case you are concerned about having to go through this every time you open a new file, I have some good news for you. The Create a New Image dialog box retains the last setting you entered. I have found that once you have a setting that is comfortable for your system and your needs, creating a new file rarely involves making any changes to those settings.

Opening an Existing Image

1. Click the Open File button on the ribbon bar or choose Open from the File menu. (See Figure 3.4.) The Open An Image dialog box appears. (See Figure 3.5.) This dialog box is fairly straightforward in its functions. Under the File Name section is a list of the files that are available in the selected directory. Highlighting any filename in this area will cause the filename to appear in the File Name box after a two-second delay. The drive/directory for the files are selected in the adjoining Directories box. Below the File Name section is the file filter selector called List Files of Type. By selecting the type of file you want to open (e.g. Paintbrush *.PCX), only the files with that extension will be shown in the filename selection area.

Figure 3.4.
Opening an existing file
using the File menu.

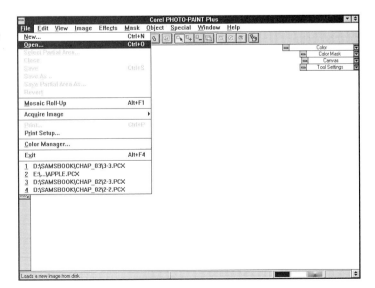

Figure 3.5.
The Open An Image
dialog box enables a
wide range of controls
on loading existing
images.

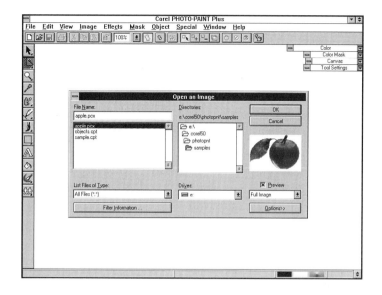

2. Click the Preview checkbox. Because a picture is worth a thousand words, PHOTO-PAINT enables you to preview files before they are opened. On the far-right side of the Open Bitmap window is the preview area. When Preview mode is selected by clicking on the checkbox, a thumbnail of the currently selected image file appears. When Preview mode is not selected, there is a large X in the area. Preview is not available for vector files that do not have a bitmap header (a thumbnail image) associated with it. An example would be a Windows Metafile *.WMF file.

Corel *TIP!*

The Preview feature provides a quick way to look through file images. By using the arrow keys to move the highlight bar in the File Name section, each file's image automatically appears in the preview area. If you want to preview a large number of files I recommend using Mosaic or some other browser program, such as U-Lead's Album.

3. Click the arrow in the List Files Of Type box. A lengthy import filter selection drop-down list will appear. (See Figure 3.6.) Selecting a specific type of image file allows only files with that extension to be viewed in the File Name section. This makes it easier to find files in a directory with hundreds of files. Select "Paintbrush (*.PCX)."

Figure 3.6.
The drop-down list
from the List Files Of
Type box shows a
partial listing of
available import filters.

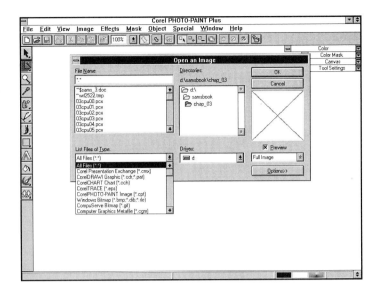

Corel *NOTE!*

With PHOTO-PAINT, you can load vector files (such as those in CorelDRAW) as well as traditional bitmap files. Vector files are converted to bitmaps (rasterized) as they are loaded. Rasterization is controlled by a separate dialog box. Selecting All Files *.* allows any file that is in a directory to be viewed (even files that cannot be opened by PHOTO-PAINT).

There are a few more features in the Open Bitmap Window that we need to explore.

Notice that the box below the preview box is the image-selection box. Clicking on the arrow in the image-selection box reveals a drop-down list containing four methods for controlling image file loading. (See Figure 3.7.) The default setting is Full Image. With Full Image selected, the entire graphic file is loaded into Corel PHOTO-PAINT. The other choices are Cropped, Resampled, and Partial Area. All of these methods are described in the section on "Options for Opening Existing Images."

Below the image-selection box is the Options button. By clicking this button, the remainder of the Open An Image dialog box opens, revealing file information about the selected file. (See Figure 3.8.) Clicking the arrow by the Sort By box gives you the choices of sorting the file list under File Name by either Date or Name. (Name is the default.) This feature is useful when you are working on a project and want to be able to find image files of various formats that you may have only recently made. Sorting the list by date displays the file list based on the file date, beginning with the newest files on the top of the list.

Figure 3.7.
The drop-down list for image selection.

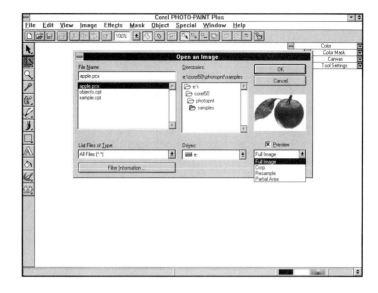

The Filter Information button (Figure 3.9) provides the revision level of the import filter. This information is helpful when working with the Corel technical support staff, but beyond that it serves no useful purpose.

Figure 3.8.
Selecting the Option button provides access to the file sort function as well as file information.

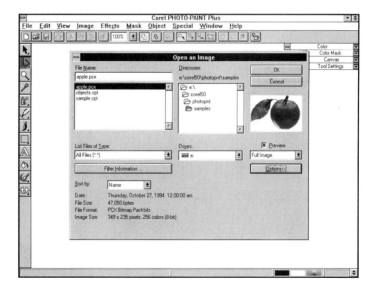

4. Click OK to load the selected image file into PHOTO-PAINT. As you open an image, you will see the bar graph in the right side of the Status bar of the PHOTO-PAINT window showing the progress of your image file being loaded.

Figure 3.9.
Filter Information
provides filter revision
information needed
when contacting Corel
technical support.

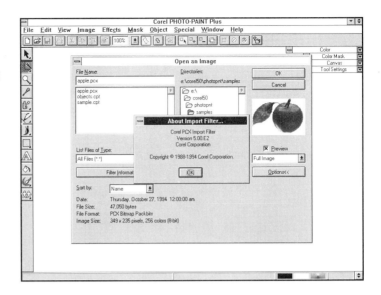

Corel*NOTE!*

> If the image you have selected is a Photo CD image, then an additional box will open. See "Opening a Photo CD Image," later in this chapter.

One of the drawbacks to using the All Files *.* setting is that some file formats share the same extension; as a result, PHOTO-PAINT sometimes doesn't know how you want the image imported. The warning message displayed in Figure 3.10 was caused by selecting an EPS image with All Files *.* selected. PHOTO-PAINT did not know whether I wanted it imported as Interpreted Postscript or as an Adobe Illustrator file. Hence I got the warning. Clicking the OK button does not return you to the dialog box but rather all the way back to the main screen. As a result, you must start the File Open process again.

Now that the image has been loaded, the ribbon bar has changed. Seven new buttons appeared when the screen changed from the opening default screen to its current mode. Also note that several buttons are grayed out (meaning their function is not available now). The Save button is grayed out because there have not been any changes made to the image because the image is an exact copy of the original. If you need to save the image at this point, you can save it using the Save As feature in the File menu.

Figure 3.10.
This warning some-
times shows up when
PHOTO-PAINT can't
determine what type of
filter to use to open
your image.

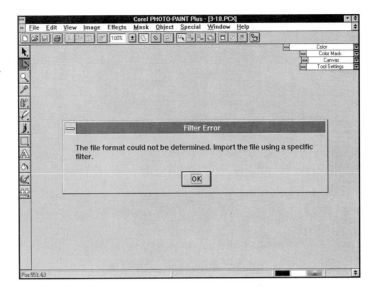

That's all that is required to open an image file. Additional options when loading standard image files and Photo CD files are explored in the following section.

Options for Opening Existing Images

PHOTO-PAINT offers three additional ways to open image files other than the
Full Image method just described. They are Cropped, Resampled Image, and
Partial Area. Each method is available through the drop-down list under the
preview window in the Open An Image dialog box.

Opening a Cropped Image

Selecting Crop in the Open Image dialog box and clicking OK opens the Crop
Image dialog box. (See Figure 3.11.) The Crop feature allows you to load only the
part of the image that is required. The cropping is permanent, creating a new,
smaller image. However, the original image is not altered. Although image
cropping can be done within PHOTO-PAINT, it is sometimes more efficient to
use the Crop function to only load the part of the image file that is required. This
is especially true with very large image files. In the preceding example, the
Corel Professional Photo CD image was great, but we only needed the diver and
the fish . We could have loaded the entire image (1.167MB) and cropped it, but it
made more sense to only load the portion of the file that we needed. The bounding box was resized and moved (see Figure 3.12), so most of the image was
excluded when it was opened. The result shown in Figure 3.13 not only is what
we wanted, but was just 397KB in size, which is easier and faster to work with.

Figure 3.11.
The Crop Image dialog
box that is used to crop
an image when it is
opened.

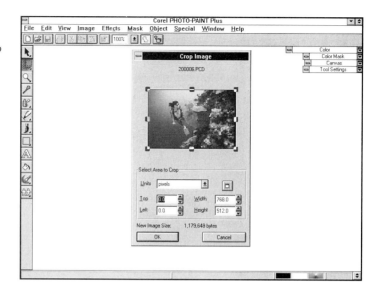

Figure 3.12.
Using the bounding box
to determine what part
of the image is cropped.

Crop Image Dialog Box Controls

Preview Window   Displays the entire image with a bounding box.
Move the nodes on the bounding box to crop the
image. Clicking and dragging anywhere inside the
bounding box produces a hand cursor. Use the
hand cursor to move the bounding box to a specific
area of the image.

Figure 3.13.
The resulting image.

Units	Choose the units of measurement from a drop-down list.
Top	Enter a number or use the scroll arrows to position the top of the cropped area.
Left	Enter a number or use the scroll arrows to position the left side of the cropped area.
Width	Enter a number or use the scroll arrows to select the width of the cropped area.
Height	Enter a number or use the scroll arrows to select the height of the cropped area.
New Image Size	Displays the file size of the cropped image based on the current size of the bounding box.

Opening a Resampled Image

Resampling may be a new term to some of you. Resampling resizes the image to a smaller size and/or a different resolution, thus creating a new file from the resampled image. The word "new" is important here, because when you resample an image, the original remains unchanged and a copy of the image, at the new size/resolution, is created. Through dialog-box commands, you can adjust the width and height of the image either by size or percentage and change the resolution.

Selecting Resample in the Open Image dialog box and clicking the OK button opens the Resample Image dialog box. (See Figure 3.14.) The units of measurement are selected in the Units box. Figure 3.15 shows an image Resampled by 50 percent, next to the original.

Figure 3.14.
The Resample dialog
box for opening an
image.

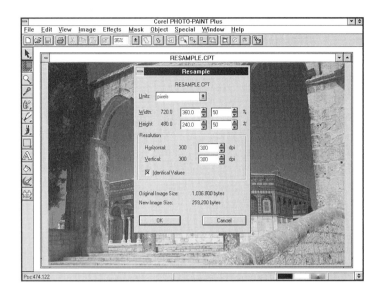

Figure 3.15.
Results of resampling
an image by 50 percent
compared with the
original image.

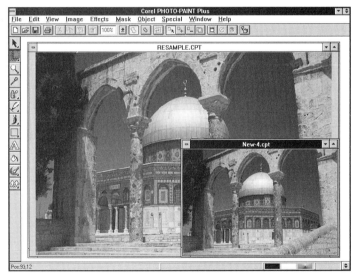

Resample Dialog Box Options (For Opening an Image Only)

Units   Choose a unit of measurement from the drop-down list box.

Width/Height   Enter a number or use the scroll arrows to choose a size
                      (entered in units of measure), or enter a percentage in the %
                      box. The dimensions of the image remain proportional to
                      the original. Any value entered in one box will cause the
                      other box to change proportionally.

Horizontal/Vertical	Enter a resolution. Resolution is measured in dots per inch (dpi).
Identical Values	If checked, any value entered will cause the other box to change to the same value.
Original Image Size	Displays the size of the original image.
New Image Size	Displays the size of the resampled version based on the values entered in the dialog box.

PHOTO-PAINT also provides a Resample command for images that have already been opened. It uses a different dialog box and can be used to increase as well as decrease the image size. Notice that the image that has been loaded is a Photo CD. When using the Resample option for loading an image with a Photo CD, the Photo CD dialog box will open first. After you have made your selections in that dialog box, the Resample dialog box opens.

Corel *TIP!*

When resampling an image, it is recommended that the Identical Values checkbox be left checked unless you have a specific requirement for mixed image resolution. Do not select a resolution that is greater than your final output device requires.

Opening a Partial Area Image.

When an image file size is larger than your system resources can handle, PHOTO-PAINT provides partial-area loading. A partial area is a selected section of an image that is displayed as a separate image. You can open a number of partial areas from the same image. This enables you to work on separate areas of an image, without the system demands of opening the entire image. You can save a partial area as a new image. Partial areas are opened automatically by PHOTO-PAINT if you have an image that is too large for your system to open. The Partial Area dialog box allows you to determine how many areas the image is to be divided into and to select the area that you want opened.

By working on selected image areas, you will be able to work on any size file regardless of existing system memory limitations. If the image file is larger than 16MB, Partial Area is enabled automatically. Lastly, Partial Area can be used to load parts of an image for purposes of special effects.

Open the Partial Area dialog box by selecting Partial Area in the Open Image dialog box (Figure 3.16) and clicking OK. Figure 3.17 shows the selected file with a 2 × 2 grid selected and Figure 3.18 shows the resulting file that was opened as a partial-area image.

Figure 3.16.
The Partial Area dialog
box with the image in
the preview window.

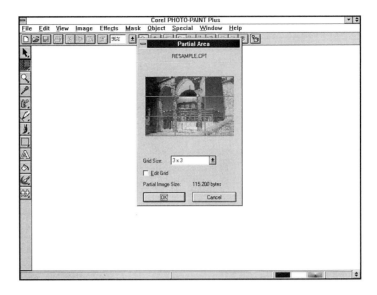

Figure 3.17.
Grid size of 2 × 2 shown
in preview window.

Partial Area Dialog Box Options

Preview

This window displays the entire image with the grid. The grid square that is blinking is the one that will be loaded. Clicking on a grid square selects it for loading.

Grid Size

This is a drop-down list box with the following preset options:

2 × 2   Two rows and two columns

Figure 3.18.
*Partial area of image
loaded in image area.*

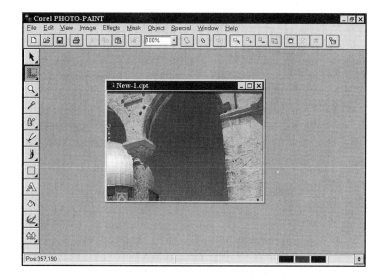

3 × 3	Three rows and three columns
4 × 4	Four rows and four columns
8 × 8	Eight rows and eight columns
Custom	Use the nodes on the grid lines to move the grid.

Edit Grid checkbox — Check this to edit the grid. When the cursor is on the nodes of the grid lines, it changes to arrows, enabling you to resize the grid. At each intersection of the grid is a control handle. Moving the corner handle resizes the grid proportionally. The side handles move the grid either horizontally or vertically without maintaining proportion. When the cursor changes to the hand cursor, you can move the entire grid around the preview window and the Grid Size box displays the word "Custom."

Partial Image Size — Displays the expected file size of the partial area.

Moving Between Partial Images

After a partial image has been opened, the Select Partial Area button becomes activated in the ribbon bar. Clicking on this button saves the partial area image back into the original file and opens the Partial Area dialog box again. The changes made to the partial image are reflected in the preview window. With the exception of filters, all effects applied to a partial area are not applied to the entire image.

35

Filters and Partial Images

In the original release of Corel PHOTO-PAINT 5, any filter that was applied to a partial area was only applied to that area. Thus, to apply a 10 percent contrast filter to a partial image that was loaded with the 2 × 2 grid required separate applications of the filter to each of the four partial areas. With the maintenance release and release of PHOTO-PAINT 5 Plus, filters are now applied to the entire image. The exception are Transformation and Mapping filters, which are only applied to the displayed partial area.

Saving a Partial Area

There are two ways to save a partial-area file after it has been opened. The normal way is to save the image is by using the standard File Save command in the File menu. This will cause the partial area you are working on to be merged back into the original file and saved as a complete image. The other method is to select Save Partial Area As from the File menu. This command allows you to save the partial area of an image that is currently open as an separate image with a different name.

Opening a Photo CD Image

If the image you selected in the Open An Image dialog box was a Photo CD image (*.PCD), the Photo CD Options dialog box opens when you select the OK button. (See Figure 3.19.) Photo CD images are images from 35mm film negatives or slides that have been converted to digital format and stored on a compact disc (CD). Although PHOTO-PAINT provides full import capability for Photo CD format, you cannot save images in .PCD format, as it is a proprietary format.

Corel *NOTE!*

Because CD-ROM drives operate at a slower data rate than ordinary disk drives, it may take noticeably longer for the preview image to appear from a CD than if it were loaded off of a hard disk drive.

Photo CD Advisory Note

Because of the popularity of Photo CD-ROMs, several products on the market today place files that are necessary for Photo CD communications in non-standard locations. As a result, you may experience system hang-up or failures when attempting to load Photo CDs. One of the most common symptoms is that when you go to preview or load a Photo CD, you are almost literally blown out of PHOTO-PAINT. No kidding—one moment you are in PHOTO-PAINT, the next you are at the Program Manager (or whatever shell you are using), wondering what happened. If this should occur, perform the following procedure to correct the problem.

1. Launch File Manager and open the \Windows subdirectory.
2. Locate a file named PCDLIB.DLL and select by clicking on it. The correct file is installed by Corel in the \Windows\System subdirectory.
3. Rename the file (using the File command in the menu bar) to PCDLIB.DLX. You can change it to any name you wish; the object is to change the extension so Windows no longer recognizes it.
4. Close File Manager.
5. Load a Photo CD again. This will resolve the problem.

Figure 3.19.
The Photo CD Options dialog box opens when a Photo CD image is opened.

Photo CD Dialog Box Options

The Photo CD dialog box allows you to specify resolution and colors, and to apply image enhancement.

Resolution   This is the name Kodak gives for the size of the image. It is a misleading term, because the settings have nothing to do with resolution. All of the images have the same resolution. However, I am glad Corel chose to stick with

the Kodak name to keep the confusion to a minimum.
When you import a Photo CD (*.PCD) file, a dialog box
will appear prompting you to choose the desired file
size, in pixels, from a drop-down list. Because the image
sizes are defined by Kodak and based on photographs,
the sizes have photographic names. The choices are as
follows:

Wallet (128 × 192)

Snapshot (256 × 384)

Standard (512 × 768)

Large (1024 × 1536)

Poster (2048 × 3072)

Colors   Color selection is another drop-down list. You are presented with three different options regarding the color
depth of the images. If you need to have the image in
grayscale, import it as 256-color and then convert it to
grayscale in PHOTO-PAINT. The following color-depth
options are available:

16.7 million colors (24-bit)

256 colors (8-bit)

16 colors (4-bit)

Image Size   The Image Size indicator will update to reflect the
choices you have made regarding resolution and color. I
always load Standard in 24-bit color, which is approximately 1.167MB.

Corel*NOTE!*

Larger file sizes require large amounts of system memory, take longer to
load, take longer to apply effects, and require more disk space for storage.
Therefore, always try to pick a resolution and color depth that is sufficient
for your application.

Apply Image Enhancement   This checkbox when clicked causes an
additional dialog box to open before the
image is opened. This is a great color-
correction system that makes some of
the not-so-great Photo CDs on the market
look much better. Image Enhancement
corrects the color of the image before
you import it into Corel PHOTO-PAINT.

The correction applied at this stage of the process is superior to any correction that might be applied in PHOTO-PAINT.

Preview

Click Preview to see a thumbnail representation of the CD image.

Loading a Photo CD Without Image Enhancement

Choose the .PCD file to be loaded. Select the resolution and color of the Photo CD image and click the OK button. After the file loads, PHOTO-PAINT issues a warning that the Photo CD is a read-only file that cannot be modified. (See Figure 3.20.) I am hoping that Corel offers a preference setting to disable the warning message in the next release. When you load a lot of Photo CD images, you get a little weary of the message box that continually states the obvious.

Figure 3.20.
The warning that
appears when a Photo
CD is loaded.

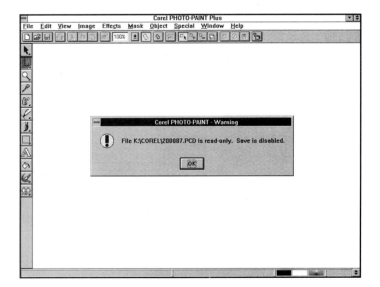

Color Correcting Photo CD Images

Selecting Apply Image Enhancement in the Open Photo CD dialog box opens the Photo CD Image Enhancement dialog box as shown in Figure 3.21. This dialog box allows you to correct the color of the image before you import it into Corel PHOTO-PAINT. The way it works is that it allows you to select neutral colors (black, white, and grays) in the image, and then the software maps these neutral colors to increase the dynamic range of the image. This increase is within the gamut system, so it doesn't go beyond the capability of color printing. The best part is that it almost always improves the overall appearance of the image if you don't need the color correction for printing purposes. The Image Enhancement dialog box is anything but intuitive. Nevertheless, after we show you how to use it, apply it every time you bring in a Photo CD and your

Photo CD images will look better. I have several Photo CD images that had black backgrounds until I applied correction, and they turned out not to be black backgrounds after all. In one, a night shot of a wolf turned out to contain a forest that had turned into mud before the correction was applied.

Figure 3.21.
The Photo CD Image Enhancement dialog box provides color-correction controls for images before they are opened. The system is great, although its operation takes some time.

Photo CD Enhancement Dialog Box Options: Color Correction Methods

GamutCD™ This color-correction method uses gamut mapping to enhance the color fidelity and tonal ranges of the CD image. Gamut mapping is a system that ensures that colors in a computer image are reproducible by a printer. Of the two methods, I have had the greatest success with this one. The Kodak system, while an excellent system, is more complicated to use.

Set Active Area Generally, the default area should be used. If you need to change the active area, use the mouse to specify an active area within the image in the view field. This ensures GamutCD will base its color correction on the area of the photo that you are going to use, and helps cut out any black borders left over from the original scan that would interfere with accurate correction.

Set Neutral Colors Define neutral colors by clicking on pure whites, blacks, and grays within the active area. The more samples that are selected, the better the color correction.

White in Image   Choose this option if you have good white elements in the photo. If you do not have a white, disable this option, as the gamut mapping will over-brighten your picture as it maps the lightest elements of your picture to white. This option will assist GamutCD in enhancing the tonal range of your image and removing color cast. If your white is not pure white, you may wish to lower the 255 setting in the number box to the right.

Black in Image   Choose this option if you have good black elements in the photo. If the image does not have blacks, disable this option, as the gamut mapping will darken your picture as it maps the darkest elements of your picture to black. This option will assist GamutCD in enhancing the tonal range of your image and removing color cast. If your black is not pure black, you may wish to raise the setting in the number box to the right from 0.

Fast Preview   Displays the effect the GamutCD settings you have chosen will have on the image. The first time you preview, you may wonder why it is called "Fast Preview." To find out, click "Best Preview" the next time. Bring a book.

Best Preview   Displays the effect the GamutCD settings you have chosen will have on the image. This method will be more accurate than Fast Preview but will take longer to build. Actually, several of the people who wrote the PAINT program think it is faster to just click the OK button to see the color correction. If you do that, you will lose your sample settings. Use the Fast Preview instead. If you are paid by the hour and need to milk the job for some more time, you will love Best Preview.

Using GamutCD Color Correction

This is all great, but how do I use it? That was my question to the people at Corel when I was writing the manual. Their answer surprised me—they hadn't used it that much themselves. So here is Dave's handy-dandy method for using the GamutCD Color Correction System, based on lots of practice and a little too much coffee. I figure the best way to show you is to use an image on the Photo CD Sampler. I picked the image because it looks like it does need enhancement.

1. Open the Photo CD image 200059.PCD on the sampler disk. In the sampler insert, it is referred to as SA59.PCD. The Photo CD Dialog box opens.

2. Pick the resolution and size suitable for your system. I selected Standard and 24-bit color.

3. Click the Apply Image Enhancement checkbox and click the OK button. Your image should look like Figure 3.21. We are going to use the default active area. (If we needed to change it, we could have clicked the Set Active Area button and dragged a rectangle in the preview window.)

4. Click on the whitest white spot you can find. Don't trust your eyes on this one. Watch the numbers on the right side of the dialog box as you move the cursor over the white area. Specifically watch the numbers by R, G, and B (which stand for Red, Green, and Blue). The whitest white will produce the highest numbers in RGB. This is basic color theory here. Pure white reads 256 on each of the RGB channels. You should be able to get in the high 240s with the snow to the lower-right side of the wolf. When you click the left mouse button, it leaves a little marker. Make several of these white samples. The more you make, the more accurate is the color correction. Don't lose your mind here—three or four samples are sufficient.

5. Click on the blackest black you can locate in the active area. "Active area" is the key phrase here—do not click on the black border. We are trying with these samples to establish the dynamic color range of the image, so shooting some of the black off of the negative border will throw the correction off. You pick the black the same way you picked the white—by the numbers. In this case, you are looking for the lowest numbers in the RGB values. You should find several good samples in the left side of the wolf's nose and in the big dark crease on his fur.

6. Find a good middle-of-the-road gray if there is one (optional). This is used to set the midtones, and finding a gray can be very subjective. Use the numbers again. In this case you are looking for RGB numbers around the 128 value. (Blue will be a little higher). There isn't a great gray in this image. Most of the grays are in the 180-185 region. If you use a gray in this image, the result will be shifted toward the warmer colors. If I was using the color correction on this image, I would forgo the gray entirely. This is strictly a matter of individual taste.

7. Click the Fast Preview button. On a good 24-bit color monitor, the difference can be very impressive. (See Figures 3.22 (before) and 3.23 (after).)

Notes on the GamutCD Color Correction System

■ There isn't a specific order to click on the colors. The computer sorts it all out.

■ If there isn't a good black (RGB less than 90) or a good white (RGB greater than 220), don't use them, and uncheck the respective White In Image or Black In Image checkbox.

Figure 3.22.
The Photo CD image
before image enhance-
ment was applied.

Figure 3.23.
The same Photo CD
image after image
enhancement was
applied.

■ If you don't like the results of the preview, click reset and choose the color
samples again. The image will appear the same, but the color values will
be correct.

■ If the preview is too dark, try increasing the value in the Black in Image
value box.

■ If the preview is too light, try decreasing the value in the White in Image
value box.

■ Experiment with it, get a feel for how it works.

The Kodak Color Correction System

This color-correction method allows you to alter color tints, adjust brightness and color saturation, as well as make adjustments to the level of contrast. This is not an automatic system like the Gamut Image Enhancement System. There are sliders to control the three tints red, green, and blue (RGB), Brightness, and Saturation (the amount of color in the image; slide it all the way to the left and all of the color is removed). There are several adjustments that are unique to Photo CD images, as follows:

Remove Scene Balance Adjustment	Turns off the Scene Balance Adjustment the photo-finisher applied at the time the original image was scanned and placed on the Photo CD disc.
Color Metric	Allows you to adjust contrast by preset amounts.
Show Out-Of-Gamut Colors	If the changes you've made are too extreme, the preview will display out-of-gamut pixels as pure red or pure blue. Colors that are out-of-gamut cannot be printed accurately, and it is important for critical prepress work for all colors to be within gamut boundaries.

Saving an Image File

Select Save from the File menu. The Save An Image To Disk dialog box (Figure 3.24) appears. The Save An Image To Disk window is pretty much self-explanatory. Below the File Name box is the Save File As Type box. The default setting is Corel PHOTO-PAINT (*.CPT extension). Clicking the arrow button to the right of the box opens a list of the types of file formats that can be saved. Below the Save File As Type box is the File Sub-Format box.

You have the option of saving your image files in compressed or uncompressed mode, depending on the file format you select. Some file formats do not allow compression. If you select one of these formats, the File Sub-Format box will be blank.

The last item on the lower right of the Save An Image To Disk dialog box is a checkbox marked Backup. Selecting this box will save the image with a ?PT extension.

Ensure that Corel PHOTO-PAINT is selected in the Save File As Type box and select the OK button.

If a dialog box appears warning that you are about to overwrite an existing image file (Figure 3.25), then the file you are saving already exists. Either click YES to overwrite the existing file, or select NO and change the name of the file to be saved.

Figure 3.24.
The Save An Image
To Disk dialog box
is used to save
and/or convert files.

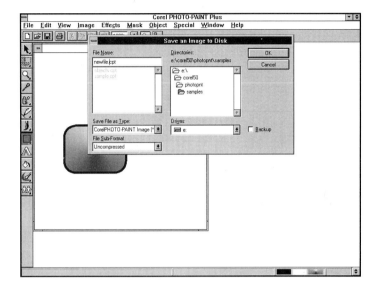

Figure 3.25.
The File Overwrite
warning box.

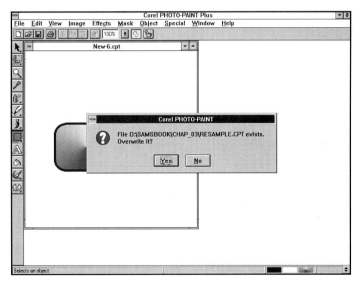

45

Corel *TIP!*

Always use the correct extensions provided by PHOTO-PAINT when naming graphics files. All filenames are restricted to eight characters with a three character extension. The import filters in most computer applications are dumb as dirt. They use the three-character extension to select the correct import filter. If a graphics image has been saved with the incorrect extension, the application may attempt to read the image with the wrong import filter and quit. Some import filters will even hang up the system trying to import it.

The Basics of Digital Image Manipulation

Now that you understand how to manage image files, the next step is to learn how to manipulate them once they have been opened. This chapter illustrates the different ways to change an image once it has been loaded into PHOTO-PAINT. All of these commands are found in the Image Menu, as shown in Figure 4.1. Note that all of the commands in the Image Menu affect the entire image and cannot be used selectively on a portion of it.

Figure 4.1.
The Image Menu
is used to apply
changes that
affect the entire
image.

Image-File Information (Bigger is not Better)

It has been said that before you can go somewhere, you first need to know where you are. Before an image is changed, it is good practice to know something about the image. What is the image size? What is the resolution? These are all questions that PHOTO-PAINT answers with the Info command, which displays information about a selected image file. The Image Information window, shown in Figure 4.2, provides file name, size (width and height in pixels), horizontal and vertical resolution in dpi, color mode, image size in bytes, number of objects, file format, subformat, and image status (i.e., whether the image has been changed since it was opened). You will find yourself using this command more than you may expect. Generally, I find myself invoking it to check what the size of my image file is before I save it.

Corel *TIP!*

The size displayed in the Image Information window rarely reflects what the file size will be like when it is saved. The reported size of the file image will always be larger than the saved size. This isn't because PHOTO-PAINT 5 can't calculate file size accurately; it is because when the image file is open in PAINT, it is using an internal 32-bit CMYK model. When the file is saved, it is saved in the selected format and color model, and therefore the file size will be smaller.

Figure 4.2
This Image Info
window doesn't always
tell the truth about
image-file size.

How to Display Image Information

Select Info in the Image menu on the menu bar or click on the control menu of the image and select Info from the dropdown menu.

Please note that the Image Information window is not a dialog box. Information is displayed but it cannot be entered or altered. The Image Information window must be closed by clicking the OK button before any other actions occur.

Making Changes to an Image

Changing Sizes

Images are rarely provided to you in the exact size that is required for your project. In the old days, when we needed to change the size of an image we made a PMT (photo-mechanical transfer) of the image, which was reduced or enlarged as required. Fortunately, PHOTO-PAINT provides several much-simpler ways to change both the size and the surrounding working area of an image. There are three general methods of changing sizes:

Resampling	Makes the image larger or smaller.
Changing paper size	Increases overall image size by increasing the size of the base image.
Resizing an image area	This really has no effect on the image; unlike the previous two methods, this only changes the viewing area without affecting the image.

Resampling

Resampling is needed when an entire image needs to be made larger, made smaller, or have its resolution changed. The Resample command doesn't just stretch or shrink the image. (That would be resizing.) When an image is resampled, PHOTO-PAINT actually examines each picture element (pixel) of the image and determines what image information needs to be added or subtracted to the image file to achieve the desired results. This is pretty incredible when you think about what is happening. For example, if we double the size of the image, PHOTO-PAINT must create a pixel to put between each existing pixel. To accomplish this, it must compare the color value for each pixel in the image with that of its adjacent pixel and calculate the color value for the new pixel. Remember that the next time you see the little hourglass spinning around.

The Resample dialog box is similar to the dialog box that is available when an image is opened using the Resample option. The major difference between the two resamples is that this Resample command can increase or decrease the image size while the Resample On Open command can only decrease image size. There are many options available to the user when resampling an image in PHOTO-PAINT.

To resample an image, first click on Resample in the Image menu bar. The Resample dialog box opens as shown in Figure 4.3.

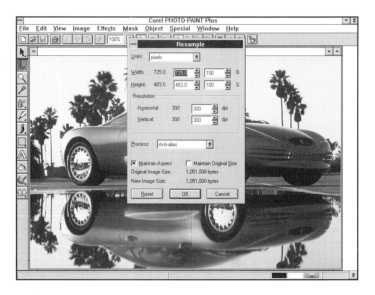

Figure 4.3.
Using the Resample
dialog box you can
change the size and the
resolution of an image.

There are two sets of images in Figure 4.4 to show the difference between resampling techniques. Both images were resampled to increase their sizes by 400 percent. The text is at 100 percent zoom. The portion of the car (in case you were wondering what it was) was then zoomed in at 250 percent. When viewed at 100 percent, even the Stretch/Truncate effect looks acceptable. Remember the purpose of this example is to show where the techniques break down. The are several things that should be evident. Black-and-white (not to be confused with grayscale) images always suffer the most when resampled. Color and grayscale images resample well, and unless you are going to increase the image size by an enormous amount, such as 1000 percent, you should see little to no image degradation.

Figure 4.4a.
An example text
resampled using
anti-alising.

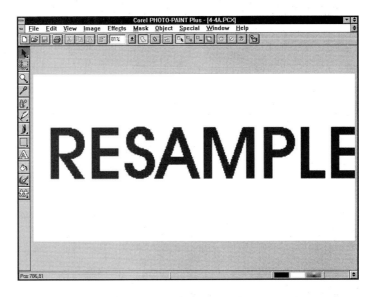

Figure 4.4b.
An example of an
image resampled
using anti-aliasing.

Figure 4.4c.
An example text
resampled using
Stretch/Truncate.

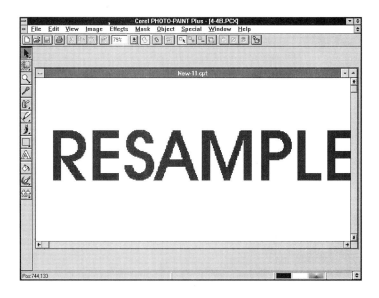

Figure 4.4d.
An example of an
image resampled using
Stretch/Truncate.

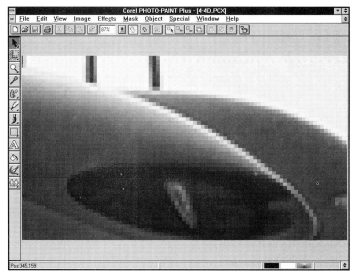

Resample Dialog Box Options

Units
Choose a unit of measurement from the dropdown list box.

Width/Height
Enter a number or use the scroll arrows to choose a size (entered in units of measure) or enter a percentage in the % box. The dimensions of the image remain proportional to the original. Any value entered in one box will

	cause the other box to change proportionally if the Maintain Aspect checkbox is checked.
Horizontal/Vertical	Enter a resolution. Resolution is measured in dots per inch (dpi). This isn't a magic system. If you have a low-resolution image with lots of jagged diagonal lines (jaggies), inserting a high-resolution value will not give you a crisp, high-resolution image. You will end up with a large, low-resolution image. (In the chapter on filters, we will see how to get rid of the jaggies.)
Identical Values	If this is checked, any value entered in one data-value box will cause the other box to change to the same value.
Process	This determines by which process the image is resampled. There are two options. Figure 4.4 shows the results of the two options on a 400 percent Resample increase.
Anti-Alias	This is the best selection. It creates a smoother image by removing jagged edges from the original. This is done by averaging or interpolating pixels. It takes longer to process, but it is worth it.
Stretch/Truncate	Only use this if you have a very slow system or you need rough approximations. It creates a rough image by stretching duplicated pixels and eliminating overlapped pixels. This process is very fast.
Maintain Aspect	When this is checked, the dimensions of the image remain proportional to the original. If you enable Maintain Aspect, values in the Width and Height boxes remain proportional to the original values. For example if you increase the height by 50 percent, the width will be increased by 50 percent. The same is true of the Horizontal and Vertical resolutions. They remain equal to each other, regardless of the values that are entered.
Maintain Original Size	When selected, this keeps the file size the same as the original, regardless of the values of resolution or Width/Height that are selected. The changes will not be reflected on screen, only when printed.

Original Image Size	Displays the size of the original image.
New Image Size	Displays the calculated size of the resampled version based on the values entered in the dialog box.
Reset	Returns all the values in the dialog box to the values of the original image when the Resample dialog box was opened.

To initiate the process, enter the values necessary to change the image to the desired size or resolution.

Click the OK button. A new image is displayed. The original image remains unchanged. Figure 4.4 shows an image resampled at 400 percent with the original image.

Notes on Using Resample

Always use anti-alaising when resampling an image unless time and/or system resources are critically short. Stretch/Truncate should be used when you need to see a quick sample of how the resampled size will fit. When changing resolution, remember: Settings that are greater than the final output device can support will result in large image files that require extra printing time without improvement in output quality. Changes to the resolution do not affect the appearance of the image on the screen. You can increase overall system performance if you close the original image after you have resampled it.

Changing the Paper Size

This command is used to increase or decrease the size of the image area by creating a new image area in the specified size and placing the original image within it. It is called Paper Size because Corel refers to the background as paper. This command takes the original image and places it **unchanged** on larger or smaller paper (background). The new image (Paper) color is determined by the PHOTO-PAINT's Paper Color setting. If the paper size is decreased to a size that is smaller than the original image, the image is cropped. If the paper size is larger than the original image, it is placed on a paper based on the Placement selection made in the dialog box.

To Change the Paper Size

1. Select Paper Size in the Image menu. This opens the Paper Size dialog box as shown in Figure 4.5.
2. Enter the values for the new paper size in the data boxes.
3. Select the desired placement and click the OK button.

Figure 4.5.
The Paper Size dialog
box can be used to
change paper size,
make a border, or
produce a precision
crop of an image. The
dialog box is shown
with the placement
dropdown list open.

Dialog Box Options

Width/Height	Enter a value for the width and height of the paper.
Units	Determines the units of measurement for width and height. The options are: inches, millimeters, picas/points, centimeters, and pixels.
Maintain Aspect	If Maintain Aspect is checked, the width and height values maintain their proportion to one another.
Placement	Determines the placement of the image on the paper. The dropdown list box has the following options: Top Left, Top Center, Top Right, Center Left, Centered, Center Right, Bottom Left, Bottom Center, Bottom Right, and Custom. If you choose Custom, use the Hand cursor in the Preview window to move the image to the correct location.
Preview Window	Displays the position of the image based on the values entered in the dialog box. The cursor changes to the Hand cursor if placed over the Preview window. The image can be moved with the Hand cursor to the desired position on the paper. If the image is moved with the Hand cursor, the placement is automatically Custom.

Tips on Changing Paper Size

The Paper Size command can be used to precisely crop an image by changing the paper size to the desired value and selecting centered placement. By moving the image with the cursor, it is possible to place the image at the exact desired position on the new paper size. Paper size provides a method of placing an image on a larger background. You can make borders around an existing image. Try using Paper Size several times on the same image with complementary colors to make a quick border.

Figure 4.6a.
The original from the
Photo CD.

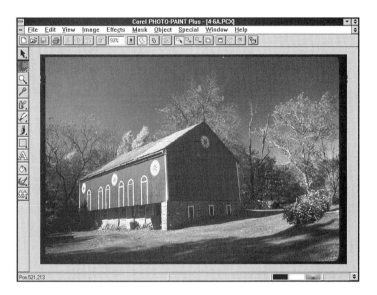

Figure 4.6b.
The original modified
using Paper Size with
Maintain Aspect
checked.

*Figure 4.6c.
A border was made by increasing the size of the paper with Maintain Aspect still checked.*

*Figure 4.6d.
The width is increased to three times wider than the vertical by turning off Maintain Aspect.*

In Figure 4.6a, we have the original from the Photo CD. Notice the irregular black border produced by the film negative. By using Paper Size with Maintain Aspect checked we were able to quickly produce 4.6b. The other advantage to cropping this way is that the original remains and a cropped copy is produced. In 4.6c, a border for our cropped image was made by increasing the size of the paper with Maintain Aspect still checked. Only one of the values needed to be increased; the other was calculated automatically. Lastly, in 4.6d, we took our new image (4.6c) and, by turning off Maintain Aspect, increased the width so that it was three times wider than the vertical.

Resizing the Image Window

Although this really has nothing to do with changing the image size, it is essential for working with images. Resizing the Image window is done by moving the cursor over the image-area window corner or side until the cursor becomes a double-headed arrow. Click and drag the image window until it is the size that fit your needs. The image remains unchanged and a gray border appears around the original image. It is very helpful to increase the image area size when working on an image close to the edge. When you are working with various PHOTO-PAINT tools near the edge of the image, the program reacts when the cursor touches the Image window's border. By increasing the view area, it prevents the cursor from changing into a double-headed arrow any time the edge is approached.

Corel *TIP!*

> For a quick resize of the image to see it better, grab the corner of the window and drag it until it is the size you desire, then depress the F4 key.

Manipulating Images

Just as images don't always come in the proper size, they also don't always come with the desired orientation. When you are laying out a newsletter, for instance, it seems that when you get the images you want, they are inevitably facing the wrong direction. You usually want them facing inward if they are on the outside edge, and facing outward if they are on the inside edge. (I knew you knew that; I just thought I would throw it in.) There are also times when you are cloning images, and by doing horizontal mirrors, the clones look a little less like clones. This trick doesn't work well with images of people, but it does work well with most natural, inanimate objects, such as trees and clouds. PHOTO-PAINT offers commands called Flip and Rotate to allow the image to be changed quickly.

Using Flip and Rotate

These commands are pretty much self-explanatory. The Flip command, accessed through the Image menu, makes either a vertical or horizontal mirrored copy of the original image. To use it, select the Flip command in the Image menu. A dropdown list appears, showing the two choices: Horizontally and Vertically. Clicking on either of these executes the function, producing a copy of the image with the selected effect.

Figure 4.7 was created using a few PHOTO-PAINT tools and techniques that you will learn about later in this book. It was actually quite simple. I took the original image (on Photo CD) and used the Paper Size command to eliminate the film border. Next I applied a horizontal flip to the image to create the duplicate. Because I knew that the resulting picture would be twice as wide as the original, I used the Info command and recorded the image size. Opening up a new file that was twice the width and same height as the original image, I copied and pasted both of the images into the new image area. Using the Text tool, the text was applied, and a duplicate of the text was made to create the drop shadow effect. That's it.

Figure 4.7.
This image represents
what can be done with
the Flip command in
the Image menu.

Figure 4.8.
The drop-down list
offers several quick
selections for image
rotation.

Rotate offers the ability to produce a rotated **copy** of the entire image. To Rotate an image, click on Rotate in the Image menu. A drop-down list appears with the choices shown in Figure 4.8. Choosing Custom opens the Custom Rotate dialog box as shown in Figure 4.9.

Figure 4.9.
When custom rotation is selected, there are several additional options available. The Maintain original image size option sometimes produces unexpected results.

The Custom Rotate Dialog Box

The Custom Rotate dialog box enables you to rotate the current image by a specified amount. A new image is created from the results of the rotation. The variables are as follows:

Degrees Enter the amount of the rotation in whole numbers. It does not accept decimal numbers.

Direction Determines the direction of rotation. Click the Clockwise or Counterclockwise radio buttons.

Maintain Original Image Size

When this checkbox is selected, the image height and width dimensions are fixed. The rotated image is cropped at the image boundaries. If this is left unselected, the dimensions of the image are automatically increased to fit the edges of the rotated image. Figure 4.10 shows examples of an original image, a rotated image, and a rotated image with Maintain/Size selected.

Working with Custom Rotation

If the original image has objects, they will all become visible in the rotated copy. They will not be merged. This includes the hidden objects. (If you are bewildered by those last few sentences, it will become clearer when you get to the chapter on objects.)

Figure 4.10a.
The original image.

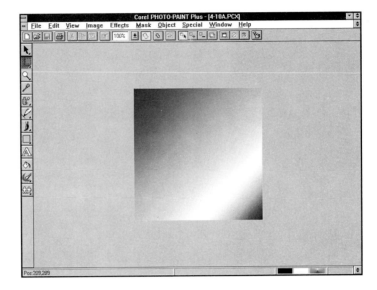

Figure 4.10b.
The same image can be rotated by 45 degrees, which makes a nice diamond.

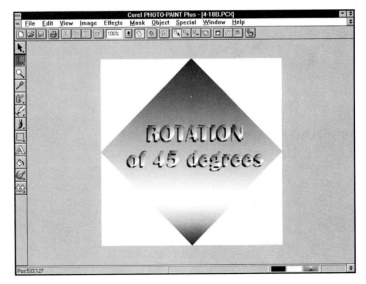

Figure 4.10c.
The original image can also be rotated with the Maintain/Size feature selected. Notice the cropping of the corners at the points where the rotated image went outside of the original border.

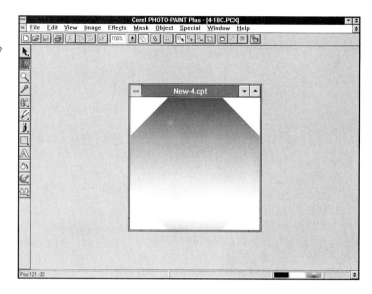

Image Conversion

PHOTO-PAINT does not have an export command. It does, however, convert images in two ways: by saving files in a wide variety of formats (.EPS, .TIF, etc.), and by converting open images to different color modes (such as 256-color, grayscale, and others) using the Convert To command in the Image Menu.

To Convert an Image

To Convert an image, select Convert To in the Image Menu. A dropdown opens with the following choices:

Black and White (1-bit) Converts the image to black-and-white (not to be confused with grayscale). This selection opens another dropdown list with the following choices:

Line Art. Use if you do not want a halftone applied.

Printer Halftone. This is for a fading halftone. Use if you are going to print the image on a low-resolution printer.

Screen Halftone: This is for a diffused halftone. Used if the image is only for display use.

16 color (4-bit) Converts the image to 16 colors.

Grayscale (8-bit) Converts the image to gray scale.

256 Color (8-bit) Opens the Convert to 256 Colors dialog box. See Figure 4.11. Converts the image to 256 colors. (See additional discussion forthwith.)

True Color (24 bit)   Converts the image to 24-bit color (also called True-Color or 16.7 million color). It uses eight bits of data for each of the three channels of Red, Green and Blue (RGB).

CMYK (32-bit)   Converts the image to 32-bit color. This is a 24-bit color image that is separated into four channels: Cyan, Magenta, Yellow, and Black (CMYK), which is the standard separation for four-color printing.

Using the Convert To Command

Choose the desired format to which the image is to be converted. (The current format of the selected image is grayed out.) The selection of a format begins the conversion process. Remember that this process creates a copy of the image being converted. For example, if a 24-bit color image is converted to grayscale (which I did a lot of while making the screen shots for this book) the result is two images: the original 24-bit color image and the grayscale image.

Corel *TIP!*

Use the Convert To command when experimenting with different file formats. When I was making the screen shots for this book, I frequently converted images to grayscale to see what they would look like when printed. Because the original was left unchanged, I was able to quickly close (delete) the copy and try another color combination.

Figure 4.11
This shows the 256 Color dialog box that appears when you are converting an image to 256-color mode. Correct selection of options can produce an image on your screen that is almost as vivid as 24-bit color.

The Convert to 256 Colors Dialog Box

This dialog box is opened by the selection of **256 Color** (8-bit) in the **Convert To** section of the Image Menu. This dialog box provides options controlling the conversion of images to 256 colors. You can select the type of dithering performed and the palette type used to display the image is converted.

Dialog Box Options

Dither Type	Three buttons determine the type of dithering per formed when the image is converted. The choices are:	
	None	No dithering performed. (default)
	Ordered	Dithering is performed at a faster rate, but the result is less attractive.
	Error Diffusion	Provides the best results, but is slower to process.
Palette Type	Two buttons determine the palette type that is used to convert the image. The options are:	
	Optimized	Uses an optimized color palette. This is a palette that contains colors centered around the image's spectrum of colors. While this option produces the best color, it is slower than the Uniform option.
	Uniform	Uses the uniform color palette. Provides a complete 256-color spectrum of color (with equal quantities of red, green and blue) regardless of whether they are used by the image.

Corel *TIP!*

Don't be too quick to dismiss the 256-color option because of previous bad experiences with a 256-color palette. Corel uses a proprietary 256-color palette that produces color that can be very close to 24-bit color but without the system overhead. (Image files in 256-color mode are two-thirds smaller than 24-bit files).

Viewing the Image: The Zoom, Locator, and Hand Tools

The Zoom Tool

The Zoom tool enables you to quickly zoom in on areas of your picture. Much of the detailed masking work that you will accomplish with PHOTO-PAINT will rely on the Zoom command. While simple in operation, it is one of the more frequently used tools in the toolbox. There are several ways to invoke the Zoom command, as follows:

- Select the Zoom icon from the toolbox. The cursor becomes a magnifying glass. Click and drag a rectangle over the area that is to be viewed. Releasing the mouse button causes the image to zoom in.

- Depressing and holding the Z key causes the selected tool to be replaced with the Zoom icon. Release the Z key after you have changed to the desired zoom level and the cursor will return to the originally selected tool.

- Select a Zoom level from the Zoom Level dropdown list in the ribbon bar using the arrow next to the Zoom Level data box.

- Enter a Zoom value in the Zoom Level data box in the ribbon bar.

- Select the Zoom selections in the View menu.

- Use the Quick keys: F4 (Zoom To Fit) or Ctrl+1 (100 percent—no zoom)

- Click the left mouse button when Zoom is selected to zoom in.

- Click the right mouse button when Zoom is selected to zoom out.

- Double-click the left mouse button on the Zoom tool in the toolbox to return the picture to 100 percent.

Tips on Using the Zoom Command

The zoom level of an image when it is created or when it is opened is determined by the Zoom State On Open data box settings in Preferences under the Special menu. The Z key is very important when you are editing or otherwise working on an image. No matter what tool you have selected, holding down the Z key changes the tool into the Zoom tool until you release the key. This tool, in combination with the Hand tool, lets you get down to the big, ugly, pixel level of an image to do precise editing and masking much faster than would normally be possible by going through the toolbox.

The Locator Tool

The Locator tool enables you to move to a specific location in an image by selecting the position in an image that is at lower zoom level. When an image is at a high level of magnification (zoom), such as 1600 percent, it is sometimes difficult to find a specific area on the zoomed image. The Locator tool only works when you have at least two windows of the same image open. Confused? I was until I had one of the PAINT team members show me how to use the thing. I have included a brief procedural description on how to use it. While it seems like a very worthwhile tool, I haven't had much need to use it. If you were doing detailed work on a very large image, it could be invaluable for navigating through a world of very large pixels.

Using the Locator Tool

To see how this tool works in actual practice, refer to Figure 4.12. To do it yourself, follow these steps:

1. Duplicate the original image using the Duplicate Command in the Window menu. A duplicate image appears.

2. Selecting the original image, set the Zoom to the appropriate zoom level (it is at 1600 percent in Figure 4.12, and the duplicate window is at a zoom level of 52 percent). It is not necessary for both images to fit neatly on the screen, as they do in the figure. (That is only necessary to make books look slicker.)

3. Select the Locator Tool in the tool box, or press down and hold the L key on the keyboard. The cursor becomes a crosshair.

4. Select the area desired on the duplicate image, and the window in the original image centers on that part of the image.

Figure 4.12.
This illustrates the
use of the Locator tool
when navigating
through an image
zoomed in at 1600
percent.

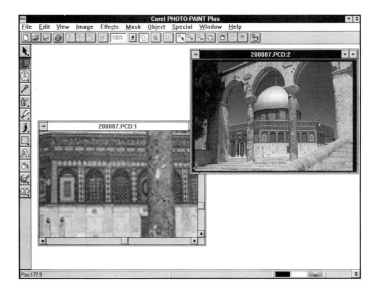

Notes About the Locator Tool

It is possible to have many windows open at various zoom levels. Selecting an area on any of the images with the Locator tool will cause all of the open images to be centered on the point selected.

The Hand Tool

The Hand tool is used to quickly pan a zoomed image inside of the image area. By selecting the Hand tool in the toolbox or holding down the H key on the keyboard, the cursor becomes a hand when it is inside the image area. Clicking the left mouse button inside the image area and dragging it causes the image to pan in the direction that the mouse is moving. The Hand tool has no effect on an image that totally fits within its image-area window. Such an image will not have any scroll bars.

Corel *TIP!*

Whenever you can, use the Hand tool to move through an image. It is much faster than the scroll bars—much, much faster. Remember, to select it you only need hold down the H key. As long as the H key is held down, the cursor remains a Hand tool.

5

The Basics of Masks

Before we can do anything substantial with Corel PHOTO-PAINT, we need to understand how some basic components of the program operate. These components are *masks*, *objects*, and *layers*. It is the creation, manipulation, and transformation of masks and objects that forms the foundation of every command and function in PHOTO-PAINT. With that said, let us begin by learning about masks.

What is a Mask?

The official Corel definition of a mask is as follows: "A Mask is a defined area that covers part of an image or the entire image." Was that as clear as mud? Another way to say the same thing is that by using a mask, we can control exactly where on the image an effect will be applied. For example, if I have a picture of a jet and I want to change the background but leave the image of the jet unaffected, I need to make a mask that protects the jet from changes.

Here's an analogy. If you have ever painted a room in a house, you know that one of the most tedious jobs is painting around the window sills and baseboards. The objective is to get the paint on the wall but not on the surrounding area, so either you paint very carefully (and slowly) or you get a roll of masking tape and put tape over the area where you don't want the paint to go. In using the tape, you created a mask.

Another example of a mask is a stencil. When a stencil is placed over an object and then painted, only the portion of the stencil that is cut out allows paint to be applied to the surface. Both stencils and masking tape are examples of masks.

Corel PHOTO-PAINT masks are much more versatile than a stencil or masking tape (and are not as difficult to remove when you are done). The masks used in Corel PHOTO-PAINT enable you to control both where and how much of an effect is applied to an image.

One further illustration may help you understand the need for masks in PHOTO-PAINT applications. Look at Figure 5.1. To our eyes it appears to be a jet flying in the sky. To the computer, there is no distinction between the jet and the sky.

Figure 5.1.
This picture of a jet
appears to be some-
thing else entirely to
the computer.

It is just a rectangle filled with pixels—some blue, some gray, and some white. (The original I am looking at is a color photo.) A bitmap image is like a large field of land. When you look at a map of an area, you can see where one lot ends And another begins. When you look at the actual property, there are no property lines, only dirt. The only way to separate the property into lots is to put up boundary markers or fences.

Masks are the equivalent of fences to PHOTO-PAINT. They inform the program where one area ends and another begins. Without masks, it would be difficult, if not impossible, to accomplish even the simplest of image-editing tasks.

Where Masks Come From

PHOTO-PAINT provides a variety of mask-creation and selection tools. Figure 5.2 shows the flyout menu of mask-creation tools. These tools, used in combination with the related buttons in the ribbon bar shown in Figure 5.3, provide the PHOTO-PAINT user an almost limitless selection of masks.

Figure 5.2.
A large selection of mask tools are shown on the flyout.

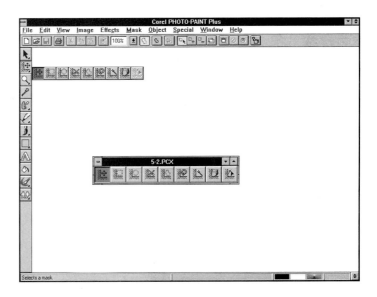

Don't be concerned about the names of tools for the moment. We will be examining each one of these so that you can understand their functions and the best times to use them.

The mask-creation tools shown in Figure 5.2 can be divided into two basic groups: *user-defined* mask tools and *computer-aided* mask tools. User-defined masks are created by the user, who defines their size and location within the image by using the mouse. The user-defined mask tools are the Rectangle, Circle, Polygon, and Freehand mask tools. Computer-aided masks are created by PHOTO-PAINT based on information entered by the user in conjunction with the color values of the image. Computer-aided mask tools are the Lasso and Magic Wand. The last button on the Mask Tool flyout is the Mask Node Edit tool, which is used to alter both user-defined and computer-aided masks.

Figure 5.3.
These buttons in the ribbon bar work with the mask-creation tools to produce an extensive selection of masks.

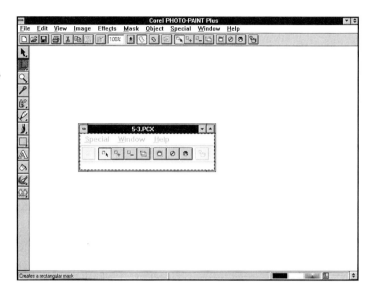

Simple and Complex Masks

Regardless of which mask tool is used, you can essentially create one of two types of masks: *simple* and *complex*. (Corel calls them "complex," but they should be called "compound.") Simple masks are masks that are made with a single operation. For example, if you take a Circle mask tool and drag it until you have a circle, you have created a simple mask. Complex masks are made up of two or more smaller masks. (Knowing the difference between simple and complex masking will save you some head scratching later on when we are discussing complex masks.)

Creating a Simple Mask

Before we can create a mask of our own, we need an image to work with. Open the Corel Professional PHOTOS CD-ROM Sampler Limited Edition (from this point on, we will call it the Sampler Photo CD) and locate the file 200032.PCD. Select the Snapshot setting on the Photo CD dialog box. If you don't have a CD-ROM drive, run out immediately and buy one. However, if the stores are already closed, open the PHOTOPAINT\SAMPLES subdirectory and select the APPLE.PCX file.

Corel *TIP!*

> A quick way to reopen a file that was recently opened or saved is to use the
> keyboard combination ALT+F and then enter the number for the file shown.

The following two steps will create a simple mask. (After completing these two
steps do not remove the image or its mask, because it will be used in the subsequent demonstration.)

1. Click and hold the left mouse button on the Mask Tool button in the
   toolbox. After one second, a flyout menu appears as shown in Figure 5.2.
   Release the mouse button (the flyout remains open) and click on the
   Rectangle Mask tool. The flyout disappears and the Rectangle Mask tool is
   now the visible button on the toolbox.

2. Move the cursor into the Image area. The cursor becomes a crosshair.
   Click at a point above and to the left of the jet and, holding down the
   mouse button, drag a rectangle ending at a point near the middle. (See
   Figure 5.4.) You have just created a simple mask. Notice that the outline of
   the mask is composed of a black-and-white line that seems to move. This is
   known as "marching ants" to Adobe Photoshop users. The color of the
   mask is used to differentiate it from other marquees used in PHOTO-
   PAINT.

Figure 5.4.
A simple mask created
by the Rectangle Mask
tool.

Corel NOTE!

Whenever a mask appears, a tiny icon appears in the lower right corner of the main screen. This informs the user there is a mask on the image. This tiny icon will save you a great deal of frustration once you train yourself to look for it. As a rule, we do not look for icons placed almost off the screen. I am working on a 17-inch, high-resolution monitor, and the icon is small; it must be a hoot to try and find on a 14-inch screen. Therefore, **make it a habit to look for the icon.**

This is important because when a mask has been placed on an image, it prevents any effect from being applied to the image *except to the area inside the mask.* Thus, if you have created a small mask or have zoomed in on a corner of the image and can't see the masked area, PHOTO-PAINT will not allow any effect to be applied to the image.

If you are unable to apply an effect to an image, check to see if the Mask icon is present. Even if you can't see the mask, the computer thinks it is there and will prevent you from applying any effect. Knowing this will save you time and money (for the cost of aspirin and tech-support calls).

The Properties of Masks

These four points summarize the general properties of masks:

- A mask "sits on top" of the image but is not part of the image.
- A mask does not contain any image information. (The only exception is a transparency mask.)
- A mask can be moved, rotated, distorted, node-edited, and even combined with other masks to achieve a desired effect.
- All masks are retained with an image when the image is saved as a PHOTO-PAINT image, or they can be saved separately as Masks.

A Quick Demonstration of Mask Properties

This work session will show how a mask works and will introduce some new PHOTO-PAINT commands. It requires the image and the mask created in the previous section, "Creating a Simple Mask." (Therefore, if you skipped it, go back and do it now.)

1. Click on the Edit menu and select Checkpoint from the dropdown list. This makes a temporary PHOTO-PAINT file of the image at this point in time. Since we have done this, we can return to this image anytime we want.

Corel *TIP!*

Get in the habit of using Checkpoint when you begin to work on an image. This is very important, because PHOTO-PAINT can only undo the most recent action. (Plus, because the image is saved to disk, it doesn't use up any system resources.)

2. Click on the Rectangle tool (not the Rectangle Mask tool!) in the toolbox or depress the F6 key.

3. Place the cursor in the upper left area of the image and, holding down the left mouse button, drag a rectangle that overlaps the mask. When the mouse button is released, the area within the mask floods with the current color and fill setting from the Fill roll-up. All of the area outside the mask remains unchanged, as shown in Figure 5.5.

Figure 5.5.
The flood fill color was only applied to the area inside the mask.

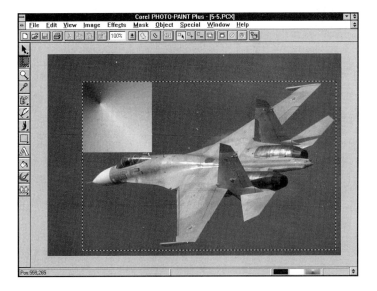

4. Click on the Mask Tools button until the flyout appears. Select the Mask Picker tool. When the picker is selected, the mask changes form. Eight control handles appear on the four corners and the sides. See Figure 5.6.

5. Placing the cursor inside the mask, click and drag the mask downward and to the right. Figure 5.7 is really ugly, but it is there to demonstrate a point. The mask moves, but the area that was filled with fill color does not. Why? Because the fill color is now part of the image. The mask has no color in it. It is like a stencil. If this were real paint, we could scrape away the fill color and the original image would be there. Unlike real paint,

bitmap colors do not cover over previous colors—they replace them. In this work session, the fill color replaced the color below it. Before we leave this session, let's clean up the mess we have made.

Figure 5.6.
The mask in this image is selected as indicated by the eight control handles. The mask is selected anytime the Mask Picker tool in the toolbox is active.

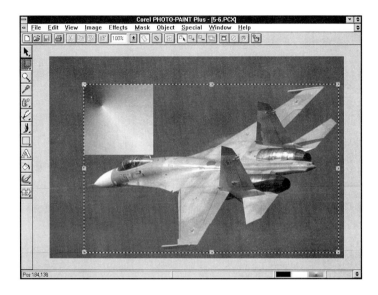

Figure 5.7.
In this figure, the mask is moved but the fill remains. This demonstrates the principle that the mask does not contain any bitmap information, and thus any color applied directly to the image remains on the image.

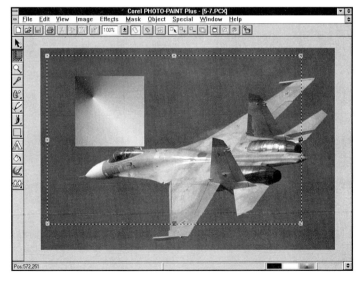

6. Remove the mask by clicking on the Remove Mask button in the ribbon bar. The mask buttons are only visible when a mask tool in the toolbox is selected. You can also remove a mask by selecting Remove in the Mask menu.

7. Restore the old image by selecting Restore To Checkpoint in the Edit menu. Did the mask come back? Remember, Checkpoint not only saves the images but any and all objects as well. Remove the mask again using the Mask Remove button in the ribbon bar.

The Basic Mask-Creation Tools

This section describes the basic mask-creation and mask-selection tools that are available in the toolbox.

The Rectangle Mask Tool

This is the tool you have already used in the quick demonstration. It is used for making square and rectangular masks. A mask is made by clicking and holding down the left mouse button and dragging until the desired shape is achieved. Holding down the Shift key produces a mask that increase or decreases proportionally from the starting point. Hold down the Ctrl key to constrain the mask to a square. The right mouse button has no effect in mask mode.

The Circle Mask Tool

The Circle Mask tool enables you to define oval or circular masks. A mask is made by clicking and holding down the left mouse button and dragging until the desired shape is achieved. Holding down the Shift key produces a mask that increase or decreases proportionally from the starting point. Hold down the Ctrl key to constrain the mask to a circle. The right mouse button has no effect in mask mode.

The Polygon Mask Tool

The Polygon Mask tool enables you to define polygonal shapes. This mask is one of several tools whose names have a tendency to mislead. It is a polygon tool. You need to be aware that the masks made by this tool are not restricted to geometrically shaped objects. Many irregularly shaped images can be masked effectively with this tool. To make a Polygon mask, click the left mouse button to anchor the starting point. Move to the next point, and click there. When you click the mouse button, a line is drawn from the last point to the cursor. A closed polygon now exists between the two points (the anchor and the second point) and the cursor. Moving the cursor continually reshapes the polygon based on the points placed and the current cursor position. If you accidentally place a point that is not where you want it to be, just use the Backspace key to remove the last point on the mask. Each successive Backspace continues to remove mask points until the starting point is reached. Holding down the Ctrl key when placing points constrains the angle of the next point to 45 degree increments. Double-clicking a point ends the last line and completes the mask. The right mouse button has no effect in mask mode.

Corel *TIP!*

Consider using the Polygon tool when creating a large and complicated mask, even if it doesn't have a single straight line in it . The advantage of the Polygon tool is the you can stop at any point and rest, whereas with the Freehand tool (discussed next), as soon as you let go of the mouse, the mask completes.

The Freehand Mask Tool

The Freehand Mask tool, like the Polygon tool, enables you to define irregular masks. Unlike the polygon mask tool, the sides are not straight lines but rather one continuous curve.

To create a Freehand mask, click and hold the left mouse button to anchor the starting point and drag the cursor around the image area to be masked. Releasing the mouse button completes the action. It is not necessary to return to the starting point before releasing the mouse button. PHOTO-PAINT will complete the mask by producing a line that is the shortest distance from the point of release to the starting point. The right mouse button has no effect in mask mode.

The Mask Brush Tool

The Mask Brush tool enables you to brush or paint the area to be masked. Instead of applying a color, you are applying a mask. The size and shape of the Mask Brush tool is set from the Tool Settings roll-up. The roll-up is accessed through the View menu or Ctrl+F8. To use the Mask Brush tool, position the cursor over the area to be masked, click the left mouse button, and drag the brush. Holding down the Ctrl key while dragging the brush produces a straight horizontal line. While the brush can be moved outside of the original horizontal line, it only has an effect on that horizontal line until the Ctrl key is released. For example, if the brush has a setting of a 10 pixels square, and you begin a line with the Ctrl key depressed, PAINT will protect every part of the image outside of a 10-pixel-wide straight line. So you could move the Brush tool all over the image and only produce a mask inside the 10-pixel horizontal line until the Ctrl is released. Holding down the Ctrl and the Shift keys produces the same effect, except in the vertical. This is one of the handiest tools in PHOTO-PAINT for doing touch up on masks.

Basic Mask Manipulation

Once a mask has been created. It can be rescaled, resized, rotated, distorted, deleted, saved, or even combined with other masks to make a compound mask. All mask manipulations use the Mask Picker tool from the toolbox. While a mask is being altered, information is continuously displayed in the lower left corner of the status bar. All of the commands and functions for the Mask tool also apply to object tools, which are explored in the next chapter. This section examines the way to control masks with a mouse and how the same mask can be controlled using the Tool Setting roll-up. This roll-up should look very familiar if you use CorelDRAW 5. In Draw, it is called the Transform roll-up. It is also called the Transform roll-up in the PAINT online help. Regardless of what it is called it still remains one of the many faces of the Tool Settings roll-up. The Tools Settings (Transform) roll-up provides precision mask manipulation, which is required for multiple operations on objects but has limited usefulness when used with masks. In the Mask section we will describe their function and exceptions. If you are looking for information on the operation and applications of this roll-up, proceed to the section on Objects.

Resizing and Scaling Masks

All of the masks can be resized (changing the size non-proportionally) or scaled (changing the size proportionally by percentage). The Mask Picker tool is used to resize masks. A mask is resized by dragging any of the four side-control handles. A mask is scaled by clicking and dragging one of the four corner control handles. When scaling a mask the opposite corner of the mask remains anchored and the size of the mask expands or contracts from that point. Holding down the Shift key while the mask is being scaled results in the mask shrinking or expanding from its center rather than from the anchor point. Holding down the Ctrl key while scaling limits the scaling to 100 percent increments. Holding down the Ctrl key while resizing (side-control handles) produces a mirror of the mask. The mirror is alongside the original mask position. (Are you bewildered yet?) See Table 5.1 for a list of the click-and-drag processes used to achieve different effects with Rectangle masks.

Table 5.1. Keyboard combination summary for Rectangle masks.

Operation	Click and drag point(s)
Scale with mask changing from center	Corner-control points with Shift key
Scale mask with far corner anchored	Corner-control handles
Make horizontal mirror	Left or right side-control handle with Ctrl key
Make vertical mirror	Top or bottom side-control handle with Ctrl key
Scale mask in 100 percent increments	Corner-control handle with Ctrl key
Resize mask	Any side-control handle

The lower-left status bar displays too much information for my liking. It reminds me of watching CNN news with the stock quotations floating across the bottom. That said, there is some valuable information in there buried among all of the rapidly changing digits: Position of Cursor (yawn) and Delta (width and height changes). It is the Delta values that tell you the size of the mask (in pixels) you create. When you are not creating masks, this information area shows the difference in the current units of measure of increase or decrease. Scale (in percentage) is a good one to watch as the mask is being scaled. All values displayed are in units of measure that are selected in Preferences under the Special menu.

A Scaling Work Session

The following exercise will introduce you to the way masks "feel." Ninety-nine percent of everything you do in PHOTO-PAINT will involve masks in one form or another. So doesn't it make good sense to learn how to use them?

1. Create a new image with a size of 300×300 pixels, 256-color capability, and 300-dpi resolution.

2. Select the Rectangle Mask tool in the toolbox.

3. Open the Tool Settings roll-up. Does it look right? It should say "This tool has no setting." Did I trick you? Yep! The Tool Settings roll-up didn't appear because (1) there is no mask; and (2) there is no tool setting for the Rectangle Mask tool. I did this for a reason. All of the user-defined mask tools are for the creation of masks and therefore have no Tool Settings roll-up associated with them. Now you know.

4. Create a square mask by clicking the left mouse button near the upper right corner and while holding down the Ctrl key drag it down to the right until you have a square mask that looks like Figure 5.9.

5. Select the Mask Picker tool in the toolbox. The Tool Settings roll-up changed so that it resembles Figure 5.8 and the mask is selected as indicated by the eight control handles.

6. Scale the mask to 50 percent of its original size as shown in Figure 5.10. Click on one of the corner control handles, hold down the Shift key and click and drag the corner in until the readout in the status bar displays 50%. If you make an error, undo the action by either selecting Undo in the Edit menu (the long way) or use Ctrl+Z. If you release the Shift key before the mouse button, the new square will be offset from the center.

7. Undo the Scale operation by selecting Undo (Ctrl+Z.)

This is all we are going to do with the Rectangle Mask tool for the moment. Keep this image open to learn the power of inverting and saving masks.

Figure 5.8.
This figure shows the
Mask Setting roll-up
with the Mask Scale
button selected.

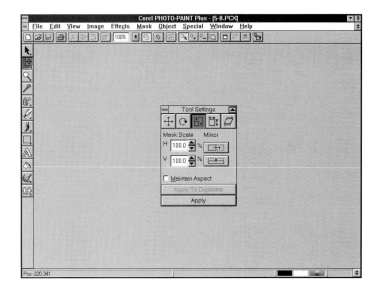

Figure 5.9.
A square mask made
by using the Rectangle
Mask tool and the Ctrl
(constrain) key.

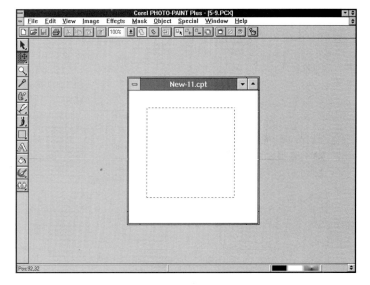

Precision Mask Scaling

For precision mask scaling, use the Tool Settings roll-up (Ctrl+F8) as shown in Figure 5.8 and select the Mask Scale Button. Values for Mask Scale are provided in percentage of original size. By clicking the Maintain Aspect checkbox, any changes in either the horizontal or vertical scale cause the value in the other scale to change proportionally. If you apply scaling to a mask, the upper-right corner of the mask becomes the anchor point, and the image is scaled to or away from that point. The Shift key option of expanding to and from the center is only available when scaling is done with the mouse.

Figure 5.10.
The same square scaled to 50 percent of its original size by dragging a control corner. Because the Shift key was depressed when it was scaled, the square mask shrunk towards its center.

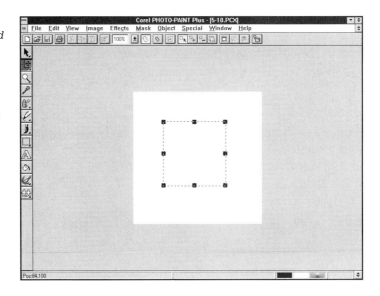

Two buttons enable the creation of horizontal or vertical mirrors of the mask. The icon on the button can be a little confusing. The icon on the button gives the appearance that the mirrored copy will be placed alongside the original. When the mirror button is applied, the original is removed and replaced with the mirrored copy in the exact position where the original was at. The mirrors can be applied individually or both at the same time. The Apply To Duplicate button in the Tool Setting roll-up is not available for masks, only objects.

Corel *TIP!*

When you make a horizontal or vertical mirror of a mask, you cannot Undo it.

Rotating and Skewing a Mask

All masks can be rotated and skewed. The Mask Picker tool is used to rotate and skew masks by clicking on the selected mask until rotation and skewing arrows replace the control handles on the mask, as shown in Figure 5.11. Grabbing a corner arrow and dragging it produces a rotation of the mask. The amount of rotation is shown in the lower-left status bar while the mask is being rotated. The point of rotation is determined by the location of the circle in the middle of the mask. Unlike in CorelDRAW, there are no constrain keys with Rotation. To change a mask's center of rotation, place the cursor over the point of rotation until the cursor becomes a crosshair symbol. Click and drag the rotation symbol to the desired position for the new rotation point. The point of rotation can be moved anywhere within the image area. The point of rotation does not have to remain inside the mask. (This last point will turn out to be one of the most important aspects of rotation. There will be a short work session to demonstrate this in the section on "Rotating Objects" of Chapter 6.)

Figure 5.11.
A mask with rotation
and skewing control
handles. Using these
handles, you can rotate
a mask around any
center of rotation, even
one that is off of the
image area.

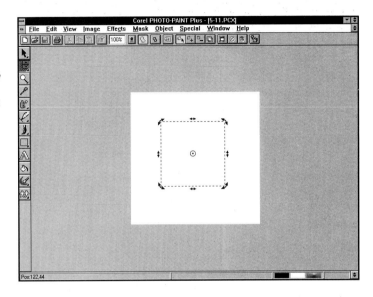

The mask can also be skewed by dragging any of the four arrows located on the sides of the mask. The status bar indicates the degree of skew as the mask is being skewed.

Corel *TIP!*

There is very little need to either rotate or skew masks, but these same processes apply to objects, which can achieve excellent 3-D appearances through skewing.

Precision Rotation and Skewing

Precision rotation and skewing is accomplished using the Tool Settings roll-up (Ctrl+F8). Figure 5.12 shows the Tool Settings roll-up with Rotation selected. The exact angle of rotation can be entered in increments as small as a tenth of a degree. The center of rotation displacement is entered in horizontal and vertical units. (The units used are determined by the settings in PAINT's Preference section.) The position of the center can be relative to the center of the mask if the Relative Center checkbox is selected. Otherwise it is an absolute value based on the distance from the upper-left corner of the image.

Use the Tool Settings roll-up for skewing (as shown in Figure 5.13) instead of the mouse when you want precise control over the amount of skew. Skewing is accomplished by selecting the Skewing button on the Tools Settings roll-up. Values are entered in degrees of horizontal and vertical skew. In both rotation and skewing, clicking the Apply button causes the mask transformation to occur.

Figure 5.12.
This figure shows the Tool Settings (Transform) roll-up with Mask of Rotation mode selected. By using this roll-up, it is possible to achieve the kind of precise control over multiple points of rotation that would otherwise be impossible.

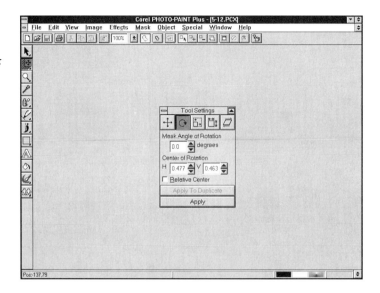

Figure 5.13.
The Tool Setting (Transform) roll-up with Skewing mode selected. By using this roll-up, it is possible to apply the same degree of skewing to multiple masks.

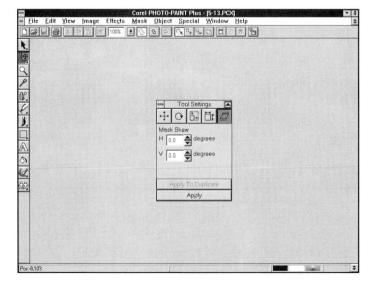

Distorting the Mask

The Distortion command enables you to select a mask and transform it into different shapes. This is different from the Node Edit tool that will be discussed later. The Distortion feature applies what could almost be called a "perspective" to the mask. To access the Distortion feature, click on the mask with the left mouse button and the rotation arrows appear. Click on the mask a second time and the Distortion arrows appear. Grabbing any of the arrows and dragging them to a new location will distort the mask as it fits the mask into position. As the arrow is being moved, the mask shape will move to show the new shape being created. This command and its counterpart in Objects provide an easy way to make very realistic three-dimensional effects and extrusions. (There is no precision command equivalent to Distortion.)

Corel *TIP!*

> There are no shortcuts to Distortion mode. You cannot double-click the mask; you must apply two single clicks. Once you are in Rotation or Distortion mode, the quickest way to return to normal selection is to click the Mask Picker tool in the toolbox.

Additional Mask Tool Setting (Transform) Commands

These commands are discussed in detail in the next chapter.

Placing Mask Mode
This is used to place masks on the base image at exact locations. This will become very handy when placing drop shadows under multiple text objects so that they all look like they are being illuminated by the same light source.

Mask Size Mode
Enables sizes of masks to be defined with digital precision.

Using the Mask Menu

All masks in Corel PHOTO-PAINT can be saved and reloaded. This is essential because (1) only one mask can be on an image at a time; (2) if you spend several hours creating a mask, it is nice to have a copy; and (3) it is a great way to copy the same size image area out of several different images. Any image that has a mask and is saved in PHOTO-PAINT format (*.CPT) will have its mask saved with it. The ability to save a mask apart from the image allows it to be loaded and applied to other images for special effects or accurate placement of objects or effects.

Saving a Mask

After a mask has been created, it can be saved by the following procedure. We are going to save the rectangular mask we made earlier.

1. Select the mask with the Mask Picker tool.

2. Choose Save from the Mask menu. The common Save an Image to Disk dialog box opens. See figure 5.14.

Figure 5.14.
The Save an Image to
Disk dialog box.

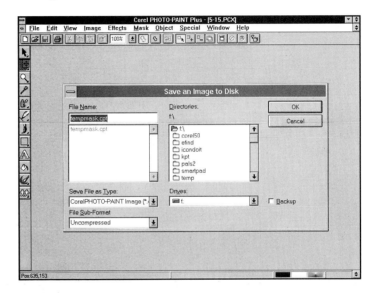

3. Name the mask TEMPMASK.CPT and click the OK button. The mask has been saved and can be recalled at a later time.

Notes about Saving Masks

When naming masks, try to create names that indicate it is a mask (e.g., MASKIMG.CPT or TREEMSK.TIF). Do not use a unique extension such as *.MSK for the mask. The three-character extension is used by PAINT and most other Windows applications to determine the correct import filter to use. Although the mask can be saved in any bitmap format (i.e. .PCX, .TIF, .BMP, etc.) it is recommended to save it in PHOTO-PAINT native .CPT format.

Loading a Mask

The Load Mask function allows a wide variety of image file formats to be loaded as masks. Loading a mask into an image involves the following procedure:

1. Select the image into which the mask is being loaded. This isn't a trivial step. If you have several images open on your screen, make sure that the one you want to load the mask into is active. If you load the mask into another image, the mask you load replaces any mask that the image may have had.

2. Choose Load in the Mask Menu. The Load a Mask from Disk dialog box opens. See Figure 5.15.

3. Select the file to be used for a mask. Notice the preview box in Figure 5.15. The mask is black outside and white inside. Click the OK button, and the mask will load into the image and the mask outline appears on the image.

Figure 5.15.
The dialog box that is used to load masks. Notice the mask in the preview box.

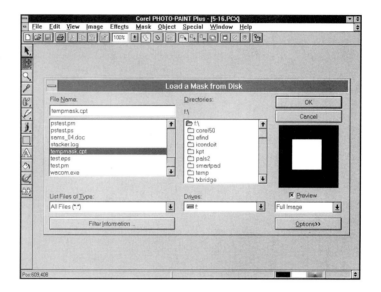

Some Suggestions about Loading Masks

Any image file can be used for a mask. I recommend that you only use genuine masks for masks. If you want to use a photograph or a vector drawing for a mask, then consider using a transparency mask, which is explained later in the book. Using non-mask files may give unpredictable results. The reason is that when a file is loaded as a mask, it is converted to a black-and-white (not grayscale) image. All shading disappears. In Figure 5.16 I have provided some examples of mask files. Using non-mask files to make masks can sometimes produce some neat effects, but it takes experimentation, because much of the process is not under your control (the conversion of the non-mask image to black-and-white, the scaling, etc.). I only recommend it to those who are looking for special effects and have lots of time on their hands.

Figure 5.16a.
The original Photo CD
from the Corel Clouds
collection.

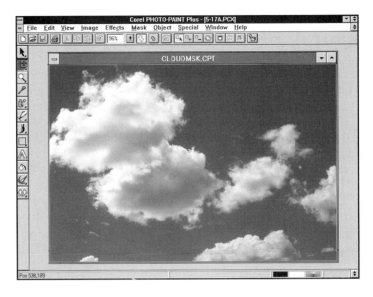

Figure 5.16b.
The mask made from
the image.

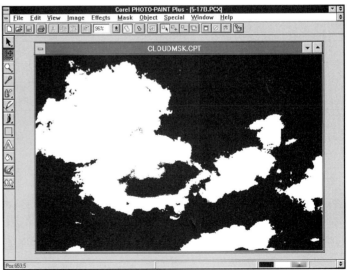

Figure 5.16c.
An example of what can be done with the resulting mask.

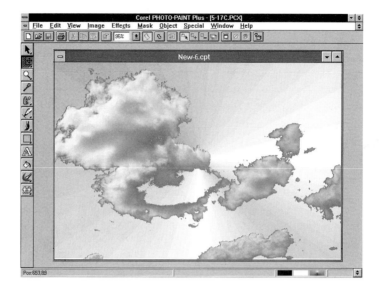

Figure 5.16d.
The mask of the jet in Figure 5.1.

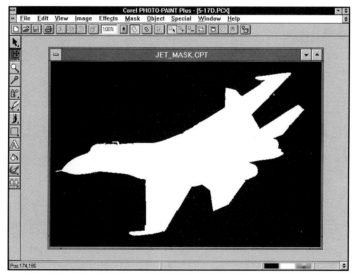

*Figure 5.16e.
Using the mask in
Figure 5.16d exten-
sively allowed the
creation of the image in
Figure 5.16e. The
intent was to make it
look as if the silhouette
of the jet was cut out of
some bristle board.*

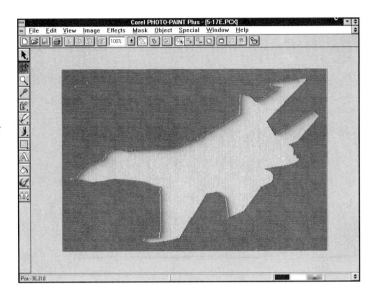

Removing a Mask

There are several ways to remove a mask. One of the quickest ways is to click
the Remove Mask button in the ribbon bar. One of the Mask tools must be
selected for the mask buttons in the ribbon bar to be available. The mask may
also be removed by selecting Remove in the Mask menu. A mask may also be
removed with the Del key if the mask is selected. The mask is selected whenever the Mask Picker tool is selected. (The mask will have control handles on it.)
If the mask is not selected, *the contents of the mask will be cleared when the
DEL key is depressed*. Therefore, use the Del key with caution.

Inverting a Mask

One of the more useful mask functions available is the Invert Mask command.
When a mask is created, the area inside the mask can be modified and the area
outside the mask is protected. The Invert Mask command reverses the mask so
that the area that was inside the mask now becomes protected and the area
outside can be modified. The Invert Mask command can be accessed through
the Mask Menu or by clicking on the Invert Mask button.

Suggestions About Using the Invert Mask Command

Some masks are so complex it is difficult to determine what part of the image
lies inside or outside the mask. A quick way to check is to select a brush and
paint across the area in question to see where the paint is applied. If it is being
applied in the wrong area, invert the mask. Immediately after applying the
paint, perform an undo (Ctrl Z) to remove the paint *before you invert the mask*.
Remember, PAINT can only undo the last action.

Mask All

To Mask the entire image, select the Mask All command from the Mask menu. The mask will encompass the entire image inside of the image window. If the image is only partially visible because you have zoomed into an area, the entire image is still masked. In this situation, you will not be able to see the entire mask. There are several shortcuts for the Mask All command: clicking the Mask All button in the ribbon bar, or double-clicking any of the basic Mask selection tools **Rectangle**, **Circle**, **Polygon**, or **Freehand** in the toolbox.

Using a Mask to Crop an Image

PAINT provides several methods to crop an image. The Crop command in the Mask menu is only one of them. To crop an image, perform the following procedure:

1. Using any of the Mask tools, make a mask that encompasses the area that is to be cropped.
2. Select the Crop command in the Mask menu. The area inside the mask is immediately copied into a new image. The original image is left unchanged.

Corel *TIP!*

While many word-processing and page-layout programs offer a Crop feature, it is always best to crop the image in PHOTO-PAINT. This is because the other programs maintain the original file size and only crop the display area. This results in very large files being sent to a printer, when only a small file was required. The printing will take much longer, and if it is too large it may not even print.

Making Complex Masks

We have discussed simple masks up until this point. In this section we will show another feature of Corel PHOTO-PAINT 5: the ability to create complex masks. A complex mask is one that is made up of several masks. It is the ability to combine several masks or types of masks into a single mask that enables the user to quickly create a very detailed and intricate mask. There are too many combinations of masks to describe each one, so you will have an opportunity to learn about them by working with some masks at the end of this chapter.

The Select Command

The Select command is the default mode of the mask tools. When it is selected, PAINT will only make simple masks. While the Select mode is active, all masks created are mutually exclusive. By that I mean, if a mask exists on the image, the creation of another mask will remove the existing mask. If one of the other buttons (Add To Selection, Remove From Selection, or XOR) is on, masks can be added to, subtracted from, or Exclusively OR'd (XORed). The Select command returns the mask tools to select mode after using the Add To Selection, Remove From Selection, or XOR commands.

The Select command is activated by clicking the Select button or by choosing Select in the Special menu.

Add To Selection Command

This command, in conjunction with the Remove From Selection command, provides a method to quickly add to or adjust an existing mask. The Add To Selection command adds areas to a mask. When this command is selected, it is possible to add to an existing mask. Where the area of mask being created intersects an existing mask, the masks are combined. When the areas do not intersect, they are still part of the original mask but in two separate areas. Regardless of the mask tool that created the mask, any tool can be used to add to the mask. The dimensions and shape of the area are determined by the new mask tool that is selected. The Add To Selection command is activated by clicking the Add To Selection button or by choosing Add To Selection in the Special menu.

Remove From Selection Command

This command, in conjunction with the Add To Selection command, provides a method to quickly "clean-up" and adjust an existing mask. The Remove From Selection command subtracts areas from a complex object or mask. The dimensions and shape of the area that is removed are determined by the mask or object tool that is selected. The Remove From Selection command is activated by clicking the Remove From Selection button or by choosing Remove From Selection in the Special menu.

Corel *TIP!*

If there is no mask on the image, make sure that the Remove From Selection button is not selected. Any attempt to create a mask with this button selected results in no action being taken by PHOTO-PAINT. You will get very frustrated until you figure out what is happening.

XOR Selection Command

This command, Exclusive OR, enables the creation of unique masks dependent on where multiple masks overlap. If the existing masks or objects and the new area do not overlap, the new area and the existing area are treated as one object or one mask and both can be manipulated. If the areas of the existing mask or object and the new one overlap, the XOR command isolates the areas in common and excludes the areas that the defined areas do not share. Only the common area can be manipulated. (This selection mode still baffles me. I know how it works, but for the life of me I can't figure out a single practical application for it. So, if you do, contact me on CompuServe.)

The XOR Selection command is activated by clicking the XOR Selection button or by choosing XOR Selection in the Special menu.

A Complex Mask Work Session

The following work session demonstrates how to use the various mask tools in combination to produce an image. It should take about 20 minutes to complete (give or take a month).

1. Create a new image with a size of 300×300 pixels, 256-color capability, and 300-dpi resolution.

2. Select the Rectangle Mask tool in the toolbox. Before doing the next step, set the Select button in the button bar on and make several masks. Notice that each time you make a mask, the previous one disappears.

3. Create a Square mask that is 0.5"×0.5" somewhere in the center of the image. Remember, to create a square with the Rectangle tool, you must hold down the Ctrl key while you drag the cursor. Read the size of the mask as you create it by watching the status bar on the lower-left side.

4. Select Checkpoint in the Edit menu. Wait a moment as the checkpoint copy is made.

5. Open the Fill roll-up (Shift+F6, or double-click the Fill roll-up color indicator in the lower-right status bar) and select the Texture Bitmap fill (the button next to the X on the top of the roll-up). The default setting of this mode should be Styles and Cosmic Clouds. This isn't critical; it is just what we use in this part of the work session.

6. Click on the Fill roll-up tool in the toolbox.

7. Click the cursor anywhere within the mask to fill it with the selected image. Try clicking outside the mask. The cursor turns into an hourglass for a moment, then nothing happens. This is because the only area in the image that can be modified is the part inside the mask. So, let's change that.

8. Select the Invert Mask button in the ribbon bar. Hey! Where is it? Sorry, I am being sneaky again. I am not trying to be a pain here—I am attempting to get you accustomed to how this program thinks. Have you figured out why the Mask buttons aren't there? It's because the Mask tool isn't selected. Select the Invert command in the Mask menu. This is always available as long as a mask is on the image. Why not change to the Mask tool to make the buttons appear? Because the ribbon bar is there to save steps. It would take longer to select a mask tool, click the button, and change back to the fill tool than it would take to select Invert in the Mask menu. (If you are really hell-bent on saving steps, next time try the keyboard sequence Alt+M+I—it's even faster.) Notice that the dashed lines that make up the mask now surround both the rectangle and the entire image area.

9. Select Fountain Fill in the Fill roll-up. While the default setting looks best, any fill will suffice. Click on the area outside the rectangle.

10. Select All in the Mask menu. The entire image becomes a single mask. If you want to see what your image looks like, Corel has provided a full-screen preview function. Just press F9 and you will see the entire image without the masks and all the other stuff on the screen.

Corel *TIP!*

> Full-screen preview is a good way to see what you are doing when working on images that use complicated masks. This is because, as you will learn in the next chapter, you can turn off the blue marquee that surrounds objects. You cannot turn off the marquee that makes up a mask.

11. Open the Effects menu. Select Mapping and choose Tile from the dropdown list. A filter preview box will open. (We won't be discussing filters for a while yet, but I thought it might be nice to make something interesting out of our mask session.) Enter a value of 3 in both data boxes and click OK.

12. (Optional) Save the image as a Windows bitmap named TILE.BMP. Save the image in your Windows subdirectory. Using the control panel (located in the Main folder), open the Desktop, and select TILE.BMP as your wallpaper. Select the Tile option button. If that doesn't wake you in the morning, nothing will.

13. Close the image and you're done.

In this chapter, we have covered a lot of information about masks. We will be doing some work sessions on compound masks in the next few chapters, after you understand objects. I suggest you get some coffee or soda and we'll move on to the next major topic.

Fundamentals of Objects and Layers

Before we can properly work with objects, we need to understand what they are and what makes them unique. To accomplish this, we must understand the fundamental differences between *bitmap* images and *vector* images. To help us, we are going to use an image from the Sampler Photo CD and a clip-art image from CorelDRAW 5.

The jet shown in Figure 6.1 is a bitmap (also called paint) image. We discussed bitmaps earlier, but the information bears repeating. The image that you see originally came from a photograph. There is only one layer to the image. While it appears to be a jet placed against a blue sky (background), it is actually composed of hundreds of thousands of tiny picture elements called *pixels*. To the computer, the jet and the background are all one image.

The jet shown in Figure 6.2 is a vector (also called draw) image. Like the bitmap, it looks like a single image, but in fact it is composed of over 146 separate elements, called *objects*. Figure 6.3 has been separated so that many of the objects that make it up can be seen. You probably noticed that the vector-based jet was in CorelDRAW while the other image was in Corel PHOTO-PAINT. DRAW is a vector-based program; PHOTO-PAINT is a bitmap-based program.

When an image is placed in a bitmap program, it becomes part of the image area. Traditionally with bitmap programs there is only one layer. If we were to take a brush from the Toolbox and draw a wide brush stroke across the entire bitmap image of the jet, every pixel the brush touches would change to the color set in the brush. If we then remove the brush color, the original image would not be there, because the brush color did not go on *top* of the original color—it replaced it. It is as if every pixel that is applied has crazy glue on it. When text is applied to an image, it "sticks" to the image and cannot be moved. This is why the Undo function can only "remember" what color(s) it replaced in the last action. Each Undo operation requires the entire affected image area to be replaced, a process which consumes vast amounts of system resources. Anyone who has spent hours and hours trying to achieve an effect will testify that the process by which bitmaps merge into and become part of the base image is the major drawback to bitmap-editing programs.

Figure 6.1.
A bitmap (also called paint) image. While to our eyes it appears to be a jet flying in the sky, to the computer the jet and the background are all one image.

Figure 6.2.
*A vector (also called
draw) image. It, like the
bitmap, looks like a
single image; it fact it
is composed of over 146
separate elements
called OBJECTS.*

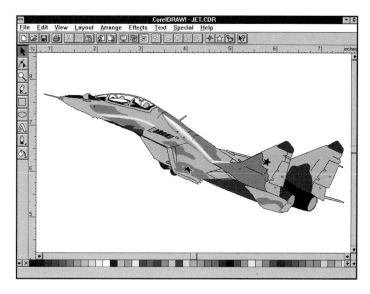

Figure 6.3.
*The image has been
separated so that many
of the objects that
make it up can be seen.*

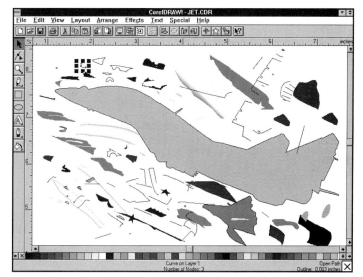

Corel *TIP!*

A solution to the single action Undo of Corel PHOTO-PAINT is to use the
Checkpoint command (which saves a temporary copy of the image to disk) and
constantly save your work to different files, so that you can quickly go back to a
previously saved version and change or correct it.

Bitmap merging is such a limitation that another solution had to be found. The solution first appeared in several applications around the same time. It showed up in a natural-media graphics program called X2 (an extension of Fractal Design's Painter) and in Micrografix's Picture Publisher. The solution was based on objects. Corel PHOTO-PAINT 5 has already incorporated object technology, and Adobe is on the verge of releasing Photoshop 3.0 with objects. So what is an object? Here is the official Corel definition:

An object is an independent bitmap selection created with object tools and layered above the base image. There are two types of objects: simple and complex. Simple objects are created using the object tools. Complex objects consist of a number of defined areas which are treated as one object.

Isn't that as clear as mud? I can't criticize the Corel documentation for the PAINT 5 Plus product (since I was the one who wrote it), so let me expand that definition. In PHOTO-PAINT, an object is a bitmap that "floats" above the base image. It is part of the base image in the same way all of the parts of the vector-based jet in Figures 6.2 and 6.3 are part of that image. Because it is not a part of the base image, but instead floats above the image, it can be scaled, resized, rotated, distorted, and moved as many times as needed without limit. In the original definition, reference was made to *simple* and *complex* objects. We are going to start by working with simple objects and work our way up to complex. Don't let the term complex give you a complex. It only refers to objects made up of several parts instead of one part. It should be called "compound," since it refers to an object made from several smaller objects, but I wasn't able to get the Corel people to change their minds on the subject.

Objects are neat, but if you have too many, they eat up system resources. (Remember that.) You are about to learn how to do some amazing things with objects. All of the rules that applied to masks in Chapter 5 also apply to objects. Since it would be redundant to repeat everything from Chapter 5, we will proceed with some technical work sessions to assist you in learning about objects.

Basic Object Creation and Manipulation

In this introductory demonstration, you will learn there are several ways to create objects: with the object-selection tools, by pasting in an image as an object, and by using the Cut and Paste commands with the Mask tools.

1. Open the APPLE.PCX file using the File Open button on the ribbon bar.
2. Click and hold the top button on the Toolbox until the flyout appears. (See Figure 6.4.) Select the Object Rectangle tool. You will notice that the tools for objects are identical to the tools used for masks. Don't get them mixed up. The object tools are for building and creating objects; the Mask tools

below it are for creating masks. Object-selection tools operate in a slightly different manner from the mask-selection tools, so we are going to spend some time in this demonstration using them both to give you a good understanding of the differences.

Figure 6.4.
The Object Selection
tool flyout.

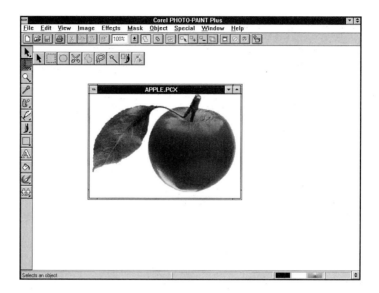

3. Ensure that the Activate/Deactivate Marquee button on the ribbon bar is on (depressed) and that the Build Mode button is in Simple mode. When Simple mode is selected, the button is up and has only one object on it. The Marquee button turns on the Object marquee when it is activated (depressed). The Build Mode determines if the objects being created are simple or complex (compound).

4. Starting near the upper left of the image area, click and drag the cursor to create a rectangle as shown in Figure 6.5. Did you notice that the marquee is blue? (This assumes that you haven't changed the system defaults in the Preferences section.) Blue tells you that the area defined by the marquee is an object. Notice that the object tool returned to the Object Picker tool as soon as you let go of the mouse button.

5. Position the cursor anywhere inside the object, click and hold the left mouse button, and move the object down a few inches as shown in Figure 6.6. What we have demonstrated is that when we created the object, PHOTO-PAINT made a copy of the area directly under the area defined by the rectangle . When we let go of the mouse button, it became an object. Because it is an object, we can move it around the image area, resize it, rotate it, flip it—almost anything we want, just like a mask. Unlike a mask, an object contains bitmap information. The object occupies its own layer at this point in time.

99

Figure 6.5.
A simple object created
with the Object
Rectangle tool.

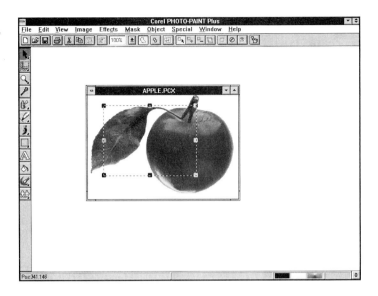

Figure 6.6.
Moving the newly
formed object shows
that the image under-
neath is unchanged.

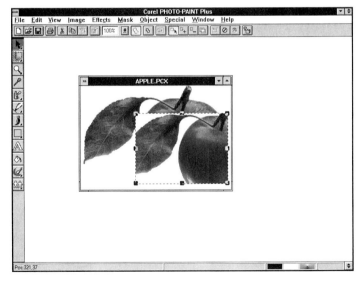

6. Click anywhere within the object, and drag the object out of the image
   area into the work area of the main screen. Don't let go of the mouse
   button until the cursor changes shape. When you release the mouse
   button, the bitmap information in the object is copied into a new image.
   (See Figure 6.7.) The new image is no longer an object but a separate
   bitmap image. Later in this demonstration we are going to learn to achieve
   some amazing effects with this feature.

Corel *TIP!*

Dragging objects out of the image area to create new images provides a quick and easy way to crop an image.

Figure 6.7.
Using the drag-and-drop capability of PHOTO-PAINT, we have created a new bitmap image from the object created in the preceding step.

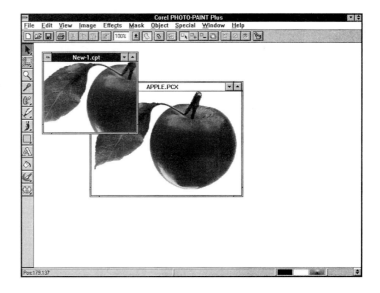

7. Close the newly created image by double-clicking its control panel. Select the No button when asked if you want to save any changes. Now, let us look at a different way to create an Object.

8. Select the Circle object tool from the Object Tool flyout.

9. Using the right mouse button, click and drag a circle anywhere over the apple in the image. Position is not critical—just get a circle over the apple. When you let go of the mouse button, the blue marquee circle indicates that you have created another object. It looks like the object made in Step 4, but there is a difference.

10. Using the left mouse button click and drag the object, and move it down and to the right of its original location. You should have a circular space where the apple used to be, as shown in Figure 6.8. What has this demonstrated?

    Using the left mouse button to create an object makes a copy of the image below it and places the copy in the object. The original image remains unchanged.

Using the right mouse button to create an object copies and removes (cuts) the image below it and places the copy into the object. The original image is altered.

To restore the cut image back into the image, select Undo from the Edit menu, or use the keyboard shortcut (Ctrl+Z or Alt+Backspace). Undo only returns the object to the precise location where it was before you moved it. While it looks like it has been restored, the object containing the removed (cut) bitmap information is still floating above the image. To restore the cut, select Merge from the Object menu. (The keyboard shortcut is Ctrl+G.) The bitmap image in the object will be merged back into the image, and the object will cease to exist. Try it out. After you have done it, we'll finish up this session.

Figure 6.8.
The results of object
creation made with the
right mouse button.

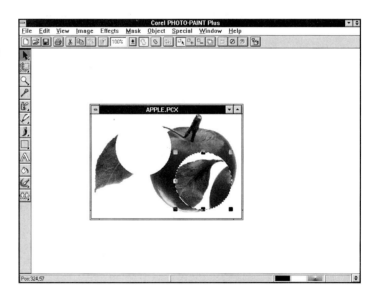

11. Close APPLE.PCX by double-clicking the control menu in the upper-left corner of the image window. Select No when asked to save changes. So now you have made a simple object. In the next demonstration, we will work with a few more tools and make some interesting objects

Advanced Object Creation and Manipulation

In this session you will be introduced to the Magic Wand and the Layers/Object roll-up, plus a few other tools. You will learn to create an object with the Cut command and how to use the Drawing mode of the Layers/Object roll-up to selectively apply effects to objects. The project is a simple one. The former Soviet Union is holding an air show. They have a very limited budget and need you to make a nice postcard for it. Unfortunately, they only have one picture of a single MIG jet, and it is decided that the postcard needs two. One top of all that, the sky is too dark and needs to be enhanced or replaced. Sound tough? It's a walk in the park.

1. Open the JET.CPT file provided on the CD-ROM.

2. Select Color Tolerance in the Special menu. This action opens the Color Comparison Tolerance dialog box shown in Figure 6.9. This dialog box sets the parameters that the Magic Wand tool uses in making a mask. Make sure the Identical Values checkbox is selected, and enter a value of 25 in one of the boxes. All of the other boxes should then have the same value. Click the OK button. (In case you were wondering, I came up with the value of 25 by trying several different settings with the Magic Wand tool; 25 worked the best.)

Figure 6.9.
This dialog box is used to give information to the Magic Wand tool, which it uses in creating a mask.

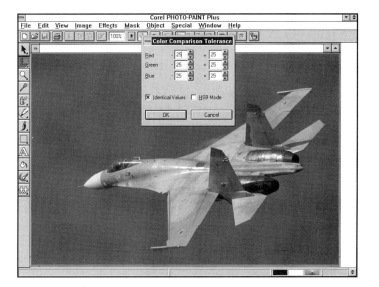

3. Select the Magic Wand Mask tool from the Mask Selection flyout of the Toolbox.

4. Click anywhere in the blue area of the sky with the Magic Wand Mask tool. You will get your best results if you click in the upper-left corner of the picture. Not too long ago, it was necessary to carefully build a mask around an image with a mouse or stylus by tracing the edge of the subject in the image. It was tedious work. Then came the Magic Wand tool, which allows the computer to define the mask for you by looking for adjacent pixels with similar colors. By clicking on the blue area with the Magic Wand tool, the mask expands until it surrounds all of the blue area as indicated by a black and white marquee as shown in Figure 6.10.

Figure 6.10.
With proper settings in
the Color Tolerance
dialog box, the Magic
Wand tool was able to
produce an almost
perfect mask of the jet.

Corel *TIP!*

If the mask doesn't look like Figure 6.10, simply remove the mask by clicking on the Remove Mask button in the ribbon bar and try again at a slightly different point. For its starting point, the Magic Wand uses the color value of the pixel under the cursor at the time it is clicked. Different starting points produce different masks.

5. To make the project in this demonstration, we need a mask that surrounds the jet and only the jet. What we have now is a mask that surrounds the background and some other things. So, before we do anything else, let's clean up the mask a little.

    Click on the Add To Selection button in the ribbon bar. We need to add to the mask created by the Magic Wand tool. This adding and subtracting can get confusing. Keep in mind what the mask is surrounding. In this case, the mask is surrounding the blue sky background. To get the little cloud in front of the right wing, we need to add it to the existing mask. (If you're still confused, just follow the directions and it will make sense. Really.)

6. Open the Mask tool flyout and select the Mask Brush tool. When the Mask Brush tool is selected, the cursor changes to the size and shape of the currently selected brush. Open the Tool Settings roll-up (Ctrl+F8) and change it to a round shape and a size of 20.

7. With the Mask Brush tool, paint over the small cloud until the mask comes even with the wing, as shown in Figure 6.11. When working with masks, you sometimes need to get in close to the area you are working on. The quick way to do this is to hold down the Z (for "zoom") key. As long as the Z key is depressed, the cursor is a magnifying glass. Continuing to hold down the Z key and the left mouse button, drag the magnifying-glass cursor over the area to be zoomed. A rectangle is created. Release both keys and wait for a moment as the image area is refreshed on the screen. Figure 6.12 shows what the little cloud looks like when we zoom in on the area. When finished with the mask, click the F4 (Zoom to Fit) key, and the image returns to its original zoom ratio.

Figure 6.11.
The mask now includes the little cloud in front of the jet wing.

Figure 6.12.
This exclusive close-up
of the little cloud is
brought to you through
the courtesy of the
Zoom tool. Learning to
use the Zoom tool will
enable you to produce
accurate masks, even
with a mouse.

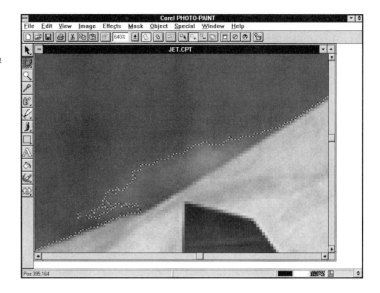

8. Click the Subtract From button in the ribbon bar. Using the Mask Brush tool remove the parts of the mask that are on the tail section of the jet. You probably won't need to zoom in to do this but if you do, use the same technique described in Step 7. At this point we have masked all of the sky. Since we need to make an object out of the jet we need to invert the mask.

9. Click the Invert Mask button in the ribbon bar or select Invert from the Mask menu. (It is the button that looks like the yin/yang symbol.) The mask has been inverted (or reversed), making the jet image selected and the background no longer selected. (See Figure 6.13.) The mask is still black-and-white, so we know that it is a mask and not an object. (Also, don't forget you can check the Mask icon in the lower right corner of the screen). From here, we will use the mask to make an object.

10. Select Checkpoint from the Edit menu. The progress bar indicator moves quickly across the bottom of the work area, indicating that a file has been made. No matter what happens to the image, we can always return the image to this point in time.

Figure 6.13.
The result of inverting
the mask. Now it is the
jet that is masked, and
the background is
protected.

Corel *NOTE!*

The file that Checkpoint creates is a PHOTO-PAINT file with a *.TMP extension. This is good to remember in case your system locks up and you must reboot out of Windows. To recover this file, you must first locate it, which is no easy task, since it could be in one of several directories. (Check the system TEMP directory, the TEMP directory used by Corel that you defined during installation, and then anywhere else.) Then, rename it with a *.CPT extension *before* restarting Corel. The reason for doing it before restarting Corel is that the Checkpoint file is automatically deleted whenever an image file is closed. When Corel starts up, it does housekeeping and looks to see if there are any stray *.TMP files that were left open (which would happen in a system lockup), and then promptly erases them.

11. Click the Cut button in the ribbon bar. The image disappears and the mask is gone, as shown in Figure 6.14. If you were to undo the Cut command, the image would return but the mask would be lost. PHOTO-PAINT can only undo the last action. When the Cut button is selected, the computer carries out two actions. It removes the mask and cuts the image, putting it into the Windows clipboard. If you use the Cut command, the mask will be lost. (This is not true of the Copy or Clear commands.)

Figure 6.14.
When the Cut com-
mand is used, the
masked object is copied
into the Windows
clipboard, the masked
area is removed from
the image, and the
mask itself is removed.

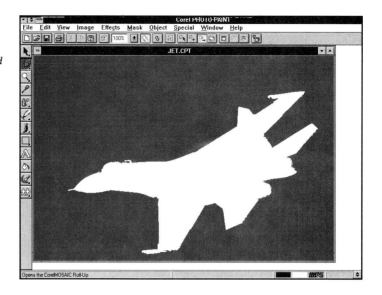

Corel TIP!

When using the Clipboard to make objects, remember that the contents of the Clipboard are stored in RAM memory, not on the disk drive. Therefore they consume system resources. In this example, putting the jet into the Clipboard reduces available memory by 718KB. Later, I will show you a way to make an object without the Clipboard.

12. Select Paste from the Edit menu. Another dialog box appears, offering a choice of pasting as a new image or as a new object. Select New Object. The image of the jet returns, with several differences. The color of the marquee is now blue (the system default), indicating it is an object, the Mask icon is no longer in the status bar of the main screen, and the whole thing looks really ugly. (See Figure 6.15.)

13. Open the Layers/Objects roll-up (Ctrl+F7). At the bottom of the roll-up, there should be two buttons with tiny images (thumbnails) on them.

Now is as good a time as any to learn about the Layers/Objects roll-up. (See Figure 6.16.)

First of all, the name is confusing: Layers/Objects. In PHOTO-PAINT 5, you work with objects. Each layer can contain one object. Instead of referring to Layers/Objects, the name of the roll-up should simply be Objects. (OK, I feel better now.)

The bottom portion of the roll-up is called the Drawing mode. No one knows why Corel chose this term. This has nothing to do with drawing. Each button on the bottom represents an object in the image. The far-left button is not an object. It is the base image. In the roll-up shown in Figure 6.16, there is a base image (the button on the left) and an object (the button on the right). The Layers/Objects roll-up is explored in greater detail in the next work session.

Figure 6.15. Because the image of the jet was made into an object using the "cut and paste" procedure, the resulting object is slightly offset from the original position

Figure 6.16. When you open the Layers/Objects roll-up, you are presented with a wide variety of controls for the objects.

14. Click the button containing the jet in the Drawing Mode section of the Layers/Objects roll-up. The button raises up (becoming lighter), and the jet disappears from the image. (See Figure 6.17.) What we did was to "hide" the object. At this point, no matter what effects are applied to the base image, it will not affect the object that is hidden. This is a very important principle to understand when working with PHOTO-PAINT.

If you can see any part of the image, any effects you apply will be applied to that part of the image. An image you can't see will not have effects applied to it.

Figure 6.17.
Using the Drawing
Mode controls, we
were able to "hide" the
object containing the
image of the jet.

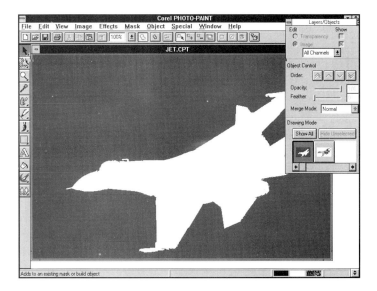

15. Select All from the Mask menu, and then select Clear from the Edit menu. The sky is now all gone and you have an empty background. Jets need a sky in order to look realistic, so we are going to quickly make one. (In the next chapter we will explore the Fill tools more thoroughly; for now, just follow the steps.)

16. Open the Fill roll-up (Shift+F6), and click the Texture Fill button. (It is between the buttons that look like a checkerboard and like an X.) The Library box should be set to Styles. (If it isn't, change it to Styles by clicking the arrow on the right side of the box and selecting it.) In the bottom box, use the down arrow and select Sky 2 Colors.

17. Select the Fill Tool (the bucket) from the Toolbox and click anywhere in the white image area. It will take a few moments to generate the sky, so be patient. Now you have some sky for the jet. Please note that if we had not hidden the jet, the jet would now be covered with blue sky as well. This is great for camouflage, but not good for pictures.

18. Click the Show All button in the Layers/Objects roll-up. (We also could have simply clicked the Object button.) We now have a jet in the sky. To see the image without the clutter of the Corel PHOTO-PAINT screen, depress the F9 key.

Corel *TIP!*

> If the full-screen preview doesn't work when you press the F9 key, you probably have a roll-up active instead of the image. If so, just click the image and try again.

To return to the PHOTO-PAINT screen, depress the Esc key. The edges look a little ragged, so let's clear it up. It is difficult to see the edges of the jet with the marquee on, so select the Marquee Activate/Deactivate button on the ribbon bar and switch it off.

19. Enter a value of 2 in the Feather value box. The result should now look like Figure 6.18. There is a lot to say at this point. First, the Feather function in Corel PHOTO-PAINT is good but slow. So the hourglass will stay with you longer than you might imagine. Next, we have asked it to feather the image for a distance of 2 pixels from the center. The smaller the image, the greater the effect of the feathering. For example, if an image is only 20 pixels in diameter, 2 pixels represents 10 percent of the image perimeter. If an image is 200 pixels in diameter, the same setting of 2 pixels only represents the outer 1 percent. Finally, notice that I didn't have you use the slider. Feel free to do so. However, the slider is an ineffective way to enter the values. For those who want to directly enter in the data values (this applies to almost every data-value box in PHOTO-PAINT), double-click the value and it becomes highlighted. Enter the value you want. To make small changes to the value, use the up or down arrow keys on your keyboard.

20. Select the Object Picker tool. The object now becomes selected, as indicated by the control handles that appear around the marquee. If there had been more than one object, the Picker tool should have been used to select individual objects, or it is possible to cycle through all of the objects using the Tab key.

*Figure 6.18.
By applying a small
amount of feathering to
the object containing
the jet image, we were
able to remove the
rough edges.*

21. Select Duplicate from the Object menu. (The shortcut is to use Ctrl+D.) You now have two jets, as shown in Figure 6.19. The duplicate is offset slightly from the original. If we had wanted it exactly on top of the original, we could have used the Transform Tool setting roll-up. Notice there are now two buttons containing thumbnails of jets in the Drawing Mode section of the Layers/Objects roll-up. We want to work on the duplicate jet. To do this, we must hide the original. Click on the far-right Object button in the Drawing Mode section. The duplicate jet disappears and its button raises. Remember that the order of the object buttons is from bottom to top, left to right. So our duplicate jet is represented by the far-right button.

22. Selecting the Object Picker tool, grab the upper-left control handle of the remaining jet. While holding down the Shift key, drag the control handle down until the scale in the lower status bar reads 50 percent. Release the left mouse button before you release the Shift key. You will see a rectangle formed as you rescale the object. When you release it, you will experience a few moments of the hourglass. Please be patient—PHOTO-PAINT is resampling the image. After a few moments (the amount of time varies with system horsepower, RAM, etc.), the progress-bar indicator will move across the bottom, indicating the progress of the object resampling. The image is now 50 percent of its original size, as seen in Figure 6.20.

    Holding down the Shift key when you scale an object (using the corner control handles) maintains the aspect ratio and scales from or to the center of the object.

    Holding down the Ctrl key when scaling an object (using the corner control handles) also maintains the object's aspect ratio, but it only allows the object to be scaled in even multiples (i.e., 100 percent, 200 percent, etc.).

*Figure 6.19.
Seeing double? By
using the shortcut key
command, we can
quickly duplicate
our jet.*

*Figure 6.20.
Although we could
have used the Tool
Settings roll-up to scale
the object, we took a
shortcut and scaled the
original object to 50
percent of its original
size by using the
control handles.*

23. Using the same Object Picker tool, move the smaller jet up and to the right, as shown in Figure 6.21. Notice that part of the object is no longer in the picture. You haven't lost any of the object; it is just off of the viewing area. Since this jet is in the background, we will make it a little lighter than the original jet. Enter a value of 90 in the Opacity value box. Remember how I told you Opacity was fast? It is slower when it must deal with feathered objects.

Figure 6.21.
The new position for
the duplicate jet.

24. Click the Show All button in the Layers/Objects roll-up. The original jet appears, and we have a nice photo of two jets in formation. (See Figure 6.22.) Now we are almost done.

Figure 6.22.
Both objects (each
containing an image of
the jet) "unhidden."

25. When working with photographic images, the juxtaposition of two identical images can look unrealistic. To make it more realistic, we will alter the background jet just a little.

    Click on the background jet (the smaller one) to select it. You can tell it is selected by the control handles surrounding it. Open the Tool Settings (Transformation) roll-up by using Ctrl+F8, and select the Rotation button (the curved arrow). Enter a value of -6 degrees and click the Apply button. The background jet is now rotated slightly. For a final touch, increase the feathering on the background jet to 4. Figure 6.23 shows the end result.

Figure 6.23.
We have created two jets and provided a brand new sky. Not bad for only 25 steps.

26. Save this image using the Save As command in the File menu. Name the file JET_2.CPT. We will use it again in a moment.

Corel *TIP!*

> When the image is saved as a PHOTO-PAINT file, all layers, objects, and masks of the image are preserved. When the image is saved as a bitmap image, such as a TIFF, PCX, or GIF format, PHOTO-PAINT displays a warning message that all of the layers/objects will be merged into the image. All layers and masks will be lost.

Options of the Layers/Objects Roll-Up

The Layers/Objects roll-up controls the placement of objects. You can also use it to isolate individual objects and apply effects; flip, invert, outline, rotate, or distort.

Edit Section

Transparency	Click on the Transparency radio button to edit a Transparency mask. You must have already created a Transparency mask in order for this option to be enabled. You can use the effects and paint tools to edit the transparency. (Transparency masks and the use of this feature are described in later chapters.)
Image	Click on the Image radio button to edit the image. By default this is checked, and it should be kept that way most of the time.
Show	Click the Show checkbox beside Transparency and/or Image to make them visible or invisible. If the checkbox is checked, the transparency and/or image is visible.
Channel Selection	Located at the bottom of the Edit section, the Channel Selection box allows you to edit specific channels by selecting them from a drop-down list box. The ability to view and work on individual channels did not seem very useful to me at first. However, I later discovered several good uses for it. In the advanced chapter on the Magic Wand tool, you will learn a way in which this selection box can put more magic into the Magic Wand. The channels available for selection depend on the color mode selected. For most color schemes, the selections are: red, blue, green and all channels. The channels can be displayed in color if you have a monitor that can display at least 256 colors. Use the Tint Channels checkbox in the General Section of the Preferences dialog box to display the channels in color. For example, you can have the preview display a red tint when you are in the red channel.

Object Control Section

The Object Control section of the Layers/Objects roll-up allows you to order the objects in your image, set the level of opacity, and set the feathering level. The Object buttons in this section are fairly self-explanatory. The first button places an object on top of all others. The second moves objects up one layer. The third moves objects down one layer, and the fourth places objects at the bottom (closest to base image).

Next are two sliders: Opacity and Feather. Opacity is the opposite of Transparency. 100 percent Opacity = 0 percent Transparency. Moving the Opacity slider controls the amount of opacity that the object has. At a 10 percent Opacity setting, the object is ghost-like. The action of this slider is pretty immediate.

Merge Mode

This is an incredibly powerful feature that was not included in the original release of PHOTO-PAINT 5. If you are a registered user (you are, aren't you?), you will have received the "B" release, which includes this feature.

The Merge Mode controls how the pixels in each layer/object will interact with the other layers below it. Each layer has its own Merge Mode settings. When you look at the drop-down list, you will find 17 possible modes for color, or 14 for grayscale. Corel choose to use the correct technical term to describe each of the modes, which unfortunately doesn't make what they do very clear. But before you think they are a bunch of bums for doing it that way, I would like to make two points. First, an alternative to the technical naming convention is a descriptive one, such as that used by Kai's Power Tools. Which of these two names best describes the effect: Logical AND, or Flaming Blue Dinner Napkins? This brings up the second point.

The effect of each mode is so interdependent on the other layers, colors, opacity, and feathering that there is no good way to describe any of them. But don't get discouraged. The folks at Corel included a nice preview feature. With the object selected, pick a Merge Mode from the drop-down list. The object in the image area now displays the effect of the Merge Mode setting. To change the settings, use the up or down arrows on your keyboard. Each time you click the arrow key, you move up or down to the next setting, and the image redisplays accordingly. Slick stuff.

Drawing Mode Section

Click the buttons to display or hide the objects in the image. If the number of objects is over three, use the scroll bar to view the other objects. Depressing the buttons displays the objects. You can have all or any combination of the objects displayed or hidden. The first button represents the base image. Effects can be applied to objects using the Drawing mode. Isolate the object you want to apply the filter to, and choose the effect from the Effects menu. The channels of selected objects can be edited using Drawing mode.

Show All	Clicking this button selects all of the layers. It is the same as depressing all of the buttons in the Drawing Mode section. It "unhides" all of the objects and the base image. It provides a quick way to select all of the buttons.
Hide Unselected	Clicking this button hides every layer/object except the one that is selected.

Corel *TIP!*

Hide Unselected is a quick way to determine which object is selected. This may not seem like much when there is only one object, but when you have multiple objects, one on top of another, it is very handy.

Each time an object is created, it is placed on it own layer. Only one object can occupy each layer. As each object is created, it appears as a square button with a thumbnail of the object in it. When the button is depressed, the layer/object in the image is displayed; when it is clicked again, the button comes up and the layer/object is hidden. If the number of objects exceeds three, then you can use the scrollbar to view all of the objects in an image. The object layers have thumbnails displayed on them so that you can see visually what is on each layer. Be aware that the buttons may not always be displaying the correct thumbnail immediately after a change is made to a layer.

Working with Layers

In this work session, we will use the Text tool and Layers/Objects roll-up to complete the postcard (and get paid before the ruble devaluates further).

Corel *TIP!*

Always insist in being paid in U.S. dollars for projects that are done in the U.S. No joke!

1. Open the file jet_2.cpt.

2. Click on the Text tool in the Toolbox. (It looks like the letter A.) When you open the Text tool, several new settings appear in the ribbon bar.

3. In real life, I would probably use a bold square font such as Futura, but we will use Times New Roman since it comes with Windows. Select Times New Roman from the Font drop-down list in the ribbon bar. Pick a font size of 24 from the font-size drop-down list, click the Bold button (marked B), and make sure the Left Alignment button is selected.

4. Click the cursor near the upper-left corner of the image and type in "Air Show '95". In case you were wondering how I got the opening single quote in front of the 95 (instead of the foot-measurement mark), I used a keyboard combination of holding down the Alt key while entering in the number 0146. Where did I get the number? In this case, I remembered it from my Pagemaker days.

Corel *TIP!*

When you don't know the Alt keyboard combination for a number, open the Character Map program in the Accessories menu and find the character in the selected font list. By selecting the desired character from the visual map, the keyboard combination appears in the lower right corner.

5. Click on the Object Picker tool. The text will turn into an object (as indicated by the blue marquee, if you haven't turned it off). Use the picker to move the text into the upper left corner as shown in Figure 6.24.

6. Ensure the text is the object selected and duplicate the text using Ctrl+D. The duplicate text (top layer) should be selected (if it is not already selected) by clicking on it. Using the Layers/Objects roll-up, hide the duplicate text object. (It is the button on the extreme right in the Draw Mode section.)

Corel *TIP!*

Since it is sometimes difficult to determine which object is actually selected when they are close together, use the Tab key to move the selection between the objects.

Figure 6.24.
In making the postcard, we have applied some text, which is now an object that can be moved, scaled, or rotated as required.

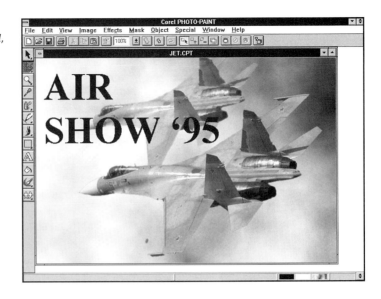

7. Select the remaining text and in the Layers/Objects roll-up enter a Opacity value of 20 and a Feather value of 1 for the selected text. (If you have the correct text object selected, it will be the top object button that is depressed. All of the other buttons, with the exception of the base image, will be hidden.) This is the down-and-dirty way to make shadows. (Later I will show you how to make great shadows with the Gaussian Blur filter.)

9. Click on the original text button (second from the top) in the Layers/Objects roll-up. It should now be selected, and you now have two text objects in view, as shown in Figure 6.25. Look closely at either your monitor or the figure in the book. It appears that the text to which we applied the 20 percent opacity is behind the black text. Actually, the faded text is on top; it just doesn't show at this point. Click the Down One Layer button. The shadow text is now behind the black text. Nothing appears to have changed, but it did.

10. Turn off the shadowed text by clicking off its button (second from the right) in the Layers/Objects roll-up.

11. After ensuring that the text is selected (with the Object Picker), open the Tools Settings (Transform) roll-up. Select the Object Position button (far-left button). Click the Relative Position checkbox and click Apply To Duplicate. We have now created a duplicate object that is precisely placed on top of the original. Because it is exactly on top of the original, nothing appears to have changed. If you look at the bottom of the Layers/Objects roll-up, you will notice that another button has appeared in the Drawing Mode section.

Figure 6.25.
It appears that the text
to which we applied
the 20 percent opacity
is behind the black
text.

12. Open the Fill roll-up (Shift+F6) and click the Uniform Fill button (far-left button). Click in the color preview square, and a palette opens. Select purple (the first purple near the top). You may call it violet, but to me it's purple.

13. Using the Layers/Objects roll-up, turn off (hide) the top text object. (It is the last duplicate we made.) Use the Object Picker to select the remaining text, and then click the Hide Unselected button. Everything but the middle layer of text should be gone. If you can't see the text against the black background, then turn on the marquee by clicking the Marquee Active/ Deactivate button.

14. Select the Rectangle tool (not the Rectangle Mask tool but the one above the Text tool). Drag a large rectangle that covers all of the text. If you don't get it right the first time, you don't have to Undo it; just do it over. If you have a black border that appears, then use the Tool Settings roll-up to set the border width to 0. You should now have text filled with purple.

15. Using the Layers/Objects roll-up, hide the purple text and select (unhide) the top text object.

16. Repeat steps 12 and 14, except use yellow instead of purple. You now have a shadow text, a purple text, and on top you have a yellow text. Make sure all of the objects are "unhidden" by clicking the Show All button.

17. Select the top text (yellow) with the Object Picker, or click the Tab key until it is selected. In the Layers/Objects roll-up, give it a setting of 100 percent Opacity, a Feather of 6, and a Merge mode of Logical XOR. The feathered yellow text gives a neon glow when it is XOR merged with the purple text behind it. Figure 6.26 shows what it should look like at this point. As an experiment, use the arrow keys to move the Merge Mode selector up and down.

Figure 6.26.
The feathered yellow text gives a neon glow when it is XOR merged with the purple text behind it.

18. Use the Object Picker tool to move the shadow text so that it is just below and to the right of the top two text objects. Click the Show All button in the Layers/Objects roll-up. Now the job needs one more thing to be finished.

19. Using the Text tool, type the word "Moscow" (Arial, 18 point, bold) and place it in the lower-right corner. Select the Moscow text and set Opacity to 100 percent, Feather at 1, and the Merge mode as Green. The Green merge means that only the contents of the Green channel in the background image will be summed with the foreground image. See Figure 6.27 for the finished product. Collect your rubles quickly.

Figure 6.27.
Your postcard is
complete.

Building Complex Objects with Object Tools and Masks

Before we can do any more advanced work with selection tools, we need to have a more complete understanding of simple and complex objects. Corel PHOTO-PAINT 5 has introduced some powerful new ways to handle bitmap images as objects, and the better we understand the way they operate, the more we can do with PAINT.

When you have the Build Mode button in Simple mode, each time you define an area with an object selection tool, you have a simple object. If the object created isn't what you wanted, the only solution is to delete it and start over. In the early days of photo-editing programs, that was the way it went. It was very difficult to mask around a complicated image. If you worked with a mouse instead of a stylus, it was almost impossible.

These simple objects are generally used for the quick creation of objects that are not complicated or detailed. Many times when you are working with images, you will want to grab a big chunk of sky or some other background from a photo. The object isn't complicated at this point because it is going to be further modified later. When the Simple Object mode is used, as soon as the mouse button is released (with the exception of using the Polygon tool), the object is created. There is no turning back. For detailed images to become objects, it is necessary to have a way to make objects in the same manner that we make complex masks. PHOTO-PAINT provides a way to make an object using several steps and tools.

To make a complex object, you must select the Complex Object mode with the Build Mode button on the ribbon bar. PHOTO-PAINT allows you to create and modify what area that will become an object, and when it is the way you want it, make it into a object with the press of a button.

Creating Complex Objects Using Build Object Mode

This session will involve a few simple exercises to acquaint you with the concept of building objects and manipulating those objects. Many times in photo-editing, you will need to modify an existing picture. With this session, it has been decided by the client that the apple needs two leaves instead of one. By creating, scaling, and rotating a simple object with the Lasso tool, we will do what Mother Nature didn't. You will also be introduced to the preview window and the Gamma filter from the Effects menu.

1. Open the APPLE.PCX file.

2. Click the Build Mode button on the ribbon bar to select Build Object mode (three objects on the button).

3. Select the Lasso object tool from the Object flyout in the Toolbox. Beginning outside of the leaf area, hold down the left mouse button and draw a line completely around the leaf, including a portion of the stem. This step is a little tricky and may take some time to get it right. If you find the line you are creating has a mind of its own at times, don't worry. It happens to all of us at one time or the other. If the mask you have doesn't look like the one in Figure 6.28, then use the Delete key (to remove it), select the Lasso tool once more (the object tools always return to the Picker tool when the button is released), and try again.

   Notice where the object marquee crosses the stem of the leaf in Figure 6.28. Try to make your selection marquee cross at around the same point. The dashed lines surrounding the leaf are now red. At this point, any adjustment to the mask can be made by using any of the object tools. The lines form a Build Object mask—which is neither a mask nor an object. If the image were saved at this point, the Build Object mask represented by the red lines would not be saved. When the Build Object mask looks like the one shown in Figure 6.28, click the Build Object Mode button. The red lines turn blue, indicating that it has become an object. The Create command creates an object from one or more areas selected with object tools while in Build mode.

   The Lasso object tool operates like the Magic Wand in that it connects areas of similar color. The Lasso tool only works within the area (freehand) defined by the boundary that is drawn with the Lasso tool. If the Build mode had been in Create Object mode, a blue marquee would have surrounded the leaf when the mouse button was released, indicating the creation of an object.

Figure 6.28.
The leaf is outlined
with a Build Object
marquee, as indicated
by its red color. (What,
you can't see the red in
this image?)

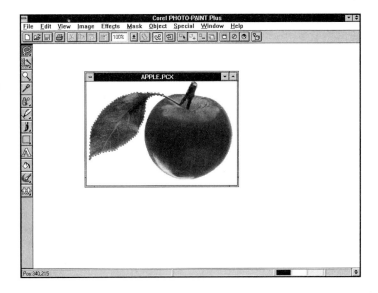

Some notes about the Lasso tool: Because the left mouse button was used, the bitmap image was copied into the object. If the right mouse button had been used with the Lasso tool, the bitmap information (the leaf) would have been removed from the original image and placed into the object.

4. Select the Layers/Objects roll-up (Ctrl+F7), and hide the base image by clicking the Hide Unselected button. (See Figure 6.29.) Only the layer with the leaf remains, because it was selected. Because nothing in nature is identical and our client wants this to look real, we must make a few modifications to this leaf to make it look less like a copy.

Figure 6.29.
The object containing
the duplicate leaf. All of
the rest of the image is
hidden.

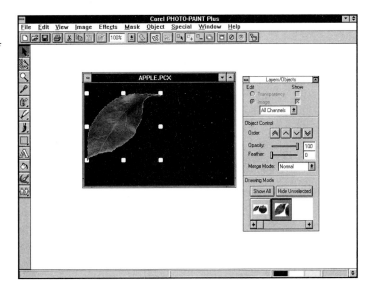

5. Open the Effects menu and select Color from the drop-down list. Select Hue and Saturation from the secondary drop-down list. The Effect Preview dialog box opens, as shown in Figure 6.30.

Corel *NOTE!*

If this is the first time you have opened Effects and you have other third-party filters installed, it may take a few moments before the drop-down menu appears.

Figure 6.30.
The Effects dialog box
shows the common
dialog box for most of
the PHOTO-PAINT
filters.

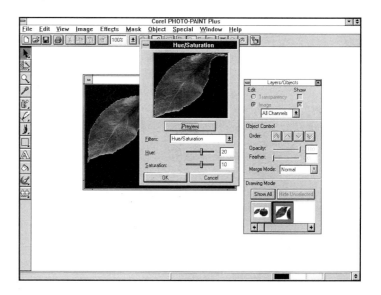

The Preview Window

The preview window allows you to see the results of various settings of the selected filter before the effect is applied to the image. Moving the cursor into the preview area causes the cursor to turn into a hand. If the object or area of the image that you desire to preview is not visible in the preview window, click the left mouse button in the area and use the mouse to drag the image until the part that you wish to preview is visible in the preview viewer. It moves very quickly.

Zooming in the Preview Window

Clicking the preview window with the left mouse button zooms in. Clicking the preview window with the right mouse button causes the preview window to zoom out.

Moving anything or zooming in or out in the preview window invokes the preview feature after two seconds, even if there hasn't been any change to the filter values.

The Preview Button

Clicking on the Preview button previews the effect. If you want to try another value, change the value and click on the Preview button again. Every time you click the Preview button, the previous preview effects are removed and the new effect values are applied. The same is true if you switch filters while in the preview window. For example, if you preview a value for Gamma, switch to Maximum, and click Preview, the Gamma effect will be removed and the Maximum effect will be previewed. The preview effects are not additive. What is additive? When we apply an effect to an object, we can go back and reapply the same effect again, and the filter acts on the previous effect to produce a greater effect. You see this used most often in Smear, Smudge, and Blur filters. Even though the preview effects are not additive, the effects that are applied to objects *are* additive.

The Filter Box

This drop-down list lets you select filters other than the one that caused the dialog box to open. Opening the Filter box with the arrow button, you will see several other effects (filters) that are available. For example, the Hue/Saturation Effect dialog box offers access to 10 other filters. These filters are mutually exclusive. If you are in the Hue/Saturation Effect dialog box and the Enhance filter is selected, only the Enhance filter will be applied.

6. Enter a value of 10 in both Hue and Saturation and click the OK button. These values were picked because they made the leaf look slightly different but not radically different. You are encouraged to try several values and see what they look like in the preview window. Hue and Saturation act like the tint and color adjustment on a color TV. Hue changes the color; saturation changes the intensity of the color.

7. Click the OK button and the effect is applied to the leaf. If we had not hidden the base image, the Hue/Saturation effect would have been applied to the entire image; but since only the leaf was visible, the effect was only applied to it, and the rest of the image remained untouched.

8. Unhide the base image by clicking on the first button in the drawing area, or click the Show All button. The leaf (object) is exactly positioned over the original image area, so you cannot see it. Because nothing in nature is identical, we are going to make the newly created leaf (object) a little smaller than the original. To do that, we need to scale the object.

9. Click and drag the lower-left control handle of the leaf object, moving toward the opposite corner until the scale in the status bar reads 75 percent. That means we reduced it by 25 percent and it is now 75 percent of its original size.

Figure 6.31.
The duplicate leaf is now lighter and smaller than the original.

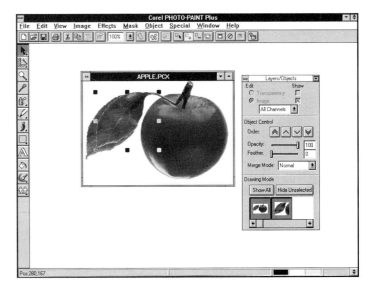

10. Click on the leaf object again to change it to Rotation mode, as indicated by the double-headed arrows in place of the control handles.

11. Place the cursor over the rotation point in the center of the leaf object. The cursor turns into a crosshair when it is over any control point on an object. Click and drag the rotation point until it is outside of the object and on the stem of the original leaf.

12. Place the cursor over the lower control handle and rotate the handle counter-clockwise until the status bar reads -20 degrees. (See Figure 6.32.) By controlling the point of rotation, we are able to make the leaf rotate at a natural connection point on the stem. You could use the custom rotation capability in the Object menu, but in real life you rotate items such as this visually.

13. Select the leaf with the Object Picker tool and enter a value of 1 in the Feather box. This is a finishing touch that removes any edges of the white background that the Lasso tool may have picked up. To put the final touch on this creation, using the default Fill setting (Conical, yellow-to-red), click on the white background with the Flood Fill tool. The result is shown in Figure 6.33. Thus we have created a second leaf on the apple, and it looks like it belongs there. Depress the F9 key to see a full-screen preview of the

results. If the F9 key doesn't produce a full-screen preview when you use it, make sure that the Image window is selected and another roll-up is not selected. To return to the regular PHOTO-PAINT screen, click anywhere on the image or use the Esc key.

Figure 6.32.
When the rotation point is shifted to the stem, the leaf appears to be attached.

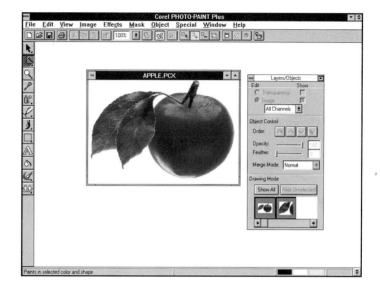

Figure 6.33.
Completed apple-leaf clone.

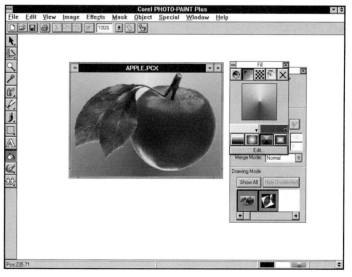

14. Close the file and do not save the changes.

Object Tool Settings Roll-Up

In the E2 release of Corel PHOTO-PAINT 5 and within Corel PHOTO-PAINT Plus, the functionality of the Transform roll-up has been added to the Tool Settings roll-up for objects. That is, when you hit Ctrl+F8 to bring up the Tool Settings roll-up, what you get is a version of the Transform roll-up for objects. The Tool Settings roll-up for objects provides a very powerful and easy way to make precise manipulations to objects.

Figure 6.34.
The new Tool Settings
dialog box for objects
adds substantial
precision and power to
objects.

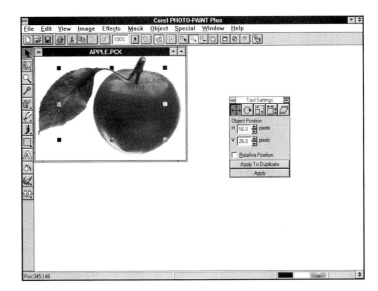

Object Position

Each of the sections within the Tool Settings dialog box for objects has an Apply To Duplicate and an Apply button, which gives users the capability to either apply the settings to a new object or to the currently selected object.

Going from left to right, clicking on the first button accesses the Object Position. These controls are accessed by clicking on the Object Position button. These controls are used to reposition or move objects. The default units are pixels, but you can change the units in the Preferences dialog box. If you attempt to move an object with a setting that will place the object outside of the image area, nothing will happen when you apply the setting. When these controls are used in conjunction with the rulers, you can position objects very precisely and quickly anywhere within the image.

When the Relative Position option is unchecked, the Horizontal listing displays the leftmost position of the object and the Vertical listing displays the topmost position of the object. Moving the object is accomplished by changing these values. If negative numbers are used nothing will happen since negative numbers would position the object outside of the image area.

Precisely positioning, such as centering an object on a page, with the Relative Position option unchecked can be a little tricky, yet quite possible. For Example, if your image area is 2 inches square and your object is 1 inch square, you could center the object by entering Horizontal and Vertical settings of .5. Objects of equal size can be positioned on top of one another by entering the same values for each object in these settings.

When the Relative Position option is checked, the Horizontal and Vertical Settings start out at zero each. Movement is applied relative to the apex of the topmost and leftmost lines of an object. Entering a positive value for the Horizontal setting moves the image to the right, and a negative value moves the image to the left. Entering a positive value for the Vertical setting moves the object down, and a negative value moves the object up. After a setting is applied, the settings both return to 0. Values that place the object outside of the image area will move the object off of the page.

Corel *TIP!*

> You can create a duplicate object exactly over another by pressing the Apply To Duplicate button without changing the Horizontal and Vertical settings.

Object Angle of Rotation/Center of Rotation

The second button from the right provides access to the Object Rotation controls. The first set of controls is for the Object Angle of Rotation. There is nothing mystical here, but it is important to note that you can enter a number for the Angle of Rotation as low as one one-thousandth of a degree. Once new values are entered into this setting, the Center of Rotation setting remains the same until it is changed, even if the file you are working on is closed and another is opened. For example, if you rotate an object 15 degrees and then close the Object Tool Settings roll-up, and then reopen it three hours later after having worked on several other files, the setting will still be 15 degrees for the Angle of Rotation. If you close and reopen PHOTO-PAINT, the setting will default back to 0.

The next set of controls is a little more exciting. With the Center of Rotation controls, you can precisely position the center of rotation. With the Relative Center option turned off, the controls for Center of Rotation report where the center of rotation is located on the currently selected object. Whenever you need to reposition the center of rotation, simply use the rulers to locate the new position and enter those values into the Center of Rotation controls. For example, if your currently selected object has a center of rotation at the Horizontal and Vertical position of 1 inch each, you could easily change that to, say, 2 inches Horizontal and 3 inches Vertical by simply entering those values in the Center of Rotation Controls.

When the Relative to Center option is turned on, the controls for Center of Rotation start off at 0. Units are controlled by the Preferences dialog box. Values entered in the Center of Rotation controls will move the center of rotation according to the values relative to its current position. For example, if you are working in inches and you enter Center of Rotation values of 1 inch for both the Horizontal and Vertical settings, the center of rotation would be repositioned one inch down and to the right of the current center of rotation.

Figure 6.35.
The Object Angle of Rotation and Center of Rotation settings provide for precision rotation.

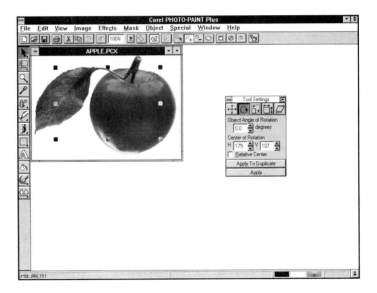

Object Scale/Mirror

Object Scale enables you to do exactly what it's name suggests—scale objects. An object can be scaled by percentages of the object's size. You cannot enter negative numbers for the Object Scaling settings. Rather, numbers larger than 100 percent scale the object larger than its current size; numbers smaller than 100 percent scale the object smaller than its current size. When Maintain Aspect is selected, the Horizontal and Vertical settings within Object Scaling remain the same. The Object Mirror buttons flip the objects horizontally and vertically. The Object Scale settings and the Mirror buttons can work in conjunction with one another. For example, if you have 50 percent Horizontal and Vertical settings for Object Scale with the Vertical Mirror button on, the selected object will be flipped vertically at 50 percent it's original size when the Apply button is pressed.

Corel *TIP!*

You can create a duplicate object exactly over another by hitting the Apply To Duplicate button with 100 percent Horizontal and Vertical Object Scale settings and the Mirror buttons unpressed.

Figure 6.36.
The Object Scale and Mirror settings allow you to resize and flip objects.

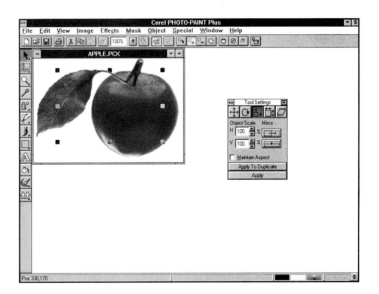

Object Size

The Object Size settings are a more accurate way to resize an object than Object Scale. The Object Size settings list the dimensions of the currently selected object. To change the dimensions of the currently selected object, simply enter in the new values and select Apply or Apply To Duplicate. Units are determined by the default setting in the Preferences dialog box. Negative numbers cannot be entered for the Object Size settings. When the Maintain Aspect option is checked, the aspect of the object will be maintained when you enter a new value in one of the Horizontal or Vertical settings. For example, if you have an object that is 1 inch horizontal and 2 inches vertical, and you enter

2 inches in the Horizontal setting with the Maintain Aspect option checked, the Vertical option will automatically maintain the aspect ratio of the object by changing to 4 inches.

Corel *TIP!*

You can create a duplicate object exactly over another by selecting the Apply To Duplicate button without changing the Horizontal and Vertical settings.

Figure 6.37.
The Object Size
settings provide a more
accurate method of
resizing objects than
the Object Scale
settings.

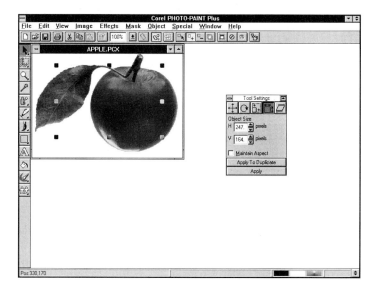

Object Skew

Object Skew allows you to numerically skew objects. Like all of the other settings in the Object Tool Settings roll-up, Object Skew simply provides a way to accurately enter in values for alterations that could otherwise be performed manually. Negative degree values can be used. Once new values are entered into this setting, the Object Skew settings will remain the same until they are changed, even if the file you are working on is closed and another is opened.

Figure 6.38.
The Object Skew
settings allow you to
skew objects accu-
rately.

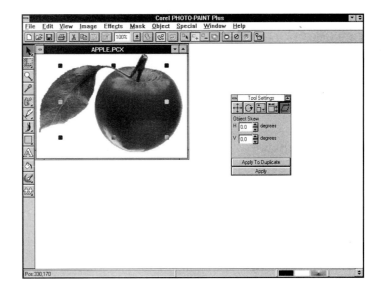

Additional Tips for Working with Objects

1. Options within the Objects menu will be unavailable when anything other than an object tool is selected from the Toolbox.

2. Objects do not have to be the same size as the page. You can paste or drag-and-drop an object that is larger than the page size.

3. While PHOTO-PAINT does not have a paste-inside feature, you can emulate this effect by creating a compound object with a hole(s) in it. For instance, if you have an image with a TV screen on it and you want to change what's on the TV, simply create an object with a hole where the TV screen is, and then position the new image behind it. With this functionality, a paste-inside feature is unnecessary.

It is the ability to create, modify and position objects that makes Corel PHOTO-PAINT 5 such a powerful photo-editing program. We have only covered the basics to this point.

Summary

- An object is an independent bitmap that is layered above the base image.
- There are two types of objects: simple and complex.
- Objects cannot be selected with mask tools, and masks cannot be selected with object tools.
- Objects are surrounded by a blue marquee.

■ There are many ways to create an object, as follows:

1. Selecting an area with an Object Selection Tool.

2. Pasting an image as an object.

3. Pasting a file into an image as an object.

■ Using the left mouse button with an object-selection tool copies the bitmap (image information) into the object. The bitmap under the selection area remains the same.

■ Using the right mouse button with an object-selection tool cuts the bitmap (image information) into the object. The bitmap under the selection area is removed.

■ A Magic Wand tool creates masks/objects by selecting connecting points of similar color.

■ Each object occupies its own layer.

■ The Layers/Objects roll-up is used to control the objects and layers by hiding or revealing them. In this way it is possible to selectively apply effects in an image composed of many layers/objects.

■ Images saved as PHOTO-PAINT format files (*.CPT) preserve their layers and objects. All other files formats lose this information as the layers/objects are merged into the image.

7

Flood Fill Tools

In this chapter we will learn everything there is to know about the Fill roll-up and the Canvas roll-up. In CorelDRAW, the Fill roll-up is a supporting player; in PHOTO-PAINT, it is a leading actor. As you work with Corel PHOTO-PAINT, you will discover that the Fill roll-up is one of the roll-ups that you use the most. The Fill roll-up controls what fill is applied when you use the Fill tool, or the Rectangle, Circle, and Polygon tools. It provides access to a wide variety of preset and custom fills, ranging from simple spot colors to complex custom bitmap fills.

The Fill roll-up, pictured in Figure 7.1, can be accessed many ways, as follows:

- Depressing the Shift+F6 key.
- Selecting Fill roll-up from the View menu.
- Double-clicking the Fill tool.

■ Double-clicking the Fill color display in the status bar (lower-right side of main screen).

When you open the Fill roll-up, you will notice that there are five buttons directly below the title bar. Each button switches the Fill roll-up into a different mode of operation. The icon on the buttons indicate the operational mode they activate.

Figure 7.1.
The five fill buttons in
the Fill roll-up.

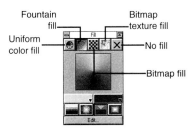

The first button selects the Uniform Color fill. From this mode, any solid (non-gradient) color can be selected either from the existing palette or from a custom palette.

The second button is the Fountain fill. It operates in the same manner as the Gradient Fill in CorelDRAW 5 to produce Linear, Radial, Conical, and Square fills. This fill comes with a large selection of presets. All of the fountain fills can be customized.

The checkerboard icon is for the Bitmap fill. Like its DRAW 5 counterpart, it can provide bitmap fills from its existing library of fills or from custom fills. Any bitmap file can be used for Bitmap fill patterns.

The Bitmap texture fill is the most unique in the Fill roll-up. Like the Bitmap fill, it can use predefined texture fills or custom fills that are created with PHOTO-PAINT or other graphics programs. You can create some unusual and exotic textures (or patterns) by using this fill.

The fifth button is the No Fill fill. When I was writing the manual for PHOTO-PAINT, it was a great temptation to make fun of this name. This choice allows the creation of closed objects without any fill being applied.

You can see the currently selected fill color/pattern by viewing the Fill Status line in the lower-right corner of the PHOTO-PAINT screen. You will notice that there are three tiny rectangles (Figure 7.2) located on the lower-right side of the status line. They are, from left to right, Paint color (foreground color), Paper color (background color), and the Fill tool color/pattern.

Figure 7.2.
Status line showing
foreground/background
and fill colors.

The Uniform Color Fill

When Color fill is selected, the preview square below the five mode-selection buttons reflects the current fill color that is selected. To change the color, click on the preview square. A palette of colors opens, allowing you to select any color you need for the Color fill. You may see additional choices on the color palette by using the gray scroll bars on the right side of the palette. To select a new color, simply click on the desired color in the palette. This action causes the palette to close and returns to the opening Fill roll-up (Uniform Color fill mode) with the selected color showing in the preview square. To select a different palette of colors based on another color model or to define a new color, either click on the MORE button below the color palette when it is open or click on the EDIT button at the bottom of the Fill roll-up. Either action opens the Uniform Fill window.

The Uniform Fill Dialog Box

The Uniform Fill dialog box (see Figure 7.3) is common throughout all of the CorelDRAW 5 suite of applications. Changes made to the palette in this dialog box are global. That means that they apply to all of the CorelDRAW suite of applications. The Uniform Fill dialog box allows you to choose colors from various color models and custom palettes, including CorelDRAW 4 (*.PAL) palettes.

You can also import and select individual colors from existing .BMP files in the Mixing area.

Figure 7.3.
The Uniform Fill dialog box.

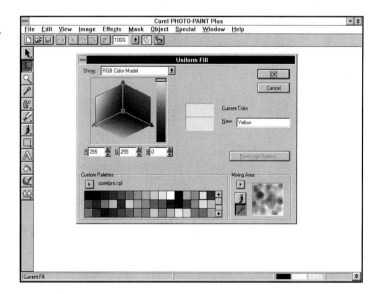

Available Color Models

The SHOW box enables you to select the color model. The options available are: CMYK, RGB, HSB, Grayscale, Uniform Colors, FOCOLTONE, PANTONE Spot colors, PANTONE Process colors, TRUMATCH, and Custom Palette. Below the SHOW box is a preview window that changes to reflect the color model selected. The color model choices are as follows:

CMYK	Shows the CMYK model and list boxes for each of the components. Cyan, Magenta, Yellow, and Black (CYMK) is the model used for the four-color printing process. A note about CMYK: When this model is selected, there may be some display irregularities if you are using blended colors. when blended colors are displayed on the monitor, they show up as banding. The printed output itself is unaffected, but the display is banded.
RGB	Shows the RGB model and value boxes for each of the components. Red, Green, and Blue (RGB) is the default color model. This is the ground zero of all color models. The human eye and the computer display are based on the RGB color model.
HSB	Shows the HSB model and value boxes for each of the components. Hue, Saturation, and Brightness (HSB) is an alternate to the RGB model. The popularity of HSB isn't what it used to be.
Grayscale	Shows the Grayscale model and the Gray Level list box. By using the arrows on the Gray Level list box, it is possible to select any of 255 possible levels of grayscale, with 0 being the lightest and 255 being the darkest.
Uniform Colors	Shows the Standard Uniform Colors model. This is a wide selection of 236 colors. It is a sampling of the entire visible spectrum at 100 percent saturation.
FOCOLTONE	When FOCOLTONE is selected, the dialog box shows the FOCOLTONE model, the Show Color Names checkbox, and a Search For box. The Search For box is used to search for specific FOCOLTONE color names. FOCOLTONE is a color-matching system. Like all color-matching systems, FOCOLTONE provides a specimen

swatch to printers and designers so there is a point of agreement as to what the color specified is supposed to look like.

PANTONE Spot
Shows the Spot Colors model, the Show Color Names checkbox, and Tint and Search For boxes. The Search For box is used to search for specific PANTONE Spot Color names. Spot colors are specific colors that are applied to an area and are not the result of multiple applications of inks. PANTONE is one of the more popular color-matching systems. As with FOCOLTONE, when using PANTONE, you pick out a specific color from a sample and then pick out the color name or number from the PANTONE list. When it goes to the service bureau to be made into film, the computer then knows what particular PANTONE color was specified.

PANTONE Process
This operate like the PANTONE Spot Colors model except that it shows Process colors. Process colors are colors that are created by multiple applications of ink. PANTONE specifies all the information that is necessary for the printer to be able to duplicate the color. When PANTONE Process is selected, it shows the Process Color model, the Show Color Names checkbox, Tint, and Search For boxes. The Search For box is used to search for specific PANTONE Process Color names.

TRUMATCH
This is another color-matching system; like PANTONE it allows specification of colors according to specific samples. When the TRUMATCH model is selected, it shows TRUMATCH colors, Show Color Names checkbox, and Tint and Search For boxes. The Search For box is used to search for specific TRUMATCH color names.

Selecting the Show Color Names checkbox will cause the preview window to change to an alphabetical listing of all of the color names for the color system selected. Each name is preceded by a color rectangle displaying a sample of the named color. Regarding the displayed colors, please remember that what you see is only a good approximation of what that actual color looks like, even when you are using a very expensive monitor and graphics card, and even when you have done all of the calibration voodoo. When using color samples from a color-matching system, always trust the sample over the screen.

The Search For box provides a quick way to locate a specific, named color in a color system. As each character is typed in, the computer begins its search. As subsequent characters are entered, the search field is narrowed. For example let's find blue. As the letters BL are entered under the PANTONE spot system, the computer goes to the first BL in the system, which is black. Then when the U is entered, the search continues to blue. The search system accepts both alphabetic and numeric characters, since many names of colors have numeric designations.

The PostScript Options button is always grayed-out (i.e., not available) in PHOTO-PAINT. The button is there because all of the Corel programs share many of the same dialog boxes. In PHOTO-PAINT, there aren't any PostScript options available.

The Current/New color box visually displays the current color on top and the new selected color on the bottom. If the color in the Current/New preview box is a custom color (that is, a color that is not named), the New field can be used for the entry of the new color name. This ability to name custom colors is important when working with many custom colors. Names assigned to colors should reflect the color, the project, or the client/company you are using the color for. Don't rename existing industry-standard colors. For example, if you are using PANTONE 1615V, don't call it Flaming Neon Ties. While you may find the nomenclature entertaining, it will not be understood by the service bureau or your printer. Another reason for sane color names is that human memory is frail, and if you give a color a cute name, there is a strong chance that when it comes time to look for it again, you may not be able to remember that specific shade of green that you created was called Aunt Fred's Toenail Clipping. Now that I have cut back on your fun, the good news is that PHOTO-PAINT gives you 20 characters with which to name your new color creation. This is a vast improvement over the terse eight-character restriction of DOS naming conventions.

Corel *TIP!*

When creating new colors, especially for company logos, be sure to give the new color a specific name. This can be critical when the job needs to be modified and you are trying to guess which color that you used out of a possible ten billion combinations.

Custom Palettes

The arrow button to the right of the Custom Palette title displays the following commands:

- **Add Color.** Adds selected color displayed in the Current/New preview box to an existing custom palette. The new color is always added to the bottom of the palette.

- **Delete Color.** Deletes selected color displayed in the Current/New preview box from an existing custom palette.

- **Create a New Palette.** This opens up an empty palette that you can fill with any combination of colors.

Corel *TIP!*

> Sometimes when you are working on a project that requires a number of exact reference colors (e.g., PANTONE), you may find it is easier to create a palette specifically for the project with the required colors.

- **Open an Existing Palette.** Opens the Load Palette dialog box. The default palette is CORELPNT.CPL, an RGB color model palette. When opening a palette, you have the choice of opening either a custom palette (*.CPL) or a CorelDRAW 4 palette (*.PAL). The loaded palette is displayed in the preview area.

- **Save a Palette.** Opens the Save Palette dialog box. Saves the current palette under the same name. This is used to save any changes made to a palette. If you do not save a palette, any change made to the palette will be lost when PHOTO-PAINT is closed or a new palette is selected.

- **Save As a New Palette.** Use this when you have modified an existing palette but do not want to apply the change to the original palette.

Corel *TIP!*

> Use the Save As command when you have made changes to the default palette. Many times, image files that you can get from various sources expect to find the default palette. If you have changed it, you may get unpredictable results.

- **Set As Default the Current Palette**. When you save a palette as default, it will be the palette that will be used when PHOTO-PAINT is made active. This is a command that is a time saver when working on a project such as this book. I make a palette that I am using for this book the default, so that

I won't have to go and load it every time. Do you know what makes the palette for this book unique? I have struggled to come up with color combinations that look good in grayscale and that also have good color in case we want use a particular image in the color section. The preview box in the Custom Palette section (lower left) displays the colors in the selected custom palette. The default custom palette for Corel PHOTO-PAINT, CORELPNT.CPL, is located in the COREL50\CUSTOM sub-directory. The only exception to this is if you used the Set As Default command in the Custom Palette dialog box.

The Mixing Area

The mixing area is something unique in PHOTO-PAINT. It is located in the lower-right side of the Uniform Fill dialog box. The mixing area is the equivalent to an artist's palette (see Figure 7.4). Lucian Mustatea, who heads up the PHOTO-PAINT team, came up with the idea of allowing the PAINT user to actually mix various colors together to make new custom colors. While I think the idea is neat, I personally do not have the necessary experience to use it effectively. Other than knowing that yellow and blue make green, and red and blue make purple, I don't know what to mix. That explained, I can still show you how it works.

The mixing area contains two buttons: a brush and an eyedropper (color picker). There is also an arrow button that opens an additional dialog box. Below the arrow button is the mixing area. By clicking on the brush button, you can select colors from the Show preview box as well as the Custom Palette preview box. Once the color is selected, it can be applied to the mixing area. Additional colors can then be selected with the brush and mixed in the mixing area by painting over the previous colors. All colors applied in the mixing area are additive. For example, if you applied a yellow and then applied a blue, the area where both colors occupied the same pixel would be green. Because it is additive, applying more yellow will cause the hue to shift toward the yellow side of the green. Applying more blue moves the green toward the darker side of the spectrum. Once you have achieved the desired color, select the color picker (eyedropper) and click on the color. The newly created color will appear in the Current/New preview box. The colors made in the mixing area can be saved.

The arrow button displays the following commands:

■ **Load a Paint Area.** This command opens the Load Paint Area File dialog box. You can load any *.BMP file into the paint area and use it for selecting individual colors from an existing image. The default Paint Area file is PNTAREA.BMP and is located in the COREL50\CUSTOM subdirectory.

Corel *TIP!*

This is an excellent way to get and keep colors from an existing image. For example, if you found a file that had a remarkable shade of ruby red, you could bring it into the paint area with the Load command and then select the color and save it to a palette. If the file you want is not a .BMP file, load it into PAINT and save it as a .BMP file.

- ■ **Save a Paint Area.** Opens the Save Paint Area File As dialog box for saving paint areas for later use.
- ■ **Clear a Paint Area.** Clears the existing paint area.

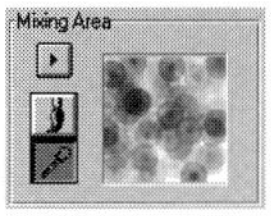

Figure 7.4.
The mixing area of the
Uniform Fill dialog box.

Using the Uniform Fill Dialog Box

So that you can get a feel for the Uniform Fill dialog box, let's do a few simple tasks.

1. Double-click on the Rectangle Draw tool with the left mouse button or depress Shift+F6. The Fill roll-up will appear. (See Figure 7.1.)
2. Click on the Uniform Color Fill button. It is first button on the top left. Because we want to get to the Uniform Fill roll-up, we could have selected the Edit button at the bottom of the roll-up. That's too easy—let's take the scenic route. Click on the preview window in the middle of the roll-up. A palette appears under the preview window. At this point you can do the following:

   You could select one of the colors that are visible or move the scroll bars on the right side of the palette to view the remainder of the palette and make your color selection there. There are 99 colors.
3. Now we'll create a custom color by selecting the More button on the bottom of the drop-down palette. The Universal Fill dialog box appears. This dialog box is composed of three major sections: model/color selection, custom palettes, and the mixing area.
4. Making sure that the show box contains RGB color model, select any color by clicking anywhere in the color preview area. The color you selected appears in the bottom (New) box. There is no name, because the RGB color model does not have named colors. The RGB values for the color you selected appear in the value boxes located below the preview box. If the

Show box does not contain an RGB color model, click on the down arrow on the right side of the box and select it from the drop-down list that appears.

5. Giving a color a name: In the new box, give the selected color a name. You can use any name as long as it doesn't exceed 20 characters in length. Names are not required by PHOTO-PAINT to save a color to a palette, but they are very useful when trying to differentiate between several similar custom colors.

6. Adding a new color: To add the new color to the custom palette, click on the arrow button in the custom palette section and select Add. The selected color is added to the custom palette. A sample square of the color appears in the Custom Palette preview box. We will now add another color.

7. Selecting spot colors by name: Using the Show drop-down list, select PANTONE Spot Colors. The preview window now contains a small portion of the PANTONE Spot Color palette. By using the scroll bar arrows on the right side, it is possible to scroll through the entire palette. Note: If the color palette did not appear but instead there was a list of names preceded by color samples, deselect the Show Color Names box by clicking on the white box in front of it.

8. Selecting a PANTONE color: Click on a color anywhere in the PANTONE palette. The name of the color appears in the New box. This is because the PANTONE color model uses named colors. Named colors make color matching much simpler. It will also make colors easier to find on large palettes (as we will see in a few more steps).

9. Selecting PANTONE process colors: Select show color names by clicking on the adjacent box. The preview window now changes into a list of PANTONE color names. Each name on the list is preceded by a small color sample of the named color. We are could also have used PHOTO-PAINT's search engine to search the very extensive PANTONE palette to find the color we need.

10. Click the OK button. This closes the Universal Fill dialog box and the Fill roll-up returns.

The Fountain Fill Tool

Next to the Effect filters, the Fountain fill tools represent the greatest tools for creating stunning backgrounds and fills. A fountain fill is a fill that fades gradually from one color to another. This is also called a "gradient" or "graduated" fill. Corel PHOTO-PAINT enables you to create linear, radial, conical, and square fountains using the Fountain Fill icon in the Fill roll-up window. To open the Fountain Tool Fill tool, click on the second button from the left on the Fill roll-up.

The resulting change in the Fill roll-up is shown in Figure 7.5. From this point, it is easy to select one of four types of fountain fills:

- Linear fill
- Radial (sometimes referred to as circular) fill
- Conical fill
- Square fill

Figure 7.5.
The Fountain Fill
roll-up.

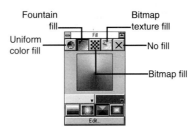

Operation of the fountain fills from this menu uses system defaults and is very simple. It involves the following three steps:

1. Select one of the four fill buttons on the bottom of the roll-up. The icons indicate the type of fill they represent. From left to right they are Linear, Radial, Conical, and Square.

2. Select beginning and ending colors for the fill using the two color-selection buttons located above the fill-type buttons. The color button on the left selects the starting color, the right button selects the end color. Each color button opens to a short color select palette with a palette of less than 99 colors.

3. You can change the angle of a Linear fill by clicking on the inside of the preview menu and dragging the point of gradient origin or direction with the mouse. You can change the offset of a Radial, Conical, or Square Fill the same way. Use the right mouse button to change the angle of a Conical fill. Use the Ctrl key to limit rotation to 15-degree increments and offsets to 10 percent increments.

If you require greater selection than the system default settings provide, clicking the Edit button on the bottom of the Fill roll-up opens the Fountain Fill dialog box.

The Fountain Fill Dialog Box

The Fountain Fill dialog box (Figure 7.6) edits and creates fountain fills. It is laid out into four sections: Type, Options, Color Blend, and Presets.

Fountain Fill Dialog Box Options

Preview Box   Shows you how the fountain fill will look with the colors you have chosen.

Type   Selects the type of fountain you want to create.

■ **Linear**   Selects a fountain fill that changes color in one direction.

■ **Radial**   Selects a fountain fill that changes color in concentric circles from the center of the object outwards.

■ **Conical**   Selects a fountain fill that radiates from the center of the object like rays of light.

■ **Square**   Selects a fountain fill that changes color in concentric squares from the center of the object outwards.

Figure 7.6. The Fountain Fill dialog box.

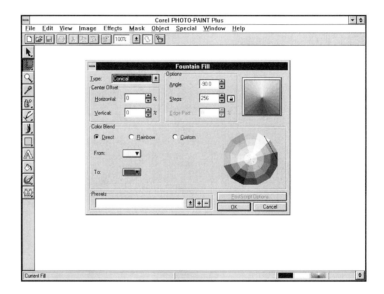

The Palette displays the colors available for creating a custom fountain.

The Center Offset repositions the center of a Radial, Conical, or Square fountain fill so that it no longer coincides with the center of the object. Negative values shift the center down and to the left; positive values shift the center up and to the right. At first appearance this seems pointless. Why would anyone in their right mind waste the time to use a value system to determine where the offset is when you can move it with the cursor to the desired position? However, the Center Offset is necessary when you need to make several fills with the exact same offset values. You can also move the center by dragging the crosshairs that appear when you click in the preview box with the left mouse button. For Conical fountains, you may either hold down the Shift key or use the right mouse button while dragging to change the direction of the fill. Holding down the Ctrl key while dragging constrains the amount of offset to 10-percent increments.

The Options section of the Fountain Fill dialog box allows you to adjust any of the settings to customize the appearance of the fountain. The choices are described in the following paragraphs.

The **Angle** box determines the angle of gradation in a Linear, Conical, or Square fountain fill. The preview box shows the effect of changing the angle. If you rotate the object, the fountain angle shown in the preview box adjusts automatically after a one-second delay. This delay prevents PHOTO-PAINT from acting on a new setting before the entire value has been entered. You can also change the angle by dragging the line that appears when you click in the preview box. Use the right mouse button (or the left mouse button and Shift) to change the angle for Conical and Square fountains. Holding down the CTRL key while dragging constrains the angle to multiples of 15 degrees.

The **Steps** box displays the number of bands used to display and print the fountain. You can change these settings for the selected object by clicking the Lock button to unlock the box and entering a value in the text box. The purpose of the lock button is to prevent accidental changing of any values. Once you have achieved the value you desire, you may lock the value by clicking on the lock button again. The preview display always shows 20 steps regardless of the Steps setting, so don't think that it is malfunctioning. The preview when you exit the Options section will correctly display the higher number of steps.

Corel *TIP!*

When increasing the value of the Steps, be aware that a large number increases the smoothness of the transitions, but the negative side of the increase is that the fountain fill becomes very complex. Very complex fountain fills take longer to display and longer to print.

Corel *TIP!*

Beware of producing too narrow a range of colors over a large area, which produces banding. For example, if a range of six shades of colors is spread over an 11- by 17-inch area, banding will result.

The **Edge Pad** increases the amount of start and end color in the fountain fill. It is used primarily with circles and irregularly shaped objects in which the first and/or last few bands of color lie between the object and its highlighting box. The effect is to take away from the smooth transition between the starting and ending colors. The Edge Pad can be used when applying shading to an object such as text. Entering in a large number into the Edge Pad box will cause a wide band to separate the top and bottom of a Linear fill. Filling the text with a fountain fill containing an Edge Pad fill produces dark shading at the very bottom of the text without having the text get progressively darker. The Edge Pad option is not available for Conical fountain fills and therefore is grayed out.

The **Color Blend** section of the Fountain Fill dialog box is where you select the colors you want to use in your fill. There are three modes of operation in the Color Blend area: Direct (default), Rainbow, and Custom.

Direct is the system default. It takes the intermediate colors along a straight line beginning at the From color and continuing across the color wheel to the To color. This is best for appearances of shading and highlights. For example, to make a circle look like a sphere, you would create a circle and do a Direct Radial fill with the light being offset away from the center. (See Figure 7.7.)

Figure 7.7. By applying an offset to a radial fill in the Fountain fill dialog box you can quickly create realistic looking spheres like the one shown. We will learn how to do shadows later in the book.

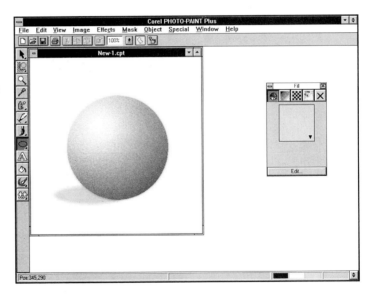

Rainbow allows you to make multicolored effects. It utilizes the spectrum of colors within a specified path around the color wheel. You can specify the direction the path takes around the color wheel by clicking the rotation buttons. The From and To colors coincide with endpoints of the path. When using the Rainbow, keep your background in mind. I have done a lot of work with this fill since it showed up in DRAW 4.

Corel *TIP!*

It is very easy to have part of the area you are filling blend into the background at the points where the background and the Rainbow fill are similar. This can result in the object being filled disappearing at those points. To avoid this, determine the colors that "blend" and make the rainbow exclude them. This is achieved by selecting a color near the "blend" color and making the rainbow fill get to the end color by avoiding the "blend" color. (It is at a time such as this that you will appreciate the rotation buttons.)

The **Custom** feature is where even more incredible effects and backgrounds come to life. When the Custom button is clicked, an additional part of the dialog box opens. (See Figure 7.8.) The Custom option allows you to select up to 99 intermediate colors from the palette at the right of the dialog box. Specify where you want the color to appear by adding markers above the preview box. The markers look a lot like the tab markers on my word-processing program. There are two ways to add markers, as follows:

- Double-click just above the preview box in the color blend area. The marker will appear, and the preview box in the color blend area and in the upper-right corner of the Fountain Fill dialog box will reflect the change after a one-second delay. (If you have a slower machine, it may take more than a second.)
- Select the "to" or "from" color squares at either end of the preview ribbon and specify a new value in the Position box.

Corel *TIP!*

Use the position box to enter precise positions for the markers. An easy way to do this is by double-clicking where you want the marker and then putting the exact position for it in the Position box. For example, by double-clicking near the middle of the fill you can get an approximate center position. To be exact, enter 50 percent in the Position box. The half-way point between the middle and the ends is 25 and 75 percent, etc.

After adding a marker, choose a color from the palette. To reposition a color, select its marker and drag it to the desired spot or edit the value in the Position box. The preview box in the color blend area and in the upper-right corner of the Fountain Fill dialog box will reflect the change after a one-second delay. To delete a color, double-click on the marker. Note: More than one color marker can be selected at a time by holding down the Shift key while selecting or deselecting.

Figure 7.8.
The Fountain Fill
dialog box with Custom
allows modification of
the fountain fills to
produce stunning fills
and effects.

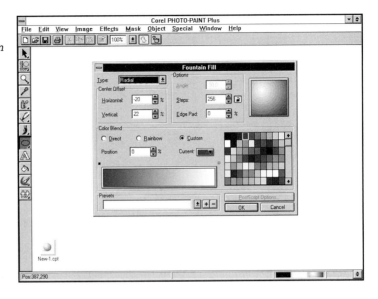

The **Presets** area lets you save the fountain settings you specified so that you
can apply them to other objects at a later time. It also contains over 100
predesigned fills that were installed with PHOTO-PAINT. To select a preset,
click on the down arrow to the right of the preset text box and a list appears.
Click on a preset name and the preset appears in the preview window. If you
want to browse through the list, just click on the first one you wish to view, and
then each time you press the down or up arrow, the next preset will be selected
and previewed. You might enjoy doing this if your cable TV is out and you are
really bored. To save a preset, type a name (up to 20 characters in length) in the
Presets box, then click the plus button. (Clicking the minus button removes the
selected settings from the Preset list.)

Corel*NOTE!*

As with the Uniform Fill dialog box, the Postscript button is not available in
PHOTO-PAINT and therefore is grayed out. This is because many Corel applications share the same user interface (UI) modules. When this UI opens up in
another application, the Postscript function is available.

The Bitmap Fill

The Bitmap fill is enabled by selecting the Bitmap Fill button on the Fill roll-up. It is the one in the center that looks like a checkerboard. The Bitmap fill allows you to fill a selected area with a bitmap image. There are a large number of images in the Corel library (located in the COREL50\PHOTOPNT\TILES subdirectory). In addition to the bitmap images provided, you can import almost any bitmap that can be read by your PC. It cannot, however, read vector-based images. (If you have a vector-based image, load it into PHOTO-PAINT 5 and export/save it as a bitmap image.) When you invoke the Bitmap fill in the Fill roll-up, you will be able to see the currently selected image in the Preview window. Unlike with the Color fill, you cannot look at the other bitmaps that are in the library by clicking on the preview window. To change the image, you must select the Load button located at the bottom of the roll-up. This will open the Import Bitmap dialog box, which should look very familiar because it is the same dialog box that is used to load files. The only difference is the title bar. In case you missed the lesson on loading files or your memory isn't what it used to be, the Import Bitmap fill dialog box allows you to use many different files for fills other than what is in the \TILES subdirectory.

Figure 7.9a.
This is an example
made using the Artistic
brush bitmaps as a fill
to produce a wallpaper
for a background.

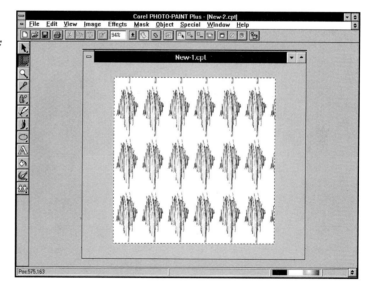

*Figure 7.9b.
While gold may be
where you find it, the
same can be said of
bitmap images. This
image was made
using the Thatch.bmp
Windows wallpaper
file to fill the text
and a canvas
(PAPER02C.PCX)
was used for the
background.*

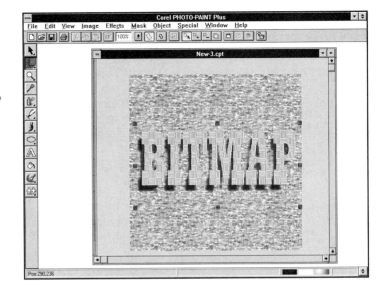

*Figure 7.9c.
This example was
created using a Photo-
CD from the Corel
Photo sampler CD as a
fill. Portions of the
letters in the word
TIGER were kept from
being filled by using an
XOR selection in the
mask.*

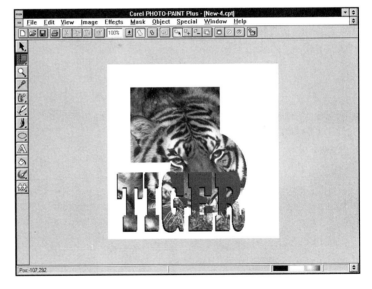

Figure 7.9d.
This is a finished piece
using four different
bitmap fills. Truth be
known, I just got a little
carried away while I
was working on the
previous example.

You have so much versatility when using bitmaps for fills that it is sometimes difficult to get a grip on all of it. Here are some pointers about using files for bitmap fills: Remember that if you use the Flood Fill tool (the bucket), the flood fill will be calculated to the boundaries of the mask. If the bitmap image is larger than the mask, it will put as much into the masked area as will fit, beginning with the lower-left corner of the original image. You can control what appears in a flood-filled area to a small degree by taking advantage of the Crop or Resample options when loading the bitmap. The Rectangle, Circle, and Polygon tools, on the other hand, will fill to the perimeter of the defined area, and only the masked area that falls within the area will be filled. In Figure 7.9c, I used the Rectangle tool to define where the overall image of the tiger would lay on the page, and only the masked areas were filled.

By using the Resample feature when you load the bitmap, it is possible to change the size of the image so that it either fits the area being filled or is small enough to act as a seamless tile.

Corel *TIP!*

When using Corel Photo CDs as bitmap fills, make sure to crop them in the Import dialog box to get rid of the black film border. If you don't, the results can be really ugly.

Import Bitmap Dialog Box

The Import dialog box (Figure 7.10) imports bitmaps for use in the Fill roll-up.

Figure 7.10.
The Import dialog box
is one of the more
powerful features in
PAINT. Through it you
can import bitmap
images from a wide
variety of sources and
tile them into your
work.

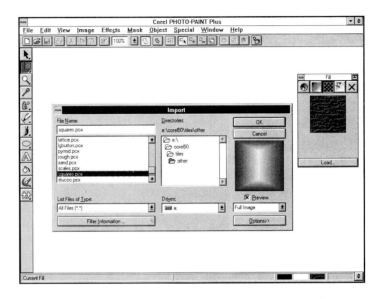

Import Bitmap Dialog Box Options

File Name. Type the name of the file you want to open. To list a different type of file, choose the type from the List Files of Type box.

File List Box. Displays files in the selected directory.

Directories. Choose the directory in which the file you want to open is stored.

List Files of Type. Use to preview and open the type of file you want. If All Files (*.*) is chosen, Corel PHOTO-PAINT will automatically select the appropriate import filter. File formats include: Windows bitmap (*.BMP, *.dib, *.rle), CompuServe bitmap (*.GIF), JPEG bitmap (*.JPG, *. JFF, *.JTF, *.CMP), Kodak Photo CD image (*.PCD), Paintbrush (*.PCX), Scitex CT bitmap (*.CT), Targa bitmap (*.TGA, *.VDA, *.ICB, *.VST), and TIFF bitmap (*.TIF, *.JTF, *.SEP).

Drives. Select the drive that contains the file you want to open.

Preview Window. If the check box is checked, it displays a preview of the image before opening. A preview will only display if there is a preview (bitmap) header available in the file. Some vector-based files, such as CorelTRACE .EPS files, do not contain bitmap preview-header information.

Preview Check Box. When checked, this activates the loading of the preview window.

Image size. A drop-down list box with four options:

    Full Image. Loads the entire file image.

    Crop. Allows you to define an area from the entire image and only load the selected part. The cropping reduces the resulting bitmap file size and is permanent.

    Resample. Reduces the size of the image by width, height, and resolution.

    Partial Image. Loads a selected area of the image.

Filter Information. Displays the developer and version number of the filter used to import the selected file type. This information is made available to help you if you need to talk with Corel technical support.

Options. Opens the lower portion of the dialog box. Displays file size, format, date, and the type of file.

Sort By. The Sort By drop-down list box allows you to sort the files by name or date.

Corel*NOTE!*

If the bitmap that you import is too small to fill the area, the bitmap is tiled. If the image is too large, the fill does not resize the bitmap, but rather it takes all of the bitmap that can fit in the area that is being filled, beginning in the lower-left corner of the original bitmap. As a result, if you have a large file you have used for a bitmap fill and a small area to fill, you might find that a large portion of the bitmap didn't make it into the fill area.

Now on to the next section of the Fill roll-up—Texture Fills.

Corel*TIP!*

There is a large selection of bitmap fills available on the CorelDRAW 5 CD-ROM Disc 01. They are buried in the CLIPART_BITMAP directory.

Figure 7.11.
This image was made
by loading the bitmap
fill MIST.TIF located in
the CLIPART_\BITMAP
\TEXTURES directory
into the bitmap fill and
then using the flood fill
tool to fill each charac-
ter. Be aware that
these bitmap textures
are not seamless tiles
and therefore if you use
them as a flood fill in an
area that is too large,
your seams will show
(no kidding!).

Texture Fills

This is the feature that makes Corel PHOTO-PAINT unique. I do not know of
another package that can do the things that can be done with Texture fills.
There are some tricks to using the fills effectively, but we will cover them. The
Texture Fill dialog box is used to select one of the 100-plus bitmap texture fills
included in Corel PHOTO-PAINT. Each texture has a unique set of parameters
that you can modify to create millions of variations. Although most of the
textures look fine on color monitors, if you are using a monochrome monitor,
you may not get a very good representation of the texture's appearance. If you
are printing on a monochrome printer, you may get good results with some of
the fills and poor results with others. The results depend on your printer, your
taste, and your willingness to experiment.

As with the effects, don't let the names of the fills confuse your thinking. As an
example, look at Figure 7.9a. The cut-metal edge of the text was created by
using the Rain Drops, Hard, 3 Color fill. I came across this effect when I was

writing the PHOTO-PAINT 5 manual for Corel. By filling each character individu- ally, the size of the "raindrops" doesn't get too large. Too large? This leads to our first general rule regarding the texture fills. As in Boyle's law of expanding gases (gas expands to fit the volume of the container), a texture fill expands to fit the volume of the masked area. In Figure 7.12 we have created squares of various sizes and filled them with the same texture fill. As you can see, as the squares increase in area the size of the fill increases proportionally. While this can be used to create some unusual effects, this can also catch you by surprise, especially when working with a large image only to find when it is applied that it doesn't look anything like the thumbnail preview. Also note the very narrow rectangle on the right side. I put it in there so you would realize the fill size is calculated by creating a square that is determined by the greatest dimension of the mask. For example, if you made a mask that was 50 pixels by 500 pixels, the resulting fill would be as if it was a 500 pixel by 500 pixel square. So how do you get around this? Not as tough as you may think. While there are several ways to do it, I will just cover a few of the basic ways.

Figure 7.12.
Squares of various sizes
filled with the same
texture fill. As you can
see, as the squares
increase in area the
size of the fill increases
proportionally.

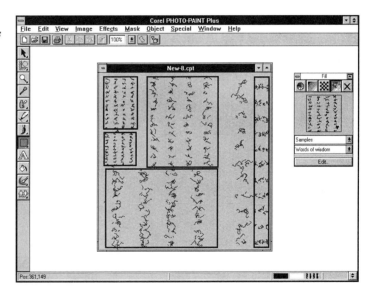

Making the Texture Fill into a Custom Bitmap Fill

This is the method that I use most often. The bitmap-fill engine does excellent tiling, and it is very simple to use. Here is all you need to do:

1. Create a new image. Size is not critical, but I recommend about 80 × 80 pixels at a resolution of 300 dpi.

2. Pick the texture fill that you want to use. After making whatever adjustments you deem necessary, click on the Flood Fill tool (the bucket) and click in the new image.

3. Save the file. The tiles are generally kept in the PHOTOPNT\TILES subdirectory, but you can put them anywhere your heart desires. Even though all of the Corel tiles are in .PCX format, any bitmap format will work.

Corel *TIP!*

Save your custom tiles in PHOTO-PAINT format. This way it is easy to locate your custom tiles in a sea of tiles by selecting the CPT filter.

4. Click on the Bitmap Fill button (checkerboard) in the Fountain Flood dialog box. Click the Load button and load your newly created custom bitmap tile.

5. Using the Flood Fill tool (bucket), click on the area to be filled. The area will flood with a non-expanding version of the texture fill.

Corel *TIP!*

Be aware that some textures don't work this way very well. They can show up as unwanted patterns. For example, I tried using this technique with the Planets fill from the Sample 5 library. The result was that the patterning of the fill showed up as a pattern in the background. This would still work if I had many objects over it, such as spaceships and planets, to break up the image. If that was not the case, then I would use the second method shown forthwith.

*Figure 7.13.
This figure was made
by filling a 400 × 400
pixel area with the
default Mercury fill
from the Sample 5
library.*

*Figure 7.14.
This figure was made
by filling the same
400 × 400 pixel area
with a bitmap of the
same default Mercury
texture fill.*

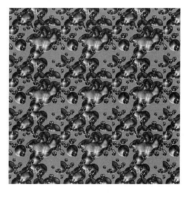

Controlling Texture Fills through Edit Modifications

So, why didn't I put this technique first? Because the texture-fill generator has some real difficulty with large (quantity) values over large (surface) areas. Sometimes it will result in a nasty little PAINT error message that says "Error Generating Texture," and then it will paint garbage on your screen. If that happens, just undo it and try it again with another tool (if possible). For example, if the error occurred using a Flood Fill tool, try laying down the fill with a Rectangle, Circle, or Polygon tool. If that option is not available to you, then just try the original process again. The error is very slippery and doesn't always repeat.

Now you know one of the deep, dark secrets of PHOTO-PAINT. The only possible damage that could be done is that your monitor may explode (just kidding). The error is completely local to the image and does not require you to close the image or close PAINT. So, if you get an error, just undo it.

Controlling the texture in a large area involves reducing the maximum values (usually expressed as percentages) to very small values (in the range of 2 or 3 percent). If the image has spots, dots, or other repeating objects, increase their value. The image in Figure 7.15 looks better than the one created in Figure 7.14, but that isn't always the case. Each texture that you use in a large area must be made on a case-by-case basis.

Figure 7.15.
The image in Figure 7.15 looks better than the one created in Figure 7.14, but that isn't always the case.

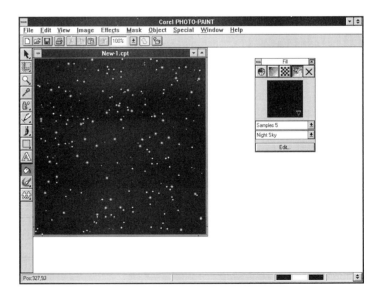

Space, The Final Frontier...

OK, here is a quick trick to make space that looks like the real thing. As we already have discussed, the Texture Bitmap fill expands to fill the area that it is put into. We are going to take advantage of that feature and put it to good use.

1. Make a new image 400 × 400 pixels. 24-bit, 96 dpi.

2. Select the NightSky fill from the Samples 5 library. Click on the Edit button and change the number of spots setting to 100. Use the Flood Fill tool (bucket) and fill the image. This results in your basic space as shown in Figure 7.16, but it doesn't have depth.

Figure 7.16.
We want to make outer space with depth which this image lacks.

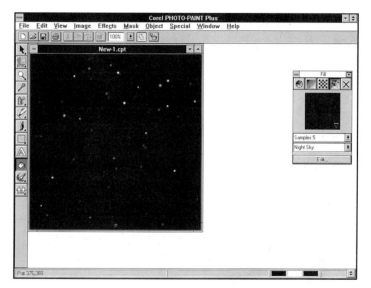

3. Select the rectangle draw tool and holding down the control key draw a rectangle inside the image. Start at a point about 25 percent in from the edge (no need to be exact). You now have more stars, and they are smaller since the area was smaller.

4. Repeat step three several more times, making each rectangle smaller than the last. You should end up with the space that has some real depth to it. For a finishing touch, use the circle draw tool and drag small ellipses in the areas toward the out edge that don't have any stars. You will end up with patches of tiny stars looking a lot like distant galaxies. The final image is shown in Figure 7.17.

Figure 7.17.
Using the variable size
feature of the Texture
Bitmap fill tool, we
were able to give our
outer space fill a little
depth in the center.

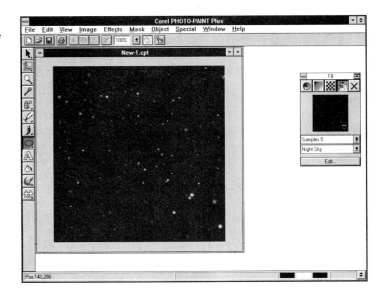

Clicking on the Texture Fill button opens its version of the roll-up. As you look at
the Texture Fill area (Figure 7.18), you will notice that it consists of the following
four components:

Figure 7.18.
The Texture Fill Mode
of Fill Tool roll-up.

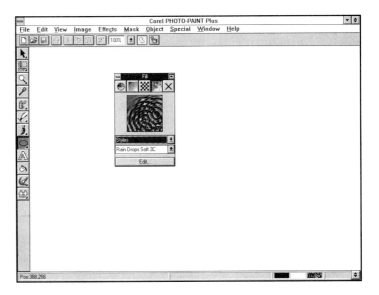

■ **Preview Box.** The Fill roll-up displays the currently selected texture fill.
  Clicking the preview box opens the Texture Library (Figure 17.19), which
  displays thumbnails of all the texture fills in the current library. A texture
  fill can be selected by double-clicking on the desired thumbnail of the fill or

by clicking on the texture (which becomes highlighted) and selecting OK from the Texture Library menu bar. The preview box only shows 12 thumbnails at a time. Additional thumbnails in the library can be viewed by using the scrollbar located on the right side the thumbnails. From the menu bar of the thumbnail display, you can select another Texture Library, Cancel, or return to the preview window by clicking on OK.

Corel *TIP!*

> This is a slow process because the preview thumbnail must be generated each time it is opened.

Figure 7.19.
Texture Library of Fill
Roll-Up showing
thumbnails

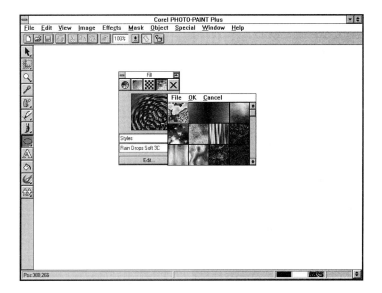

■ **Textures Library**. This list box displays the names of the texture libraries. Corel PHOTO-PAINT ships with three libraries: Styles, Samples, and Samples 5, described forthwith.

Styles: These are the building blocks of the bitmap texture fills. It is from the textures in this library that all of the other samples in the other two libraries are made. This library is a read-only library. If you modify a texture and want to save it, you will not be allowed to save it in this library. You must either create a new library or save it in Samples or Samples 5 (see Figure 7.20).

Samples: This is the original set of samples that were made with the Texture generator in the Styles library (see Figure 7.21). For example, Sky, Midday was created with Sky, 2 Colors. It is a quick way to get a texture without having to wade through all of the texture parameters to make it. The Samples library shipped with the original version of Corel PHOTO-PAINT 5.

Samples 5: This library is like Samples except that there are more variations. Some of my personal favorites are in this library (see Figure 7.22). I find that I use the Night Sky and Planets textures in this library more than almost any other texture. This library first shipped with the maintenance release of Corel PHOTO-PAINT 5.

Figure 7.20.
Nine texture fills from
the Styles library.

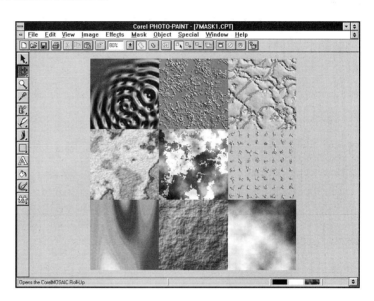

- **Texture List.** Lists the texture fills available in the currently selected library. Clicking on a texture in the Textures list will select it and the default setting for the texture will display in the preview window.

Corel *TIP!*

Each time a library is selected, the texture list returns to the default texture for that library. For example, if you were in Samples 5 and had been working with Night Sky and then you switched over to look at something in Styles, when you returned to Samples 5, it would have returned to the default texture.

Figure 7.21.
Nine more from the
Samples library.

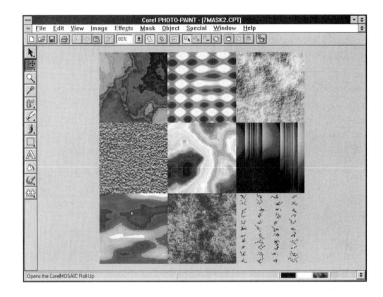

Figure 7.22.
The Samples 5 library.
In many cases these
samples were selected
because of they looked
better in grayscale.
Some of the best color
ones looked like the
pits in grayscale.

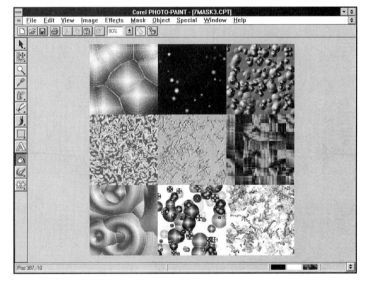

■ **Edit.** This button opens the Texture Fill dialog box. This dialog box allows you to edit and create an unlimited number of new texture fills from existing fills. Unlike bitmap fills, you cannot import files for use as texture fills. The texture fills are actually fractals that are created as they are applied. This goes a long way to explain why textures sometime malfunction or take a long time to load.

If you cannot find the exact file that you want in the 100+ default textures that were shipped with PHOTO-PAINT, you can edit the existing textures by clicking on the Edit button. This opens the Texture Fill dialog box shown in Figure 7.12.

The Texture Fill Dialog Box

Don't let all of the values and number boxes in this dialog box intimidate you. The Texture Fill dialog box is, for the most part, logically laid out (see Figure 7.23).

Figure 7.23.
The Texture Fill Dialog
Box looks scary, but it
provides incredible
control over a very
powerful phrasal
generator.

Texture Fill Dialog Box Options

■ **Texture Library.** Textures in the Samples and Samples 5 libraries can be altered and saved. Textures in the Styles library can be modified but not saved in the Styles library. You can save them, however, in any other existing library or in a new library.

■ **Texture List.** Displays textures in the selected library. Click the one you want. When you switch between libraries, the Texture list always returns to the default texture selection.

■ **Preview.** Varies the appearance of the selected texture by randomly changing all unlocked parameters. This button does more than is apparent at first. There are over 15,000 textures with several million possible combinations for each one. Rather than requiring you to wade through a sea of permutations, Corel PHOTO-PAINT textures have certain variables unlocked by default. The unlocked parameters are the ones that the graphic engineers at Corel thought provided the best way to modify the textures.

Every time the Preview button is depressed, the unlocked parameters change randomly. This is especially important for the texture pattern settings.

You can lock and unlock a parameter by clicking the Lock icon next to it. You can also use the Preview button to update a texture after changing the parameters yourself.

Corel *TIP!*

Until you get used to using a texture, I recommend using the default settings for the locks. They generally provide the best results the quickest.

■ **Save.** After changing the parameters of a texture in the library (or a new library you created), choose Save to overwrite the original.

Corel *TIP!*

Don't overwrite the original textures. Leave the originals alone, and use the Save command for saving custom textures that you have created.

■ **Save As.** Opens a dialog box for naming (or renaming) a texture you have created. The texture name can be up to 32 characters (including spaces). The Library Name option allows you to create a new library in which to store the textures. You can type up to 32 characters (including spaces). The Library List displays libraries where you can store the modified texture. (Note: You must save any modified Style textures in a library other than the Styles library, because Styles is a read-only library.)

■ **Delete.** Deletes the selected texture. You can only delete textures from libraries you create.

■ **Style Name Section.** This part of the Texture Fill dialog box allows you to change the existing textures into almost anything you can imagine. Because each texture has different value assignments, methods, colors, and lights, it would take a separate book just to list a few of the combinations. The value boxes in this area list parameters for the selected texture. Changing one or more of these parameters alters the appearance of the texture. The changes are displayed in the preview box whenever the Preview button is depressed. The Style Name fields list numeric parameters. All textures have a texture number, which ranges from 0 to 32,768. The names of the other parameters vary with the texture selected and have ranges from 0 to 100 or -100 to 100.

To change a numeric parameter, enter a value in the text box or use the cursor and click on either the up or down arrow.

Corel *TIP!*

If you are going to ascend or descend very far on the list, you can use a speedup feature of the up and down arrows. Place the cursor between the up and down arrows. The cursor will change into a two-headed arrow cursor with a line between the two arrowheads. After the cursor changes, click and drag either up or down, and the selection list will move rapidly up or down the list (depending on which way you choose). To see the change entered, click the Preview button.

The right side of the field lists up to six color parameters, depending upon the texture selected. To change a color, click on the color button and select a new color from the pop-up palette. If you desire a specific color or named color that is not on the color palette, click on the More button. The More button opens the same dialog box as the Uniform Fill dialog box. (See the Uniform Fill section for specific details regarding the use of this dialog box.) After you have made the desired changes, click the Preview button to see the effect the new color has on the selected texture.

The No-Fill Fill

This isn't a joke—there really is a No-Fill fill. It is rarely used, but there are times when it is necessary. Using the No-Fill fill in combination with the Rectangle Draw, Circle Draw, or Polygon Draw tools provides a way to make empty rectangles, circles, or polygons. To use it, select the No-Fill Fill button or "button X" and select one of the aforementioned drawing tools. If the Tool Setting roll-up is not open, double-click on one of the drawing tools, and it will appear.

With the Tool Settings roll-up you can control the size of the border made by the Rectangle, Circle, or Polygon tool (in points). The "roundness" of the corners is determined by the Roundness slider. A rough representation of the rounded curve is continuously updated as the slider is moved. Make sure the Settings value box is set to a value other than zero, or you will end up making nothing. (Think about it: What does a rectangle with a border width of 0 points and no fill look like? That's reserved for the Zen masters.)

The Canvas Roll-Up

Introduction

The Canvas roll-up is a simple roll-up that will allow you to achieve some professional looking effects with little experience or effort. A PHOTO-PAINT Canvas can be any color (mono or gray scale images have to be converted to color first) image. The Canvas bitmap is used to load a bitmap pattern that is applied to the background of an image to give the appearance of a canvas. The canvas can also be used with a high transparency to overlay an existing picture. The canvas shows through the image and any future application of paint. You can set the transparency and the level of embossing. A low transparency value allows you to view more of the canvas. Embossing creates a relief effect.

The Canvas roll-up

The Canvas roll-up is opened by selecting Canvas roll-up in the View menu or depressing the Ctrl+F3 key. Figure 7.24 shows the Canvas roll-up with system default settings. The roll-up consists of the following options:

Roll-Up Options

- **Preview**
  The Preview box displays the selected canvas. If no canvas has been loaded or if the **None** button has been selected the Preview window will be blank except for a large X in the center of it.

- **Transparency**
  Sets the level of transparency expressed in percentage. High levels make the canvas more transparent and the underlying image more visible. Lower levels make the canvas opaque and less of the image is visible.

- **Emboss**
  Emboss gives the canvas a raised relief effect. Use the slider to change the percentage of embossing or enter the number directly into the value box.

Figure 7.24.
The Canvas roll-up.

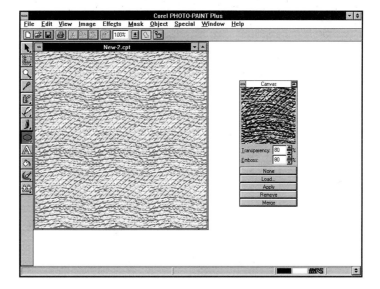

■ **Remove**

Selecting this removes the canvas from the image area if it has not been merged.

■ **None**

Removes the canvas from the Preview box.

■ **Load...**

Displays the Load a Canvas from Disk dialog box. (See Figure 7.25.) Select a canvas from the PHOTOPNT\CANVAS directory, or choose another image.

■ **Apply**

Applies the selected canvas to the image. It only applies it to the base image. A canvas cannot be applied to an object. If you have depressed the None button, selecting the Apply button removes the canvas from the image if it has not been merged.

■ **Merge**

Merges the canvas with the image. The canvas becomes part of the image and can no longer be removed. *Note: Canvases are merged automatically with all files when they are saved. The only exception to that is Corel PHOTO-PAINT (*.CPT) files. An applied canvas in a *.CPT file can still be modified after the file is saved and reopened. Once the canvas has been merged, it cannot be changed regardless of what format the file structure is in.*

Figure 7.25.
The Load a Canvas
from Disk dialog box is
opened from the
Canvas roll-up.

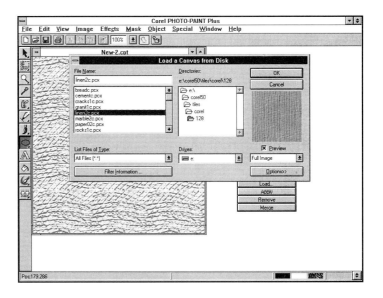

Figure 7.25 shows the Load a Canvas from Disk dialog box. PHOTO-PAINT installs 10 .PCX files as your initial selection for Canvases. They are located in the COREL50\PHOTOPNT\CANVAS subdirectory. There are a total of 120 canvases located on the CD-ROM Disk under COREL50\PHOTOPNT\CANVAS. Now the 120 additional canvases are actually 40 canvases that each come in three different sizes. The different size files are identified by the last letter of the file name (not extension.) The files are designated as follows:

- Coarse -*filename*C.*PCX* (128 × 128 pixels) Example - PAPER01C.PCX
- Medium *filename*M.*PCX* (96 × 96 pixels) Example - PAPER01M.PCX
- Fine *filename*F.*PCX* (64 × 64 pixels) Example - PAPER01F.PCX

Figures 7.26 through 7.28 are examples of each of the three types of canvases, coarse, medium, and fine, applied on top of the same image.

Figure 7.26.
The Coarse canvas
applied at 80 percent
transparency and
80 percent emboss.

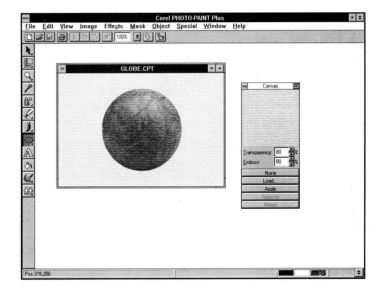

Additionally, you can use any color bitmap file that can be imported by PHOTO-PAINT to create a new canvas by loading it into the Canvas roll-up through the Load a Canvas from Disk dialog box. (This dialog box is identical to the File Open dialog box covered in previous chapters) This includes files from Photo-CDs and the files that you create with PHOTO-PAINT 5. If you have a vector-based file that you want to import. Load it into PHOTO-PAINT and save it as a color bitmap file. If you attempt to load a non-color bitmap file (black/white or grayscale) you will get a warning message and the file will not load.

Figure 7.27.
This figure demon-
strates the Medium
canvas applied at 80
percent transparency
and 80 percent emboss.

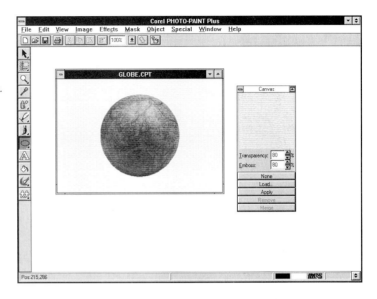

Figure 7.28.
The fine canvas applied
at 80 percent transpar-
ency and 80 percent
emboss.

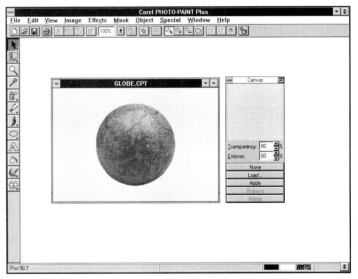

If the bitmap image that is selected for use as a canvas is too small to fit the image area where it is being applied, the image will be tiled by PHOTO-PAINT to fit the image area. Note: if the image is going to be tiled you may want to consider cropping the bitmap with the Object rectangle tool, feathering the edge of the object with a small value, and dragging the image into the PAINT workspace to create a new cropped image. The feathering will reduce the lines and therefore the "kitchen tile" look. If the Image used for a canvas is too large to fit into the image area, it will be cropped to fit the image area.

Considerations About Using Canvases

Canvases can either be placed on top of an image or be used as the base image. If you are going to place the canvas on top of the image, be aware that it will make the image more opaque to some extent. The best canvases for placing on top of an image are those with little color, lots of white area and contrast. Cement is a good example of a canvas to place on top. It is a high contrast canvas and therefore the effect of the embossing really stand out.

Do not let the names of canvases fool you. In Figure 7.29 I have applied a canvas to one of the photographs that is included in the Europe section of the Plus edition of PAINT. As you can see, the canvas I used looks like a painter's canvas. It is PAPER01C.PCX. It is the same one used in the previous examples with the globe. Corel provides two canvases called Linen, but both of them are too dark for most applications. Bottom line, don't go by the name, go by what it looks like in the preview window.

There is good news and bad news. The bad news is one of the effects of applying the canvas is that the resulting image looks washed out. The good news there is a cure. After you have applied the canvas, apply the Equalize filter (located in the Effects menu, under the Tone setting) using the default setting. Applying this filter restores most of the color depth that is lost when the canvas is applied.

Figure 7.29.
A canvas applied to a photograph to produce the appearance of a painting.

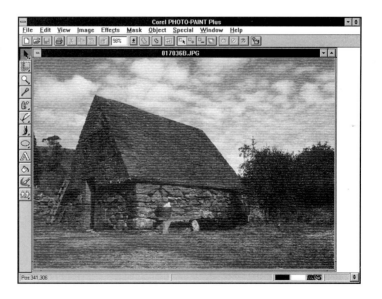

Figure 7.30.
The wash out caused
by the application of a
canvas.

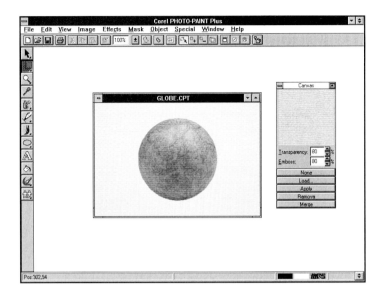

Figure 7.31.
The restoration of some
of the original color
depth by use of the
equalize command.

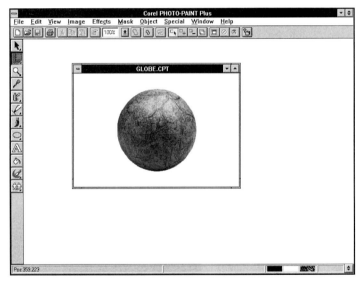

Canvases can be placed on top of and behind images. Canvases can be applied to objects. In fact, the canvas provides a way to add texture to just an object.

Adding texture to text. Figure 7.32 shows the application of a canvas to text (or any object) when the background is hidden. Only the objects that are visible have the canvas applied to them. Remember to merge the canvas before showing (unhiding) the base image or any other objects.

Figure 7.32.
This was created by
hiding the base image
(background) and
applying a cement
canvas to the text.

Any bitmap file can be imported and used as a canvas as long as it is a color bitmap. A Canvas remains separate from an image (like an object) until it is merged using the merge button on the roll-up. If an image is saved as a PHOTO-PAINT file (*.CPT) the canvas will not be merged when it is saved. If it is saved as any other format file, the canvas is merged in the image. A canvas can be removed by selecting the Remove button. When a Canvas is merged, it cannot be removed.

Working with Text

The Text tool, used in combination with the Flood fill capabilities and layers/objects, can produce stunning effects quickly.

Basics of the Text Tool

The Text tool (the icon with the letter A on it) is located in the toolbox. The best way to quickly get through the basics of this tool is to participate in a quick demonstration. In this session you will learn how all of the associated buttons work and some general principles about working with the text tool.

1. Open a new image file by either selecting New in the File menu or by clicking on the New File icon in the ribbon bar. Either accept system defaults for the new image or select 400 pixel width by 200 pixel height, 256 colors with a white paper color. Resolution is not important, mine is set for 96 dpi.

Corel *TIP!*

> The Text tool will not work unless you have an image selected.

2. Click on the Text tool in the toolbox. The text-editing section of the ribbon bar appears as shown in Figure 8.1. If you have worked with recent versions of Windows word processors, everything on the ribbon bar should be familiar to you. The first box shows all of the available fonts that are installed in Windows. The second box displays the selected font sizes in points. While the drop-down list shows a long list of available sizes, you can select any size you need by typing the desired font size (in points) in the Font Size box. The system default settings for the Text tool's font selection and font size are the first elements of their respective lists. The last settings entered into the text-editing section of the ribbon bar remain until they are either changed again or PHOTO-PAINT is shut down.

The next three buttons are controls for the bold, italics, and underline attributes. The last three buttons are for left alignment, centering, and right alignment.

Figure 8.1.
Text-editing command buttons in ribbon bar.

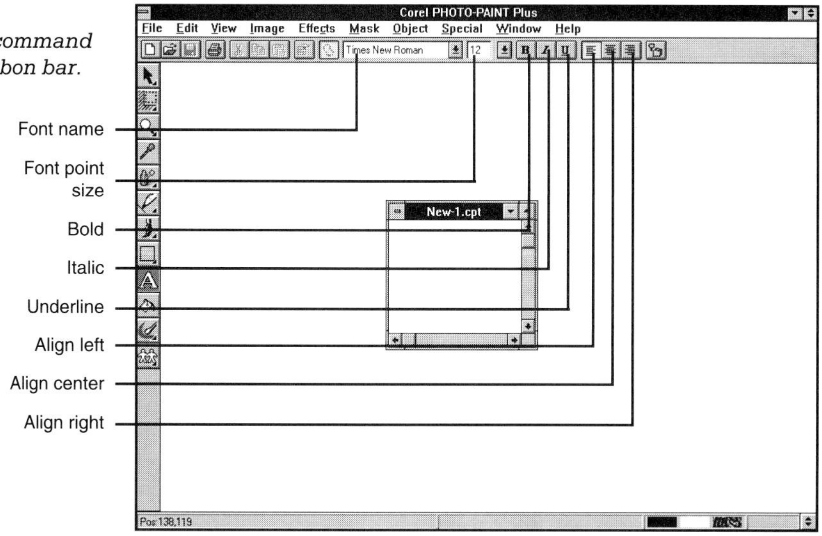

Font name
Font point size
Bold
Italic
Underline
Align left
Align center
Align right

3. Select Times New Roman from the Font drop-down list, a font size of 48 and click on the Center text button. As you move the cursor inside the image area it changes into a Text tool bar. Click near the middle of the image and type in the word "TEXAS." You now have the word "TEXAS" surrounded by a rectangle. Before we go further, here are the facts about the PHOTO-PAINT Text tool:

   ■ Character, word, and line spacing (leading) are controlled by PAINT.

   ■ The color of the text is determined by the setting of the paint (fore-ground) color.

   ■ To correct text, use the backspace or Delete key.

   ■ The selected alignment of text (left, center, or right alignment) occurs when the Enter key is pressed.

   ■ There is no automatic line wrap (soft carriage returns) of text.

4. Change the name of the Font to PLAYBILL (it is one of the fonts provided by Corel; if you do not wish to install it, keep the Times New Roman font but be aware that the font sizes will be different). Change the Font Size to 72 and click the Bold button. The word "TEXAS" is still to small for this typeface, but 72 points is as large as the preset list goes to. No problem, it is easy to fix. In the font size window highlight the 72 point value and type in 140. Notice that the font size did not change. Now hit the enter key and the font now reflects the requested size. The word "TEXAS" may have gone off of the screen when you changed sizes. Do not be concerned, it is still there. It is only out of the image area. Notice the font, font size, and characteristics can all be altered at this stage. Any change you make in the Ribbon Bar is instantly reflected in the text displayed in the image area. You can move the rectangle containing the text by clicking on it and dragging it with the left mouse button.

Corel*CAUTION!*

> Make sure the text is correct before it is made into an object. After the text becomes an object, its font, characteristics (**bold**, *italics* and <u>underline</u>) and alignment (left align, center, and right align) cannot be altered. Only the size can be changed.

5. Click on the Object Picker (Top button of the Tool Box). The text becomes an Object, as indicated by the blue marquee that surrounds it. Because it is an object, it will be on its own layer. Depress CTRL+F7 key to open the Layers/Objects roll-up box. (See Figure 8.2.) Since it is an Object, we can do anything to it that we can do with any Object. We can resize it by

dragging the control handles, rotate it, or distort it. Next we will add some color to this text, but not to the background. We first must deselect (hide) the base image.

Figure 8.2.
Text (Playbill) as an
Object. Layers/Objects
roll-up shows it on a
layer.

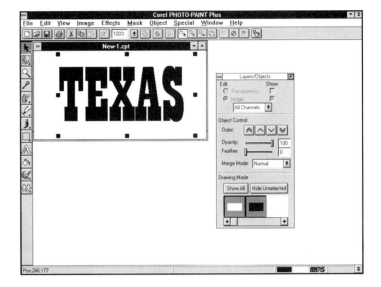

6. Click on the base image button in the Layers/Objects roll-up to deselect (hide) the base image (background). All that remains is the text with the word "TEXAS" enclosed with a blue marquee. Open the Flood Fill roll-up (double-click the Flood Fill color display in the lower right part of the display) and select Uniform Color Fill (first button on the left). Pick the color blue for the Fill color.

Corel *NOTE!*

> If you cannot see the text/marquee, the Marquee Select/Deselect button in the ribbon bar is off. Click it to activate it.

7. Select the Rectangle tool in the toolbox. Open the Tool Settings roll-up by depressing Ctrl+F8. Set both the Size and Transparency boxes in the Tool Settings roll-up to 0 and move the Roundness slider to the far left.

8. Starting above and to left of the word "TEXAS" drag a rectangle that covers the entire word. When you release the mouse button, the text fills with blue. Let us examine what you have just done. This is an important principle of applying fills to text. When the Rectangle tool was used, it did not make a rectangle. We filled an area with the selected fill color that was

defined by the rectangle drawn. After the area was filled with the fill color, the rectangle boundary ceased to exist. An object on the layer under the rectangle is filled with color. If multiple layers are selected, then all objects under a defined area are also filled with color. The black area on the layer is like a black hole. Anything applied to it is lost. So, when we filled the rectangle area, only the text could be filled with the fill color. This is how we apply color to text.

9. Select the Fountain Fill mode in the Flood Fill roll-up. Click on the button for Linear fill. Select red for the start color and blue for the end color. The left button in the Fountain Fill roll-up is the "from" color. The angle of the fill should be 90 degrees (default), which puts red on the bottom and blue on the top.

10. Drag the Rectangle Draw tool over the entire word again, beginning with the uppermost corner of the word and ending at the bottom-right tip of the S in "TEXAS." Now the entire word is filled with one radial fill, with the center being around the letter X. The radial fill floods the rectangle area without regard to what objects are being filled with color. This means the center of the fill will be in the center of the rectangle. This principle works to our advantage, as we will see in the next few steps. Whenever you want to see what the fill of text looks like against the base image (background), click on the base image button in the Layers/Objects roll-up. To see a full-screen preview without the marquee, depress the F9 function key.

Corel *NOTE!*

If you unhide the base image to see how the text-color fill looks against it, don't forget to deselect it; otherwise, the next time you apply a fill color, you will paint both the text and the background.

11. Drag the Rectangle Draw tool over the word "TEXAS," beginning at the extreme upper-left corner of the image area and ending at the far-right corner of the word. The result is shown in Figure 8.3. Because the rectangle was offset in relationship to the word "TEXAS," the center of the fill is somewhere below the letter X in "TEXAS." Did you also notice that the fill colors are not additive? Any existing color is wiped out by the application of a new color; the two fills (colors) are not combined.

There are other ways we can control the fill. Before we do the next step, we must return the text-color fill to a uniform color. In the Fountain Fill roll-up, select the Uniform Fill button (any color will work) and drag a rectangle over the entire word "TEXAS." (We applied the Uniform Fill before the next step because the Flood Fill tool will only fill until it reaches a color boundary that is determined by the Color Tolerance command setting, thus filling only part of each character.) Return the Flood Fill dialog box to Fountain fills and while keeping your original setting, click the edit button and set an Edge pad of 40 percent.

Figure 8.3.
Text with offset linear
fill of text. The object
marquee is deselected
for clarity.

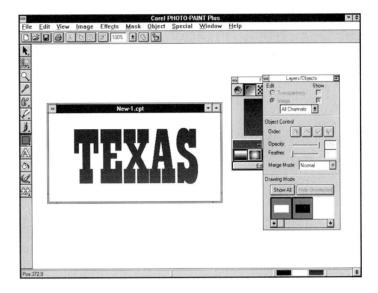

12. Select the Flood Fill tool from the toolbox. Click the Flood Fill icon on the center of each letter. Now each letter in the text exhibits an individual linear fill, as shown in Figure 8.4. Close the file and do not save any changes.

The possible combinations of fills and tools are almost infinite. Rather than spend more time running over combinations, let us learn some effects that can be done with the Text tool in combination of the other tools of PHOTO-PAINT 5.

13. Select Uniform color, pick white from the color palette and using the Draw Rectangle tool make a white rectangle across the word "TEXAS" as shown in Figure 8.5.

14. Hide the text and select the base image. Open the Fill roll-up and select the Bit Map fill mode (the button that looks like a checkerboard). Click the Load button. When the dialog box opens, select the Wood3.TIF from the Corel CD-ROM Disk 1 in the COREL50\CLIPART_BITMAP\TEXTURES directory.

Figure 8.4.
"TEXAS" is now a blue top with a red base so to finish up the project, we need a touch of white—don't forget the Texas flag is red, white and blue. The base image (white background) is only being shown so that is it visible in this grayscale image. On your image the base image should be hidden (black).

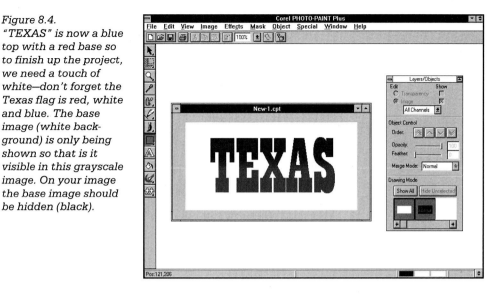

Figure 8.5.
Whoa! What happened to the characters when we turned on the base image? We need to change the base image so the white in the text stands out.

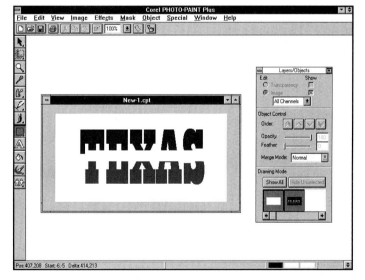

15. Use the rectangle draw tool to fill the entire base image. Notice that the image area is larger than the bitmap image we are using so visible tiling is apparent. Since the word "TEXAS" will be in front of it, it doesn't matter that much.

16. Click the Show All button in the Layers/Object roll-Up and we are done.

185

Figure 8.6.
The completed
"TEXAS" sign.

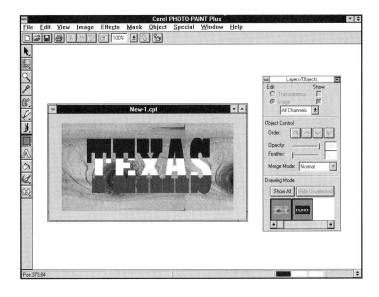

Figure 8.7.
The result of applying a
cement canvas (with
the base image hidden)
to the word "TEXAS"
and then hiding the
text and applying a
light (setting of 2)
Gaussian Blur to the
base image.

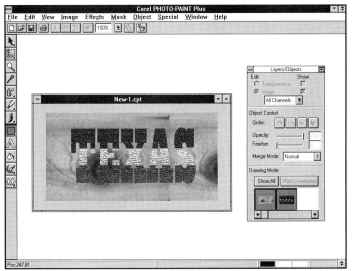

17. Close the file. You do not need to save any changes since we won't be
using this again.

Now we will learn to combine text with the Emboss filter to make what appears
to be embossed paper and a few other effects.

186

Simulating Embossed Paper

This demonstration uses several filters, the Canvas roll-up, and text to achieve several different effects.

1. Open a new file that is 300 pixels wide and 150 pixels in height. Set the resolution at 150 dpi (identical values box checked) and the Color Mode at 24-bit color.

2. Select the Text tool in the Toolbox. Click on the far left side of the image with the cursor. Type the word "ACE Papers." Using the Ribbon bar, make the typeface Times New Roman with a size of 48 points; click off the Bold button if it is on. You may also want to turn off the marquee.

3. Click on the Object Picker (located on the top of the toolbox). This action changes the text into an Object. Using the Pick tool, move the word "ACE Papers" to the center of the image area, as shown in Figure 8.8.

Figure 8.8.
The text to be used for embossing is centered in the image area.

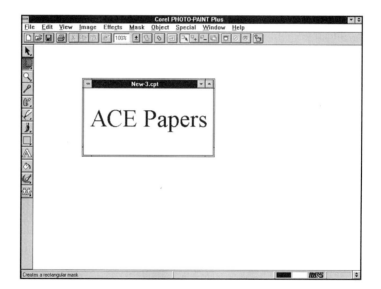

4. Save the file as ACEPAPER.CPT, using the Save As command in the File menu.

5. Click on the Checkpoint command in the Edit menu. This provides a quick method to get back to here later in the session.

6. Select the Emboss filter from the Fancy submenu under Effects. When the filter preview window opens, change the Emboss Color to Gray. Click on the lower-right direction arrow and select OK. When the filter is finished, it should look like Figure 8.9. Now the embossed image has crisp, sharp lines. However, in the real world, when paper is embossed it doesn't have the distinct sharp lines. In the next step we will create the soft transitions.

Figure 8.9.
Text after application
of the Emboss filter.

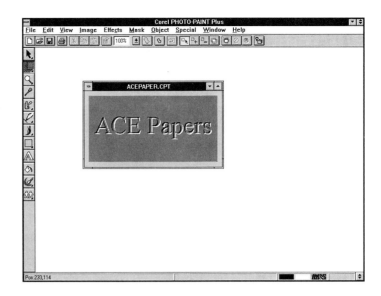

7. Select the Gaussian Blur filter from the Fancy subgroup in the Effects menu. When the Preview dialog box opens, enter a value of 1. Click on OK. After the filter completes, repeat the same filtering by selecting Ctrl+F. Now we have a slightly blurred image. The reason for using the blur twice at a setting of 1 instead of doing it once at a setting of 2 is related to the way the filter is designed. In some cases, it achieves a smoother effect with multiple passes of small values.

8. Open the Canvas roll-up (Ctrl+F3). Click on the Load button. Select PAPER13C.PCX on the CorelDRAW CD-ROM Disc 1 (COREL50\PHOTOPNT\CANVAS directory).

9. Set the Transparency to 50 percent and Emboss to 100 percent. Click the Apply button. Don't click the Merge button yet. At this point you have a nice embossed-paper effect, but it isn't as visible as it could be, so we will improve it.

Corel *TIP!*

The value of both Transparency and Emboss are a function of the type of bitmap being used for the canvas. If the bitmap is dark, use a higher transparency value. If it is light (bright), as in the case of PAPER13C.PCX, then use a lower transparency value. The Emboss value used with the canvas should be based on the selected canvas contrast. On a low-contrast canvas, such as PAPER13C.PCX, emboss will have little effect, even when set to 100 percent. On a high-contrast image, it works better to use lower emboss values.

10. From the Effects menu select Tone Map from the Color subgroup. Select Solarized Response Curve under Presets. (See Figure 8.10.) Click on OK. Watch as the filter is applied to the image. What we have done is apply the Solarize effect to the embossed image "under" the canvas. Remember, the canvas hasn't been merged yet. Now the embossed image is looking pretty good. But because of the Transparency effect, we lost some of the richness of the canvas. Let's fix that now.

Figure 8.10.
The Tone Map filter
dialog box showing the
Solarized Response
curve.

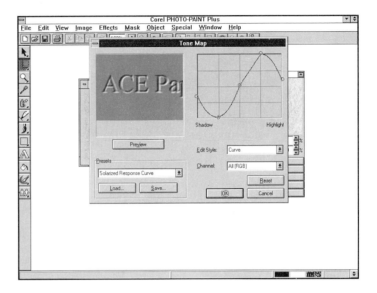

Figure 8.11.
Embossed text after
the Solarization filter is
applied and the canvas
is merged.

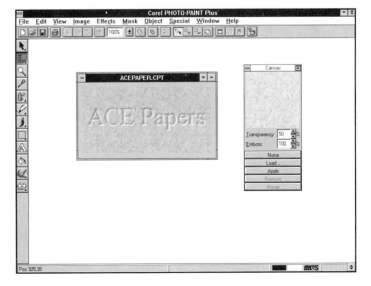

11. Click the Merge button on the Canvas roll-up. If you do not click on the Merge button, the canvas "floats" above the base image and is not seen in the filter preview window. (See Figure 8.11) You should not see any changes in the image when you merge the canvas.

12. Select Tone from the Effects menu. Click on Equalize in the drop-down list (which is the only choice). This action opens the Histogram Equalization dialog box. (See Figure 8.12.) This is a very powerful tool for applying corrections to photographs.

    The Equalize filter from the Tone flyout menu (Histogram Equalization) redistributes shades of colors. Equalize can change the dynamic range of an image, moving the darker colors toward black and the lighter colors toward white. This action "stretches" the colors in between. The histogram that is displayed represents the shades in the image. The height of each bar shows the number of pixels with that amount of shading. The distance between the three triangle-shaped markers at the bottom of the histogram shows the range of shades in your image. The markers represent dark (low), medium (midtones) and high (highlights), and the equivalent values are shown numerically in the three boxes at the bottom of the chart. We are going to make the colors in our image look more like the original canvas with this filter.

Figure 8.12.
The Histogram
Equalization dialog box
is where we correct
some of the canvas
"washout."

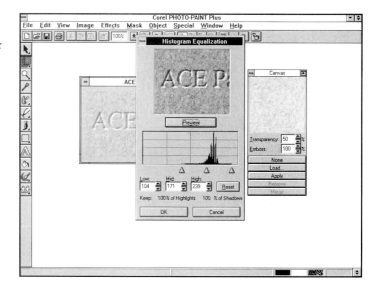

13. Do not change the markers yet. This is your starting point for equalizing the picture. Let us see the effect the default setting makes. Click the preview button. Look at the color and contrast of the preview. Does it match the color and contrast of the original canvas in the Canvas roll-up? If not, adjust the top two markers until they do. Notice that all of the high-lights (brighter colors) are near the very edge of the dynamic range of the histogram. Moving the markers redistributes the area of concentration of shading over a larger area. By moving the top marker further to the right we have increased the dynamic range of the entire image. Moving the mid-tone (middle) marker until it almost touches the area of the image where all of the shading is centered, increases the mid-tone values in that region and has the visual effect of increasing contrast. This same function is also called quarter-tones in other photo-editing applications. You are encour-aged to move all of the markers around to see the effects that they have. Click preview after each change to see the effect. After you have done that, return the markers to their default position by clicking the Reset key so that the canvas image in the preview window looks as close to the canvas image in the Canvas roll-up windows as possible. Figure 8.13 shows what the finished product should look like.

Corel *NOTE!*

Equalization does not control color shading, although it sometimes gives the appearance of doing so. Color shading is controlled through Hue and Saturation.

Figure 8.13.
The finished product,
embossed paper for the
ACE Paper Company
logo.

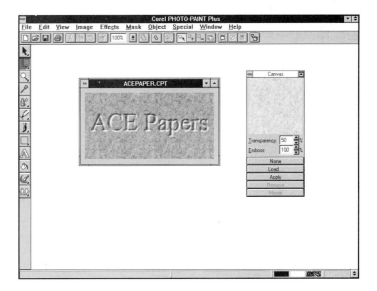

14. When you are satisfied with the image in the Preview window, click the OK button. Depress F9 (full screen preview) and see how you like your Embossed text. If you want to save your embossed text at this point use the File, Save As... command and save it under a different name.

The Color Mask

The Color Mask is one of PHOTO-PAINT's computer-aided masks. The Color Mask that is applied to the image is created by the computer based on user-selected colors. The colors are selected using the color picker (eyedropper) in the Color Mask roll-up. The selected colors can be either modified or protected. Doesn't sound like a tool that would serve much purpose, right? However, once you get comfortable with using the Color Mask, you will save yourself literally hours of time in retouching and recreating photographic images.

Simply put, the Color Mask lets you use color to mask portions of an image. The masking affects all colors within a certain range of the selected color, as defined by values selected in the Color Mask roll-up.

The original CorelDRAW 5 documentation for PHOTO-PAINT illustrated some unusual effects that could be achieved by using the Color Mask. It has been my experience that unusual effects are fun to look at but rarely of any practical benefit in the day-to-day work of photo-editing. The strength of the Color Mask is its ability to either protect or allow modification of a sets of colors that define an area. Figure 9.1 is a picture from the Corel Professional Photos CD-ROM Sampler. The tree in the image looks great, but the sky is too dark. We could use the Magic Wand Mask tool and make a mask to isolate the sky from the rest of the image. The problem with this approach is that the sky is visible in literally hundreds of spots throughout the tree. The Magic Wand tool, if you recall, works with similar colors that are contiguous (connected to each other). To make a mask for the tree with the Magic Wand would require individually selecting almost one hundred little spots and including them in a mask. It would take several hours. With the Color Mask, I was able remove all of the sky in a few minutes as shown in Figure 9.2. Using the Texture fill (Morning Sky in the Samples library), I was able to add a very realistic-looking sky as shown in Figure 9.3. (If the images were printed here in color, you would be much more impressed.) This is only one use of the Color Mask. There are several other uses, which we will discuss and learn in this chapter.

Figure 9.1.
This is the original image of a tree and a dull, cloudless sky from the Corel Photo Sampler CD. Our goal is to replace the sky with something less dark and gloomy.

Figure 9.2.
Here the same image
has had the sky
removed using the
Color Mask roll-up.

Figure 9.3.
The image with dark
sky replaced with a
cloud picture from the
Corel Photo CD clouds
collection. The dark
area under the tree was
also color masked and
slightly lightened.

The Color Mask Roll-Up

I will be honest with you—when I first opened the Color Mask roll-up, my first instinct was to close it again. I would have never used it again if it hadn't been for the encouragement of the PAINT development team, who assured me that once I got the hang of the thing, I would use it all the time. They were right. While it looks like a numerical nightmare, once you understand it, it won't be nearly as intimidating. The Color Mask roll-up is shown in Figure 9.4.

Corel *NOTE!*

If you are using the original PHOTO-PAINT 5 that was shipped with CorelDRAW 5, your roll-up will look and operate differently. We will note the differences in the text.

Corel *TIP!*

If you are still using the original version, upgrade. It is available free to all registered users. If you have an illegal copy, shame on you.

Figure 9.4.
The Color Mask roll-up.

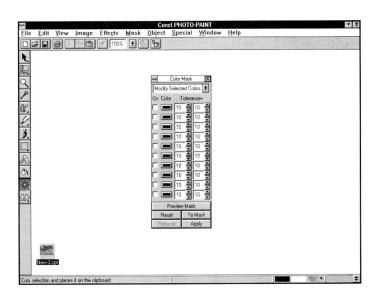

The Color Mask roll-up is opened by depressing Ctrl+F5 (F5 in the original version) or selecting the Color Mask roll-up in the Mask menu. The drop-down list on the top of the Color Mask roll-up is the mode-selection area. There are two modes: Modify Selected Colors and Protect Selected Colors. The name of the first mode, Modify Selected Colors, might be misunderstood. The Color Mask is just that, a mask. A mask does not modify anything. Its function is to allow the modification of selected colors. Anything selected by the mask in this mode can be modified; anything not selected cannot have any effects applied to it. Clear?

Modify Selected Colors isolates the selected color(s) so that any changes applied affect only the selected color(s).

Protect Selected Colors. This is the inverse of Modify Selected Colors. It protects the selected color(s) so that the changes affect only the colors that are not selected.

Below the Mode drop-down list are three columns of functions. There are 10 rows. Each row of selected color or range of colors has three components: On, Color, and Tolerance. The descriptions of each follows:

On	Turns the protection or modification mode for specified colors on or off. When color protection is turned on, there is an X in the checkbox.
Color	The color contained within the button is a sample of the color selected. Colors are selected either from the image or from the Select Color dialog box (see Figure 9.5). The color to be included in the mask is chosen by selecting desired colors from the image. Clicking on the color button causes the cursor to become an eyedropper tool, which is used to select a color from the image. Holding down the Shift key while clicking on a color button opens the Select Color dialog box.
Tolerance	Determines the range of color that is either protected or can be modified. The numbers entered in the - and + boxes control the range. Higher values create a greater range of color; lower values create a small range of colors. (We will explore this concept in greater detail forthwith.)
Preview Mask	Displays a preview of the mask. Colors that are protected or to-be-modified are displayed. The color of the preview mask is selected in the Advanced section of the Preferences dialog box.
Apply	Applies the mask to the image. The mask covers the entire image. Because it is a mask, you cannot see any change in the image after it is applied. When a Color Mask has been applied, an icon appears in the status bar of the Main screen. Masks are not additive. When the Apply button is depressed, any existing Color Mask is wiped out.
Reset	Resets all of the Color Mask values to their default values.
To Mask	Allows the Color Mask to be saved as a standard mask.
Remove	Removes the Color Mask.

Figure 9.5.
While it is wonderful that Corel provides a method to isolate a precise color based on several possible color models, in normal use you will hardly ever use this dialog box with the Color Mask.

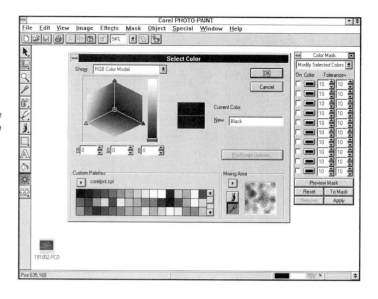

Color Tolerance

At this point we could go into a long-winded explanation of color models, which would leave you more confused than ever. Instead let me oversimplify a few concepts for the sake of clarity. (So if you are a color expert, don't send me letters. OK?)

The Color Tolerance values represent color ranges using the selected color as a starting point. This works as follows:

- The maximum number of shades that can exist on either side of the selected color is 256. This means the largest value that can be entered is 255. (In the computer world, 0 is a number, so 0 through 255 represents a total of 256.)

- If we select a color and enter 255 on the + and the - side of the Tolerance column, we will have selected every pixel in the image.

- A small number indicates a narrow range of colors centered around the selected color.

- A large number indicates a wide range of colors centered around the selected color.

- Numbers entered on the positive (+) side of the Tolerance column have a greater effect on the lighter shades of the selected color.

- Numbers entered on the negative (-) side of the Tolerance column have a greater effect on the darker shades of the selected color.
- A maximum of 10 color ranges can be masked.
- A Color Mask can be used in conjunction with other masks to allow even further fine tuning of the color ranges.

This last point is important. If you are selecting a range of colors, many times you will find that some of the colors that you want to include also exist in an area you want excluded. To accomplish this, make the Color Mask as specific as possible (many colors/narrow range, i.e., small numbers). After you have applied the Color Mask, use the masking tools to isolate further the areas of the image you want modified or protected.

Selecting a Range of Colors

1. Choose Color Mask roll-up from the mask menu or depress the Ctrl+F5.
2. Choose Modify Selected Colors or Protect Colors Mode from the drop-down list box.
3. Click the first button in the Color column. The cursor changes to the eyedropper tool.
4. Select the desired color to be masked in the image by clicking on it with the eyedropper cursor. The point at the tip of the eyedropper is where the color pixel is selected. As the cursor is moved around, the color under the cursor is displayed within the button.
5. Enter a number or click and drag the Tolerance scroll arrows to set the tolerance. Higher values allow for greater range (more shades) of the selected color; lower values narrow the range (the number of shades).
6. Check the On checkbox to allow modification of the selected color. Only the colors with the checkbox set to On will affect the mask.
7. Click Preview Mask to view the mask. The mask color appears red (default) wherever the colors fall within the ranges of all the selected colors. If you have a lot of the mask color in the image, go into the Advance Preferences section under the Special menu and change the mask color to one that does not blend easily into the image. When the Preview Mask is on the screen, any keyboard or mouse action clears it. However, the action that clears it is lost. Remember this if you can't figure out why the mask did not apply or why something didn't happen when you clicked it. (I mention this because it has taken me some time to get used to it.)

Corel *NOTE!*

When you see the Preview Mask on the screen, make note of where the mask does not cover the desired area. There are two methods to increase the coverage. Either increase the range of the color(s) near the area, or select an additional color (if you have a another color button available). The disadvantage of increasing the range is that the color may spread into parts of the image you did not want included. If some of your Preview Mask is covering a part of your image that you do not want masked, you can reduce the Tolerance value of the color nearest to the area. If that does not work, then turn off the color and select several similar colors with narrow ranges. This should do the trick. If not, you can always use the mask tools and place a mask over the area (although this is the least desirable solution).

8. To apply the Color Mask, click on the Apply button. The only visual indication you have that the mask has been applied is that the Color Mask icon appears in the status bar of the main screen. The mask will remain until one of the following occurs:

The Remove button is clicked.

The To Mask button is clicked.

The File is closed.

Modifying an Image with the Color Mask

To get a feel for using the Color Mask tool, we will learn how to modify an image using the Color Mask in combination with several other masks. For this project we start with an excellent photo. The client wants to use the photo in his brochure, but all of the colors in the photo are "cool," so he wanted this to be a sunset shot. There are several ways to remove the sky, but in this work session we want to use the Color Mask tool. Looking at the photo we observe that the sky and the ocean are the same color near the horizon. This makes it difficult to use the Color Mask tool, because if we Color Mask the sky, it will include the ocean. No problem—let's get to work.

1. Open image 2000039.PCD from the Sampler Photo CD. If loading the image 2000039.PCD, we need to crop off the crummy black border, so select Paper Size in the Image menu and enter a value of 1.60 inches in the Height setting. Click OK. After the new image is drawn, double-click the control menu on the original and it will redisplay and disappear. (Because it was a read-only image, PHOTO-PAINT doesn't ask you if you want to save the image.) Click the F4 (Zoom to Fit) key.

2. Open the Color Mask roll-up (Ctrl+F5, or F5 in the original version). If it already has values other than the default settings as shown in Figure 9.4, then click the Reset button.

Figure 9.6.
The original photo we must change for the brochure.

3. Click the topmost On checkbox and then click the Color button. The cursor becomes an eyedropper. Find a spot that is an average blue in the sky. Don't waste time looking for the "right" blue—just pick an average blue. Notice that as you move the eyedropper cursor around, the button you clicked changes color to represent the color that the cursor is currently on. Once you have the average blue color selected, click on it and the cursor returns to its original shape. You have just selected your first color.

4. Click the Preview Mask button. PHOTO-PAINT will work on it for a few moments, and the progress bar in the status bar will indicate the action of the Color Mask. When complete, all of the areas that have been selected by the Color Mask will be colored with a solid red. Note that red is the default color for the mask; it can be changed in the Preferences section under the Special menu. (I recommend that you do not change the mask color unless the image you are working on has a large areas of red.) I have shown what the first pass of my image looked like in Figure 9.7.

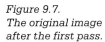
Figure 9.7.
The original image
after the first pass.

At this point you have two choices: Increase the value of the Tolerance or add an additional color to the mask. The disadvantage of increasing the Tolerance value is that when the value gets too large, it starts covering colors other than the range you selected. In Figure 9.8 the Tolerance value of the originally selected color was increased from 10 to 100. You can see that it not only covered the blues but was working its way into the greens and grays. Next we selected a value of 50 for both Tolerance values. Figure 9.9 was the result. The mask is still going into the water; but we will learn that this is not a problem.

Using more colors in the mask takes longer but achieves the best masks. With this image, we are going to use both techniques. Click anywhere on the screen to remove the Preview mask.

Corel *TIP!*

When the Preview Mask is visible, any action (keystroke or mouse action) takes the image out of Mask Preview mode. The action that removed the Preview Mask is lost. This gets frustrating when you are doing a lot of work locating colors that didn't mask. You must take an action to remove the mask, and then you can take your next step. What you end up doing is clicking on a Color button and then realizing that the action was lost.

Figure 9.8.
In Figure 9.8 the
Tolerance value of the
originally selected color
was increased from 10
to 100.

Figure 9.9.
The figure after
selecting a value of 50
for both Tolerance
values.

5. Increase the Tolerance value of the first selected color to 50 in both boxes
   and click the Preview Mask button. Depending on your first color selected,
   you should have a Color Mask that looks somewhat like Figure 9.9. Now
   we have increased the Tolerance value about as much is as reasonable, so
   we need to add a second color. Look for an area of the sky that is not
   masked, and make note of where it is in the image. In Figure 9.9, it is the
   dark blue in the upper-right corner. Click anywhere to remove the Preview
   Mask.

6. Click on the second On button from the top, then click on the Color button. The cursor becomes an eyedropper. Click on an area that was missed by the mask based on the first color settings. In Figure 9.9 it is the dark blue in the upper-right corner. Click the Preview Mask button to see if all of the sky is masked. If there are still areas that are not masked, try either selecting additional colors or increasing the Tolerance values of the selected colors. I was able to produce the mask shown in Figure 9.10 with three colors. I set the Color Tolerance values for the dark blue in the upper-right corner at 30-30. For the third color, I chose the whiter portion of the cloud (which was quite blue) at a value of 40-40. Continue to repeat this step with additional colors or different values of Color Tolerance until the entire sky is masked. As I said before, don't worry if the mask bleeds into the ocean or the rest of the image. When you have masked the entire sky, remove the Preview Mask and go on to the next step.

Figure 9.10.
The resulting mask.

Before we go further, I need to explain that we are entering a portion of the program that changed greatly between the OVA (the original release) and all other versions. The OVA would allow the mask, once it was applied, to be inverted. All versions since that release re-evaluate the image before changing modes. While this is the superior approach, when the colors that define the mask are changed, the mask changes. This does not present a problem, because we now have the ability to save the Color Mask.

7. Click the To Mask Button. A mask appears on the image that coincides with the boundaries of the Color Mask and looks like Figure 9.11. So how do we remove the sky without taking part of the ocean with it? There are two ways. One is to apply the Color Mask and then place a mask on top of the image that covers only the sky area. This would be a very crude mask made with a Polygon Mask tool, because all of the edge details of the mask are being controlled by the Color Mask. The crude mask keeps any effect from being applied to the parts of the image that are to remained unaltered, such as the ocean, the boats, etc. That said, we are going to use a different method. Looking at the image, we see that the line which separates the ocean from the sky is a relatively straight line. So in the next step we are going to subtract a big, fat rectangle from the mask.

Figure 9.11. Click the To Mask Button. A mask appears on the image that coincides with the boundaries of the Color Mask.

8. Select the Rectangle Mask tool from the toolbox. Click the Subtract From Selection button in the ribbon bar. At this point, anything that the Rectangle Mask covers will be removed from the mask we made with the Color Mask tool. Draw a Rectangle Mask over the lower half of the image at the horizon line.

Corel *TIP!*

Trying to make the Rectangle Mask align with the horizon from the side of the image is difficult. I made two passes, beginning at the middle horizon line and going out toward the edge and down.

9. Use the Rectangle Mask tool or the Brush Mask tool to remove any other remnants of a mask that may be floating around the image. Your resulting mask should look like the one shown in Figure 9.12. From this point it is all meat and potatoes. There are several ways to replace the sky at this point. We can get the greatest control of the image if the foreground (everything except the sky) is copied to the clipboard and placed over the new sky as an object.

*Figure 9.12.
Use the Rectangle
Mask tool or the Brush
Mask tool to remove
any other remnants of a
mask that may be
floating around the
image.*

10. Select the Brush Mask tool from the toolbox. Holding down the Z key, draw a rectangle over the area where the ocean meets the sky. When you release the Z key, the cursor returns to the Paint Brush tool. Use the Brush Mask tool to add the faint blue islands that sit right on the horizon as shown in Figure 9.13. I tried to avoid this step, but the flat horizon doesn't look natural in the final picture. Click on the F4 (Zoom to Fit) key to return the image to the original size.

11. Invert the mask by clicking the Invert Mask button on the ribbon bar. After the mask has inverted click the Copy button in the ribbon bar. Click the Minimize button in the upper-right corner of the image.

Figure 9.13.
Use the Brush Mask
tool to add the faint
blue islands that sit
right on the horizon.

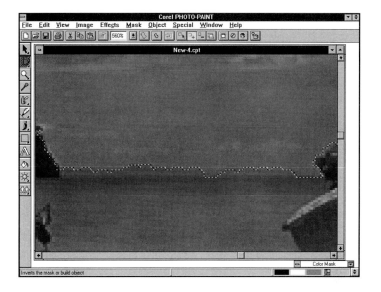

12. Open the image of the sunset 191028.PCD (from the Corel Photo CD clouds collection). Use the same size setting that was used for the original, i.e., if you used Snapshot for the boats, then use Snapshot for the sunset. I used Standard on my system, but then again I have a large monitor. When loading the image 191028.PCD, you will need to crop off the black border, so select Paper Size in the Image menu and enter a value of 1.59 inches in the Height setting. Click OK. After the new image is drawn, double-click the Control menu on the original and it will redisplay and disappear. (Because this was a read-only image, PHOTO-PAINT doesn't ask you if you want to save the image.)

13. Click the Paste button on the ribbon bar, or select Paste and choose As A New Object. Our boats appear as an object on top of our sunset. Align the boats so they look like Figure 9.14. Technically, we are done at this point. The sky has been changed. If we give this to the client to put into his brochure, he will never come back, because it looks like a fake. Why? The boats are bathing in bright sunlight, while the sun is setting behind them. So how do we solve this one? The are several ways. Because the image of the boats is an object, we could reduce the Opacity of the objects and make it blend in into the sunset and it would pick up some of its tint. I tried that, and while it looked good, the trees that were part of the original image began to show through. On to Plan B: Give the object a tint that matches the sunset.

*Figure 9.14.
Click the Paste button
on the ribbon bar, or
select Paste and choose
As A New Object. Our
boats appear as an
object on top of our
sunset.*

14. Holding down the E key and the cursor turns into an eyedropper. Place it in the lighter part of the sunset, right above the clouds, and click the right mouse button. Release the E key. You just made the fill color the same as the lighter part of the sunset sky.

15. Select the Rectangle tool (not the Rectangle Brush tool) out of the toolbox. Open the Tool Settings roll-up (Ctrl+F8, or just F8 for OVA). Set the Size to 0, set the Roundness slider all of the way to the left, and set the Transparency to 75. We are going to place a 75 percent sunset-orange tint over the boats. We don't want to include the sunset, because it is already the right color, so we must hide the base image.

16. Open the Layers/Objects roll-up (Ctrl+F7, or F7 for the OVA) and hide the base image by clicking on the far-left button in the Drawing Mode section. Now draw a rectangle that covers all of the object that remains. When that is finished, click the Show All button on the Layers/Objects roll-up. Because the edges on the object are kind of ragged, we need to feather the object just a little.

17. Select the Object Picker from the toolbox. The object is now selected. Enter a value of 1 into the Feather value, and wait for the hourglass to complete. It will take a few moments. (See Figure 9.15.)

Figure 9.15.
Select the Object Picker from the toolbox. The object is now selected. Enter a value of 1 into the Feather value, and wait for the hourglass to complete.

18. Now there is one last thing to do. The image looks washed out, so let's correct that now. Pick Tone from the Effects menu and select Tone (the only choice). This opens the equalization curve dialog box. (See Figure 9.16.) You could see an improvement by just using the default setting. To make this the best possible, let's tweak it just a little. Change the setting of the Low value to 50. (Don't worry about what we are doing at this point. When we get to the chapter that deals with this filter it will all make sense.) The finished image is shown in Figure 9.17.

Figure 9.16.
The equalization curve dialog box.

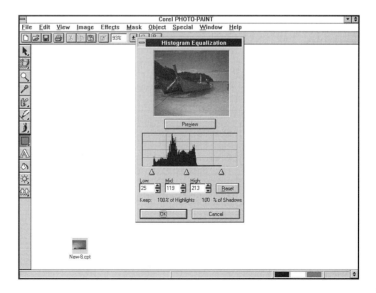

Figure 9.17.
The finished image.

Improving an Image with the Color Mask

Now that you have changed a photo into something that it wasn't, we are going to make a dull and drab photo look better with the help of the Color Mask and some other tools. This exercise is very similar to a job I recently had to do for a company newsletter. The original photo was 24-bit color. The picture was taken on a blustery day. (I have got to quit watching Winnie the Pooh with the kids.) In this exercise, we will use the Color Mask to remove the drab sky and replace it with an improved sky. We will also increase the overall clarity of the image so that it looks better.

1. Open the file 200053.PCD. (See Figure 9.18.) If you are loading the image 200053, you need to crop off the black border, so select Paper Size in the Image menu and enter a value of 1.60 inches in the Height setting. Click OK. After the new image is drawn, double-click the Control menu on the original and it will redisplay and disappear. (Because this was a read-only image, PHOTO-PAINT doesn't ask you if you want to save the image.) Click the F4 (Zoom to Fit) key.

2. Open the Color Mask roll-up (Ctrl+F5, or F5 for OVA). If it already has values other than the default settings as shown in Figure 9.4, click the Reset button. (OVA does not have a Reset button.)

Figure 9.18.
The original image
lacks contrast, detail
and is a generally poor
photograph.

3. Click the topmost On checkbox, and then click the Color button. The cursor becomes an eyedropper. Find a spot that is an average gray in the sky. Don't waste time looking for the "gray" blue. I lucked out and found a gray in the cloud that was directly above the Sphinx. Remember that as you move the eyedropper cursor around, the button you clicked changes color to represent the color that the cursor is currently on. Once you have the gray-blue color selected, click on it and the cursor returns to its original shape. You have just selected your first color.

4. Click the Preview Mask button. PHOTO-PAINT will work on it for a few moments, then the progress bar in the status bar will indicate the action of the Color Mask. When complete, all of the areas that have been selected by the Color Mask will be colored with a solid red. Note that red is the default color for the mask and can be changed in the Preferences section under the Special menu. I recommend that you do not change the mask color unless the image you are working on has a large areas of red. I have shown what the first pass of my image looked like in Figure 9.19. I had a Tolerance setting of 23 and 30.

   This is a good time to talk a little bit more about the Tolerance settings. Up until now we have always set them identically. Now here I go rushing off and making them different.

Figure 9.19.
The image after the
first pass.

To clarify what is going on, I will explain how I came up with that setting. We need to remember that the place where we click the eyedropper establishes the point from which the tolerance is measured. The - numbers are darker shades than the color selected, and the + numbers are lighter shades than the selected color. In this case, after I saw the Preview Mask, with a setting of 30-30, I decided that I wanted fewer of the darker shades included in the mask and no more of the lighter shades. I dropped the minus setting to 20 and left the plus setting alone. It was an improvement, but with a couple of more adjustments, I was able to make the mask as good as possible considering the uniformity of the color spectrum in this image (all drab). Ultimately you want a mask that covers the sky and as little of anything else as possible.

5. Repeat steps 3 and 4 until you have the sky completely masked. Use the Rectangle Mask tool or the Brush Mask tool to remove any other remnants of a mask that may be floating around the image. Click the Apply To Mask button. Your resulting mask should look like the one shown in Figure 9.20. There are several ways to replace the sky at this point. In the previous exercise we copied the foreground to the clipboard and placed it over the new sky as an object. In this exercise we are going to use the Texture fills to create a sky.

6. Open the Fill roll-up (Shift+F6) and select a texture fill that looks like a sky. I used Clouds: Midday out of the Samples library, but you should find one that you like.

7. Select the Rectangle tool out of the toolbox and click and drag a rectangle over the sky area. Only the sky is replaced with the Texture fill. Your image should look like Figure 9.21. The sky looks much better, but we need to clean up Old No-Nose and his surrounding area.

Figure 9.20.
Repeat steps 3 and 4 until you have the sky completely masked. Use the Rectangle Mask tool or the Brush Mask tool to remove any other remnants of a mask that may be floating around the image. Click the Apply To Mask button. Your resulting mask should look like this one.

Figure 9.21.
Select the Rectangle tool out of the toolbox and click and drag a rectangle over the sky area. Only the sky is replaced with the Texture fill.

8. Invert the mask using the Invert button in the ribbon bar. (If you have the original version, you must do the following: Change the mode in the Color Mask roll-up to Modify Selected Colors, and click on the Preview button. You need to do this because the original version could not change the Color mask to a regular mask. Click the Apply To Mask button. It is not necessary to remove the first mask, because each time the Apply button is clicked, the old mask is removed as the new one is applied.) The image should look like Figure 9.22.

Figure 9.22.
The resulting image.

9. In the Effects menu, under Color, select the Brightness and Contrast filter. Enter a value of 35 in Intensity and 25 in Contrast. Leave Brightness untouched. Click the OK button. The effect will only be applied to the masked part of the image; the sky remains unchanged. (See Figure 9.23.)

Figure 9.23.
The effect will only be applied to the masked part of the image; the sky remains un-changed.

10. To finish up, in the Effects menu, under Sharpen, select Directional Sharpen. Enter a value of 100 and click on OK. The picture (Figure 9.24) now looks much better than when we started and is ready for publication. The difference in color is much more dramatic than the grayscale that is printed on this page.

Figure 9.24. The final image. Contrast and detail have been enhanced. The new sky helps to make the Sphinx stand out.

A Quick Final Session

I stuck this exercise in here because I felt we needed an exercise that actually used the Color Mask as a *color* mask and not as a mask generator. The job is simple. Change the skier's clothes from red to another color.

1. Open the file 200023.PCD. (See Figure 9.25.) If you are loading the image 200023, we need to crop off the black border, so select Paper Size in the Image menu and enter a value of 1.60 inches in the Height setting. Click OK. After the new image is drawn, double-click the Control menu on the original and it will redisplay and disappear. (Because this was a read-only image, PHOTO-PAINT doesn't ask you if you want to save the image.) Click the F4 (Zoom to Fit) key.

2. Open the Color Mask roll-up (Ctrl+F5, or F5 for OVA). If it already has values other than the default settings as shown in Figure 9.4, click the Reset button.

3. Click the topmost On checkbox and then click the Color button. The cursor becomes an eyedropper. We have two ranges of colors we want to mask: the light red on his suit that is being hit by the sunlight, and the dark red of his suit. Find a spot that is an average light red on the back side of his suit.

Set the Tolerance value to 40-40. Find a dark red spot on the front of his snow suit for the second color. The Tolerance setting for the darker red is 40-35. The reason for the lighter plus setting is that if it is any higher on my system, the Preview Mask starts moving into his face. Don't forget this is a quick session, so neatness doesn't count for much.

Figure 9.25.
The original image.

4. Click the Preview Mask and see what, if anything, needs to be touched up. There will be a few spots left uncovered, but don't spend the time to correct them now.

5. Select the Rectangle Mask tool from the toolbox and draw a large rectangular mask around the skier as shown in Figure 9.26.

Corel *TIP!*

Using a mask to restrict the area affected by the next application is done for the sake of speed. If the mask is not there, it will take longer because the filter will be applied to the entire image rather than to the smaller area defined by the mask.

6. Select Color in the Effects Menu, and choose Hue/Saturation from the drop-down list. The Filter dialog box opens. Enter a value of -122 in the Hue box, and click the OK button. The results should look like Figure 9.27, except for the color. The skier's clothes turn blue. There will be a few tiny spots of red, but not to worry. This was merely a quick demonstration exercise.

Figure 9.26.
Select the Rectangle
Mask tool from the
toolbox and draw a
large rectangular mask
around the skier.

Figure 9.27.
The final image.

Summary

- Entering a value of 255 in the + and the - sides of the Tolerance column selects every pixel in the image.

- A small number indicates a narrow range of colors centered around the selected color.

- A large number indicates a wide range of colors centered around the selected color.

- Numbers entered on the positive (+) side of the Tolerance column have a greater effect on the lighter shades of the selected color.

- Numbers entered on the negative (-) side of the Tolerance column have a greater effect on the darker shades of the selected color.

- Color masks are not additive. Each time a Color Mask is applied, the previous mask is wiped out.

- A maximum of 10 color ranges can be part of the mask.

- A Color Mask can be used in conjunction with other masks to allow even further fine tuning of the color ranges.

- A Color Mask cannot be saved, either as part of a *.CPT file or as a mask.

10

Painting and Drawing Tools

Some of the tools we will be looking at in this chapter are among those we have already used. Here we will explore PHOTO-PAINT's drawing and paint tools. PHOTO-PAINT 5 is not classified as a "natural media" program. A natural-media program is designed to faithfully reproduce the effect of charcoal, oils, etc. Programs that are natural media include Fractal Design's Painter and Fauve Matisse. Although it isn't a natural-media program, PHOTO-PAINT does have both drawing and painting tools that provide the user with a limited ability to create original images and effects.

The painting tools are used most often to create or touch up masks. They can also be used to create images or add special effects to existing images. The Tool Settings roll-up is used to control the large selection of variables available with each painting brush.

The drawing tools enable you to create lines, curves, ellipses, rectangles, and polygons.

Corel *NOTE!*

After the initial shipment of PHOTO-PAINT 5 with the CorelDRAW 5 release in May 1994, Corel released a maintenance version in September. This maintenance version is a free upgrade to all registered users of CorelDRAW 5 and has many changes both to the user interface and the product features. Where there are differences between the operation of the two versions, they will be indicated in this text as Original Version (OV) or Subsequent Releases. Although the stand-alone version of PHOTO-PAINT 5 Plus contains a large assortment of additional filters and libraries of photographic clip art, it contains the same PAINT program as the maintenance version and is treated as a subsequent release. The additional "Plus" filters are covered in a separate chapter of this book.

Painting Tools

The Paint Brush Tool

The Paint Brush tool paints an area in the current paint color. Remember that the Paint Brush works by replacing (not covering) the pixels underneath the brush tool with the currently selected paint (foreground) color.

Corel *TIP!*

Corel refers to the foreground color as the "paint" color and the background color as the "paper" color. While this is logical enough, it is difficult to change old habits of calling them foreground and background.

Paint Brush Color

The Paint Brush color is selected through the Color Fill roll-up. The Color Fill roll-up is opened in the original version of the software by pressing F2. In all subsequent releases, it is selected by double-clicking the Paint square in the status bar or by using the keyboard combination Ctrl+F2.

Paint Brush Settings

The size, shape, and about a million other parameters of the Paint Brush are controlled in the Tool Settings roll-up. The Tool Settings roll-up is opened in the original version of the software by pressing F8 and in all subsequent releases by double-clicking the Paint Brush tool button or using the keyboard combination Ctrl+F8. While the Tool Settings roll-up might seem a little intimidating at first sight, it isn't so difficult once you understand how it works with the brushes.

Controlling the Brush

In all versions of the software, using the Ctrl key constrains the brush to a vertical or horizontal direction. The constraint methodology used by PHOTO-PAINT is unique—so much so that you may not think at first that it is working. In other products, most horizontal or vertical constraint keys keep the cursor from moving outside of a fixed line. You can move the mouse anywhere you want, but the cursor is going to stay right on that line. With PHOTO-PAINT, the constrain key does not constrain cursor movement—it only controls where the effect is applied.

For example, if the brush width is set to 5 pixels, and we begin to draw a line with the Ctrl key held down, PHOTO-PAINT internally makes a 5-point-wide horizontal mask across the page at the point where the line was started. As long as you hold down the Ctrl key, the cursor can be moved anywhere around the image area, but the paint color will only be applied in that 5-point-wide horizontal line. (I originally thought this was pretty dumb. However, before this chapter is finished, I will show you some tricks that can be accomplished using this method of constraint.) The constraint applied with the Ctrl key does not prevent the brush from moving outside of either the vertical or horizontal direction—it only prevents them from having an effect outside of the chosen direction.

In all subsequent releases, PHOTO-PAINT added the feature of pressing the Shift key to change the direction of constraint.

Corel *TIP!*

> When using the Ctrl-activated constrain key multiple times, remember to first click the left mouse button on the place you wish to begin. If you hold down the Ctrl key first, the brush will return to the last constrained line. (A neat little gotcha!)

Controlling the Paint Brush with the Tool Settings Roll-Up

Shape Buttons	Sets the shape of the brush. The three available shapes are **Round, Square**, and **Custom**. If Custom is chosen, a different dialog box appears and the outline image of the currently selected Custom brush shape appears as the cursor.
Flatten	The Flatten slider controls the height of the Round and Square brushes. Values are in percentage of height. You can see the effect of the flattening in the preview window as the change is being applied. The Flatten control does not effect the Custom brush.
Rotate	Rotates the Round or Square brush by the amount entered. You can see the effect of the rotating in the preview window as the change is being applied. The Rotate control does not effect the custom brush. Value is in degrees, up to a maximum of 180 degrees. Obviously, rotating a Round brush serves no purpose, but rotating a flattened Round brush does.
Size	Allows adjustment of Round or Square paintbrush sizes from 0 to 100 pixels. The size of brush selected is shown in the preview box. The size of the Custom brush is not adjustable.

Figure 10.1.
Tool Settings roll-up for
Paint Brush.

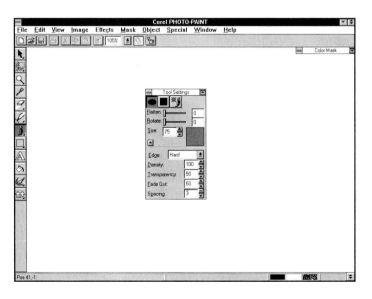

Edge	Sets the edges of the brush to **Hard**, **Medium**, or **Soft**. Soft edges make the brush stroke the least dense at the edges; Hard edges are dense up to the edge, with little to

no softening, depending on the brush size and other brush settings. The preview box displays the edge selected. The edge has no effect on the Custom brush, even though the text is not grayed out. I have shown several settings in Figure 10.2

*Figure 10.2.
The different brush
Edge settings. Each set
starts with Hard on the
top, Medium, and Soft.
Here, the Brush Size is
50 pixels, Density was
set to 25, Transparency
set to 50, Spacing 2,
and Fade Out 25.*

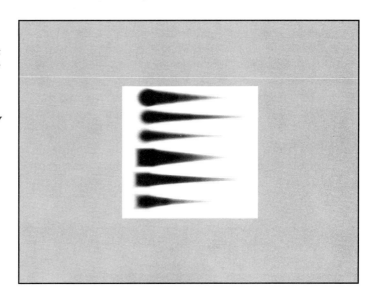

Corel *TIP!*

You can only see real differences in this setting when the Density is below 80 and the Transparency is at least 45 to 50.

Density

This control sets the overall density of coverage from the center of the brush stroke through the edges. To understand how this setting works, think about working with a tapered paintbrush. A low density is like applying a small amount of pressure to the brush. The resulting stroke is dense in the center and lighter towards the edges. A high Density setting is the equivalent to pressing the brush hard against the paper. This results in uniform density across the entire stroke. The result is that the Density and Transparency values interact with one another. The Edge setting also has an effect on these two, but it is only slight. When this setting gets above 80 or more, Edge has little effect. Density controls how solid the brush stroke is, beginning at the center.

The lower the number, the finer the brush stroke, with smaller, softer edges. The higher the value of the Density setting, the greater the density throughout the width of the brush stroke, resulting in a bolder stroke. Figure 10.3 shows the effects of different Density settings.

Figure 10.3.
shows the effects of changing the Density settings on a Round brush. The Square brush size is 75 pixels, the Transparency is set to 50. Fade Out is 60 and the Spacing is 3. From left to right, the density settings are 0, 25, 50 , 75, and 100 percent.

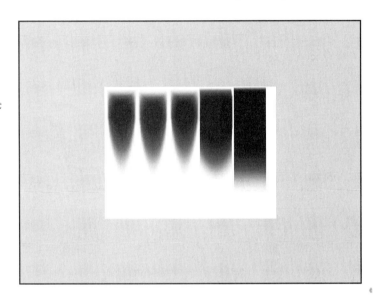

Transparency   Sets the level of transparency of the brush stroke. It is similar to adjusting the amount of water mixed with watercolors. The higher the setting, the more transparent the brush stroke. At a very high setting, the color acts more like a tint. A setting of 0 has no transparency, whereas setting the brush to 100 makes the brush stroke invisible regardless of any other settings.

Fade Out   This setting determines the length of the brush stroke before it fades entirely by adjusting the rate at which the brush stroke disappears. This is similar to adjusting the pressure of the brush against the canvas as the paint is applied. The greater the Fade Out value, the more fade out is applied and the quicker the fade out of the brush stroke occurs. As the Fade out value decreases, the amount of fade out applied to the brush stroke diminishes; a value of 0 turns off the Fade Out function completely.

Fade Out works by counting the number of brush applications to determine when to begin applying the gradual fade-out function. This is important for the following reason: Spacing, the next parameter, controls the distance between brush applications. Increasing spacing between brush application increases the distance that the brush stroke will go before Fade Out begins.

Corel *TIP!*

Spacing affects Fade Out. Increases in Spacing increase the distance before Fade Out occurs.

Spacing   Sets the distance, in pixels, between applications of the brush. To create a brush stroke, the pointing device draws a line across the image. At a frequency determined by the Spacing setting, the brush is applied to the line. For example, if a brush stroke is made with a setting of 5 (pixels), PAINT will produce the selected brush on the image area at a spacing of every 5 pixels. While it may seem that a setting of 1 would be desired, a lower setting slows down the generation of the brush stroke considerably. It can be really slow on some systems. When a large brush is being used, the setting can be larger (and this is recommended) because of the overlap caused by the larger brush.

Figure 10.4.
Tool Settings roll-up for
Custom Brush.

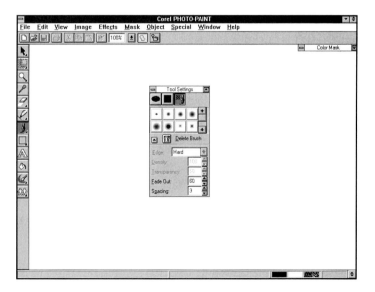

Custom Brushes

Custom brushes offer a large selection of different shapes to use. They work well in the role of a border creation tool, a rubber stamp, or for replacing repeating patterns in an image.

Selecting a Custom Brush

When the Custom Brush button is selected, the Tool Setting roll-up changes to show the selection of custom brushes that are available. PHOTO-PAINT comes with 35 custom brushes to choose from. Use the scroll bars to navigate through the Custom Brush library. Because of the way the thumbnails of the brushes are created, navigating through the Custom Brush library is less than speedy. Only Fade Out and Spacing adjustments are available for custom brushes. All of the other settings in the Brush Settings dialog box are ignored.

Figure 10.5 was created with two different custom brushes. In the first row on the top, the plane was placed by painting across the page with the constrain key (Ctrl) held down. The Spacing was set at 80 pixels and the Fade Out was set to 90. On the next row down, the Spacing setting was decreased to 60 and in the last plane row the Spacing was set to 40 pixels. Notice that even though the Fade Out setting remained constant, the fade changed with the different Spacing settings. Remember that the fade "counts" the number of times a brush is applied and begins to fade based on that count. When the Spacing setting is smaller, there is a greater number of brush applications in the stroke; therefore, the fade appears more quickly. Look at the notes. They are set at a Spacing of 60, 40, and 20, the bottom row setting being 20. The bottom row with the smaller spacing is almost completely faded by the time it reaches the paper's edge. The top row of notes is still going strong at the edge of paper.

Figure 10.5.
This figure was created
with two different
custom brushes.

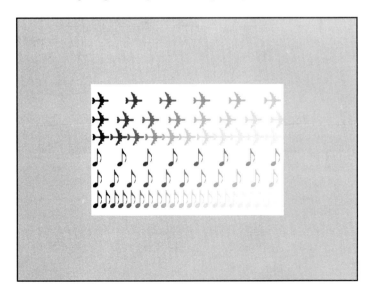

One more point about this figure: The bottom row of planes begins to overlap at the 40-pixel setting, and the bottom row of notes still have some space between them at a setting of 20. Conclusion? Each brush can be a different size—and most are. The only limitation is that the longest side of a brush cannot exceed 100 pixels. Knowing this fact will come in handy when we make custom brushes later in this chapter.

Figure 10.6 shows an anomaly of using the constrain (Ctrl) key with a custom brush. As you can see, the brush strokes on the left side of the figure are uniform, while those on the right do not exhibit the same uniformity of spacing. What made the difference? Speed. The brush strokes on the left side on the figure were made s-l-o-w-l-y, and those on the right were made with average speed. Notice that as the spacing increases, the effect of the speed diminishes.

Figure 10.6.
Here we see an anomaly of using the constrain (Ctrl) key with a custom brush. As you can see, the brush strokes on the left side of the figure are uniform, while those on the right do not exhibit the same uniformity of spacing.

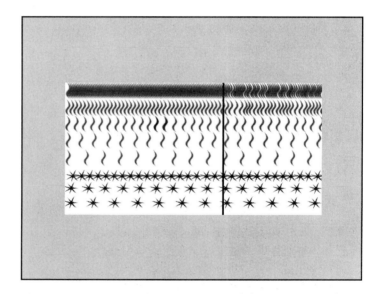

One last point: The type of brush determines how apparent this non-uniform stroke appears. The vertically oriented brushes make the irregularities stand out like a sore thumb. The star in the bottom half of the figure doesn't show it at all.

Figure 10.7 is a sample file I made in order to show all of the brush effects we have already discussed. The star border was made with a star-shaped custom brush using the constrain key and the shift function to turn the corners. The fade was a nice touch for the border. The word "FADE" was made using the same brush that was at the top of Figure 10.6. It took two passes to make the texture on the text. With the constrain key, I was able to line up the effects the first time. The other text was made with overlapping combinations of custom brushes with different shades of gray. The shadow is a Gaussian blur of a 50 percent gray.

Figure 10.7.
A sample file to show
all of the brush effects.

Although you may have thought that Spacing was one of those settings that a graphics engineer came up with on a cold Ottawa winter evening with nothing else to do, you now know that there are a lot of things that can be done with this control. Almost all of it has to do with custom brushes—which happens to be the next subject.

To select a brush, click on the button. The button representing the custom brush selected depresses and the cursor becomes an outline of the custom brush.

To delete a brush, select the brush to be deleted by clicking on the brush button and click the Delete Brush button. The Delete Brush button looks like a trash can. When you click the Delete Brush button, you receive a warning message as shown in Figure 10.8.

Using Custom Brushes

I told you that are some neat things to do with custom brushes. Here are a just few that I have found while working with them over the past few months.

Creating an Unusual Screen Background to Highlight Text

All it takes is the following steps:

1. Create a new image. I used 450×300 pixels (grayscale) at 300 dpi. Using the Text tool, enter the text. I used Futura Xblk BT at 36 points.

CHAPTER 10

2. Use the Magic Wand Mask tool and click inside each letter to create a mask around every letter.

3. Select the text with the Object picker and use the Delete key to delete it. You now have a mask that you can use to do several things.

4. Invert the mask. With the mask inverted, we can draw on everything except the area of the letters.

5. Pick the Paint Brush tool and select a custom brush. In this case, I used the star that looks like an X.

6. Set the Spacing for about 30 and Fade Out to 0. (No need to worry about the brush size, because all custom brushes are fixed sizes.)

7. Drag the mouse back and forth across the background until you have the desired effect.

8. Invert the mask again and fill it with any fill that suits your fancy. In the sample in Figure 10.9 I used a custom radial fill.

Figure 10.8.
Corel gives you a
warning before
sending your custom
brushes into the trash
can.

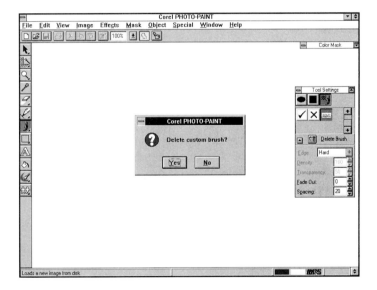

Creating Custom Textures with a Custom Brush

(I was wondering if I could get a few more words beginning with the letter C into the topic title.) The texture applied to the text shown in Figure 10.10 was created using a custom brush with a little help from a few filters. This little piece of magic is simple, and the process is useful in many other projects.

Figure 10.9.
A simple background
created with a custom
brush.

Figure 10.10.
This image was created
using a custom brush
with a little help from a
few filters.

1. Repeat Steps 1 through 3 from the previous procedure. In this example, I used the word "CUSTOM" for the text.

2. Pick the Paint Brush tool and select the Custom brush. I used the brush that looks like a herd of ants milling around. (I wish they had names.) If you are willing to slowly scroll through the list, it is the first brush on the left, sixth row from the top.

3. Set the Spacing to about 30 and Fade Out to 0. There is no need to worry about the brush size, because all custom brushes are of fixed size.

4. Beginning outside the masked area, place the cursor so that as it moves horizontally it will fill the bottom part of the characters. Click and hold the mouse button and then the Ctrl key. Now move the mouse horizontally until the bottom of the text looks like Figure 10.11. (That's the easy part. Now for the tricky part.) If you actually read the part of this chapter that talked about the constrain key, you may have noticed that if you use the Ctrl (constrain) first, the brush will jump back to the last constrained brush stroke. (This only applies to multiple constrained brush strokes.) Follow the next step carefully.

Figure 10.11.
Fill in the bottom part
of the text.

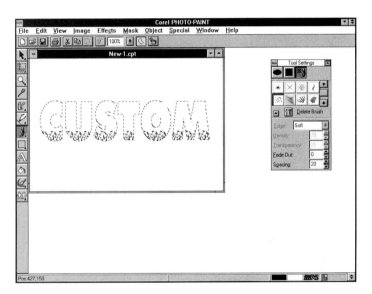

5. Click the left mouse button at a point that is outside of the text and slightly above the top of the last brush stroke. (This brush has a slight tendency to paint lower than its cursor would indicate.) Still holding down the left mouse button, depress the Ctrl (constrain) key and move the brush horizontally across the text for a second time. It's not unlike mowing a lawn. You should now have something that looks like Figure 10.12. If your brush stroke is either too high or too low, simply use the Undo function (Ctrl+Z) and try again. Repeat this procedure until all of the text is covered.

Figure 10.12.
*The text after the
second pass with the
brush.*

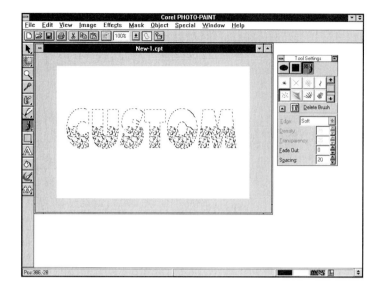

6. Click the Copy button and then the Paste button in the ribbon bar.

7. Open the Layers/Objects roll-up and hide the object you just created.

8. Select the Rectangle tool (not the Rectangle Mask tool) and, after ensuring that the fill color is black, draw a rectangle over all the text.

9. Save the mask using the Save Mask command in the Mask menu. I gave mine the name brushmsk.cpt. Invert the mask using the Invert Mask command in the Mask menu.

10. Change the fill to Plastered Wall from the Samples 5 Library. (If you have the original version, use Putty 2C. When applied to this large of an area, it is as close as you're going to get.) Using the Rectangle tool, apply the fill to the entire image. Don't use the Flood Fill tool, because then the inside (called the counter) of the O won't be filled. This will take a few moments to create. Be patient. Next we make the shadow.

11. Remove the mask using the Remove command in the Mask menu. Select the Rectangle Mask tool and draw a rectangle around the text as shown in Figure 10.13.

12. Select the Gaussian Blur filter from the Fancy group in the Effects menu. As soon as the dialog box opens, make sure that the setting is 5, and click the OK button. You now have made a lovely shadow like the one shown in Figure 10.14. We are done with the mask, so click the Remove Mask button in the ribbon bar.

Figure 10.13.
Select the Rectangle
Mask tool and draw a
rectangle around the
text.

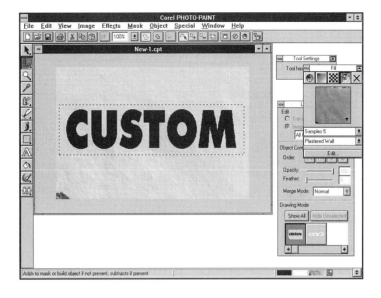

Figure 10.14.
Creation of the
shadow.

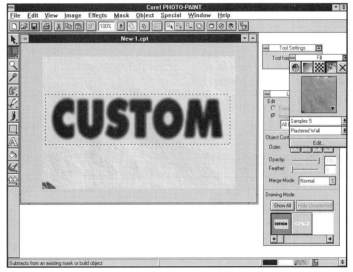

13. In the Layers/Objects roll-up, hide the base image and select the Text object.

14. In the Effects menu, select Fancy and choose the Emboss filter from the dropdown list. Make the following settings: Direction: Down-Left arrow, Emboss Color: Light Gray. Click the OK button. We are almost there.

15. Select the Mapping Group in the Effects menu, choose Wind from the dropdown list, and using the default settings (which should be Opacity: 75, Strength: 50), click the OK button.

16. Click the Show All button in the Layers/Objects roll-up. Use the Object picker to move the top layer of text until you get it where it looks best to you in relation to the drop shadow.

You can use this same technique (the constrained custom brush) to create an entire world of textures. Now that we have created crazy custom creations with custom brushes, let's learn how to construct custom brushes of our own. (That's seven words beginning with the letter C!)

Creating a New Custom Brush

You can create a custom brush using the Mask tools and the Create Brush command in the Special menu. The new brush is saved and can be used in conjunction with all of the Paint Brush tools, the Mask Brush, and the Object Brush. The Paint Brush tools paint the image with the custom brush. When used with the Mask Brush, the new brush creates masks; when used with the Object Brush tool, the new brush creates objects.

1. Pick the image to be used for the custom brush and surround it with a mask.

2. Select Create Brush from the Special menu. The Create a Custom Brush dialog box opens. (See Figure 10.15.)

Figure 10.15.
The Create a Custom
Brush dialog box.

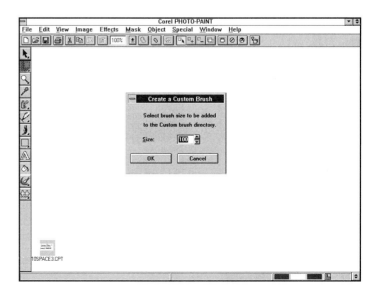

3. Enter the size of the brush in pixels. The maximum size is 100 pixels. If the image has any dimension larger than 100 pixels, PHOTO-PAINT resizes the image, maintaining the aspect ratio. When you have created a custom brush, a thumbnail of the brush is displayed in the Custom Brush section of the Tool Settings roll-up. All new brushes are added to the bottom row of the Custom Brush library.

The Ins and Outs of Making and Using Custom Brushes

■ Any masked area that is converted to a custom brush is converted to grayscale image. Although the color of the custom brush is determined by the paint color when the brush is being used, if the image being used for the custom brush began as a neat little color image, it is now either grayscale or a colorized grayscale.

■ The masked area is resized so that its largest dimension does not exceed the value set in the Create a Custom Brush dialog box or 100 pixels, whichever is smaller. This means if you have an image such as Figure 10.16, you will get a better brush if you make the mask tightly fit around the image rather than masking the entire image.

Figure 10.16.
If you have an image such as this, you will get a better brush if you make the mask tightly fit around the image rather than masking the entire image.

■ The resulting brushes, when applied, are transparent. This means that you faintly can see the background through the brush impression.

■ One way to use a custom brush is as a kind of rubber stamp. Instead of dragging the brush, just click it, and a copy of the image appears. If you paint a long stroke with a custom brush at a low Spacing setting, you will end up with a large, solid black line.

■ Masks can be any shape. In Figure 10.17 a circle mask was drawn around the tiger's face. In Figure 10.18 the magic wand was used to isolate the apple. If you look at Figure 10.19 you will see that only the apple and not the background was included in the brush.

Figure 10.17.
A circle mask drawn
around the tiger's face.

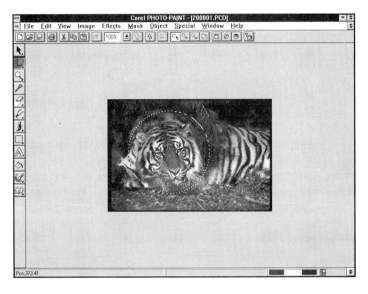

Figure 10.18.
The magic wand used
to isolate the apple.

■ Using the Custom brushes and the constrain tool makes wallpaper as shown on the left side of Figure 10.19.

Figure 10.19.
Using the Custom
brushes and the
constrain tool makes
wallpaper.

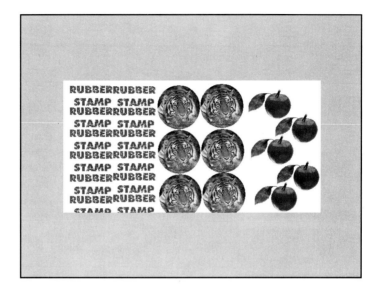

The Impressionism Brush Tool

The Impressionism brush tool produces brush strokes that appear like those used in Impressionist art. (At times I think the real purpose of the Impressionism rush is to place a serious load on your CPU and give you some time to write friends, catch up on your reading, and feed the goldfish while the CPU is sweating its brains out—assuming that CPU's had brains or could sweat.)

The brush stroke incorporates a selected number of lines in colors that are similar to each other. For example, it turns a single shade of red into eight shades of red. The size, shape, and qualities of the Impressionism brush tool are set by our old friend the Tool Settings roll-up.

Using the Ctrl key constrains the brush to a vertical or horizontal direction. Pressing the Shift key changes the direction of constraint. The constraint applied with the Ctrl key does not prevent the brush from moving outside of either the vertical or horizontal direction—it only prevents them from having an effect outside of the chosen direction. (For a detailed discussion on the constrain key, see the "Brushes" section earlier in this chapter.)

Figure 10.20.
*Tool Settings roll-up
with only the Artistic
brush settings shown.*

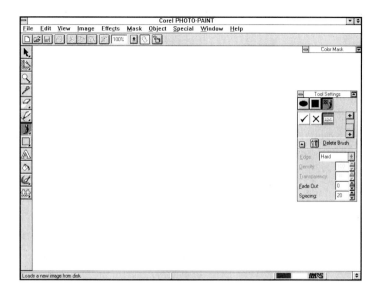

Impressionism Brush Tool Settings Roll-Up

(For an explanation of the settings for Shape Buttons, Custom Brush, Flatten, Rotate, Size, Edge, Density, Transparency, Fade Out, and Spacing, see the discussion of Paint Brush Tool Settings roll-up, earlier in this chapter.)

H Variance Determines the variation of color in the brush. The Impressionism-brush style incorporates a number of colors. The **H Variance** (Hue Variance) determines the difference between the colors of the lines. For example, if you set the value to a higher number, the variation is greater. The difference between the colors is determined by this setting. The actual number of colors is determined by the setting of the **# of Lines** box. If you are working on a grayscale image, H Variance varies the shades of gray. (Don't forget that gray is a color.)

Corel *TIP!*

Use this setting with some caution. The default setting is 5, and when you take it to the maximum setting, you will have samples from just about every color in the rainbow. I made a sample with a custom brush (star shape) and set the H Variance to 50. The result was blue, purple, green, and yellow stars. (This brings up a neat feature that we will discuss later.)

S Variance   Sets the variation for the purity of the color. Purity is the number of colors used to mix a specific color. Lower values decrease the number of colors used in the mix; higher values increase the number of colors used to produce the selected colors. The greater the number of colors used to mix a color, the duller the final color looks.

Corel *TIP!*

The default value of this setting is 5. That is a great setting. I recommend you leave it alone.

L Variance   Sets the variation of light colors to dark colors that are used in the brush. Higher values make the variation of light greater, giving a greater range of light-to-dark variation in the brush strokes. Confused? What it means in practice is that the greater the amount of light variance (which, in the HSL model, this brush is built on), the greater the differences in the colors themselves. I have made a sample file shown in Figure 10.21 to show the effect of L Variance. The left side had all its values set to default, and the right side was made with all of the values unchanged except for L Variance, which was set to the maximum. The solid color area represents the brush color used. If you are looking at the grayscale version of the figure, the top is red and the bottom is blue.

Figure 10.21.
L variance.

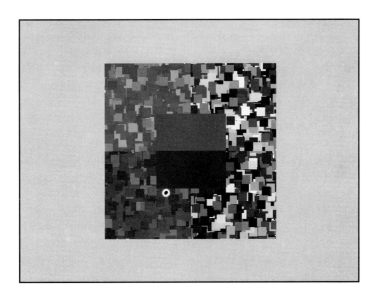

Brush Spread Sets the distance between strokes. Higher values make the distance between strokes greater.

# of Lines Sets the number of lines created in brush strokes. This value, like the Spacing value, can have a significant effect on the speed at which your computer renders an image. It is recommended that you keep the number of lines low and the spacing as high as practical.

Applications for the Impressionism Brush Tool

If you were expecting me to use this tool to paint a portrait, you were wrong. I have said this many times before, but I am going to repeat it again: Don't be limited by the name of the brush or filter; just ask yourself what the brush or filter actually does. You might say that the Impressionism brush tool produces brush strokes that look like those used in Impressionist art, and that would be technically correct. But what does this brush actually do to make the brush strokes? It creates duplicates of the original brush in random colors and locations. This answer suggests that there are other things that can be done with it besides imitating Impressionist art. The following are several examples.

Making Wallpaper with the Impressionism Brush

This is simple. Select either a Custom brush (one of the 35 presets, or one of your one making), a Square brush, or a Round brush. Set both the size of the brush (unless it is Custom) and the brush spread to a large value and click (don't drag) the brush all over the area that needs a random background. I just took two custom brushes that came with PHOTO-PAINT and, by clicking the background several times, I was able to quickly make a backdrop.

Simulating a Fabric with the Impressionism Tool

Figure 10.22 was made using several Impressionism brushes. The fabric of the serape was made by creating a bitmap tile (100×100 pixels) with the Impressionism brush. The following is the procedure for making the bitmap tile. It is a little complicated, so I numbered the steps.

1. Create a new image of 100×100 pixels, with 24-bit color and a resolution of 300 dpi.

2. Select the Impressionism brush from the Toolbox and open the Tool Settings roll-up (Ctrl+F8, or simply F8 if you have the original release).

3. Adjust the Spacing value to 7 pixels. The objective here is to simulate the separate threads of the fabric. You may have to adjust your spacing further. Keep the H Variance at 25. (Twenty-five to 30 are good values for many colors in the fabrics; 3 to 8 are good settings for fabrics containing fewer colors.) Put the L Variance at the maximum setting for good contrast.(You could use a lower number if a more subtle pattern were desired.)

4. Select a Square brush (no kidding) with a size of 40, and rotate it 45 degrees. Next, flatten it to about a value of 93. Set the Fade Out value to 0. This turns off the Fade Out effect.

5. Keep the Density to 60 and the Transparency at 50. This setting removes the square edges of the Square brush and also gives us some "depth" as the brush patterns overlay one another.

6. Set the # of Lines setting to 8 and the Brush Spread at a low number such as 2 or 1. The # of Lines is going to determine how many lines are created with each pass. The colors of each line and where they are put is determined randomly. The maximum setting for the # of Lines is 20. I didn't choose a large number because the Brush Spread is a low number and the result of a higher number would be multiple lines repainted one over another. The reason we kept the Brush Spread setting low was to prevent the brush strokes from going all over the image. It was also to make sure that all of the brush strokes began at or near the same spot. If a higher number is used, some of the Impressionism strokes would begin in the middle of the image (which is not good for the effect we are trying to obtain).

Figure 10.22.
Simulating fabric with
the Impressionism tool.

Corel *TIP!*

In the remaining steps, we will be working very close to the edge of the image window. To prevent PHOTO-PAINT from getting confused when the cursor approaches the edge of the image window, grab one of the corners of the image window and enlarge it. This makes it much easier when you are working close to the edge of an image.

7. Holding down the constrain key (Ctrl), draw your line outside of and below the bottom of the image, and slowly drag the mouse across the bottom of the image. The result of this action when the computer finally gets finished is a group of cloth-like lines as shown in Figure 10.23. Because the output of this brush setting is random, you will sometimes get results you don't care for. Don't hesitate to use the Undo function (Ctrl+Z) if you don't get the results desired.

Figure 10.23.
The result of this
action is a group of
cloth-like lines.

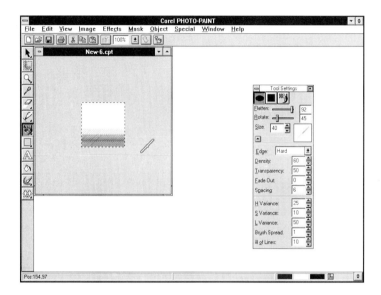

8. Change the Rotate value to 135. Beginning at a point outside of the image, click the left mouse button at a point where the brush cursor is about halfway down over the previous brush stroke, then click the constrain (Ctrl) key. Drag the mouse slowly across the image. You should end up with something like Figure 10.24.

9. Return the Rotate setting to 45 and repeat step 8. This should have filled the entire image. (See Figure 10.25.)

10. Save the image as CLOTH1.PCX. You now have a bitmap fill that, when loaded through the Bitmap Fill roll-up, makes a great cloth. By the way, to make the horizontal version of the cloth as used in Figure 10.22, just rotate the image before saving it.

The Pointillist Brush Tool

This tool operates much like the Impressionism brush. The Impressionism brush paints strokes; the Pointillist brush tool paints dot patterns that are similar to those used in Pointillist art. This brush stroke incorporates a selected number of dots in colors that are similar to each other. The size, shape, and qualities of the Pointillist brush tool are set from the Tool Settings roll-up.

Figure 10.24.
The result after
additional brush
strokes.

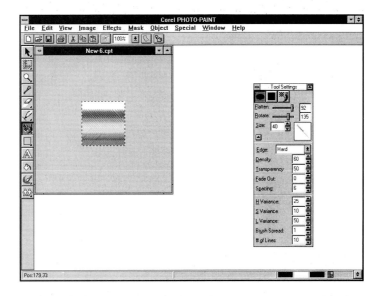

Figure 10.25.
The end result.

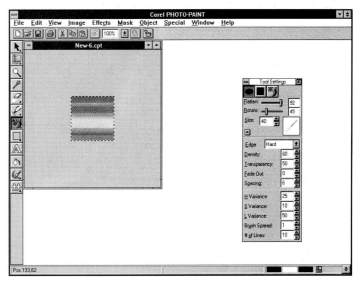

Using the Ctrl key constrains the brush to a vertical or horizontal direction. Pressing the Shift key changes the direction of constraint. Note that the constraint applied with the Ctrl key does not prevent the brush from moving outside of either the vertical or horizontal direction; it only prevents it from having an effect outside of the chosen direction.

(For a detailed description of the settings options, see the section on the Impressionism Brush Tool Setting roll-up.)

The Artist Brush Tool

This could be another one of those "Why did they put it in here and what can I do with it?" brushes, but it isn't. I will show you some tricks to make this tool of some use to you.

The Artist brush is actually a bitmap of a brush stroke that applies the current paint in a specific pattern. The length of the bitmap pattern is, for all intents and purposes, fixed. The only factor you can vary is the proportional size. For example, if I want a really long stroke of a particular pattern, you must increase the brush size. The result will be a really long and really wide stroke. The shape of the Artist brush is set from the Tool Settings roll-up by selecting one of the 25 bitmap patterns. You cannot create your own brushes.

Using the Ctrl key technically constrains the brush to either a vertical or horizontal direction. Pressing the Shift key changes the direction of constraint. I say "technically" because there isn't much to constrain. Because this brush is applying a fixed bitmap pattern, you cannot change directions while painting as you can with a normal brush. This brush acts strangely, to say the least—so much so that I have gathered some observations about working it, as follows.

Strange Facts About the Artist Brush

- The direction of application operates as a mirror control for the brush. When the mouse is dragged from left-to-right, the bitmap image is applied as it appears in the preview display. When the same brush is applied from right-to-left, the mirror image of the bitmap brush appears.

- How fast the mouse is dragged effects the bitmap image length. If the mouse is dragged slowly the bitmap is applied to its full length (depending upon the length of the stroke and the setting of the fade). If the mouse is dragged the same distance in a fast motion, the bitmap application of the Artist brush is shortened considerably.

- If you change direction while making the stroke, you drive PHOTO-PAINT crazy and God only knows what the final outcome will be. For example, if you attempt to drag a large curve with the brush, the program ignores the changes after it passes some internal preset number of degrees and waits until you release the mouse button. Then it figures out where the brush would have been if you had stayed on the straight lines and it subtracts a 20-pixel penalty for illegal lane changing. (Hey, that makes more sense than it seems.)

The Artist Brush Tool Settings Roll-Up

Brush Style	Selects the type of brush (bitmap pattern) to be used, out of a palette of 25 predefined brush styles.
Size	Sets the size of the brush's height. The length of the brush pattern is proportional to the height.

Fade	Sets the amount of fade that occurs over the entire brush stroke. Higher values create more fading. If the fade value is too small, the brush bitmap will end before the fading begins.

Using the Artist Brush

While the brush styles are of a predefined size, some of them are really good bitmap images.

One application of this Artist brush is to create a mask around text and then use the Artist brush to fill it. Another use of this brush is to make a border around an image or a subject. (Remember when you do this last one that the brushes cannot be rotated, so pick your brushes carefully.)

In Figure 10.26 I have made a crude painting using the Artist brushes, some Texture Bitmap fills, and the Canvas (Paper2). This is 20 minutes worth of work, tops. (It would have taken less time had not the system crashed and made all of my work go into the great Windows Black Hole of Doom halfway through the project.) Some notes about making the picture. First, I am not an artist and I have never watched the guy with the bowling ball afro who teaches dummies like me to paint. I took the freehand drawing tool and made the tree trunk. Next I created some leaves primarily with the Graphic Pen 2 artist brush. The empty spaces were filled in with several other Artist brushes. Now for the most important part. Using the Magic Wand masking tool, I masked the tree and made it into an object. From there on it was just pasting, scaling, and using different Hue and Transparency settings to make the individual trees look different. The sky and the lake are both Texture bitmap fills. The last thing I did was apply a canvas to the image.

Figure 10.26.
A crude painting using the Artist brushes, some Texture Bitmap fills, and the Canvas (Paper2).

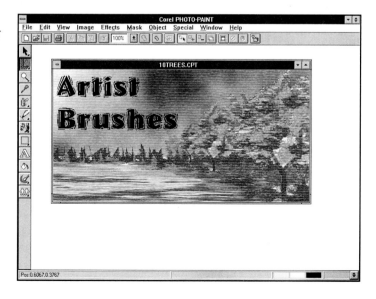

Corel *TIP!*

When I applied the paper canvas to this image, it washed it out (even at 90 percent). No problem. Use the Tone Equalize filter, and the washed-out look will go away.

A fact that bears repeating is that regardless of the fade setting and the length of your brush stroke with the mouse, the Artist brush pattern cannot exceed the size of the predefined bitmap pattern.

The Air Brush Tool and the Spraycan Tool

The Spraycan tool and the Airbrush tool are identical in every aspect except for their respective patterns. Unlike the smooth pattern that comes out of an airbrush, the Spraycan pattern more closely resembles the uneven pattern from a can of spray paint. In actual operation, it is difficult to tell them apart except at the most extreme settings. The Air Brush and Spraycan tools spray the current paint (foreground) color like an airbrush/spray can—the center of the spray has more concentrated color, and the color lessens in intensity as it gets near the edge of the tool shape. The size, shape, and qualities of the Air Brush and Spraycan tools is set from the Tool Settings roll-up.

Using the Ctrl key constrains the brush to a vertical or horizontal direction. Pressing the Shift key changes the direction of constraint. Note that the constraint applied with the Ctrl key does not prevent the Air Brush/Spraycan pattern from moving outside of either the vertical or horizontal direction; it only prevents them from having an effect outside of the chosen direction.

The Air Brush Tool Settings Roll-Up

Shape Buttons	Sets the shape of the brush. The three available shapes are Round, Square, and Custom. If Custom is chosen a different dialog box appears and the outline image of the currently selected Custom brush shape appears as the cursor.
Flatten	The Flatten slider controls the height of the Round and Square brushes. Values are expressed in percentage of height. You can see the effect of the flattening in the preview window as the change is being applied. The Flatten control does not effect the Custom brush.

Rotate   Rotates the Round or Square brush by the amount entered. You can see the effect of the rotating in the preview window as the change is being applied. The Rotate control does not effect the Custom brush. Value is expressed in degrees, up to a maximum of 180 degrees. Obviously rotating a Round brush serves no purpose, but rotating a flattened Round brush does.

Size   Allows adjustment of Round or Square paintbrush sizes from 0 to 100 pixels. The size of brush selected is shown in the preview box. The size of the Custom brush is not adjustable.

Edge   Sets the edges of the brush to Hard, Medium, or Soft. Soft edges make the brush stroke the least dense at the edges; hard edges are dense up to the edge, with little to no softening, depending on brush size and other brush settings. The preview box displays the edge selected. The edge has no effect on the Custom brush, even though the text is not grayed out.

Density   This control sets the overall density of coverage from the center of the brush stroke through the edges. A low density is like applying a small amount of pressure to the brush. The resulting stroke is dense in the center and lighter towards the edges. High density is equivalent to pressing the brush hard against the paper. This results in uniform density across the entire stroke. The result is that the Density and Transparency values interact with one another. The Edge setting also has an effect on these two but it is only slight. When this setting gets above 80 or more, Edge has little effect. Density controls how solid the brush stroke is, beginning at the center. The lower the number, the finer the brush stroke, with smaller, softer edges. The higher the value of Density, the greater the density throughout the width of the brush stroke, resulting in a bolder stroke. (See Figure 10.3 in the description of the Paint brush, which shows the effects of different Density settings.)

Transparency   Sets the level of transparency of the brush stroke. It is similar to adjusting the amount of water mixed with watercolors. The higher the setting, the more transparent the brush stroke. At a very high setting the color acts more like a tint. A setting of 0 has no transparency, and setting the brush to 100 makes the brush stroke invisible, regardless of any other settings.

Fade Out   This setting determines the length of the brush stroke
                    before it fades entirely by adjusting the rate at which the
                    brush stroke disappears. This is similar to adjusting the
                    pressure of the brush against the canvas as the paint is
                    applied. The greater the Fade Out value, the more fade
                    out is applied and the quicker the fade out of the brush
                    stroke occurs. As the Fade Out value decreases, the
                    amount of fade out applied to the brush stroke
                    diminishes, until the value of 0, which turns off the Fade
                    Out function completely.

                    Fade Out works by counting the number of brush
                    applications to determine when to begin applying the
                    gradual fade-out function. This is important because
                    Spacing, the next parameter, controls the distance
                    between brush applications. Increasing the space
                    between brush applications increases the distance that
                    the brush stroke will go before Fade Out begins.

Corel *TIP!*

Spacing effects Fade Out. Increases in Spacing increase the distance before
Fade Out occurs.

Spacing   Sets the distance, in pixels, between applications of the
                    brush. To create a brush stroke, the pointing device
                    draws a line across the image. At a frequency deter-
                    mined by the Spacing setting, the brush is applied to the
                    line. For example, if a brush stroke is made with a set-
                    ting of 5 pixels, then PAINT will produce the selected
                    brush on the image area at a spacing of every 5 pixels.
                    While it may seem that a setting of 1 would be desired, a
                    lower setting slows down the generation of the brush
                    stroke considerably. When a large brush is being used,
                    the setting can be larger because of the overlap caused
                    by the larger brush.

Rate of Flow   This is the major control for these brushes. This setting
                    determines the speed at which the color is placed. In
                    effect, these tools act like real air brushes and spraycans.
                    A rate of flow of 0 makes the color flow slowly; there-
                    fore, to create a denser color, the tool must be held at the
                    same position for a longer period of time. At a rate of

100, the color is applied so fast, the effect is very close to that of a brush.

Using the Airbrush and Spraycan Tools

Let me restate something I mentioned earlier. Although their patterns are slightly different, don't spend too much time choosing the Air Brush or the Spraycan. The difference isn't enough to be concerned about.

That said, when applying minor touch-up to an image, you can't beat the Air Brush tool. It is also great for making shadows behind an image.

There are a few tricks to using these tools effectively. First, be patient when using these tools. Start off using a low setting for Rate of Flow. It will seem like the paint doesn't go on fast enough at first, but remember that you can go back over an area several times and apply more paint. And unlike the real thing, this paint will not run if you put on too much of it.

Corel *TIP!*

Remember that these brushes work like a real air brushes or spray cans; that is, the longer you remain over a spot, the denser the paint applied under the cursor becomes. This is unlike any of the other brushes.

Drawing Tools

The drawing tools are located on two different flyouts on the Toolbox. The first flyout, shown in Figure 10.27, consists of the Line, Curve, and Pen tool. The second flyout, shown in Figure 10.28, contains the Rectangle, Ellipse, and Polygon tools. Of these two flyouts, you will rarely use the first and constantly use the second. That said, we still need to describe how these tools are used, just in case.

The Line Tool

The Line Tool is used to create single and joined lines. This tool can only produce straight lines. Holding down the Ctrl key while drawing a line constrains lines to 45-degree angles. The size and shape of the Line tool is set from the Tool Settings roll-up. (The description for the Line Tool Settings can be found in the Paint Brush Tool Settings roll-up section.)

> **To draw straight lines:** Choose Color (from the Color roll-up), Line Width, Spacing, and Transparency from the Tool Settings roll-up. Click and hold the left mouse button at the point where the line is to begin. Drag the

cursor to the point where the line is to end and then release the button. To start over, erase the line by pressing the Esc key **before** releasing the mouse button.

To draw joined lines: Make line-parameter choices, as described for standard straight lines. Click the right mouse button. Continue to add lines, each joined to the end of the previous line. Double-clicking the left mouse button completes the line.

Figure 10.27.
The Drawing tool flyout
showing the Line,
Curve, and Pen tools.

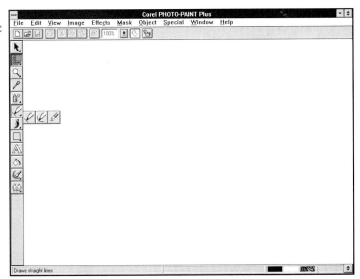

Figure 10.28.
The second flyout
contains the Rectangle,
Ellipse, and Polygon
tools.

The Curve Tool

The Curve tool is used to create freehand lines. Immediately after a line has been created, nodes appear that enable its shape to be altered. By clicking and dragging a node, it can be moved. Clicking on the image area will complete the painting of the freehand tool.

Corel *TIP!*

This tool has a few quirks—namely, PHOTO-PAINT cannot always correctly read where you are clicking the cursor. There is no way to return to the node-edit part of the freehand line once you leave it. The best way to handle inadvertent exiting of the node-edit mode is to Undo and try it all again.

The size and shape of the Line tool is set from the Tool Settings roll-up. (The description for the Curve Tool Settings can be found in section on the Paint Brush Tool Settings roll-up.)

To Draw a Curve: Set the Line Color, Width, Spacing, and Transparency as described under the Line Tool. Click the cursor at the starting point and draw the line desired. When the button is released, the line is not immediately painted; rather, a jointed line with a series of nodes appears. These nodes can be adjusted to fine tune the line so that it is exactly as you want it. Clicking on anything other than a node causes the nodes to disappear, and the line is painted.

The Pen Tool

The Pen Tool paints freehand shapes and lines. Holding down the Ctrl key constrains the Pen tool to either horizontal or vertical movements. Holding down the Shift key changes the direction of the constraint. The size and shape of the Pen tool is set from the Tool Settings roll-up. (The description for the Pen Tool Settings can be found in the section on the Paint Brush Tool Settings roll-up.)

The Rectangle Tool

The Rectangle tool is used to draw hollow or filled rectangles and rounded rectangles. Without the tools in this flyout, we wouldn't be able to control the fill of masked areas as well as we do. Here are the Rectangle drawing tool facts:

If the Ctrl key is held down while defining the shape, the rectangle is constrained to a square. Holding down the Shift key while creating a rectangle will cause the rectangle to shrink or grow (depending on the direction of the mouse movement) from the center. When the Rectangle is produced, it is filled with the current fill setting in the Fill roll-up. If the No-Fill setting is

251

selected, a hollow rectangle is created. It doesn't consume system re-sources, it doesn't do anything. Sounds Zen. Very good, Grasshopper.

Figure 10.29.
The Rectangle, Ellipse
and Polygon flyout.

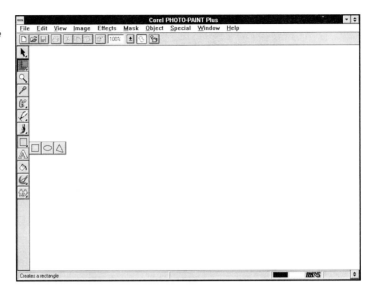

Figure 10.30.
The Rectangle Tool
Settings roll-up. Watch
out for the trans-
parency setting. If it is
set between 40 and 70
you will go crazy trying
to figure out why all of
your fill colors are
faded.

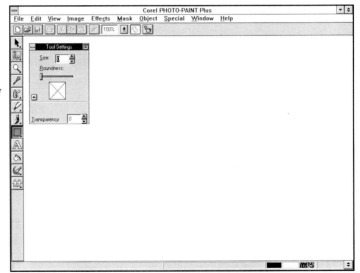

Rectangle Tool Roll-Up Settings

> **Size**   The size of the border in pixels is entered in this value box. A value of 0 produces a rectangle with no border.

Roundness	This slider determines how round the corners of the rectangle will be. The preview box shows the effect of changing the Roundness slider setting. If the size is set to 0, the preview box is inactive. The roundness setting is still seen in the rectangle that is produced.
Transparency	Sets the transparency of the color that is applied. The lower the value, the lesser the transparency (and the denser the color). A setting of 100 is the highest value of transparency and produces an invisible effect.

To draw a rectangle or rounded rectangle: Click the Rectangle tool and choose the border color from the Color roll-up. (Paint Color determines Border color.) The rectangle is filled with the Current Fill color. The rectangle is hollow if No-Fill is selected in the Fill roll-up. Specify the width and roundness of the border in the Tool Settings roll-up. Press the left mouse button to anchor the rectangle and drag until you have achieved the desired size. If the rectangle is not what you desire, it can be erased by pressing the Esc key **before** releasing the mouse button.

Notes on the Rectangle Tool

The Rectangle tool is one of the most-used drawing tools in the Toolbox. It is used to apply fill colors to masked areas and objects. For an example of how it is used, see Chapter 8 "Working with Text."

The Ellipse Tool

The Ellipse tool draws hollow/filled ellipses. If the Ctrl key is held down while defining the shape, the ellipse is constrained to a circle. Holding down the Shift key will shrink or grow the ellipse/circle from the center.

To draw an ellipse: Click the Ellipse tool and choose the border color from the Color roll-up. (Paint Color determines Border color.) The ellipse is filled with the Current Fill color. The ellipse is hollow if No-Fill is selected in the Fill roll-up. Specify the width of the border in the Tool Settings roll-up. Press the left mouse button to anchor the ellipse and drag until you have achieved the desired size. If the circle is not what you desire, it can be erased by pressing the Esc key **before** releasing the mouse button. Holding down the Shift key produces a circle.

The Polygon Tool

The Polygon tool produces closed multi-sided figures. By selecting different Joint settings in the Tools Settings roll-up, the Polygon tool can provide a wide variety of images.

Figure 10.31.
The Polygon Tool
Settings roll-up.

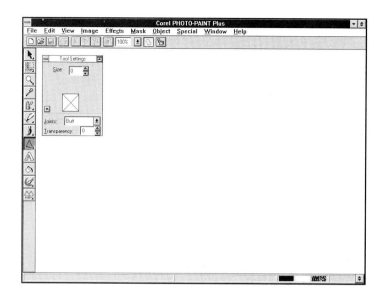

The Polygon Tool Roll-Up Settings

Size
Changes the size of the outline. The size of the outline is displayed in the Preview box.

Joints
Sets the types of joints used in the Polygon, as follows:

Butt
The squared ends of the lines meet and overlap.

Filled
The open areas caused by the overlap are filled.

Round
The corners are rounded.

Point
The corners end in points.

Transparency
Sets the level of transparency of the fill and border. Higher levels are more transparent

To draw a Polygon: Click on the Polygon tool. Choose Color, Width, type of joints, and Transparency of the border and fill. Click where the polygon is to begin in order to anchor the starting point. Move the cursor where the first side of the polygon is to end. As the cursor is moved, the closed shape of the polygon is continually redrawn on the screen to assist the user in what the final shape will look like. Click the left mouse button again to complete the first side. Continue moving the cursor to define the remaining sides. Double clicking the end of the last line completes the polygon. Holding the Ctrl key down while moving the cursor constrains the sides of the polygon vertically, horizontally, or at 45-degree angles.

11

Artistic, Color, Fancy, and Mapping Filters

Well, here is the chapter some of you have been waiting for. This is the magic locker. One of the first things mentioned when people talk about the new release of PHOTO-PAINT 5 is the ability to use plug-in filters. PHOTO-PAINT 5 contains the many software filters that can completely change a bitmapped image with the click of a button. The Sample image (Figure 11.1) that introduces this section was enhanced with several different filters.

Plug-in filters (located under the Effects menu in the menu bar) are new with Corel PHOTO-PAINT 5. PHOTO-PAINT 4 offered a large selection of filters, but did not have the ability to install third-party plug-in filters. Filters and plug-in filters are small programs, selected from the Effects menu, that call up a pre-defined series of commands to produce a specific effect. These filters automatically calculate the values and characteristics of every pixel in the selected area of an image and then alter each pixel according to the filter selected. As an example, if the Motion Blur filter is applied to a picture of a parked bus, it gives it the appearance of moving down the street at high speed. The filter determines where the edge of the bus is, analyzes the relative traits of the pixels adjacent to the bus, and changes them so the neighboring dots are more similar to one another. All of these calculations occur automatically. You, the user, never see the millions of individual calculations that go on when you click the OK button, only the results.

Figure 11.1.
Sample image en-
hanced with several
PHOTO-PAINT Filters.

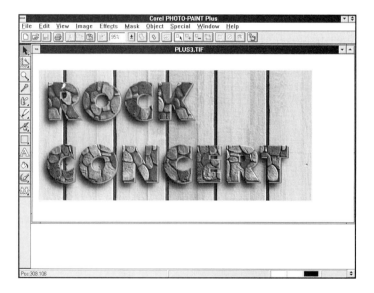

The filters can be applied to an entire image, or just a part that has been masked off. They can be applied to a single object or multiple objects in the image. Once you open Corel PHOTO-PAINT's Effects menu you are presented with a drop-down menu grouped either by the type of filter or by the filter software developer name, if you have third-party plug-in filters installed. In Figure 11.2, the drop-down menu shown is the default Effects menu drop-down list with no third-party filters.

Let's take a few moments to look at each group of filters. We'll discuss the operation of the filters that will allow the best possible performance both in speed and in the effects they produce.

Additional third-party plug-in filters may be easily installed and configured with Corel PHOTO-PAINT 5.

Figure 11.2.
Effects drop-down
Menu showing default
Filters installed.

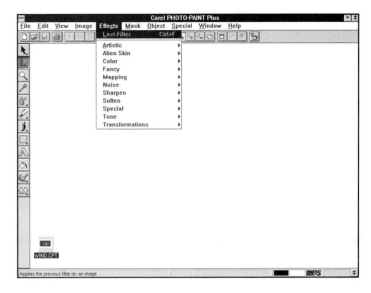

Corel *TIP!*

> If several third-party filters are installed, you will experience a slight delay the first time the Effects menu is opened. Once they have been used, the menu opens instantly as long as PHOTO-PAINT remains on.

Installing Third-Party Plug-In Filters

I put third-party plug-in filters first in the chapter because many of you have plug-in filters that are personal favorites. PHOTO-PAINT 5 makes the installation of the plug-in filters very simple. Most of the filters on the market have their own installation procedures. Some of these packages recognize Corel PHOTO-PAINT and will install their filters directly into the Corel PHOTO-PAINT plug-in subdirectory. After the filters are installed on your hard disk, you still need to configure PHOTO-PAINT to use them.

1. Install the third-party plug-in filters according to vendor's directions. After you have installed the filters use File Manager (or your favorite equivalent program) and examine the directories where the filters were installed. You are looking for files with an extension that is .8BF. The only exception is Aldus Gallery Effects, which use an .EFF extension. Make note of the locations of any files with an *.8BF or *.EFF extension.

257

2. Select preferences under the special menu on the menu bar (the keyboard shortcut is Ctrl+J). The Preferences (General) Window will open. (See Figure 11.3.) Click on the advanced tab (it looks like the tab on an index card). The Advanced Preferences section will open (see Figure 11.4). The default location for all of the built-in Corel PHOTO-PAINT filters is COREL50\PLUGINS. If you haven't installed any other filters that is all that should be in the Plug-in Directories portion of the Advanced Preferences Section.

Figure 11.3.
The Preferences
(General) Window is
where you control
many of the settings in
PHOTO-PAINT 5.

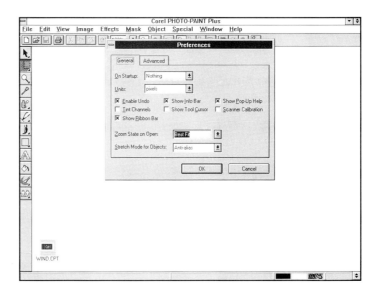

Figure 11.4.
The Advanced Prefer-
ences section is where
you list the location of
any third-party filters
you have installed. The
default location for all
of the built-in Corel
PHOTO-PAINT filters is
COREL50\PLUGINS.

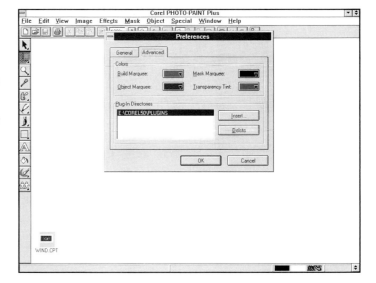

3. Click on the Insert... button of the plug-in directories section of Advanced Preferences. A Select Directory window will open, enabling you to select the location of any installed plug-in filters that you made note of in Step 1.

4. Select the location of the plug-in filters that were installed in Step 1 and click the OK button.

5. Repeat Step 4 if you have additional filter sets. Click the OK button when you are finished. After you select OK, the message appears in the status area (lower left of the screen) "Searching for plug-ins..." This can take up to a minute, so be patient.

6. Open the Effects menu to see if the filters were installed properly. Remember, the first time that Effects is opened after you have added new filters, PHOTO-PAINT must read through the entire plug-in list, so it will take a few moments to open.

Exploring the Filters

When you open the Effects drop-down menu you are presented with a long list of the filters that are available. They are grouped either by type or by software vendor. Before we can use some of the more exotic filters we must first learn to use the basic editing filters effectively. Most of the image manipulation that you will do with PHOTO-PAINT will require you to use one or more of the editing filters. The first group of filters we will explore are grouped under Color in the Effects drop-down menu. The filters are Brightness and Contrast, Gamma, Hue/Saturation, and Tone Map. We will begin by discussing Brightness and Contrast.

Brightness and Contrast

Brightness and Contrast represents one of the most basic tonal controls in any bitmap editing program. Almost every image that you work with will benefit from a slight increase (about a 10 percent increase) in both brightness and contrast. That slight increase can give dull and flat pictures a little more pizzazz.

You will always find Brightness and Contrast controls together in photo-editing programs. Tradition? No, their actions are complementary (although the controls work independently). You will probably never adjust brightness without making an adjustment to contrast, or vice versa. This is because if you increase brightness, it has a tendency to wash out both shadows and highlights of the image. To counter the "washout effect" you need to increase contrast. If you decrease brightness, darkness increases. (I know this stuff. I used to watch Mr. Wizard.) When darkness increases Contrast must also be decreased or all of the details of the image will look like a close-up of the LaBrea Tar Pits in Los Angeles at midnight.

If the photograph that you are working with is too dark, due to improper exposure or poor lighting conditions, Brightness and Contrast might be able to salvage what would be an unusable picture.

Corel *TIP!*

There will be some pictures that you can't fix. Filters have their limitations.

Be careful not to develop a disease called Contrastus-Maximus. This is a disorder suffered by newer PHOTO-PAINT users when they discover the Contrast tool. Too much contrast makes the picture look grainy. The deceiving part of this disease is that many times, too much contrast will look good on the monitor, but the printed result will be disappointing. Another recommendation for when you are working with scanned images is to make as many initial corrections as you can when you scan the image into the system.

Now that you have been properly warned... where do you find Brightness and Contrast? It's located in the Effects menu under Color—Brightness and Contrast.

In Corel PHOTO-PAINT Brightness, Contrast, and Intensity are grouped together in a single window. This filter arrangement allows the user to see what the combinations of these three filter functions will produce on the image. You can use Corel PHOTO-PAINT to modify the brightness of an image. This is a particularly powerful capability that can make changes to an image without affecting the overall color (hue) of the picture.

Use the Brightness and Contrast filter to lighten or darken a picture (brightness), or change the distinction between the light and dark areas of an image. Intensity affects (brightens) the light areas of an image without washing out the darker ones.

Brightness is the only component in the color model that has nothing to do with a color value (Brightness can also be used with a grayscale image). Brightness can destroy an image when it is increased or decreased too much. When mismanaged, this component can wipe out a subject's detail and shading, or turn a lovely sunset into a faded blob. The Brightness filter expresses values as a percentage. The extremes are -100 percent (solid black) and +100 percent (white). Brightness affects every pixel equally.

Contrast works by **adjusting the difference in the degree of shading between pixels** causing pixels that are separated by a small difference in shading to be separated by an even greater amount of difference. When taken to an extreme, you can darken a color image to a point where you will be unable to distinguish any features. On a grayscale photograph you can end up with an effect called posterization where all of the shades of gray are polarized to just black or white. Always remember, the goal with Contrast is to enhance, not distort the image. The Contrast filter expresses values as a percentage. The extremes are -100 percent (no contrast—image is solid gray) and +100 percent (extreme contrast—image too dark, almost black). Contrast only affects adjacent pixels of differing shades.

Intensity is like a combination of both Brightness and Contrast. It isn't, but it has the effect of the two. Intensity increases the brightness of the lighter pixels and applies less brightness to the darker mid-tones and dark pixels. The result is the image looks brighter without being washed out. The Intensity filter expresses values as a percentage. The extremes are -100 percent (Zero intensity—the image is black) and +100 percent (the image doesn't look bad on the screen but tends to print grainy). Intensity mainly affects lighter pixels, making them brighter.

In Figure 11.5, image SA21.PCD of the Waterfowl collection from the Corel Professional PHOTO CD-ROM Sampler is shown loaded into PHOTO-PAINT without any image enhancement. Figure 11.6 is the same image with 15 percent Brightness and 10 percent Contrast applied. You will hear many rules about ratios of Brightness to Contrast. Ignore them, use the preview window and find what works for you and your output device. Many of the rules are carryovers from disciplines other than digital imagery. In Figure 11.7, the image has had 10 percent Brightness, 20 percent Contrast and 30 percent Intensity applied. How about Figure 11.8? Have you figured out what was done to it? I cheated! Earlier in this chapter I told you to make as many initial corrections as you can when you bring the image into the system. The image in all of these figures is in Photo CD format. By taking a few moments and applying the Image Enhancement correction when the image was loaded, I was able to achieve an even greater improvement in the image quality.

*Figure 11.5.
The original image
200021.PCD from the
Corel Professional
Photos CD-ROM
Sampler.*

*Figure 11.6.
Image with only
Brightness and
Contrast filters
applied.*

Figure 11.7.
Image with Brightness,
Contrast, and Intensity
filters applied.

Figure 11.8.
This image was
corrected before
being loaded
using the Gamut
CD color correction.

Using the Brightness, Contrast, and Intensity Filters

Figure 11.9 shows the Filter dialog box for Brightness, Contrast, and Intensity. The basic functions of this dialog box are identical in all Corel PHOTO-PAINT filter dialog boxes.

Figure 11.9.
Filter Dialog Box for
Brightness, Contrast,
and Intensity.

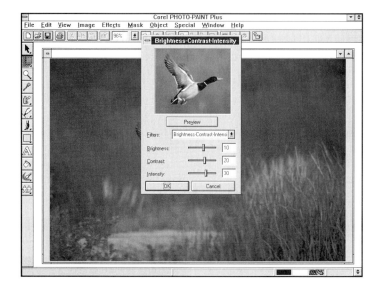

Preview Window

This area presents a thumbnail of the entire image allowing you to experiment with various filter settings and combinations of settings. Because of the small preview area involved, filter effects are applied rapidly. This can be very helpful, especially when the image you are working on is very large and the filter is complex. When the dialog box initially opens, the preview area is set to the upper left corner of the image. To change the view area, click and hold down the left mouse button in the preview area. The cursor becomes a hand. While holding down the mouse button, drag the image until the part of the image you need to see is in the Preview window. One second after you release the mouse button PHOTO-PAINT applies the current setting of the filter(s) to the image, even if the filter setting hasn't changed.

There is also a zoom function that allows you to zoom in or out of the Preview window. This allows you to see the effect on either the entire image or on a very small portion of the image. To zoom in, left-click the preview window. To zoom out, right click inside the preview window.

Preview Button   Clicking on this button causes PHOTO-PAINT to apply the selected filter to the image in the Preview window.

Filters Drop-Down   Clicking the arrow on this drop-down list provides many other filters that can be accessed directly without leaving the current dialog box. A few points to make note of concerning this box are:

- It only shows PHOTO-PAINT filters.

- It only shows a portion of the PHOTO-PAINT filters. The PAINT filters are grouped together in Dynamic Link Libraries (DLLs). You will only see the filters that are in the DLL for the selected filer.

- You can preview many filters by using this box but only one filter set (Brightness, Contrast, and Intensity, for example) can be applied. Once the filter is applied, the dialog box closes.

The remainder of the Filter Dialog box is either Filter specific or self-explanatory. The Brightness, Contrast and Intensity filters allowed us to enhance an image. Now, we will learn to use the Hue and Saturation filters to change colors in the image and produce some exciting effects.

Hue and Saturation

This is a filter you are more familiar with than you realize. You have both of these "filters" on your color television. You know them by a different name. Hue acts like the Tint control and Saturation acts like the color control.

Hue is a term used to describe the entire range of colors of the spectrum. In HSB and HSL color models, hue is the component that determines just what color you are using. The Hue filter changes the selected color from shade to shade until you have gone through the entire spectrum. Remember the color wheel when a rainbow function is selected in the Fill roll-up? When you went all of the way around the color wheel you were back at the color where you started. The Hue filter expresses values in degrees of rotation around the color wheel. The extremes are -180 degrees and +180 degrees (a value of 180 degrees in either direction selects a point exactly half way around the color wheel). This means that every pixel that has the Hue filter applied to it will have its color value changed. Hue affects all pixels by changing their color value. Every pixel that the Hue filter is applied to will have its color value changed.

Saturation is the strength or intensity of color applied to the image. Did you ever take the color control knob on the TV set (back when they had control knobs) and turn it all the way up? If you did, the colors became saturated and began to look surreal (actually, in the 1960s they looked psychedelic). The Saturation filter expresses values as a percentage. The extremes are -100 percent (no color—the image becomes grayscale) and +100 percent (image gets an unreal, comic strip look). Saturation affects very pixel in an image, increasing the amount of color in each one to its maximum.

What can you do with hue and saturation? That's the question I had when I began working seriously with color. While it's possible to use both hue and saturation for color correction, with Corel PHOTO-PAINT's advanced color management system, the need for correction is not practical. The demonstration you usually see is someone taking a color photograph of a rose and turning the red roses on green stems into blue roses on purple stems. Now, as I said earlier, there are many effects that look great, or at least interesting, but have no practical application, The color-shifted rose falls into that category. The good news is that there are several useful things that you can do with both hue and saturation. The secret of both hue and saturation is to apply them selectively to parts of the image. Let's first look at hue. I have a hard time with the word hue, it reminds me of the *Star Trek* episode where they find this Borg who they name... sigh... back to work).

In the first session you'll learn to selectively change the color of something in a photograph.

1. Open the image 200021.PCD (that's the duck picture we just looked at in Figures 11.5 – 11.9) from the Sampler of the Corel Professional Photos CD-ROM Sampler. Select standard size if your screen resolution can fit most of it. If the standard size is too large select snapshot.

2. Select the Brightness and Contrast... filter under color in the Effects menu.

3. Enter the values of 10 percent brightness, 20 percent contrast and 20 percent intensity and click the OK button. There is nothing magic about these settings. I came up with the figure by experimenting with several different settings.

4. Select the Circle Mask tool in the toolbox.

5. Drag a circle mask that covers the duck as shown in Figure 11.10. Notice the mask did not cover the entire duck. Our goal is to slightly alter the color of the background toward a warmer color. We will not apply the color shift to the duck because it causes an unacceptable effect on the white parts of the duck. The feathers that are outside of the mask are mainly gray and therefore will not be significantly altered by the hue filter.

Figure 11.10.
The duck surrounded by a mask made with the Circle Mask tool.

6. Invert the mask by either clicking the Invert Mask button or select Invert Mask in the Mask menu.

7. Select the Hue/Saturation filter under Color in the Effects menu.

8. Enter a value of +6 in the hue value box. Change the saturation value to 20. Click inside the Preview window with the right mouse button (zoom out) to bring the entire image into view. Two seconds after you let go of the image in the Preview window, the value will take effect. The entire image takes on a warmer tone. You may have wondered why everything in the Preview window changed colors. The Preview window doesn't always read masks and acts on the entire image area.

   As proof that Hue really does go half way around the color wheel, drag the slider all the way over to the left (-180) and click preview. Make a mental note of the color. Now drag the slider all the way over to the right (180). Click the Preview button. Same color. That is because it doesn't matter which direction we go, we will end up at the same spot on opposite sides of the color wheel. Return the value to -100 or find another setting to give you a color that you like better.

9. Click the OK button. The effect is applied to the entire image except for the duck. There are some other things we could do to this picture to sharpen it up, but we have accomplished what we need to do with the Hue/Saturation filter.

10. Close the file and save the changes as DUCK2.CPT.

Figure 11.11.
Although the change
doesn't show up much
in grayscale, it looks
very good on your
display when you do
the work session.

This feature is very powerful. There are many times that colors will need to be changed and the Hue/Saturation filter is the best way to accomplish this quickly. I have one last note on Hue. Theoretically, you can get every color in the rainbow using the Hue filter. However, I find that in practice it is sometimes difficult to get an exact match, even using one degree steps in the filter. Now we'll move on to Saturation and a special effect that is becoming very popular in advertising.

Saturation Exercise

In this session we will work with the Saturation filter and show that absence of color can be very effective in some applications.

1. Open the file BFLY.CPT. This file has been provided in *.CPT format so you won't have to make a mask in this session. If you want practice making the mask, remove the mask by clicking on the Remove Mask button in the ribbon bar (circle with a line through it). Using the Polygon Mask tool, outline the butterfly (just on the inside of its wings). Don't do the antennas. Next make sure the Add Selection button is active and fill in the areas on the wings that the Polygon tool missed using the Brush Mask tool. (Brush too big? Open the Tool Settings Rollup with the F8 key and change the size.) All done? Now invert the mask (Ying-Yang button) and move on to step 2.

2. Select the Hue/Saturation filter under Color in the Effects menu.

3. Slide the Saturation filter all of the way to the left (-100 percent). Click on OK. You do not need to preview. You now have an image that would make any perfume company proud. Nothing stands out like color in a black-and-white (grayscale) ad. That's it for this session. Before you cast off the butterfly you may want to try applying some different Hue values to it. To make it look realistic, you would need to mask the body and head separate from the wings and give them a darker color than the wings.

4. Close the file and don't save the changes.

On to Gamma

The Gamma Filter

I wish there was a quick and slick way to explain gamma. Many people work with gamma and don't know what it is. Australians refer to sunbathing as "catching gammas." Gamma Hydra 4 is one of the more popular names for a planet in the old *Star Trek* series. Monitors have gamma settings and scanner hardware, and software offers gamma correction. Corel PHOTO-PAINT offers a Gamma filter. What is gamma and what does it do?

What Gamma Is

A gamma curve is the name for a mathematical function that describes the nonlinear tonal response of many printers and monitors. That is the best and most concise official technical description I have been able to find. What does it say? Gamma is a mathematical curve that describes how inaccurately scanners, monitors, or printers reproduce a tonal range. Still fuzzy? A color original often has a large tonal range. The tonal range is the difference between the lightest and darkest tones. This range of difference is expressed in a logarithmic density scale. Such a wide tonal range cannot be reproduced in printing. As a point of reference, the tonal range of a color slide (the best) is 2.7. The best range possible for printing (on very high quality paper) is about 1.9, and the worst is newsprint with a range of 0.9. So what happens when a color image with a tonal range of 2.7 is printed on newsprint? Similar tones merge into a single tone resulting in undesired and uncontrolled color range reduction.

One method of controlling tonal range is to restrict the range by setting limits. A common setting is to have all tonal values below 5 percent made white and all values above 95 percent set to black. This has an unfortunate side effect of increasing the image's contrast. The best method is to compress the range. Gamma values indicate the relationship.

The Gamma filter controls the Gamma curve of an image in a very simplistic manner. The Gamma curve is a graphical representation of the balance of shadows, midtones, and highlights. Use the Gamma filter to enhance detail by adjusting middle grayscale values (mid tones). This will not affect shadow areas (darkest black areas), or highlight areas (lightest white areas). Visually it will look and act like a combination of Brightness, Contrast, and Intensity. It will pick up some additional detail in low contrast images without the graininess of the Contrast filter. For those experienced users who are accustomed to working with gamma values, a gamma value of 180 represents a normal gamma of 1.8.

So that's great and all but, what can I do with it?

Color correction is one thing you can do with it. Bored yet? Figure 11.12 shows my favorite use for the filter. In the special projects chapter I show how to make letters stand out like this.

Figure 11.12.
When you have a dark photograph, using the Gamma filter on the text can make it stand out. In the special projects chapter you will learn this very simple but effective technique.

Tone Map

The Tone Map (Figure 11.13) is the last filter in the Color Group of the Effects menu. The Tone Map allows you to adjust the response curve of selected images. In some situations it provides finer adjustment of gamma, contrast and brightness than can be obtained with the previously described filters. The various response curves of the Tone Map are powerful and complex image-adjustment tools. For users not familiar with response curves and their use, PHOTO-PAINT provides seven preset options that will help improve image quality without having to manually adjust the response curves.

With the Tone Map dialog box it is possible to customize response curves for the entire image and for individual color channels as well. While this is intended for specialized correction, by applying different curves to individual channels it is possible to create some unusual special effects.

Figure 11.13.
The Tone Map dialog box is very powerful and also very confusing to the faint of heart.

Preset Options	Drop-down list provides choice of seven PHOTO-PAINT preset response curves.
Load	Opens Load Tone Map dialog box. Provides access to preset or customized response curves with *.MAP extensions.
Save	Opens Save Tone Map As dialog box for saving customized response curves.
Edit Style	Used to select one of four sets of Tone Map controls.
Curve	Smooths distribution and fine-tunes other Styles. Clicking on any of the handles and dragging them allows adjustment of the response curve.
Freehand	Allows the creation of any shape of response curve.
Linear	Provides adjustment of brightness and contrast of either an individual channel or all channels. Clicking on the handles on either end of the line and dragging the line to a new location provides a wide range of contrast and brightness adjustments.
Gamma	Used to make fine adjustments in the image gamma by providing visual adjustment of the middle grayscale component of the image.

| Preview | Provides preview of changes made to the image. Note that change made to response curves do not automatically activate preview function. |
| Reset | Resets the dialog box to its default values. |

Artistic Filters

Here is a set of filters that you may need if your job is getting done too quickly. Both of these filters are designed to make existing images look like oil paintings. There are two of these filters in the Artistic filter sub-group, Pointillism and Impressionism. These filters transform existing images into representations of classic artistic styles, but you have to have a very powerful machine and plenty of time.

| Pointillism: | Use the Pointillism filter to add a dot-like appearance to the picture. I had to look up Pointillism in an art book. So sue me, I wasn't an art major in school. The effect can vary between a very subtle patterning to extreme distortion, and if you don't keep your brush size small you can count on distortion. Pointillism can also be used to create special effects to a limited degree. The greatest disadvantage of the effects of a large brush setting is that you no longer can recognize the original work. |

Corel *TIP!*

Change your brush size before you begin. This filter and the Impressionism filter use the current brush size for their filter and you must exit the filter to change the brush size. I expect this will be improved in the next version of PHOTO-PAINT.

About Brush Sizes...

All brush size settings are in pixels. I have made a comparison of the Pointillism with a brush size of 5 pixels on four different Photo-CD sized images to make my point (bad pun). In Figure 11.14 there are images loaded off the Sampler Photo-CD at four different sizes (Wallet, Snapshot, Standard, and Large). The Pointillism filter was applied to all four images with identical settings. POINT3.CPT was the smallest (wallet) and the result of applying a 5-pixel brush to that small of an image is to make it unrecognizable. POINT1.CPT was applied to a Snapshot size, POINT2.CPT to a standard size and it is now almost recognizable, and POINT4.CPT to a Large size which is clearly a tiger (it also took 5 minutes to process).

Figure 11.14.
Too many tigers?
This collection of four
different settings
shows the effect
applying the same
size brush (in pixels)
to four different sizes
of Photo CD images.

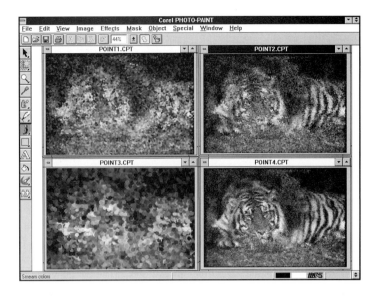

Figure 11.15.
The Pointillism dialog
box. Sure it looks scary,
but wait until you use
it. Remember, the
Pointillism filter takes
time so make sure you
have a book before you
click the OK button.

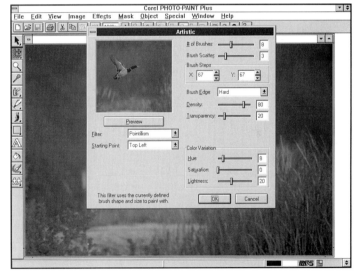

Pointillism Dialog Box Options

Starting Point: Choose a starting point from the drop-down list. Defines the direction the dots are applied. I have tried several settings here and cannot see any significant difference other than an almost imperceptible shift in the position of the finished image.

# of Brushes	This setting determines the number of brushes that apply the dots. The greater the number the more diffused the picture appears.
Brush Scatter	Distance (in pixels) between the dots of each brush.
Brush Steps	Distance (in pixels) in both X and Y axes between each repeat application of the brush.

Corel *TIP!*

> Brush step settings, more than any other variable, affect the amount of time it takes to process the image. Smaller values produce the greatest effect on the image but take the longest amount of time to apply.

Brush Edge	Drop-down list with selections of soft, medium, and hard. Soft produces an image that is more blurry. Hard produces sharper harder dots.
Density	Determines the width of color applied with a brush stroke. Range 0 percent = invisible; 100 percent = maximum to edge of brush stroke. Density's affect is like that of a paintbrush. When it is set to 100 percent it is like a brush that is pressed hard against the paper. The color goes clear to the edge of the brush. When set to a lower value, the color is applied mainly to the center of the stroke or dot as if the brush were pressed again the paper with little pressure.
Transparency	Sets the transparency of brush colors—Range 100 percent = invisible; 0 percent = maximum

Corel *TIP!*

> Watch out for this setting. If it is set at 60 percent or more you may not be able to see any changes in the image you are apply the pointillism to other than a mild blurring.

Color Variation Box

Almost all of the variations introduced in the Color Variation box control the overall appearance in the area of color variation, color versus grayscale, and general contrast and brightness.

Corel*NOTE!*

If you own PHOTO-PAINT 5 (including the maintenance release "B"), the Hue and Saturation sliders will be reversed. A quick way to confirm this is by applying 50 to the Hue and clicking the Preview window. If the image becomes grayscale, it is reversed. No big deal, just thought you should know.

Hue

A higher number increases the number of colors introduced by filter. This is operational even if the image is grayscale. A very large number looks a lot like a Gaussian noise filter was applied (distortion with random color as a bonus). Any colors applied are overridden by very high Saturation settings.

Saturation

Controls the number of grays in applied colors— Higher number moves toward all grayscale. At the maximum of 50 the image is totally grayscale. What if the image is already grayscale? It acts like contrast. At a setting of 0 it is higher contrast, and at a maximum setting of 50 it is a lower contrast.

Lightness

The amount of light (intensity) applied to colors— it increases the difference between colors. At the maximum setting the maximum amount of intensity is applied to each pixel. The result is there are a greater number of shades of color visible and a greater contrast between the shades (in other words, the dots are much more vivid). At the lowest setting the intensity is decreased to each pixel and the colors move toward each other. There is a lot of averaging and generally lower contrast.

Preview

Allows the effect to be seen on a thumbnail of the image. Because of the small preview area involved filter effects are applied rapidly. This can be very helpful, especially when the image you are working on is very large and the filter is complex (and Pointillism is very complex and Impressionism is worse). When the dialog box initially opens, the preview area is set to the upper left corner of the image. To change the view area, click and hold down the left mouse button in the preview area. The cursor becomes a hand. Still holding down the mouse button drag the image until the part of the image you need to see is in the Preview window.

No Auto-Preview

On all of the other filters except Pointillism and Impressionism, one second after you release the mouse button PHOTO-PAINT applies the current setting of the filter(s) to the image, even if the filter setting hasn't changed. This Auto-Preview function wasn't put in due to the complexity of the filter and the time that previews could take. The only way to see the preview is to press the button.

Zooming in the Preview

There is also a zoom function that allows you to zoom in or out of the Preview window. This allows you to see the effect on either the entire image or on a very small portion of the image. To zoom in, left-click the Preview window. To zoom out, right-click inside the Preview window.

Things to Do with Pointillism

If your intent is to produce images that really look like the classic art style oil painting and you are going to do it more than a few times, I recommend that you get Fractal Design's Painter program. This type of work is referred to as natural media effects, and it is what Fauvve's Mattise and Painter do best. If you are not willing to shell out several hundred dollars for either of these programs, then there are ways to make Pointillism do some neat tricks. Before we look at ways you can make Pointillism earn its pay, we need to cover the minimum image requirements.

Before You Begin

First and foremost use clearly defined images. If the subject of the image is vague or indistinct, you will not be satisfied with the results. If the subject is not easily recognizable in its original form, it will be impossible to distinguish what it is after the Pointillism effect is applied. Dark or blurred images can become unrecognizable when using this filter. What a bummer! You might be thinking that you can't use Pointillism with anything. WRONG! I am just telling you what I have learned the hard way. When someone gives you a photo of a large black man in a black suit against a dark background, that is not a candidate for using this filter. I didn't make that up; I really had such a photo.

Corel *TIP!*

Pointillism achieves a more realistic effect if a small brush size is used with an X/Y Step setting about 2 pixels greater than the brush size.

Effects with Pointillism

The first effect is basic Pointillism. The Pointillism filter was applied and the result is Figure 11.17. No tricks here. Keep the brush size below 4 or 5 pixels. To get something that looks like a charcoal and chalk sketch is easy. Take the image in Figure 11.17 and convert it to a grayscale image using the Convert to... command in the Image menu. Apply Motion Blur (under the Fancy group in the Effects menu) with a value of 1 using the down-left arrow direction. To complete the picture apply Edge Enhance (from the Sharpen group in the Effects menu) with a value of 50. The result is shown in Figure 11.18. I also increased the paper size and, for a final touch, applied a canvas as explained in previous chapters.

Figure 11.16.
The barn was chosen because it would still be recognizable after applying the Pointillism effect to it.

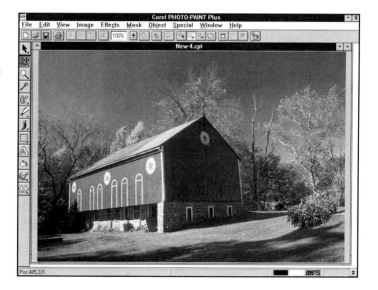

Figure 11.17.
This was created
by applying the
default setting of the
Pointillism filter at a
brush size of 5. The
image size was
Photo-CD Standard.

Figure 11.18.
The barn is now a
pencil sketch thanks
to the magic of the
Pointillism, Motion
Blur, Edge Enhance
filters, and the
Canvas roll-up.

The next effect is shown in Figure 11.19. This is another example of using a filter
for something other than what it was designed for. The word point was made
with the FUTURA Extra Bk typeface. The background was hidden using the
Layers/Objects roll-up, and the Pointillism filter was applied with a large brush
size (10 pixels) and a lightness setting of 50. The shadow was made by duplicat-
ing the text object and applying a Gaussian blur to it.

*Figure 11.19.
Another example
of using a filter for
something other than
what it was designed
to do. In this case the
Pointillism was used to
give the colorful scaling
effect to the text.*

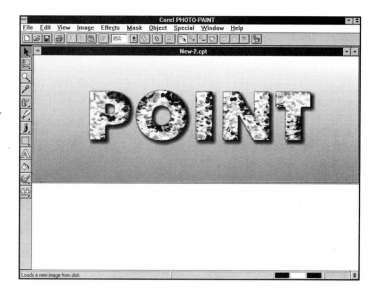

*Figure 11.20.
A hand behind a
shower door. To make
opaque glass distortion
use a 2:1 ration (X/Y-
Step to Brush size).
For the image shown I
used a photo of a hand
from the Just Hands
collection by CMCD
and applied Pointillism
with a brush setting of
9 (try flattening and
rotating the brush just
a little). Use a Light-
ness setting of 2 and
make Hue and
Saturation zero.*

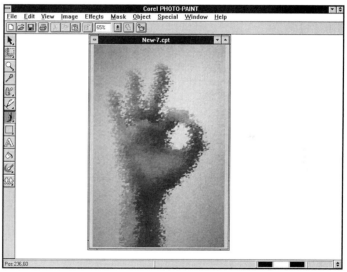

Enough already. Get the idea? Experiment with the filter or combinations of
these filters, and don't let their names get you into a rut.

Impressionism

The Impressionism filter can give an image the look of an oil painting. Depending on the settings in the Impressionism dialog box, the result can vary from
subtle enhancement of a photograph to extreme distortion. Images that have
large clearly defined objects work best with this filter. Dark or blurred images
do not always produce optimum results.

Figure 11.21.
*Impressionism
dialog box.*

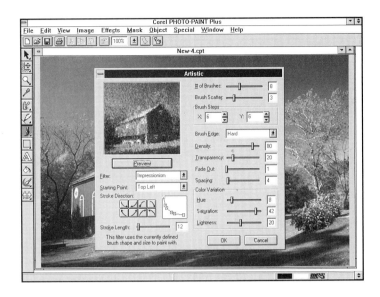

Impressionism Dialog Box Options

Many of the settings in the Impressionism dialog box are identical in function
to the Pointillism dialog box. Where the functions are identical they are so
indicated.

Starting Point	See Pointillism dialog box.
Stroke Direction Buttons	These eight buttons provide control of the direction of the stroke as indicated by the arrows on each button.
Stroke Direction preview box	The nodes in the preview allow the user to alter the path followed by the stroke.
Stroke Length Slider	Controls the length of the stroke. Stroke length readout is in pixels.
# of Brushes	See Pointillism dialog box.
Brush Scatter	See Pointillism dialog box.
Brush Steps	See Pointillism dialog box.
Brush Edge	See Pointillism dialog box.
Density	See Pointillism dialog box.
Transparency	See Pointillism dialog box.

| Fade Out | Sets the length of the brush stroke before it fades out entirely. A value of zero has no fade out. Higher values cause the fade to occur closer to brush stroke origin. |
| Spacing | Adjusts the spacing (in pixels) between points on a brush stroke. A setting of zero or one creates a solid line. It also increases filter processing time. |

Fancy Filters

This collection of filters covers a wide variety of effects. The Fancy sub-group menu has the following filters:

Edge detect, Emboss, Gaussian Blur, Invert, Jaggy Despeckle, Motion Blur and **Outline**.

Edge Detect

The Edge Detect filter is used to add a variety of outline effects to an image. Use the Edge Detect filter to add different outline effects to an image. You can set sensitivity, color, and edge.

Sensitivity	Enter a value from 1–10. The value determines the amount of edge enhancement. The higher the number the more edges are enhanced.
Color	A drop-down list allows selection of the color of the non-outlined areas. The color selected in this drop-down box will be used to fill all of areas of the image that are not part of the outline both inside and outside of the outline.
Edge	Determines the following:

> **Auto** automatically adjusts the outline.
>
> **Light** For a grayscale image, choose Light. For white outlines or for a 24 bit color image, choose Light to produce light colored outlines.
>
> **Dark** For black outlines, choose Dark or for a 24-bit color image, also choose Dark to produce dark colored outlines.

Notes on using **Edge Detect**.

For best results, use Edge Detect on high-contrast images including text.

Figure 11.22.
Our barn after the
application of the
default settings of the
Edge Detect filter. Even
though it was designed
primarily to work with
solid colors, it does well
with some images.

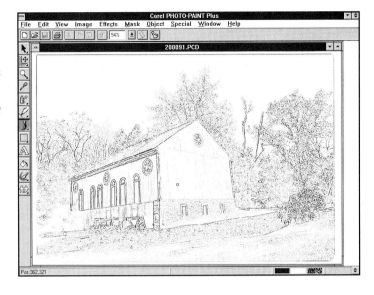

Figure 11.23.
This image was created
using the Edge Detect
filter in combination
with the Object Merge
feature of PHOTO-
PAINT.

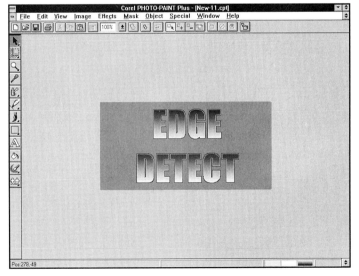

Emboss

Embossing creates a three-dimensional relief effect. Directional arrows point to the location of the light source and determine the angle of the highlights and shadows. The Emboss filter has its most dramatic effect on images that have medium to high contrast. Several filters can be used in combination with the Emboss filter to produce photo-realistic effects.

Figure 11.24.
This figure was
originally created for
the PHOTO-PAINT
manual, and I have
included it here to
show what can be
done with the
Emboss filter.

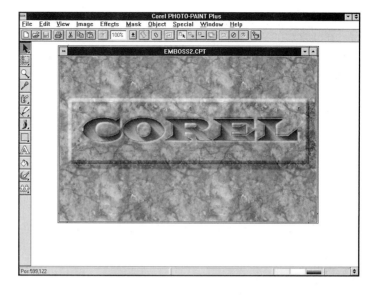

Figure 11.25.
Another example from
the PHOTO-PAINT
manual that uses
the Emboss filter.

Figure 11.26.
Gives you an idea of
some of the variations
that are possible with
the Emboss filter. The
butterfly was masked
and then a standard
Emboss filter was
applied.

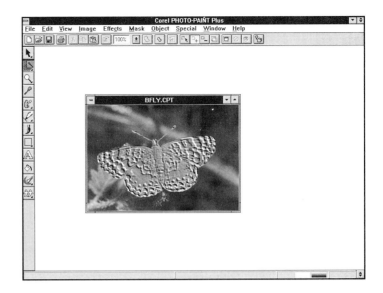

Emboss Dialog Box

Direction buttons: Selecting one of the eight buttons determines the location of the light source for the embossing effect.

Emboss Color: A drop-down list provides selection of one of three shades of gray, the paint (foreground) or paper (background) color for the Emboss color.

Gaussian Blur

This filter, although deceptively simple, is used in many of the effects that are created with PHOTO-PAINT. The Gaussian Blur filter produces a hazy effect giving the appearance that the image is slightly out of focus. The filter can improve the quality of images with sharp edges. If the image has "jaggies," the Jaggy Despeckle filter is a superior choice. The term Gaussian refers to the bell-shaped curve that is generated by mapping the color values of the pixels in the selected area. There is only one setting with the Gaussian Blur. It is Radius. It refers to the radius (in pixels) that is affected. The greater the Radius Slider setting, the greater the amount of blurring of the image occurs.

Notes about the Gaussian Blur filter—the filter is best used with small values. If a large amount of blur needs to be applied, a more uniform blur is obtained by applying small values (<5) several times using the Apply Last Filter command (CTRL+F). Gaussian Blur is very useful in creating a neon glow effect, and making embossed images look more realistic.

Figure 11.27.
The basic shadow.

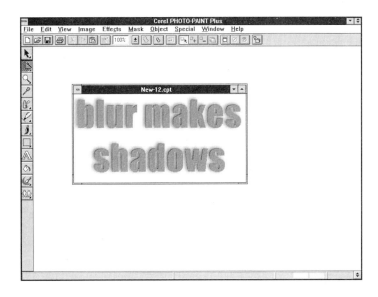

Figure 11.28.
The Gaussian Blur
creates the glow
effect around the text.

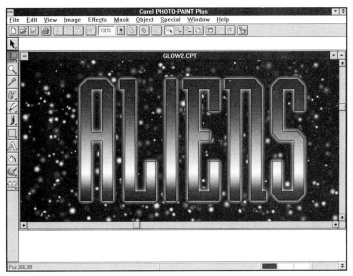

Figure 11.29.
The shadows under the text were created in another image area with the Gaussian Blur, and then an object merge was used to make the shadows an object. This is impor-tant since using the blur to make shadows on a detailed back-ground can cause loss of detail on the background.

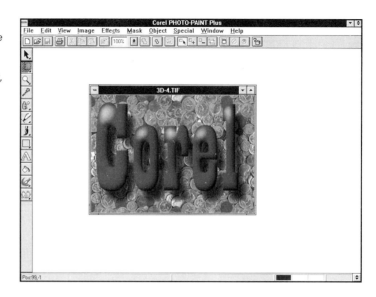

Invert

The Invert command changes the colors so they appear as if they were a photographic negative. While the ability to make a photographic negative is rarely needed, the invert can be used to reverse a portion of an image. There are many uses for the "reversal" effect with the Invert filter. In the sample shown, the Invert filter was used before the Embossing was applied to create a raised effect. There are no variables available with the Invert filter.

Figure 11.30.
This poster took less than 3 minutes to make. I just made a rectangle mask of the right side, applied the Invert filter and then typed the text and filled with the MIST.TIF fill from Corel CD-ROM Disk1.

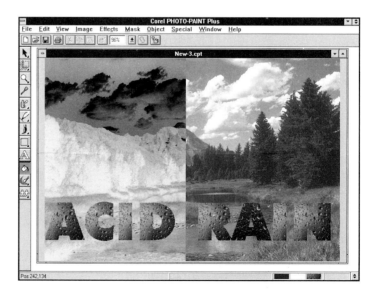

Jaggy Despeckle

The Jaggy Despeckle filter scatters colors in an image creating a soft, blurred effect with very little distortion. It also smooths out jagged edges (jaggies) on images. It is most effective in removing "jaggies" on line art or high contrast images. The Jaggy Despeckle dialog box offers options to control Height and Width values of diffusion separately or keep the values identical if the Identical Values checkbox is selected. Setting the values independently offers a mild diffusing of the image while keeping image detail loss to a minimum.

Figure 11.31a.
The original text.

Figure 11.31b.
The same text
stretched by
400 percent.

Figure 11.31c.
The text from 11.31b
after application of the
Jaggy Despeckle filter.

Motion Blur

Motion Blur creates the impression of movement in an image. It achieves this effect by determining the edges of the image for the direction selected and smearing them into the adjacent pixels. Direction of the motion is selected in the Motion Blur dialog box using one of the eight direction arrow buttons. A slider provides speed value selection. The higher the speed number, the more blurring is applied.

Notes on the Motion Blur Filter

The Motion Blur filter has uses other than what its name describes. In the sample shown, the shadow on the engraved type was created by applying the Motion Blur filter to the text while it was the only object not hidden. The result was black being pulled across the leading edge (shadow), and the blurring of the trailing edge was lost because the text was the only layer/object selected. The result is a very realistic depth to the text. This is only one example. Do not let the name of a filter limit its function. The only way to find out what the large variety of filters included in PHOTO-PAINT can do is to experiment with them.

Figure 11.32.
The cutout effect of the text was created by using the Motion Blur filter and then applying it using Object Merge mode to the original copy of the text. A canvas filter provided the texture.

Outline

The Outline command applies an outline to selected objects or images. Objects of solid color will be outlined with the color of that object. The inside of objects and the background areas of the image will be filled with a gray color.

Mapping Filters

Glass Block

This filter creates the effect of viewing the image through thick transparent blocks of glass. The width and height of the glass blocks can be set independently of each other. The setting range is 5 through 100. The lowest setting (5) produces 5 complete glass blocks in the image area. The width and height values are based on a percentage of the image and are therefore constant regardless of the image size.

Notes on Glass Block

Using larger numbers (>25) produces an diamond glass pattern look. While lower numbers produce a unique appearance, the best effects will be obtained using numbers in the 25–75 range. Setting the width on the lowest number (widest block) and the vertical value on the highest number (smallest block) creates a visual effect like the image was being viewed through 5 vertical mirrors.

Figure 11.33.
A radial fill Image
(purple02 preset) with
Glass Block filter
applied and then the
invert filter applied
makes a stunning
background that looks
like gold wrapping
paper.

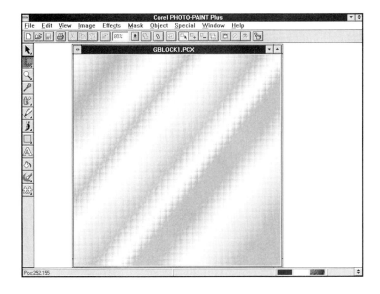

Impressionist

This filter is applied to an image to give the image the appearance of an impressionist brush. The amount of effect can be applied independently as Horizontal or Vertical values. The range is 1–40 and is measured in the amount of displacement in pixels. For example, a setting of 10 in the Vertical will diffuse the image over a 10-pixel region in the vertical. The greater the setting the greater will be the blurring of the original image, to the point where the original image can become unrecognizable.

Figure 11.34.
A sample image with
Impressionist filter
applied. The back-
ground image has a
default setting of the
Impressionist filter
applied. The boots are
objects from the Plus
version of PAINT.

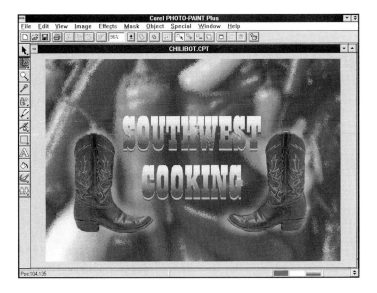

Map To Sphere

The Map to Sphere filter creates the impression that the image has been wrapped around a sphere, vertical cylinder or a horizontal cylinder.

Drag the Percentage slider to choose the amount of wrapping. Negative values wrap the image toward the back and positive values wrap the image toward the front. For most applications values between 15–30 percent provide the best effects. Clicking Sphere, Vertical Cylinder or Horizontal Cylinder allows selection of the model used for wrapping.

While the filter can be applied to the entire image, some of the most dramatic effects are achieved by applying the effect to a smaller area of the image that has been defined by a mask. The effect is more pronounced and effective if the object has horizontal and vertical lines.

Pinch/Punch

The Pinch/Punch filter either squeezes the image so the center appears to come forward (pinch) or depresses the image so the center appears to be sunken (punch). The results make the image look as if it has been either pulled out or pushed in from the center.

In the dialog box, moving the slider in a positive (+) direction applies a Pinch effect and moving it in a negative direction (-) produces a Punch effect. While the filter can be applied to the entire image, some of the most dramatic effects are achieved by applying the effect to a smaller area of the image that has been defined by a mask. The effect is more pronounced and effective if the object has horizontal and vertical lines.

Figure 11.35.
The background image is one of the uninteresting bitmap fills that comes with CorelDRAW. I put a circle mask in the center and applied the Map to Sphere filter to make the shape appear.

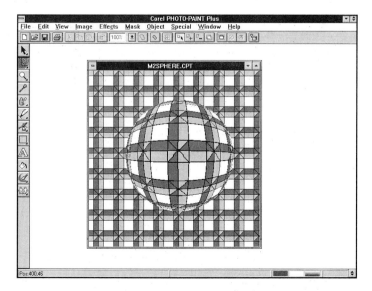

*Figure 11.36.
This is so simple to
make. Make a circle
mask. Fill it with the
Texture Bitmap fill
Satellite Photography
(Styles library). Apply
the Map to Sphere filter
with a setting around
22–26. Invert the mask
and apply the Night
Sky Texture Bitmap fill
from the Sample 5
library. The clouds on
the planet edge are
airbrushed; those on
the planet are created
by the fill.*

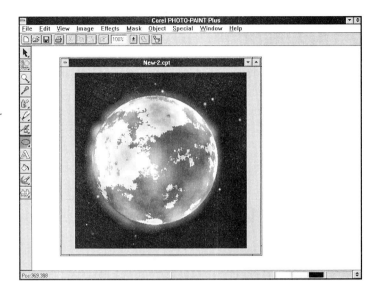

*Figure 11.37.
This was created by
applying the Pinch/
Punch filter fill to a
bitmap fill as a starting
point. The Map to
Sphere filter was
applied to the result.*

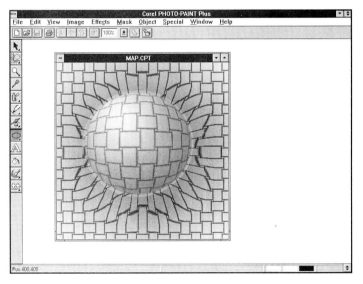

Figure 11.38.
Figure 11.38 was made much in the same way as Figure 11.37 except the Brick Bitmap fill pattern was used and some object merges were applied to make the shadows (which are a little too dark to suit my fancy).

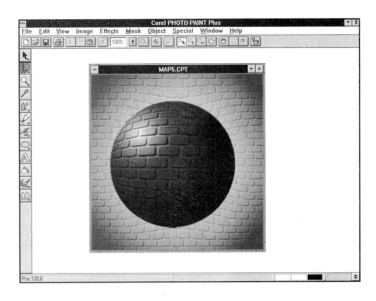

Figure 11.39a.
A photo of a model from the original Sampler Photo CD.

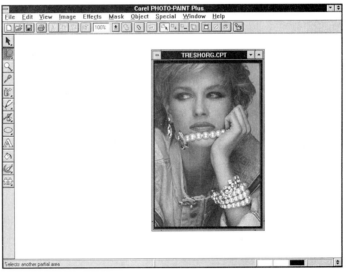

*Figure 11.39b.
An example made by
applying the Pinch/
Punch filter to parts of
the photo with a mask.*

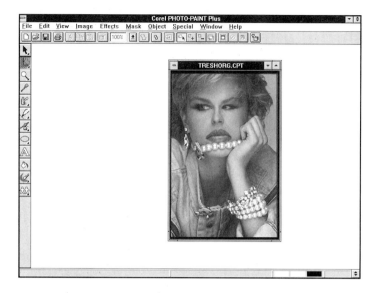

*Figure 11.39c.
An example made by
applying the Pinch/
Punch filter to parts of
the photo with a mask.*

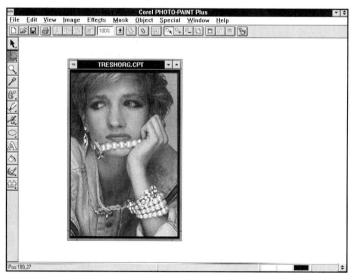

Figure 11.39d.
An example made by
applying the Pinch/
Punch filter to parts of
the photo with a mask.

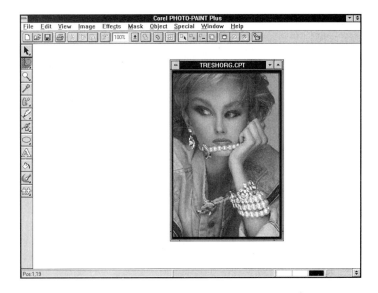

Pixelate

The Pixelate filter adds a block-like appearance to the image. You can vary the effect by selecting either circular or rectangular mode and changing the size and opacity of the blocks. This filter can be used to created backgrounds that have the appearance of mosaic tiles.

Horizontal and vertical values (in pixels) for the size of the Pixel blocks can be entered independently. The effects of pixel block size are dependent on the image size. A value of 10 in a small image will create large pixel blocks. A value of 10 in a very large image will produce small pixel blocks. Use the Opacity Slider to control the transparency of the pixel blocks. Lower values are more transparent. The shape of the blocks are controlled with the Mode buttons. Rectangular arranges the pixel blocks on horizontal lines. Circular bends the pixel blocks and arranges them on concentric circles beginning at the center of the image or the masked area.

Ripple

The Ripple filter creates the effects of waves vertically, horizontally, or both. In the Ripple dialog box the Period slider selects the distance between each cycle of wave. A value of 100 creates the greatest distance between each wave, resulting in the fewest number of waves. The Amplitude sets the amount of displacement the wave creates. The greater the number, the greater the displacement. The Ripple filter can be used to create rippled edges on an image.

*Figure 11.40.
The butterfly in this
photo was masked, and
then the mask was
inverted and a circular
setting of the Pixelate
filter was applied.*

*Figure 11.41.
This was created by
making a rectangle
filled with the Gradient
Bitmap fill (my favor-
ite). Text was placed
on top; then the Ripple
filter was applied. A
duplicate of the text
was then laid on top.*

Smoked Glass

The Smoked Glass filter applies a transparent mask over the image to give the
appearance of smoked glass. You can determine the color of the tint, the percentage of transparency, and the degree of blurring.

The color of the tint is determined by the paint (foreground) color. This is set using the Color roll-up (Ctrl+F2). The Tint slider controls the Opacity of the tint being applied. Larger values produce greater amounts of color tint being applied to the image. A value of 100 fills the area with a solid color. The Percentage slider controls the amount of blurring applied to the image to give the appearance of the distortion caused by glass. A value of 100 percent produces the greatest amount of blurring and 0 percent produces no blurring of the image.

Figure 11.42.
This one took some time to make. The Smoked Glass filter provides two things: tinting and blurring (distortion). The result only looks like smoked glass if the paint color is set to a dark color.

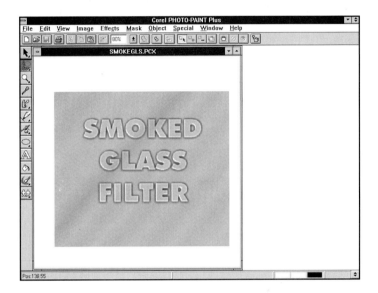

Swirl

The Swirl filter rotates and drags the image in the angle designated. The image appears to swirl around the center. The direction of the movement is determined by whether the angle is a negative or a positive value. Click and drag the Angle slider to set the amount of rotation. Negative values rotate counterclockwise, and positive values rotate clockwise.

One suggested use is to apply Swirl to a sky texture fill pattern many times, thus creating a pattern that is similar to a satellite photograph of a hurricane. While one rarely needs that particular effect, by using different images many excellent background images can be created.

Figure 11.43.
In this one I have taken the Map to Sphere and Pinch/Punch filter base work and added a swirl component to the center circle. Several fills and layers were added for effect. Looks interesting and I had fun making it, but unless it wins an art contest, I can't see much use for it.

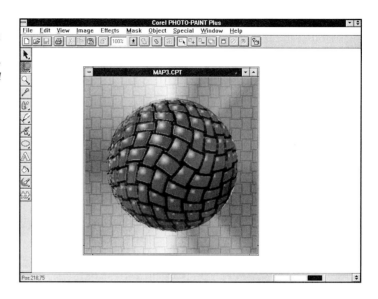

Tile

The Tile filter creates blocks of the image in a grid. You can adjust the height and width of the tiles using the Width and Height sliders in the dialog box. The values entered represent the number of images duplicated on each axis. For example, the default setting of 10,10 results in 100 copies of the images (10 × 10).

The Tile filter can be used in combination with floodfills to create backgrounds as well as making wallpaper for Windows.

Figure 11.44a.
You begin with a basketball object (Plus edition).

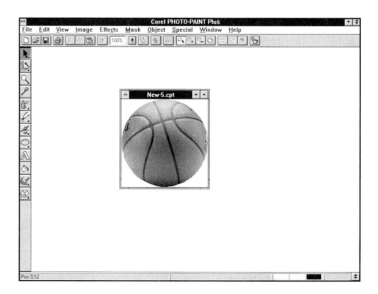

Figure 11.44b.
Tile the object
as shown.

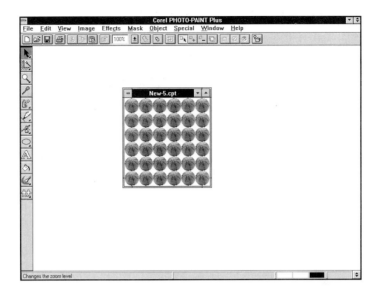

Figure 11.44c.
Apply the new tile
using the bitmap fill
as shown.

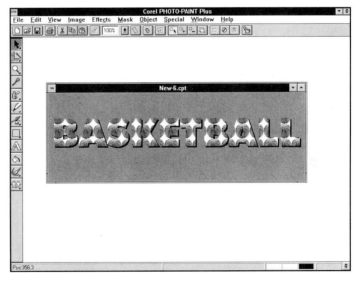

Vignette

The Vignette filter applies a mask over the image that has a transparent oval in the center. The remainder of the mask is opaque. It is designed to appear as an old style photograph when the image was placed in an oval.

A Vignette can be applied to the entire image or just a masked area. By clicking and dragging the Offset slider you can control how large the oval is in the center of the image. The larger the percentage, the larger the transparent oval.

The Fade slider controls the fade (feathering) at the edge of the oval. Using the Vignette dialog box you can determine the color of the mask by selecting black, white, or Pen color. If Pen color is chosen the Paint Color must be selected in the Color roll-up. The Paint color must be selected before applying the Vignette filter.

Figure 11.45.
Remember our attractive model in the Pinch/ Punch filter? Here she is again, but this time in a more Victorian motif thanks to our Vignette filter. In the original, I made it a pseudo-duotone and it is all browns and tans.

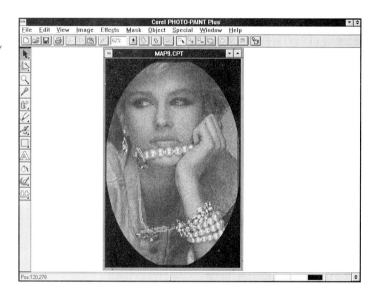

Wet Paint

The image is given the appearance of wet paint. You can set the percentage and the degree of wetness. Percentage refers to the depth to which the wet paint look is applied. For example, if you set low percentages, the amount of wetness appears to affect only the surface of the image.

Technically, Percent controls the amount (how far down) the drip travels. The wetness determines which colors drip. Negative (-) wetness values cause the dark colors to drip. Positive (+) wetness values cause light colors to drip. The magnitude of the wetness values determines how large of a range of colors drip. Maximum values are +/- 50 percent.

Wet Paint can be used to provide many different effects. Several combinations of positive and negative wetness can be applied to the same object to produce drop shadows giving a three-dimensional appearance to rounded text.

Figure 11.46.
This filter provides a "cute" effect with limited usefulness. All that is necessary is to apply the filter to an object. In the case of this figure, it was text.

Wind

The Wind filter creates the effect of wind blowing on the objects in the image. You can set the opacity and the strength of the wind. Click and drag the Opacity slider to determine the visibility of the wind effect. Higher values make the effect more visible, and lower values make a more subtle effect. The amount of the wind effect (distortion) applied is controlled by the Strength slider.

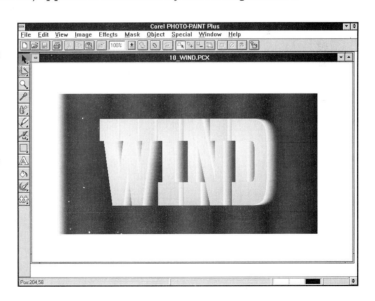

Figure 11.47.
In the Corel manual I used this filter to create the three-dimensional effect shown here. It isn't what the original he had in mind when they made it, but it is a slick effect. Just take some text, make a duplicate of it, and hide the bottom layer. Apply the wind filter several times and then show both layers. Instant 3-D!

Figure 11.48.
This is what they had in mind when they made the filter. While this works great if your object appears to be traveling from right-to-left, it does not let you change the direction of the wind. This is appropriate since, to quote Mark Twain, "Everyone talks about the weather but no one ever does anything about it."

Summary

- Use the Brightness and Contrast filter to lighten or darken a picture (brightness), or change the distinction between the light and dark areas of an image.

- Intensity affects (brightens) the light areas of an image without washing out the darker areas.

- Ignore "rules" about contrast to brightness ratios and find a combination that works best with each picture.

- Always use Image Enhancement correct (if available) on Photo-CD images.

- Move images in the Filter dialog box Preview window by clicking and dragging the image.

- Every time an image is moved in the Preview window the currently selected filter is applied to the Preview image one second after the image is released.

- Zoom in on an image in the Preview window by left-clicking on the image.

- Zoom out on an image in the Preview window by right-clicking on the image.

- Hue is a term used to describe the entire range of colors of the spectrum.

- The Hue filter is used to change the color on selected areas of the image.

- Saturation is the amount or intensity of the color applied to an image.

- The Saturation filter provides control of color image saturation from -100 percent (grayscale) to +100 percent (gross).

- The Gamma filter enhances detail by adjusting middle grayscale values (mid-tones) on a color image. It does not affect shadow areas (darkest black areas) or highlight areas (lightest white areas).

- The Tone Map filter provides more specific control over lighting/shading in an image through the manipulation of Gamma and other response curves.

12

Basic Filters

This chapter describes the remaining PHOTO-PAINT 5 Basic filters in the Effects menu. The first subgroup to be examined is the Noise filters.

Noise Filters

The Noise filters can be used to add or remove random pixels from an image or masked area. Too much noise in an image can result from badly scanned images or the scanning of an image that was received on a FAX machine (always a poor choice). Whether noise needs to be removed or even added, Corel PHOTO-PAINT 5 provides the necessary filters to accomplish it.

The Noise subgroup has the following filters:

Add Noise

Why would you want to add noise? Actually, adding noise has more uses than you would first imagine. Noise (random pixels) can give the effect of grit and texture to a picture. It can add a dusting of pixels to an image in a way that emulates film grain. When the grain color is not quite compatible with the image, adding noise can be helpful in softening the look of stark image areas. When you are retouching photographs that have existing film-grain texture, it can be helpful to add noise so the blending is less apparent. If you are an old hand with Photoshop, you probably know much of this already.

There are several neat tricks that can be done with this filter. Let's begin with the technical description of the filter, which I wrote for the manual.

The Add More Noise filter creates a granular effect that adds texture to a flat or overly blended image. Three types of noise are available. They are Uniform, Gaussian, or Spike method.

Uniform   Provides an overall grainy appearance. Use this option to apply colors in an absolutely random fashion, with the range specified by the Noise Level percentage slider.

Gaussian   Using this option prioritizes colors along a Gaussian distribution curve. The effect is that most colors added by the filter either closely resemble the original colors or push the boundaries of the specified range. The results are more light and dark pixels than with the Uniform Noise option, thus producing a more dramatic effect.

Spike   This filter uses colors that are distributed around a narrow curve (spike). It produces a thinner, lighter colored grain.

Noise Level Percentage

This slider increases or decreases the amount of noise applied.

Noise Filter Effects

Backgrounds

The Noise filters are used to create a wide variety of background effects. In this book we can only show a few of them.

Noise and Embossing

The first use of Gaussian noise is shown in Figure 12.5. To get the effect, we first typed in the word "NOISE" (using Futura XBLK BT). Next we applied the Emboss filter in the Fancy subgroup of the Effects menu. We used dark gray, and after it was applied, we applied a Gaussian noise at a setting of 50. Using the Layers/Objects roll-up, hide the base image, leaving only the text. Apply a Motion Blur (down-right direction with a setting of 5). Click the Show All button in the Layers/Objects roll-up.

Figure 12.1.
Radial fill enhanced
with addition of noise.

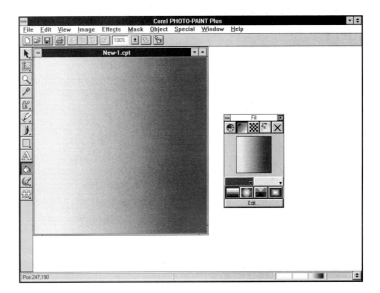

Removing Banding from a Radial Fill

Many times if a radial fill (or any gradient fill, for that matter) is applied to a large area, some banding occurs. (Banding is the phenomenon wherein the changes of color or shades appear as bands in the image.) This effect is more pronounced in grayscale or 256-color fills than it is in 24-bit color.

Not only can the Noise filter add some very interesting visual effects, but when used in combination with other filters, it can produce unusual backgrounds. (See Figure 12.1–12.4.)

Additional effects using noise are discussed in the special-effects section of the book.

Figure 12.2.
This is a more tradi-
tional application of
noise. The original
photograph of the man
climbing the rock was
subdued by the
addition of the noise so
as not to distract from
the text.

Figure 12.3.
This is the same idea as
the previous figure. The
noise helps to make
backgrounds stay
where they belong, in
the background.

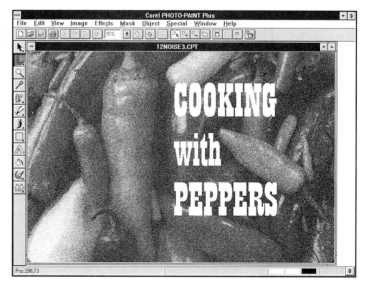

Figure 12.4.
In this example, noise was used to accent the characters in the text. To achieve the effect the text was masked, a transparency mask with a linear gradient was created and then noise was applied.

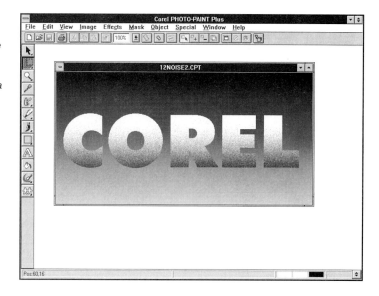

Figure 12.5.
To achieve this texture, noise was applied only to the text and the text was embossed. The rest of the image was protected from the noise and embossing by hiding it through the Layer/Objects Roll-Up.

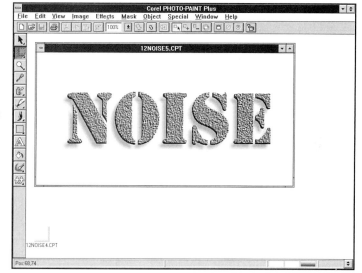

The Maximum Filter

The Maximum filter is not a traditional noise filter. In truth, it is a bit of a mystery what it is even doing in the Noise subgroup. The Maximum filter lightens an image by adjusting the pixel values of the image, decreasing the number of colors. By using the slider, you can control the percentage of filtering that is applied. This filter provides a method of lightening an image without washing it out (as would happen with brightness or intensity adjustments). If you are an experienced Photoshop user, the Maximum filter that you are already used to does something different. (See Figures 12.6a–12.6c.)

Figure 12.6a.
The original image.

Figure 12.6b.
The original image with the Maximum filter set at 50 percent.

Figure 12.6c.
The original image with
the Maximum filter set
at 100 percent.

Fundamentally, Maximum as used in Photoshop creates a spread trap. In layman's terms, the Maximum filter spreads the white areas and chokes the black areas. Spreading and choking is used to compensate for minute misalignments in the printing process. While the Maximum filter in PHOTO-PAINT can be used as a traditional Maximum (Choke) filter, it doesn't do it as well as other programs. The effect is applied along a radius rather than on the pixel edge. (If you didn't understand the last sentence, don't bother re-reading it. It will not become any clearer the second time around. If you live and breathe digital imaging and pre-press, you understood it.)

Notes on Using the Maximum Filter

The Maximum filter does reduce the number of colors in an image area to achieve the lightening effect. In addition to color depth reduction, it also causes a mild blurring of the image if applied in large percentages or multiple times. This blurring should be taken into consideration when using it.

The Median Filter

This filter reads the brightness of the pixels within a selection and averages them. Median simplifies an image by reducing noise (produced when pixels of different brightness levels adjoin one another) and by averaging the differences out of the selection.

The Median filter is used to smooth the rough areas in scanned images that have a grainy appearance. This filter uses a slider to set the percentage of Noise removal that is applied. The filter looks for pixels that are isolated and, based on the percentage setting in the dialog box, removes them.

Notes on Using the Median Filter

There is nothing magic about the Median filter. Its ability to remove noise is dependent on the type of noise (sharp and high-contrast or blurred and low-contrast) that is in the image. The Median filter tends to blur the image if it is set too high. Use the preview window to experiment with various settings. If a particular area of the image has noise, mask it off and apply the filter to the noisy areas rather than to the entire image.

The Minimum Filter

The Minimum filter, like the Maximum filter, is not a traditional noise filter. This filter darkens an image by adjusting the pixel values of the image, decreasing the number of colors. By using the slider, the percentage of filtering applied can be controlled. This filter provides a method of lightening an image without washing out the image (as would occur using brightness or intensity).

Converse to the Maximum filter, this filter spreads out black or dark areas into the white or light areas of an image. (See Figures 12.7a and 12.7b.)

Notes on Using the Minimum Filter

The Minimum filter reduces the number of colors in an image area to achieve the darkening effect. In addition to color depth reduction, it also causes a mild blurring of the image if applied in large percentages or multiple times. This should be taken into consideration when using it.

Figure 12.7a.
The original image.

Figure 12.7b.
The Minimum filter at
100 percent.

What's Really Going on with Maximum, Median, and Minimum

These filters are each taking a look at an image's brightness values, pixel by pixel, and replacing adjacent pixels with the maximum or minimum brightness value of the neighboring pixel. Thus the names Maximum and Minimum. (The Median filter is, obviously, named after that thing in the middle of the highway.)

Remove Noise

This filter acts like a combination of the Jaggy Despeckle and Median filter. The Remove Noise filter softens edges and reduces the speckled effect created by the scanning process. Each pixel is compared to surrounding pixels and an average value is computed. The pixels that then exceed the threshold set with the slider control in the dialog box are removed. This operates in the same manner as the Jaggy Despeckle does on objects (it reduces jaggies by softening edges), but, unlike Jaggy Despeckle, it also removes random pixels (noise) in the image.

This filter is good for cleaning up faxes and poor scans. Like the other Noise filters, it cannot take a real garbage scan and make it look pristine. It can, however, take a poor scan and make it better.

Corel *TIP!*

To improve the performance of this filter, mask the areas to which you want to apply the Remove Noise filter. This speeds up the operation (because the area is smaller) and also keeps the filter from modifying areas that do not need to have any noise removed.

The Sharpen Filters

The Sharpen subgroup contains six filters that provide a wide range of sharpening effects that both improve image quality and produce special effects. By increasing the contrast between neighboring pixels, sharpening filters enable you to compensate for images or image elements that were photographed or scanned slightly out of focus. The Sharpen subgroup menu has the following filters:

Adaptive Unsharp

This filter has nothing to do with "unsharpening." It is named after a traditional film compositing technique that highlights the edges in an image by combining a blurred film negative with the original film positive, which results in a sharper image.

Use the Adaptive Unsharp filter from the Sharpen flyout menu to accentuate edge detail without affecting the rest of the image or defined area.

Using the Adaptive Unsharp Filter

Set the percentage slider in the dialog box to a value between 1 and 100 percent to specify the degree to which you want to sharpen the selected image. Higher values produce more pronounced effects. Use the preview window to see the effects of different slider settings.

Notes about Adaptive Unsharp

The effect of the Adaptive Unsharp Masking filter is very subtle and may only be apparent in color images at high resolutions.

Directional Sharpen

The Directional Sharpen filter from the Sharpen flyout menu analyzes values of pixels of similar color shades to determine the direction in which to apply the greatest amount of sharpening.

Using the Directional Sharpen Filter

Set the percentage slider in the dialog box to a value between 1 and 100 percent to specify the degree to which you want to sharpen the selected image. Higher values produce more pronounced effects. Use the preview window to see the effects of different slider settings. (See Figures 12.8a and 12.8b.)

Figure 12.8a.
The original image.

Figure 12.8b.
The original image with
100 percent Directional
Sharpen filter applied
to entire image.

Edge Enhance

The Edge Enhance filter sharpens the outlines of the image. You can determine the degree of enhancement by entering a percentage.

Using the Edge Enhance filter

Set the percentage slider in the dialog box to a value between 1 and 100 percent to specify the degree to which you want to sharpen the selected image. Higher values produce more pronounced effects. Use the preview window to see the effects of different slider settings. (See Figures 12.9a and 12.9b.)

Enhance

The Enhance filter can either smooth or sharpen an image. Set the percentage slider in the dialog box to apply either Smooth or Sharp effects. Enter a value between -200 percent and +200 percent to specify the degree to which you want to sharpen or smooth the selected image. Higher values on either end of the slider produce more pronounced effects. Use the preview window to see the effects of different slider settings. (See Figures 12.10a–12.10c.)

Corel *TIP!*

> When you need to smooth an image, the Enhance filter works as well at smoothing as it does at sharpening. Remember, however, that it is here in the Sharpen subgroup.

Figure 12.9a.
The original image.

Figure 12.9b.
*100 percent Edge
Enhance filter applied
to entire image results
in a little too much
contrast in the areas of
naturally occuring high
contrast.*

Sharpen

The Sharpen filter sharpens the resolution of the image or the defined area by intensifing the contrast of neighboring pixels. This filter acts as a general image enhancer.

Figure 12.10a.
The original image.

317

*Figure 12.10b.
Minus 200 percent
Enhance applied to the
image creates a
blurring (smoothing) of
the original.*

*Figure 12.10c.
Plus 200 percent
Enhance results in a
too-grainy picture.*

Using the Sharpen Filter

Set the percentage slider in the dialog box to a value between 1 and 100 percent to specify the degree to which you want to sharpen the selected image. Higher values produce more pronounced effects. Use the preview window to see the effects of different slider settings. Use this filter at higher settings with some degree of caution. (See Figures 12.11a–12.11g.)

The Unsharp Mask Filter

The Unsharp Mask filter is similar to the Sharpen Edges filter, except you have more control over what gets sharpened and by how much it gets sharpened. The Unsharp filter accentuates edge detail as well as sharpening a certain amount of smooth areas in the image. The difference between this filter and the Adaptive Unsharp filter is how the smooth areas of the image are treated.

Using the Unsharp Mask

Set the percentage slider in the dialog box to a value between 1 and 100 percent to specify the degree to which you want to sharpen the selected image. Higher values produce more pronounced effects. Use the preview window to see the effects of different slider settings.

Figure 12.11a.
The original image.

Figure 12.11b.
The same image with
20 percent Sharpen
applied.

Figure 12.11c.
The image with 100
percent Sharpen
applied. (This setting is
far too high for a high-
contrast image such as
this one.)

Figure 12.11d.
The original of a low-contrast image.

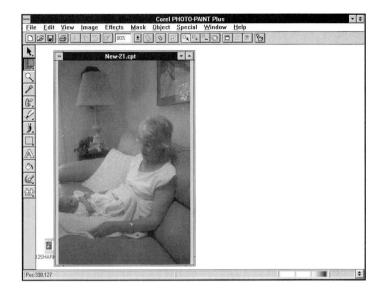

Figure 12.11e.
80 percent Sharpen applied to the entire image. Notice that the contrast of the wall and pillow becomes a distraction.

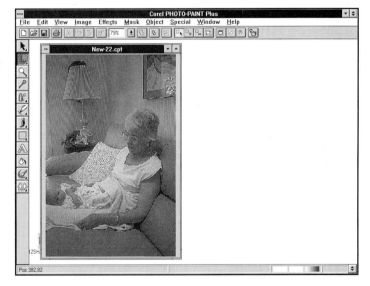

Figure 12.11f.
A quick mask around
the lady and the baby
with the Polygon Mask
tool.

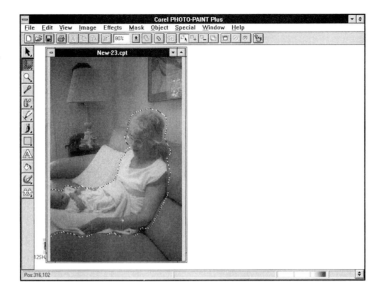

Figure 12.11g.
Figure 12.11f with the
80 percent Sharpen
filter applied.

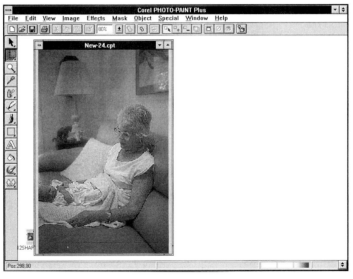

The Soften Filters

The Soften subgroup offers four different filters that soften images or selected areas of images. Generally, soften filters work by taking adjacent pixels that have high contrasting values and adjusting them so that their values are closer to each other. Soften filters give the effect of blurring an image as the adjacent pixels blend into one another. The Soften subgroup menu has the following four filters:

The Diffuse Filter

The Diffuse filter from the Soften flyout menu scatters colors in an image or a selected area creating a smooth appearance.

Using the Diffuse Filter

Set the level slider in the dialog box to a value between 1 and 255 to specify the degree to which you want to diffuse the selected image. Higher values produce more pronounced effects. Use the preview window to see the effects of different slider settings. (See Figures 12.12a–12.12f.)

Notes on Using the Diffuse Filter

When selecting a level setting, watch the preview window for the appearance of an edge. When some objects are diffused at too high of a setting, they develop an outline which may be undesirable. To overcome this, do multiple applications of the diffuse filter at lower settings.

Directional Smooth Filter

The Directional Smooth filter from the Soften flyout menu analyzes values of pixels of similar color shades to determine in which direction to apply the greatest amount of smoothing.

Using the Directional Smooth Filter

Set the percentage slider in the dialog box to enter a value between 1 and 100 percent to specify the degree to which you want to apply directional smoothing to the selected image. Higher values produce more pronounced effects. Use the preview window to see the effects of different slider settings.

Figure 12.12a.
The orignal text image.

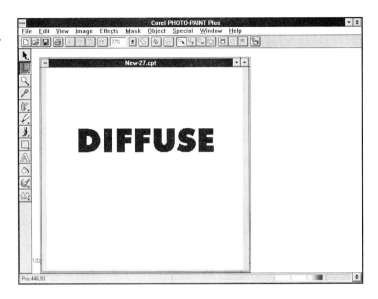

Figure 12.12b.
A Diffuse value of 80
applied.

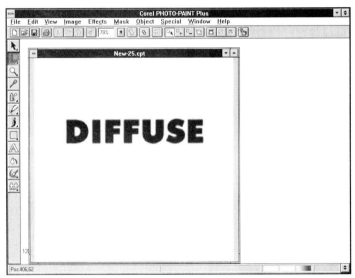

Figure 12.12c.
The same text with a
value of 255 applied.
The resulting outline
can be used for a
special effect but is
otherwise undesirable.

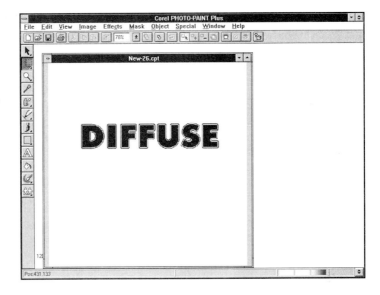

Figure 12.12d.
The original photo-
graph.

Figure 12.12e.
The application of a
Diffuse value of 128.
(The image is blurred
but not distorted.)

Figure 12.12f.
The application of a
Diffuse value of 255
causes distortion that
acts like a special
effect.

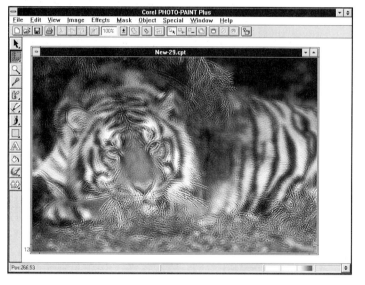

The Smooth Filter

The Smooth filter from the Soften flyout menu tones down differences in adjacent pixels, resulting in only a slight loss of detail while smoothing the image or the selected area. The differences between the effect of the Smooth and Soften filters is subtle and may only be apparent on a high-resolution display.

Using the Smooth Filter

Set the percentage slider in the dialog box to enter a value between 1 and 100 percent to specify the degree to which you want to smooth the selected image. Higher values produce more pronounced effects. Use the preview window to see the effects of different slider settings.

The Soften Filter

The Soften filter from the Soften flyout menu smooths and tones down harshness without losing detail. The differences between the effect of the Smooth and Soften filters is subtle and may only be apparent on a high-resolution display.

Corel _TIP!_

> When you need to smooth an image, the Enhance filter works as well at smoothing as it does at sharpening. Remember, it is in the Sharpen subgroup.

Using the Soften Filter

Set the percentage slider in the dialog box to enter a value between 1 and 100 percent to specify the degree to which you want to soften the selected image. Higher values produce more pronounced effects. Use the preview window to see the effects of different slider settings.

So what is the difference between the way that each of these filters work? Very little. Don't waste a lot of time trying to determine if you need to use soften or smooth. The results will appear to be identical in most cases. See Figure 12.13.

Figure 12.13.
The best way to show the effect of the soften filter was to show its effect on text. The text in the center is the original, the text on top was softened with a setting of 100 percent, and the text on the bottom had a setting of 50 percent applied to it.

Special Filters

The filters in the Special subgroup are a set of five unique filters that provide unusual effects. While these filters would not normally be used on a regular basis, they do provide the user with effects that could not be achieved any other way. The Special subgroup contains the following five filters:

Contour

The Contour filter outlines the edges of an image or the selected part of an image. Use the slider in the dialog box to set the edge threshold level. The range of the threshold level is 0 to 255. A lower setting leaves more of the image intact. A higher setting reduces the amount of the original image that is left after the filter is applied.

Using the Contour Filter

This filter can be used to create some unique and useful effects. The best effects are achieved when the subject matter is easily recognizable. (See Figures 12.14a–12.14c.)

Figure 12.14a.
The original image of a
barn from the Photo CD
Sampler.

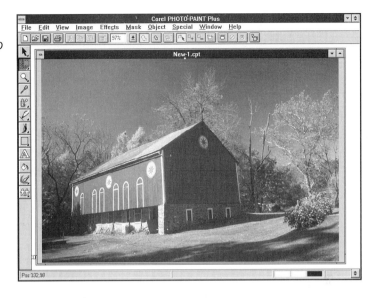

Figure 12.14b.
The Contour filter
applied at a setting
of 40.

Figure 12.14c.
The contoured image
was made to look like a
pen rendering by
applying a Motion Blur
of 1 at a down-left
direction and then
applying an Edge
Enhance filter at a
setting of 50.

Posterize

The Posterize filter removes gradations, creating areas of solid colors or gray shades. This is useful when there is a need to simplify a complex color image without converting it to 256- or 16-color mode. Another way to use this filter is to apply the Posterize effect selectively to individual channels through the Layers/Object roll-up. Posterizing an image to something like two, three, and four images is a standard use of this filter. (See Figures 12.15a–12.15c.)

Figure 12.15a.
The original PCD image
from the Sampler CD.

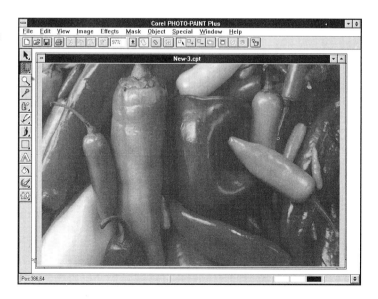

Figure 12.15b.
Posterize applied at a
level of 6.

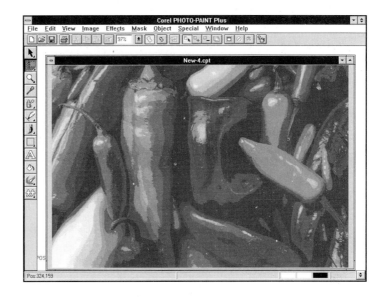

Figure 12.15c.
Just to make some-
thing out of it, Spike
noise was applied at
100 percent, two times,
and the text was
added.

Psychedelic

If it isn't bad enough that the 60s are showing up in the fashion world, we now
have this filter in the PHOTO-PAINT program. (It has been said that if you
clearly remember the 60s you weren't really there. Perhaps this filter will bring
it back to you.) The Psychedelic filter changes the colors in selected areas or
image to bright, electric colors such as orange, hot pink, electric-banana yellow,
cyan, lime green, etc. Use in small amounts to achieve some almost useful
effects. Used in large doses, it can induce flashbacks. (See Figures 12.16a–12.16c.)

Figure 12.16a.
The original image.

Figure 12.16b.
The Psychedelic filter
applied at a setting of
128. The grayscale
image in these figures
does not do justice to
the effects achieved.

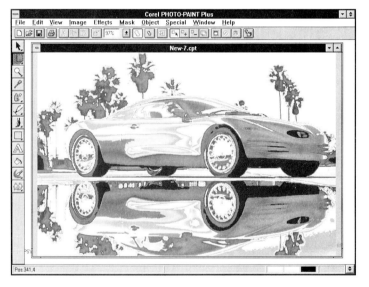

Figure 12.16c.
The Psychedelic filter
applied at a setting of
200.

Solarize

The Solarize filter enables you to make an image look like a photographic negative. The effect will be more pronounced in color images. Solarize is an effect that, when applied to its maximum (255 shades), results in a negative or inverted image. It simulates an old photographic technique that required the photographic plate to be briefly exposed to sunlight outside of the camera. This resulted in the darkest areas being washed out. How washed out they were was determined by how long the plate was exposed. (The emulsions they had in the old days were a very low speed.)

The PHOTO-PAINT Solarize filter operates in a similar fashion—except that instead of entering in the time the image is in the sun, you can control the shades of color that will be affected by the filter (0 through 255). (See Figure 12.17.)

Figure 12.17.
This figure had a light
application of the
Solarize filter. The
reason it is so strange
looking is because I
used the Object Merge
and Added another
copy of the same image
on top.

Threshold

Use the Threshold filter to gradually darken an image. RGB component values below the threshold will become 0. Component values above the threshold are not altered. For grayscale images, pixels below the threshold value become black; lighter shades remain unaltered.

Threshold effects are very popular in printed ads. They provide the effect of the subject matter—be it a human model, a car, or other easily recognizable form—without any distracting detail. The images shown represent making a color Photo CD image look like a comic book character when applied to a color image and like an album cover when applied to the same image that was converted to a grayscale image. (See Figures 12.18a–12.18b.)

When considering an image to apply the filter to, be cautious about images that have shadows or large dark areas. Those shadows or areas will grow very large and reduce the overall effect of the Threshold. It generally doesn't work to mask the dark areas or shadows because they then look like a light spot in the shape of the mask. The only way a mask will work is if it is a Transparency mask with a Gradient fill. See Chapter 15 for advanced techniques on Transparency masks.

Figure 12.18a.
The original island
photo.

Figure 12.18b.
The island photo with a
Threshold filter applied
to it at a level of 90. The
major difference is in
the posterization of the
colors which do not
show up well in
grayscale.

Tone

In this release of PHOTO-PAINT, the Tone subgroup contains one filter, called
Equalize.

335

The Equalize Filter

Use the Equalize filter from the Tone flyout menu to redistribute shades of colors. Equalize makes the darkest colors black and the lightest colors white and stretches the colors in between. In some programs, this filter is called Quarter-Tone. The histogram that is displayed when the filter dialog box is opened represents the shades in the image. The height of each bar shows the number of dots with that amount of shading. The bottom of the histogram shows the range and distribution of shades in your image.

Using the Equalize Filter

1. Select Equalize from the Tone flyout on the Effects menu.
2. Click the Preview button to see the effect of the default Equalize settings.
3. Click and drag the arrows below the histogram to adjust the Low, Mid, and High values. (See Figure 12.19.)

   Shades to the left of the Low arrow are black.

   Shades to the right of the High arrow are white.

   Highlights are the shades between the High and Mid values.

   Shadows are the shades between the Low and Mid values.

   Reset returns the Histogram to its original values.
4. Click Preview to see the effect of the changes.

A very effective way to get a feel for how the Equalize filter works is to try different variations with the Equalize filter on a file that has a basic Linear Gradient Fountain fill from black to white. (See Figure 12.20.)

The effect of an adjustment using the Equalize filter is relatively evident with a Linear Gradient Fountain fill because the tones are as equally spread out as possible, so the redistribution of tones that a given Equalize setting applies is clearly evident. As long as you keep in mind that most images do not have an equal distribution of tones the way a Linear Gradient fill from black to white does, it can be useful to learn about the Equalize filter in this way.

1. Open a new file, 1 inch high, 2 inches wide, at 150 dpi. Fill the file with a Linear Gradient fill from black (left) to white (right) at 0 degrees and 256 steps.
2. From the Effects menu, choose Tone and then Equalize. Notice that the histogram shows an even distribution of tones.

Figure 12.19.
A histogram of a Linear
Gradient Blend from
black to white shows
that the tones are
evenly distributed.

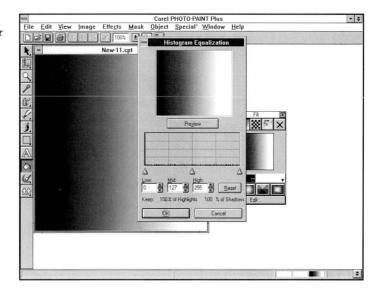

Figure 12.20.
This shows the original
Linear Gradient Blend.

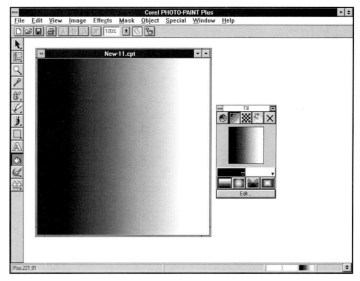

3. Enter in a value of 63 for the Mid setting and 127 for the High setting, then hit OK. The Equalize filter will redistribute the tones according to these settings by taking all of the values from 127 to 256 and making them white and then redistributing the gradient from black to white so that it goes from 0 to 127, with the midpoint being at 63. (See Figures 12.21 and 12.22.)

Figure 12.21.
The Linear Gradient
Blend from black to
white affords a clear
view of the results of
the Equalize filter.

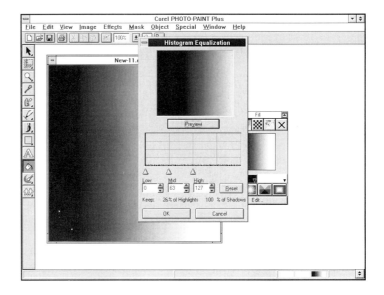

Figure 12.22.
The result of the
changes applied to the
Linear Gradient Blend.

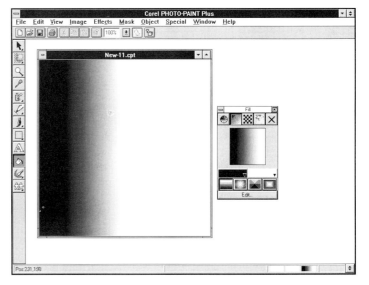

4. In order to get a handle on the Equalize filter, select Undo and try different variations.

While there is a science to using the Equalize filter, it takes a significant amount of experience to use it effectively. Generally, though, if you have an image with a lot of dark tones and you need to lighten it up, you could try adusting the High and Mid tones as explained in the preceding steps (though not quite as radically, of course) to bring more light tones into the image. Conversely, if the image is too light, you can adjust the Low and Mid tones to ease more dark tones into the image. If the midtones are where the problem is, you would just adjust the Mid setting to redistribute midtones to correct the image.

Notes on Using the Equalize Filter

Equalize provides some of the most powerful controls to adjust the overall appearance of the image. The other filters deal with specific areas of the image—i.e., special effects, adjustment of softness/sharpness, etc. The Equalize filter enables you to take a dark murky image and make it bright and clear, or to make a washed out color appear more vivid. All of these effects are best accomplished through experimentation with the filter. A good starting point (after you have used the Preview button to see the effects that the default settings made) is moving the midtone arrow a small amount to the left or right and checking the preview window to see the results. Don't be concerned with the numerical data presented on the bottom when you are making adjustments, although the numerical data is useful for commercial applications where critical adjustments are required. Keep moving the arrows, making note of the effects. All of the settings interact with one another, so moving the High arrow to the right has an effect that is different depending on where the Mid arrow is located. It bears repeating: Experiment with the settings on the histogram. The time invested will pay great dividends later on. Expertise comes from repeated use and familiarity with the results of different settings on the Equalize filter. The following are some more hints on using the Equalize filter:

- It is often best to equalize a scanned image first to improve its appearance before using other filters.
- Use Equalize when you have applied a Canvas that has been washed out from applying it at a high Transparency value.
- The Equalize filter can be used several times on the same image until the right effect is achieved. It can be done, but don't make a habit of it. Be sure to use Checkpoint before attempting this approach.
- If you get lost while moving the arrows around, click the Reset button to return to the original values.
- Experiment! Experiment! Experiment!

Transformation Filters

This subgroup contains three filters that provide various degrees of image manipulation to give the selected image a three-dimensional appearance. These filters are very limited in their functionality, but they can be used to provide some interesting effects.

3-D Rotate Filter

The 3-D Rotate filter rotates the image according to the horizontal and vertical limits set in the 3-D Rotate dialog box. The rotation is applied as if the image were one side of a three-dimensional box.

Using the 3-D Rotate Filter

The preview window shows the perspective of the image with the current slider settings. The plane of the box in the preview window that is shaded represents the image. By moving the vertical and horizontal sliders, the preview box can be oriented into the correct position. The preview window shows the result of the application of the 3-D Rotate filter. Checking the Best Fit checkbox results in the image size being changed to fit into the existing image window. If it is not checked, the image size will be increased to fit the rotated image. (See Figure 12.23.)

Notes on the 3-D Rotate Filter

There are no zoom or automatic preview functions in the preview window of the dialog box. Applying the 3-D Rotate filter to objects is not recommended, as the results may be unpredictable. I recommend that you merge any objects before applying the filter to them. Hide objects that the filter is not being applied to. The part of the image you want rotated should be masked, or the filter will ignore it.

There are some real limitations to this filter. Although you can apply rotation to both the horizontal and vertical axes simultaneously, it is not recommended. The resulting images lose varying degrees of prespective. The preview reads out incorrectly. Don't worry about it.

Figure 12.23. 3-D rotation. This image was taken from the Sampler Photo CD. Using the 3-D Rotate filter, the two sides were created. After it was created, each side was made into a separate document, and later the two were combined to produce the 3-D look. The final touch of shading was done by applying the Smoked Glass filter to the left side at 40 percent.

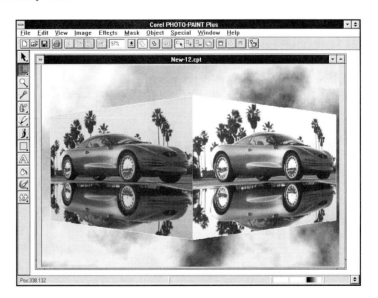

Perspective

The Perspective filter creates the impression of three-dimensionality in an image. There are two modes in the Perspective filter: *Perspective* and *Shear*. Perspective applies the look of three-dimensionality to the image according to the movement of the four nodes in the preview box. The nodes are moved by clicking on them with the mouse and dragging them to the desired location. Shear applies perspective as well; however, it holds the original size and shape.

Using the Perspective Filter

Select the type of perspective to be applied: Perspective or Shear. Select Best Fit if the original image size must be maintained. (See Figure 12.24.)

Notes on Using the Perspective Filter

This is another filter that I first considered rather pointless. However, after much messing around with this filter I have been able to obtain some good 3-D perspectives. There are still some rough edges in using it, and there is even (dare I say it?) a bug. But it is a *great* bug and produces a neat effect, so here's hoping they don't change it.

You can only move the nodes along the horizontal and vertical planes in Shear mode. There are no zoom or automatic preview functions in the preview window of the dialog box. Applying the Perspective filter to objects is not recommended, because the results may be unpredictable; therefore merge objects before applying the filter. Hide objects that the filter is not being applied to.

Figure 12.24. Perspective. This Photo CD image of a tiger has had the Perspective filter applied to it.

Mesh Warp

The Mesh Warp filter distorts the image according to the movement of the nodes on a grid in the Mesh Warp dialog box. Higher settings of the mesh grid create more nodes for distortion. The individual nodes move independently of each other.

Using the Mesh Warp Filter

When the Mesh Warp dialog box opens, click and drag the Mesh Grid slider to set the number of nodes that will appear on the image. Lower values have fewer nodes, higher values have more nodes. Use the Preview button to see the results of the node placement. (See Figure 12.25.)

Notes on the Mesh Warp Filter

The greater the number of nodes, the smoother the transitions on the image. Because each node is independent, each node must be individually moved. There is a trade-off between the smoothness of the transition and the time to move all of the nodes necessary. Since there are no constrain keys to keep the grid lines on the horizontal or vertical planes, use the grid lines themselves as your guide. As long as the line in the preview window appears straight, the line is still in line with its respective plane. The Mesh Grid value represents the number of nodes on each line of the grid. (The two end nodes on each grid line are out of view and not adjustable.) There are no zoom or automatic preview functions in the preview window of the dialog box. Applying the Mesh Warp filter to objects is not recommended as the results may be unpredictable; therefore merge objects before applying the filter. Hide objects the filter is not being applied to.

Figure 12.25.
Sample image using
the Mesh Warp filter.

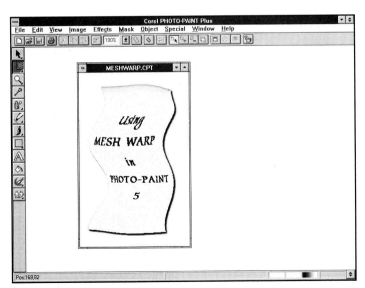

13

Exploring the Power of the Plus Release

When Corel was putting together the Plus stand-alone release of PHOTO-PAINT 5, they searched all over the country for unique filters and applications that would make people want to buy the product. Well, Corel not only succeeded, they may have gone overboard. The Plus release contains plug-in filters from several independent sources, as follows:

Xaos Tools:

- Paint Alchemy
- Terrazzo

HSC (Kai Power Tools 2.0):

- 3D Stereo Noise
- Page Curl
- Fractal Explorer

Alien Skin (the Black Box):

- Drop Shadow
- The Boss (an embossing filter)
- Glass Filter
- Swirl (the poor man's Terrazzo)

Corel also added a large collection of seamless tiles (over 250), 50 floating objects from CMCD, and 1,000 photographs.

When putting this book together, we felt it was important to spend some time explaining how to use these filters, since they are not documented in the manual I wrote for Corel to be shipped with the Plus release. Before you shake your finger at Corel, remember that the production cycle for documentation is 4–5 weeks. Several of these filters didn't come online until just before the software was released. That said, let's learn about these marvelous filters.

Paint Alchemy

This filter and its counterpart Terrazzo were only available for the Macintosh until their release on PHOTO-PAINT. They are both incredible filters. To provide the most accurate documentation, I have been assisted greatly by Xaos Tool's Mac documentation and their tech-support people, who have been a world of help. Acknowledgments and kudos given, let's play with Paint Alchemy.

Paint Alchemy applies brush strokes to selected areas of your image, in a precisely controlled manner. As with all filters, you can apply Paint Alchemy on part of an image or the entire image. You can use pre-existing brushes or create your own brushes. It is not hard to create effects and control Paint Alchemy. The key to using and enjoying this filter is experimentation.

Corel *TIP!*

> When making changes to the Paint Alchemy filter styles, try limiting your changes to one at a time so that you can keep track of the effects.

Starting Paint Alchemy

The filter is located in the Special subgroup (category) of the Effects menu. Clicking Alchemy in the drop-down list opens the Paint Alchemy dialog box as shown in Figure 13.1.

Corel*NOTE!*

Paint Alchemy is only available in one of the color modes: 16-color, 256-color, 24-bit color, or 32-bit color. If a grayscale or back-and-white image is open, the Alchemy filter is grayed out.

Figure 13.1.
The dialog box for the
Paint Alchemy filter in
PHOTO-PAINT 5 Plus.

The Paint Alchemy Dialog Box

The dialog box is divided into three sections: control cards, style controls, and preview controls.

The Control Cards

The controls that let you customize Paint Alchemy are arranged on five control cards. Only one card is visible at a time, but the controls on all five cards are always active. To switch between cards, click on the labeled tabs at the top of the cards.

The Style Controls

The style controls let you create new styles, remove old ones, or select one of the preset styles to use. Corel has included 75 standard styles with Paint Alchemy. While you may think it would be a neat idea to begin changing these styles right away, I encourage you to work with the basic styles to get a feel for them before you begin changing them. If you do change a style and like the results, you can save these settings as a style. (We will discuss this in greater detail later in the chapter.)

The Preview Controls

The preview controls work just like all of the other Corel features. Left-clicking in the preview area zooms in, right clicking zooms out, and clicking and dragging produces a hand for moving the image around in the preview window. Two seconds after any change in the preview window, the filter preview is automatically invoked.

If you have used Paint Alchemy on the Mac, this is an area where you will notice a difference. The Mac version shows a before-and-after thumbnail, whereas Corel opted for the larger display area.

After you click the OK button to apply the Paint Alchemy filter, clicking the Esc key at any time before the filter has completed its action will cancel the filter action.

A Quick Tour of Paint Alchemy

Paint Alchemy is fun. That said, here is a quick tour of the filter to help you get familiar with how it works.

1. Open a existing image. For this quick tour, I have selected a photo of a barn from the Photo-CD Sampler. (See Figure 13.2.)
2. Select the Special subgroup (category) in the Effects menu.
3. Click on Alchemy. The Paint Alchemy dialog box opens. (See Figure 13.1.)
4. Click on the down arrow and select any of the styles.
5. Click the Preview button to see the results of the selected style. If the image is zoomed in too closely, right-click the mouse button in the preview window to zoom out.
6. Select the Dabble style and click the OK button. The results are shown in Figure 13.3.

Figure 13.2.
Your average barn
before we apply Paint
Alchemy to it.

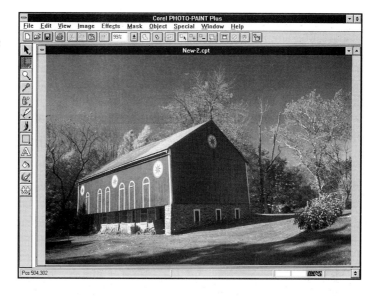

Figure 13.3.
The result of applying
the Dabble Paint
Alchemy filter to the
picture of a barn. (It
looks a lot better in
color.)

7. Either select Undo from the Edit menu or use Ctrl+Z to undo the filter action.

8. Open the Paint Alchemy dialog box again.

9. This time, select the style called Brush Stroke Random. The default setting for the style is a density of 100 percent. (The number of strokes for all the settings at 100 percent density is also calculated in the space above the density slider.) Click the Preview button and you should see an effect similar to Figure 13.4.

10. Change the density to 50 percent and click Preview. The result is more subtle, but it still looks like an Impressionist oil painting.

Corel *TIP!*

> If you need to apply an Impressionism effect to an image, use this filter. It is one hundred jillion times faster than the Impressionism filter in PHOTO-PAINT 5.

11. Repeat Step 10, except use 25 percent and then 0 percent, clicking Preview after each setting.

12. Return the filter to its default density setting and click Cancel to return to PHOTO-PAINT.

Figure 13.4.
Here are four variations of the number of brush strokes (i.e., the density) applied by the Paint Alchemy filter. The density setting is only one of 50 settings available with this filter.

Corel *TIP!*

> A quick way to return to the default setting for any style is to click on the style name. Then use either the up- or down-arrow key to move to an adjacent style, and then, using the opposite arrow key, return to the original setting.

Figure 13.5.
*A variation of the
original image.*

Figure 13.6.
*A variation of the
original image.*

Using Styles

You can use Paint Alchemy to create an enormous variety of different effects.
With 30 parameters to change and the ability to use custom brushes in addition
to the one provided, the number of possibilities is virtually infinite. To keep
track of favorite settings, the Paint Alchemy filter offers the ability to record all
of the filter settings as styles.

*Figure 13.7.
A variation of the
original image.*

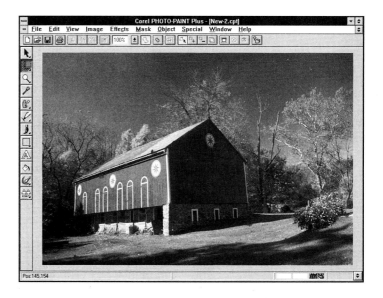

Each style is a complete record of the settings of all the controls. By loading a style, you can recreate an exact reproduction of that incredible filter effect that so wowed your client.

Loading a style is very simple. You only need to click on the down arrow to the right of the Style box, and a drop-down list of 75 predefined styles appears, as shown in Figure 13.8.

*Figure 13.8.
Clicking the arrow on
the Style box opens a
drop-down list that
here shows six of the
75 predefined styles
that come with Paint
Alchemy.*

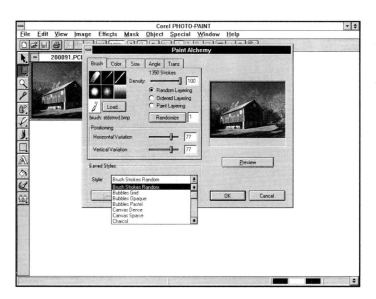

You can use the styles that Corel provides with Paint Alchemy, or you can create your own. The styles can be customized using any of the Paint Alchemy controls.

Corel *TIP!*

> Altering existing styles is often the best way to begin creating your own styles.

Creating A Custom Style

Paint Alchemy, like many paint-oriented filters, can take a long time to apply to an image. When you begin experimentation in search for the custom look that is going to win the Corel Design contest for you, either select a small area of the total image by using a mask or pick one of the smaller image configurations, such as snapshot or wallet, if you are working from a Photo CD. Smaller image areas can be processed much faster. When you find the style you want, you can then apply it to a larger image to make sure all of the settings work before you save it as a style.

The people at Xaos Tools have a wealth of experience making custom styles. I have extracted the following procedural approach from their Mac manuals and from suggestions I received from Mac Paint Alchemy users via online services.

1. Find the existing style that is closest to the style you want to create. Use the settings from that style as your starting point.

2. Reduce the number of brush strokes (the density) until you can see what the individual brushes are doing. Using the Zoom feature of the preview window, zoom in on individual brush strokes and make necessary adjustments to appropriate parameters (e.g., size, transparency, etc.).

3. Change the color attributes until you can see how the controls change each brush stroke. Once you are comfortable with the color controls, adjust your colors.

4. Increase the density (number of brush strokes) until the angle of application becomes clear. Now you can adjust the brush stroke angle.

5. To save a new custom style, click the Save As button. You are asked to enter a name for the new file (it can seemingly be a name of endless length, but you can only see the first 40 characters in the Style box. See Figure 13.9). The current settings are saved with the name you provide, and the new style is added to the Style Controls drop-down list in alphabetical order.

When you create a custom style, all of the style information is stored in the ALCHEMY.INI file located in the COREL50\CONFIG directory.

Figure 13.9.
This box opens when
you want to save a
custom style in Paint
Alchemy.

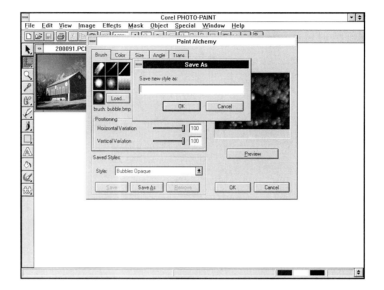

Corel *TIP!*

If the style name's length exceeds 80 characters (which would be dumb), it causes the name to wrap in the .INI file, and thus the filter (1) doesn't work, and (2) can't be removed using the Remove button. The only way to remove it is to go into the ALCHEMY.INI file and manually delete it and the description of the setting near the bottom of the file.

Changing a Custom Style

To change a custom style, do the following:

1. Select the style to be changed.
2. Make the changes desired.
3. Click the Save button. You cannot change and save a preset style. With preset styles, only the Save As button is available.

Saving a custom style will substitute the current style settings for those of the Paint Alchemy style with the same name.

Removing a Custom Style

To delete a custom style, you need only select the style you want to delete and click the Remove button. A warning box (I like to call them "second chance" boxes) asks you if you are sure that you want to remove the style. If you click OK, it's all over.

The Brush Card

The Brush card is the card you see when Paint Alchemy is first opened. This card is the heart of Paint Alchemy. The description that is in the Xaos Tool's Paint Alchemy manual can't be beat, so I will quote it: "The simplest description of what Paint Alchemy does it this: It applies a whole bunch of brush strokes to your image. As a result, the shape of the brush has a profound effect on the look that is produced."

The Brush card displays six of the standard brushes. When I first began working with this program, I thought that they displayed the best brush for the application, and then they showed brushes that were also likely candidates for the effects. Wow, was I ever wrong! The six standard brushes that are displayed never change, regardless of the current brush that is loaded. The currently selected brush has a highlighted border around it. (On my system it is red.)

Loading a Custom Brush

There are 30 custom brushes included with Paint Alchemy. They are located in the COREL50\PLGBRUSH directory.

Click on the Load button and the Load Brush dialog box opens. (See Figure 13.10.) It allows you to select any *.BMP file as a custom brush. Here are the general rules regarding brushes:

- You can load any size of .BMP file as a brush. That said, if it is too large, then the brush will overwhelm the image. The recommended size is around 128 × 128 pixels.
- The best brushes are grayscale (256 shades) with a resolution of 96 dpi. If a color .BMP file is loaded, it will be converted to grayscale.
- Brushes are completely opaque where white, invisible where black. Gray areas of the brush are transparent; the darker they are, the more transparent they are. Black portions of your brush will not change your image, while the white portions define the area in which your selected effect is applied.

Corel *TIP!*

When making brushes in PHOTO-PAINT, it is not necessary to paint white-on-black. Do all of your work in black-on-white, and then use the Invert filter.

- Styles that are built around custom brushes depend on the brush remaining the in COREL50\PLGBRUSH directory. If the brush that a selected style needs is not available when the style is selected, a default brush is loaded in its place.

Figure 13.10.
Click on the Load
button and the Load
Brush dialog box opens.

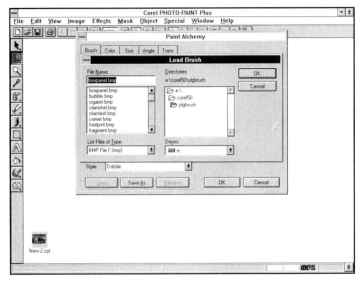

Density

The Density slider controls the number of brush strokes that will be applied to the selected area. The density is a factor that is used to calculate how many brush strokes should be used for a given image size. The absolute number of strokes that will be used with the current image size is displayed above the slider. All of the calculations are based on the image size, not the mask size. Unlike the Texture Bitmap fills, the size of the brush effects does not increase or decrease as a result of the image size or the mask size.

Corel *TIP!*

The time required to apply the effect depends directly on the number of brush strokes—the more strokes, the longer the effect will take. The other factor that determines the amount of time that it takes to apply an effect is the size of the image or the size of the mask. If the image is large and the mask is small, the processing will still occur more quickly because the effect is only calculated for and applied to the masked area.

Positioning

These sliders are far less than self-explanatory. They add randomness to the position of the brush strokes. When the sliders are both set at 0, the strokes are placed on a regular grid. The Horizontal Variation slider controls side-to-side brush stroke deviation. The Vertical Variation slider controls the up-and-down motion of the brush stroke deviation. With most of the styles applying brush strokes one on top of another multiple times, there are many styles that seemed to be changed very little by the positioning controls.

Figure 13.11a.
This is the style called
Ordered Molecules,
(set to the default, with
both Horizontal and
Vertical Variation set to
0), applied to a Radial
fill.

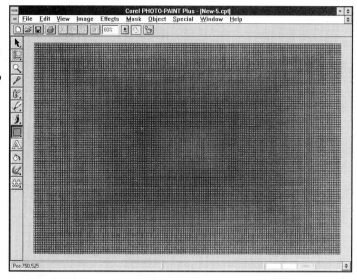

Figure 13.11b.
The same image with
the Horizontal variation
set to 100 and the
Vertical Variation kept
at 0.

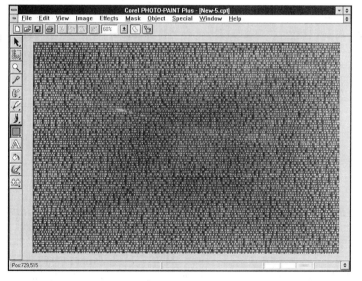

Layering Methods

There are three choices for layering methods in the Brush card. (See Figure 13.12.) The choices are Random, Ordered, and Paint layering.

*Figure 13.11c.
Shows horizontal at 0
and Vertical at 100.*

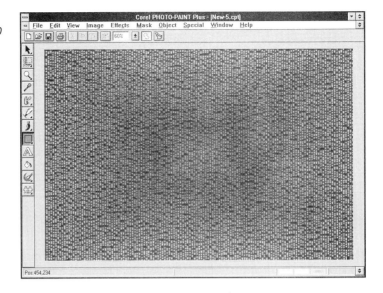

*Figure 13.11d.
Shows both Horizontal
and Vertical Variation
set to 100.*

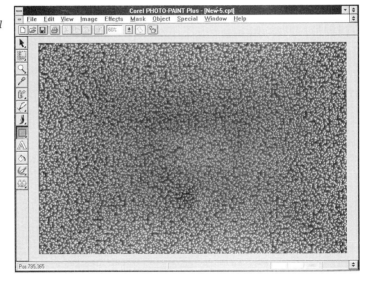

Random Layering

The brush strokes are applied so that they randomly overlap each other.

Ordered Layering

The brush strokes are applied so that strokes that are above and to the left always overlap those that are below and to the right. With a square brush, this can look like roofing shingles. With a round brush, it can look like fish scales.

Figure 13.12.
The Brush card.

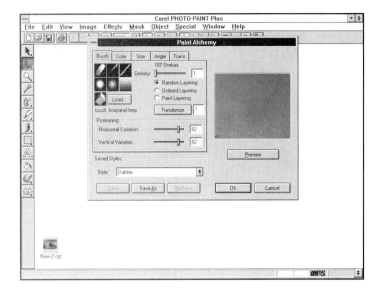

Paint Layering

With Paint Layering, the brightest portions of each brush stroke take priority in the layering. The effect it produces is highly dependent on the shape and coloring of the brush. You will need to experiment with Paint Layering to find out what it can do.

Corel *NOTE!*

This method of layering can cause aliasing (the dreaded "jaggies") when a brush that has hard black-and-white (or bright) edges is used.

Paint layering can also cause brush shape to be lost when brushes overlap too much. The overlapping brush problem is resolved by lowering the brush-density setting or reducing the brush size to reveal more of the brush.

Randomize

Before you read this, click the Randomize button and see if you can figure out what it does. For all of you who understand techno-babble, it is a random-seed generator. For those who do not speak the language, it is Randomize that lets you set the initial value used in the random-number generation, a value that is called the seed number.

Clicking the Randomize button will randomly change the seed. You can also type a number directly into the box that is adjacent to the button. As a rule, forget the button. The fine folks at Xaos Tools, however, give two examples where you might actually want to use this function, as follows:

Changing the seed to subtly change the effect

You may want to change the seed if you like the general effect that Paint Alchemy is producing but there are some brushes that don't quite work the way you would like them to. Changing the seed puts the brush strokes in slightly different random positions, and this may produce that final correction you were looking for.

Maintaining the seed to ensure repeatability

Using the same seed number guarantees that the same series of random numbers will be used for Paint Alchemy's internal calculations and thus all of the effects will be identical. This application, however, sounds a little fishy to me. How can it be a true random-number generator if identical results occur every time you use it?

Bonus: Picking the numbers for your state lottery

This is my idea. The numbers that you get each time you click the Random button are indeed random, so you can use this function to pick lottery numbers in much the same way that they are picked by the state, untainted by the sentimental and unscientific "favorite numbers" technique. The only hitch is that most big-money lotteries are based on two-digit numbers. No problem—just use the last two digits of the random number for the lottery. By the way, if you win using this method, it is only fair for you to split the winnings with myself and the editors who let this piece of nonsense get into print.

Creating Your Own Brushes

Creating brushes is one on the slicker things you can do with Paint Alchemy. It is easy to make a brush, but it is a little more difficult to make a brush that looks great when it is used in Paint Alchemy. Here is a summary of brush-making tips from Xaos Tools and from my own experience working with PHOTO-PAINT and Paint Alchemy.

- You can open the existing brush files in PHOTO-PAINT 5. (The brushes are .BMP files located in the COREL50\PLGBRUSH directory.) You can then use PHOTO-PAINT to alter the appearance of the brushes. If you change one of the original brushes that came with PHOTO-PAINT 5 Plus, make sure you only save it under a new name. All of the styles in Paint Alchemy were designed to use one of these brushes. If you change the brush, you will need to reinstall PHOTO-PAINT Plus to restore the original brushes. If you want to save some changes you made, use the Save As feature of PHOTO-PAINT.

■ When you create a new brush from scratch, try using an image size of 96 × 96 pixels with a resolution of 96 dpi. Also, remember to make the image a grayscale. If the brush you create is too large, it will not load into Paint Alchemy.

■ For more texture in the effect, create brush designs with a lot of gradation between black and white. I have included several samples from a Xaos Tools collection called Floppy Full Of Brushes. This collection is only available at this time for the Macintosh. However, the brushes on the Mac side are PICT files (.PCT in DOS lingo), so I took the Mac disk to a copy center, where we copied my original to a high-density disk (it comes from Xaos on a low-density disk which cannot be read on a PC) and had the .PICT files saved in a format that my IBM could read. Finally I loaded each one into Corel PHOTO-PAINT as Mac .PCT files (did you remember that we could read Mac files?) and saved them as .BMP files. I know that may seem like a lot of work, but it's worth it.

Corel *TIP!*

To change the brush that is used by a style, select the style before you select the brush. This is because every style has a brush associated with it. If you load the brush and then the style, the style will load its own brush, forcing you to reload your brush.

The Color Card

Brush Color

Each brush stroke is a single, solid color. To determine the color of your brush strokes, use the Color card. (See Figure 13.13.) You can set the colors of your brush strokes by using the colors of the image you are working on or by selecting a specific color using the Brush Color controls.

From Image

The color of each brush stroke is based on the color of the image at the center of each brush stroke.

Solid Color

The color of all the brush strokes is based on the color that you select. To select the color, click on the color preview window to the right of the Solid Color button to open up the standard color-selection palette.

Figure 13.13.
The Color card.

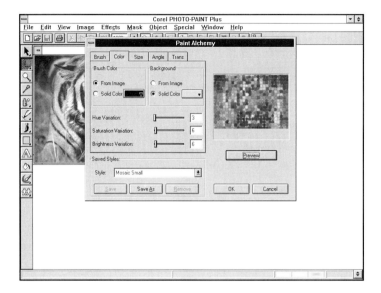

Background

You can choose to apply Paint Alchemy brush strokes to a Paper (background) of solid color using the Background controls.

From Image

The brush strokes are applied to your image based on the color of each brush stroke.

Solid Color

The brush strokes are applied to a Paper (background) of a solid color. To select the color, click on the color preview window to the right of the Solid Color button to open up the standard color-selection palette.

The Hue, Saturation, and Brightness Variation Controls

These controls operate in a similar manner to the Impressionism or Pointillism brush tools. They allow you to vary from the initial Brush Color settings. The amount of variation can be controlled independently for the hue, saturation and brightness of the brush color. These controls affect the brush stroke of both the From Image and the Solid Color settings.

Hue Variation controls how much the color varies from the starting color. A small setting causes the colors in the brush to vary just a few shades to either side of the original color. A large setting produces a rainbow of colors, producing a confetti-like effect.

Saturation Variation has the least noticeable effect of the three. It controls the amount of gray level in the image. It isn't a simple relationship; for example, 100 percent gives lots of gray. It has a greater effect in images where the color scheme of things contains large quantities of gray. Play with this control, but expect subtle rather than great changes in the image.

Brightness Variation has the effect of controlling contrast. Officially it controls the amount of variance there is in brightness between the starting color and the additional colors that are created by Paint Alchemy.

Further Suggestions for Using the Color Card

Following are some tips about using the Color card and what you can expect to be able to do with it.

Image Enhancement

As with many of the other filters, you can increase the effectiveness of the Color card by using the other controls and filters in PHOTO-PAINT to modify the image before working on it with the Paint Alchemy filter. If you have a low-contrast image you should consider applying the Equalization/Tone filter to stretch the dynamic range of the image or increase the contrast of the image to produce more dramatic results.

Color Effects

You can use the Color control to create effects such as pastel-like colors or even create improved black-and-white styles.

If you use a single color for your brush (instead of using the From Image setting), you can vary hue, saturation, and brightness controls to get a range of colors.

To create pastel-like colors using the Color card, set the Brush Color to From Image and the Background color to Solid Color (white). Then set your brush strokes to be partially transparent.

The Size Card

The Size card does just what it says: It enables you to vary the size of the brush strokes that are applied. There is only one control immediately available on this card: Vary Brush Size. The setting for Vary Brush Size then determines what controls are available in the rest of the Size card. When I first opened the Vary Brush Size drop-down list, I was greeted by a lengthy list of, shall we say interesting, names. However, once you understand the thinking behind the designers at Xaos, these might make a little more sense.

The Vary Brush Size Control

Clicking on the arrow button to the right of the name box produces a list of eight sets of brush variations. What follows is a description of the action of each of these variation sets.

■ **No Variation**

Here's the only one that is self-explanatory. (Well, sort of.) When this option is selected, all of the brush strokes will be the same size. The size of the brush is set using the Size slider. The size is scaled from the actual size of the brush image selected. In practice, it is a percentage of the size of the original. For example, if the .BMP file that makes up the brush is 100×100 pixels, a size value of 100 would produce brush strokes of the same size. If the value was set for 50 (50 percent), the brush strokes would be 50×50 pixels in size. Most of the brushes included in Paint Alchemy are 128×128 pixels. Now for the weirdness. What does a Variation slider do in a No Variation setting? It overrides the No Variations In Size option, of course. Thus, larger numbers cause larger variations in brush size in the No Variation setting. Is that clear? I think I'm getting a headache.

■ **Randomly**

When this option is selected, the brush strokes vary in size randomly. I love the two settings for this one: This and That. You use This and That to set the minimum and maximum size allowed. It doesn't matter which is which. The larger setting will be the Maximum and the smaller setting will be the Minimum. Look at the bottom of the card. Another Variation slider! This one does the same thing as the Variation slider in No Variation: It overrides the This and That slider settings.

■ **By Radial Distance**

With this option, the brush strokes will change smoothly in size, in a circular manner. The brush strokes start out one size in the center and gradually change to another size at the edge of the circle.

Center slider:	Determines the size of the brush at the center of the circle.
Edge slider:	Sets the size of the brush at the edge of the circle.

To set the location of the center point, click the Set Center button. This brings up a rather large thumbnail of the area selected by the mask. If more than one area is masked, an area of the image that is determined by the boundaries of the various masks makes up the preview image. By clicking on the place that you want to be the center of the circle, a small crosshair is placed on the image at the point where you clicked.

Below the thumbnail is exact X/Y-position information (in pixels) for the point where the circle is centered. Actually, I haven't got a clue why this information is provided. It wasn't in the Mac version, and when I asked some members of the Paint development team, they didn't know either, except that it had been requested from higher up in the command chain.

Corel *NOTE!*

The Set Center point determines the center of the circle used by the Size, Angle, and Transparency cards.

*Figure 13.14.
This little dialog box lets you determine the starting point of the circle for the Radial Distance function. The X and Y numbers at the bottom indicate the location of Russian submarines in the Baltic Sea. Or something like that.*

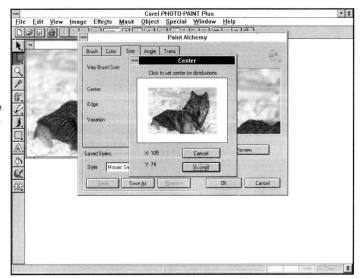

■ By Vertical Position

With this option, the brush strokes change smoothly in size from the top to the bottom of the image. You set the sizes using the Top and Bottom sliders.

■ By Horizontal Position

With this option, the brush strokes change smoothly in size from the left to the right of the image. The sizes of the brushes are set using the Left and Right sliders.

■ By Hue

With this option, each brush stroke is scaled according to the hue of the image at the location of each brush stroke. You set the minimum and maximum sizes using the Warm and Cool sliders. For example, the default setting for the Spatula style is Warm 5, Cool 30. The warmer colors will be limited to variations of up to 5 percent of the brush size, while the cool colors will be allowed to become up to 30 percent of brush size. So what do we mean by cool and warm? On a color wheel, the dividing line between cool and warm runs through red. Therefore, by using the By Hue option for determining brush size, brush strokes that are applied to areas of the image that contain colors on the yellow side of red are given the Warm size values. Those colors that fall on the magenta side of red are given the Cool size values. (This detailed explanation is so that you know how it works. I have yet to sit down with a color wheel that can calculate this stuff. Experiment on small images or the preview window.)

By Saturation

With this section, each brush stroke is scaled according to the saturation of the image color at the location of the brush stroke. You set the minimum and maximum sizes using the Saturated and Unsaturated sliders. If you are very health-conscious, you can use these setting to make images that are high in unsaturates. Setting the values for Saturated to be larger than the value for Unsaturated results in brush strokes over richly colored areas that will be larger than the brush strokes over black, white, or gray areas.

Corel *TIP!*

While working with this larger/smaller brush stroke thing, remember that smaller brush strokes retain more detail of the original image and may be more desirable than larger brush strokes.

By Brightness

With this option, each brush stroke is scaled according to the brightness of the image color at the location of the brush stroke. You set the minimum and maximum sizes using the Bright and Dark sliders. Setting the values for Bright to be larger than the value for Dark results in brush strokes over bright areas of the image that will be larger than brush strokes over dark areas.

Size Variation

The Variation slider lets you set a range within which brush stroke size is chosen randomly. The higher this value, the more your strokes will vary from their set sizes. That is all you need to know. However, for those of you who are like me and desire a more detailed explanation, here goes: The variation is calculated as a percentage of the full-sized brush. Thus, if you set Vary Brush Size to No Variation, set the Size to 50, and set the Variation to 10, you will get brush strokes that range in size from 40 to 60. The variation size is determined after you set the range or distribution with the sliders associated with the Vary Brush Size option you have selected.

The Angle Card

You use the Angle card to set the angle of your brush stroke and to change brush angle based on its position in your image. You can also control brush angle based on the color content of your image, or you can change brush angle randomly. This card is similar in operation to the Size card.

Vary Brush Angle

The Vary Brush Angle drop-down list lets you specify what should control the orientation (the amount of rotation) of your brush strokes. You can apply all of the brush strokes at the same angle, or you can have them vary randomly, according to information in the image, or by their position. The following is what each option does.

- **No Variation**

  When this option is selected, all of the brush strokes will be rotated by the same angular amount. The amount of rotation is set using the Angle slider. If the Angle is set to 0, the brush strokes will not be rotated at all; they will have the same orientation as the picture of the brush that is displayed on the Brush card. If the angle is set to 180 degrees, the brushes will be upside-down.

- **Randomly**

  With this option, the brush stroke angle varies randomly. You use This and That to set the minimum and maximum angles. It doesn't matter which is which. The larger setting will be the Maximum and the smaller setting will be the Minimum.

- **By Radial Distance**

  With this option, the brush strokes will change their orientation smoothly in a circular manner, starting at one angle in the center and gradually changing to another angle at the edge of the circle.

Center slider:	Determines the angle of the brush at the center of the circle.
Edge slider:	Sets the angle of the brush at the edge of the circle.

  To set the location of the center, click the Set Center button. This brings up a large thumbnail of the area selected by the mask. If more than one area is masked, an area of the image that is determined by the boundaries of the various masks makes up the preview image. By clicking on the place that you want to be the center of the circle, a small crosshair is placed on the image at the point where you clicked.

Corel *NOTE!*

> The Set Center point controls the location of the center of the circle for the Size, Angle, and Transparency cards.

■ **By Vertical Position**

With this option, the brush strokes change their angle smoothly from the top to the bottom of the image. You set the angles using the Top and Bottom sliders.

■ **By Horizontal Position**

With this option, the brush strokes change their angle smoothly from the left to the right of the image. The angle of the brushes are set using the Left and Right sliders.

■ **By Hue**

With this option, each brush stroke is rotated according to the hue of the image at the location of each brush stroke. You set the minimum and maximum angles using the Warm and Cool sliders. Therefore, when using By Hue for determining brush stroke, angles that are applied to areas of the image that contain colors on the yellow side of red are given the Warm size values. Those colors that fall on the magenta side of the red are given the Cool size values. If you set the angle for Cool to be larger than the angle for Warm, brush strokes over the blue areas of the image will be rotated more than brush strokes over yellow areas. (You should feel free to experiment on small images or the Preview window.)

■ **By Saturation**

With this option, each brush stroke is rotated according to the saturation of the image color at the location of the brush stroke. You set the minimum and maximum angles using the Saturated and Unsaturated sliders. Setting the values for Saturated to be larger than the value for Unsaturated results in brush strokes over richly colored areas that will be rotated more than brush strokes over black, white, or gray areas.

■ **By Brightness**

With this option, each brush stroke is rotated according to the brightness of the image color at the location of the brush stroke. You set the minimum and maximum angles using the Bright and Dark sliders. Setting the values for Bright to be larger than the value for Dark results in brush strokes over bright areas of the image that will be larger than brush strokes over dark areas.

Angle Variation

The Variation slider lets you add randomness to the stroke angles. The higher this value, the more your strokes will vary from their set angles.

The variation is calculated as degrees of offset from the brush angle. Thus, if you set Vary Brush Angle to No Variation, set the Angle to 90, and set the Variation to 10, you will get brush strokes that range in angle from 80 to 100 degrees.

The Transparency Card

The Transparency card is used to control brush stroke transparency and to change the transparency based on brush position in your image. It is also used to change the level of transparency based on color content in the image or the selected area of the image as well as changing the level of transparency randomly.

Figure 13.15.
The Transparency card.

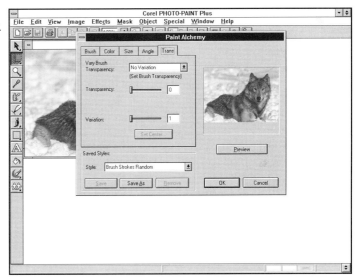

The Vary Brush Transparency Controls

The Vary Brush Transparency drop-down list lets you specify what controls the transparency of your brush strokes. The following are brief explanations of what each option does.

■ **No Variation**

With this option, all of the brush strokes are equally transparent. You set the degree of transparency using the Transparency slider. If the Transparency is set to 0, the brush strokes will be completely opaque. If it is set to 100, the brush strokes will be completely transparent (in other words, invisible).

Corel *NOTE!*

> The gray areas of the brushes are partially transparent when the Transparency is set to 0. The transparency that you set with the slider is added to the normal transparency of each pixel in the brush.

■ **Randomly**

The transparency of your brush strokes can vary randomly. The maximum and minimum transparency is set using the This and That sliders. It doesn't matter which is larger or smaller.

■ **By Radial Distance**

With this option, the brush strokes smoothly change their transparency in a circular manner, starting at one angle of transparency in the center and gradually changing to another at the edge of the circle.

Center slider: Determines the degree of transparency of the brush at the center of the circle.

Edge slider: Sets the degree of transparency of the brush at the edge of the circle.

To set the location of the center, click the Set Center button. This brings up a large thumbnail of the area selected by the mask. If more than one area is masked, an area of the image that is determined by the boundaries of the various masks makes up the preview image. By clicking on the place that you want to be the center of the circle, a small crosshair is placed on the image at the point where you clicked.

Corel *NOTE!*

> The Set Center point is used to position the center of the circle for the Size, Angle, and Transparency cards.

■ **By Vertical Position**

With this option, the brush strokes change their degree of transparency smoothly from the top to the bottom of the image. You set the degree of transparency using the Top and Bottom sliders.

■ **By Horizontal Position**

With this option, the brush strokes change their degree of transparency smoothly from the left to the right of the image. The degree of transparency of the brushes are set using the Left and Right sliders.

■ **By Hue**

With this option, each brush stroke is rotated according to the hue of the image at the location of each brush stroke. You set the minimum and maximum degree of transparency using the Warm and Cool sliders. Thus, by using By Hue for determining brush stroke, the degree of transparency that is applied to areas of the image that contain colors on the yellow side of red are given the Warm size values. Those colors that fall on the magenta side of the red are given the Cool size values. If you set the degree of transparency for Cool to be larger than the degree of transparency for Warm, brush strokes over the blue areas of the image will be rotated more than brush strokes over yellow areas. Experiment on small images or the preview window.

■ **By Saturation**

With this option, each brush stroke is rotated according to the saturation of the image color at the location of the brush stroke. You set the minimum and maximum degree of transparencies using the Saturated and Unsaturated sliders. Setting the values for Saturated to be larger than the value for Unsaturated results in brush strokes over richly colored areas that will be rotated more than brush strokes over black, white, or gray areas.

■ **By Brightness**

With this option, each brush stroke is rotated according to the brightness of the image color at the location of the brush stroke. You set the minimum and maximum degree of transparencies using the Bright and Dark sliders. Setting the values for Bright to be larger than the value for Dark results in brush strokes over bright areas of the image that will be larger than brush strokes over dark areas.

Transparency Variation

The Variation slider lets you add randomness to the degree of brush stroke transparency. The higher this value, the more your strokes will vary from their set degree of transparencies.

■ The variation is calculated as degrees of offset from the brush's selected degree of transparency. Thus, if you set Vary Brush Transparency to No Variation, set the Transparency to 90, and set the Variation to 10, you will get brush strokes that range in transparency from 80 to 100 degrees.

Now that you have all the grimy details on operating this set of filters, I urge you to experiment, experiment, and experiment some more.

Application: Preserving Detail When Using Paint Alchemy Filters

The following real-world application contains some Paint Alchemy tricks I learned while working on this chapter.

Let's say you get this sweet assignment from a travel agency to make their new Bahamas cruise-package brochure. It is going to be printed in four colors on some nice textured paper. It is decided that the owners of the travel agency are tired of the sterile stock photo shots of swimmers and divers. The owner's wife considers herself a patron of the arts and wants something more "artsy" for the brochure. Suddenly you remember that you have your new copy of PHOTO-PAINT 5 Plus with the slick Paint Alchemy filters. "No sweat," you say, shaking hands with the departing clients. As soon as they leave, you fire up the old computer with a copy of this book in your hand.

The original source image is the scuba diver picture from the Corel Sampler Photo CD. (See Figure 13.16.) Now, using Paint Alchemy, you apply a Spatula style to it. The result is almost unrecognizable. While the colors looks great, you remember the old adage that images in publications are like jokes: They don't work if you have to explain them. Meanwhile, any thoughts of making money on this job are floating out the window as you try several other settings, each resulting in a similarly beautiful-but-puzzling look. As you are looking up the number of your friend who does pricey oil paintings on canvas, you remember something that might help.

Making an object from the original image, you place it on top of the resulting Spatula-style filter. After trying several different object-merge modes, you discover that by using the Lighter Than or the Color Merge modes you get the Impressionism look while still being able to recognize the subject matter without calling the Psychic hotline. The image is finished by applying some Unsharp and a little Equalization Tone to enhance the image.

So the travel agency people come back and are so thrilled with the artwork that they not only pay your bill on time, but they throw in a free cruise. Actually, in the real world, this is the point where you are likely to find that the wife of the owner prefers Picasso to Impressionism. "No problem," you say with a smile as you step into the back room and pull Figure 13.17 from the trashcan. "I love it," she purrs.

Terrazzo

The next plug-in filter we will discuss from PHOTO-PAINT 5 Plus is called Terrazzo. (The name comes from the Italian word for "terrace" and originally referred to a kind of mosaic floor covering.) I again acknowledge my gratitude to the fine folks at Xaos who have let me borrow heavily from their manual so that the material in this chapter would be accurate (and available before the release of PHOTO-PAINT 6).

Figure 13.16.
The original image.

Figure 13.17.
After application of
several styles from the
Paint Alchemy filter the
subject was difficult to
see.

Terrazzo is a filter that enables you to create beautiful, regular patterns taken from elements in existing source images. With Terrazzo, the patterns are very easy to create—and infinitely repeatable. The best part is that Terrazzo is simple to use. Xaos Tools ships a wonderful manual with their product that covers Terrazzo in incredible detail. I will try to give you in this part of the Plus chapter a compromise between their manual and the scant information you received with the Plus release. I have included several images here (in grayscale) that were created by using some bitmap fills and applying Terrazzo to them.

Figure 13.18.
By applying a copy of
the original image on
top and using various
merge modes, this
image resulted.

Some Terrazzo Examples

Figure 13.19.
A boring Conical fill
changed into a tile
pattern.

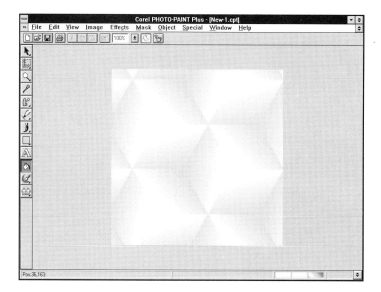

Figure 13.20a.
I deliberately chose
this bitmap fill
(Cheetah) because
I hate it, and yet
made it into a
pleasant pattern.

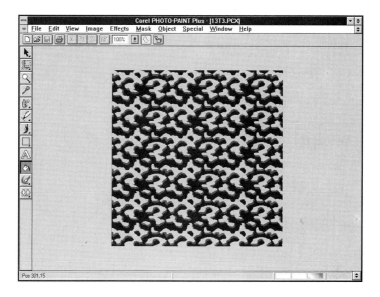

Figure 13.20b.
The resulting pattern.

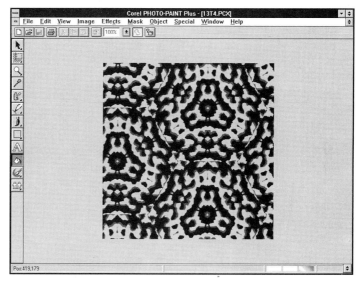

An Overview of Terrazzo

The regular patterns you can create with Terrazzo are based on 17 symmetry
groups, which are known in the math and design worlds by several names,
including "planar," "ornamental," or "wallpaper" symmetry groups. You choose
the symmetry you want to use from a Symmetry selection box from the Terrazzo
dialog box.

Figure 13.21a.
A texture fill to which
we applied two differ-
ent types of Symmetry
to show how varied
the results can be.

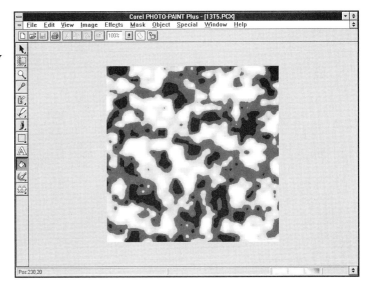

Figure 13.21b.
An additional pattern.

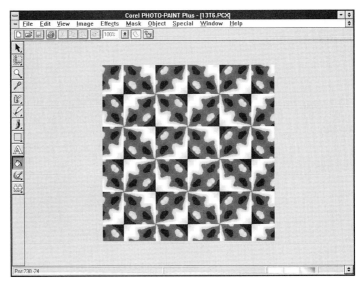

The 17 symmetries in the Terrazzo filter are named after common American patchwork quilt patterns. Each of these symmetries also has a mathematical name. Because these mathematical names (such as p-4m) aren't very exciting or as easy to remember as the quilt names (such as Sunflower), Xaos has only used the quilt names in the interface.

Figure 13.21c.
An additional pattern.

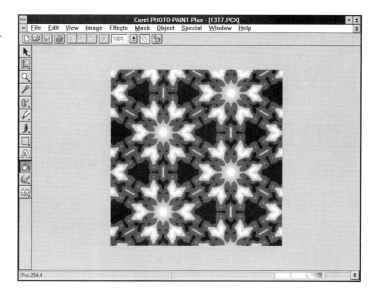

Figure 13.22a.
A photo from the Corel
Sampler Photo CD
collection.

Tiles, Motifs, and Patterns

Each Terrazzo-generated pattern is made from a **motif**, which is the shape that builds a **tile** when a **symmetry** is applied to it. The tile in turn, repeats to build a regular pattern. These three terms will be used throughout this discussion.

Following are simple examples of a motif, a tile, and a pattern. The rectangular outline shown in Figure 13.24 is a motif. The motif in Terrazzo is very similar to the masks in PHOTO-PAINT. The area that is enclosed by the motif is the foundation of the tile. There are eight different motif shapes. Different symmetries use different motifs.

Figure 13.22b.
I used a small part of the banner in the back-ground to achieve the four different patterns. (It looks much better in color.)

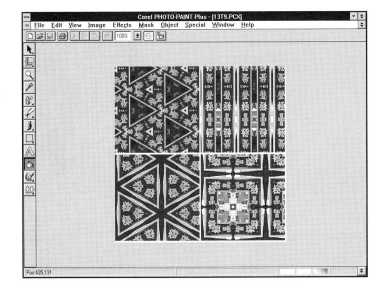

Figure 13.23a.
This is the result of taking a tiny piece of sky and applying the Sunflower Symmetry to it.

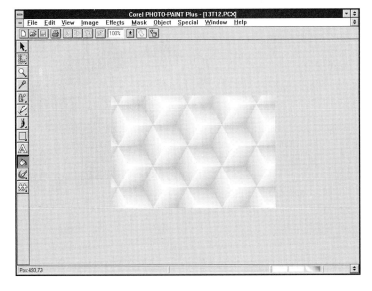

Figure 13.25 is a portion of the tile produced when the footprint in Figure 13.24 has the Wings symmetry applied to it. The Wings symmetry creates a mirror

reflection of the contents of the motif. This is one of the simplest of the 17 symmetries in Terrazzo. Figure 13.26 is the actual pattern made from the original footprint.

Figure 13.23b.
I used the pattern in
the background of this
figure.

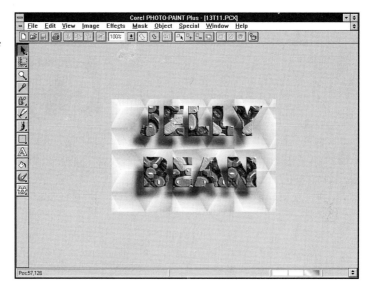

Figure 13.24.
A basic footprint
surrounded by a motif.
The little door in the
lower right corner is
the control handle.

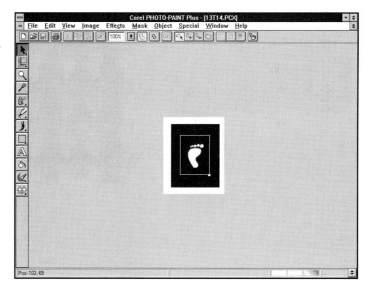

Figure 13.25.
A portion of the tile
produced by applying
the Wings symmetry
to our lonely little foot.
We now have two feet.

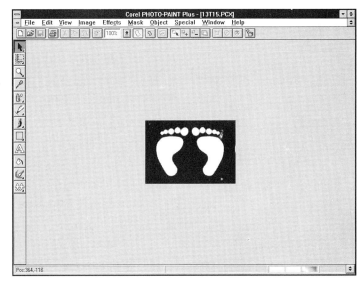

Figure 13.26.
The happy patter of
little feet when Wings
is applied to Mr. Foot.

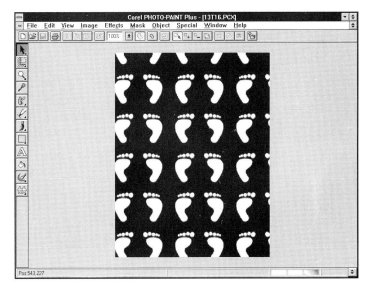

Symmetries

Although each of the 17 symmetries produces different results, all of the symmetries perform one or more of the following operations:

■ *Translations*, which move the motif up, down, right, left, or diagonally without changing the orientation. Figure 13.27 is an example created with the Gold Brick pattern which performs a simple translation on the motif.

*Figure 13.27.
An example created
with the Gold Brick
pattern which per-
forms a simple
translation on the
motif.*

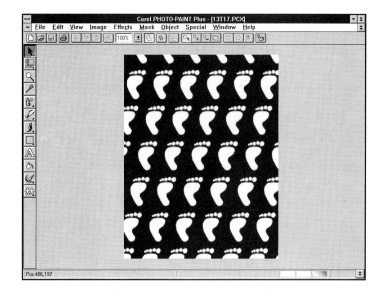

■ *Rotations*, which turn the motif one or more times around a center at a
specific angle. An example of a rotation is the following pattern shown in
Figure 13.28. This was created with the Pinwheel symmetry, in which the
motif is rotated by 90 degrees, three times.

*Figure 13.28.
An example of a
rotation.*

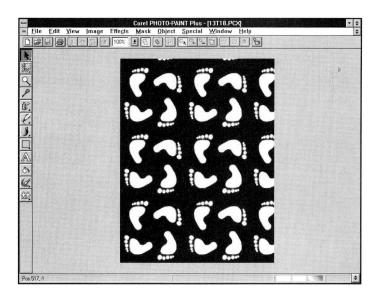

■ *Mirror Reflections*, which create one or more mirror images of the motif. An example of a mirror reflection is shown in Figure 13.29. It was created with the Prickly Pear symmetry, which produces mirror reflections in two directions.

Figure 13.29.
An example of a mirror reflection.

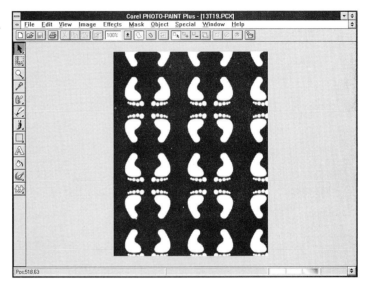

■ *Glide Reflections*, which create one or more mirror images of a motif and move the motif up, down, right, left, or diagonally. Figure 13.30 shows a glide reflection as produced by the Hither & Yon symmetry.

Figure 13.30.
An example of a glide reflection as produced by the Hither & Yon symmetry.

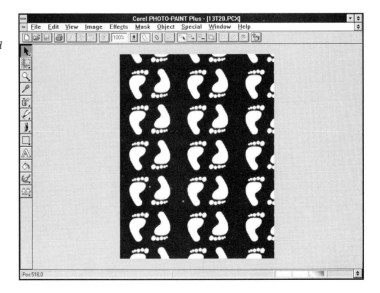

Using Terrazzo

Terrazzo is located in the Effects menu under the Special subgroup (category). When Special is invoked, a long drop-down list appears, and at the bottom is Terrazzo. Clicking on the name produces an hourglass for a moment. (Of all of the filters that were available at the time this book was written, Terrazzo takes the longest to initialize. Still, on my system we are only talking about 10 seconds. And after it is initialized, Terrazzo operates very fast.)

Unlike Paint Alchemy, Terrazzo operates on grayscale and color images, but not on black-and-white (1-bit) images. Like Paint Alchemy and all of the other filters, you must have a image open before you can access the filter.

When you first open Terrazzo, you will see the opening screen as shown in Figure 13.31. Let's take a closer look at it.

The large image on the left side of the Terrazzo dialog box displays the masked area of the image, or the entire source image if you haven't selected any areas with a mask. (Transparency and Color masks don't count.)

The large image on the right of the dialog box displays the source image with the current symmetry applied to it. We'll refer to the image on the right as the *destination* image.

Figure 13.31.
The Terrazzo opening screen.

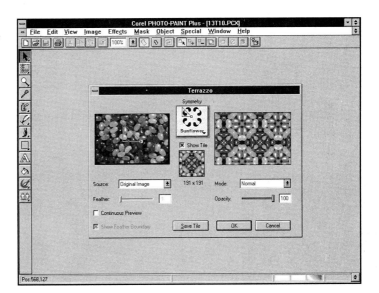

Corel *NOTE!*

> The destination image is the one to which you are applying a pattern. Although you can open a new source image from within Terrazzo, you cannot open a new destination image without closing Terrazzo and returning to PHOTO-PAINT 5's main screen.

The Continuous Preview Option

When the Continuous Preview checkbox is checked, the destination image is continuously updated as you change any of the settings in the Terrazzo dialog box. This allows you to see the effects of your adjustments in real time as you are making them.

Corel *TIP!*

> Leaving the Continuous Preview options selected may slow down some systems. This is especially true if you are using a large motif one of the triangular motifs such as Sunflower, or a kite-shaped motif such as Whirlpool. If you experience system slow down, you may want to consider switching off the Continous Preview option. That said, I find that having it on really helps in finding some nice patterns quickly.

By default, Continuous Preview is turned off in the Terrazzo dialog box.

When the Continuous Preview checkbox is not selected, the destination image is updated only when you release the mouse button after making an adjustment to one of the controls in the Terrazzo dialog box.

The Terrazzo Motifs

When you first open the Terrazzo dialog box, the motif is positioned in the center of the source image; if you have already opened the Terrazzo dialog box, the motif is in the position where you last placed it.

Adjusting a Motif

You can change the tile you are creating by moving the motif to a new position on the source image, thus selecting a different part of the image to make into a tile.

In addition to moving the motif, you can also adjust the size and, in the case of the Gold Brick symmetry, the shape of the motif. Each motif has a handle on it that enables you to resize the motif.

To adjust the motif's position:

Place the cursor anywhere inside the motif and hold down the left mouse button. The cursor becomes a hand, and while you hold down the mouse button you can drag the motif anywhere inside the source image.

If the Continuous Preview option is on, the destination image on the right side is constantly updated to show the results of repositioning the motif on the source image.

To adjust the motif's size:

Place the cursor over the motif control handle and drag it to increase or decrease the size. The only exception to this is the Gold Brick, which has two handles. The handle in the upper-right corner of the motif resizes the width and the handle in the lower-left lets you resize the height of the motif and skew its shape.

Corel *TIP!*

> To constrain the Gold Brick motif to a rectangular shape, or to return to a rectangular motif after you have skewed the motif, hold down the Shift key as you drag the lower-left handle. The motif automatically becomes rectangular as long as you hold down the Shift key.

Selecting a Symmetry

The first time you open Terrazzo, the active symmetry is Pinwheel. This symmetry is displayed between the source and the destination images in the Terrazzo dialog box. Each symmetry swatch displays a simple representation of the selected symmetry.

To select a different symmetry, click on the currently displayed symmetry swatch and the Symmetry selection box opens as shown in Figure 13.32. Clicking the desired symmetry causes it to be highlighted with a blue border. Click the OK button when you are satisfied with your selection, and the selected symmetry appears between the source and destination image.

Figure 13.32.
The selection of 17
symmetries available
to use with Terrazzo.

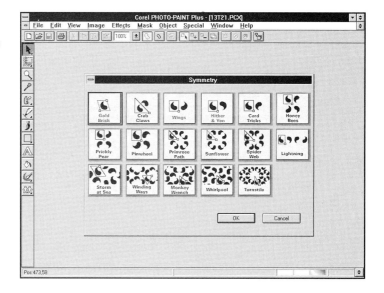

Creating Seamless Patterns

With most of the Terrazzo symmetries, you may notice a visible edge or seam between the tiles. The feather option in the Terrazzo dialog box allows you to feather the edge of a motif so that the seams between tiles fade away.

When you turn on feathering in Terrazzo, an area outside the motif (called the feather boundary) is selected; the pixels inside the feather boundary are dispersed, thus creating a gradual transition between motifs.

Figure 13.33a.
An image that had
a symmetry applied
with no feathering.

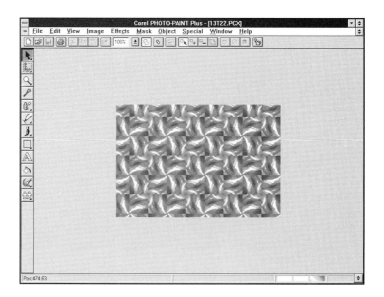

*Figure 13.33b.
The same image with
the same settings,
except that a feather
value of 20 was used.
The result is the ab-
sence of the fine lines
that separated the
tiles. In other words,
feathering makes
seamless tiles.*

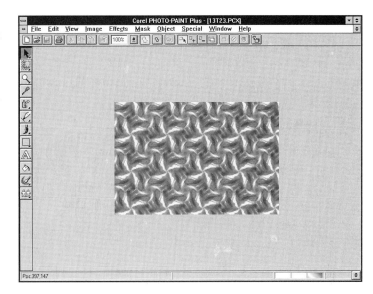

Corel *TIP!*

> Sometimes there *is* such a thing as too much of a good thing. With certain pat-
> terns, using too large a feathering value causes faint black seams to develop.

Using the Feather Option

You use the Feather option in the Terrazzo dialog box to set the width of the
feather edge around the motif. The feather option is dimmed (not available)
if you have selected the Sunflower, Prickly Pear, Turnstile, or Winding Way
symmetries. The option is not available because these four symmetries are
kaleidoscopic and therefore always seamless.

To adjust a motif's feather edge, drag the slider to increase or decrease the
feather edge around the motif, or enter a value directly into the data box to the
right of the slider. The value is a percentage based upon the size of the image.
For example, setting the Feather value to 25 creates a feather with a width of 25
percent of the distance from the edge of the motif to its center.

When you set the feather value above 0, you will notice that a second border
appears around the motif in the source image, as shown in Figure 13.34. This
border represents the area included in the feather edge of the motif.

Figure 13.34.
When you set the
feather value above 0,
you will notice that a
second border appears
around the motif in the
source image. This
border represents the
area included in the
feather edge of the
motif.

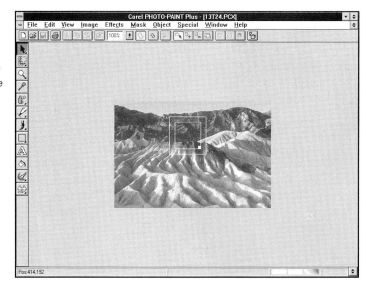

Corel *TIP!*

> You cannot move the motif by clicking-and-dragging inside the feather border.
> You must be inside the motif itself to move a feathered motif. (This little jewel
> drove me crazy till I figured it out.)

If you don't want to see the feather boundary around the motif, you can turn it
off by clearing the Show Feather Boundary checkbox in the Terrazzo dialog box.
This only turns off the visible border; if you have feathering selected, the feathering is still applied.

You may notice that setting a Feather value slows down your system a wee bit.
The folks at Corel have done a wonderful job of speeding up these filters in
comparison to the Mac versions. However, if you noticed that the feathering is
slowing down your system, keep it off until you are ready to fine-tune your
image.

Corel *TIP!*

> Some symmetries create mirror lines as they reflect a motif to create a pattern.
> Feathering does not occur on mirror lines, because these are "seamless" lines;
> feathering only appears on edges with visible seams.

Feather Boundary Constraints

If the Show Feather Boundary is off and you have some value of feathering entered, you will discover that you cannot position the motif any closer to the edge of the source image than the feather boundary.

If the motif is already positioned near the edge of the source image and you attempt to enter a value for Feather that would create a boundary that goes beyond the image edge, the maximum allowable value is automatically entered in the Feather value box, and the slider or values will not exceed that value unless the motif is moved.

One last feathering note: If you have a very small motif, you may not be able to see the feather boundary, even if you have the Show Feather Boundary option turned on. Although you can't see it, the feather will still appear when you apply the pattern.

The Mode Settings

The Mode drop-down list in the Terrazzo dialog box lets you control the way a pattern is applied to a selection. The following sections contain explanations for each of Terrazzo's mode choices. In each of the accompanying figures, the same tile was applied to the same image. The only setting that was changed was the mode.

Unfortunately, the examples that follow don't do justice to what some of the modes can be used for. The purpose of the examples is to demonstrate the differences between the modes rather than to demonstrate impressive applications of them.

Normal

This mode applies the pattern uniformly to all the pixels of the destination image.

Darken

This mode applies only to those pixels in the pattern that are darker than those in the destination image. The pixels in the destination image that are darker than those in the pattern remain unchanged.

Lighten

This mode applies only to those pixels in the pattern that are lighter than those in the destination image. The pixels in the destination image that are lighter than those in the pattern remain unchanged.

Figure 13.35a.
The original image.

Figure 13.35b.
Tile made using
Sunflower at the
Normal mode setting.

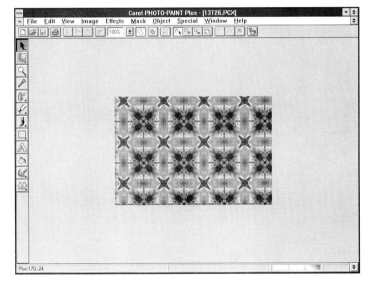

Hue

This mode applies the pattern by changing only the hues (colors) of the destination image, without affecting the saturation (intensity of colors) or the luminosity (lightness and darkness) values of pixels in the destination image. This mode is not available if the destination image is in grayscale.

*Figure 13.35c.
Darken mode.*

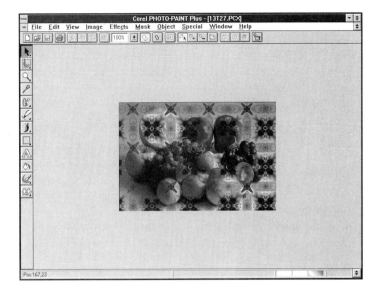

*Figure 13.35d.
Lighten mode.*

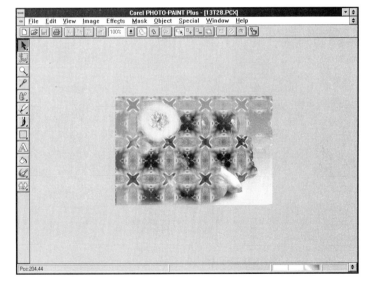

Saturation

This mode applies the pattern by changing only the saturation values of the destination image, without affecting the hue or the luminosity values of the pixels in the destination image. This mode is not available if the destination image is in grayscale.

Figure 13.35e.
Hue mode.

Figure 13.35f.
Saturation mode.

Color

This mode applies the pattern by changing both the hue and saturation values of the destination image without changing the luminosity values of pixels in the destination image. This mode is not available if the destination image is in grayscale.

Figure 13.35g.
Color mode.

Luminosity

This mode applies the pattern by changing only the luminosity values of the destination range, without affecting the hue or saturation values of the pixels in the destination image. This mode is the inverse of Color mode. (It can also produce some surprising results.)

Figure 13.35h.
Luminosity mode.

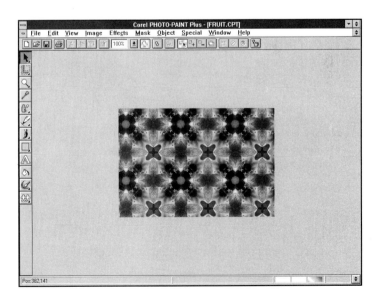

Multiply

This mode causes the color pattern to combine with the color in the destination image, creating colors that are darker than those in either the pattern or the destination image.

Figure 13.35i.
Multiply mode.

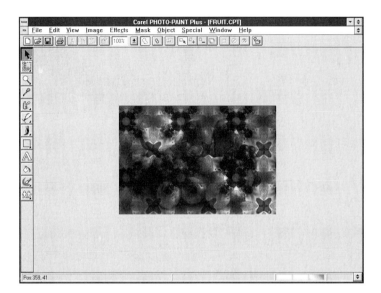

Screen

This mode causes the colors in the pattern to combine with the colors in the destination image, creating colors that are lighter than those in either the pattern or the destination image. This mode is the inverse of Multiply mode.

Opacity

The Opacity slider in the Terrazzo dialog box lets you adjust the opacity of the pattern when you apply it to a selection. You may want the effect of an almost invisible pattern (low opacity), or you may want a bold application of a pattern, covering the destination image entirely (high opacity). An opacity value of 100 (100 percent) means that the pattern is completely opaque; an opacity value of 0 means that the pattern is invisible (which is not very useful).

Previewing and Saving Tiles

When the Show Tile option in the Terrazzo dialog box is enabled, a preview of the current tile appears below the symmetry swatch. The pixel dimensions of the current tile are also displayed below the tile.

Figure 13.35j.
Screen Mode.

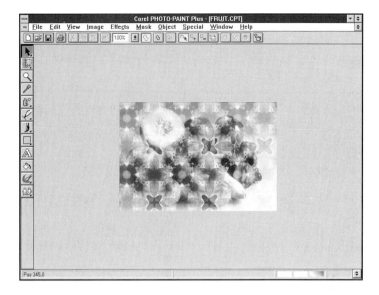

While the Show Tile option is enabled, you are provided with a constant pre-view of the tile you are creating. You may find it helpful to keep this option turned on, especially if you plan to save the tile later on. It does not slow down the system as far as I have been able to detect.

Saving a Tile

One of the benefits of having the Terrazzo filter integrated into PHOTO-PAINT 5 is that the saving a tile button becomes a real time-saver. The Save to Tile feature saves the tile created by Terrazzo (this is the tile that is displayed when the Show Tile option is enabled) as a .BMP file in the default location for the Bitmap Fill tiles. This way you can quickly use Terrazzo to make a tile, and by saving it as a tile, you can use it immediately as a bitmap fill.

To save a Terrazzo tile:

- Choose the symmetry, and position the motif where you want it in the source image.
- Click the Save Tile button in the Terrazzo dialog box. The Save Tile dialog box opens as shown in Figure 13.36.
- Name the file and confirm where you want the file saved. Click the OK button. When you return to the Terrazzo, click Cancel if you do not want the pattern applied to the image.

Figure 13.36.
This dialog box allows you to name the tiles you create and put them in either the default tile directory or a directory of your own choosing.

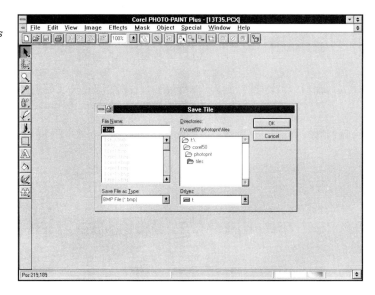

3D Stereo Noise

This filter from the Kai Power Tools collection is my least favorite, because it has become such a fad. The 3D Stereo Noise filter takes an image and converts it to something akin to a printer failure all over your paper. By staring at the paper, you can see the original image with depth effect. (It is rumored that if you can stare at it for over an hour, just before the onset of a major migraine, you can see Elvis.) 3D Stereo Noise is what produces those posters that have gained such popularity at suburban shopping malls in recent seasons. If you stare at them, you can actually see an embedded image with depth perception.

The method was discovered a long time ago at Bell Laboratories. The researchers observed that when certain points on an image where shifted, it gave the appearance of depth. As used here, the term "stereo" should not be confused with music. We as human beings were designed with stereoscopic sight—two eyes that render a single image from two slightly different angles, thus producing depth perception.

The images that produce the best results with the 3D Stereo Noise effect use gray levels, are slightly blurred, and do not have extreme contrast. Don't waste precious system resources by using 24-bit color. The result will be grayscale. The 3D Stereo Noise filter generates a pixellated noise pattern that has horizontal frequencies that correspond to the gray levels of the initial image. This means that white will map to the highest frequency and appear closest to the viewer; black will map to the lowest frequency and appear furthest away.

Making an Image

First, create a grayscale image that uses text and simple objects. Although the filter will apply in all modes, the best images initially use gray levels. The smaller and more detailed the image you choose, the harder it will be to focus the stereo image. Apply a standard Blur filter. This will soften the edges of the image for easier viewing. Open the Effects menu and under the Special subgroup, click on the 3D Stereo Noise filter. This opens the preview dialog box. (See Figure 13.37.) The only option with this box is depth control, with a relative depth range of 1–10. At the bottom of the dialog box is a checkbox to enable the creation of two dots in a box near the bottom of the image to help the user focus on the 3D image. Apply the filter to the entire image. The results will appear to be a random array of black and white noise.

Figure 13.37.
The preview box for the
3D Stereo Image filter.
Unlike with the Kai
Power Tool version,
you can control if the
dots are printed at the
bottom with a check-
box in this filter.

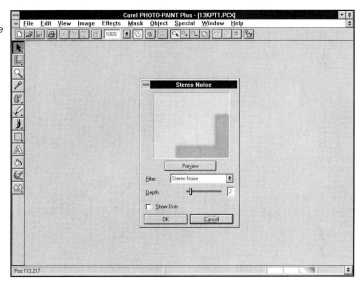

Viewing 3D Stereo Noise Pictures

After you have created a stereo noise picture, it is time to focus your eyes and energies to see the image. I was never able to view the depth on-screen. Maybe you can do better here than I did. Don't feel bad if you don't see the image right away; it may take a few tries. There are several ways to view the image in-depth. Try enabling the Show Dots checkbox to produce black dots about a half-inch apart at the bottom of the image. De-focus your eyes and gaze through the image as if you were looking into the distance. The dots you placed at the bottom will separate into four. If you focus so that the middle two dots fuse, depth should pop in or out. Another way is to try crossing your eyes to fuse the four dots into three. You may also try holding the edge of a thin object such as a floppy disk or your hand between your eyes in order to separate each eye's vision.

Figure 13.38.
An image that is a good
candidate for 3D Stereo
Noise. It is simple and
easily recognizable,
and it has low contrast
with lots of gray.

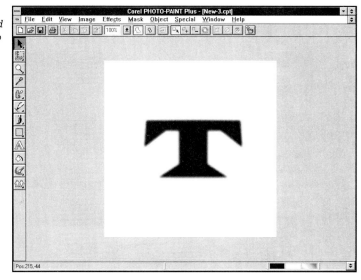

Figure 13.39.
The result when the
filter is applied.

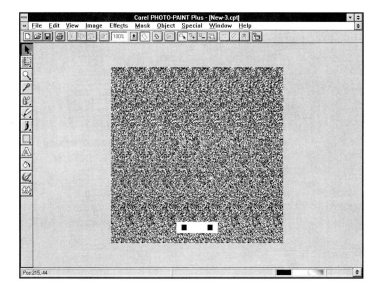

Controlling Depth in Stereo Images

When you see a 3-D object up close, the object seems to be in a slightly different
place depending on which eye looks at it. For instance, hold your finger about
five inches from your computer monitor and look at it with one eye, then the
other. Observe how it seems to move left and right with respect to objects on
the screen. This discrepancy gives your brain information on how far away the
object is. Against the background of your screen, your finger that is five inches
away is displaced about one inch, depending on which eye views it.

The background was made using a bitmap fill of some coffee beans. The steaming coffee cup from the CorelDRAW clipart library was used as a mask in combination with a Transparency mask to produce the effect. For more detailed information, I show how to make this in Chapter 18.

When the new seamless tiles appeared in the Plus release of PHOTO-PAINT, I had to try them out. The stones and the wood in the image are made from seamless tiles. Can you see the seams? Now you know why they call them seamless.

This is the same image with the background hidden and the text shadow inverted. It shows what great changes can be accomplished with only a few adjustments to the objects in an image.

I originally created this for the PHOTO-PAINT User manual. Using the Aldus Gallery Effect Emboss filter and a floating shadow, I was able to improve on the original.

This simple project, done with DRAW and PAINT, is created by following the directions in Chapter 18. I began working with PHOTO-PAINT 5 to make stained glass images by scanning in Titfany stained glass images from a coloring book series by Dover press. By using the Bitmap Texture fills with the flood fill tool, I was able to quickly achieve some realistic looking glass. The lead in between the glass was solid black and didn't look very real. I experimented with using the emboss filter to make the leading look three-dimensional with disappointing results. The major problem with using any embossing filter are lines that are parallel to the light source either fade or disappear entirely. This fading of lines presents two problems, it doesn't look very good and, more importantly, the flood fill tool begins to fill in the wrong areas as it "leaks" through the faded lines. Along come the PAINT maintenance release with Object Merge Mode. It took many hours of experimenting, but the procedure will show you how to make leaded glass that looks very realistic.

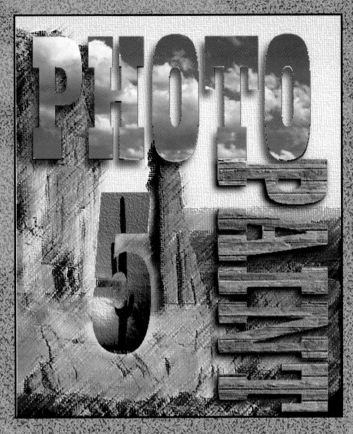

Corel PHOTO-PAINT began its life as a software product called Photofinish created by Z-Soft. It was introduced as Corel PHOTO-PAINT 3 in May of 1992. It was then an interesting bitmap editing package of limited usefulness. Now you may find this hard to believe, but there are many unfounded rumors that float around the computer industry. One of these rumors is that Corel PHOTO-PAINT 5 is still made by Z-Soft and is actually their current product, Photofinish 3. This is not true. When Corel PHOTO-PAINT 4 was released in May 1993, there were many improvements and only a small amount of the original Z-Soft Photofinish program remained in it. PHOTO-PAINT 4 still had limitations in the size of image files it could handle and the absence of several other key features prevented it from being a first-class product. Now Corel PHOTO-PAINT 5 is emerging as a product that can be regarded as a serious photo-editing program in its own right.

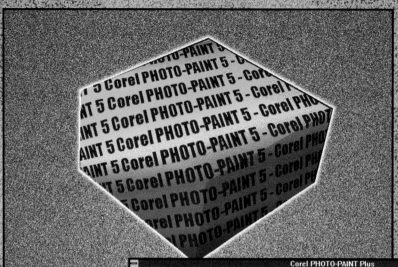

The text was imported from CorelDRAW. The rainbow effect was added with PHOTO-PAINT and the 3-D box was made with Andromeda's Series Two 3-D Plug-in filter. The glow was with Alien Skin's Glow filter.

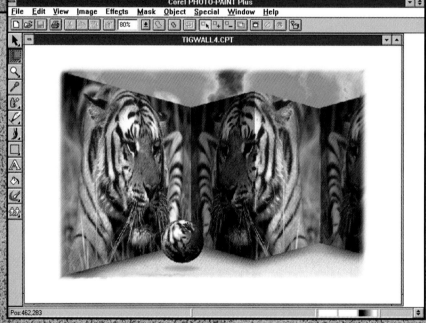

This began as an exercise to learn how the transformation filters worked. I got a little carried away. The sky and floor are texture bitmap fills. The wall was made from a single tiger photo. I applied the Perspective filter to the photo and then mirror duplicated the photo and added shading. The sphere is the same photo scaled down and with the Map to Sphere filter applied.

This poster was very simple to create. The left side was masked and the image was inverted. A glow was added to the text and it was filled with a Corel Bitmap texture.

An experiment with Layers produced this effect. The material of the background was created with a canvas fill. The cutout are objects that have been shaded to give them depth.

The idea with this figure was to highlight the building, which blended in with the background too much. So I masked the building, and applied a -100 percent saturation effect. In the end result, the building really stands out.

SCAN1.TIF (Left) Original photo.

SCAN2.TIF (Right) Enhancements made to photo using the PHOTO-PAINT 5 editing tools and filters.

This was a tiny experiment in 3-D objects. The rug is made of seam-less tiles. The result then had a ripple filter applied. The shading was done with an airbrush.

Using the impressionism brush I made a bitmap pattern that looked like cloth. I used it to make a serape. Shadow was made by duplicat-ing and applying a Gaussian blur.

Above: This is a postcard that was created using several combinations of masks and noise filters.

Below: This image is from a proposal for a poster. The wooden Texas flag was created with seamless tiles. The star originally came from the CorelDRAW symbol library.

The neon butterfly began as a real photograph of a butterfly. The result is made of 4 layers and many applications of filters. The background is a Fractal explorer fill that comes with the Plus release.

Personal favorite. This was done entirely with PHOTO-PAINT 5. In Chapter 18 I show how to make this image.

A sunset photo was "sandwiched" between a raindrop photo as a transparency mask and as an object to produce the drops on the glass look. The frame is a seamless tile with some airbrushing for shading.

It is one thing to go where no man has gone before, it is another to create worlds. Everything in this image was created with PHOTO-PAINT 5.

This began as a photograph of a young girl and was changed through the application of several filters.

This is a composite image of the five principle designers of PHOTO-PAINT 5. In the background is a photograph of Mars. The other planets, stars, and color effects were created with PHOTO-PAINT.

This began as a single shell object from the Objects collection in the PAINT 5 Plus release. By making a mirror duplicate of the shell and embossing it, I was able to get the cast bronze look.

Here the two originals were composited together to make one. The photo of the young girl was cut out, scaled and then put into clone1.tif using the clone tool. Editing tools were used to correct shading and remove unwanted parts of clone2.tif.

This image shows a realistic shadow and the text has a 3-D quality to it that is achieved by merging several layers in different merge modes.

The background was created with the new Paint Alchemy filter in the Plus release. The 3-D looking number 5 was created using several object layers merged together. The Page Curl filter was used in the corner and the stones are the same stones used in the Rock Concert sign.

The basic background shot for a exotic car flyer was created entirely with PHOTO-PAINT 5.

Page Curl

This is a really excellent filter. The only drawback to it is that everybody and his uncle seems to be using it. I have seen a lot of flyers recently that have used the Page Curl filter. I wouldn't let that deter you, however; I just want to warn you in case your client seems less than enthusiastic when you show them something with the Page Curl filter. Page Curl simulates the effect of a page being peeled back, with a highlight running along the center of the curl and a shadow being thrown from beneath the image (if your image is light enough to contrast with a shadow).

The curl begins in one corner of your selection and follows a perfect diagonal line to the opposite corner of the selection. You may also notice a slight transparency to the curl if there is any pattern or texture in the selected portion of your image.

The filter is accessed through the Effects menu under the Special category. Select Page Curl to open the Page Curl dialog box. The origination point of the curl is controlled by using one of the four keys in the Page Curl dialog box, as shown in Figure 13.40. The Vertical and Horizontal orientation check boxes determine which side of the image appears to curl. If the Opaque button is not selected, the page curl has a slightly transparent quality.

Figure 13.40.
The dialog box used to control the Page Curl filter.

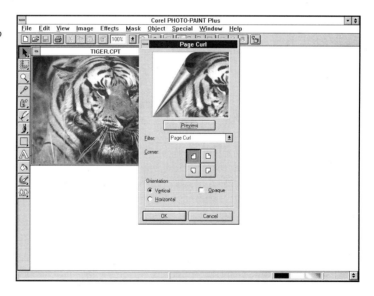

Fractal Explorer

Here is the big mama of all the filters from from HSC. This filter reminds me of a U.S. highway that runs near my house—the filter and the highway have several different names, depending on where you are at the time. When you open the Effects menu and select Special, you are presented with a drop-down list that we have seen before, which includes the Julia Set Explorer. Clicking on the Julia Set opens the Fractal Explorer 2.0. Confused? No need to be; this filter is a hybrid of the Julia I Explorer from Kai Power Tools (KPT) 1.0 and the interface from KPT 2.0.

If you are a old hand at using KPT 2.0, read on. If you have never heard of Kai Power Tools, skip to the next paragraph. If you currently have KPT 2.0, I am going to recommend that you either reinstall it or just copy the files from your KPT directory (or wherever you have installed it) into the COREL50\PLUGINS directory. Be prepared to see double when it comes to Page Curl, 3D Stereo Noise, and Julia Set Explorer. If you don't want to see double, rename the files for Page Curl (PAGECURL.8BF) and 3D Stereo Noise (NOISE3D.8BF) to PAGECURL.OLD and NOISE3D.OLD. This will prevent PHOTO-PAINT 5 from seeing them. If you have other programs that use these filters, then move the files as previously discussed, keep the originals in the KPT directory, but don't include the KPT directory in the Advanced Preferences. This way PHOTO-PAINT won't know where the originals are located, and you won't see double.

If this is your first time with the Kai Power Tools (KPT) user interface... Welcome to Hell! Just kidding. I have heard this user interface (UI) called everything from the best UI on the planet to a Klingon Control Panel. I opt for the latter. Whether you hate it or love it, you have to use it, so to get the most out of this very powerful fractal generator, we need to spend some time learning our way around. A friend of mine who is a big fan of KPT insists that it is really easy to learn. On the other hand, he believes that Neil Armstrong's moonwalk was a fake and that wrestling is real, so judge accordingly.

Fractal Explorer Basics

The Fractal Explorer UI, you may have already noticed, doesn't look like your average Windows dialog box. The dialog box can be moved around the screen by clicking on the title bar and dragging the dialog box anywhere on the screen. When you exit the filter by either clicking on OK or Cancel, the filter will remember its placement on the screen for the next time it is called up within that session. When you leave PHOTO-PAINT and return, all positioning information is lost and the UI restarts in the center of the screen.

Temporary Resizing

Clicking on the button in the upper-left corner with the Kai circular logo on it brings up the program credits for Kai Power Tools. Double-clicking this button reduces (i.e., minimizes) the Fractal Explorer to its preview window. Double-click on the preview window and the Explorer is returned to its original happy self.

Help

Clicking on the Help button (to the immediate left of the title bar) brings up the Help menu for Kai Power Tools 2.0. Be aware that it is going to make references to things that are not in the Corel version of this product. You can also get help by pressing the F1 key, which turns the cursor into a question mark. Clicking on any part of the UI brings up context-insensitive help. No matter what you click, you are going to get the opening help screen.

Options Menu

In the upper-right corner is the Options button. Clicking on this button brings up menu choices that deal with apply modes, which are discussed in detail later in this chapter.

Keyboard Shortcuts

Knowing several of these keyboard shortcuts will save you time when exploring images.

When Launching Julia Set Explorer from the Effects/Special Drop-Down List:

Control	Holding down the Ctrl key while clicking on the words Julia Set prevents the image from being loaded into the preview window. This can be a real time saver with very large image files.
Space bar	This brings up the UI with a black background. The underlying image cannot be seen.

Shortcuts Within the Fractal Explorer UI:

Up arrow	Previous preset (in current category)
Down arrow	Next preset (in current category)
Page Up	First preset (in current category)
Page Down	Last preset (in current category)
Home	First category (also first preset in category)
End	Last category (also first preset in category)
Ctrl+right arrow	Moves apply mode to next mode
Ctrl+left arrow	Moves apply mode to previous mode
Ctrl+Z	Undo
S	Shuffles parameters (user-defined apply mode, color, etc.)
OK	Enter key

NO	ESC key
F1, **?**, or **Shift** + **?**	Help

A Quick Tour of Fractal Explorer

To do Kai Power Tools justice would take volumes and (1) we still wouldn't scratch the surface, and (2) it wouldn't do you much good. The real secret is to experiment. That said, let's take this baby for a trip around the block and see what she does.

Making a Background with Fractal Explorer

1. Open a new image of 300 × 300 pixels, 150-dpi resolution, 24-bit color.

2. Open the Fractal Explorer by clicking on Julia Set in the Special drop-down menu in the Effects menu. The Fractal Explorer dialog box opens. (See Figure 13.41.) Now for the tricky part. Presets on this dialog box are not the same as normal drop-down lists.

Figure 13.41.
The Fractal Explorer
dialog box.

3. On the bottom preset box, click and hold the tiny arrow in the right corner until another pop-up menu opens. When it opens, don't let go of the mouse button. You have two choices at this point. The top choice is Corel Presets. While still holding down the left mouse button, move the cursor over to select it.

4. Still holding down the mouse button, move back over to the new drop-down list that just appeared and move the cursor down the list to the

bottom. As you do this, the list will begin to scroll downward. Keep going down until you get to Totally Tubular. Now let go of the mouse button. After a moment the preview window should look like Figure 13.42.

Figure 13.42.
Scroll until you reach
Totally Tubular.

5. Click the down-arrow key and watch the preview window. The preview window changes almost instantly to a new shape. Keep watching. The first image you see in the preview window is a really "rough" approximation of what it will look like. If you give it a moment, the preview window will be "refreshed" three more times, giving it more detail each time.

6. Now look at the preset window. It says "Tropical Island." The down-arrow key selects the next preset. By using the up- and down-arrow keys, you can move quickly though all of the presets and see what they look like.

7. Click the up-arrow key and return to the Totally Tubular preset. Now we are going to make a change. We like this effect, but the color is wrong. I picked this preset because the Inside Color setting has no effect, so we only need to concern ourselves with the Outside Color.

8. Place the cursor over the box that says "Color Outside." When the cursor is over where it is supposed to be, the cursor will change into a tiny representation of a drop-down box. Click on the box and a very long drop-down list will appear.

9. Holding down the left mouse button, move down the list until you reach "Metallic." As you pass some of the names on the list various-sized drop-down lists will appear. When you get to Metallic, the drop-down list

associated with that setting will appear. The default setting for Totally Tubular is Blue Green Metal Cone, which is checked at the top of the list.

10. Still holding the left mouse button, move the cursor down the secondary list to "Gentle Gold" and release the mouse button. The lists disappear and Totally Tubular changes from a blue-green to a lustered gold.

11. Click the OK button on the lower-right and you have created an excellent gold background for a presentation. (See Figure 13.43.)

Figure 13.43.
One of thousands of
possible fractal fills
made with the Fractal
Explorer.

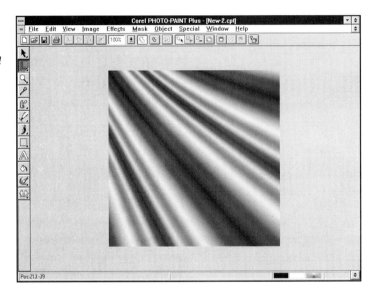

12. Open the Fractal Explorer again. This time select the 60s Wallpaper preset. A faint rainbow-colored fractal is now sitting on top of our golden background in the preview. We are going to use one of the apply modes to change the look of our golden background.

13. Click on the Options button and another drop-down list appears. This time select Darken Only and view the results after you let go of the mouse button. Now it looks like we have rolls of wrapping paper. (See Figure 13.44.)

Corel *TIP!*

> A quick way to preview the apply modes is to hold down the Ctrl key and use the right arrow key to move down the list and use the left arrow key to move up the list.

14. Click the OK button to apply the fractal to the original. You can save it if you want. It will not be required for another work session.

Figure 13.44.
Now it looks like we
have rolls of wrapping
paper. This was
created by merging
another fractal using
the Darken Only apply
mode to achieve a
multicolored wrapping-
paper look.

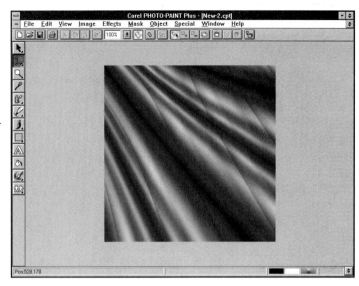

The Apply Modes

Now that you have played with them a little, it is time to discover what those apply modes really do. The apply mode determines how the fractal you create with Fractal Explorer is going to be merged with your existing image, if there is one. It is similar in operation to the way the Object Merge mode works in the Objects/Layers roll-up. The apply modes appear on a drop-down list when the Options button is clicked. The apply modes are as follows:

Normal Apply

This is the mode that is used most often. What you see in the preview window is applied to the image or to the masked (selected) area of the image. Normal mode applies the fractal without regard to the underlying image. All underlying image data is destroyed by this process. Transparency in general is not available in this mode unless the gradient, texture, or fractal has some level of transparency. Those areas underneath the transparency will show through, while everything else will be covered with the selected gradient, texture, or fractal.

Procedural Blend

This is a killer application that produces stunning effects with a fractal. Each pixel is evaluated and acted upon based on its luminance value. If the original pixel has a luminance value in the medium range (128 +/- on a scale from 0–255), the apply is normal. If the luminance value is brighter (200 +/-), the apply effect will be brightened by that amount. If the original pixel is darker, the apply effect will be proportionately darker. The effect is to wrap a fractal around the underlying grayscale image, based upon luminance values. Any areas of pure white or pure black will show through as pure white and pure black, as the luminance values dictate a full brightening or darkening to maximum values, black and white. The Procedural Blend results in the effect "following" the intensity of the original image and appears to be wrapped around.

Reverse Blend

This is applied in the same way as Procedural Blend, except the image and the effect are reversed (which is probably why they called it Reverse Blend). Wherever the effect is a medium intensity, the image is added normally. Wherever the effect is brighter or darker than the image, the effect will be modified proportionally before it is added. The real-time preview window is really necessary to be able to use this filter effectively.

Lighten Only

The Lighten Only mode reads the luminance values of both the original image and the fractal image and compares them. It then adds the fractal only in those areas where the fractal is lighter than the underlying image.

Darken Only

The Darken Only mode reads the luminance values of both the original image and the fractal image and compares them. It then adds the fractal only in those areas where the fractal is darker than the underlying image.

Unusual effects can be achieved with multiple applications of Lighten Only or Darken Only.

Add

The Add mode sums the numerical values of the underlying image and the fractal you wish to apply and clips them when the values reach the maximum (white). Remember that the Add apply adds the numerical value of colors. Thus, while yellow plus blue will make green on a real palette, the result of adding their numerical values together is white. In many cases the results of the Add apply mode may resemble a Blend function, wherein the brighter areas tend to wash out to white, but not always. Add is more difficult to predict than Blend or Multiply, so the best results are achieved with time and experimentation with the real-time preview window.

Subtract

The Subtract apply mode compares the underlying image and the fractal, and then combines them using subtractive color theory. For instance, if the image is white and a green effect is applied, the Subtract mode will yield a magenta. (Subtracting green from RGB yields red plus blue, or purple.) While it would be nice to say that Subtract gives the opposite results of what you get with the Add apply, it doesn't work that way. The color theory behind it gets ugly, so you should experiment with this mode.

Multiply

The Multiply apply mode takes only the dark components of the fractal and adds only those dark components to the underlying image. Everything that is white is ignored, and everything that is black is added proportionally according to its luminance values.

Screen

The Screen apply mode measures the light components in both the underlying image and the fractal. The lighter components are added to the image, and the darker components are discarded or ignored. Everything in-between appears to be blended.

Both Multiply and Screen will provide more predictable results than the other apply modes we have discussed so far (except Normal).

Difference

The Difference apply mode is probably the most dramatic of the apply modes. Before you start using it, you should be warned that it is also one of the most difficult apply modes to predict. The Difference apply mode uses both the underlying image and fractal color ranges to their fullest, and it measures the difference between the two. This difference is what is applied.

For example, if a black-to-white gradient (such as a Fountain fill) is applied over an image, wherever the gradient is black, the image stays the same. Wherever the gradient is white, the image is inverted to negative colors. In-between, the effect is somewhere in-between the two. The Difference mode can create very abstract and colorful images. The downside of this is the inability to predict the results ahead of time. This means that a lot of time is needed for experimenting with various combinations in order to get an effect you want.

Tie Me Up/Tie Me Down

If there was ever any question that KPT comes out of California, I think the names of these two apply modes should erase any doubts. Tie Me Up and Tie

Me Down use "modulo arithmetic" for color manipulation. (You are probably wondering what modulo arithmetic is. So am I.) Their function is similar to Add and Subtract, with the distinction that instead of clipping to black or white, the result which would have been clipped is retained and used as color data. When dealing with a lot of black or white within either the underlying image or selection, or within the gradient itself, Tie Me Up/Tie Me Down will not yield anything surprising. On the other hand, some results will be astonishing, with polarized sheens and kaleidoscopic type effects.

As a group, the apply-mode options take what is already a wide variety of fractal effects and increases their variety exponentially. Since it is easy to experiment with the apply modes by using the Ctrl+Up or Ctrl+Down arrow keys (see the preceding section on keyboard command shortcuts), the apply modes are well worth investigating while you are working with different fractals.

Fractal Explorer Controls

Preview Window

The real-time preview window shows the fractal while it interacts with the underlying image. The initial preview window displays a rough idea of the fractal very quickly, followed by three steps of increasingly refined views. Repeat clicks preempt the preview computation, allowing fast exploration of the fractal space. Color choices are instantly mapped onto the set.

Opacity Selector

The Opacity selector on the UI controls the underlying image view. It is useful when there is a special apply mode or transparency in the gradient that is part of the fractal. Click on it to sample a test image, to view the underlying image, or to view the contents of the Clipboard.

Fractal Map

The fractal map is represented by the shape of a traditional Mandelbrot set. When the cursor is over the fractal map, it changes to a small hand. Click-and-drag the small circle around the fractal space inside of the fractal map. The real-time preview window displays the changes immediately, without having to manually input any numbers. As you move around the fractal map, you may stop to zoom in or zoom out, using the controls on the preview window, at any time.

Corel *TIP!*

> If you are used to working with Kai Power Tools 2.0, you'll find that this fractal map operates differently. The Fractal Explorer in Corel PHOTO-PAINT 5 has only the Julia Set I included with it, while KPT 2.0 has all of the fractal generators available in a drop-down list that would normally appear in this area.

Zoom Controls

Zooming within the Fractal Explorer is accomplished in a number of different ways. The easiest method of zooming is to simply place the cursor in the real-time preview window and click. The zoom controls on the top of the preview-window frame allow centered zooming, and clicking on the preview window enables direct zooming.

Centered Zooming

For centered zooming, use the two controls on the upper left of the preview-window frame. The plus sign (+) zooms in; the minus sign (-) zooms out; the center of the window stays constant. If you click on the word "Zoom" on the interface, a pop-up slider will appear. Drag the slider in either direction to zoom in large steps. This is a fast way to zoom all the way in or all the way out.

Direct Zooming

Whenever the cursor is over the preview window, the arrow changes to a magnifying glass with a plus sign. Click on the spot you wish to magnify inside the preview window, and it zooms in to that spot and makes it the new center of the preview. Holding down the Alt key changes the magnifying cursor to "magnify-minus." Clicking with the Alt key held down will zoom out from that point.

Panning Control

The Panning control allows 360 degrees of continuous panning of the fractal through the preview window.

How to Pan

On the outside edge of the preview window are eight small arrows. Click on any of the arrows to move the main preview window in that direction. Clicking anywhere on the frame surrounding the preview (in-between the arrows) moves the fractal in that direction.

Drag Panning

A Ctrl+click-and-hold turns the cursor into a hand which allows the fractal to be "dragged" around the preview window for precise positioning. Limitations don't end at the preview-window boundaries. Drag as far away as the screen allows.

Detail Settings

Increasing the detail settings on any fractal set adds new elements to the fractal set. Repeated zooms on a fractal set seem to eventually zoom "through" the fractal to nothing. Increasing the detail settings fills the space by increasing the ability to discern small changes, particularly inside the fractal's interior. The higher the detail is set, however, the more computational time is required for rendering. Use the two controls on the lower-left of the preview-window frame to control the detail in the fractal image. The plus sign (+) increases detail; the minus sign (-) decreases detail. Clicking on the word "Detail" shows a slider for more precise detail settings.

Gradient Preview/Pop-Up Menu

On the right-hand side of the Fractal Explorer dialog box are two gradient preview/pop-up menu dialogs. The top gradient dialog governs the interior of the set, and the bottom one governs the exterior of the set (which is most often the dominant area). The pop-up menu for gradients is the same menu that is used by the Gradient Designer, complete with hierarchical categorization of gradient presets. The triangle/sawtooth icon shows the looping control and further affects the way that the gradient is mapped to the fractal set.

Gradient Wrapping Control

The fractal set may be colored with any gradient you choose. You can obtain more interesting renders with the same gradient by controlling the repetition of the gradient as it applies to the set in two different directions. There are two controls for mapping the gradient frequency to the fractal set. The Spiral setting, on the upper-left, controls how fast the color cycles as it moves from one potential line to the next. (The lines are expressing the potential of any point in four-dimensional space to fall toward the attractors, roughly analogous to space around an electric charge with equal attraction to their electrostatic center. Within a ring, the electrostatic pull is the same and there can be many such rings moving toward the center of the charge.) The Spoke setting, on the lower-right of the Wrapping control, determines how often the gradient will be repeated over the entire 360-degree circle around the set. This is the Radial control. These two settings interact with each other. Variations in the Spiral setting will result in widely divergent effects.

The Preset Menu

The Preset Menu is where all of the named or saved fractals are stored. When you press the letter A or click on Add, a dialog box will allow options for item names, category names, and preset files.

Shuffle Button

The Shuffle Button allows selection of different Fractal Explorer parameters to randomize. You may check All, None, or select from the list. Each time the shuffle button is clicked, the selected parameters are shuffled. The parameters that can be shuffled are:

- Exterior Colors
- Interior Colors
- Exterior Looping
- Interior Looping
- Apply Mode
- Test Image
- Potential Speed
- Radial Speed

Options Button

Clicking on the Options Button displays a menu with the apply mode and three other options. Those options are

Wrap Image Instead of Gradient

This option allows the user to grab color data from an opacity preview mode, which can be the underlying image, the Windows clipboard, or a selection. The Fractal Explorer uses the color data contained in the selection, image, or clipboard, and wraps that color around the gradient.

Numerical Input

Numerical Input enables the experienced "fractologist" to find previously explored spaces or to explore new fractal spaces by "hard coding" the algorithm variables.

Draw Gradient Across Top

This feature only works if you have a complete copy of Kai Power Tool 2.0 installed.

Alien Skin's Black Box Filters

The Black Box is a unique collection of filters, and their author, Jeff Butterworth, has made some remarkable enhancements for their inclusion in PHOTO-PAINT 5 Plus. The filters that come with Corel PHOTO-PAINT 5 Plus are an Emboss filter (called The Boss here, so you don't have to keep track of which Emboss is the Alien Skin Emboss and which is the original PHOTO-PAINT Emboss), a Glass filter, a Swirl filter, and a filter called Drop Shadow. (The Drop Shadow filter is different from the rest in that it comes with a free commercial every time you use it.)

Before You Begin

One of the things that makes the Black Box filters unique is that they require a Transparency mask before they can operate. So here is a brief procedure on how to prepare the image to be used with the Black Box filters.

1. Create a mask surrounding the image that is to have the filter applied to it. If it is text, use the Magic Wand and click on each letter. If it is an object against a background, hide all of the object except the part to be masked, use the Magic Wand tool, and then invert the mask to mask the object.

2. Select Create Transparency Mask from the Mask menu. When prompted by the next drop-down list, select From Mask.

3. When the Transparency Mask Creation dialog box appears, click OK and the Transparency Mask icon appears in the status bar in the lower-right corner. One item you may want to change is the Remove Mask checkbox. If this is checked (which it is by default), then the mask you just used to create the Transparency mask will be removed. If you want to keep the mask, then uncheck the box.

Corel *TIP!*

> If you are using the Drop Shadow filter, the Transparency mask will be lost when the filter is applied. Since there is no preview capability with these filters, I recommend that you temporarily save the Transparency mask before using it so that you can undo and reapply the Drop Shadow if necessary. This removal of the Transparency mask does not occur with the other three filters (The Boss, Glass, and Swirl).

Black Box Overview

All of the Black Box filters from Alien Skin have a few options in common, so I thought it best to discuss them now to save repeating them later on in the chapter.

Saving Preferences

One of the first things you will notice about these filters is that they have lots and lots of choices. This is both good news (lots of flexibility) and bad news (lots of decisions). To keep the selection process under control, there are preference sets. At the bottom of each filter's dialog box is a group of controls that allow you to load, save, and delete named sets of preferences.

Loading a Preference

To load a preference, click the arrow button to the right of the box under Preferences. This produces a drop-down list from which to select the preferences for that filter. Each filter comes with a set of commonly used preferences that act as starting points. Experiment with these settings to get a feel for some of the effects that can be achieved with a particular filter.

Saving a Preference

You can save a preference set by clicking the icon that looks like a camera after you have made the changes to the settings for the dialog box. After you click the camera, a dialog box (Figure 13.45) appears that allows you to name the preference set you are saving. From that point on, unless you remove it, the new preference will appear in the preference-set list. The name of the preference set can be up to 40 characters long, but you can only see the first 24 characters from the list. All saved preferences are added to the list alphabetically. Preferences are not saved globally; in other words, if I save a preference set in Emboss, I will not see it in the set that is available for the Drop Shadow filter.

Deleting a Preference

You can delete a preference set by selecting it in the Preference list and clicking on the trashcan icon. A dialog box appears, asking you if you really want to delete the preference set. Once a preference set is deleted, it cannot be retrieved. Think twice before eliminating these sets, since they take up almost no disk space.

Drop Shadow

Drop shadows are the things that graphics designers like to turn their nose up at, saying the effect is "overused" and a "cheap visual trick." You will probably find out that these same designers use drop shadows several times a week. Drop shadows are one of the most commonly used techniques for giving a three-dimensional quality to a flat surface, particularly text. The effect gives an object the appearance of floating above the surface of the document.

One of the things to remember when making a drop shadow is to select an object that already stands out from the background.

Figure 13.45.
The dialog box that
appears when Save
Preference Set is
selected by clicking on
the camera icon. It also
shows the author
needs to start listening
to some newer songs.

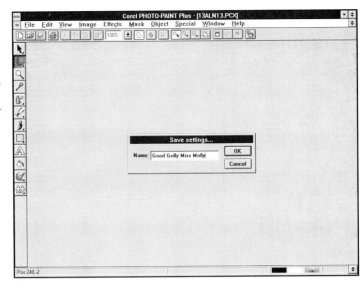

You will find the Drop Shadow filter under Alien Skin in the Effects Menu.
Clicking on Drop Shadow will open a dialog box (after the mini-commerical
splashscreen) as shown in Figure 13.46.

Figure 13.46.
Clicking on Drop
Shadow will open a
dialog box.

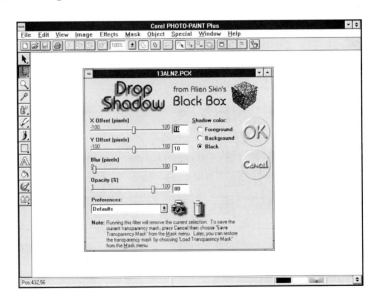

Drop Shadow Dialog Box Options

Shadow Placement

The X- and Y-Offset sliders let you control where the shadow falls in relation to the selection (masked object). The further the X-offset is to the right, the further the shadow will fall to the right. Likewise, the Y-offset controls how far down the shadow will fall toward the bottom of the image, based on how far to the right the slider is moved.

Blur

Blur is how soft the edges of the shadow appear. A blur of 0 usually results in an aliased sharp edge (that is, one with jaggies). It also creates a sharp shadow, which is indicative of harsh light and makes for distracting shadows. Large blur values make a shadow more subtle.

Opacity

Opacity is a measure of how solid the shadow appears. This operates exactly like the Opacity setting in the Objects/Layers roll-up. If Opacity is 100 percent, the shadow is solid and totally obscures any image that lies beneath it. The lower the opacity, the more the background detail can be seen through the shadow.

Shadow Color

You can specify the color of the shadow by using one of the three buttons in the dialog box. The choices are black, the current Paint (foreground) color, or the current Paper (background) color.

Figure 13.47.
The text example.

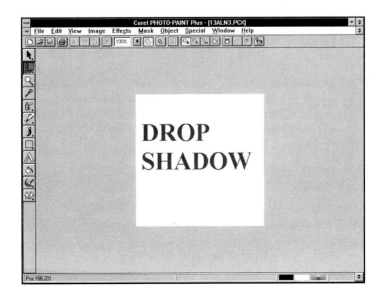

Figure 13.48.
The result of applying
the Drop Shadow filter
to the text, giving it the
appearance of floating
above the surface of the
paper.

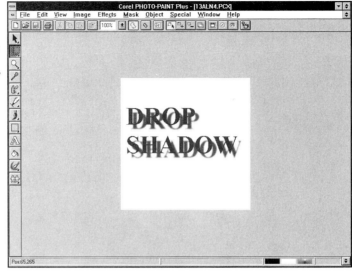

The Boss (Emboss)

The Emboss filter included with the Black Box set makes the selected area look as if it is pushed out of the image. The effect is achieved by putting what appears to be a slanted bevel around the selected area.

The Emboss is located in the Special category of the Effect menu. When included with Corel PHOTO-PAINT 5 Plus, it is called The Boss (so as not to create confusion with the original Emboss filter). This opens the Emboss dialog box as shown in Figure 13.49. Like the Drop Shadow, this filter does not have a preview box. Unlike the Drop Shadow, this filter does not delete the Transparency mask after it is applied. This means that you can apply it, look at it, undo it (if necessary) and then try, try again. While I would prefer a preview box, this beats having to recreate or reload the Transparency mask each time.

Corel *TIP!*

If you are going to apply the filter to the entire image, then select All from the Mask menu to quickly mask the image, and then create the Transparency mask from it.

Figure 13.49.
The Emboss dialog box. Although it lacks a preview function, it can still provide some very effective effects.

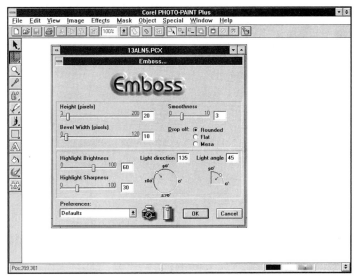

Corel *TIP!*

When applying Emboss to objects, you must mask the object. For example, in Figure 13.50, the text "The Boss" is an object. The first time Emboss was applied, the entire image was masked. There were no results, because the filter only saw the masked white background, not the object. The second time it was applied, the text was masked, which resulted in the Figure 13.51.

Figure 13.50.
This version was created using the default setting of the Emboss filter.

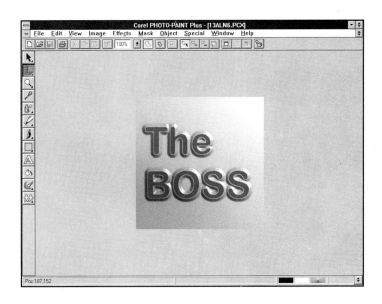

Figure 13.51.
This version was
created by masking the
text before the second
application of the filter.

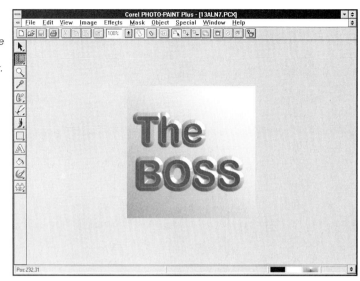

Emboss Dialog Box Controls

Bevel Shape

The controls at the top of the Emboss dialog box affect the shape of the bevel around the selection. The Height slider controls how far the selection pushes out of the screen toward the viewer. This is the primary way to control the amount of the 3-D effect. The Width slider controls how much of the image is taken up by the bevel. Be aware that the bevel grows around the area selected by the mask. Therefore, if it gets too wide or the objects selected are too close together, they will begin to merge into one another. Thin bevels appear steeper than wide ones, so this setting also controls the strength of the 3-D effect. Drop Off controls the general shape of the bevel. The default setting for Drop Off is Rounded, which has already been seen in Figure 13.50. The Flat bevel is slightly different and shown in Figure 13.51. Figure 13.52 shows the Mesa bevel.

Jeff really worked hard trying to work a compromise in the use of "aliasing" in both this filter and the Glass filter. The basis of the problem was that if there were no "jaggies," there would also be no sharp lines. So instead of deciding how much his filter would "melt" the bevel, he added a smoothing slider, so you can make the decision yourself. When Smoothing is set low, the edges will be sharper but little steps in the bevel will be more noticeable. In Figure 13.53, the Smoothing was set to 0, resulting in an almost chiseled appearance. When Smoothing is high, the edges will be more rounded, and it will look like your objects are floating on marshmallows, as shown in Figure 13.54.

Figure 13.52.
The Mesa bevel.

Figure 13.53.
The first version of the
text.

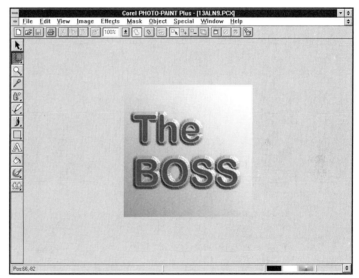

Highlight

The Highlight is the bright reflection of the light off the 3-D surface. The Highlight Brightness slider can make the highlight disappear at the lower settings, or it can wash out part of the image at the higher settings. The Highlight Sharpness slider lets you control how small and crisp the highlight is. Sharper highlights tend to make the surface look shinier or even wet. Dull highlights are more spread out and make the surface look chalky.

Figure 13.54.
The two figures are
identical except that
Figure 13.53 had a
Smoothing factor of 0
and Figure 13.54 had
a Smoothing factor
of 10.

The shape of the bevel interacts with the highlights. Sharper bevel corners (low width, high height, low smoothing) will make sharper highlights, so you will have to experiment to see how all these parameters combine to make the final 3-D effect.

Lighting Controls

You can control the direction that the sun or light source comes from using the Light Direction and Light Angle controls. High light angles light the selection from directly above the surface, which tends to cause lighting that is bright and even. Low light angles tend to make shadows stronger, thus accentuating the 3-D effect.

Making Plastic Letters with the Boss Filter

1. Make a Transparency mask of the text.

2. Invert the Transparency mask using the Invert Transparency Mask command in the Mask menu. (Don't use the Invert Mask button.)

3. Apply the Emboss filter with a Highlight Brightness and Sharpness setting of 75 or greater. When setting the lighting direction, remember that since the Transparency mask is inverted, it will result in the apparent light direction being reversed also.

4. Hide the text using the Layers/Objects roll-up, and remove the background (base image). This is an optional step since there will be very little applied to the base image. The result is shown in Figure 13.55.

Figure 13.55.
These are plastic letters made using the previously described technique. For a finishing touch, I added a light Radial fill background (white to 40 percent gray), and then I dusted it with 20 percent Uniform Noise. When doing this, make sure that the apparent source of your background matches the light direction applied to your characters.

Making Transparent Objects with the Boss Filter

This is an easy process. Emboss an object as previously described, select the object that was embossed with the Object Picker in the Toolbox, and move the Opacity slider in the Objects/Layers roll-up until the desired level of transparency is achieved. The letters in Figure 13.56 represent a Opacity setting of 20 percent.

Figure 13.56.
This shows how the Boss filter can be used to make transparent text.

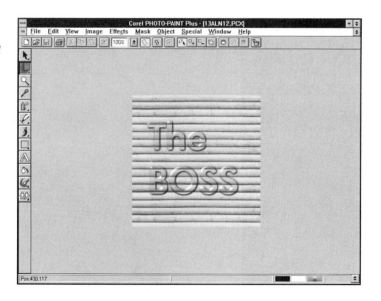

419

Corel *TIP!*

> Remember that you must have made a Transparency mask for the area to which the filter will be applied. The good news is that the Corel version of these filters does not remove the Transparency mask, so you can reuse it. The bad news is that this removal can drive you batty later on when you're wondering why the last fill or effect acted so oddly. So, when you are finished with the Transparency masks, remove them!

Glass

Unlike The Boss, the Glass filter does not make the underlying image look three-dimensional. Instead, the Glass filter seems to put a layer of glass on top of the image. Keep in mind that the sheet of glass is the three-dimensional part, while the image remains flat. The bevel of the glass is very similar to the bevel of the Boss filter. By adjusting the combination of light filtering, refraction, and high-lights, you can achieve some striking effects with this filter.

Like the previous filters, this filter requires a Transparency mask to do its job. The shape of the glass sheet is controlled by the shape of the Transparency mask. The top edge of the glass bevel occurs along the mask. Like the Boss filter, Feathering the transparency mask has no effect on this filter's operation.

Glass Filter Dialog Box Controls

The Glass filter dialog box is opened by selecting Glass in the Special category of the Effects menu. The dialog box is shown in Figure 13.57.

Bevel Shapes and Highlights

The Bevel and the Highlights operate identically to the Emboss filter's Bevel and Highlights. See the description of these in the preceding discussion of the Emboss filter.

Refraction

The most striking 3-D effect of the Glass filter is refraction. When the direction of light rays is changed (bent) as a result of passing through a material such as glass, water, etc., it is called refraction. Since here we are looking directly at the glass sheet, refraction only occurs at the bevel edges. You control how much the light rays are bent using the Refraction slider.

Figure 13.57.
The Glass filter dialog
box has many controls
in common with the
Emboss Filter.

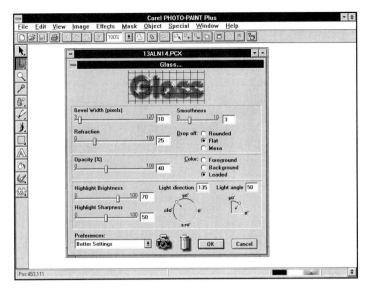

Corel *TIP!*

> To make the refraction effect more noticeable, try using a wider bevel. This will
> increase the area of glass that does not directly face the viewer.

Opacity

Colored glass filters light, and it filters it more where the material (the glass) is
thicker. Therefore, when you have a non-zero opacity and non-white filter color,
Glass will filter the light the strongest in the masked area and the least where
the glass is thin in the bevel region. The higher the Opacity setting, the stronger
the underlying setting will be tinted to look like the glass color.

Glass Color

The glass can be the Paint (foreground) color, the Paper (background) color, or
leaded. Leaded is really the same as dark gray, but it makes it somehow seem a
little more "real" to call it leaded. Dark glass colors the underlying image
stronger than light glass does, so if you are experiencing difficulty in getting a
noticeable glass effect, try darkening the glass color.

Lighting Controls

You can control the direction from which the sun comes by using the Light
Direction and Light Angle control. High light angles illuminate the selection
from directly above the surface, which tends to cause lighting that is bright and

even. Low light angles tend to make shadows stronger, thus accentuating the 3-D effect.

Figure 13.58.
Figures 13.58 and 13.59 show the effect of applying the glass filter on text with different Bevel Width settings.

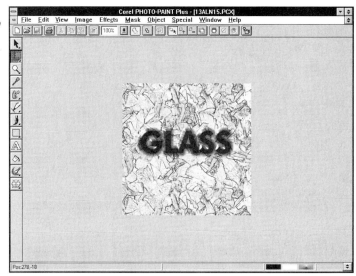

Figure 13.59.
An additional version.

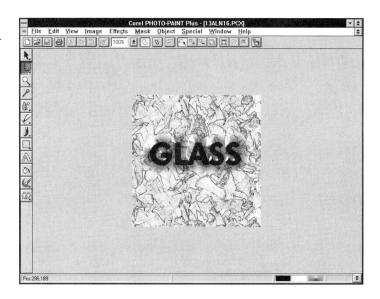

Corel *TIP!*

I have found most of the default or preference-set settings to be way too large for Bevel Width and Refraction. The text in Figures 13.58 and 13.59 was changed from a Refraction of 80 to 25 and from a Bevel Width of 20 to a setting of 10.

Swirl

I have referred to the Swirl filter as a poor man's Terrazzo. (I have also called it the Smear tool on steroids, which may be a more accurate description.) Since Terrazzo is now part of this release, one would assume that there is no need for this filter. That is not quite true. Instead of making tiles, the Swirl filter does a blender operation on the selected area and creates some nice textures for use as backgrounds. In the manual that comes with the Black Box filters, Jeff Butterworth states, "We just couldn't resist throwing in something fun. Swirl uses state-of-the-art scientific visualization techniques for examining complex fluid simulations. This technique smears the image along artificial fluid streamlines."

The Swirl filter is located in the Special subgroup within the Effects menu. By clicking on Swirl, you open the Swirl Filter dialog box as shown in Figure 13.60.

Figure 13.60.
The Swirl Filter dialog box.

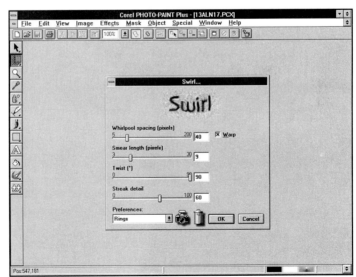

Corel *TIP!*

> This is the only Alien Skin filter in Corel PHOTO-PAINT 5 Plus that does not require a Transparency mask to operate.

Whirlpool Spacing

All you really need to understand about Swirl is that it randomly places whirl-pools in the selection and then smears the selected area with them. The Whirl-pool Spacing slider controls approximately how far apart these whirlpools are from one another. A large spacing setting creates more of a "painterly" effect. Smaller settings make the whirlpools close together and create effects that are reminiscent of the 1960s.

Smear Length

Smear Length controls how much the underlying image is blurred. Low values create noisy results, while large settings create smoother results. This is the one setting that has the greatest effect on how long the filter will take to process the image. A longer Smear Length setting results in longer processing time.

Whirlpools Versus Fountains

The Twist slider controls whether the flows flow *around* the whirlpools or *out* of the whirlpools. Twist angles near 0 degrees make the whirlpools act more like fountains, because the fluid flows outward in a star-like pattern. Twist angles approaching 90 degrees flow around in rings.

Streak Detail

Swirl is a form of blurring, so it can remove detail from your image or make your image altogether unrecognizable. To recover some of the image detail, increase the setting of Streak Detail.

Warp

When the Warp toggle is on, the simulated fluid stretches the image "down-stream" along the stream lines. Warping makes the swirl effect more striking, but it may not be desirable if you want the original image to remain recogniz-able. Turning the Warp toggle off causes smearing without moving the under-lying image.

Creating Strange New Worlds with Swirl

When I first got the Swirl filter (without documentation), I discovered a fun thing to do with it. I thought you might enjoy it too. Here goes:

1. Create a new image and, holding down the Ctrl key, use the Circle Mask tool to make a circle that almost fills your image area.

2. Using the Fill roll-up, fill the circle with a Radial fill (60 percent to 10 percent), and offset the lighter spot so that it is in the upper left of the circle.

Figure 13.61.
This is a basic sphere,
which is one of the
most important
ingredients when
making a planet.

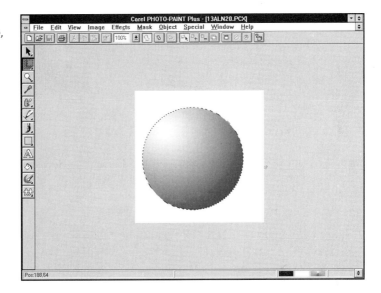

3. Copy the contents of the circle to the clipboard using the Copy button in the ribbon bar. The sphere we just made will still be there.

4. "Dust" the sphere with 30 percent Uniform Noise. This gives our planet some texture for the Swirl filter to grab on to. Your image should look like Figure 13.62.

5. Apply the Swirl filter (default setting). You should now have something that looks like Figure 13.63.

6. Apply Map To Sphere (in the Mapping category of the Effect menu) with a setting of between 20 and 30. The setting for your planet will vary with the size of the image you are making. Watch the preview window on Map To Sphere. You want it to look like a sphere without too much distortion. Be warned that the preview in Map To Sphere leaves a lot to be desired.

7. Click on the Paste button and your original copy of the circle will appear on the scene slightly offset. Grab it with the Object Picker and move it so it

is directly on top of the "swirled" planet. Did you notice that you cannot see your swirled planet anymore? Not to worry.

Figure 13.62.
Using the Uniform
Noise filter, we have
"dusted" our sphere.

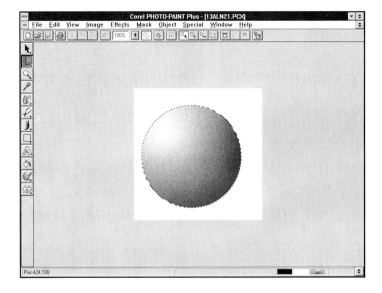

Figure 13.63.
Now our little planet is
coming to life. We still
need to add a few more
touches to make it a
new planet.

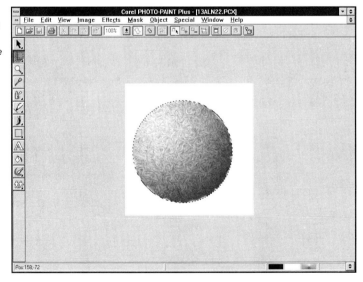

8. In the Object/Layers roll-up, select Texturize in the Merge Mode drop-down list. This will only allow the darker portions of our pasted object to show through, resulting in Figure 13.64.

*Figure 13.64.
With the help of several filters we now
have a dark side to
our little planet.*

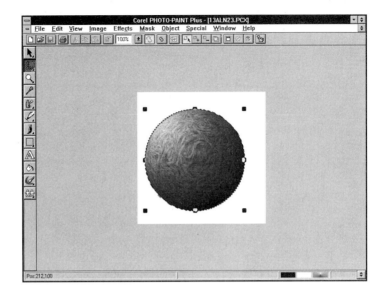

9. After it looks like Figure 13.64, merge the object. Invert the original mask using the Mask Invert command in the Mask menu.

10. Open the Texture Bitmap fill in the Fill roll-up and select Night Sky in the Samples 5 library. Using the Flood Fill tool, fill in the background as shown in Figure 13.65.

*Figure 13.65.
One genuine brand-
new world—and it only
took ten steps.*

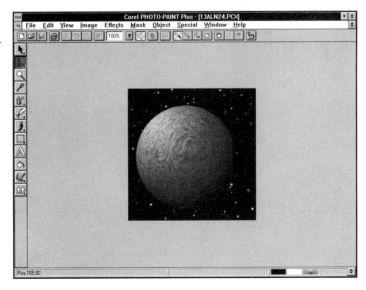

That's all there is to it. (Beam me up, Scotty.) However, if you don't have the maintenance release of PHOTO-PAINT 5, then you may not have the Samples 5 library. And if the image you are working on is too small, your night sky may be a little too much night and too little stars. To correct that, simply click the Edit button in the Fill roll-up and change the # of Spots setting to 400, the Max Height percentage to 10 percent, and the Max Width setting to 4 percent.

Floating Objects

This has nothing to do with pollution. It is about 50 common ordinary items that are produced by a wonderful little company called CMCD. Corel went through the CMCD library of objects that were photographed against a white background and selected 50 of them to be included in the PHOTO-PAINT 5 Plus release.

I had already used the CMCD objects before. They have six libraries of around 100-plus objects on each CD. Corel took these photographs and converted them into objects, saving them as .CPT files. This means that you can use them just like clip art. Need a picture of a boot? Then all you have to do is open the image called BOOT.CPT, grab the boot object, and drag it into your existing picture. There is a better way, but you have to be aware of the following process or it will make you think that you broke something.

Since these are .CPT files, I can bring them into an existing image by using the little-talked-about Paste From File command in the Edit menu. All you need do is select Paste From File, and when it asks for the name of the file, locate the COREL50\OBJECTS directory and select the object you want. The preview window shows you what it looks like before you load it. After you have selected the object, click the OK button and the objects are pasted into your image as objects. Objects? I thought we wanted an Object (as in singular). Here is the tricky part. All of the floating objects consists of two parts: the object that you want, and a white background object. The first time the white background fell into my existing image, I thought I had lost part of my image somehow. To get rid of the white background, select it with the Object Picker and either select Delete Object from the Object menu or use the Delete key.

Seamless Tiles

Now I know that new seamless tiles may sound as interesting as five pounds of fertilizer, but these tiles are a lot more exciting than you might first expect. Seamless tiles are used to create canvases and fills in PHOTO-PAINT. A company called Artbeats was the source for 25 of the marbled paper and marble seamless tiles. I have their Marble and Granite collection, and their tiles were made from high-resolution photographs of real marble and marbled paper. So these are not your average look-what-we-scanned-in-today Kodak moments. The photographs were scanned on a drum scanner and are incredible.

Visual Reality has provided a large selection of seamless images as well. The PHOTO-PAINT 5 Plus version now has a large assortment of tiles to choose from.

14

Editing and Retouching Tools

This chapter examines the tools that are used to edit and retouch images. Several of the tools referenced in this chapter accomplish filter functions and menu commands already discussed in previous chapters. These tools enable you to apply the filter functions selectively to small areas to achieve effects such as increasing contrast in a small part of an image or removing a shadow. By using these tools, you will also be able to access quickly some commands and functions without going through multiple menus and drop-down lists.

The Eyedropper Tool

The first tool we are going to talk about has been mentioned before, but now we will explore it in depth. It is the Eyedropper tool, and it is not part of a flyout.

The Eyedropper tool is used to pick a specific color from an image by clicking on it. This tool has more uses than might first be apparent. For instance, while the Eyedropper tool is active, the color value of the pixel under the cursor is displayed in the status bar. I'll explain the usefulness of this in a moment. First let's go through the basics of how to use the Eyedropper.

The are three color areas that can be picked using the Eyedropper tool: the paint color, the paper color, and the fill color.

> To select the paint (foreground) color, click on the desired color with the left mouse button.

> To select the paper (background) color, click on the desired color with either mouse button while holding down the Ctrl key.

> To select the fill color, click the right mouse button or click the left mouse button while holding down the Shift key.

To temporarily select the Eyedropper tool without leaving your currently selected tool, hold down the E key. This turns the cursor into an Eyedropper as long as the E key is held down. (All of the key combinations just described work with the E key; although, you may feel like you are playing the keyboard version of Twister when selecting the background color.)

Corel *TIP!*

> The E key shortcut is a quick way to get a numerical color value for a spot or area. This information is very helpful when setting Color Comparison Tolerance values.

The Eyedropper Tool Settings Roll-Up (Ctrl+F8)

This roll-up first appeared in the E2 Maintenance release. It is used to set the sample size of the Eyedropper tool. With the Eyedropper tool selected, select the Tool Settings roll-up in the View menu, or enter Ctrl+F8. The roll-up shown in Figure 14.1 has three preset sample sizes—1 pixel (1×1, or Point), which is the default setting; 9 pixels (3×3); and 25 pixels (5×5)—as well as the Custom Area setting. The Custom Area setting enables you to use the Eyedropper tool to define any size sample area.

With every sample size (except 1×1), the color selected when the mouse button is clicked represents the average of all the colors in the sample area. Obviously with the 1×1 setting, it represents the color value of the single pixel underneath the cursor. Be aware when using samples larger than the default setting of 1 pixel on areas of high contrast that the averaged color may be different than any individual color in the sampled area. The settings made in the Tool Settings roll-up only effect the Eyedropper tool, and they have no effect on other tools that may use an Eyedropper to define colors, such as Color Mask.

Figure 14.1.
The Tool Setting roll-up for the Eyedropper tool with the drop-down list open. This roll-up, which was introduced with the "B" version of PHOTO-PAINT, gives the user even greater flexibility when doing retouching.

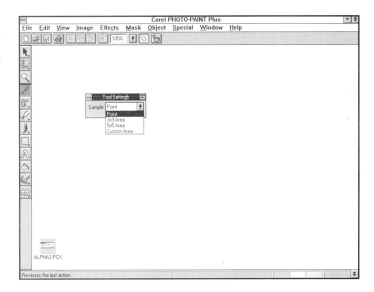

Notes on Using the Eyedropper Tool

If there are multiple objects on the image, the Eyedropper tool can only read the colors on the top object. Good rule of thumb: If you can't see it, the Eyedropper can't see it either.

When a large area is sampled and averaged, the result may be a color that, while representing the average color in the image, may not exist in the image. An example of this would be an area that had the same number of white and red pixels. The resulting color would be pink, even though there was no pink in the image.

Use the Eyedropper quick key (E) when you want to see what the color value(s) are for a part of the image to help set the Color Comparison Tolerance Values. Remember that the E key (or any other key or tool for that matter) doesn't work when the Color Comparison Tolerance Values dialog box is open. Thus it is best to check color values before opening the dialog box. An example of using this is when determining where a Magic Wand mask in an image is to be created. I use the quick E key to see what the color value is of the starting area (where I click to start the mask).

Corel *TIP!*

Use the quick key (E) when retouching images. It provides a quick and easy way to pick up adjoining colors, which is critical when touching up an imperfection on a picture of someone's face.

The following three tools are located together on the same flyout: **Local Undo, Color Replacer**, and the **Eraser** tool.

The Local Undo Tool

The Local Undo tool enables you to paint over areas where you wish to undo the last action performed by the previously used paint tool. There are two reasons to use this tool: to correct a mistake, or to create an effect.

Holding down the Ctrl key while using the Local Undo tool constrains the movements of the tool to the horizontal or vertical. Depressing the Shift key changes the direction of constraint. The shape, size, rotation, and flatten characteristics of the Local Undo tool are determined by the Tool Settings roll-up (Ctrl+F8). See Figure 14.2.

Figure 14.2
The Tool Settings roll-up.

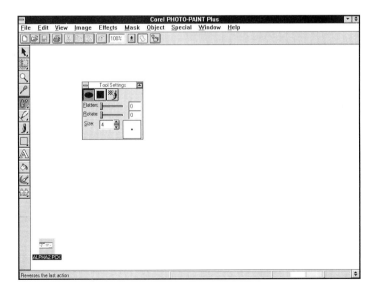

Local Undo Tool Setting Roll-Up Options

Shape buttons	Sets the shape of the brush. The three selections are Round, Square, and Custom brush. If you select Custom brush, a thumbnail of the brush is displayed as a button. To select one of the custom brushes, click on the button.
Delete Brush	You can delete a custom brush by clicking on the brush button and then clicking the Delete Brush button.
Flatten	If you select the Round or Square brush button, you can flatten the brush using the Flatten slider.
Rotate	Rotates either a Round or Square brush by the amount entered.
Size	Changes the size of either a Round or Square brush. The size of the brush is displayed in the preview box.

- The Transparency of the Local Undo function is fixed at 0 percent.
- Double-clicking the Local Undo tool button acts the same as the Ctrl+Z keyboard command—that is, it toggles the Undo/Redo function for the entire image or selected area.

Corel *TIP!*

> The Local Undo tool only works on fill and paintbrush applications. It does not partially undo filter effects or object merges.

Notes on Using the Local Undo Tool

The Local Undo tool is very useful for removing part of whatever effect was last applied. Many times a filter will effect more of the image than was desired. By using the Local Undo tool, it is simple to remove "extra" effects.

The Local Undo tool can also be used for effects. The image in Figure 14.3 was created by placing the brick bitmap flood fill over the Photo-CD image of the building. Then using the Local Undo tool (Square brush), some bricks of the flood fill were removed to give the appearance of looking through a hole in a brick wall. The whole image took less than three minutes to complete.

Local Undo only operates on the last effect or last paint that was applied, so exercise care to ensure that additional steps are not unintentionally performed either before or while the Local Undo tool is being used.

Figure 14.3.
A hole-in-the-wall image was created by applying a brick bitmap fill over the photo and then using the Local Undo Tool to selectively remove parts of it. This was a real "quickie" job (less than five minutes). To make it work effectively you use the Tool Settings roll-up to make the brush size the same as the brick.

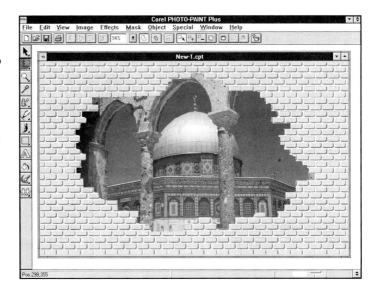

The Eraser Tool

Big secret: The Eraser tool doesn't erase anything. Instead, the Eraser tool paints over the image with the current paper color. Remember that the way PHOTO-PAINT and all other bitmap editing programs operate paints, they don't cover each pixel with a color but rather replace an existing color with a new color. This has the desired effect of "erasing" the image underneath it.

Hold down the Ctrl key to constrain the Eraser tool to horizontal/vertical movements and hold down the Shift key to change the direction of constraint. The size and shape of the Eraser tool is set from the Tool Settings roll-up in the View menu. Transparency of the Eraser Tool is fixed at 0 percent, and there is no fade available. When the Eraser tool is applied to an object, only the object is effected—the image under the object remains unchanged. The rule remains: If you can't see it, PHOTO-PAINT cannot affect it.

The Color Replacer Tool

The Color Replacer tool replaces a range of colors using the current paint (foreground) color as the reference point with the paper (background) color. The advantage of the Color Replacer tool is that it can be applied selectively to an area of an image.

The size and shape of the Color Replacer tool is set from the Tool Settings roll-up in the View menu (Ctrl+F8). Transparency of the Color Replacer tool is fixed at 0 percent, and there is no fade available. Holding down the Ctrl key constrains the tool to horizontal/vertical movements. Holding down the Shift key changes the direction of constraint. Double-clicking the Color Replacer tool will cause a color replacement for the entire image.

Notes on Using the Color Replacer Tool

While this is a useful tool to selectively go into an image area and replace one color with another, be careful in using it. Remember that this tool replaces a range of colors (the range of colors selected is determined by the setting in Color Tolerance) with a single color. Unless the image you are working on is composed of solid colors or a limited number of shades, it is difficult to get all of the shades correctly matched and replaced. If it is your desire to change the color of an object that is composed of many shades of color, you may want to use the Hue tool instead.

Although the color of paint (foreground) to be replaced can be selected from the Color roll-up, a more accurate (and practical) way is to use the Eyedropper to pick out the exact color that needs to be replaced. To date I can't recall someone ever giving me a project and saying, "Please replace all of the TRUMATCH 10-b2 with 11-a." That doesn't happen in real life.

As said before, the range of colors that will be replaced is determined by the Color Comparison Tolerance setting in the Special menu. A greater number of shades increases the colors that are replaced by the Color Replacer tool. You could think of it as a quick color-mask/paintbrush combination.

So what can you do with this tool? Good question. I really had to scratch my head on this one. It makes great silhouettes, and it does a nice but limited job of posterization. Other than that, I couldn't really figure out any eye-popping applications for this one. (We are both on CompuServe, so if you find an application for this tool, please send us a message.)

Freehand Editing Tools

The next nine tools constitute the freehand editing tools and are on their own flyout. The effects of the first five of the nine tools can also be applied through various menu commands. These are *Contrast*, *Brighten*, *Sharpen*, *Hue* and *Saturation*. The remaining four tools—*Tint*, *Blend*, *Smear*, and *Smudge*—are unique to the Toolbox and not available elsewhere in PHOTO-PAINT. We will explore these tools in the order they appear on the flyout, beginning with the Smear tool.

However, before we can do anything worthwhile with the Editing tools, we need to review some tools and techniques that will make your photo-editing and photo-touchup work more productive.

Most work in photo-manipulation requires the ability to zoom in real close to catch some fine detail in the work. Corel has provided some excellent tools that give us the ability to zoom in and zoom out quickly; they have also provided a means that lets us zoom in and remain zoomed in until we are finished. Let's review these magnification tools as they would be used with the freehand editing tools. The three tools are the Zoom tool, the Hand tool, and the Locator tool.

We'll examine an actual job. The photo in Figure 14.4 is one we received to make a brochure for a gospel singer in Houston named Kenny Rodgers. Like most photos we receive, it needed a little touch-up after it was scanned. After it was scanned in, we applied a 100-percent Adaptive Unsharp mask to it, which made the soft fuzzy images (which photo studios love to create) a little sharper. Also notice that some white spots appear on Kenny's coat. They were always there—the Unsharp filter just made them more obvious. (See Figure 14.5.)

Figure 14.4.
The original photo-
graph as it was
scanned.

The first thing we are going to do to illustrate the use of the tools is to show how we would approach the removal of the bright shiny spot on his forehead.

After selecting the appropriate editing tool, holding down the "Z" key transforms the selected tool cursor into a Magnifying glass cursor. While still holding down the Z key, click and drag a rectangle area over the area to be edited. Release the mouse button and the Z key, and after a few moments the image has been zoomed in 440 percent, as shown in Figure 14.6

Figure 14.5.
By applying the
Unsharp Mask filter we
are able to make it
appear a little more in
focus, but at the same
time all of the dust and
scratches have also
been enhanced.

Figure 14.6.
Now that we have
zoomed in this close it
is difficult to see any
effects we are produc-
ing. Not to worry, there
is a solution.

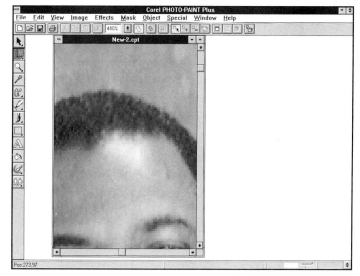

Corel *TIP!*

> You can zoom in or out with the Z key depressed. Each *left* mouse click zooms *in*
> 100 percent while the Z is held down. Each *right* mouse click zooms *out* 100
> percent while the Z is held down.

The great part about being close is that you can see precisely what you are doing. The problem with being this close is that you can't see what you are doing to the image as a whole. To see what you are doing both close-up and far away, select the Duplicate command in the Windows menu. A duplicate of the zoomed image appears. It probably won't look as nicely laid out as mine does in Figure 14.7, so click on Tile Vertically in the Windows menu. Hey, where did the spot go? Sorry, I got a little ahead on myself and removed it already. Don't worry about how we did it. Like summer reruns, it will appear again when we are talking about the Smear and Smudge brushes. Let's move a short distance to the glare on the singer's nose.

Figure 14.7.
Now with the duplicate
window open we can
see the changes we
make in perspective.

The best way to move short distances is not the scroll bars. To move short distances, hold down the "H" key and the cursor becomes a hand. Isn't that handy? (Sorry about the pun.) While still holding down the H key, click and drag the cursor. It is as if the hand were attached to the image, and it will move in the direction you drag it. It is a lot faster than the scroll bars. OK, so much for short-distance work, about the long haul? See that white spot on Kenny's suit? We could try and move down there with our Hand tool, or zoom out and zoom in again. You know that's not the answer, don't you? Click on the duplicate image to make it active. Hold down the "L" key and the cursor becomes a cross hair. Click on the white spot, and the zoomed-in image is now centered on that spot. When you release the L key, the Locator tool is no longer active, but you must click on the zoomed-in image one time to make it active.

To recap: Use the Z key to zoom in or out of an area without needing to change tools. You can watch the effect of your close-up work on a 100 percent image by selecting Duplicate in the Window menu. Use the H key (the Hand tool) to move short distances rapidly and the L key (the Locator tool) to move to another part of the image without changing the zoom ratio.

The Smear Tool

The Smear tool smears colors. The same tool in Adobe Photoshop is called Smudge (which can get confusing, because there is a Smudge tool in PHOTO-PAINT). The smudge tool is covered later in this chapter.The Smear tool spreads colors in a picture, producing an effect similar to dragging your finger through wet oil paint. The size and shape of the Smear tool is set from the Tool Settings roll-up in the View menu. Use the Ctrl key to constrain the tool to a vertical or horizontal direction. Pressing the Shift key changes the direction of constraint. Use the Smear tool Settings roll-up to change shape, size, spacing, transparency, density, fade out and edge.

Figure 14.8.
The Smear Tool
Settings dialog box.

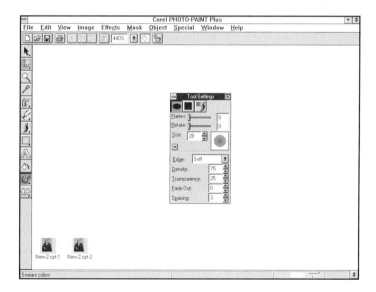

Smear Tool Settings Roll-Up Options

Shape Buttons   Sets the shape of the Smear tool. The three available shape choices are Round, Square, and Custom. If Custom is chosen, a different dialog box appears and the outline image of the currently selected custom Smear tool shape appears as the cursor.

Flatten	The Flatten slider controls the height of the Round and Square tool. Values are in percentages of height. You can see the effect of the flattening in the preview window as the change is being applied. The Flatten control does not affect the custom Smear tool.
Rotate	Rotates the Round or Square Smear tool by the amount entered. You can see the effect of the rotation in the preview window as the change is being applied. The Rotate control does not affect the Custom Smear tool. Value is in degrees, up to a maximum of 180 degrees. Obviously, rotating a standard Round Smear tool serves no purpose, but rotating a flattened Round Smear tool does.
Size	Allows adjustment of Round or Square Smear tool size from 0 to 100. The size of the Smear tool selected is shown in the preview box. The size of the Custom Smear tool is not adjustable.
Edge	Sets the edges of the Smear tool to Hard, Medium, or Soft. Soft edges make the Smear tool's stroke the least dense at the edges. Hard edges are dense up to the edge, with little to no softening, depending on the Smear tool size and other Smear tool settings. The preview box displays the edge selected. The edge has no effect on the Custom Smear tool, even though the text is not grayed out.

Corel *TIP!*

You can only see real differences in this setting when the Density is below 80 and the Transparency is at least 45 to 50.

Density	This control sets the overall density of coverage from the center of the Smear tool stroke through the edges. A low density is like applying a small amount of pressure to a brush—the resulting stroke is dense in the center and lighter towards the edges. High density is the equivalent to pressing the brush hard against the paper. This produces uniform density (a smear effect) across the entire stroke. The result is that the Density and Transparency values interact with one another. The Edge setting also has an effect

on these two, but it is only slight. When this setting gets above 80 or more, Edge has little to no effect. Density controls how solid the Smear tool is, beginning at the center. The overall softness of the Smear tool is controlled by the settings of the density values. The lower the number of density, the finer the Smear tool with smaller, softer edges of the smearing. The higher the value of density, the greater the smearing (density) throughout the width of the Smear tool, resulting in a bolder stroke.

Transparency Sets the level of transparency of the Smear tool. It is similar to adjusting the amount of water mixed with watercolors. The higher the setting, the more transparent the smear. At a very high setting, the smear is very faint. A setting of 0 creates the maximum smear effect and setting the Smear tool to 100 makes the smear action invisible, regardless of any other settings.

Fade Out This setting determines the length of the Smear tool before it fades entirely by adjusting the rate at which the smear effect disappears. This is similar to adjusting the pressure of the brush against the canvas as the paint is applied. The greater the Fade Out value, the more fade out is applied and the quicker the fade out of the Smear tool occurs. As the Fade Out value decreases, the amount of fade out applied to the Smear tool stroke diminishes, until the value of 0, which turns off the Fade Out function completely.

Fade Out works by counting the number of Smear tool applications to determine when to begin applying the gradual fade-out function. This is important. Spacing, the next parameter, controls the distance between Smear tool applications. Increasing the spacing between smear applications increases the distance that the Smear tool will go before the fade out begins.

Corel *TIP!*

Spacing effects Fade Out. Increases in the Spacing value increase the distance before fade out occurs.

Spacing

Sets the distance, in pixels, between applications of the Smear tool. To create the smear effect, the pointing device draws a line across the image. At a frequency determined by the Spacing setting, the Smear tool is applied to the line. For example, if a smear is made with a setting of 5 pixels, PAINT will produce the selected smear effect on the image area at a spacing of every 5 pixels. While it may seem that a setting of 1 would be desired, a lower setting slows down the generation of the Smear tool considerably. When a large Smear tool is being used, the setting can be larger because of the overlap caused by the larger Smear tool. Too large of a setting causes the gaps between applications of the Smear tool.

Working with the Smear Tool

The purpose of this tool is to smear colors. I know I said that before, but it's worth repeating, because many first-time users of PHOTO-PAINT misuse the Smear tool—to soften color transitions. That is the purpose of the Blur tool. Think of it this way: The results of using the Smear tool are not that much different from finger painting (except you don't have to wash your hands after you're done).

Corel *TIP!*

Make a practice of using the Checkpoint command (which makes a temporary copy of the image that can be quickly restored) before you begin application of the Smear tool or any other freehand editing tool.

Have the Smear Tool Settings roll-up open when you work with this tool. For retouching, Density/Transparency should be adjusted to produce the greatest effect without being obvious. Remember that a lower density setting causes the edges of the Smear tool to appear more feathered, which is desirable for most Smear tool applications. Fade Out and Spacing are not the critical settings. That said, you might want to play with the Fade Out settings for applications where you do not want the effect to end abruptly. The effect of the Smear tool is additive. Every time you apply it to the image, it will smear the pixels, no matter how many times you apply it. For retouching, you may end up "scrubbing" the area with the tool to get the effect desired. When retouching a photo, you do not want a solid color after you are done—you need to have texture for the subject to look real (and also to make the subject look like it is in focus). I will explain this in more detail later.

Corel *TIP!*

If you start the Smear tool well off of the image, it pulls white pixels unto the image. This can be used to give the brush-stroke effect on the edge.

The last application of the tool can be removed with the Undo command (Ctrl+Z), provided it was applied with one continuous stroke without letting go of the mouse button.

If you must be zoomed in at great magnification to do your work, keep a duplicate window open to a lower zoom value so you can see the effect in perspective.

Using the Smear to Do Touch-Up

I am going to use the Smear tool on our friend Kenny in order to smear the glare on top of his head. Again, the purpose of this tool is to smear colors. I am going to smear the colors from around the patch of glare on his head into the glare spot. (There are several other ways to do this, which I will show you later on in the chapter. I choose this method in order to demonstrate this tool and another tool with it.) Using a Density setting of 40 and a Transparency of 30, I dragged the color from around the patch of glare (including the hair) until the glare is gone, as shown in Figure 14.9. Great—the glare is gone, but what is left has no texture. While the picture looks fine, if this picture was blown up to make a poster, it would look like scar tissue. Thus we will take care of the smoothness with the next tool.

Figure 14.9.
We have toned down, but not completely removed the glare on his forehead. The smear tool is more effective for this type of work since if we used the Clone tool we would lose the highlights on the forehead, which would make the final photo look flat.

Corel *TIP!*

> Never count on an image being small enough to cover the sins of touch-up. With all of the fancy equipment in the world today, it is too easy for people to get their photo blown up to poster size, and that is when they get real touchy about your touch-up work.

The Smudge Tool

Maybe it is just me, but the first time I began exploring the freehand editing tools, I thought Smear and Smudge sounded like they did the same thing. The Smudge tool in PHOTO-PAINT is different from the tool with the same name in Adobe Photoshop. As it turns out, the Smudge tool adds texture by randomly mixing dots in a selected area. It is like a can of spray paint that sucks up color from the area that it is currently over and then sprays it back onto the subject. I am not aware of any equivalent of this tool in Photoshop.

The size and shape of the Smudge tool is set from the Tool Settings roll-up in the View menu. Use the Ctrl key to constrain the tool to a vertical or horizontal direction. Pressing the Shift key changes the direction of constraint.

The Smudge Tool Setting roll-up is identical to the Smear tool with one exception. Smudge uses Rate of Flow in place of Spacing.

Smudge Tool Settings Roll-Up Options

Shape Buttons	Sets the shape of the Smudge tool. The three available shape choices are Round, Square, and Custom. If Custom is chosen, a different dialog box appears, and the outline image of the currently selected custom Smudge tool shape appears as the cursor.
Flatten	The Flatten slider controls the height of the Round and Square tools. Values are expressed in percentages of height. You can see the effect of the flattening in the preview window as the change is being applied. The Flatten control does not affect the custom Smudge tool.
Rotate	Rotates the Round or Square Smudge tool by the amount entered. You can see the effect of the rotation in the preview window as the change is being applied. The Rotate control does not affect the Custom Smudge tool. The value is expressed in degrees, up to a maximum of 180 degrees. Rotating a standard

Round Smudge tool serves no purpose, but rotating a flattened Round Smudge tool does.

Size   Allows adjustment of Round or Square Smudge tool size from 0 to 100 pixels. The size of the Smudge tool selected is shown in the preview box. The size of the Custom Smudge tool is not adjustable.

Edge   Sets the edges of the Smudge tool to Hard, Medium or Soft. Soft edges make the Smudge tool stroke the least dense at the edges. Hard edges are dense up to the edge, with little to no softening, depending on Smudge tool size and other Smudge tool settings. The preview box displays the edge selected. The edge has no effect on the Custom Smudge tool, even though the text is not grayed out.

Rate of Flow   This setting is in place of the Spacing setting for the other brushes and acts like the Rate of Flow setting for the Airbrush/Spraycan tools. It determines how fast the color is placed on the image. A rate of flow of 0 causes the color to flow very slowly; therefore, to create dense color, the tool has to be held at the same location for a longer period.

Notes on Using the Smudge Tool

The Smudge tool adds texture, the Smear tool removes it. I will explain. Whenever you use the Smear tool, you end up with these wonderfully smeared pixels. If you have been working on a photograph that has any tonal range to it, you have pixels that may be similar in color, but they are not smeared.

Corel *TIP!*

> Make a practice of using the Checkpoint command (makes a temporary copy of the image that can be quickly restored) before you begin application of the Smudge tool.

The effect of the Smudge tool is additive. As long as you hold the button down, the effect is being applied, *even if the brush is not moving.*

Any application of the tool can be removed with the Undo command (Ctrl+Z), as long as it was applied with one continuous stroke without letting go of the mouse button. If you must be zoomed in at great magnification to do your work, keep a duplicate window open to a lower zoom value so you can see the effect in perspective.

Corel *TIP!*

One of the little known advantages of texture in a photo is that it gives the illusion of being in sharper focus. Professionals sometimes add a little noise to a "soft" photograph to give it a sharper look.

Using the Smudge Tool for Touch-Up

Remember the smooth spot on Kenny's head? This is a place where the application of the smudge tool adds some of the texture that the Smear tool removes. In this case, we added just a little texture. It still stands out too much, but that can be corrected with the Blend tool.

Corel *TIP!*

Always remember when working with the Smudge tool that it acts like a airbrush/spraycan brush. That means that you do not need to drag it across the image unless you have a high Rate of Flow setting. Just put it over the area you want hold down the mouse button until you get the effect you want.

The Sharpen Tool

The Sharpen tool sharpens selected areas of the image by increasing the contrast between neighboring pixels. It operates in the same manner as the Sharpen filter except that it can be applied without the need to create masks. The size and shape of the Sharpen tool is set from the Tool Settings roll-up in the View menu.

Use the Ctrl key to constrain the tool to a vertical or horizontal direction. Pressing the Shift key changes the direction of constraint.

Sharpen Tool Settings Roll-Up Options

Shape Buttons — Sets the shape of the Sharpen tool. The three available shapes are Round, Square and Custom. If Custom, is chosen a different dialog box appears and the outline image of the currently selected custom Sharpen tool shape appears as the cursor.

Flatten — The Flatten slider controls the height of the Round and Square tools. Values are in percentages of height. You can see the effect of the flattening in the preview

	window as the change is being applied. The Flatten control does not affect the Custom Sharpen tool.
Rotate	Rotates the Round or Square Sharpen tool by the amount entered. You can see the effect of the rotation in the preview window as the change is being applied. The Rotate control does not affect the custom Sharpen tool. The value is in degrees, up to a maximum of 180 degrees. Rotating a standard Round Sharpen tool serves no purpose, but rotating a flattened Round Sharpen tool does.
Size	Allows adjustment of Round or Square Sharpen tool size from 0 to 100 pixels. The size of the Sharpen tool selected is shown in the Preview box. The size of the Custom Sharpen tool is not adjustable.
Sharpen	Sets the amount of sharpening. Enter a number in the Sharpen box or drag the slider. The greater the amount of sharpening desired, the greater the percentage entered. Visually it appears that as the amount of sharpening increases, the slider approaches the sharp point of the graphic.

Notes on Using the Sharpen Tool

Avoid overusing the Sharpen tool, which results in exaggerated white spots (specular highlights) wherever the white component of the image approaches its maximum value. You also may have noticed that this tool does not offer the control of the previously discussed freehand editing tools. It does not offer Density, Transparency, Fade Out or Spacing controls. While this doesn't make the tool unusable, it does limit its ability to work subtly in some areas.

Unlike the previous tools, the effect of this tool is not additive. It will apply the Sharpen effect to the Sharpen level set in the Tool Settings dialog box the first time it is applied. This tool will apply the value set, and the only way to get it to apply more or less effect is to change the settings in the Tool Settings roll-up. Progressive applications cannot produce additional changes unless the Tool Settings are changed.

Any application of the tool can be removed with the Undo command (Ctrl+Z) as long as it was applied with one continuous stroke without letting go of the mouse button. If you must be zoomed in at great magnification to do your work, keep a duplicate window open to a lower zoom value so you can see the effect in perspective.

The Contrast Tool

The Contrast tool intensifies the distinction between light and dark. It operates in the same manner as the Contrast filter except that it can be applied to small areas without the need to create masks. The size, shape and level of the Contrast tool is set from the Tool Settings roll-up in the View menu. This tool does not offer Density, Transparency, Fade Out, or Spacing controls. Even though some of the Custom Brush settings show a Density or Transparency-like setting, the brush applies a solid 100 percent density Contrast based on the Tool Settings roll-up value. While this doesn't make the tool unusable, it does limit its ability to work subtly in some areas. To achieve subtle effects in areas that have no naturally occurring visual boundaries, you must be prepared to apply the brush in several stages to reduce the sharp transition of the contrast effect. You can also achieve this feathered or faded transition by using a Transparency mask, which involves a little more work.

Use the Ctrl key to constrain the tool to a vertical or horizontal direction. Pressing the Shift key changes the direction of constraint.

The Sharpen tool has only one setting that is only found in the Sharpen Tool Dialog box.

Contrast Tool Settings Roll-Up Options

Shape Buttons	Sets the shape of the Contrast tool. The three available shapes choices are Round, Square and Custom. If Custom is chosen, a different dialog box appears and the outline image of the currently selected Custom Contrast tool shape appears as the cursor.
Flatten	The Flatten slider controls the height of the round and square tool. Values are in percentages of height. You can see the effect of the flattening in the preview window as the change is being applied. The Flatten control does not affect the Custom Contrast tool.
Rotate	Rotates the Round or Square Contrast tool by the amount entered. You can see the effect of the rotation in the preview window as the change is being applied. The rotate control does not affect the Custom Contrast tool. Value is in degrees, up to a maximum of 180 degrees. Rotating a standard Round Contrast tool serves no purpose, but rotating a flattened Round Contrast tool does.
Size	Allows adjustment of Round or Square Contrast tool size from 0 to 100 pixels. The size of the Contrast tool selected is shown in the preview box. The size of the Custom Contrast tool is not adjustable.

Contrast	Sets the level of contrast. Enter a number in the Contrast box or use the slider. The slider visually indicates the amount of contrast being applied by the differences between the top and bottom band. On the right side is the greatest contrast between the top and bottom band. On the left is the least amount of contrast. The range is -100 percent to +100 percent.

Notes on Using the Contrast Tool

Be careful not to overuse the Contrast tool, which can result in exaggerated white and dark areas. At the maximum setting (100 percent), the areas become much lighter and the almost all shades are lost. At the minimum setting (-100 percent), the areas affected have no contrast, resulting in a gray image.

The effect of the Contrast tool is not additive. It will apply the effect at the level set by the Tool Setting dialog box the first time it is applied. Progressive applications cannot make any additional changes until the Tool Settings options are changed. Any application of the tool can be removed with the Undo command (Ctrl+Z) as long as it was applied with one continuous stroke without letting go of the mouse button. If you must be zoomed in at great magnification to do your work, keep a duplicate window open to a lower zoom value so you can see the effect in perspective.

The Brightness Tool

The Brightness tool lightens or darkens areas of the image. The size, shape, and level of the Brightness tool is set from the Tool Settings roll-up in the View menu. This tool does not offer controls for Density, Transparency, Fade Out, or Spacing. Even though some of the Custom Brush settings show Density or Transparency-like settings, the brush applies a solid 100 percent density contrast based on the Tools Settings roll-up value. To achieve any subtle effects in areas that have no naturally occurring visual boundaries, you must be prepared to apply the brush in several stages to reduce the the sharp transition of the contrast effect. You can also achieve this feathered or faded transition by using a Transparency Mask, which involves a little more work

Use the Ctrl key to constrain the tool to a vertical or horizontal direction. Pressing the Shift key changes the direction of constraint.

The Brighten tool has only one setting that is unique to its function. It is the Brightness value.

Brighten Tool Settings Roll-Up Options

Shape Buttons	Sets the shape of the Brighten Tool. The three available shapes are Round, Square, and Custom. If Custom is chosen, a different dialog box appears and the outline image of the currently selected custom Brighten tool shape appears as the cursor.
Flatten	The Flatten slider controls the height of the Round and Square tools. Values are expressed in percentages of height. You can see the effect of the flattening in the preview window as the change is being applied. The Flatten control does not affect the Custom Brighten Tool.
Rotate	Rotates the Round or Square Brighten tool by the amount entered. You can see the effect of the rotation in the preview window as the change is being applied. The Rotate control does not affect the Custom Brighten tool. The value is expressed in degrees, up to a maximum of 180 degrees. Rotating a standard Round Brighten tool serves no purpose, but rotating a flattened Round Brighten tool does.
Size	Allows adjustment of Round or Square Brighten tool sizes from 0 to 100 pixels. The size of the Brighten tool selected is shown in the preview box. The size of the Custom Brighten Tool is not adjustable.
Brighten	Sets the level of brightness. Enter a number in the Brightness box or use the slider. The slider visually indicates the amount of Brightness being applied by the differences between the top and bottom band. The range is from -100 percent to +100 percent.

Notes on Using the Brighten Tool

When using this tool, remember that you want the changes to be subtle, so make them in small increments using a Round Brighten tool unless you are working near straight lines, as in a geometric figure. The effect of the tool is not additive. It will apply the effect at the level set by the Tool Setting dialog box the first time it is applied. Progressive applications cannot make any changes unless the Tool Settings options are changed. Any application of the tool can be removed with the Undo command (Ctrl+Z) as long as it was applied with one continuous stroke without letting go of the mouse button. If you must be zoomed in at great magnification to do your work, keep a duplicate window open to a lower zoom value so you can see the effect in perspective.

The Tint Tool

The Tint tool tints an area in the current paint color. This may seem the same as painting with a high-transparency paintbrush, but it is not. The paintbrush is additive. That is, when the same area continues to have the brush applied to it, the paint builds up until it reaches 100 percent. The Tint tool will apply the paint color as specified by the Tint setting, regardless of how many times it is applied.

The size, shape, and level of the Tint tool is controlled from the Tool Settings roll-up in the View menu. Use the Ctrl key to constrain the tool to a vertical or horizontal direction. Pressing the Shift key changes the direction of constraint.

Tint Tool Settings Roll-Up Options

Shape Buttons	Sets the shape of the Tint Tool. The three available shapes are Round, Square, and Custom. If Custom is chosen, a different dialog box appears and the outline image of the currently selected custom Tint tool shape appears as the cursor.
Flatten	The Flatten slider controls the height of the Round and Square tools. The values are expressed in percentages of height. You can see the effect of the flattening in the preview window as the change is being applied. The Flatten control does not affect the Custom Tint Tool.
Rotate	Rotates the Round or Square Tint tool by the amount entered. You can see the effect of the rotation in the preview window as the change is being applied. The Rotate control does not affect the Custom Tint tool. The value is expressed in degrees, up to a maximum of 180 degrees. Rotating a standard Round Tint tool serves no purpose, but rotating a flattened Round Tint tool does.
Size	Allows adjustment of Round or Square Tint tool size from 0 to 100 pixels. The size of the Tint tool selected is shown in the preview box. The size of the Custom Tint tool is not adjustable.
Tint	Slider controls the amount of tint that is applied with the brush. The range is from 0 to 100 percent.

Using the Tint Tool

The first thing to remember with the Tint tool is that 100 percent tint is a solid color without any transparency. The Tint tool provides a way to highlight a selected area with a color. You can also achieve the same effect over larger areas by using the Rectangle, Ellipse, or Polygon Draw tools and controlling the Transparency setting through the Tool Settings roll-up.

Another use of the Tint tool is for touching up an image. The technique is simple. When you have a discoloration to cover, pick an area of the image that is the desired color. Using the Eyedropper tool, select a large enough sample to get the average color that is needed to match the adjoining areas. Now apply the tint to the area with progressively large percentage settings until the discolored areas disappears into the surrounding area. If the resulting tint application looks too smooth, use the Brush to add texture. You can also use the Blend tool to reduce spots where there are large differences in the shades.

The Blend Tool

This is a better tool to use for retouching than the Smear tool. The Blend tool enables you to blend colors in your picture. Blending is the mixing of different colors to cause less distinction among them. For example, if you have two areas of different colors and they overlap, it is possible to blend the two different colors so that the separation of the two areas is indistinct.

The size and shape of the Blend tool is set from the Tool Settings roll-up in the View menu. For a detailed explanation of the settings in the Blend Tool Setting dialog box, see the earlier section of this chapter on the Smear tool. The Blend tool has only one setting in the Tool Settings roll-up that is unique to the Blend function: the Blend setting.

Use the Ctrl key to constrain the tool to a vertical or horizontal direction. Pressing the Shift key changes the direction of constraint.

Blend Tool Settings Roll-Up Options

Shape Buttons — Sets the shape of the Blend tool. The three available shapes choices are Round, Square And Custom. If Custom is chosen, a different dialog box appears and the outline image of the currently selected custom Blend tool shape appears as the cursor.

Flatten — The Flatten slider controls the height of the Round and Square tools. The values are expressed in percentages of height. You can see the effect of the flattening in the preview window as the change is being applied. The Flatten control does not affect the Custom Blend tool.

Rotate — Rotates the Round or Square Blend tool by the amount entered. You can see the effect of the rotation in the preview window as the change is being applied. The Rotate control does not affect the Custom Blend tool. Value is in degrees, up to a maximum of

	180 degrees. Rotating a standard Round Blend tool serves no purpose, but rotating a flattened round Blend tool does.
Size	Allows adjustment of Round or Square Blend tool size from 0 to 100 pixels. The size of the Blend tool selected is shown in the preview box. The size of the Custom Blend tool is not adjustable.
Blend	Sets the level of blend. Enter a number in the Blend box or use the slider. The slider visually indicates the amount of Blend being applied by the differences between the top and bottom band. The range is 0 to 100 percent. At 0 percent, no blending occurs. At 100 percent, the maximum blending between adjacent pixels occurs. Adjacent pixels must be different shades for the blend to operate.

Notes on the Blend Tool

While the Blend tool acts like applying water to a watercolor, the effect of the tool is not additive. It will apply the effect at the level set by the Tool Setting dialog box the first time it is applied. Progressive applications will not make any changes unless the tool settings are changed or another tool is selected and then the Blend tool is re-selected. Any application of the tool can be removed with the Undo command (Ctrl+Z) as long as it was applied with one continuous stroke without letting go of the mouse button.

The Hue Tool

The Hue tool adjusts the amount and type of color in an image. It acts in the same manner as the Hue filter, described in the chapter on Filters. The size, shape, and color of the Hue tool is set from the Tool Settings roll-up in the View menu. For a detailed explanation of the settings in the Hue Tool Setting dialog box, see the section on the Smear tool. Use the Ctrl key to constrain the tool to a vertical or horizontal direction. Pressing the Shift key changes the direction of constraint.

Hue Tool Settings Roll-Up Options

Shape Buttons	Sets the shape of the Hue tool. The three available shape choices are Round, Square, and Custom. If Custom is chosen, a different dialog box appears and the outline image of the currently selected Custom Hue tool shape appears as the cursor.
Flatten	The Flatten slider controls the height of the Round and Square tools. The Values are expressed in percentages of height. You can see the effect of the

	flattening in the preview window as the change is being applied. The Flatten control does not affect the Custom Hue tool.
Rotate	Rotates the Round or Square Hue tool by the amount entered. You can see the effect of the rotation in the preview window as the change is being applied. The rotate control does not affect the Custom Hue tool. The value is expressed in degrees, up to a maximum of 180 degrees. Rotating a standard Round Hue tool serves no purpose, but rotating a flattened Round Hue tool does.
Size	Allows adjustment of Round or Square Hue tool size from 0 to 100 pixels. The size of the Hue tool selected is shown in the preview box. The size of the Custom Hue tool is not adjustable.
Hue	Sets the level of hue. Enter a number in the Hue box or use the slider. The value range of the Hue tool is from +180 to -180 degrees.

Notes on the Hue Tool

The Hue tool actually changes the color of the pixels it touches by the amount of the setting. The number of degrees entered in the Tool Settings roll-up relates to the color wheel. The maximum setting is half-way around the color wheel—180 degrees—which represents the complementary color of the changed pixel. The effect of the tool is not additive. It will apply the effect at the level set by the Tool Setting dialog box the first time it is applied. Progressive applications will not make any changes unless the tool settings are changed. Any application of the tool can be removed with the Undo command (Ctrl+Z) as long as it was applied with one continuous stroke without letting go of the mouse button.

The Saturation Tool

The Saturation tool acts in the same manner as the Saturation filter, as discussed in the Filter chapter. Saturation refers to the purity of a color. Purity is the number of colors used to mix a specific color. The more colors that are used to mix a color, the duller the color looks. The Saturation tool adjusts the purity of the color in an image by reducing the colors in an image. When it is reduced to -100 percent, the result is a grayscale image. The size, shape, and level of the Saturation tool is set from the Tool Settings roll-up in the View menu.

Use the Ctrl key to constrain the tool to a vertical or horizontal direction. Pressing the Shift key changes the direction of constraint.

Saturation Tool Settings Roll-Up Options

Shape Buttons	Sets the shape of the Saturation tool. The three available shape choices are Round, Square, and Custom. If Custom is chosen, a different dialog box appears and the outline image of the currently selected custom Saturation tool shape appears as the cursor.
Flatten	The Flatten slider controls the height of the Round and Square tools. The values are expressed in percentages of height. You can see the effect of the flattening in the preview window as the change is being applied. The Flatten control does not affect the Custom Saturation tool.
Rotate	Rotates the Round or Square Saturation tool by the amount entered. You can see the effect of the rotation in the preview window as the change is being applied. The Rotate control does not affect the Custom Saturation tool. The value is in degrees, up to a maximum of 180 degrees. Rotating a standard Round Saturation tool serves no purpose, but rotating a flattened Round Saturation tool does.
Size	Allows adjustment of Round or Square Saturation tool size from 0 to 100 pixels. The size of the Saturation tool selected is shown in the preview box. The size of the Custom Saturation tool is not adjustable.
Saturation	Changes the level of Saturation. The range value is -100 percent to +100 percent. A setting of -100 percent changes color pixels into grayscale.

Notes on the Saturation Tool

The Saturation tool actually removes the color of the pixels it touches by the amount of the setting. The effect of the tool is not additive. It will apply the effect at the level set by the Tool Setting dialog box the first time it is applied. Progressive applications will not make any changes unless the tool settings are changed. Any application of the tool can be removed with the Undo command (Ctrl+Z) as long as it was applied with one continuous stroke without letting go of the mouse button.

Cloning Tools

Clone tools are what was used to make the dinosaurs in *Jurassic Park*. (Did you know that the Tyrannosaurus Rex that attacked the cars wasn't just a model but a whopping 23-ton model? There is a little fact to chew on.) In our little world of PHOTO-PAINT, Clone tools are used to take part of an image and apply it to another part of the image. This is extremely important when part of an image needs to be removed and something is needed to replace the removed section. Another use is to duplicate an area of one image into another. A clone is an identical duplicate of an area on the image. The Clone tool creates an identical replica, whereas the Pointillism Clone tool and the Impressionism Clone tool create a duplicate in the style of Pointillism (dots) and Impressionism (lines).

How the Clone Tool Works

The Clone tool reproduces an area of a picture identically. The area to be reproduced is determined by establishing a clone source point and then moving the tool to a destination where the cloned image is to be placed. The source area to be cloned can be on the same image or a different image in another image window. The movement of the tool over the area determines what is cloned. By placing the cursor over the area to be used as the source and clicking the right mouse button re-anchors the clone point. The cursor shape for the anchor point is a "plus" symbol and the cursor shape for placing the cloned image is dependent upon the brush selected (Circle, Square, or Custom). The size of clone placement cursor is dependent upon the brush size in the Clone Tool Settings roll-up.

Clicking the right mouse button while holding down the S key will cause the anchor point to snap back to its original location when the mouse button is released.

Holding down the Ctrl key constrains the Clone tool to horizontal/vertical movements. Holding down the Ctrl and the Shift key changes the direction of constraint. The size and shape of the Clone tool is set from the Tool Settings roll-up in the View menu.

Clone Tool Settings Roll-Up Options

Shape buttons	Sets the shape of the brush. The three selections are Round, Square, and Custom brush.
Custom Brush	If you select the Custom brush, a thumbnail of the brush is displayed as a button. To select one of the Custom brushes, click on the button.
Delete Brush	You can delete a Custom brush by clicking on the brush button and then clicking the Delete Brush button.
Flatten	If you select the Round or Square brush button, you can flatten the brush using the Flatten slider.
Rotate	Rotates either a Round or Square brush by the amount entered.

Size	Changes the size of either a Round or Square brush. The size of the brush is displayed in the preview box.
Edge	Sets the edges of the brush to Hard, Medium or Soft. Soft edges make the brush stroke the least dense at the edges. Hard edges have the densest. The preview box displays the effect.
Density	Sets the overall density of coverage, which includes the center of the brush stroke and the edges. Higher values make the brush stroke densest. The preview box displays the effect.
Transparency	Sets the level of transparency. Lower levels are less transparent. The preview box displays the effect.
Fade Out	Sets the length of the brush stroke before it fades out entirely. A value of 0 sets the Fade Out to none.
Spacing	Sets the spacing between dots. A spacing of 0 creates a solid line.

Using the Clone Tool Effectively

Remember when using the Clone tool that the area under the cursor becomes the anchor point when the right mouse button is clicked. This is sometimes easy to forget if you are doing a lot of cloning work. One of the more important settings when using the Clone tool is the Transparency setting. By using a high Transparency setting and a low Density setting, it is possible to clone a "ghost" of a selected image.

To effectively use the Clone tool, it will help you to understand what is going on "under the hood." When the anchor point is selected, the clone source is the image at the moment the mouse button is first clicked. As the image is modified by the Clone tool, the original clone source image does not change.

Corel *TIP!*

> Be careful where you drag your Clone tool. If you go over an area that you have just cloned, you will read (clone) the original image rather than the newly cloned image.

Here is a little trick to demonstrate the point.

1. Open the file Apple.pcx in the PHOTOPNT\SAMPLES library.
2. Mask the entire image by selecting All in the Mask menu.
3. Select the Clone Tool. Make a Square brush size about 50 points.

4. Place the Square brush in the lower right of the image and click the right mouse button. This will anchor the source for the clone tool. It also sets the image plane that the clone tool operates on.

5. Either select Clear from the Edit Menu or click the Del key to remove the apple. The image area is now clear. Or at least it looks clear.

6. Hold down the left mouse button and beginning in the lower right corner drag it across the image area. The apple begins to reappear. If you continue drag the mouse across the image area you will eventually get the entire image back.

Corel *TIP!*

The clone tool source image remains fixed until you change tools or use the Undo function.

The starting point of the cloned image is determined by where the initial point is established. In the apple example, if you had starting dragging the clone tool in the middle of the image, the apple would be off the page. This does not apply to the Impressionism and Pointillism Clone Tools.

Remember that the effects of the clone tool are additive. Repeated cursor movement over the same area will reduce the Transparency effect (if you have any selected). Using the Checkpoint command in the Edit menu is highly recommended before starting to clone an image. Be aware when cloning between two separate images. When you clone the image the first time, you click the button that selects the image window. So before you begin to clone, click the left mouse button in the image are that is receiving the clone before beginning. The title bar of the image will indicate that it is selected.

Impressionist Clone Tool

The Impressionist tool reproduces an area of a picture using Impressionist-style brush strokes. You identify the area that you want to reproduce and then move the tool to the new location. The movement of the tool determines the area to clone. Use the Ctrl key to constrain the tool to a vertical or horizontal direction. Pressing the Shift key changes the direction of constraint. The size and shape of the Impressionist Clone tool is set from the Tool Settings roll-up in the View menu.

Impressionism Clone Tool Settings roll-up options

This roll-up is identical to the Clone Tool Setting roll-up, with the addition of H Variance, S Variance, L Variance, Brush Spread, and # of Lines. Only these five options are described herein. For information on the other options, see the Tool Setting description for the Clone Tool.

Impressionism Clone Tool Settings Roll-Up Options

H Variance   Determines the variation of color in the brush. The Impressionism brush style incorporates a number of colors. The H Variance (Hue Variance) determines the difference between the colors of the lines. For example, if you set the value to a higher number, the variation is greater. The difference between the colors is determined by this setting. The actual number of colors is determined by the setting of the # of Lines box. If you are working on a grayscale image, it varies the shades of gray. Please don't forget that gray is a color.

Corel *TIP!*

Use the H Variance setting with some degree of caution. The default setting is five; when you take it to the maximum setting, you will have samples from just about every color in the rainbow.

S Variance   Sets the variation for the purity of the color. Purity is the number of colors used to mix a specific color. Lower values lower the amount of colors used to mix; higher values increase the amount of colors used to produce the selected colors. The greater the number of colors used to mix a color, the duller the final color looks.

Corel *TIP!*

The default value of this setting is five. That is a great setting and I recommend you leave it alone.

461

L Variance	Sets the variation of light colors to dark colors used in the brush. Higher values makes the variation of light greater, giving a greater range of light-to-dark variation in the brush strokes. Confused? What it means in applications is that the greater the amount of Light Variance (which in the HSL model this brush is built on), the greater the difference in the colors themselves.
Brush Spread	Sets the distance between strokes. Higher values makes the distance between strokes greater.
# of Lines	Sets the number of lines created in brush strokes. This value, in combination with the Spacing value, more than any other will bring your system to its knees. Keep the number of lines low and the spacing as high as practical.

Notes on Using the Impressionist Clone Tool

This tool wins the big prize—I have been unable to find any practical use for this tool whatsoever. Think about it for a moment. A clone is an exact copy of the original, right? The Impressionist Clone tool makes randomly distorted copies of the original. Am I missing something here?

In the original manual I wrote, "Use this tool to create unusual or special effects." True enough.

In using the tool, remember that by keeping your brush size and number of Line settings small, your result will more closely approximate the original. At least the outcome will be recognizable. The results with this tool are rather unpredictable, so be sure to use the Checkpoint command before beginning your work.

Pointillist Clone Tool

The Pointillist Clone tool reproduces an area of a picture using Pointillist-style brush strokes (i.e., the dot effect). For my opinion of this tool, see the description of the Impressionist Clone tool. You identify the area that you want to reproduce and then move the tool to the new location. The movement of the tool determines the area to clone. Use the Ctrl key to constrain the tool to a vertical or horizontal direction. Pressing the Shift key changes the direction of constraint. The size and shape of the Pointillist Clone tool is set from the Tool Settings roll-up in the View menu.

Pointillism Clone Tool Settings Roll-Up Options

H Variance   Determines the variation of color in the brush. The Pointillism brush style incorporates a number of colors. The H Variance (Hue Variance) determines the difference between the colors of the lines. For example, if you set the value to a higher number, the variation is greater. The difference between the colors is determined by this setting. The actual number of colors is determined by the setting of the # of Lines box. If you are working on a grayscale image it varies the shades of gray. Gray is considered a color.

Corel *TIP!*

As with the Impressionist Clone tool's H Variance setting, you should use this setting with some degree of caution. The default setting is five. When you take it to the maximum setting, you will have samples from just about every color in the rainbow.

S Variance   Sets the variation for the purity of the color. Purity is the number of colors used to mix a specific color. Lower values lower the amount of colors used to mix; higher values increase the amount of colors used to produce the selected colors. The greater the number of colors used to mix a color, the duller the final color looks.

Corel *TIP!*

The default value of this setting is five. I recommend you leave it alone.

L Variance   Sets the variation of light colors to dark colors used in the brush. Higher values makes the variation of light greater giving a greater range of light-to-dark variation in the brush strokes. The greater the amount of Light Variance (which in the HSL model this brush is built on) means greater differences in the colors themselves.

Brush Spread	Sets the distance between strokes. Higher values makes the distance between strokes greater.
# of Lines	Sets the number of lines created in brush strokes. This value, in combination with the Spacing value, can bring your system to its knees. Keep the number of lines low and the spacing as high as practical.

Notes on Using the Pointillism Clone Tool

Experiment with this tool when you have lots of time on your hands and no deadlines. Use this tool to create unusual or special effects. Keeping the brush size very small (a setting between 2 and 5) enables the creation of a clone that looks vaguely similar to the original. As with the Impressionism filter, use objects that have definite shapes, making them easily recognizable as the Clone tool distorts their appearance. The results with this tool can be rather unpredictable, so use the Checkpoint command before beginning your work.

Advanced Masks, Tools, and Techniques

The Magic Wand and the Lasso

In previous chapters, we examined the Mask and Object flyout menus and the tools they contain. These are two nearly identical sets of tools—one set is found in the Mask flyout and is used to create masks, and the other is located in the Object flyout and is used to create objects. We use the mask-creation tools all of the time, whereas the object-creation tools have limited usefulness.

All the mask tools that have been discussed so far create masks that have boundaries defined by the user with the mouse and without the aid of the PAINT program. In this chapter, we will explore the Magic Wand and the Lasso, which produce computer-aided masks whose boundaries are determined by the PHOTO-PAINT program.

The Magic Wand and Lasso functions take color information supplied by the user and pass it to PHOTO-PAINT for generating the mask. The boundaries of the mask are based on the color similarities of adjacent pixels. The color-sensitivity level is set using the Color Comparison Tolerance dialog box. (See Figure 15.1.)

The Color Comparison Tolerance dialog box is opened with the Color Tolerance command in the Special menu. The dialog box is used to enter color-tolerance values representing the range of colors that are to be included inside the mask. A higher number means that more colors will be included in the mask. The plus and minus values displayed in the dialog box indicate the range of color values from 0 to 255, which represent brighter and darker shades of each primary color. The chosen values take effect the next time you use the Magic Wand or Lasso tools.

The Magic Wand Mask Tool

The Magic Wand Mask tool is used to create masks both quickly and automatically. The ability of the tool to make an accurate mask is dependent upon the settings in the Color Comparison Tolerance dialog box and the actual color-value composition of the image. In other words, it takes a little time to get the hang of using this tool correctly. However, once you do, it is a very handy tool to have. The Color Mask tool, which was discussed in a previous chapter, masks all colors in the image that match the values entered. The Magic Wand Mask tool differs in that the mask expands from a starting point until all of the adjacent colors that meet the selection criteria are included.

Two simple facts about the Magic Wand tool are (1) there is nothing magic about it; and (2) it is very simple to use once you understand the concept behind its operation. In theory you simply click on the area that needs to be masked or the area that surrounds the area to be masked, and PHOTO-PAINT does the rest. There are actually times when this will work as intended.

PHOTO-PAINT treats the pixel under the cursor when it is clicked as the starting point. The program reads the color value of the pixel, then, using the limits entered in the Color Tolerance Comparison dialog box, expands a mask pixel-by-pixel until it can no longer find pixels that are within the limits. For example, if the starting pixel has a hue value of 60 and the Color Comparison Tolerance Command has been set to 50, the mask will continue to expand from its starting point until every adjacent pixel with a value between 10 (60 minus 50) and 110 (60 plus 50) has been included in the mask.

Figure 15.1.
The Color Comparison
Tolerance dialog box.
(It may not look like
much, but it is a vast
improvement over the
one that shipped with
the original release of
PHOTO-PAINT 5.)

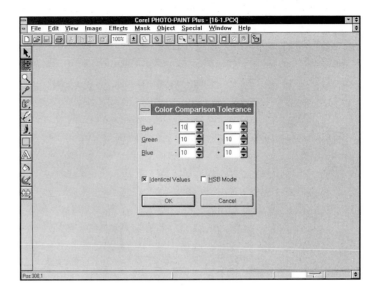

Corel *TIP!*

When using the Magic Wand mask tool the most important decision to make is the choice of whether to mask the object or the area around the object. If the area to be masked is filled with a wide variety of colors or the colors in it have a wide tonal range (like the apple), then look at the area surrounding it. Remember, it only takes one click of the button to invert the mask.

How about some real-life situations? Fair enough. I'll walk you through several photos that are representative of different ways to use the Magic Wand tool.

Let's begin with an easy one. Look at Figure 15.2. The sky needs some clouds in it. No problem—Corel has an entire collection of Clouds on CD-ROM. The preferred way to accomplish this is to make the foreground an object and place it on the cloud picture. However, making a mask of the foreground could be complicated, because it has a wide range of tonal qualities. So we will mask the sky and invert the mask.

Figure 15.2.
A professional photo of the area. The lack of clouds in the picture makes it seem uninteresting.

1. Open 200020.PCD. The size of PCD isn't important, except you need to use the same size when you open the cloud picture. If your system has a small display, a slow graphics card, or a limited amount of RAM, I recommend that you use the snapshot size rather than standard.

2. Isn't the black border charming? Let's get rid of it with Paper Size. After selecting Paper Size in the Image menu and making sure the Maintain Aspect box is checked, enter a value of 1.5 in the Height value box. Click OK. A new cropped image is created.

3. Close the original image by double clicking its control menu button (in the upper-left corner of the image). It should close without asking you if you want to save any changes because PAINT knows that it cannot be saved. If it asks you, say no. We are closing the image to save system resources.

4. Select Color Tolerance in the Special menu, thus opening the Color Comparison Tolerance dialog box. Make sure Identical Values is selected and HSB isn't selected. Enter a value of 40. Click the OK button. Did you wonder where the number 40 came from? In a way I wish there were some complicated mathematical formula I could lay on you here, but experience and some experimentation is my only explanation for where the number came from.

Corel *TIP!*

> The best overall starting number for the Color Comparison Tolerance dialog box seems to be 40.

6. Select the Magic Wand tool in the toolbox and click just about anywhere in the blue sky.

7. The sky that is under the arch is not part of the mask, and it needs to be included. Click the Add To Selection button in the ribbon bar and click the Magic Wand cursor in the center of the arch. Figure 15.3 shows the completed mask. We want the foreground as an object. To do this we must invert the mask of the sky.

    Click the Invert Mask button in the ribbon bar. The image should look like Figure 15.4.

Figure 15.3.
The completed mask.

Figure 15.4.
With the foreground
removed, we are now
ready to haul some
rocks (remove the
foreground).

8. Now comes the scary part. We need to cut the masked area into the clipboard. We could copy the image into the clipboard. I generally cut the image because when it is removed (cut), it enables you to see if the mask missed anything. The negative side of doing it this way is that you will lose your mask in the process. If you spent a lot of time constructing the mask, it would be advisable to save the mask before cutting it to the clipboard. Click the Cut button in the ribbon bar. All that should be left of the original image is the sky. (See Figure 15.5.) Close the image and do not save any changes when asked.

Figure 15.5.
The rocks are gone and
we are about to
dispatch the original
image.

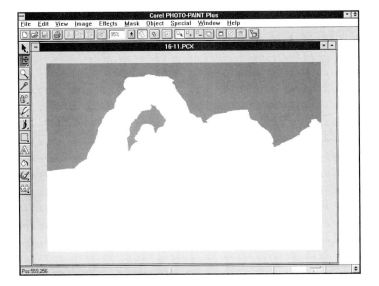

Corel *TIP!*

If you have a system with limited amounts of RAM, you could be experiencing some technical difficulties at this point. The first thing to do to speed up the process is to temporarily turn off the Enable Undo function in the General Preferences section of the Special Menu. Undo is nice, but it slows everything down. (Don't forget to turn it back on when we are through.) Next, close any roll-ups that are open. (These consume system resources.) Close any Windows applications you are not currently using. My system pulled a little surprise on me. While making the many screen-capture screen shots for this book, I forgot that the screen capture utility uses the same clipboard as my example. Imagine my surprise when I clicked the Paste button and had one of my screen capture shots appear instead of that nice stone arch.

Speaking of clipboards, the image we just put into the clipboard is very large and it also takes up system resources. Since they didn't put a "drain" in the clipboard, the next best thing to do is to open the clipboard viewer and select Delete from the Edit menu. Make sure you are done with the contents of the clipboard first.

9. Open the Image 191084.PCD and repeat steps 2 and 3 for this image.
10. Click the Paste button in the ribbon bar. The resulting image should look like Figure 15.6.

Figure 15.6.
Now we have an image that will look much better in the brochure than the original.

Corel *NOTE!*

If this were a real image and we were working to make money, there are several finishing touches that would need to be considered. First, if the object isn't completely aligned, use the arrow keys and nudge it into the proper position. (The nudge capability in PHOTO-PAINT is fixed at one-pixel-per-nudge and cannot be changed.) Next, open the Layers/Objects dialog box (Ctrl+F7) and set feathering at 4. This action removes any last pixels of the original sky that may have been stowaways on the arch object. I think the foreground is a little washed out, so I would go into the Tone/Equalize filter and put a little more sparkle into it. For a little fun, don't use clouds. Instead, flood the background with the bitmap texture fill called Night Sky in the Sample5 library. To keep the stars small, edit the settings so the maximum height and width are 3. Make the number of spots 200-300. The result is shown in Figure 15.7.

Figure 15.7.
With a little imagination and PHOTO-PAINT 5, it is easy to create something completely different from the original.

That was an easy mask. Now let's try something a little more adventurous. At first appearance, the next photo appears easy. The background is dark, so it will be easy to mask. Well, maybe.

In this session we will combine several techniques from this and previous chapters to build a Complex Object. Our goal is to take a photograph of a wolf, extract the wolf from its dark and brooding background, and change the background into something lighter for use in a later session. We will be customizing the power of the Magic Wand tool using the Color Tolerance command and learning a few advanced techniques to make the Magic Wand Mask tool more magic for us. We will give some of the effect filters a serious workout as well.

For this work session, let's say we have a client that wants to advertise a real-estate development called Lone Wolf Estates. (He watches a little too much *Northern Exposure*.) All you have to work with is this Photo CD of a wolf. Let's see what we can do with it.

1. Open the file labeled 42080.PCD (200021.PCD on the Corel Photo-CD and 42080.PCD on the Predators CD). If the wolf does not fit in your display, use the Zoom To Fit command (F4). The wolf in this picture is great, but the background is dark. We could lighten it up, but instead it has been decided that we need to replace the background altogether. If we were to click a Magic Wand tool on the background, we would end up with a mess as the computer attempted to create a mask from all the similar colors in this photo. We can use the Magic Wand tool to help us, but we are going to have to help it out.

2. Select Color Tolerance from the Special menu. The Color Comparison Tolerance dialog box appears on the screen.

3. Click the Identical Values button on the Color Comparison Tolerance dialog box. This forces the values in all of the boxes to increase or decrease when one of the boxes is changed. For now, this is a good setting. Change the value to 40 using the arrow buttons. Click on OK. All of the values should change to 39. So, how did I come up with 39? I divide the line screen frequency by the average tidal depth in Calcutta during monsoon season. OK, there is no formula—I did some experimenting and this is a good value for what we are attempting to demonstrate.

4. Select the Magic Wand and click on the background. Depending on the part of the image you clicked the cursor on, you will have a map that requires a lot of adjustment. The one we came up with is shown in Figure 15.8. Now, before you decide that the Magic Wand is only good on white backgrounds, let me show you a trick. Remember the first rule: Look for the area with the narrowest range of colors and the highest contrast. Well, you can look at the image all day and you won't see either a narrow range of colors or particularly high contrast. What we need is in there, it is only a question of displaying it.

5. Open the Layers/Objects roll-up (Ctrl+F7) and click the arrow to the right of the value box that says All Channels. When the dropdown list appears, select the red channel, then the green, and finally the blue. Figures 15.15a, 15.15b, and 15.15c show what all three channels look like. As you can see, the appearance of two of the channels are similar, but the blue channel is different. While the red and green offer higher contrast, the blue offers a uniform background.

Figure 15.8.
No, the wolf is not
suffering from some
horrible sort of disease.
This is what happens
when you apply a
magic wand tool to an
area with a lot of
similar colors.

Figure 15.9a.
The red channel.

Figure 15.9b.
The green channel.

Figure 15.9c.
The blue channel.

Color Basics: The image is composed of three channels: red, green, and blue. Each of the three channels contain grayscale information that is applied to a color gun in the monitor. Therefore an RGB color image is, in truth, composed of three channels of grayscale information. Kinda spooky, huh? The grayscale information for each color channel is applied to the appropriate color gun of the display. For example, in an image comprised of a blue square the grayscale information applied to the blue gun will be a white square. Larger grayscale values (white is 255, black is zero) in a color channel produce greater amounts of the color. With PHOTO-PAINT 5, we are able to look not only at individual channels, but apply effects to them.

6. Select Color Tolerance from the Special menu, deselect the Identical Values button and select a value of -24 and +16. What happened to the dialog box? Because each channel is a grayscale, the dialog box changes to reflect that we are now working with grayscale. Any changes made to the dialog box in grayscale mode will not affect the settings we had in RGB color mode. About the -24 and +16, the minus values have their effect on the lighter shades and the plus values have determine the darker shades. This setting works well with our wolf picture.

7. With the Magic Wand cursor, click on the dark area just above the wolf's back. Don't drag the Magic Wand; just click it on the spot. Wait a few moments while the computer figures out the boundaries of the mask. When it finishes, we will have a mask that's looks something like Figure 15.10. The Magic Wand did a fairly good job outlining our wolf, but we are going make it better.

Figure 15.10.
With a little adjust-
ment to the color
tolerance the Magic
Wand does a much
better job of outlining
the wolf.

8. Click on the Add To Selection button on the button bar. This will enable us to add additional areas to the mask that we will eventually use to make the wolf into an object.

9. Select the Object Brush tool from the Object Selection tools. The cursor now becomes a circle or a square (depending on what is selected in your Tool Settings roll-up—Ctrl+F8). Anything that you touch or drag across that

is outside of the wolf will be added to the area selected by the mask. If you need to change the size or shape of your Object Brush tool, select the Tool Settings roll-up with the Ctrl+F8 key and change the shape or the size of the brush.

10. Use the Object Brush tool to remove any partial masked areas that remain outside of the wolf image. Now that we have cleaned up the outside of the wolf, you noticed that our Magic Wand tool got a little confused about where the wolf was, especially around his mouth. Because we are selecting the background and we have parts of the wolf that were also selected as background, we need to subtract these areas from the mask.

11. Click on the Subtract From Selection button on the button bar. This will enable us to subtract additional areas from the mask. Use the Object Brush tool to remove any partial masked areas that remain inside of the wolf image.

12. Now our wolf is pretty much cleaned up. Next we must invert the mask. Why? you ask. Because now that we have selected the background with the mask, we need to select the wolf. Click on the Invert Mask button on the ribbon bar. Now the marquee only surrounds the wolf.

13. Before we can make the wolf into an object, we must return to all channels. Select All Channels in the Layers/Objects roll-up. The mask remains! A mask that is applied to an individual channel will affect them all.

14. Click on the Copy button in the ribbon bar. The contents of the mask are copied to the Windows clipboard. Click the Paste button on the ribbon bar. A copy of our wolf appears.

Corel *TIP!*

> Don't be too quick when performing the copy/paste operation. PHOTO-PAINT returns the cursor too quickly to suit my fancy. I wait until the drive light quits flickering before using the Paste button.

Down in the Drawing Mode section, we see that there are two buttons. One button represents the Base image and the second button represents our wolf object. We now have two copies of the wolf. We could have removed the wolf from the base image by using the Cut command instead of Copy. If we had done so, the background would have had a wolf-sized white hole in it. We could have then pasted the wolf we cut out back into the image as an Object. We could have done it that way, but we need the original image of the wolf as part of the new improved background.

15. Click on the wolf-image layer in the Layers/Objects roll-up in order to hide it. We are going to be working on the background, and we do not want the effects that we are applying to affect our wolf object. If you think you are looking at the unmodified original image again, you're right.

16. Click on the Checkpoint in the Edit menu and remove the mask by clicking the Remove mask button on the ribbon bar. The former is necessary just in case something goes haywire with our effects. We would not want to lose the wolf object. The latter is necessary because we need to apply effects to the entire image.

17. Under the Effects menu, select Color, Brightness, and Contrast. We need to lighten up the background first. Using the sliders or entering values directly into the boxes, enter a brightness of 70 and a contrast of 55. Leave the intensity unchanged. Select OK. This washes out our wolf and the background. (See Figure 15.11.) There are two important terms that we will be using interchangeably from here on: *filters* and *effects*. Technically, a filter is used to achieve an effect. In the digital photo-editing world, the two terms have come to mean the same thing.

Figure 15.11.
This is the beginning of the transformation of the original wolf picture into an arctic background.

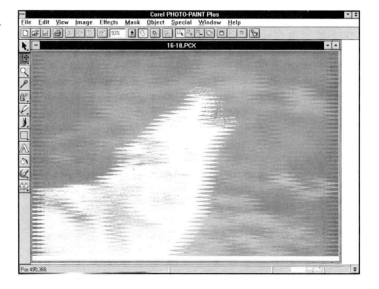

18. Under the Effects menu, select Mapping, and pick Ripple from the dropdown menu. Enter a period value of 10 and an amplitude of 20. Leave the ripple-type set to Horizontal. Select OK. (See Figure 15.12.) We have now grossly distorted the wolf and made an interesting background pattern.

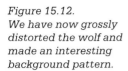

Figure 15.12.
We have now grossly
distorted the wolf and
made an interesting
background pattern.

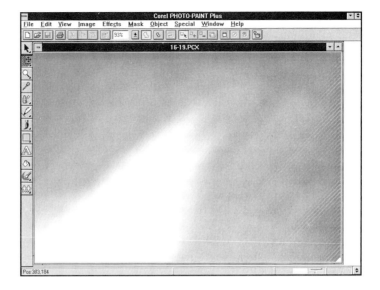

19. Select the Effects menu, pick Fancy, and click on Motion Blur from the dropdown menu. Enter a value of 50 for speed and click on the downward left-corner arrow for direction. Motion Blur is a filter that people tend to underestimate because of the name. They think it must only be good for showing that something is moving real fast. But it is also good for streaking a background, as we have done here. Select OK.

20. Unhide the wolf-object layer by clicking on the Layer button in the Drawing Mode section of the Layers/Objects roll-up. The wolf looks good, but we need to make a few adjustments before we are done with this session.

21. Click and drag the upper-right control handle to scale the wolf (object) to about 80 percent. (Look at the status bar in the lower-left portion of the screen to see the percentage of scale.) Click on the object and drag it partially out of the image area.

22. Ensure that the object is selected and enter a feather value of 7 and an opacity value of 85 in the Layers/Objects roll-up. The feathering takes away the cutout look to the image. The value of 7 represents the feathering effect being applied to the outer seven pixels of the object. The opacity helps the coloration of the object blend into the background. Opacity is expressed as a percentage and is the opposite of transparency. If we have a value of 85 in the Opacity box, it means that the object is 85 percent nontransparent. All the other roll-ups employ a transparency setting. An 85 percent Opacity setting would be the same as a 15 percent Transparency setting. Confused yet? This is a good time to experiment with different values of Opacity and Feathering. If the blue marquee is annoying or obscuring your view, turn it off with the Activate/Deactivate Marquee button in the ribbon bar.

479

23. Add the text "Lone Wolf Estates" and you are done. Figure 15.13 shows the final product. Press the F9 key to see what the image looks like.

Figure 15.13.
The final product.

Corel *TIP!*

If the Full Screen preview (F9) doesn't work when you use it, make sure that the Image window is active and not the Objects/Layers roll-up.

Suggestions for Using the Color Comparison Tolerance Dialog Box

A simple way to determine the best Color Comparison Tolerance Command settings without calculating color mathematics is to pick an arbitrary setting (the default is 10) and click the Magic Wand tool and see where the mask is created. If the mask does not fit the desired area, you may (1) remove the mask with the Remove Mask button in the ribbon bar; (2) change the settings (greater numbers include more in the mask and smaller numbers reduce the size of the mask); or (3) edit the newly created mask using the Mask Node Edit tool.

Corel *TIP!*

To quickly find the color value of any part of an image, hold down the E key and the cursor will become an eyedropper tool. The color-value readout will appear in the status bar (lower right) when the cursor is moved. The readout values are dependent upon the type of image, i.e. color, grayscale, etc.

Using the Magic Wand with CorelDRAW Files.

I couldn't leave this chapter without showing you some neat tricks that can be done with images from CorelDRAW 5. If you haven't tried it yet, you can import CDR files directly from CorelDRAW without the need to export them as bitmap images. The result is the image bound with a rectangle. This is where the Magic Wand mask tool really shines. The following is a brief work session to show how this is done.

1. Open the picture of fireworks (file 2000083.PCD from the Photo CD). Select Standard size if your system can support it.

2. Open the enclosed file MAGICWND.CDR. When presented with the Import Into Bitmap dialog box, select "1 to 1" for the size and 300 dpi for the resolution. Click the OK button and go get a cup of coffee—it's going to take a few minutes to convert the file to a bitmap. (It took about one and one-half minutes on my system.)

Figure 15.14.
Extruded text imported
from CorelDRAW.

3. Select the Magic Wand mask tool (almost any setting for Color Tolerance will work) and click on the white background of the image below the word "TOOLS." The mask will cover everywhere but the upper-left corner because the text touches the border edge. It also doesn't mask the inside of the letter O in the word "TOOLS" and the inside of the R and E in "incredible." This is very easy to fix.

4. Select the Add To Selection button in the ribbon bar. Using the Magic Wand, click inside the O in "TOOLS" and the inside of the R and E in "incredible." I recommend zooming in on the R and E by holding down the Z key and selecting the area. Place the mask and depress the Zoom To Fit (F4) key.

5. Invert the mask by clicking the Invert Mask button in the ribbon bar. All of the text should now be masked as shown in Figure 15.15.

Figure 15.15.
All of the text is now
ready to be pasted into
an image as an object.

6. Cut the image to the clipboard using the Cut button in the ribbon bar. Make sure none of the image remains behind when you cut it. Close the image and do not save any changes when asked.

7. Click the Paste button in the ribbon bar to paste the text as an object in the fireworks image. You should now have a picture that looks like Figure 15.16.

*Figure 15.16.
Now we have the
extruded CorelDRAW
text as an object in
PAINT.*

Finishing Touches: There are several things you can do at this point to add finishing touches. You have completed the Magic Wand portion at this point. Everything from here is fluff—the fun stuff.

8. Select the object and make a duplicate (Ctrl+D). Click the base-image button and the top-layer button in the Layers/Object roll-up to hide them. Only the button in the middle should be depressed at this point.

9. Apply a Jaggy Despeckle filter (under the Fancy group in the Effects menu) with a value of 5 in both width and height.

10. Open the Fill roll-up and select a Uniform Fill color that is a muted yellow. (It is at the end of the greens in the color palette.)

11. Select the Rectangle tool (not the Rectangle mask tool) and draw a rectangle covering all of the text object.

12. Click the button in the Layers/Object roll-up to unhide the base image.

13. Select the Freehand mask tool, ensure the Add To Selection button on the ribbon bar is still selected, and draw a freehand mask around all three text blocks. The object here is to apply a Gaussian blur to the yellow text block but not blur the fireworks. (In case you were wondering why we didn't hide the base image and apply the blur filter, the answer is because all of the blurring would be lost if we did it that way.) Figure 15.17 shows the mask I made.

Figure 15.17.
The mask I made. It
isn't very pretty but it
does the job.

14. Select the Gaussian filter from the Fancy group in the Effects menu. Apply a Gaussian blur setting of 7 and click OK.

15. Remove the mask using the Remove Mask button in the ribbon bar.

16. Select the Show All button in the Layers/Object roll-up. Using the Object Picker tool in the toolbox, move the top text over and slightly above the blurred text. At this point you can go crazy with the Object Merge mode in the Layers/Objects Roll-up. Figure 15.18 was done by selecting Multiply for the blurred object and Lightness for the top layer of text. It doesn't look like much in grayscale, but it is really stunning in color.

Figure 15.18.
This figure was done by
selecting Multiply for
the blurred object and
Lightness for the top
layer of text.

Additional Suggestions for Using the Magic Wand Mask Tool

Consider the image you need to mask. If the image has many colors in it and the area outside the image does not, try masking that part with the least complex color patterns and invert the resulting mask. Remember that the point where you click the Magic Wand cursor is the starting point. If the pixel you click on is very light, the program makes all of its calculations based on the color value of that point. Sometimes you can achieve better results just by clicking on a different starting point. It isn't necessary to have the Magic Wand produce the entire mask. If the mask is correct for a majority of the image, click on the Add To/Subtract From Selection buttons in the ribbon bar and use another mask tool (such as the Brush Mask tool, or you can even use the Magic Wand Mask tool again) to add to or subtract from the mask as required. Remember, when you find it difficult to create a mask with the Magic Wand, you can use the Layers/Object roll-up and look at the individual channels (red, green, and blue) for the image. Many times, one of the three channels has a higher contrast than the other. Any mask applied to an individual channel is applied to the entire image.

The Magic Wand Object Tool

The Magic Wand Object tool (not to be confused with the Magic Wand Mask tool) is used to create objects both quickly and automatically. The ability of the tool to make an accurate object is dependent upon the settings of the Color Comparison Tolerance command values and the color-value composition of the image. The Color Mask tool, which was discussed in a previous chapter, masks all colors in the image that match the values entered. The Magic Wand Object tool differs in that the Objects boundaries only goes from the starting point until it runs out of adjacent colors that meet the selection criteria. Once the object is created, it cannot be edited with the Node Edit tool the way a mask can be modified.

As with all of the Object tools, there are two types of objects that can be created with the Mask Object tool: Build objects and Simple objects. By depressing the Build Mode button (it is active when the button has three shapes in it instead of one) in the ribbon bar, this tool does not make an object immediately when used. Instead it creates a sort of "work-in-progress" mask called a build-object mask. The result is not a mask and not an object. If you close the image file with a build-object mask on it, the build-object mask will not be saved. The build-object mask is indicated by a red marquee. It acts like a mask in every sense of the word. That is, you can add to it, subtract from it, node edit it, etc. When you have finished modifying the build-object mask, click the Create Object button in the ribbon bar and then everything in the build-object mask becomes an object, as indicated by the blue marquee. The entire "build-object function" is redundant. The only difference between doing it this way and using the mask tools is that with the mask tools you must cut/copy and paste, whereas with the build-object method you create an object. (For what it's worth, I believe that this entire function will be absent in PHOTO-PAINT 6.)

Like the Magic Wand Mask tool, the Object tool is very simple to use. Simply click with the left mouse button on the area that needs to be made into an object. PHOTO-PAINT treats the pixel that is under the cursor when it is clicked as the starting point. The program reads the color value of the pixel, then, using the limits entered in the Color Comparison Tolerance dialog box, expands the Object marquee pixel-by-pixel until it can no longer find pixels that are within the limits. When the left mouse button is used to start the Magic Wand, the contents of the area under the marquee are copied into the object. If the right mouse button is used to create the object, the image area under the blue marquee is cut (removed) from the original and placed into the object.

If the resulting object was created with the left mouse button and is not what was desired, the user can remove it with the Remove command in the Object menu. If it was created with the right mouse button (cut from the image), the user can select Merge from the Object menu to return the contents of the object to the image.

Notes on Using the Magic Wand Object Tool

This is one of those tools that asks the question, "Why am I here?" The object-creation tools, of which this tool is one, all have very limited usefulness. Because the area selected by the tool in simple-object mode immediately becomes an object, and in build-object mode it acts like a mask, the best use of this tool is for applications that have many clearly defined areas that need to be made into objects. For example, if you have a lot of images to convert into objects that are solid shapes with little-or-no tonal variation in the interior, this would be your tool of choice. You cannot use it with the sample file APPLE.PCX because, if you recall, our ability to use the Magic Wand with it relied on selecting the background and inverting the resulting mask. With this tool, whatever you create in simple-mask mode becomes an object that cannot be altered. Therefore I would be interested to know if anyone can find a legitimate use for it.

The Lasso Mask Tool

If you are an experienced PhotoShop or PhotoStyler user, you might think you know what this tool does, but you're probably wrong. The Lasso Mask tool is a very handy tool that unfortunately bears the same name as a different tool in both of the aforementioned programs.

The metaphor of a lasso is perfect for this tool. (You may think that because both of the authors live in Texas, we use lassoes all the time. Nothing could be further from the truth. Our knowledge of lassoes primarily comes from watching

City Slickers a few too many times.) On a ranch, a lasso surrounds an object, and when you pull on the rope the lasso closes until it fits tightly around the object. The Lasso tool works very much in the same way, but without the rope.

The Lasso Mask tool enables you to define a mask that is irregular in shape in much the same way as the Freehand tool. When the mouse button is released, the mask shrinks until it surrounds an area of colors that fall within the limits set in the Color Comparison Tolerance dialog box. The mask will contain the area surrounded by the Lasso Mask tool. The Lasso tool acts as a localized version the Magic Wand Mask tool. It is used when it is necessary to restrict the region where the mask is to be placed.

Whereas the Magic Wand Mask begins at the pixel starting point and *expands* until it reaches its limits, the Lasso Mask *shrinks* until is reaches its limits. The range of color sensitivity is set using the Color Comparison Tolerance command on the Special menu.

How to Use the Lasso Mask Tool

The Lasso Mask tool operates much like the Freehand Mask tool. Click and hold either mouse button to anchor the starting point for the mask. Still holding the mouse button, drag the cursor around the area to be masked. This causes a line to be drawn around the object. The pixel underneath the cursor when the line is started determines the starting color value. Continue to drag the cursor around the area until you are near the starting point. When the button is released, the computer will complete the line and compute the masked area.

Following is a brief work session to show how to use the Lasso Mask tool.

1. Open the APPLE.PCX image.
2. Select the Lasso Mask tool from the toolbox.
3. Starting between the leaf and the apple, click and drag a line completely around the leaf, making sure to include most of the stem. Don't be too concerned about staying near the shape of the leaf—just stay outside of it. It you leave the image area, it is all right as well. I had you start between the leaf and the apple because drawing with a mouse is not easy and I find that you have greater control over the mouse in its starting position than at the end of the line. Remember that PAINT will complete the line for you, so make sure that when you release the left button, a straight line between where you let go and the beginning point of the line doesn't cross the leaf. Figure 15.19 shows the completed mask. Now that we have made this silly thing, let's do something with it.

Figure 15.19.
The completed mask.

4. Copy the masked area to the clipboard with the Copy button in the ribbon bar. Now remove the mask with the Remove Mask button on the ribbon bar.

5. Paste the leaf copy onto the image with the Paste button on the ribbon bar.

6. Using the Object Picker (which should be selected automatically), click and drag the leaf so it is exactly on top of the original leaf.

7. Click the leaf object, and rotation arrows will replace the control handles.

8. Click and drag the rotation circle so that it is at the top of the stem of the leaf object.

9. Click and drag the lower-left rotation handles and rotate the leaf counter-clockwise (-25 degrees). I told you in an earlier chapter, there are several advantages to being able to move the center of rotation. This is one of them. The leaf is rotating on its stem and therefore it looks natural and much easier to position.

10. Select the Object Picker (which returns it to normal mode) and, grabbing the lower-left corner, reduce the size of the leaf (its scale) by 25 percent. The status bar will read 75 percent, meaning it is now 75-percent of its original size. Now the apple and its two leaves look natural..

Clean-up procedures:

11. Add a feather value of 1 to the leaf object. This removes the little white pixels that weren't picked off by the Lasso Mask tool.

12. Hide the base image with the Layers/Object roll-up and apply a Hue filter (from the Color group in the Effects menu) of -10. This makes the leaf a slightly different shade than the original leaf.

13. Use the Airbrush and paint a little black under the leaf object to produce a shadow where the top leaf lays on top of the original.

14. The last step is to take the Clone tool and remove the little gold-colored highlight at the top of the duplicate leaf. You need to merge the leaf before you can use the Clone tool. Figure 15.20 shows the final apple with a radial fill background that I threw in for good measure.

Figure 15.20.
The final apple.

The Lasso Object Tool

The Lasso Object tool enables you to create objects that are irregular in shape and surrounded by colors that fall within the limits set in the Color Comparison Tolerance dialog box. The resulting object is composed of the area surrounded by the Lasso Mask tool. The Lasso tool acts as a localized version of the Magic Wand Object tool. It is used when it is necessary to restrict the region from which the Object is created. Whereas the Magic Wand begins at the pixel starting point and *expands* until it reaches its limits, the Lasso Object tool *shrinks* until is reaches its limits. The range or color sensitivity is set using the Color Comparison Tolerance command on the Special menu.

How to Use the Lasso Object Tool

The Lasso Object tool operates like the Freehand Mask tool. The starting point of the Object is determined by clicking and holding the *left* mouse button. Still holding the mouse button, drag the cursor around the area to be masked. This causes a line to be drawn around the object. The pixel underneath the cursor when the line is started determines the starting color value. Continue to drag the cursor around the area until you are near the starting point. When the button is released, the computer will complete the line. The computed masked-image area will be copied into the object. Performing the same operation with the *right* mouse button will cause the same image area to be *cut* (removed) and placed into the newly created object.

If the resulting object was created with the left mouse button and is not what was desired, the user can remove it with the Remove command in the Object menu. If it was created with the right mouse button (cut from the image), the user can select Merge from the Object menu to return the image.

Mask Node Edit Tool

The Mask Node Edit tool enables you to edit the shape of a mask by adjusting nodes on the mask's outline. When the Mask Node Edit tool is chosen, the selected mask is displayed as a series of connected Bézier curves. Each node on the curved lines has Bézier control points that can be used to control the shape of the lines, enabling fine adjustments of the mask for a more perfect fit.

Using the Mask Node Edit Tool

By selecting the Mask Node Edit tool from the Mask Tool flyout, the mask becomes a series of lines and curves connected by control nodes. The number of nodes in the mask is determined by the Node Edit Tool Setting roll-up (Ctrl+F8). The roll-up provides a list of five possible Precision options for the Mask Node Edit tool. Each of these Precision settings controls the number of nodes on the mask. By increasing the number of nodes on a mask, for the purposes of editing, it is possible to produce a very accurate mask.

Options from the Mask Node Edit Tool Setting dropdown list.

Very Good	Maximum number of nodes, highest degree of precision
Good	Fewer number of nodes, but still excellent precision
Medium	Average number of nodes; curves follow mask well
Loose	Low number of nodes; should be used for masks with lots of straight lines
Very Loose	Lowest number of nodes; use only for very gross mask-adjustment

To move a node in the mask, click on it and drag the node to the desired position. The attached lines and curves in the mask move to adjust to the new position. To change the shape of the line in a mask, click on a node and two control handles appear. Click and drag either handle and the shape of the curve changes interactively as the handles are moved. To remove a node, click on the node to be removed and depress the Delete key. To insert a node, click on an existing node nearest to where a node is to be inserted and depress the Insert key.

Notes on the Node Edit Tools

There are some surprises in using these tools if you are not careful. First, the only way to zoom in on one of the mask nodes is to use the Z key. If you go to the toolbox and select the zoom button, the image drops out of mask-edit node. Next, every time that either of the Node Edit tools are selected, PHOTO-PAINT regenerates the nodes as controls by the Tool Settings roll-up for Node Edit. This means that if you perform all kinds of node removal and node additions, as soon as the Node Edit tool is closed, all of that information is lost. That is not to say that the mask or build-object thing won't reflect the changes, because they will. Lastly, it is not a very accurate mechanism. The nodes and their Bézier curves are very rough and many times do not exactly coincide with the points on the mask. It is a tool for fine mask editing, not precision. To get precision, I recommend that you zoom to a higher level and use the Brush Mask tool.

The Object Node Edit Tool

The Object Node edit tool enables you to edit the borders of Complex Objects. Complex objects are created when the Build mode button is in Build Mode and is distinguished by a red marquee. In every respect, it operates identically to the Mask Node Edit tool.

Transparency Masks

This section explores the Transparency Mask commands. As you know, a mask is a defined area that covers part or all of the image. The mask can be either transparent or opaque. Masks can be used to protect areas from change or to isolate an area and limit the effects to within the boundaries of the mask. Transparent masks enable you to control the amount of protection.

A transparency mask covers the entire image. If the image used for the transparency mask is smaller than the image onto which it is loaded, PAINT will stretch the mask to fit the image. This may distort the mask. A transparency mask can be created from any importable image, such as a Photo CD image or a CorelDRAW file.

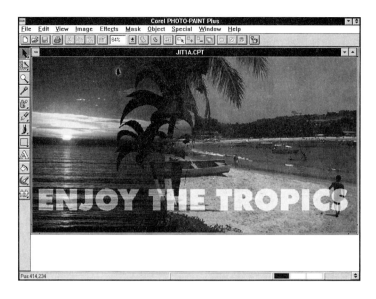

Figure 15.21.
Several different
transparency masks
were used to create the
image shown.

When creating transparency masks using the Create Transparency Mask command, the amount of transparency of the mask is determined by the value of gray chosen in the Transparency Mask Creation dialog box or the Color roll-up. If you increase the transparency of the mask, the mask acts as if it is thinner, and any changes applied (brush strokes, filters, etc.) have more effect on the underlying image. If you decrease the transparency of the mask, the mask acts as if it is thicker, and the changes have less effect on the underlying image. Black (numerical value = 0) provides 100 percent protection for the underlying image and thus no transparency. Lighter shades of gray (higher numerical values) provide less protection and higher transparency. White (numerical value = 255) provides 0 percent protection.

When an image is loaded as a transparency mask using the Load Transparency Mask command, the image is converted to grayscale (if the image isn't grayscale already). Darker areas of the image are converted to dark grays and black, while lighter areas of the image are converted to light grays and white. The resulting transparency mask otherwise works exactly as described previously.

That is how a transparency mask operates. Now what can you do with it? Several different transparency masks were used to create the image shown here. A transparency mask and a regular mask both define area boundaries. Where a transparency mask differs from a regular mask is that the transparency mask controls not only where the effect is applied, but also how much effect is applied. There are a vast number of ways to use the transparency mask. The only restrictions are time and imagination. In this book, we can only begin to show you what this powerful tool can accomplish.

Creating a Transparency Mask from a Regular Mask

When a transparency Mask is created from a regular mask, the masked area is transparent and the area outside the mask fills to the edges of the image boundaries. Once a mask has been created, it can be named and saved as a file. The saved mask can then be loaded and used whenever required. If you want to save the mask with the file, you must save the file in the PHOTO-PAINT format (*.CPT).

A transparency mask can be created from a previously defined regular mask by using the following procedure:

1. Define a mask using any of the mask tools.
2. Select Create Transparency Mask from the Mask menu.
3. Choose the From Mask option. This opens the Transparency Mask Creation dialog box. The dialog box choices are listed forthwith.

   Transparency Mask Creation dialog-box options.

Opacity Slider	Determines the opacity of the Transparency mask. Range of 0-100 percent.
Feather	Allows the feathering of the mask. This feature is provided for use with third-party plug-in filters that require feathering of masks or paths.
Remove Mask	This checkbox, if selected, removes the original mask when the transparency mask is created.

4. Click the OK button. The Transparency Mask icon appears in the lower-right corner of the status bar.

Figure 15.22.
The Transparency
Mask Creation dialog
box.

Creating a Transparency Mask from a Mask

This method is used when an effect is needed in a specific area. It is especially useful when text is involved. For example, when a mask for text needs to be created, the text is typed in, and after it becomes an object, the Magic Wand mask tool is used to create a mask around the text. The Create Transparency mask function in the Mask menu is selected, and From A Mask is chosen. Taking defaults, the resulting mask allows the hand-drawn effect shown in the accompanying image.

Figure 15.23.
This is a mock CD cover that used three different transparency masks.

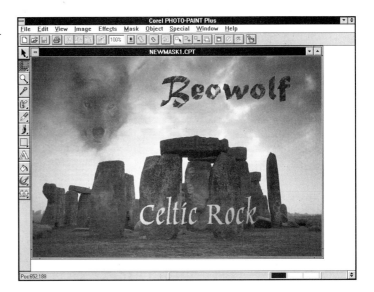

Creating a New Transparency Mask

This method uses the entire image area for the Transparent Mask area. Once a mask has been created, it can be named and saved as a file. The saved mask can then be loaded and used whenever required. If you want to save the mask with the file, you must save the file in the PHOTO-PAINT format (*.CPT).

A New Transparency Mask is created using the following procedure:

1. Choose Create Transparency Mask from the Mask menu.
2. Select New from the drop-down list. The Transparency Mask Creation dialog box opens.
3. After the choices in the dialog box are made, click the OK button. The Transparency Mask icon appears in the lower-right corner of the status bar.

Transparency Mask Creation Dialog Box

The Transparency Mask Creation dialog-box options enables you to customize the new transparency mask.

Transparency Mask Creation dialog-box options.

Uniform	Enables uniform transparency. A uniform transparency mask provides equal transparency coverage over the image.
Transparency	Enter a value from 1 to 255. Lower values provide more protection. Higher values allow more of the effects and the paint to show through.
Gradient	Enables gradient transparency. A gradient transparency provides a range of coverage over the image, depending on which type of gradient fill is chosen.
Type	This is a dropdown list box displaying the types of gradient transparencies. The options are: Rectangular, Linear, Circular, and Conical.
Preview box	Displays the selected gradient or uniform transparency. If you have chosen Gradient, you can use the cursor to change the origin of the gradient by clicking inside the preview box and dragging the origin point to the desired position.

Figure 15.24.
Transparency Mask
Creation dialog box
with a circular gradient
selected.

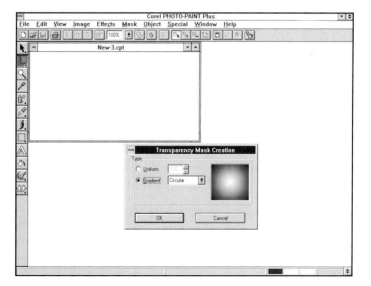

Viewing a Transparency Mask

1. Open the Objects/Layers roll-up (Ctrl+F7).

2. Click the Show checkout to the right of the word Transparency. The transparency becomes visible as a red mask. Red is the default color for transparency tint and is controlled in the Preferences section of the Special Menu. If the image you are working on has a lot of red in it, the transparency mask may not show up very well. You can change the transparency mask tint in the Advanced section of Preferences. The transparency mask and the image are visible. Where the transparency tint color (red) is darkest is where the least amount of effect can be applied. Where there is no tint color, effects will be applied at 100 percent.

Editing a Transparency Mask

Once a transparency mask has been created, the masks can be edited using the normal PHOTO-PAINT tools.

1. Open the Objects/Layers roll-up (Ctrl+F7).

2. Click the Transparency button under the word Edit. The button next to the label "Image" goes out when Edit Transparency is selected. The transparency mask and the image are visible. Where the transparency tint color (red) is darkest is where the least amount of effect can be applied. Where there is no tint color, effects will be applied at 100 percent.

3. Edit the transparency exactly as you would any other image. All of the tools can be applied to the transparency mask just as with normal images, with the following exceptions: the Text tool, Mask tools, and Object tools are disabled (grayed out) whenever Edit Transparency is selected.

Notes on Editing Transparency Masks

By using the show button next to the image button, you make the image that is in the image area visible or invisible. It is sometimes useful to be able to see the image so as to position some areas of the mask. At other times you may find it confusing to have both on at the same time. You can turn the image off if it becomes difficult to edit the transparency mask with the image on. To edit a gradient fill, you must replace it with another from the Fill roll-up.

Corel *TIP!*

> The Remove Transparency Mask option is grayed out under the Mask menu when the Edit Transparency Mask option is selected in the Layers/Options roll-up. You must select Edit Image in order to remove the Transparency Mask.

Other Transparency Mask options in the Mask menu.

Save Transparency Mask	Selecting this option opens the Save Image To Disk dialog box. Transparency masks are saved as *.CPT files, just like any other PAINT image.
Remove Transparency Mask	This option removes an existing transparency mask without saving it. There is no warning dialog box telling you that the mask will be lost.
Invert Transparency Mask	This inverts the mask so that the areas that were protected can now have effects applied to them. This is very useful when working with an image wherein the effects must be applied to both sides of the mask.
Load Transparency Mask	This command opens the Load Transparency Mask From Disk dialog box. Any image that PAINT can import (bitmap or vector) can be used as a transparency mask. Vector bitmaps are converted to bitmap images (rasterized). Color images are converted to grayscale.

Transparency Masks in Action

Let's look at a few examples of transparency-mask applications. One of the main strengths of transparency masks is that they enable the application of effects and operations with variable degrees of transparency. With the Opacity setting for objects, you can vary opacity; but transparency masks go a step further, allowing you to vary the opacity at any given point within an image. Since it is easier to demonstrate this than to explain it, let's merge two images together to get a feel for what transparency masks can do.

First, let's create the transparency mask. We will need to make our transparency masks the same size as the images that we will be using them on. In this case, we will use Photo CD images from the Corel Professional Photos CD-ROM Sampler Limited Edition. We will be using the Stonehenge image (200000.PCD on the CD) from the Sacred Places series and a trees image (200007.PCD on the CD) from the Trees and Leaves series. We will be using standard-sized images, which are 512×768 pixels (or 2.560 inches wide by 1.707 inches high) at 300 dpi, so open a new grayscale image with those settings.

Corel *TIP!*

Even though you can create transparency masks using the Create Transparency Masks command in the Mask menu, there are many good reasons to simply create your transparency mask as a separate file. Since you can load a transparency mask from a bitmap file, you can create a transparency mask as a separate file and then you will no longer be prevented from using Mask, Object, and Text tools. Furthermore, if you will only be using the file as a transparency mask, it is best to create transparency masks in grayscale, because no matter what other color mode you use to create the file it will be converted to grayscale when you load it as a transparency mask. So, if you will only be using the file as a transparency mask, it is always better to work in grayscale. Your work will be faster in grayscale, not only because its file size will be smaller than CMYK or RGB, but also because if you load a CMYK or RGB file as a transparency mask, PHOTO-PAINT will have to convert it to grayscale on the fly, which takes longer then merely loading a grayscale image.

1. Open the Fill roll-up and select a linear blend from black to white with a 180-degree angle and 256 steps. To fill the entire file with the linear gradient fill, simply click anywhere on the image with the Fill tool. (See Figure 15.25.)

Figure 15.25.
Fill the entire image
with a linear gradient
fill from black to white.

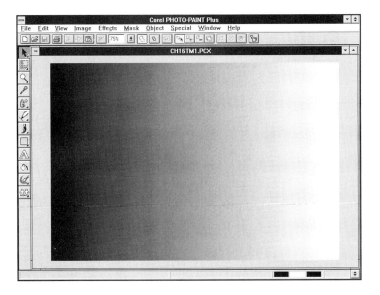

2. Add a Noise filter at a setting of Gaussian level 20. Even with 256 steps, the linear blend can be banded. This helps create a smoother transition. Then save the new file with a recognizable name in a familiar directory, and close it. (See Figure 15.26.)

Figure 15.26.
Add Noise to smooth
out the blend.

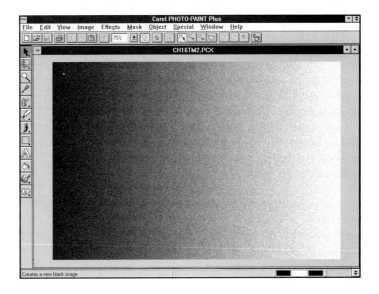

3. Open the Stonehenge image (200000.PCD on the Sampler CD) and select Load Transparency Mask from the Mask menu. Load the file with the linear blend as a transparency mask. (See Figure 15.27.)

Figure 15.27.
Click on the Show
option by Transparency
in the Layers/Objects
roll-up to observe the
Stonehenge image with
the transparency mask.
(Note: It's not easy to
see in grayscale.)

4. Open the Mosaic roll-up, locate the trees image (200007.PCD) on the Sampler, and drag-and-drop it onto the Stonehenge image. (See Figure 15.28.) When you drag-and-drop an image from Mosaic, PHOTO-PAINT automatically makes a floating object out of it. When the trees image is loaded as an object into the Stonehenge file, it may not be positioned perfectly over the Stonehenge image. Notice that when you open the Layers/Objects roll-up, you now have the Stonehenge image as your base image and the trees image as a floating object.

Figure 15.28.
Drag-and-drop the tree-image file from Mosaic to create an object with the tree image within the Stonehenge image.

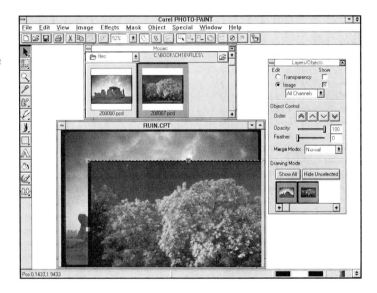

Reposition the tree object so that it is exactly over the Stonehenge image. Select the Object Picker tool from the Object tools in the toolbox and hit Ctrl+F8 to bring up the Tool Setting (Object Transform) roll-up . Select the Icon Object Position, make sure the Relative Position option is not checked, and enter a 0 value in both the Horizontal and Vertical settings. Hit Apply. Because the tree file is exactly the same size as the Stonehenge file, this positions the tree object exactly over the Stonehenge background. The Stonehenge background is not gone—it is just underneath the tree object. (See Figure 15.29.)

Figure 15.29.
Use the Tool Setting
roll-up to reposition the
object over the back-
ground.

5. Select Merge from the Object menu or hit Ctrl+G. Using the linear blend as a transparency mask will create a merging effect between the two images, because the linear-blend transparency mask will protect the base image at the darker points of the linear blend and allow the tree object to seep through at the lighter points of the linear blend when it is merged. Because the transparency mask is darker at the left, less and less of the tree object seeps through as you go further left; because the transparency mask is lighter to the right, more and more of the tree object seeps through as you go right. Using the linear-blend transparency mask smoothly blends the Stonehenge image into the trees.

This is a basic example of how transparency masks work to create transparency effects, but merging two images together is easy as long as they are the same size. Now let's look at how to merge parts of images with transparency masks using advanced masks.

1. Open image 23048.PCD from the companion CD in standard size. Crop the black outline from the Photo CD image and save the file with a recognizable name in a familiar directory. (See Figure 15.30.)

Figure 15.30.
Sheesh, doesn't this
guy know about
escalators?

2. Select the Magic Wand Mask tool, hit Ctrl+F8 to bring up the Tool Settings dialog box (if it isn't already open), and click on the Color Tolerance button in the Tool Settings dialog box. Make sure the Identical Values option is on, enter 100 into any value of the RGB tolerance values, and click OK. Click on the Add To Selection button on the ribbon bar. We are going to create a mask of the rock to exclude the climber, the shadow, and the sky. It will take some tedious masking to accomplish this, but the effect is worth it, and practicing advanced-mask creation is always valuable. (See Figure 15.31.)

3. There are four isolated sections of rock in the image: on the left of the climber and his shadow, between his legs, between his left arm and his shadow, and to the lower right of the climber. Click the Magic Wand somewhere within each one of the sections. The section between the climber's arm and shadow has a dark area of the rock that cuts between that section, so click the Magic Wand on both sides of the dark line. Select the Save option under the Mask menu and save the mask with a recognizable name in a familiar directory. This has given us the majority of what we want, as well as a little bit we didn't want. We will have to add parts of the rock to the mask and subtract parts of the climber's sweater, head, and sock. This is the tedious part. (See Figure 15.32.)

Figure 15.31.
While it does not show
up well in grayscale,
the mask covers the
majority of the rock.

Figure 15.32.
In this grayscale close-
up, you can see (albeit
not very well) that the
Magic Wand has
selected parts of the
sock, while missing
parts of the rock.

4. Select the Mask Brush tool. There's a lot to do here, so we can't take you through step-by-step, but there are a few touchstones. The object here is to add the parts of the rock that have been missed to the selection. You want to avoid adding parts of the sky, shadow, or climber to the selection. When you use the Mask Brush tool with the Add To Selection button on, parts of the image that are already selected remain selected, while parts of the image that are not selected are added to the selection when you brush over them with the Mask Brush tool. (See Figure 15.33.)

There are plenty of random parts of the rock that have not been selected, so here's a few tricks that you can use to make this a little easier. Some parts of the rock have big areas where you can easily miss small parts of the rock with the Mask Brush tool. To avoid this and to make selecting these areas a little easier, make your brush size as big as possible and simply make one or two clicks to select large chunks at a time. For instance, the bottom left and right sides of the image are all rock. You can take the your brush size up to 100 and click in the corners of the image to select a chunk of those nasty little unselected areas. Don't worry if the brush goes outside of the image. For smaller areas, make the brush size as large as possible to select as much as possible without selecting the shadow, climber, or sky. For the touchy areas around the shadow, climber and sky, you will likely have to make your brush size fairly small. If you are unsure whether you have all of the rock selected, simply hit the delete button (make sure your have Undo enabled first), to observe what portions of the rock are still unselected. If there are parts of the rock still unselected, they will remain undeleted. Undo the deletion and select those areas with the Mask Brush tool. When you have finished selecting the rock, save the selection or mask. If your computer crashes or you need to take a break, you can simply reopen the image and load the mask at any time.

Figure 15.33.
This shows how the image looks when you are temporarily deleting the selection to ascertain what portions are selected and what portions are not. Make sure Undo is disabled before you use this technique.

5. Click on the Remove From Selection button on the ribbon bar. Brush over the portions of the sweater, head, and sock that are selected in order to remove them from the selection. Save the mask.

6. Click on Paper Size in the Image menu, make a note of the size of your climber image (the size is dependent and where you have cropped the image), and open a new image with those dimensions. Close the original image for the time being, convert the new image to grayscale, and close the RGB version. Load the Mask you have just created by selecting Load from the Mask menu. Select Invert from the Mask menu. At long last, we are finally creating the transparency mask in earnest. You may be wondering why we didn't create the transparency mask from the existing mask. This will become apparent in the next step.

Figure 15.34.
With the mask inverted in the new file, use a black fill for the area where the shadow, climber, and sky will be.

7. Hit Shift+F6 to open the Fill roll-up, click on the Color Fill button, and click on the Edit button. Click on the Color box in the middle of the roll-up and select Black. Select the Fill tool from the toolbox and fill the masked area with black. Select Invert from the Mask Menu. (See Figure 15.34.) Hit Shift+F6 to open the Fill roll-up, click on the Fountain Fill button, and click on the Edit button. Create a custom linear fountain fill of 270 degrees with 256 steps going from black on the right to white on the left. Enter an intermediate position at 75 and color it white. Hit OK to exit the Fill roll-up. Select the Rectangle tool and hit Ctrl+F8 to bring up the Tool Setting roll-up (if it is not already open). Enter a 0 value in the Size and Transparency options. Draw a rectangle over the entire image. You can draw the rectangle larger than the image to make sure that you cover everything. Save the file with a recognizable name in a familiar directory. Close the transparency-mask file and reopen the original cropped color image of the climber. The mask protects the blacked out areas from the fountain fill.

You cannot use masks when editing transparency masks via the Edit Transparency Mask option in the Layers/Objects roll-up, so that is why we didn't create the transparency mask from the mask back in Step 6.

Figure 15.35.
It may not look like much, but this advanced transparency mask is the key to some very cool stuff.

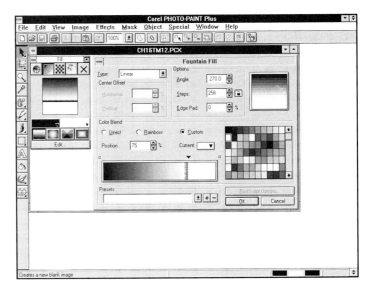

8. Select Load Transparency Mask from the Mask menu and select the file you just saved. Select Paste From File from the Edit Menu, locate 250015.PCD from the companion CD, and click on OK to load the circuit-board image as an object into the climber file. Select the Object Picker tool from the toolbox and move the circuit-board object so that only the circuit board covers the image (not that pesky black outline). Remember, you can use the arrow keys to nudge objects pixel by pixel. Choose Rotate 180 Degrees from the Object Menu. Hit Ctrl+G to merge the circuit board to the climber image. We did not use the Mosaic roll-up this time to demonstrate an alternate method of loading an image as an object. Mosaic takes up quite a bit of resources, so this alternate procedure is often the preferred method of loading objects.

The preceding examples are only the beginning of what you can accomplish with transparency masks. (There are many other exciting techniques using transparency masks covered in the Special Effects chapter and the Dynamic Duo chapter.)

Figure 15.36.
Climbing a mountain of
technology.

Splitting and Combining Channels

This set of tools should be included in a new category in the art contest I have been trying to get Corel to start. The category is "best use of an obscure or pointless tool or command." Scott and I have been asking everyone we can find what they have found they can do with this command. In the original manual, which I had nothing to do with, they give the example of splitting the channels to apply an effect to one channel and not the other. While that sounds great, the fact is that the easiest way to do this is to select the respective channel in the Layers/Objects menu, thus saving you the work of splitting and recombining the channel. Therefore, if you find a unique and important use for the channel-splitting functions, please let us know. (Really.) If it is valid, we will pass it along to the PAINT team at Corel, since they are not sure what purpose the tool has either. Nonetheless, so that this book will be as complete as possible, the following sections represent a comprehensive description of these functions.

Split Channels To (Image Menu)

The Split Channels To command separates an image into channels corresponding to the different components of each color model. (See Figure 15.37.) Corel PHOTO-PAINT can split channels for five different color models: CMYK (cyan, magenta, yellow, black), RGB (red, green, blue), HSV (hue, saturation, value), HLS (hue, lightness, saturation), or YIQ (luminance, chromaticity).

CMYK Model

The CMYK model, as its name suggests, is based on the colors of the inks used in four-color printing. By combining percentages of cyan, magenta, yellow and black, you can reproduce virtually any color you want.

RGB Model

The RGB color model uses percentages of red, green, and blue to create colors. Each component has 100 levels of intensity, ranging from black to the component's full intensity.

HSV (HSB) Model

The HSV model, creates color by varying three parameters: hue, saturation and value (brightness). Hue refers to the quality which makes a particular color different from another. Blue, red, and green, for example, are all hues. Saturation refers to the purity or intensity of a color. By varying the intensity, you can make the color lighter or darker. Value refers to the percentage of black in a color, where 0 percent is black and 100 percent is white. Value (brightness) refers to the perceived intensity of a self-luminous object.

HLS Model

HLS refers to hue, lightness, and saturation. Hue, again, refers to the quality which makes a particular color different from another. Blue, red, and green are all hues. Lightness is the perceived intensity of a reflecting object. Saturation refers to the purity or intensity of a color. By varying the intensity, you can make the color lighter or darker.

YIQ Model

YIQ is the color model used in television broadcast systems (NTSC standard). Only the Y component of this color model would be seen on black-and-white television systems. The Y component of this splitting process produces a grayscale image that is often superior to results obtained with a grayscale conversion using the Convert To command from the Image menu. The Y component is luminance, and chromaticity is encoded in the I and Q components.

Each channel can be edited without affecting another channel. When you split an image, a new grayscale file is created for each component. When you split the channels of an image, the component files created have a .TIF extension. For example, if the image is split into an RGB image, it results in three separate grayscale images, as shown in Figure 15.37.

Figure 15.37.
The original has been
spilt into an RGB image
using the Split Chan-
nels command,
resulting in three
grayscale images.

Combine Channels (Image Menu)

The Combine Channels command recombines an image that has been split. You can also reassign the channels to different destination files (components of the color models) to create unusual special effects when the components are recombined. For example, you can combine the red channel into the green channel. Doesn't that sound like something you do every day? (I shouldn't knock it. It does provide some extra flexibility and doesn't cost anything.)

Combine Channel dialog box options.

Mode	The mode determines what the composite channels are. Channels represent color information about the image. For example, RGB is made up of three channels: red, green, and blue. Each channel contains specific color information for the image. The Mode options are: RGB, CMYK, HSB, HSL, and YIQ.
Channel	Displays each channel of the chosen mode. The Channel buttons work in conjunction with the Images list box. Click a channel button beside to assign the channel to the .TIF images.
Images	Displays the .TIF images created when the image was split. The mode of the image determines the number of channels and the .TIF name. For example, if the image is an RGB image, the Images list box displays the following: RED-0.TIF, GREEN-0.TIF, and BLUE-0.TIF. Click on the image and then choose a channel from the list of Channels that appears.

Figure 15.38.
This dialog box is only
available after an
image is split into
separate channels.

How to Combine Channels

1. Click the Combine Channels command in the Image menu. The Combine dialog box opens. (See Figure 15.38.)

2. The component files are displayed in the Images box.

3. Verify that the image files displayed in the Image box correspond to the correct channels in the Channel box. For example, the GREEN.TIF file should be highlighted when the green button is selected, unless it is your purpose to reverse the channels. To reverse channels, click the channel button and then click the channel image you want assigned to that channel. To check that the channel assignments are correct, click the individual channel buttons and the channel assigned will be highlighted.

4. Click the OK to combine the component image into a new .TIF file. Continue to combine the channels until all of the channels have been added.

Using the Split/Combine Channels Commands

There are some commercial applications that require the ability to split and recombine channels. The average PAINT user will not often have need for these commands. Actually, Scott and I haven't found anyone that uses it either. But I have faith there is some application for this besides making images that look like bad flashbacks from the '60s.

Corel *TIP!*

If you need a quick way to apply an effect to one channel and not the others, use the channel selector in the Objects/Layers roll-up. Select the desired channel and apply the effect.

Bringing Images into PHOTO-PAINT

There are many ways to bring images into PHOTO-PAINT.

Opening an Image file

The most direct method is to load an image file by opening the file with the File Open command in the File Menu. This was explained in Chapter 2.

Dragging and Dropping Image Files

PHOTO-PAINT allows the opening of image files by dragging and dropping them from the File Manager or similar program into the PHOTO-PAINT workspace.

To open a file with drag-and-drop, do as follows:

1. Choose Tile from the Program Manager Window menu. (This step may not be required. The object is to have the File Manager or a similar program open but not occupying the entire display area.)
2. Open File Manager and click on the desired file. It must be an image file.
3. Click and drag the file into the PHOTO-PAINT window and release the button.

Notes on Dragging and Dropping Files

This feature requires that PHOTO-PAINT be open to operate properly. PAINT can either occupy part of the display screen or it can be reduced to an icon. If it is an icon, drag the file on top of the icon at the bottom of the display.

Dragging and Dropping Graphics from a Graphics Program

It is possible to drag-and-drop a graphics image from another application (one that supports OLE 2.0) into Corel PHOTO-PAINT.

To drag-and-drop graphics, do as follows:

1. Size the windows of Corel PHOTO-PAINT and the application that created the graphics so that both are visible.
2. Click on the graphic and drag it into Corel PHOTO-PAINT.

Notes on Dragging and Dropping Graphics

There are several items to consider when using the drag-and-drop feature to move graphics into PHOTO-PAINT. The item that is grabbed is removed from the original application, so you need to make sure it is saved before you drag it across to PAINT. The graphic is rasterized if it is a vector image (i.e., one from CorelDRAW). Even though you may have only dragged some text across, it will come into PAINT as an image square (not text) with a rectangular background. One of the best ways to get graphics from CorelDRAW into PHOTO-PAINT is to save the file as a .CDR file and open it with PHOTO-PAINT.

Setting Preferences

The Preferences section is used to customize Corel PHOTO-PAINT to fit your working environment. It is located under the Special menu and is divided into two sections: General and Advanced.

Preferences Dialog Box—General Section

The General section of the Preferences dialog box enables you to set startup preferences and to customize the Corel PHOTO-PAINT screen.

General Preferences dialog-box options.

On Startup	Determines whether a file is open on starting Corel PHOTO-PAINT. The options are: Nothing, New File, and Open File. The default for this option is Nothing. You may want to change it if you always open an existing file (with this option selected, you are always presented with the Open Existing Bitmap dialog box) or if you are always creating a new file when starting PAINT. Otherwise, leave it set to Nothing.
Units	Determines the units of measurement used for rulers, the status bar, and dialog boxes. The options are: Inches, Millimeters, Picas/Points, Points, Centimeters, Didots, Ciceros/Didots, and Pixels. The default is Pixels. There is an American tendency to want to use Inches. I have slowly gotten used to using Pixels and recommend you try and use it also. Just a suggestion.

Enable Undo

This checkbox enables the Undo command on the Edit menu. If unchecked, Undo is not available. If system memory becomes too low to complete an operation, PHOTO-PAINT will present a warning box that it is disabling Undo. Undo will remain disabled until you go into the General Preferences section and click on it again. This is a good-news/bad-news option. Which do you want first?

The good news: When Undo is not enabled, most operations in PHOTO-PAINT speed up. To understand the reason for the speed improvement when Undo is disabled requires knowledge of how Undo works. When enabled, Undo makes a copy of the image into memory before performing the operation. The copy is into RAM memory, not to the disk.

The bad news: When Undo is not enabled, you cannot undo the last operation.

I have found that when doing the examples, where there is little need for the Undo feature, the speed improvement is noticeable.

Corel *TIP!*

When you have limited system resources, disable the Undo option. When you perform an operation that you may want to Undo, use the Checkpoint feature, which writes a copy of the image to the disk and not to memory. It takes a little longer, but overall the speed improvement is worth it.

Tint Channels

Checkbox enabling the display of channels in color on the Layers/Objects roll-up. This makes the grayscale of the red channel have a red tint to it, the green channel have a green tint, etc. The default is Off.

Show Ribbon Bar

Checkbox enabling the display of the ribbon bar. When checked, the ribbon bar is visible. Why would you want to disable the ribbon bar? I have spent a good part of the book encouraging you to use the ribbon bar. Leave it on.

Show Info (Status) Bar	Checkbox enabling the display of the status bar. When checked, the status bar is visible. I have no idea why this is called an Info bar. I wrote the manual for Corel and could not get an answer to this one. You need the status bar. Leave it on.
Show Tool Cursor	Checkbox enabling the display of the tool cursor. When checked, the cursor is a replica of the type of tool selected. For example, if the paintbrush is selected, the cursor is a miniature paintbrush. The default is Off. This feature is like some of the screen savers I have seen recently. They seem neat for a short while, and then you turn them off. This feature, when enabled, is really cute for about a minute. When you begin to use these "picto-cursors," you realize the "hotpoint"(active point of the cursor) is different on each one. In summary they are difficult to use. Leave it off.
Show Pop-Up Help	Checkbox enabling the display of pop-up help. When checked and the cursor passes over menus and tools, pop-up help is displayed. The default is Off. Although it takes some system resources, it is a nice feature while you are learning your way around PAINT.
Scanner Calibration	Checkbox enabling the calibration of a scanner. Calibrating the scanner is covered in Chapter 17.
Zoom State on Open	Determines the level of magnification when files are opened. The options are: Best Fit, 25, 33, 50, 100, 200, 300, 400, 600 and 1600 percent. The default is 100 percent. Best Fit is recommended unless you have a very slow graphics board.
Stretch Mode for Objects	Determines the mode for stretching objects. The options are: Anti-Alias/Average and Stretch/Truncate.
	Anti-Alias/Average creates a smooth image by removing jagged edges from original and averaging duplicated pixels.
	Stretch/Truncate creates a rough image by stretching duplicated pixels and eliminating overlapped pixels.
	So why would you want to use Stretch/Truncate when the other gives better results? Because sometimes on large images it is desirable to do it

quick and dirty to see an approximation of what
the finished product will look like. Other than
that, always use anti-alias.

Preferences Dialog Box—Advanced Section

The Advanced section of the Preferences dialog box allows you to set the colors
of marquees and specify plug-in directories.

Advanced Preferences dialog-box options.

Build Marquee	Determines the color of the Build marquee. The Build marquee is displayed when creating complex objects. When you are defining the areas for a complex object before building it, the Build marquee is displayed. Click the drop-down palette button. Choose a color or click More. The Select A Color dialog box opens. Choose a color. The default color is red. Leave it alone unless you really believe it somehow violates your fashion sense. This marquee is rarely used in day-to-day applications.
Object Marquee	Determines the color of the Object marquee. Both complex and simple objects have the same colored marquee. Once a complex object has been built, it displays the Object marquee. Click the drop-down palette button. Choose a color or click More. The Select A Color dialog box opens. Choose a color. The default color is blue. There is little reason to change this one.
Mask Marquee	Determines the color of the Mask marquee. Click the drop-down palette button. Choose a color or click More. The Select A Color dialog box opens. Choose a color. Believe it or not, you may need to change the color of the mask now and then. If the color of the transparency and the color of the object are the same or close to the same, it is difficult to see where the mask is in comparison to the subject matter. It is critical when using the Color Mask to see where the boundaries are. I have changed the Mask color several times on a project.

Transparency Tint	Determines the color of the Transparency mask when displayed using the Layers/Objects roll-up. Click the drop-down palette button. Choose a color or click More. The Select A Color dialog box opens. Choose a color. The only reason to change this is because the color of the transparency and the color of the object are the same or close to being the same. When this happens, it is difficult to see where the mask is in comparison to the subject matter.
Plug-In Directories	Determines the plug-in directories to be used. You can insert a directory or delete an inserted directory. For detailed instructions about the installation of additional third-party plug-in filters, refer to Chapter 11.

The Dynamic Duo: Corel PHOTO-PAINT and CorelDRAW!

Corel PHOTO-PAINT and CorelDRAW enjoy
a new relationship with the release of the 5.0
versions. Corel PHOTO-PAINT now imports
CDR and CCH files as well as other industry-
standard vector files, not the least of which is
interpreted Postscript. Futhermore, Corel
PHOTO-PAINT can export with clipping paths,

creating increased flexibility with bitmaps in programs like CorelDRAW and Corel Ventura. This chapter explores the powerful relationship between CorelDRAW and Corel PHOTO-PAINT.

While Corel PHOTO-PAINT's capabilities have increased dramatically, CorelDRAW is still much better suited for layout, shape creation, and non-standard gradients. Most of the following techniques follow this principle. Utilizing CorelDRAW's strengths, we will first prepare the illustrations in CorelDRAW and then use Corel PHOTO-PAINT to take the image to dynamic new heights.

Moving Between DRAW and PHOTO-PAINT

Before we begin demonstrating all of the neat tricks and effects, we must cover some basic rules about transferring images between these two programs. It is a highly advertised fact that the entire Corel line of products, beginning with DRAW 4, supports OLE 2.0 (Object Linking and Embedding). Corel PHOTO-PAINT and CorelDRAW both support dragging an image from one application and dropping it into another. This is great, right? Well, sort of. The drag-and-drop method does work. Our only reservation is that the image quality isn't as good with this method as it is with others. So, is there a better way to get something from CorelDRAW to Corel PHOTO-PAINT? Glad you asked.

There are three different ways to transfer images between CorelDRAW and PHOTO-PAINT. The first method is drag-and-drop. This method is the quickest of the three. The second method is the traditional approach. An image is exported as a .TIF file from CorelDRAW. The third—and best—way to transfer images between the two programs is to save the image as a Corel CDR format file and then open it with PHOTO-PAINT. Each method offers advantages and disadvantages. Let's look at the rules for each one and explore the options and limitations for each method. To save a lot of explanation further down the page, here are a few concepts that are common to all three methods.

When we go from CorelDRAW to PHOTO-PAINT (or any other bitmap application), it is necessary to convert the vector (or line) format into bitmap (or paint) format. This process is called *rasterization.* It is how the rasterization is accomplished that determines what the object we imported into Corel PHOTO-PAINT ultimately looks like. When a color in the original image cannot be produced precisely (either because of display or mode limitations), the computer does its best to make an approximation of the color through a process called *dithering.* Dithering is the mathematical averaging of the color values of adjacent pixels. The use of dithering is another factor in the process of getting from DRAW to PHOTO-PAINT.

That's enough prelude for now. Let's look at drag-and-drop.

The Drag-and-Drop Method

Don't let image quality put you off on the drag-and-drop method. The real loss in image quality results from the way the fountain fill information is rasterized. One of the big advantages of using the drag-and-drop method is the speed at which it operates. Without going into the technical details of how rasterization is done with drag-and-drop, let's simply say that it is not the best choice for importing images that have fountain fills or other images that have a large number of colors (because of the dithering method). So what good is it? It is an excellent way to import items with solid or no colors, such as symbols, or items with a limited number of diagonal lines. (Diagonal lines are a particular obstacle to the rasterization of drag-and-drop.)

Using Drag-and-Drop

If you do decide that drag-and-drop is the best choice for your project, you should follow these guidelines:

- Both applications must be open. This means that neither one can be reduced to a little icon at the bottom of the screen.

- PHOTO-PAINT does not need to have an image area open. If an existing image is not open, a new image will be created.

- To drag an image from CorelDRAW, you must click on it and drag it into the PAINT application. When you are over the paint application, the icon will turn into an arrow coming out of a rectangle. When you let go, two things happen: (1) The image is rasterized and placed into PAINT, and (2) the image in CorelDRAW disappears.

- To restore the image that was dragged kicking and screaming out of CorelDRAW, just click anywhere in the CorelDRAW window (which makes it active again) and select Undo Delete from the Edit Menu or press Ctrl+Z.

As an example, let's start with something fairly simple from CorelDRAW. (This book is mainly about Corel PHOTO-PAINT, so the CorelDRAW files have already been created and are located on the companion CD.) We will be taking something fairly bland from CorelDRAW and making it shine in Corel PHOTO-PAINT, as follows:

1. Open a new document in Corel PHOTO-PAINT that is 3×3 inches at 200 dpi. Open the Fill roll-up by pressing Shift+F6. Select the Noise, Rainbow, Blended Texture options from the Texture list, then change the Background color to Blue and the Foreground color to Cyan. Hit OK to accept the changes. Select the Fill tool from the Toolbox and click it anywhere within the new file to fill it with the new texture. (See Figure 16.1.)

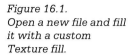

Figure 16.1.
Open a new file and fill
it with a custom
Texture fill.

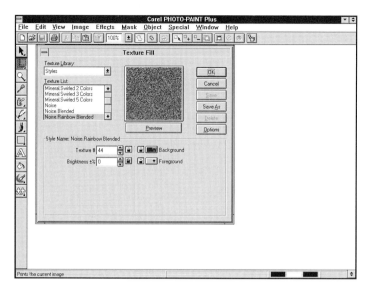

2. Locate WAVEMSK1.CDR from the companion CD and load it as a Transparency mask. When the Import To Bitmap dialog box comes up, make sure that the size option is set at 1 to 1, and then enter 200 for each resolution setting. Select Invert Transparency Mask from the Mask menu. From the Effects, Color menu, select the Brightness and Contrast filter and apply a -50 brightness to the entire file. Save the file with a recognizable name in a familiar directory. Close the file. The CorelDRAW file you loaded as a Transparency mask was created by blending a series of two wavy lines together in CorelDRAW from white to 60 percent black. The blended lines were PowerClipped into a 3- by 3-inch square with no outline and no fill. This non-standard gradient would be difficult to create in Corel PHOTO-PAINT, but it is very easy to create in CorelDRAW. (See Figure 16.2.)

3. Select Open from the File menu and open WAVEMSK2.CDR from the companion CD as a Corel PHOTO-PAINT file. Enter 200 in the Import To Bitmap dialog box for Resolution. If 1 to 1 is selected as the Size setting, the pixel ratio of the image will be adjusted automatically when you change the resolution—which is what we want. The shape we are importing is one of CorelDRAW's symbols from the Transportation library. It has been resized and centered into a 3- by 3-inch square with no fill and no outline. Centering the symbol within the square assures that the CorelDRAW file will import in the correct dimensions.

Figure 16.2.
Load the CorelDRAW
file WAVEMSK1.CDR
from the companion CD
as a Transparency
mask, Invert, and apply
Brightness.

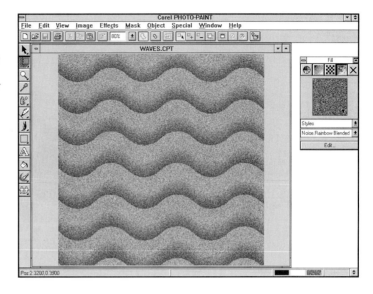

Figure 16.3.
Enter 200 as the
Resolution in the
Import to Bitmap dialog
box, and enter 1 to 1 as
the Size setting.

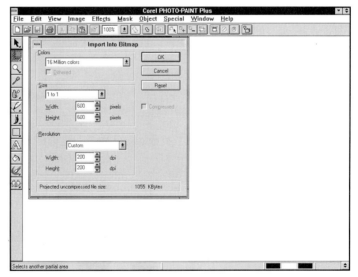

Figure 16.4.
Open the
WAVEMSK.CDR
file from the
companion CD.

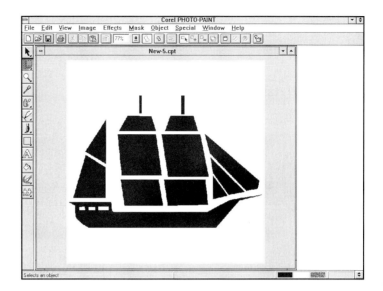

4. Click on the Build Mode button on the ribbon bar. Click on the Add To
    Selection button on the ribbon bar. Select the Object Magic Wand tool
    from the Object Tools flyout on the Toolbox and click within each black
    area of the ship symbol. When you have all sections of the ship selected,
    click on the Create Object button on the ribbon bar.

Figure 16.5.
Open the
WAVEMSK.CDR
file from the
companion CD.

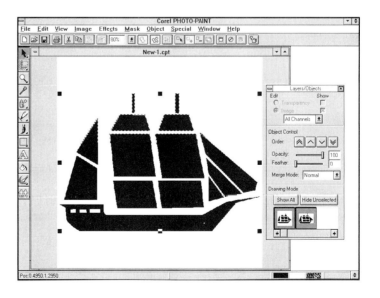

5. Press Ctrl+F7 to open the Layers/Objects roll-up and turn off the base layer under Drawing Mode so that only the newly created object is showing. Press Shift+F6 to open the Fill roll-up and click on the Color Wheel icon and change the color to white. Select the Rectangle tool from the Toolbox and draw a rectangle over the entire picture area to fill the ship with white. Now click on the checkerboard or Bitmap Fill icon in the Fill roll-up. Click on the Load button and locate the WOOD.CPT file on the companion CD. After the wood fill is loaded, select the Fill tool from the Toolbox and click within the boat and mast white areas as shown in Figure 16.6. The wood texture was created using Pixar 128. Pixar 128 is a great resource for realistic textures that tile seamlessly.

Figure 16.6.
Turn off the base layer
in drawing mode, fill
the ship object with
white, and then fill the
boat and mast portions
with a wood texture.

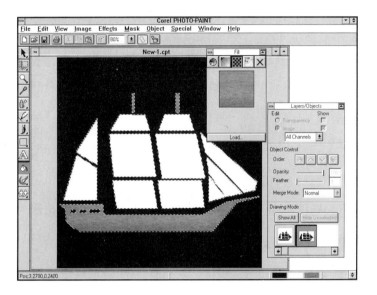

6. Select Load Transparency Mask from the Mask menu, locate WAVEMSK3.CDR from the companion CD, and load it as a Transparency mask. Select Invert Transparency Mask from the Mask menu. When the Import To Bitmap dialog box comes up, make sure that the size option is set to 1 to 1 and then enter 200 for each resolution setting. Select the Brightness and Contrast filter from the Effects, Color menu and apply the Brightness and Contrast filter with a setting of -70 for Brightness. Here we have used custom blends created with the Blend and Contour tools in CorelDRAW as intricate Transparency masks for our ship in Corel PHOTO-PAINT. Again, these custom gradients would be very difficult to create in Corel PHOTO-PAINT, but in CorelDRAW they are a snap.

Figure 16.7.
Load WAVEMSK3.CDR
from the companion CD
as a Transparency
mask, Invert the
Transparency, and add
-70 Brightness with the
Brightness and
Contrast filter.

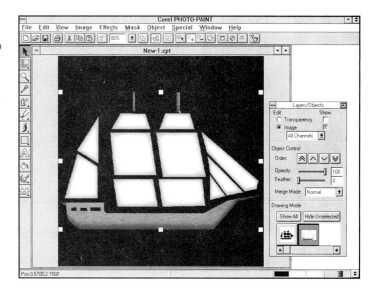

7. With the ship file still open, reopen the waves file you created in step 2. Arrange the files so that the paper areas are visible for both files as shown in Figure 16.8. Select the ship object and drag-and-drop it onto the waves file. Figure 16.8 shows the two files before dragging and dropping. Close and do not save the ship file. The Layers/Objects roll-up for the ship file is shown in order to illustrate what happens when the object is dragged into the new file. Figure 16.9 shows that the ship has been dragged and dropped into the wave file and the Layers/Objects roll-up of the ship file shows that now only the original base remains and that the ship object is now only in the wave file.

8. With the Object Picker tool, position the ship object approximately as shown in Figure 16.10.

9. Load WAVEMSK4.CPT as a Transparency mask from the companion CD. When the Import To Bitmap dialog box comes up, make sure that the size option is set to 1 to 1, and then enter 200 for each resolution setting. With any object tool selected, press Ctrl+G to merge the ship with the wave file. The WAVEMSK4.CPT file was created from a CorelDRAW file by importing the CorelDRAW file and applying Gaussian Blur to create a slightly blended transition between the black and the white areas. With WAVEMSK.CPT loaded as a Transparency mask, the ship looks like it is in the water when it is merged with the wave background. Thus, what was once a very basic image in CorelDRAW has been easily transformed into a vibrant image in Corel PHOTO-PAINT.

Figure 16.8.
Open the wave file created in Step 2. Arrange the wave file and ship file so that their paper areas are both displayed side by side.

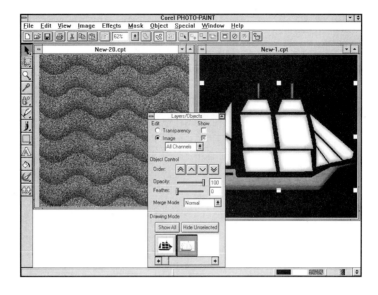

Figure 16.9.
Drag-and-drop the ship object into the wave file.

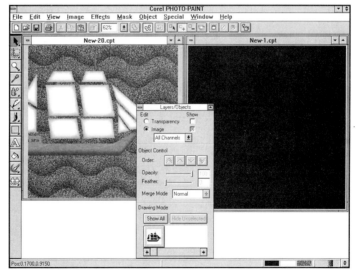

Let's move on to something a little more focused. In this case, we will use CorelDRAW to create Transparency masks that will be used to create a beveled look. In the real world the beveled look is achieved by chipping out letters with a chisel. If you are an old Dragnet fan, the bevel effect was done with a stamp, a hammer and a large sweaty arm.

Figure 16.10.
Reposition the ship over the third set of waves from the bottom

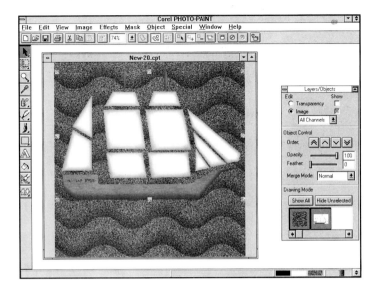

Beveling

1. This mask, for a beveled roman-numeral VI, was created in CorelDRAW. A separate shape was created for each individual bevel. Again, because this book is mainly about Corel PHOTO-PAINT, the CorelDRAW files are simply included on the companion CD. But here's a little background on how the bevel shapes were created in CorelDRAW: Two squares were drawn with the help of the Transform roll-up, one inside of the other. The bevels were drawn by using the Bezier Pencil tool, with the Snap To Objects setting on. For the roman-numeral VI, a sans-serif font was used, with lines drawn down the center of the font. Again, the bevels were drawn by using the Bezier Pencil tool with Snap To Objects on.

   Each bevel was filled with the same linear gradient fill from 50 percent black to white. Then each bevel that faced the same way was given the same angle for the linear gradient fill. Left: 90 degrees. Right: -90 degrees. Up: 180 degrees. Down: 0 degrees. All of the outlines were removed.

2. After the overall bevel mask was created in CorelDRAW a separate file was saved for each direction. For example, a duplicate of the original image was created and set aside. Then all of the bevels, except those facing left, were turned to black. To create the left mask, all of the shapes for the left mask were selected by drawing the marquee around them, and then the image was saved as a separate file with the Selected Only option on. This step was repeated for each direction.

*Figure 16.11.
Each bevel shape is
shown here in
wireframe mode within
CorelDRAW. The
shapes have been
spread out to show
each shape clearly.*

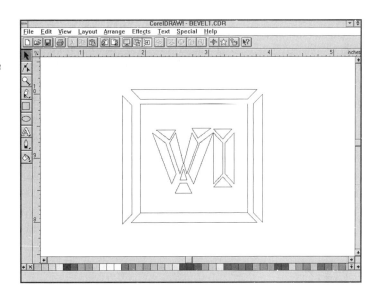

*Figure 16.12.
The original image was
duplicated, and then
the left bevel was
isolated by turning all
other directions to
black and saving only
the new image as a file
with the Selected Only
option on.*

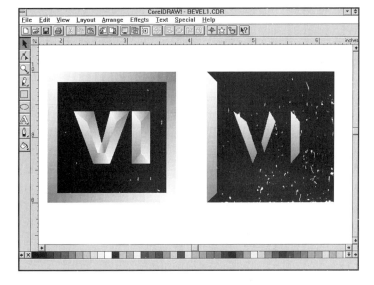

3. Open the MARBLE.TIF file from the companion diskette. The
   MARBLE.TIF file was cropped from an image in Image Club's Backgrounds and Textures volume. Because the .CDR files will be imported as
   Transparency masks, the bitmap file should be the same size or proportional. The .CDR files are 2×2, so the Marble file was cropped to 2×2 at 200
   dpi. If the MARBLE.TIF file were 4×4, the .CDR files would work just fine
   as masks, because they are proportional. If the MARBLE.TIF file were 2×3,
   the .CDR file would be forced into the 2×3 space, and the effect would be
   distorted.

Figure 16.13.
This image was
cropped from Image
Club's Backgrounds
and Textures volume.

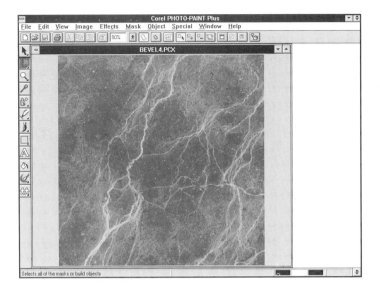

4. Select Load Transparency Mask from the Mask menu and locate the LEFTBEV.CDR file on the companion CD. Load the .CDR file as a Transparency mask. When you load a vector file as a Transparency mask, the Import Into Bitmap dialog box comes up. Change both Resolution settings to 200. Notice that the Size, measured in pixels, changes to 400 when you enter 200 into the Resolution. That's because 1 to 1 is the default for the Size settings. If this option is set to Custom, you will have to enter the Size values separately from the Resolution values. In general, it is best to simply import the Transparency mask at the same size and resolution as the file you are loading it into.

5. Select Color from the Effects menu and choose the Brightness and Contrast filter. Enter a value of +30 in the Brightness setting.

6. Repeat Steps 4 and 5 for the right (Brightness -30), up (-20) and down (-20) masks.

*Figure 16.14.
The Size and Resolution of the Transparency mask should be the same as the image the Transparency mask is being loaded into.*

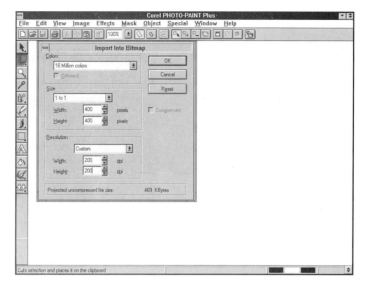

*Figure 16.15.
This dialog box is useless. It does not matter if you answer Yes or No.*

Figure 16.16. Increase the Brightness setting to +30. Brightness is applied only to the left bevels in the image. The linear gradient blends in the Transparency mask give the brightness a gradiated effect.

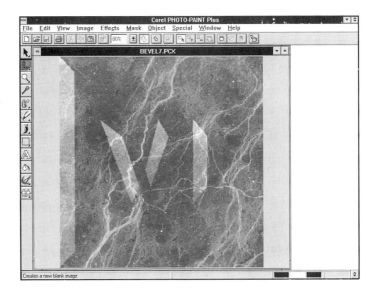

Glowing with Contour

CorelDRAW can even help Corel PHOTO-PAINT with some of its weaker points. For instance, the Gaussian Blur filter is sort of an afterthought filter that was added to Corel PHOTO-PAINT in the maintenance release (E2). Unfortunately, the Gaussian Blur filter is a little weak. It does not evenly distribute blurs the way it should, so, consequently, it cannot accomplish the same tasks as filters with the same name in most other image-editing programs. Here's where CorelDRAW comes to the rescue.

You can accomplish a glow effect with the Contour tool in CorelDRAW. The Contour tool can be a little touchy and slow, but with a little patience and determination, you can accomplish a neat effect. For this, a little bit of explanation is necessary.

1. Open CorelDRAW and type an uppercase G in a large sans-serif font such as Futura Extra Bold, in 72 point. If the G does not already have a black fill, fill it with black. Press Ctrl+Q to convert the G to curves and hit Ctrl+F9 to open the Contour roll-up. Zoom in on the G to get a better view. Draw a 2-by 2-inch box and center the G inside of it. Remove any fill and outline from the box. Save the file with a recognizable name in a familiar directory.

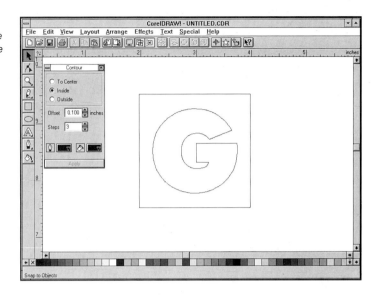

Figure 16.17.
Open CorelDRAW, type the letter "G," open the Contour roll-up, draw a 2-inch-square outline with no fill or outline, and save the file. This screen shot was taken in wireframe mode for clarity.

2. Now fill the G with white and give it a black 1-point (.0014-inch) outline. In the Contour roll-up, change the direction to Outside, the Offset to .003, the Steps to 45, and the outline and fill colors to white. Select Apply. Notice that the Contour does not create a perfect shape of the G as it blends. This actually turns out to be nice, since it creates a certain randomness that is similar to glow effects in reality. Unfortunately, Contour can get overwhelmed from time to time. When using Contour on text, it is often better to convert the text to curves and even break the text apart (combining any text with holes, such as the "o" or the "e," back together), and then apply the contour to each letter individually. Save the file with a new, recognizable name in a familiar directory. Close CorelDRAW and open Corel PHOTO-PAINT. The key here is to go from the solid black line from the original shape to a white line in the last contour step. We use a white fill in the contour dialog box so that Contour will only have to calculate the changes between the lines and not the fills. Contour always puts the contours below the original, so it really doesn't matter what color the fill is if the offset is small enough to create a smooth blend with the lines. You can vary the distance of the glow by varying the offsets and the steps of the Contour. Just remember that you shouldn't make your offsets any larger than half of your line width.

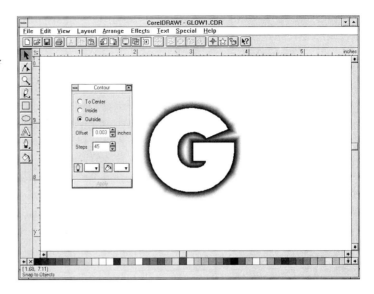

Figure 16.18.
Turn the G to white,
apply a Contour, and
save the file with a new
name.

3. Open the CorelDRAW file you created in Step 1 at 300 dpi. (The gradients show up better in higher resolutions.) Press F4 to Zoom to Fit. Select the normal Magic Wand Mask tool (as opposed to the Object Magic Wand tool) from the Toolbox and click it within the black G. Cut the resulting mask and paste it in as an new object by pressing Ctrl+V.

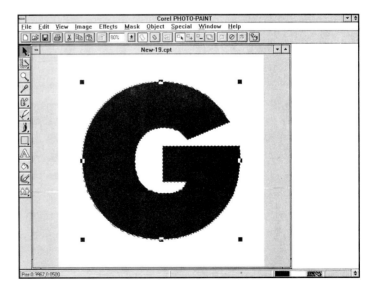

Figure 16.19.
Open the CorelDRAW
file created in Step 1 at
300 dpi and make an
object out of the G.

4. Hit Ctrl+F7 to open the Layers/Objects roll-up and turn off the base layer in drawing mode. Hit Shift+F6 to open the Fill roll-up, click on the Texture fill icon, and change the texture fill to Mineral, Speckled, 3 Color. Fill the G with the fill. Turn off the G object and turn on the base layer in drawing mode. Change the fill to Mineral, Speckled, 5 Color and fill the base layer with the fill.

Figure 16.20.
Fill the Object with a
texture fill and then fill
the base layer with
another fill.

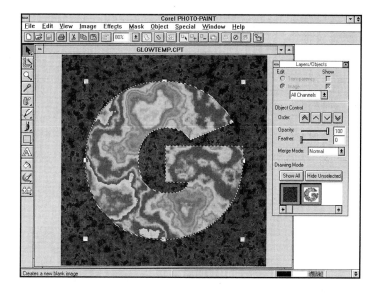

5. Load the CorelDRAW file that you created in Step 2 as a Transparency mask at 300 dpi resolution. Select Invert Transparency Mask from the Mask menu. Apply a 100 percent brightness value with the Brightness filter located in the Effects, Color menu. If you want to add a little yellow, use the Hue and Saturation filter, with a Hue value of 15 and Saturation at 100 percent. (To get a yellow, you will have to use different Hue values with different images, because the Hue values depend on the colors of your base image.) Select Remove Transparency Mask from the Mask menu.

6. Turn the G object back on in the drawing mode within the Layers/Objects roll-up. Hit Ctrl+G to merge the G to the image.

Figure 16.21.
Load the CorelDRAW
file from Step 2 as a
Transparency mask,
Invert the Transpar-
ency Mask, and apply
Brightness with the
Brightness filter.

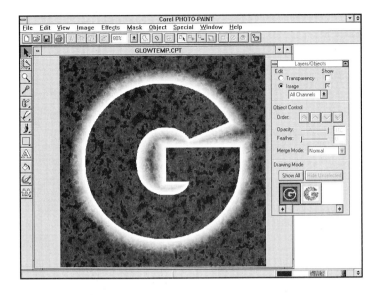

Figure 16.22.
The finished product.

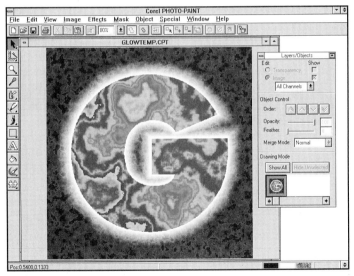

Drag-and-Drop

While you can drag-and-drop from CorelDRAW to Corel PHOTO-PAINT and vice-versa, there is a catch. When you drag-and-drop an image from CorelDRAW into Corel PHOTO-PAINT, it is rasterized at 72 dpi. To get an idea of the problem let's try a quick example.

1. Open CorelDRAW and Corel PHOTO-PAINT. In CorelDRAW, use the Symbols roll-up to drag-and-drop the snowflake (#104) from the Stars1 symbol library, and use the Transform roll-up to resize the snowflake to exactly 2- by 2-inches.

Figure 16.23.
Use the Symbols roll-up to drop a snowflake from the Stars1 library into CorelDRAW and resize it with the Transform roll-up.

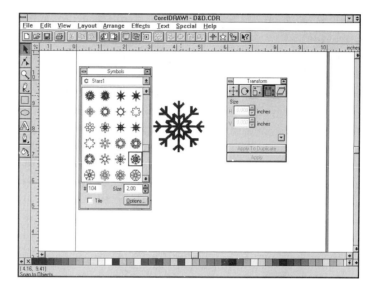

2. Position CorelDRAW and Corel PHOTO-PAINT so that you can drag-and-drop the snowflake from CorelDRAW into Corel PHOTO-PAINT.

Figure 16.24.
Reposition CorelDRAW and Corel PHOTO-PAINT to drag-and-drop snowflake.

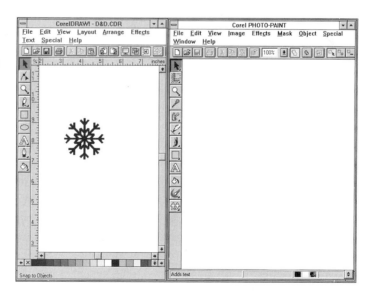

535

3. Minimize Corel PHOTO-PAINT. Notice that the snowflake is gone from CorelDRAW. When you drag-and-drop something from CorelDRAW, it is cut and pasted into Corel PHOTO-PAINT. Press Ctrl+Z or Alt+Backspace to undo, and the snowflake will reappear. (Don't worry, it's still in Corel PHOTO-PAINT.) Save the file with a recognizable name in a familiar directory. Maximize Corel PHOTO-PAINT and open the file you just saved, choosing a Resolution of 300 dpi and a Size of 1 to 1 in the Import To Bitmap dialog box.

Figure 16.25.
Save the snowflake in CorelDRAW and import it into Corel PHOTO-PAINT at 300 dpi.

Notice that the two snowflakes are different sizes. If you have 100 percent as your setting for Zoom State On Open in Preferences, each snowflake will open/import at 100 percent. The snowflake that was dragged and dropped is .48-inch square at 300 dpi, and the snowflake that was imported is 2- by 2-inches at 300 dpi. This is because CorelDRAW rasterizes an image that is cut at 72 dpi, and Corel PHOTO-PAINT assumes you want high resolution, so the image is shrunk to a size that allows it to achieve the high resolution with the information that it receives from the Clipboard. If you divide 2 inches (the size of the imported snowflake) by .48 inches (the size of the drag-and-drop snowflake), you will get 4.1666667. Multiply 4.1666667 by 72 (the dpi at which CDW rasterizes cut images), you will get 300.

So, when you drag-and-drop an image from CorelDRAW to Corel PHOTO-PAINT the image will be shrunk to about 1/4 its original size. Unless you want to draw you image 4.1666667 times the size you want it in Corel PHOTO-PAINT, it is therefore, better to import your CorelDRAW image into COREL PHOTO-PAINT than to drag-and-drop it.

Pumping Up CorelDRAW Artwork

The preceding tutorials are examples of some of the more exciting and powerful techniques that you can accomplish using CorelDRAW with Corel PHOTO-PAINT. Some other, more obvious techniques bear mentioning, though. Because you can import CorelDRAW files directly into Corel PHOTO-PAINT, you can easily liven up vector-based artwork created in CorelDRAW by using Corel PHOTO-PAINT.

The image in Figure 16.26 was created by importing the CorelDRAW file into Corel PHOTO-PAINT and adding basic PHOTO-PAINT filters. With Corel PHOTO-PAINT 5.0 Plus, the possibilities are increased even further with the Alchemy filter. With very little effort, Corel PHOTO-PAINT can add a lot of punch to a relatively static CorelDRAW image.

Figure 16.26.
Add a filter or two to a CorelDRAW image and make the image come alive.

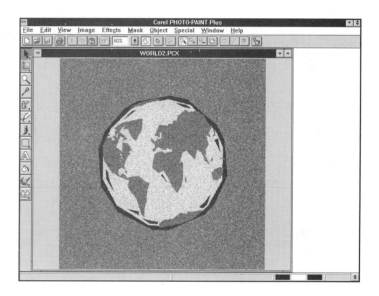

Additional Tips

Clipping Paths from Corel PHOTO-PAINT to CorelDRAW

You can use any mask from Corel PHOTO-PAINT to create what is known as a clipping path. Normally, when you import a bitmap image, the bitmap is in a square or rectangular shape, even if the image you want does not occupy the entire square. Clipping paths allow an image to print out in CorelDRAW and other applications that import EPS images. Clipping paths allow you to print only the portion of the bitmap image you want to. Clipping paths will only work if you are printing to a Postcript printer. Let's try a quick example to get the idea.

1. Open a new image in Corel PHOTO-PAINT that is 2- by 2-inches square at 150 dpi, then type the letter T in Futura Extra Bold at 140 points with the color set to black and the paper set to white. We are using a simple shape to keep this example simple. The T represents any bitmap shape that you might wish to isolate by a clipping path in order to print just that shape in another program like CorelDRAW.

Figure 16.27.
Open a small Corel
PHOTO-PAINT file and
type a black T in a
large, sans-serif font.

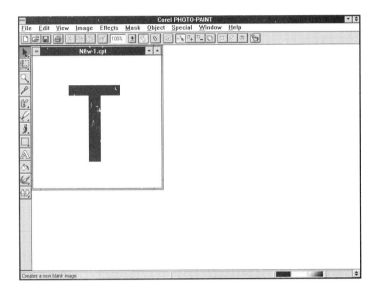

2. Select the Magic Wand tool from the Masking Tools in the Toolbox, and click anywhere within the white portion of the image. Select Invert from the Mask menu.

3. Export the bitmap as an .EPS file with a recognizable name in a familiar directory.

4. Open CorelDRAW and use the EPS import filter to import the T .EPS image. Do not use the .EPS Interpreted import filter; it will not import the .EPS file correctly. Because there are two EPS filters, it is best to actually select EPS (Placeable) from the Import dialog box, than to double-click on the .EPS file choice with All Files *.* setting selected under List Files of Type.

5. Draw a red box over the T image and send it to the back, behind the T image. The T still seems to be surrounded by a white box, but that is only how it looks in CorelDRAW. Print the image to a PostScript printer and you will see that only the T prints over the red box.

Figure 16.28.
Import the .EPS file
with the EPS
(Placeable) import
filter.

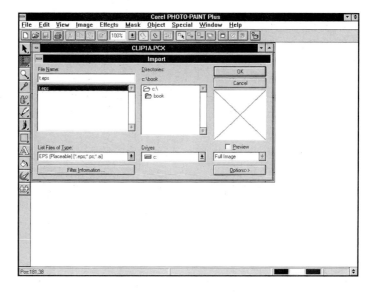

Figure 16.29.
The imported T still
looks like it has the
surrounding white box
when it is imported
into CorelDRAW, but
when the image is
printed to a Postcript
printer, you will see
that only the T prints,
because the clipping
path crops out the rest
of the image.

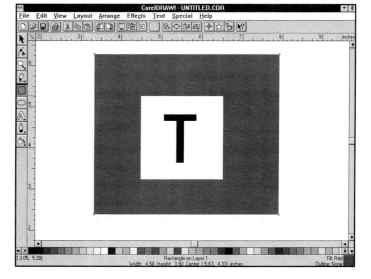

CorelDRAW Bitmap Export Limit

This is undocumented, but CorelDRAW has a bitmap-export limit of 4800×4800 pixels. Admittedly that is a very large file, but if, for instance, you have created a standard poster-sized image at 18 by 24 inches, you will not be able to export it from CorelDRAW at 300 dpi. If you want the file converted to a bitmap format such as TIFF, you can open it up in Corel PHOTO-PAINT. Corel PHOTO-PAINT cannot open a file that big, but it will open a partial file and convert the whole file to a bitmap image in the process. If you want to work with images of that size from CorelDRAW, your only option is to open the file into Corel PHOTO-PAINT.

System Resources

If you do not need to use CorelDRAW, it is usually best not to have it open while doing work in Corel PHOTO-PAINT, even if this means you have to open and close CorelDRAW several times. Corel PHOTO-PAINT is a system-resource hog, so unless you have a lot of RAM, you'll save yourself time by running it alongside other applications as rarely as possible.

Text Handling in CorelDRAW Versus Corel PHOTO-PAINT

Corel PHOTO-PAINT is excellent for creating astonishing text effects, but if you need to set more than a few words of plain text, such as body text for an ad, you will usually be better off importing the bitmap image into CorelDRAW and setting the type from there. Not only is text far easier to work with in CorelDRAW, text will also print better as a font than as a font converted to a bitmap. When doing commercial work, text is often changed at the last minute. If the text is set in PHOTO-PAINT, this could require hours of extra work or even starting over, whereas if the text is set in CorelDRAW, the changes can be made quickly and easily.

Printing

Now that you've spent hours and hours creating your dazzling image, it's time to print it. There's no reason at this point to break into a cold sweat and start searching for an unblemished white lamb to sacrifice. While printing is not a subject for the timid, Corel has taken great lengths to make things as easy as possible.

Print Setup

The first step before you can print is to make sure that the program knows which printer you will be using. When you print from Corel PHOTO-PAINT, your image is automatically sent to the default printer. If you have installed other printers, you can specify which one you want Corel PHOTO-PAINT to use through the Print Setup command. The printer that you specify remains active until you exit Corel PHOTO-PAINT. The Print Setup dialog box is shown in Figure 17.1. The dialog box is accessed by selecting Print Setup in the File menu. Using the dialog box, you can select the printer options as well as the printer. Using Print Setup is not mandatory, because PHOTO-PAINT allows you to make both printer and option selections from the Print dialog box.

Corel *TIP!*

> Print setup is the only option available if an image file is not currently open.

Figure 17.1.
The dialog box that is used to select the output device and options you will be using for the printed output.

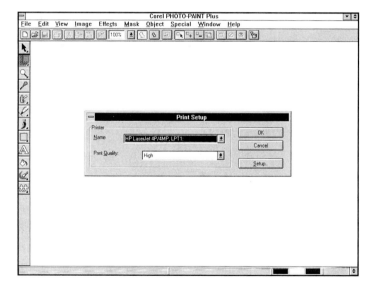

Print Setup dialog-box options

Printer Name   Select the printer to be used from the drop-down list that is available when the arrow button is clicked. When you select a printer it will take PHOTO-PAINT a few moments to read the associated printer files and make the necessary change to the Print Quality selection list.

Only printers that are installed in the Windows system appear in the list. To install a new printer, use the Windows Control Panel and Microsoft Windows documentation for instructions. A new printer cannot be installed by PHOTO-PAINT.

Print Quality The drop-down list available with this option is dependent upon the printer selected.

Setup This button opens up the option dialog boxes that are specific to the printer selected. Figure 17.2 shows the diversity of options that are available with different printers. All of them offer the same basic paper orientation (portrait or landscape) and print quality.

Cancel This button does what it says, it closes the dialog box without taking any action and returns you to the PHOTO-PAINT main screen. If you have opened this dialog box in error, use it.

OK Completes the selection and returns you to the PHOTO-PAINT main screen.

The Print Command

There are several ways to begin the process of printing. You can click on the Print button in the ribbon bar, select the Print command under the File menu, or use Ctrl+P. Using any of these methods opens the Print dialog box. If you're experienced with printing in other Corel applications, you will recognize the Print dialog box right away.

Figure 17.2.
This is a sample of the printer option dialog box you might see when the Setup button is used in the Print Setup dialog box.

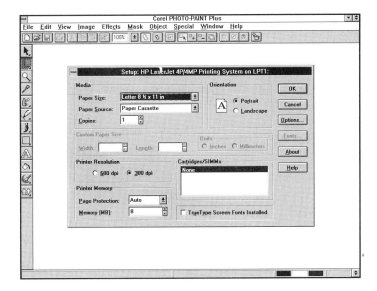

Figure 17.3.
This may be the first
thing to greet you
when you select the
Print command. It is
easy to disable this if
you get tired of seeing
it.

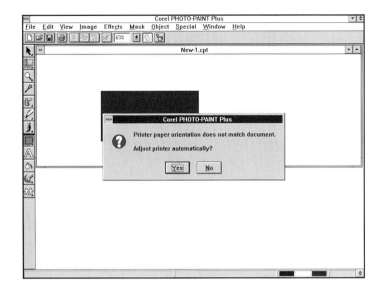

There is a text file in the CONFIG subdirectory of Corel called CORELPRN.INI
that contains all the printing-related information. This file is used by PHOTO-
PAINT and shared by any installed Corel applications. In it are many lines that
you can change and inadvertently mess up your system. That said, the following is a safe change you can make. This change will make the warning box go
away, and whenever Corel detects that the orientation is incorrect, it will
automatically correct it without the warning box. Here is how to make the
change:

1. Using the Windows File Manager, open the file CORELPRN.INI. The
   Notepad opens with the text file in it. (See Figure 17.4.)
2. Under the [CONFIG] section, locate the line that says `WarnBadOrientation=1`
   and change the 1 to a 0.
3. Save the file and exit Windows File Manager.

Congratulations, you are now a certified Windows power user. (Sorry, no
certificate.) More importantly, you will not see the warning box again unless
you go back into the file and return it to its default settings. (In case you are
wondering what you are giving up by disabling your choice at this point, the
answer is nothing.)

Figure 17.4.
The insides of the
CORELPRN.INI file,
which controls all of
the printing-related
functions in PHOTO-
PAINT.

Figure 17.5.
The Print dialog box.

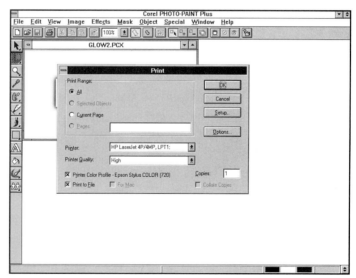

Print dialog-box options

Print Range

Only two of the four buttons are active in PHOTO-PAINT. Whether you click on All or Current Page makes no difference, PHOTO-PAINT will still only print the image you are currently working on. The Selected Objects option does not refer to objects in PHOTO-PAINT. This dialog box is a carry-over from the CorelDRAW print engine, and the Selected Objects and Pages options are permanently grayed out for PHOTO-PAINT because you cannot print selected objects nor create multiple page documents in PHOTO-PAINT.

Printer

The printer option shows the active printer. If other printers are installed, choose the one you want to use from the list. If the printer driver you need is not loaded, you will need to load it via the Printer dialog box in the Windows Control Panel. If you are printing at a service bureau, consult your service bureau operator for what device driver you will need as well as the settings.

Printer Quality

This option enables you to choose a level of resolution depending on the printer chosen. Resolution is measured in dots per inch (dpi). This can be a little confusing. This setting does not change the resolution of the image you are working on. Printer Quality changes the resolution at which your printer prints. So if you have a 72-dpi image printing on a printer set at 300 dpi, the printer will print its best attempt at a 72-dpi image at a printer resolution of 300 dpi.

Corel *TIP!*

It is important to realize that the size of your output is unlikely to match the size of the image on your screen. Monitors have constant resolutions of somewhere between 72 and 93 dpi. Your image may fill up the screen on your monitor and yet only be a couple inches square when printed. The image will print at the Width and Height setting at which you have Image set. You can see what size the image will be by selecting the Preview Image button after you have clicked the Options button. The image will be displayed in the Page Window at approximately the size it should print out.

Printer Color Profile This option indicates the current Color Profile. Having this checked tells Corel PHOTO-PAINT to use the Color Profile you have selected in the Color Manager. For a more in-depth discussion on color management, see Appendix A; here we will just go into it a little. The Color Profile is simply a way to link up an input device (scanner), monitor, and output device (printer). The main purpose of a Color Profile is to ensure that what you see on your monitor matches (as closely as possible) what was scanned and/or what will be printed. Although it is complicated and somewhat difficult to accomplish, the color-management options provide this capability for the first time to the Corel application set.

Corel *TIP!*

The Printer Color profile switch affects both vector and bitmap information on color output devices. In most cases, the color profile should be used, and it is enabled by default. Some printer drivers, such as the HP1200C, perform their own color correction, and Corel's color profile should be disabled to avoid conflict. This switch enables the Color Profile, i.e. color circuits on your printers. If colors need to be converted at print time —for example, if the file contains an RGB bitmap and you are printing to a CMYK color printer—using the color profile will improve color integrity. If you are unsure about this, contact your printer manufacturer's technical support to see if they provide color correction.

Besides color management, one of the main ways to accomplish accurate color is by using color matching systems such as Pantone or TRUMATCH. If the Color Profile option is not checked, you will be dependent on color matching, third-party color-profile software, or hardware-based monitor-calibration systems for color accuracy. Having said all of this, many users find they don't need a high level of color accuracy. It is unlikely that the blue you see on your monitor will print out red. The blue may print out lighter or darker than you thought, but if you can live with this, then there is no need to feel inferior. The Printer Color Profile feature has been provided for those who need it. When you are getting paid to create artwork and your blue prints out too dark to contrast properly with your black and you end up losing your customer, *then* it becomes important.

Print to File

This creates a file that can be printed from DOS. This option is usually used to print files from systems that do not have Corel PHOTO-PAINT installed or when sending files to a service bureau for high-resolution printing. When you click OK, a dialog box opens, prompting you to type a filename.

Figure 17.6.
The Print To File
dialog box.

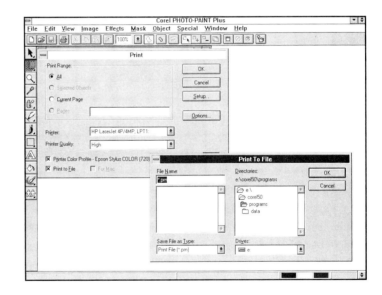

For Mac

You should select this option if you are printing on a device controlled by a Macintosh computer. This option is only available when the Print To File option is checked and only then when it is going to a PostScript printer.

Setup

Clicking on this button takes you to the same dialog box as selecting the Setup button for Print Setup under the File menu. (For details on its operation, see Print Setup section earlier in this chapter.) It allows you to select specific printer options, such as orientation, paper size, paper source, and other options that are unique to the printer selected.

Options	This is where the trickiest controls are. Use the Print Options dialog box for more advanced options for controlling the way an image prints. If you are printing to a black-and-white laser printer, you may not need to use these options.
Copies	If you have no scruples about all of the trees and owls you are destroying, you can print up to 999 copies with this option. Presumably your conscience (and your budget) will ordinarily limit you to just one copy.

Corel *TIP!*

If you do need more than one copy, this is the best place to do it. Most all of the printing time on laser printers is consumed in placing the image on the drum. So by telling PHOTO-PAINT you need several copies, it passes that information to the printer and it only takes a few more moments for the additional copies. This is not true of thermal-wax or ink-jet printers.

The Print Options Dialog Box

Although the Print Options dialog box (Figure 17.7) is largely used for four-color output controls, there are several reasons why you might use this section with a laser printer. For instance, you may need to check your separations on your laser printer by clicking on Print Separations, or you may need to change where the image prints on the page. The point is that even if you are not going to print four-color output, it can still be useful to learn about the Print Options dialog box.

The first thing that you will probably notice when you click in the Print Options dialog box is the Page window. This window shows how an image will look when it is printed. Notice the bounding box surrounding the preview image. This bounding shows the non-printable area, which is dependent on the printer and paper size you are using. Usually this is about a quarter of an inch. Any portion of your image that is outside of this bounding box will be clipped off. How accurately PHOTO-PAINT determines the printable area is dependent on the printer driver. For example, if you use the Fargo Primera Color printer it has a printable area that is smaller than the 8-1/2" × 11" sheet that is loaded into it. PHOTO-PAINT knows what the printable area is, because the Fargo paper selection has the correct information built into it. Most color printers that work with Windows have the necessary information to enable this feature to work accurately.

Figure 17.7.
The Print Options
dialog box. Even if you
are just printing to a
black-and-white
printer, the Screen
Options dialog box has
a lot to offer.

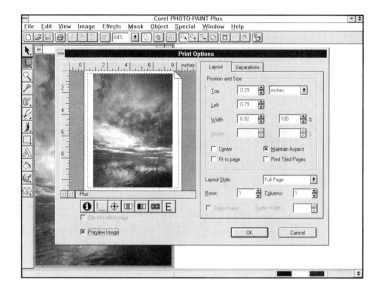

Rulers help you judge the relative size and placement of the image. You can change the rulers' units by clicking on the Units box under the Layouts tab and selecting a new unit from the list. It is important to note that changing the image's size or position will not affect the image file. It will only affect how it is printed.

Reference Buttons

Directly underneath the Page Window are several handy buttons (Figure 17.8). These are different features that add useful information to your image, such as standard printers' marks and file information. In order for the references to appear, the size of the printable page (as set in the Page Setup dialog box) must be smaller than the size of the page you are printing on. Many image setters have an "extra" page setting ("letter extra" is 9 1/2" × 12", for example) that allows for crop marks and file information, etc. If you click on each, you will notice that the result is displayed in the Page window.

Info button

The first button is the Information button. When this button is depressed, information about the image file will be printed along with the file. If you are printing a composite image (an image that is not separated), clicking the Information button results in the following information being printed: filename, the date and time that the file was printed (if it was printed to a file it will show the time of file creation), and a composite header. All of this information will be printed outside the image area if there is sufficient space. If there is not enough space or the Fit To Page option is selected, nothing will be printed, regardless of the button settings. When printing separations, the following will be printed with the image: the color of the plate, the filename, the date and time that the image was printed, and which plate the separation is.

If the File Info Within Page option is selected, all of the file information is printed inside the image area, regardless of the effect. The operation of File Info Within Page is dependent upon the size of the image and if the Fit To Page option is enabled. PHOTO-PAINT will attempt to print the information and the image separately if possible. Clicking this option is useful if you need the information, and the image doesn't take up the entire page.

Figure 17.8.
Reference buttons.
These buttons are
made available when
the Option button is
selected in the Print
dialog box. They offer
useful options at the
click of a button.

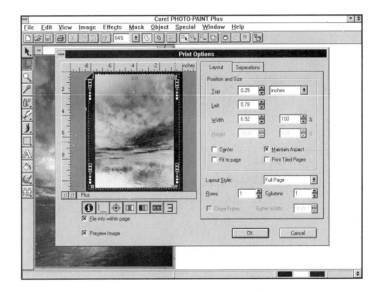

Figure 17.9.
The Print dialog box
(with option button
enabled) showing the
Preview image area
enabled.

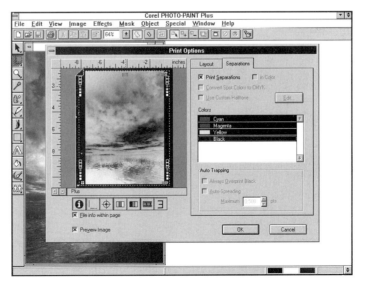

551

Crop Mark Button

When this button is depressed, crop marks will print with the image. Crop marks indicate where the printer should trim the image. Use Crop marks when you want the image to bleed to the end of the page. No printing device can print to the edge of any page, so if you want the image to print to the edge of the paper, the image must be printed on an oversized page and then the paper must be cut off. Printing to the edge of the paper is referred to as *bleeding*. (Bandages are rarely necessary.)

Registration Marks Button

Depressing this button results in registration marks being printed. Printers use registrations marks to align color separations. Registration marks look like little bull's-eyes and are not to be confused with crop marks, which are simple straight lines.

Corel offers three different registration marks. By default you will get the little bull's-eye. Here is how to get the other two:

1. Using the Windows File Manager open the file CORELPRN.INI. The Notepad opens with the text file in it.

2. Under the [CONFIG] section locate the line that says PSRegistrationMarkType=1 and change it to one of the three available options:

   0 = Corel logo registration mark

   1 = Standard bull's-seye registration mark

   2 = Half inverted bullseye

3. Save the file and exit Windows File Manager.

The PSRegistrationMarkType=<0,1,2> setting determines what style registration marks are used when printing PostScript separations. The default setting is 1.

Calibration Bar Button

Press this button to have a calibration bar print with the image. The calibration bar consists of six colors: red, green, blue, cyan, magenta, and yellow. You can use these color bars in conjunction with the Color Manager to calibrate your monitor by printing a test page and then using the resulting calibration bar as a reference.

Densitometer Scale Button

This option prints a densitometer scale on each page of a color-separated image. A densitometer scale is used to gauge the accuracy, quality, and consistency of the four-color output. This reference is only available if you are printing separations.

Negative Button

The Negative button is much like the Invert filter except it does not change the image file; it only affects the output. Many American printers prefer color separations to be shot as a negatives. Ask your printer what they prefer.

Emulsion Button

The last button indicates the position in which the emulsion is facing: up or down. Depress this button when printing to film emulsion-side down. Check with your service bureau or printer as to whether they prefer the emulsion side up or down. Emulsion refers to the photosensitive layer on a piece of photographic paper or film. By default the emulsion is up. Again, ask your printer what they prefer. Generally you're safe with the default. FYI, if you examine a piece of film after it has been developed, the emulsion side is the dull side (the shiny side is referred to as the base). Usually the orientation of the emulsion is related to whether the image is printed to film as a negative. That is, a printer will tell you whether they prefer positive emulsion up, negative emulsion up, positive emulsion down, or negative emulsion down.

Preview Image

Clicking on this button displays the current drawing in the Page Window instead of the default gray box. Use this option only if you need to see the image; otherwise the gray box is much faster. Be advised that when previewing a large image (larger than 14MB in size), the Preview image can take a very long time to generate and it really doesn't offer that much in the way of information.

Objects Appearing Black in Print Preview

If you encounter problems with objects appearing black in the Print Preview when using Windows For Workgroups 3.11 and the Super VGA (SVGA) 256-color driver, you can change the setting in the CORELPRN.INI file, as follows:

1. Using the Windows File Manager, open the file CORELPRN.INI. The Notepad opens with the text file in it.
2. Under the [CONFIG] section, locate the line that says `BadPreview = 0` (the default) and change the 0 to a 1.
3. Save the file and exit Windows File Manager.

Print Options Layout Dialog Box

Position and Size

This section of the Layout dialog box gives you the ability to adjust the size and position of an image. The image will default to print in the center. The Center options is available if you play with different position settings and then later decide you want it back in the center.

Top and Left

These options adjust the position of an image on page. The value in the Top box controls the location of the top of the image. While the Left value surprisingly represents the location of the top left corner of the image (don't ya hate it when these things make sense).

Width and Height

Most of the time you will want to print your image at 100 percent. Caution should be used when adjusting the size of the image. If you increase the size or percentage you will lose resolution, whereas if you decrease the size or percentage you will gain resolution. When the value in one box is changed, the value in the other changes proportionately to maintain the image's aspect ratio when the maintain aspect option is on.

Center

When this option is on, the image is converted into a purple Martian eating a banana, uh, that is... it centers the image on the page.

Fit to Page

This option reduces or enlarges the image to fit on the size of paper in the printer. Again, if the image is smaller than the paper size you will lose resolution if you select fit to page. The reverse is true if the image is larger than the page size. This feature is mainly handy if you need to proof large drawings that exceed the printer's maximum paper size.

Maintain Aspect

This option allows you to keep the aspect ratio when resizing. For instance, if you resize an image that is one-inch wide by two-inches high to 50 percent, the Maintain Aspect ratio keeps you from inadvertently resizing the image to .5-inches wide by 10-inches high (Ouch!) instead of .5-inches wide by one-inch high.

Print Tile Pages

If your image is larger than your page size and you want to proof it in full size, this option allows you to print tiles of the image that you can assemble to puzzle the piece together in full size. The Maintain Aspect Ratio option should be on when using this feature. With careful cutting and pasting, it is possible to use this feature and the Fit to Page option to make larger prints than your printer could normally handle.

Layout Style

These options allow you to adjust the size and position of an image according to various printing needs. For instance, if you need to print an image that you want to fit to a two-column format that you will later add text to, you can adjust the columns (and rows) here to print the image on one column.

Rows	Sets the number of vertical rows on the page.
Columns	Specifies the number of horizontal columns on the page.
Gutter Width	Sets the size of the gutter between Columns.
Clone Frame	Clones the frame.

This can also be pretty spiffy if you've used PHOTO-PAINT to create something that you need to print multiple copies off of one sheet of paper, such as a business card. It is as simple as increasing the number of rows and columns and then clicking on Clone Frame. You shouldn't feel too bad about all those typesetters you will be putting out of business—I'm sure their families don't need too much to eat.

Corel *TIP!*

You can inadvertently scale an image by putting them into columns and rows that are smaller than the actual image, so some thought should be put into the layout before using this feature.

Print Options Separations Dialog Box

This dialog box is used to prepare an image for color separations. If you are not familiar with printing four color output, it is important to consult your printer about these settings.

Print Separations

When this option is on, PHOTO-PAINT prints the color information of your image in grayscale separations. Typically, these are the four process colors (cyan, magenta, yellow and black). You can also individually choose the colors you want to separate.

Color Separations are necessary for four color output. Printers cannot render images like photographs (continuous tone images). In order to print full color images, printers utilize combinations of tiny dots (called *halftones*) from four colors (cyan, magenta, yellow, and black). Individual color separations are referred to as *plates*. Each plate has the color printout for each color. When these plates are printed in combination with each other, the illusion of full color output is created. It's an illusion because the image is made up of tiny dots that the human eye blends together at a comfortable reading or viewing distance.

In Color

When checked, prints the separations in color rather than grayscale. This option is available if you are printing to a color printer or to file. This option gives you the ability to print on transparencies allowing you to check any trapping you've applied to objects in your image.

Convert Spot to CMYK

Clicking this option converts spot colors in the image to their process color equivalents. It is functionally unnecessary since PHOTO-PAINT cannot print spot color. That's right, PHOTO-PAINT automatically converts spot colors to CMYK whether this option is checked or not.

Use Custom Halftone

This option is only available if you are printing separations to a PostScript device. When you check this option the Edit Button becomes active. Clicking on the Edit button brings up the Advanced Screening dialog box. This option gives you access to advanced screening options such as, custom halftone screen angles and line frequencies for each of the CMYK colors. If unchecked, your image prints using Corel's default angle and frequency. Since the default angles are already optimized for a very large majority of four color output needs, you will almost always want to use the defaults. Again, consult your printer if you have questions on this.

Corel *TIP!*

What do you do if you have a PostScript printer that Corel PHOTO-PAINT doesn't recognize as a PostScript printer?

As new PS printers appear there is a possibility that you will install a PS printer that Corel will not recognize as PS. There is a simple solution: The PSDrivers section of CORELPRN.INI lists PostScript printer drivers that can be used by Corel. The number 1 after the driver name tells PHOTO-PAINT that the printer is a PostScript device. If a 0 follows the driver name, PHOTO-PAINT treats the printer as a non-PostScript device, which will lead to the inability to use some of the screening and other advanced options. To recognize additional PostScript drivers, add their filename to this section. For example, to include the HP4P/4M driver, open the WIN.INI file and search for the [Devices] section. You will find the driver name, HPWINPS, here. Add it to the list below and make it equal to 1.

```
MGXPS=1
PSCRIPT=1
AGFAPS=1
```

Figure 17.10.
Advanced Screening dialog box.

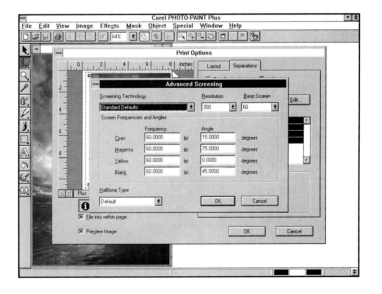

Advanced Screening

Clicking the Edit button opens the Advanced Screening dialog box. These options require a high level of expertise for desirable results. Control screening technology, output resolution, line screen, screen angles and frequencies for the four process colors. Set halftone screen type. The look-up table in CORELPRN.INI defines the default screen frequency and angle for different resolution devices.

Screening Technology

Resolution

This option allows you to manually set the resolution. This does not mean that you can select an arbitrary resolution, for instance, print 301 dpi on a 300-dpi printer. Resolution is printer dependent. Logic suggests that if you have a 300-dpi printer you will not be able to print at 400 dpi. Furthermore, you can't arbitrarily pick a number lower than the printer's maximum and expect it to print at that lower setting. If, for instance, you set your 300-dpi printer to print at 93 dpi, it may or may not default to a different setting, such as 75 dpi or 150 dpi.

Corel *TIP!*

A good rule of thumb with resolution to remember is that resolution settings should always be evenly divisible into the resolution of the printer. For example, for a 600-dpi printer, some of the acceptable setting should include 75, 100, 150, 300, and 600.

Basic Screen

The screen setting measures the fineness of the halftone screen in lines per inch (lpi). The higher the number the finer the screen the crisper the output. Laser printers generally print at about 60 lpi, while imagesetters can print up to 200 lpi. This setting is also referred to as the Screen Frequency setting.

Screen Frequencies and Angles

This area allows you to set screen frequencies and angles for individual colors. When printing color separations, the angles of each color plate are very important. Each plate is printed at a different angle to avoid a major printing problem referred to as moiré. *Moiré* is an undesirable pattern caused by the tiny dots (halftones). Printing each color plate at a different angle reduces moiré to the point that it is usually undetectable at a comfortable reading distance.

Halftone Type

In the previous example, we have referred to the halftones as tiny dots, which implies round dots. In fact, you can print halftones in many different shapes. Some of these shapes can help reduce various printing problems, but mainly these have been used for special effect printing. At low screen frequencies, these different Halftone types can create interesting visual effects.

Colors

Lists four process colors (cyan, magenta, yellow and black) and any spot colors used in the image. Click to choose the colors to separate.

Auto Trapping, Always Overprint, and Auto-Spreading

These options are another carry over from the CorelDRAW engine. There is no Auto Trapping available for Corel PHOTO-PAINT.

Print Options, Options dialog box

This dialog box is used to specify screen-frequency settings.

This determines the halftone screen frequency used to print your image. The screen frequency is measured in lines per inch. If your printing company tells you that they print at a screen frequency of 150 lpi, this is where you would specify that value. Unless you specified a new halftone screen in the PostScript Options dialog box, objects will print using the screen frequency selected here. If you are printing color separations, adjust the screen frequency of each CMYK color in the Separations dialog box in the Use Custom Halftone option.

A good portion of the time, most users will not need to worry about these printing options, but they are available if you need them.

Tips for Printing to a PostScript Device

If you are encountering problems printing to a PostScript device, the following information may help you in isolating and correcting the problem.

Verifying the Postscript Printer Driver

To date, the most current revision of the PostScript printer driver is version 3.58. To check the version of the driver, double click on the Windows Control Panel in the Main group. Select the Printer icon and then the PostScript printer you are currently using. Go to Setup, then choose the About box. The version is stated here. If your driver is not the most current, you should contact Microsoft to get the update. The easiest way I know to do this is to get on CompuServe and download it from one of several sources.

Using The Error Handler

Before you can determine the best approach to getting your file to print, you need to find out exactly what is causing the problem.

Corel PHOTO-PAINT makes use of the error-handler option in your Windows printer driver. The error handler is enabled by default; therefore, if you want to take full advantage of this feature do not disable its function. You will find the Print PostScript Error Information option at the end of the following menu chain: Windows Control Panel, Printers, Setup, Options, Advanced.

Downloading an error handler in advance of the print job will force it to print out an error message giving some indication of the source of the problem. If you don't have this loaded, your printer will simply go idle. Essentially, an error handler is a memory resident program in your printer that intercepts PostScript errors and prints them.

Common Printing Problems

A Few Suggestions to Avoid Error Messages

- Open the WIN.INI file that is located in your Windows directory. In the [Windows] section, scroll down until you find the line that says:

  ```
  TransmissionRetryTimeout=45
  ```

  Change the value 45 to 999. (This sets the time that Windows waits for the printer to report that it is ready to receive more data.) A value of 999 is equal to an infinite amount of time. Once this is changed, you must restart Windows for the change to take effect.

- Corel PHOTO-PAINT uses temporary (.TMP) files to store data while it is running. These files contain image information that does not fit into available memory. Your temporary area can run over several drives, which will make it easier to work with complex drawings. CorelDRAW.TMP files begin with the characters ~CPT and are deleted at the end of each session. If your system hangs, Corel PHOTO-PAINT will automatically search and remove any .TMP files it created during startup.

- Check to see how much RAM is resident in the printer. A minimum of 1.5MB is required in order to print a full page of graphics to a 300-dpi device. To print fairly complex files, we recommend a minimum of 4MB of RAM in the printer. (Note: Some files may require more than 4MB of memory.)

- Depending on the type of PostScript device, some devices allow the user to set a WAIT TIME amount, specifying how long the printer should wait to receive data from the computer. Set the WAIT TIME to equal INFINITE, if possible. (Please refer to your printer documentation for settings on your printer.)

■ Disable the Print Manager when working with large or complex images. To do this, you must open the Control Panel, double click on the icon for printers, then click on the option at the bottom-left corner indicating whether to use the Print Manager or not.

Some non-PostScript printers will run out of memory when sending bitmap information. Some printer drivers allocate enough space in printer memory to hold the entire bitmap, but they send only one line of information at a time. After the driver allocates this memory several times, as the individual lines are being processed, the printer runs out of memory. This switch controls whether bitmaps will be sent to non-PostScript printers one line at a time or as a single unit. Setting this switch to 1 means that the entire bitmap information is sent to the printer at once. To make the change, do as follows:

1. Using the Windows File Manager, open the file CORELPRN.INI. The Notepad opens with the text file in it.

2. Under the [CONFIG] section, locate the line that says `DumpEntireBitmap=0` and change the `0` to `1`. The default setting is `0`.

    `0` = Sends one raster line at a time

    `1` = Sends entire bitmap at once

3. Save the file and exit Windows File Manager.

Special Effects, Projects, and Other Wow Stuff

Work Session: A Display Placard for Joe's Coffee Company

The inspiration for this placard came from the Image Club's miniature *Tips & Tricks* magazine, which is embedded into every issue of their monthly catalog. The making of this placard involves several procedures we learned in previous chapters and some extensive applications of the Tone/Equalize filter. The techniques that are used to make the placard can be applied to many other similar projects.

1. Open a new image at 400 × 600 pixels, 24-bit color, 96 dpi.
2. Type in "JOE's COFFEE CO." (without the quotes) using Futura XBlk BT at a font size of 55 points.

Corel *TIP!*

To make the apostrophe, hold down the Alt key and enter 0146 on the keypad of the keyboard.

Figure 18.1a.
The beginning of the project. Placement of the text in the image area is not critical.

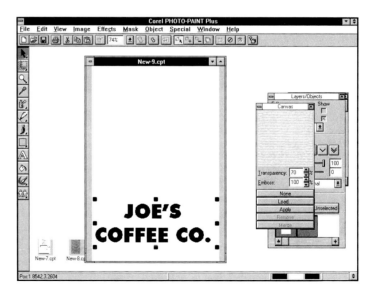

Making a Drop Shadow

Drop shadows can be made using a duplicate of the object and then reducing the opacity and adding feathering. The problem with this approach is that real shadows tend to be larger than the object being illuminated. Feathering an object makes the resulting shadow smaller, because PAINT's feathering only goes in and not out. An alternate method is to apply a Gaussian Blur filter to the shadow duplicate. This works great on a solid background. Applying the filter to an object on a detailed background results in the background being blurred as well as the shadow. Don't despair about using the Merge mode; we will be able to make a realistic shadow without sacrificing background detail.

3. Select the Rectangle Mask tool from the Toolbox and create a Rectangle mask around the text, as shown in Figure 18.1b. The mask should surround the text, but not closely. We are going to blur the text in the next step; therefore we don't want the mask to be so close that it prevents the blur from spreading. The purpose of the mask is two-fold. First, it will speed up the blur filter we are about to apply by "localizing" the effect to the area surrounding the text. The second purpose will become evident in the next few steps.

Figure 18.1b.
The mask defines the outer edge of our shadow.

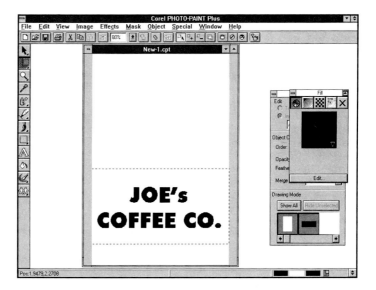

4. Apply the Gaussian Blur filter with a setting of 5. After it is complete, apply it again using the Ctrl+F keyboard combination. Figure 18.1c. shows the result.

*Figure 18.1c.
This illustrates how
well the Gaussian Blur
filter makes the text
into a realistic shadow.*

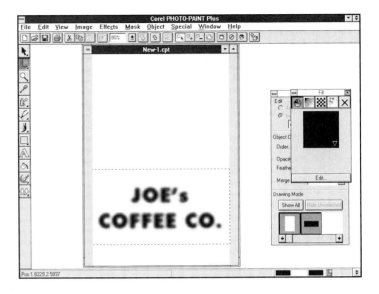

5. Copy the masked area to the Windows Clipboard using the Cut button on the ribbon bar. I told you we were going to use the mask again. You now have an empty image area.

6. Open the Fill roll-up (Shift+F6) and select the Bitmap Fill button (the button that looks like a checkerboard), then click the Load button. This will open a dialog box. This project requires a custom tile called COFFBEAN.BMP for a finished image like the one shown. I created the COFFBEAN.BMP file by masking off a square of a photo of some coffee beans and saving it as a .BMP file. Subjects like the coffee beans are perfect for seamless tiles because they have no definite pattern to indicate to the viewer when they are tiled. Load COFFBEAN.BMP.

Corel *TIP!*

> When making a seamless tile, try to make the image at least 100 × 100 pixels. The larger the image (within reason), the less chance the "edges" of the tile will make themselves known.

7. Paste the contents of the Clipboard onto the image using the Paste button in the ribbon bar.

Figure 18.2.
Coffee anyone? Using the Bitmap Fill tool, we now have 240,000 pixels of coffee beans.

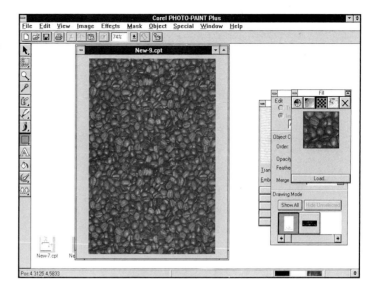

Figure 18.3.
The shadow returns. (Bet you're wondering what we are going to do with the white rectangle, aren't you?)

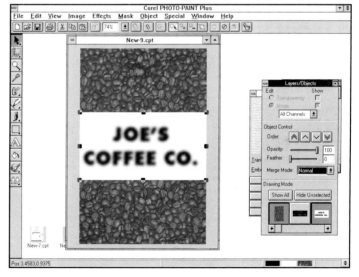

8. Open the Layers/Objects roll-up (Ctrl+F7) and select Texturize from the drop-down list of Merge modes. The white rectangle disappears, leaving only the shadow. The Texturize Merge mode removes anything with a high value. (White is as high as you can get with RGB values of 256,256,256.) I have also found that the Multiply mode also works well for most shadow work. While the shadow here is great, it blends into the dark background of the coffee beans. We will take care of that later. For now, let's make the text look better.

Figure 18.4.
The white rectangle
disappears through the
magic of Merge mode,
leaving only the
shadow.

9. Select the Object Picker in the Toolbox. This automatically selects the text, because it is the only object available at the moment. Use the object-control arrows and click the up arrow so that the text is the top layer and the shadow is the bottom. Click the Hide Unselected button on the Layers/Objects roll-up. This leaves only the text.

Corel *TIP!*

If you are sick of looking at that blue border around the text object, click the Activate/Deactivate Marquee button in the ribbon bar. It is the button with the icon that looks like a fuzzy amoeba on it, located to the right of the Zoom value setting on the ribbon bar.

10. Open the Canvas roll-up (Ctrl+F3). Click the Load button and select PAPER01M.PCX, which is located on CD-ROM Disk 1 of the CorelDRAW 5 release. It is in the COREL50\PHOTOPNT\CANVAS directory.

Apply the Canvas with a 0 percent Transparency setting and any Emboss setting. With 0 percent Transparency, the Emboss setting has no effect. The Canvas will appear over the entire image area. Click the Merge button on the Canvas roll-up. Now only the text has the Canvas texture applied.

Figure 18.5.
We have applied some
texture to our text, but
it looks washed out.

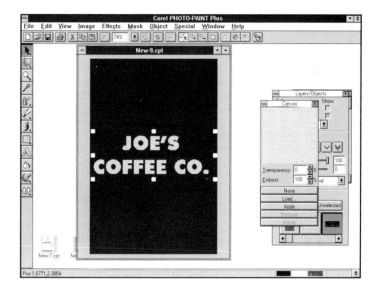

11. Select Tone in the Effects menu and choose Equalize. (It's your only choice.) Move the right (high) and middle (midtone) setting arrows to the two extremes of the histogram line, as shown in Figure 18.6. The low arrow has no effect in this setting. Don't worry too much about the numerical settings. Our goal is to set the midtones at the bottom of the range and the highs at the top. Click OK.

Figure 18.6.
This figure shows the
histogram for making
the texture colors stand
out more.

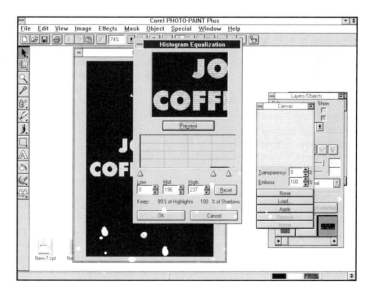

Figure 18.7.
Our color and texture is
more pronounced now
that we have applied
the Tone/Equalize filter.

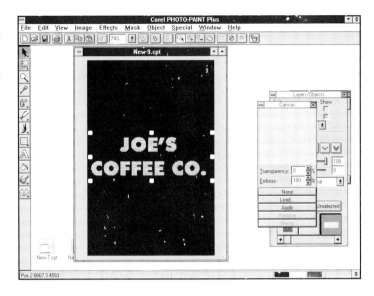

12. In the Layers/Objects roll-up, hide the text (to make the image look less cluttered while we work), and "unhide" the coffee-bean background.

13. Select Paste From File in the Edit menu, and when the dialog box opens, select COFFECUP.CPT. The image will be pasted into our beans. Please make note of the fact that there are two objects: the base image and the actual coffee cup.

    COFFECUP.CPT was created by importing a clip-art image of a coffee cup from the Corel clip art library. I used Mosaic to import it into PHOTO-PAINT, which converted it from its original vector-based format into the bitmap format. Next I used the Magic Wand Object tool and made the elements of the clip art into a single object. The result was saved as a .CPT file.

14. Using the Object Picker, select the white background and delete it using the Delete key. Now position the remaining coffee-cup object as shown in Figure 18.9.

15. Click the Hide All button in the Layers/Objects roll-up. Only the coffee cup object should be visible. Take the Rectangle tool (not the Rectangle Mask tool) and drag a large rectangle over the entire cup. The coffee-cup object fills with beans. While they look OK now, let's make them look rich and hearty, like in the commercials. To do that, we need to use the Tone/Equalize filter again.

Figure 18.8.
This shows the image as it appears when pasted as an object onto our coffee beans.

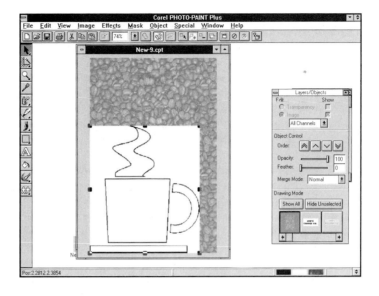

Figure 18.9.
The coffee cup with the original base image removed.

16. Select Tone in the Effects menu and choose Equalize. (It's your only choice.) This time, move the right (high) and left (low) setting arrows to the two extremes of the histogram line, and move the midtone arrow to the middle, as shown in Figure 18.10. Again, don't worry too much about the numerical settings. Click Preview and adjust the image until the beans look like you want them to look. Click OK. The beans look much better now. We are almost finished.

Figure 18.10.
This time we are using
the Tone/Equalize
histogram to make the
coffee beans in the clip
art look more robust.

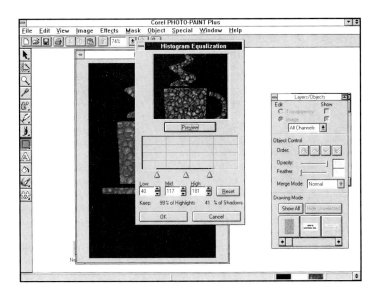

17. The image only needs a border to be complete. So, using the buttons in the Layers/Objects roll-up, hide everything except the base image (coffee beans). Select All in the Mask menu. This creates a mask around all of the coffee beans.

18. Select Create Transparency Mask from the Mask menu. When the drop-down list appears, select From Mask. Enter a value of 30 for the Feather setting in the Transparency Mask Creation dialog box. Make sure the Remove Mask checkbox is checked, and click the OK button. The only indication that a Transparency mask is in place will be the icon in the lower-right corner of the status screen. Select Invert Transparency Mask from the Mask menu.

19. For the last time, select Tone in the Effects menu and choose Equalize. Move the right (high) and middle (mid-tone) and left (low) setting arrows as shown in Figure 18.11. Our goal is to set the tonal balance so that the dynamic range is spread uniformly across the part of the histogram line where the colors are distributed. Click OK.

20. Click the Show All button in the Layers/Objects roll-up. Use the Object Picker tool to position the parts so that they look like Figure 18.12.

Figure 18.11.
Now we are using the Tone/Equalize histogram to make the coffee beans on the border look more robust.

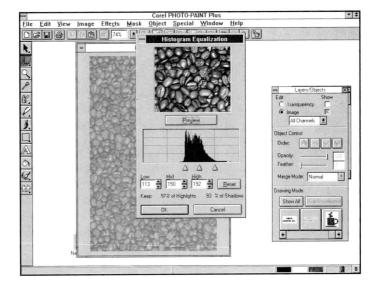

Figure 18.12.
The finished product.

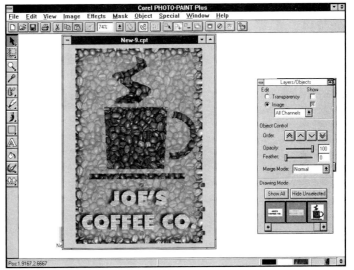

Modifying a Photo for Placement on a Page

Here is a quick project that will look as if you spent some serious time on it. The job is to produce a graphic to go at the top of a restaurant's wine list. Since this is a high-dollar restaurant, they type in the names of the premium wines available that evening. It is decided to use a photo from the Corel Photo CD, Wine and Grapes Series. While the image looks fine as is, we need to modify it for this application. We want to blur the image slightly and make the edges fade rather than have a sharp border.

When I thought about how I was going to make this, I had all these ideas about using an inverted Transparency mask (as was done in the previous work session) to blur the edges. The solution I chose instead turned out to be very simple.

1. Load the PCD image 157076.

Figure 18.13.
This is our starting
point. It is a crisp clear
photo of wine, cheese,
and bread. We are
going to change that.

2. Select the Rectangle Object tool and drag the tool across the entire image so as to make the entire image an object.

3. In the Layers/Objects roll-up, hide the newly created object by clicking on its button in the Drawing Mode section.

4. Click on Mask All in the Mask menu and then click the Delete key. The original image is gone. Click the Show All button in the Layers/Objects roll-up.

5. Apply a Feather value of 40 in the Layers/Objects roll-up. That is a large feather value, so it will take some time to complete. Notice at the corners that the feathering tends not to be as uniform This is when you feather first.

6. Select Fancy in the Effects menu and choose Gaussian Blur from the drop-down list. Use a setting of 5 (default) and click the OK button. After the effect is complete, apply the same amount of blur filter again, using the Ctrl+F keyboard combination.

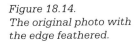

Figure 18.14.
The original photo with
the edge feathered.

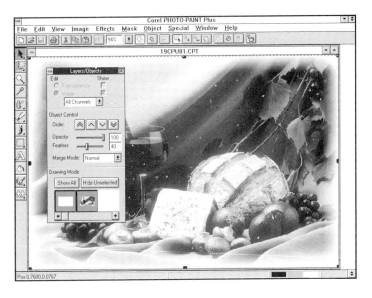

Corel *TIP!*

When you need to apply a large value of Blur (greater than 5), I recommend several smaller applications. This seems to provide a more uniform blurring effect.

Figure 18.15.
After two applications
of blur, the photo is
ready to use.

7. Save the file as WINELIST.CPT. Open CorelDRAW and import WINELIST.CPT into the page. Position it as shown and add the text.

Figure 18.16.
The finished product.

Making a Stained-Glass Image for a Book Plate

I began working with PHOTO-PAINT 5 to make stained-glass images by scanning in pictures of Tiffany stained glass from a coloring-book series by Dover Press. By using the Bitmap Texture fills with the Flood Fill tool, I was able to quickly achieve some realistic-looking glass. The lead between the panes of glass was solid black and didn't look very real. I experimented with using the Emboss filter to make the lead look three-dimensional, with disappointing results. The major problem with using any embossing filter is that the lines which are parallel to the light source either fade or disappear entirely. This fading of the lines presents two problems: It doesn't look very good, and, more importantly, the Flood Fill tool begins to fill in the wrong areas as it "leaks" through the faded lines. Now along comes the PAINT maintenance release, with Object Merge mode. It took many hours of experimenting but the following procedure will show you how to make leaded glass that looks very realistic. Since I wrote this near the holiday season, I thought it would be appropriate to make something that looks like the front of a Christmas card.

Some Considerations Before Beginning

First of all, to do this project you must have the E2 maintenance release of PHOTO-PAINT 5 (which was shipped free to all registered users of CorelDRAW 5) or have the version of PAINT 5 that came with the Ventura bundle or that was sold as PHOTO-PAINT 5 Plus (a stand-alone product). Second, I highly recommend a 486-DX based computer with 8MB of RAM at the very least. I am using a 486-DX2/66 with 16MB. If you have a 386-SX and 2MB of RAM, just read along. Throughout the chapter I will offer suggestions on how to save system resources, suggestions that have very little negative impact on the quality of the finished product. I have divided the operation into three stages: (1) making the image, (2) getting the lead (to stand) out, and (3) making the glass.

Stage One: Making the Image in DRAW

Corel*NOTE!*

> If you don't have CorelDRAW 5, we have included a copy of the file FLOWER.CDR on the companion CD.

1. Use Mosaic to import from the Plant clip-art collection any flower that you like. The one in this example is FLORAI4.CMX.

Figure 18.17.
Our project begins in CoreIDRAW. This is one of the flowers from the clip art collection on the Corel CD-ROM.

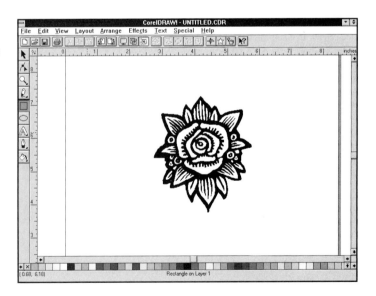

2. Create a rectangle in Draw using a four-point outline pen. I don't recommend making the rectangle any larger at this point, as the resulting bitmap image in PAINT will be approaching Godzilla-like proportions. Later I will show you how to make it bigger.

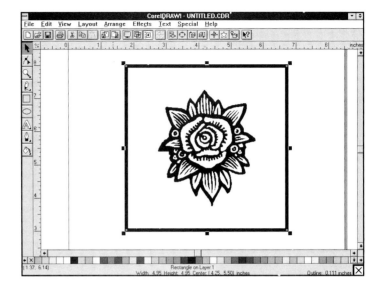

Figure 18.18.
We have created the
outline for our stained-
glass image.

3. Using the Align command, center the flower in the rectangle.

4. Using the PowerLines roll-up, with a setting of WoodCut4 and an outline pen size of 1.3 points with rounded corners, draw lines from the edge of the rectangle to the flower, as shown. Use your imagination with the lines. Because PowerLines tend to take considerable time to redraw, I recommend that you change your view to wireframe until you have completed all of the lines you wish to draw. After you have created the lines, make another rectangle (without the PowerLines) inside the first, as shown in Figure 18.18.

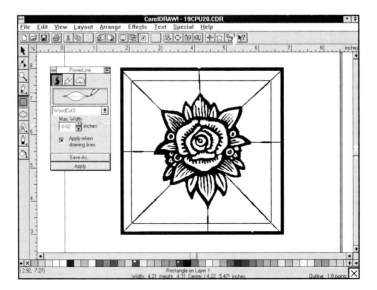

Figure 18.19.
This is all we can do in
CorelDRAW. Now we
need to save it.

5. When you are satisfied with the result, choose the Select All command in the Edit menu and save the image as FLOWER.CDR. Make sure to use the Select Only option in the Save To File dialog box. This keeps the image file we save limited to the image area rather than the entire page. Surprised that we didn't export it as a bitmap image? PHOTO-PAINT does a better job of importing the .CDR files than DRAW does exporting them. This doesn't make sense when you consider that the two products use the same programs for the rasterization; but that's the way it is.

6. Close DRAW. We no longer need it; we do need the system resources that closing it will free up.

Stage Two: Getting the Lead (to Stand) Out

7. Using Corel PHOTO-PAINT, open the file FLOWER.CDR. The Import Into Bitmap dialog box opens. Use the settings shown. This will take a little longer than you may expect because of all the processing necessary to convert the PowerLines into a bitmap image. Be patient; the results are worth it. Here is an area where you can save system resources by changing the resolution to a lower value, such as 75 dpi (you won't see any difference on the screen, only in the printed output). Another way to save resources is by importing the image as a 256 grayscale and converting it to 256 color (8-bit) after it has been imported. PHOTO-PAINT has an optimized 256-color palette scheme that produces excellent results with little or no loss in image quality. It also reduces image file size by two-thirds compared to 24-bit color images.

Figure 18.20.
This is the dialog box
that controls how the
image will be converted
into PAINT.

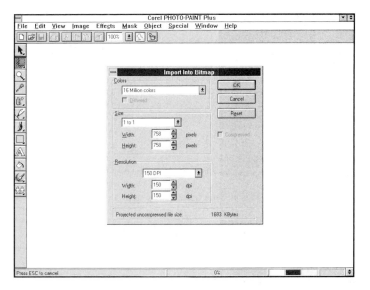

8. Open the Fancy subgroup in the Effects menu and select Jaggy Despeckle from the drop-down list, opening the Jaggy Despeckle dialog box. Use a setting of 3 for Width and Height, and click on OK.

   This is a great filter with a really odd name. It is good for removing the jagged edges from the lines in the image and doing so with the least amount of blurring.

9. Now it is time to copy the image into the Clipboard. Select All in the Mask menu. A dashed line should surround the entire image. If you cannot see the entire image, click the F4 key (Zoom to Fit). The entire image is now masked. To copy the contents of the mask into the Clipboard, click the Copy button in the ribbon bar or select Copy in the Edit menu. After the image has been copied, remove the mask by selecting Remove from the Mask menu. This last step is just an example of good housekeeping procedures that help to keep as much system resources available as possible.

   Wait until the image has been transferred into the Clipboard before proceeding. One way to tell when it has transferred is when the drive-activity light quits blinking.

10. Click on the Paste button in the ribbon bar, or select the Paste command in the Edit Menu. If you use Paste from the Edit menu, you will be presented with an additional choice. When asked, select Paste As An Object. The contents of the Clipboard are pasted on top of the existing (base) image as an object, as indicated by the blue marquee surrounding it.

11. Open the Layers/Objects roll-up (Ctrl+F7). First we must "hide" the object we just made. Remember, when an object is hidden, it is protected from any effect being applied to it. Hide the top layer/object by clicking on the right button of the two large buttons in the Draw Mode section of the roll-up. After you click the button, it will rise up, leaving only the base image (the one on the left) showing. The image doesn't appear to have changed because we "hid" an exact copy of the base image. Next we will emboss the base image.

12. Select the Fancy subgroup again in the Effects menu. This time, select Emboss and the Emboss dialog box opens. Click on the upper-right arrow button, and from the Emboss Color drop-down list, choose Gray. Click the OK button. The Emboss filter is applied to the base image. Look carefully at the diagonal line that goes from the tip of the flower to the upper-right corner of the rectangle. This line is parallel to the direction of the light source. Compare the Emboss effect on this line with the adjacent lines. While the line is still visible, it does not have the same quality of Emboss effect as the other lines. To correct, this we must apply the Emboss effect in a different direction to the top object that is currently hidden, and to do that, we need to "unhide" it first.

Figure 18.21.
Our Emboss filter did
not do a complete job.
Lines that were parallel
to the light source
faded out of existence.

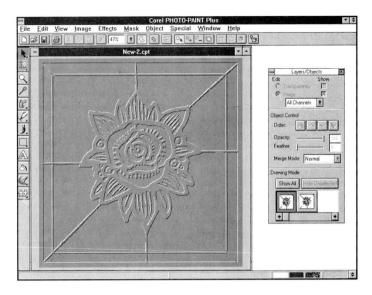

13. Click the Show All button in the Drawing Mode section of the Layers/ Objects roll-up. Because the top object completely covers the base image, we can apply the Emboss filter to it without needing to hide it.

14. Select the Fancy subgroup again in the Effects menu. Choose Emboss, opening the Emboss dialog box. Click on the upper-left arrow button to keep the Emboss color gray. Click the OK button. The Emboss effect is applied to the top object/layer in a different direction. The same problem with parallel lines exists, but the direction has changed. The solution is found in the Mode Merge part of the Layers/Objects roll-up (new with the maintenance release). Using Mode Merge, we can get the Emboss effect without the parallel-line fade by merging the top layer with the base image.

15. Click on the Object Picker tool (the top button on the Toolbox). Click the Mode Merge arrow in the Object/Layers roll-up. From the drop-down list that appears, select Multiply.

There are 20 different Mode Merge functions. The names are not very descriptive unless you are a graphics programmer, and the effects are not fixed but rather a function of the images being merged. Before you criticize the programmers for not being imaginative with the Merge Mode function names, take a look at the other extreme, Kai's Power Tools. How descriptive is "Flaming Blue Dinner Napkins?" There isn't any good middle ground here. The only way to get the best use out of this powerful feature is to experiment with the functions. Select one of the functions, and, using the arrow keys, move up or down the list to observe the results.

Figure 18.22.
The top layer has been
embossed from a
different direction for
the light source.

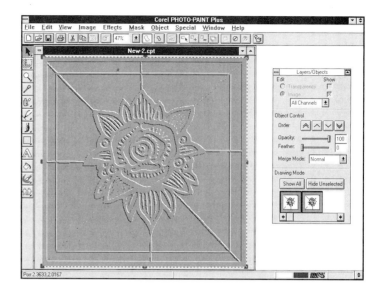

Figure 18.23.
Notice the three-
dimensional quality of
the lines.

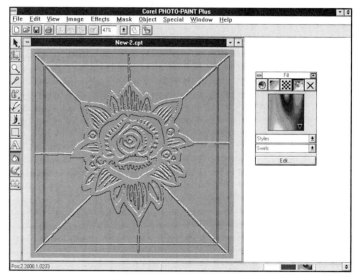

16. The last step to finish the leading is to merge the top object into the base image. Select Merge from the Object menu in the menu bar. The result will probably be too dark, so use the Tone/Equalize filter and adjust it until the lines look firm but the overall darkness is decreased. After a few moments, the image will become much darker (not to worry). The top object merges into the base image. Now we can make some glass. This is the fun part.

Stage Three: Making the Glass

17. Open the Fill roll-up (Shift+F6) and select Bitmap Texture fill by clicking on its button (the one next to the X button).

18. Click the OK button on the Texture Fill dialog box. Open Color Tolerance in the Special menu. Click the Identical Values checkbox and enter a value of 3 into any of the data values, then click OK. This setting of Color Tolerance keeps the Flood Fill tool from filling areas that are more than three shades greater or lesser than the starting pixel (the point where you clicked the cursor).

19. Select the Styles library and the Swirls preset from the drop-down list. The image in the Fill roll-up preview window should be a blue-colored swirl. We need to change it to make it look like green glass.

20. Click the Edit button. The Texture Fill dialog box opens, which allows modification of the Texture Fill patterns. One of the great little-known features of this dialog box is the way the preview window works. If the lock button next to a setting is clicked and put in the unlocked position, each time the Preview button is clicked, the unlocked value is randomly changed. Before you yawn, consider what makes stained glass look real: the non-uniformity of the glass. By using this random feature of the Preview button, many complementary patterns can be created, simulating the effect of real glass. Look at the dialog box in Figure 18.24.

Figure 18.24.
This is the box where
we "make" our glass.

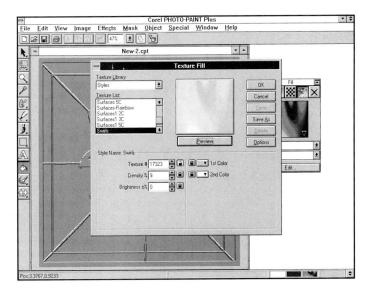

21. To make a fill that is identical to the one displayed in Figure 18.24, use the values shown in the dialog box. The first color green is the bright green located on the right side of the palette two squares above the brown. The second green is a dark green on the left side of the palette. It is the first green in a series of green. Play with different colors and find a combination you like. When you find a pattern you like, lock it by clicking on the pad-lock button next to the Texture # value. If you don't lock it, every time you preview a new color combination, the pattern will change. When you are satisfied with both color and pattern, save it using the Save As button.

    Note that you cannot save custom textures in the Styles directory, so as you see in Figure 18.24, I made a custom library of stained glass textures called SGLASS.

22. Now let's use the glass texture we have made. Click on the Flood Fill tool in the Toolbox (located under the button with the letter A on it.) The cursor now changes to a paint-bucket icon. Place the cursor in the area located in the lower-left corner of the image, and click the left mouse button. (The active part of the cursor is located under the tip of the paint pouring out of the icon bucket.) The selected area fills with the selected texture. This really puts paint-by-numbers to shame.

23. Continue to pick several non-connected areas on the images, and fill them with the same texture fill.

24. Repeat Steps 5 and 6, selecting different colors and patterns until all of the areas are filled, as shown in Figure 18.25.

Figure 18.25.
This is the final image for the stained-glass portion of the book plate. In addition to the steps described, I used the Magic Wand tool to mask the gray leading and applied a large amount of noise to give the leading some texture. I also put some shading under the leading by using the Air Brush tool.

Well, that's all there is to it. Did your computer work up a sweat? Bitmap images can be real demanding on system resources.

So what do we do with this little stained-glass wonder? I saved it as a .CPT file and imported it into CorelDRAW. After making a rectangle behind the stained glass, I filled it with a wood texture out of the clip art library. I then made a white rectangle below the glass and inserted the text.

Figure 18.26.
The finished book
plate.

Special Effects Using PHOTO-PAINT 5

Using the Impressionism and Pointillism Brushes to Make Fabric

When it came time to write about the Impressionism and Pointillism brush tools for the Corel PHOTO-PAINT manual, I tried to explain what they did, but I honestly couldn't figure out any practical use for either of them. The reason I wasn't able to think of anything was that I violated my own personal rule concerning PHOTO-PAINT tools and filters. The rule is: *Never let the name of the tool or filter mislead you: concentrate instead on what it does.* Disobeying my own rule I tried to think of applications that needed an Impressionistic or Pointillist touch. I drew a complete blank.

Time passed, and as I was writing this book for Sams, I came across the dreaded Impressionism and Pointillism brush tools again. This time, I took the opportunity to explore the brushes and found some incredible things to do with them. If you're not familiar with these brushes (perhaps because you didn't read the chapter on these brushes), a quick review follows.

Basics of the Impressionism and Pointillism Brushes

The Impressionism Brush tool creates brush strokes that appear like those used in Impressionist art, although sometimes I think the real purpose of the Impressionism brush is to place a serious load on your CPU. The Impressionism brush stroke produces a selected number of lines in colors that are composed of similar shades. (For example, it turns a single shade of red into eight shades of red.) The size, shape, and qualities of the Impressionist effect is set from our old friend the Tool Settings roll-up (which is now activated through Ctrl+F8).

The Pointillism Brush tool operates exactly like the Impressionism brush. The only difference between the two is that the Impressionism brush produces strokes and the Pointillist brush tool paints dots that are similar to those used in Pointillist art. At least that is what the designers had in mind when they created these brushes. The following is my description of what these two brush tools accomplish.

The Impressionism and Pointillism (I&P) tools create multicolored, randomly placed copies of the currently selected brush (including the custom brush) when the brush is *clicked on* (not dragged across) the image area. Since any image can be made into a custom brush (bet you didn't know that), we have a powerful random-pattern generator. The stars represent several of the 35 built-in custom brushes. The Impressionism brush placed them randomly each time I clicked the brush.

The brush-application process is not as random as you might first imagine. There are five unique settings that control this randomness in the Tool Settings roll-up (Ctrl+F8) for the I&P brushes. What follows is a brief description of what each one does.

H Variance	Determines the variation of color in the brush. The I&P brush style incorporates a number of colors. The H Variance (Hue Variance) determines the difference between the initial brush color and the colors created. For example, if you set the value to a higher number the variation is greater. The difference between the colors is determined by this setting. The number of colors painted each time the brush is applied is determined by the setting of the # of Lines box. If you are working on a grayscale image, the H Variance varies the shades of gray. Please don't forget that gray is a color.

Corel *TIP!*

> Use this setting with some degree of caution. The default setting is 5, and when you take it to the maximum setting, you will have samples from just about every color in the rainbow.

S Variance Sets the variation for the purity of the color. Purity is the number of colors used to mix a specific color. Lower values lower the number of colors that are used to mix; higher values increase the number of colors used to produce the selected colors. The greater the number of colors used to mix a color, the duller the final color looks.

Corel *TIP!*

> The default value of this setting is 5. That is a great setting, and I recommend you leave it alone.

L Variance Sets the variation of luminosity in the colors applied by the brush. Higher values makes the variation of light greater, giving a greater range of light-to-dark variation in the brush strokes. Still confused? This explanation is correct. What it means in real-life application is that the greater the amount of luminosity variance (which, in the HSL model, this brush is built on) means greater differences in the colors themselves. The result is that a higher setting produces greater contrast. (It took me a long time to figure this one out.)

Brush Spread Sets the distance between strokes. Higher values make the distance between strokes greater. This is the setting that determines how far apart each of the brush applications will be from one another. When working on images where the brush strokes begin at the edge of the paper, this setting also determines where the brush strokes begin.

# of Lines Sets the number of lines created in brush strokes. This value, in combination with the Spacing value, can sometimes bring your system to its knees. But for clicking the image to produce random patterns, it isn't that bad.

Making a Fabric with the Impressionism Tool

In this procedure we are going to make a bitmap tile that looks like woven cloth. It isn't complicated and it also makes use of the Bitmap Fill tool, which many users don't realize is an excellent tiling engine.

1. Create a new image of 100 × 100 pixels, with 24-bit color and a resolution of 300 dpi.

2. Select the Impressionism brush from the Toolbox and open the Tool Settings roll-up (Ctrl+F8).

3. Adjust the spacing to 7 pixels. The objective here is to be able to see the separate threads of the fabric. You may have to adjust your spacing. Keep the H Variance at 25. (25 to 30 are good values for fabrics containing many colors, and values of 3 to 8 are good settings for fabrics containing fewer colors.) Put the S and the L variances at the maximum setting for good contrast. You could use a lower number if a more subtle pattern is desired.

4. Select a Square brush (no kidding) with a size of 40, and rotate it 45 degrees. Next, flatten it to about 93. Set the Fade Out value to 0. This turns off the Fade Out effect.

5. Keep the Density setting at 60 and the Transparency setting at 50. This setting removes the square edges of the Square brush and also gives us some "depth" as the brush's patterns overlay one another.

6. Set the # of Lines setting to 8 and the Brush Spread at a low number such as 2 or 1. The # of Lines is going to determine how many lines are created with each pass; the color of each line and where they are put is determined at random. The maximum setting for the # of Lines is 20. For this project, I didn't choose a large number because the Brush Spread is set to a low number and the result of a higher number would be multiple lines repainted one over another. The reason we kept the low Brush spread setting was to prevent the brush strokes from going all over the image and, more importantly, to make sure that all of the brush strokes began at or near the same spot. If a higher number is used, some of the Impressionism strokes would begin in the middle of the image (not good for the effect we are attempting to obtain). Select a bright primary color for the cloth, such as red or blue. We are finally done with the brush settings.

Corel *TIP!*

In the remaining steps we will be working very close to the edge of the image window. To prevent PHOTO-PAINT from getting confused when the cursor approaches the edge of the image window, grab one of the corners of the image window and enlarge the image windows. This makes it much easier when working close to the edge of an image.

7. Holding down the constrain key (Ctrl), draw your line outside of and below the bottom of the image, then slowly drag the mouse across the bottom of the image. The result of this action, when the computer finally gets finished, is a group of thread-like lines, as shown in Figure 18.27. Because the output of this brush setting is random, you will sometimes get results you don't care for. Don't hesitate to use the Undo key (Ctrl+Z) if you don't obtain results that you like.

Figure 18.27.
The first row of threads
for the cloth.

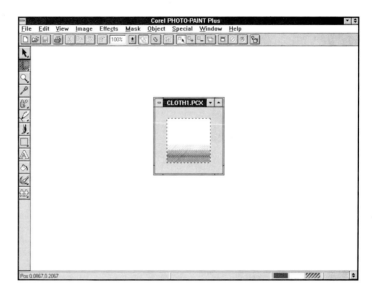

8. Change the Rotate value to 135. Beginning at a point outside of the image, click the left mouse button at a point where the brush cursor is about halfway down over the previous brush stroke, and then click the constrain (Ctrl) key. (Don't click the Ctrl key first or you will reapply the next stroke over the first.) Drag the mouse slowly across the image. You should end up with something like Figure 18.28.

9. Return the Rotate setting to 45 and repeat Step 8. This should fill the entire image. (Figure 18.29.)

10. Save the image as CLOTH1 in the TILES subdirectory of COREL50\PHOTOPNT. You now have a bitmap fill that, when loaded through the Bitmap Fill roll-up, makes great cloth. By the way, to make the horizontal version of the cloth, just rotate the image by selecting Rotate from the Image menu before saving it.

Figure 18.28.
The second row of
threads for the cloth
tile.

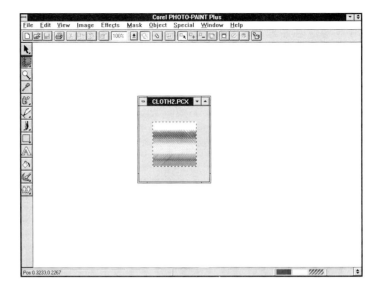

Figure 18.29.
The finished cloth.

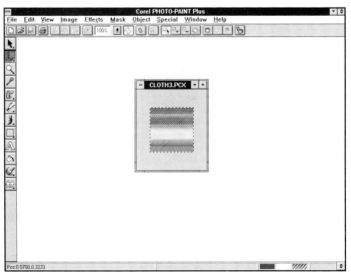

Figure 18.30.
The serape was made using the cloth we just made and applying a ripple filter to it.

To use the bitmap we just made, do as follows:

1. Open the Fill roll-up and select the Bitmap Fill button (the checkerboard button in the center).

2. Click the Load button and select the file we just created.

3. Open a new image and, using the Text tool, type in the word COREL. (I used a large broad font, FUTURA XBLK.)

4. Select the Magic Wand Mask tool in the Toolbox, click the Add To Selection button in the ribbon bar, and click on each letter until there is a mask over each character.

5. Select the Rectangle Draw tool (it's above the letter A) from the Toolbox, and draw a rectangle over the entire word. The Text fills with the cloth texture.

The Corel Flower text was made as described in the exercise just concluded. The little flowers on the letters (I know it looks like a leftover from the original Woodstock) were created by selecting the Flower custom brush included in Paint and clicking judiciously on the text a couple of times.

Figure 18.31.
The text was made
with the cloth bitmap
fill, and the flowers are
a custom brush that
was applied (by
clicking, not dragging)
with the Pointillism
brush.

The Mexico sample was made by drawing a rectangle with the cloth fill (rotated 90 degrees), applying a ripple filter to it, making an object out of the result, duplicating the object, and using the original to make the drop shadow. The text was entered and then the resulting object was duplicated twice (making 3 objects). The bottom object was blurred to make the shadow. The middle object was given a radial fill to give it a metallic gold look, and the top object was actually painted with the Impressionism brush. The resulting object was feathered to pull the Impressionism strokes in from the edges of the text.

Again, don't forget the golden rule of PHOTO-PAINT: *Never let the name of the tool or filter mislead you; concentrate instead on what it does.*

Work Session: Making Water Droplets on Pictures for a Postcard

This is an effect that you cannot use very often, but every time I have looked at similar effects in the *Photoshop WOW!* book (Peachpit Press), I have wanted to re-create the effect with PHOTO-PAINT. Well, several headaches later, here is how you make water drops on a picture. The images that are used in this work session are located on the CorelDRAW CD-ROM Disk 1. I have resampled both of the images by 200 percent and made them available on the companion CD.

1. Open the file MIST2.CPT, located on the companion CD.
2. Click the Build Mode button on the ribbon bar. Build mode is indicated by the button having three shapes on it instead of one.

3. Select All in the Object Menu. This action causes a red marquee to surround the entire image. Click the Create Object button (the button to the immediate right of the Build Mode button). The masked area becomes an object, as indicated by the red marquee turning blue.

Figure 18.32.
This is the image we
will use to create the
water drops.

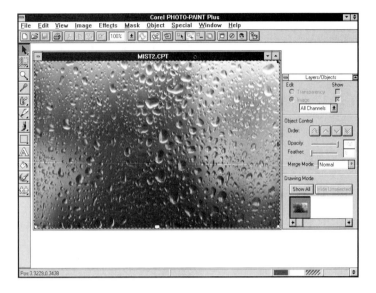

4. Hide the newly created object by clicking the Layer button in the Drawing Mode section of the Layers/Objects roll-up. The image appears unchanged since the original MIST image part of the base image.

5. Select Paste From File in the Edit menu. When the dialog box appears, choose the file PLANT-2.CPT from the companion CD. The new image is placed as an object on top of the original image.

6. Merge the PLANT-2 object by using the keyboard combination Ctrl+G. You will have noticed that there is an object/layer between the newly pasted object and the base image. We do not need to change the layer order to merge the top object because we had previously hidden the MIST object.

7. Select Load Transparency Mask from the Mask menu. When the dialog box opens as shown in Figure 18.35, select the MIST-2.CPT file from the companion CD. Click the OK button. Nothing seems to have changed, with the exception that the Transparency Mask icon has appeared in the lower-right side of the status bar.

8. Unhide the MIST-2 object by clicking on its button in the Layers/Objects roll-up. The PLANT-2 image is covered completely.

9. Merge the MIST-2 object by using the keyboard combination Ctrl+G. There you have it—water droplets on a photograph.

*Figure 18.33.
The subject of the
postcard after it has
been pasted as an
object. Notice it is the
top layer in the Layers/
Objects roll-up.*

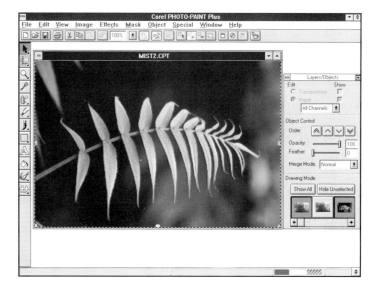

*Figure 18.34.
The subject of the
postcard after it has
been merged into the
base image.*

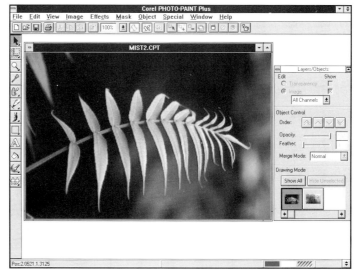

Corel *TIP!*

For this technique to work effectively, both the merged image and the Transparency mask must be identical and aligned. If either image is slightly off in either area, the resulting image will be blurred.

Figure 18.35.
The secret to this
technique is merging
an image in combina-
tion with an identical
image as a Transpar-
ency mask.

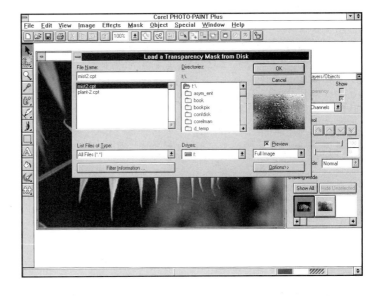

Figure 18.36.
The water drops on the
photograph make an
appropriate backdrop
for our little postcard.

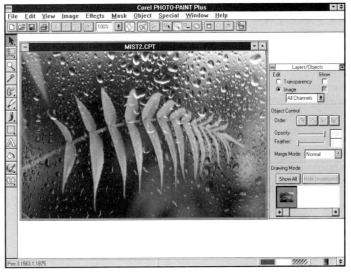

For the final touch, I added the text, as shown in Figure 18.37. After the text was first applied, a mask was made of the text. The text was then removed and a gamma value of 400 was applied to the mask. Nothing to it.

Figure 18.37.
The finished postcard.

Making Engraved Text in Marble

The technique demonstrated here makes what looks like engraved type in marble. You can do it even if you don't have the Plus version of PHOTO-PAINT. To achieve the effect, we have included a great marble seamless tile from Artbeats.

1. Open PHOTO-PAINT by clicking on the icon.

2. Create a new file by clicking on the New File button in the ribbon bar. (It is the one to the far left.) I made my file with 24-bit color, 3-inch width, 2-inch height, 200 dpi resolution, and a paper color of white. You can use 256 color if your graphics card slows down or does not support 24-bit color.

3. Click on the Text Tool button. It is the button that has the letter A on it. The cursor turns into a text-insertion tool bar. Notice that up in the ribbon bar a new series of text-related buttons has appeared.

4. Click anywhere near the middle-left in the image area, and type the word COREL (all caps). In the font box in the ribbon bar, use the drop-down list and pick TMS RMN (Times Roman). Highlight the type size selector and change it to 60. Click the Bold button . Don't worry about any of the other settings.

5. Select the Object Picker tool. It is the button at the top of the Toolbox, just as in Draw. Notice that the text is now surrounded by a blue marquee and eight control handles. The blue marquee is important. This indicates that the text is now an object. Click and drag the word COREL so that it is in the center of the image area, as shown in Figure 18.38.

Figure 18.38.
The word COREL has now become an object so it can be manipulated.

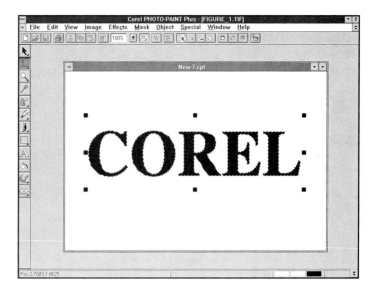

6. Click on Effects in the menu bar and select Soften from the drop-down list. This opens another drop-down list. Select Diffuse. The Diffuse Filter Preview dialog box opens. Let's take a brief moment and review the way the Preview dialog box works.

   Put the pointer into the preview window and it becomes a hand. Click and drag in the preview window and you can move (very rapidly) a thumbnail of the image. One second after you release the mouse button in the preview window, the selected effect is applied. Each left-click on the preview window zooms in on the preview image. Each right-click of the mouse zooms it out. All of these actions are common to all of the effects (filters) supplied with PHOTO-PAINT 5.

7. Enter a value of 80 in the Level box to the right of the slider and click the OK button. The value of 80 was the highest number I could enter with my setting to get a blurring of the text without a distinct edge beginning to appear on the text outline. We also could have used the Gaussian Blur filter, but that filter "scatters" the pixels, producing a more grainy pattern. The text is now slightly blurred, as shown in Figure 18.39. (I have turned off the blue marquee so the text is easier to see.)

Corel *TIP!*

> You also could use the slider to select the level of diffusion, but I have discovered it is easier to enter the value directly.

597

Figure 18.39.
No, your eyesight is not
getting fuzzy. This is
the effect of the Diffuse
filter.

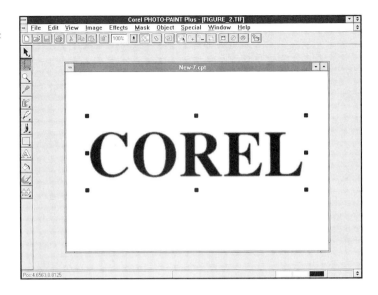

8. Click on Effects in the menu bar and select Fancy from the drop-down list. This opens another drop-down list. Select Emboss. The Emboss Filter Preview dialog box opens.

9. From the drop-down box for Emboss Color, select Gray. Click on the arrow button that points down and to the right. Click on the OK button. The Emboss effect is now applied to the image area, as shown in Figure 18.40.

Figure 18.40.
This is the result of
applying the basic
Emboss filter to the
text.

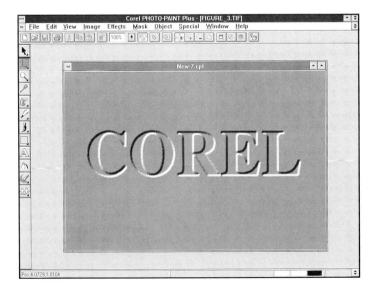

10. Open the Canvas roll-up by depressing the Ctrl+F3 function key. In the Canvas roll-up, click on the Load button. When the Load a Canvas From a Disk dialog box opens, select TEMPLE.TIF, located on the companion CD. (If you do not have the disk, you can use the MARBLE02C.PCX. file, located in the COREL50\PHOTOPNT\CANVAS subdirectory.) Click on OK to return to the Canvas roll-up.

11. In the Canvas roll-up, enter a Transparency value of 40 percent and an Emboss value of 80 percent. Click the Apply button and then the Merge button. The results of this action are shown in Figure 18.41.

Figure 18.41.
Our embossed text now
has a marbled appear-
ance.

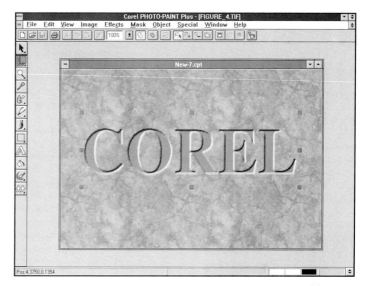

12. Open the Layers/Objects roll-up (F7 function key). On the bottom of the roll-up is a section called Drawing Mode. It has nothing to do with Drawing; it controls what layers/objects are activated. Since we want to work on the text, we will deselect the base image by clicking its button. All that remains is the text. (See Figure 18.42.) Any effect we apply will only affect the text.

13. Open the Fill roll-up. Select the Bitmap Fill button. It is the one in the center with the checkerboard on it. Click the Load button and load the same file you loaded in Step 10. If your screen is getting crowded, close all of the roll-ups.

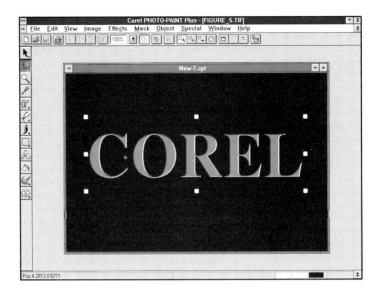

Figure 18.42.
The base image is
hidden so that we can
apply an effect to only
the text.

14. Select the Fill tool by clicking its button in the Toolbox, located under the Text tool. The cursor now becomes a Fill Tool icon. Click on each character in the word COREL. As you click on each character, it will fill with the marble pattern selected in Step 13. If the letter doesn't fill completely, click on the part that didn't fill. Continue until all of the characters are filled with the marble pattern.

15. Select Effects, Mapping, and Smoked Glass. Enter a value of 20 for the Tint value of the Preview dialog box. The image will darken slightly.

16. Select Effect, Fancy, and Motion Blur. Click on the lower-right arrow button and leave the Speed value set to 1. Click the OK button. This is a case of using a filter for something other than what the designer had in mind. Motion Blur was designed to make an image look like it had motion; we are using it to create the slight shadow of engraved text.

17. From the Layers/Objects roll-up, select the base image again by clicking on it in the Drawing Mode section. The marble reappears under the text and should look like Figure 18.43. That's it—you have made real marble engraving, and you don't even have any marble chips on the floor.

What you have just done can be applied to any object. Experiment with the direction of the embossing filter. By selecting up-left instead of down-right, the image appears to be embossed instead of engraved. Instead of marble, use a solid fill to make embossed letters that look like a license plate.

Figure 18.43.
This is the finished
product.

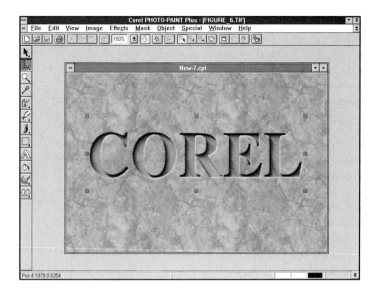

Tinting and Duotone Effects

While you cannot print spot colors from Corel PHOTO-PAINT, you can use Transparency masks to create a tint or duotone effects. The process is actually very easy. The results do not show up very well in grayscale, so you'll have to try it yourself to see the effect.

Corel *TIP!*

> Actually, you can print one spot color: black. If you print grayscale or line-art images to film from Corel PHOTO-PAINT, CorelDRAW, or a layout program such as Pagemaker, you can tell your printer to print another spot color in place of the black.

1. Open the retro image of the couple at the beach, located on the companion CD. This image is from PhotoDisc's Retro Americana volume and is unlike most stock photography in that it is a grayscale image. Select All from the Mask menu and, with a masking tool selected, delete the image. Open the Layers/Objects roll-up. Select Convert To RGB color (24-bit) from the Image menu and close the original image without saving.

Corel *TIP!*

Delete an image when you don't need to paste the image back in. Cutting an image is useful if you want to paste it into something else, but it takes up more system resources because the Windows Clipboard has to store it.

Of course, if you are going to print this on a four-color press, you'd need the image to be in CMYK (32-bit) format. Since RGB files are smaller than CMYK files (because RGB files have one less channel), we'll use RGB for this example. You can always change an RGB to CMYK before printing, but beware of color shifts if you go this route. We opened the image and deleted its contents because we need the page size to be the same size as the Transparency masks we will be using. In this case, the Transparency mask will be the actual image itself. So, conveniently, we can use its file-size information as the basis of our image.

You do not have to start from a grayscale image. You can convert a full-color image to grayscale if you like. The key is to use an image that has a fairly even distribution of tones from dark to light or, when converted to grayscale, black to white.

Figure 18.44.
This grayscale image is from PhotoDisc's Retro Americana volume. Your image should be blank after finishing Step 1.

2. Select Load Transparency Mask from the Mask menu, and load the image of the couple at the beach from the companion CD as a Transparency mask. Select Invert Transparency Mask from the Mask menu. You should be looking at a blank page. To see the Transparency mask, click on the Show option by the Edit Transparency section of the Layers/Objects roll-up. Notice that the Transparency mask looks like a negative, especially if you change the default color of the Transparency mask from Red to Black in the Advanced Preferences dialog box. This is no mistake. We will be applying color just like photographic negatives do. Negatives work by protecting the paper from the ink where the negative is black and applying ink where the image is white. In the case of negatives, though, there is only black or white information. Transparency masks work along the grayscale, as you will see. Uncheck the Show option by the Edit Transparency section of the Layers/Objects roll-up.

Figure 18.45.
Load the image of the couple at the beach as a Transparency mask, and then invert the Transparency mask.

3. Select Blue, or any other medium-to-dark color you wish, from the Fill roll-up, then click on the blank page with the Paint Bucket tool. This will tint your image. Too easy, isn't it? Notice how each color in the grayscale from the original picture has been replaced with a corresponding shade of blue. That is, 100 percent black has been replaced with 100 percent blue, 60 percent black has been replaced with 60 percent blue, and so on. This is a tint. Again, traditional tints would usually be printed with spot colors. The spot colors would simply use varying shades of the one color to print the image. Still, you can create a tinting effect with this technique.

Figure 18.46.
Select a color and fill
the image with it using
the Fill tool. Again, it is
not visible in grayscale,
but the shades of black
in the grayscale image
have been replaced
with equal shades or
densities of Blue.

4. Now we'll create a duotone effect. Select Remove Transparency Mask from the Mask menu. Make sure the Edit Image option is selected in the Layers/Objects roll-up. With an Object Picker tool, go under the Object menu, make sure Build Mode is on, and select All. To create a floating object the exact size as the base image, select Create, Copy from the Object menu. Now you should have two images in the Layers/Objects roll-up: the base layer and the object. Turn off the base layer with the Drawing Mode option within the Layers/Objects roll-up. (Click on the thumbnail image so that the border is light gray.) Select Invert Transparency Mask. Now select Orange as the second color (or any other color you wish to use) from the Fill roll-up.

5. Now we will change the color of the object to 100 percent orange. Select the Rectangle tool (with no outline and square corners), click outside of the canvas on the gray area surrounding the image, and drag from the upper-left corner to the lower-right corner over the entire image. With the Pick tool active (remember, you can only change the attributes of an object when you have an Object tool selected), change the Opacity setting of the object to 20 percent from within the Layers/Objects roll-up. Twenty percent is somewhat arbitrary; experiment with different Opacity settings. In this case, 100 percent would be way too overpowering—unless, of course, that's the effect you're looking for.

Figure 18.47.
Make an object out of the entire image and chose the second color for the duotone.

Figure 18.48.
Change the color of the object to a different color, orange in this example, and change the Opacity setting of the object to 20.

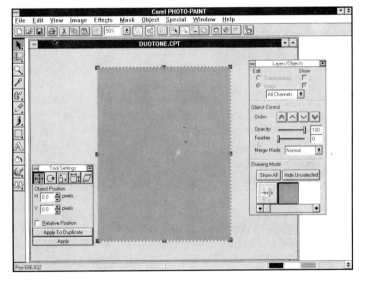

6. Now, with the floating object filled with the second color for the duotone, select Load Transparency Mask again and load the image of the couple at the beach from the companion CD. This time we don't want to invert the Transparency mask because we want the orange to be applied to the opposite areas and with the inverse shades in the grayscale areas, as the blue was. Notice that the thumbnail of your second image has added the yellow tint. It takes the Drawing Mode icons in the Layers/Objects roll-up

a while to catch up. In Drawing mode, turn on the base layer. With the Pick tool active, merge the two images by either selecting Merge from the Object menu or hitting Ctrl+G. Notice that the Drawing Mode preview now shows only one image: the duotone.

Figure 18.49.
Load the original image again as a Transparency mask, and merge the orange object to the base layer.

Glow Effects

There are so many wild and crazy things you can do in the area of glow effects, it would be difficult to keep from getting sidetracked. Let's do a simple glow first. To do that we need to understand a feature and a limitation of the Gaussian Blur filter in PHOTO-PAINT. Each time the Gaussian Blur filter is applied to an object, some of the color of the original object is depleted and replaced with the background color. This results in repetitive applications of the Gaussian Blur having less effect each time you apply the Repeat Last Filter (Ctrl+F) command. Figure 18.50 had the Gaussian Blur filter applied four times, and then the text was hidden, producing a basic glow. Figure 18.51 had the same filter applied the same number of times. The only difference between the two figures was that Figure 18.51 had the text "recharged" between each application. This results in a stronger, more-defined glow.

To "recharge" an object, hide everything except the object being blurred using the Layers/Objects roll-up. Reapply the original color over the object with a Rectangle Draw tool. What if the object isn't a solid color? Make as many duplicates as required to get the job done. Use the Tool Settings roll-up to make the duplicates. This way they will be precisely on top of one another. Don't make too many duplicates in advance; it takes up system resources and slows things down. After you use one of the objects, delete it.

Figure 18.50.
The Gaussian Blur filter
applied four times, and
then the text was
hidden, producing a
basic glow.

Figures 18.51.
The same filter applied
the same number of
times. The only
difference between the
two figures was that
Figure 18.51 had the
text "recharged"
between each applica-
tion. This results in a
stronger, more defined
glow.

Now that we have covered the basics, let's learn some tricks to make glow effects. First, let's learn a quick way to make great back-lit text, like in the title sequence of the movie "Aliens." James Cameron, who directed that movie, loves objects that are back-lighted with a blue aura. Here's how to do it.

1. Create a new file. Any size will do; I used 400 × 200 pixels at 300-dpi resolution, 24-bit color.

2. Set the Paint (foreground) color to Red. (Trust me on this.)

3. Pick a narrow typeface (I used a typeface called Teknik by Fontek), and type in some text.

4. Apply the Gaussian Blur filter (I used the default setting of 5) several times, "recharging" the text object with red after each application. Now we do some color magic.

Corel *TIP!*

> Narrow characters can't take very much blur because they are so close to one another. For condensed (narrow) typefaces, just do it 2 or 3 times. For wide typefaces, apply up to 6 times.

5. Apply the Invert filter from the Fancy subgroup in the Effects menu. The inverse of white is black. If you look at a color wheel, you will see that the inverse of red is the ghostly light blue we are looking for. Like it? We are not done yet.

Figure 18.52.
The Invert filter turns our red blurred type into blue type with a ghostly blue effect.

6. Hide the base image by using the Hide Unselected button on the Layers/Objects roll-up.

7. Change the Fill roll-up to a solid black, and, using the Rectangle Draw tool, paint the text black.

8. Click the Show All button on the Layers/Objects roll-up. (Figure 18.53.) That's all there is to it, although there are other things that could be done. By duplicating the text again, you can make the middle text a radial fill going from a dark blue to an inner light blue. Dust the top type with 20 percent uniform noise, and then feather the top copy, producing an effect like Figure 18.54. Don't worry about the background; I will show you how to do that in a moment.

Figure 18.53.
We now have text with a glow.

Figure 18.54.
Here is the effect of adding a second text layer and dusting it with noise.

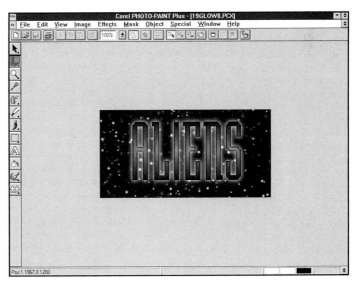

Corel *TIP!*

Determining which object layer you are on when the layers are precisely on top of one another is difficult. Here are a few hints that may help. First, move between layers with the Tab key, and watch the control handles. The control handles on the top object are almost always the shortest distance from one another. Second, you can turn off the layer you want to work with by clicking on its button and then clicking it on again. When you add an object, it comes into the image selected. A last resort, when you have a whole herd of objects, is to hit the Hide Unselected button and then click the object that you want.

Placing a Glow Effect on a Different Background

Having a neat glow effect is good, but being able to do something practical with it is another story altogether. There are several ways to place glows against different backgrounds, so we will talk about each one separately. The first one we will deal with is the simple one, where the background matches the background of the glow effect. If you haven't made the original glow figure, go back and do it now.

We first need to make a background for this effect. So let's make some space.

1. Hide all of the objects except the base image by using the Layers/Objects roll-up.
2. In the Fill Tool-roll-up (Shift+F6), select Night Sky in the Samples 5 library and click the Edit button.
3. In the Texture Fill dialog box, make the # of Spots 300. Change the Max Width % to 2 and the Max Height % to 3. Click OK.
4. Using the Rectangle Draw tool, draw a large rectangle over the entire base image. You should end up with a rectangle of space like that shown in Figure 18.55. (There is a slick way to make the space look more realistic, which I will show you later.)

*Figure 18.55.
The Texture Bitmap Fill
feature can be used to
make some wonderful
fills.*

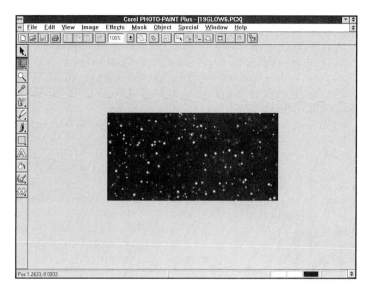

5. Select (Unhide?) the glow-effect layer, which should be the top layer. (If it is not, select the image and make it the top layer by using the Object Control arrow buttons. There should remain a middle layer of black text that is hidden.) The image we just selected is on top, so it covers the space we just made. To be able to see through this image to the base image, we will have to use Object Merge Mode in the Layers/Objects roll-up.

6. After you ensure that the Object Picker in the Toolbox is active, click on the Merge Mode arrow and select Add from the drop-down list that appears. The glow effect and the space-base image both appear as shown in Figure 18.56. Why does this happen? You need to understand this if you are going to create variations of this look. We have added the color values of the top image with the bottom images. The rules are as follows: Dark + dark = dark; dark + light = light; light + light = light. Notice that the "stars" not only shine through the glow, but they shine through the letters as well. (Light + dark = light.) The solution to this is simple. Did you remember we still had the original text hidden?

7. Select (unhide) the text (top object). Now the letters should fit precisely on top of the glow-effect layer. Because this layer is set to normal, it prevents any of the "stars" from shining through.

Figure 18.56.
We have the space and
we have the text, but
the problem is that we
can see the stars
through the letters.

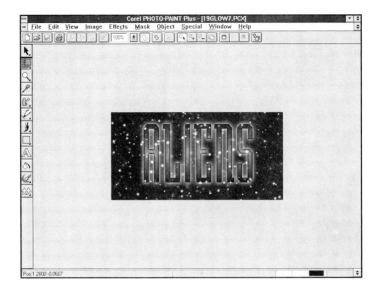

Figure 18.57.
The finished product.

19

Setting Up Your System (or "Do You Have What it Takes?")

This is more than just a cute title. Corel PHOTO-PAINT 5 requires some substantial systems resources in order to work properly. To make sure that you have sufficient system resources, it is necessary to spend a little time understanding what is "under the hood" with the system you already have. (Good news for you techno-wizards: If you already know everything about hardware, go directly to the next chapter).

Fear not—we are not going to go crazy with technical information in this section. However, after you finish this chapter, you will have enough information to outshine the man selling computers at your local computer outlet. (Of course, there is a good chance that that same computer clerk was selling wide-screen televisions only a week ago.)

The CPU

When I was growing up, a long, long time ago, computers were called "electronic brains." However, they were far from being "brains"—they were more like adding machines on steroids. Then, when real computers came along, it was the Central Processing Unit (CPU) that was called the brains of the computer. This term isn't being used as much anymore, however, and for that we can be thankful.

Figure 19.1.
The Intel Pentium.

The CPU performs all of the data processing on your computer. Nearly everything inside your computer is under the control of this chip. CPUs come in many varieties—and this an area where many people are misled by sometimes well-meaning salespeople.

At the time this book was being written, IBM, Apple, and Motorola were swamping us with news of how the new PowerPC is the most incredible chip in the world and that you'd better get yours now to beat the Christmas rush. For the time being, the PowerPC runs nicely when it's in the Macintosh. And that's all. Corel does not have a Macintosh product, so if you're primary interest is in using Corel products, ignore all of the hype about the PowerPC.

When IBM introduced the first PC, it used an Intel-designed architecture for its CPU. Microsoft, then a very small company, designed the first DOS (Disk Operating System) to work with that architecture. As time passed, new CPU chips were introduced (with progressively larger identifier numbers). The numbers we see in computer ads reflect the last three digits of those chips. For example, the correct nomenclature for a 386 CPU is an i80386. At this time, there are only three sets of chip nomenclature to know: the 386 family, the 486 family, and newest chip family, the Pentiums. (Intel got tired of the numerical 86 handle and is now giving its CPU names. It is also known as the P-5.) What about the 286 CPU? Well, there are millions of them out there, but if you are running Windows 3.1, you aren't (or shouldn't be) running it on a 286. (Note to all the techno-wizards that are running Windows 3.1 on their overheated 286s: Don't send me mail. Upgrade!) The 386 and 486 CPUs additionally come with different letters behind their name. You have seen them advertised—they are called SX and DX, and those subcategories can further be divided by clock-speed factors, such as DX2 or DX4. Now, let's put this all together.

Here is the pecking order of Intel microprocessors, from the most powerful to the least powerful:

1. 90, 60, 66 and 100 MHz Pentium (P5)
2. 100MHz 80486DX4
3. 66MHz 80486DX2
4. 50MHz 80486DX
5. 33MHz 80486DX
6. 25MHz 80486DX
7. 80486SX
8. 40MHz 80386DX
9. 33MHz 80386DX
10. 80386SX

Just as a point of information, you may see some of these numbers with lower case "i" in front of the chip number (i.e., i486). The "i," which stands for Intel, replaces the "80" prefix and does not represent a special product.

If you are confused, read on and we will sort out all of the numbers.

Rule number one: The Pentium CPU is faster (better) than the 486 CPU, and the 486 CPU is faster than the 386 CPU.

Rule two: DX is always better than SX.

CPU Processing Power

This section is for those who want to know more about how the CPUs got listed in that order. (You can jump to the next subtopic if you want. Follow just those two rules I gave you and you can't lose.)

The numbers in the front of the CPU number (i.e., 25MHz) refer to the clock speed of the computer. There are two ways in which we measure a CPU's power specification. One, the amount of data (that is, how many bits of information) that the CPU can process; and two, the clock speed of the CPU (that is, how fast it operates on the data that it has). The amount of data a CPU can move is determined by the width of the data path. A 64-bit computer can move more bits per second than a 16- or 32-bit computer. Although the 386 and 486 CPUs are all 32-bit CPUs technically, it is how they handle the data inside the chip that determines which is the fastest. I could go on here at length about internal data structures, but it wouldn't be necessary to your understanding. Remember Rule One: 486 CPUs are faster than 386 CPU. The DX and SX suffixes have to do with data bus structures. Remember Rule Two: DX is better than SX.

Clock speed is measured in millions of clock cycles per second. Therefore a CPU that operates at 50 million clock cycles per second is said to be a 50MHz CPU. The speed of the CPU indicates how many instructions per second that the CPU can process. Now here is the deceiving part about clock speed. Logically, it would seem that a 50 MHz CPU would be twice as fast as a 25MHz CPU, right? It seems that way, but that's not the case. The 50MHz machine will be faster, but not twice as fast. In fact, based on the type of performance testing you do, it would be about 40-percent faster in this example. It is in the area of clock speed that many people who are buying a computer get mislead by salespeople. Easy rule: Faster clock speed computers work faster; but the difference in speed is not linear—i.e., a 50MHz machine is not twice as fast as a 25MHz machine.

I can't leave clock speed without a discussion about the DX2 and the DX4. These are clock-doubled CPUs. That is, the CPU runs externally at a speed that is half of the internal speed. Why would they do that? Because when Intel released the 50MHz CPU, the systems operated at such high frequencies that systems were becoming unstable; they were difficult to design and meet FCC emission requirements. Then one day someone remembered that only the CPU needs to run at the high clock speed, so why not let all of the hardware outside of the CPU run at half the speed while the CPU ran internally at the higher speed? Thus came what has been called the Overdrive CPU. If you have a 80486SX-based CPU with an overdrive socket, you can put the 80486DX2 in the computer and have a faster machine. As of the time I am writing this, the 66 MHz 80486DX2 is the most popular high-performance CPU on the market—and yet in a period of less than 12 weeks, the newest "I've-gotta-have-it" chip has become the 60 and 66Mhz P5 chips. Why are they suddenly so popular? Because Intel started dropping the prices to keep the other CPU chip makers at bay.

Now holding second place for performance is the 486DX/4 (100MHz) CPU. This is a screamer of a CPU. It is being priced just below the P5 chip and should be a strong price performer.

CPU Summary

- The faster the clock speed, the faster the computer. (Faster is better.)
- DX is faster and more expensive than SX.
- 80486 is faster and more expensive than 80386.
- The Pentium is the fastest and the most expensive.

So what kind of CPU do you need? To run Corel PHOTO-PAINT 5, you should have a 80486DX. While a 40MHz 80386 or any 80486SX will operate, it will be slow if you are working with 24-bit color (also called true color). If most of the images you will be using in Corel PHOTO-PAINT are grayscale or black-and-white, then any CPU on the list should work nicely.

Corel *NOTE!*

None of the Corel applications make use of a math co-processor chip. So, if you own a 386, don't think that by buying a co-processor (math) chip, it will improve the performance, no matter how sincere the salesperson is.

Computer Memory

Computer memory is often confused with disk-storage-device memory. Many times when I am helping someone with their system, I will ask them how much memory they have installed. The most common response I get is "I don't know." The second most common one is that they will tell me how big their disk drive is. Memory on the computer is called RAM (for Random Access Memory). It is in RAM that the computer loads and stores its programs when it is running. RAM is volatile. This means that when the power is turned off, anything left in RAM disappears forever. RAM used to be sold in little chips that were installed in endless rows of sockets in a computer. The original nightmare was in trying to find the memory chip that was going bad somewhere in a vast sea of them. Fortunately, they are now sold as small boards called SIMMs (Single In-line Memory Module.) They are sold in blister packs in some computer retail stores and are very easy to install.

Photo-editing programs such as Corel PHOTO-PAINT require lots and lots of RAM memory. They will never give you an error message telling you that you have too much RAM memory. Although you can assume that the practical limit for a PC using Windows 3.1 is 32MB, with the release of Windows 4.0/Chicago (scheduled for release sometime near the end of time) that will all change. Any RAM above 16MB cannot be effectively used by most Windows applications.

So, how much memory do you need? There is not a precise way to determine the amount, but I would recommend 8MB as the minimum for working with 24-bit color or really large grayscale images scanned at high resolutions. I use 16MB on my system and would bump it to 32MB if I could afford it. This is a good time to talk about motherboard memory organization and how it affects both how much and in which combination your computer can accept memory.

Memory modules (SIMMs) comes in several sizes. The most popular sizes are 1, 2, and 4MB, with 8MB SIMMs becoming more attractive as their prices begin to come down. The best way to explain some of the challenges you may face is to explain what happened to me when I upgrading my system from 8MB to 16MB. The 8MB on my system was composed of eight 1MB SIMMs. This filled all of the available slots; there wasn't any room for more SIMMs. Therefore, to upgrade I would have to sell my existing 1MB SIMMs and replace them with four 4MB SIMMs. This can be a real pain. Fortunately, there is a computer repair shop in Austin through which I was able to trade in my existing memory. (This will not work at your local national reseller.) A second consideration, called the inter-leave factor, may effect in what increments you may upgrade your memory. Interleave has to do with the way the CPU addresses your RAM memory. An older system of mine had an interleave factor of four. That meant that whatever size of SIMM I used, it had to be in groups of four. This can get pretty ugly, so it is best to get a professional to do the upgrade, although on newer systems, interleave is getting to be much less of a problem. The only reason I thought it was important for you to know about this stuff is so you didn't think some technician is trying to rip you off. Not all SIMMS are created equal—there are standard SIMMS, and then there are the newer 72-pin SIMMS. This isn't a question of which is better—it is a question of which your computer uses. I have only seen the 72-pin SIMMS in newer computers.

Corel *TIP!*

> Beware of playing with SIMMS. They are extremely static sensitive and can be damaged or destroyed if the proper precautions are not taken when handling them. If you buy them pre-packaged, read the precautions thoroughly!

Drives and Their Controllers

Every PC has a hard drive. I used to sell hard drives. We called them Winchester disk drives in those days. Why? IBM invented the first hard drive using what later became known as Winchester technology. Why did they call it Winchester? Because it was for an IBM product called the 3030 (pronounced thirty-thirty). So, since the Winchester rifle is a 30-30, it seemed natural. Back then, all drives were of the 5 1/4-inch full-height type. My company, Rodime, had just created the first 3 1/2-inch drive. In fact, I sold the first 3 1/2-inch drives in the United States. (As long as we're telling stories here, one of my customers was a little shop here in Austin called PC's Limited. It had about six employees at the time. They sold computer peripherals and gray-market Compaq computers. They were just beginning to assemble and sell their first PC clone. That little outfit today is called Dell Computer. Times have changed.)

When Michael Dell was getting his start in the business, a 30MB disk drive was a monster. The average was 10MB. Today, there are computer games that will ask for 50MB of disk space or you can't install them. The CorelDRAW package will take more than 30MB of drive space if you do a full install. Not only are the applications getting bigger, but the images you will be working with can get extremely large as well. A common disk size now is around 300-400MB. With disk compression, it can hold almost one gigabyte of data. A gigabyte is 1000MB. (This is pronounced *giga*byte, not *jiga*byte.)

If your system has less than 100MB of hard drive, you may experience some challenges by the time you give Windows a good-sized permanent swap file. I'm not saying it can't be done; it's just a little tight.

Controllers

A controller is the interface card that allows your computer to talk to your hard drive. There are four controller interfaces for hard drives. They are, in order of desirability:

1. SCSI (Small Computer Standard Interface). Everyone calls it *scuzzy*.
2. IDE (Integrated Drive Electronics). The most popular today.
3. ESDI (Enhanced Small Disk Interface). An older interface, pronounced *ez-dee*.
4. ST-506. The original hard disk interface. Very old and very slow.

In many cases you have no choice of controller. There is no performance value to justify changing an existing drive or its controller unless they have malfunctioned or you have a very small drive. If you are buying a new system, I recommend getting a SCSI drive if possible. If you are purchasing a new drive, consider upgrading your controller at the same time.

The IDE drives used to be limited to approximately 500MB because of the IDE interface specification. There are now IDE drives on the market with capacities of up to 1 gigabyte and more.

There are two things that increase the data throughput of a controller. The first is the use of a caching (pronounced *cashing*) controller. There are heated arguments as to whether a hardware caching controller is as fast or faster than just using software caching (such as Microsoft's Smartdrive caching program) alone. The people who make caching controllers can prove without a doubt that hardware caching is superior. Unfortunately the software caching companies can prove the opposite. The second way to increase throughput is to use a local-bus controller card. This does make a difference in the speed of your system. (I explain how the two different local-bus structures work in the video controller section of this chapter, because local-bus was designed by the video people for video applications.)

I maintain that you will get the best performance out of a SCSI controller and SCSI hard drive. There are two general classifications of SCSI drives. They are SCSI and SCSI-2. SCSI is the original specification. SCSI-2 is the updated specification. A SCSI-2 drive will, on the average, achieve a noticeably higher throughput than the original SCSI drive. Most new SCSI drives today are SCSI-2.

Another advantage of the SCSI controller is that the same controller can be used to control your CD-ROM drive, scanner, tape drive, removable drives, and some printers—all from one card. If you have heard that SCSI cards are difficult to install and configure, I can say that this used to be true. These days, they are easy to install, and SCSI makes the installation of additional devices very simple. Corel makes a great collection of SCSI software and utilities called Corel SCSI 2.

CD-ROM Drives

CD-ROMs are the greatest thing to come along in years. They can not only hold programs, they can also be used to play video, animation, and sound. With the new Kodak Photo-Disc standard, several hundred color images can be stored on a single disk. The CD-ROM drive looks like the CD players that have taken over the music industry during the past few years. In many ways the CD-ROM drive and the home-stereo CD player (also called CD Audio) are similar. However, before you run over to your boom box and try to load the Corel CD-ROM onto your system with it, we need to understand that there are a few differences between CD-ROM and CD Audio. The CD-ROM is a read only device that can hold up to 660MB of uncompressed data on a disk that looks identical to a CD music disk. It is called a Read-Only Memory (ROM) because you can't record on it. (There are recordable CD-ROM machines that are, as I write this, in the $2,500-14,000 price range.)

When a CD player plays a music CD, it is reading digitally sampled music and converting it to an analog (non-digital) signal that can drive your headset or speaker. If there is one bit of music on the disc that is missed when the player reads the CD, you lose 1/22,000 of a second in one channel. I doubt that you would miss it. When it comes to program data, one bit missing out of 30 million will cause a program to be corrupted and the application will probably not load or run. I only mention this so that when you are at the computer store and are wondering why CD-ROMs cost more than their musical cousins, you understand that the CD-ROM drive must be much more precise in its mechanics and electronics than an audio CD player.

Figure 19.2.
A CD-ROM drive.

When CD-ROM drives first hit the street, they were modified versions of the CD-Audio mechanisms. The spindle speed worked out to a transfer rate of approximately 150K characters per second. Now, that figure may sound pretty fast to you, but remember that a good hard-disk drive can move data at rates up to several million characters-per-second. Still, in the beginning it was sufficient. In the early days of CD-ROMs, there was maybe one new title a month that would be released. I remember one of the first titles available was The Constitution Papers. I believe it was a listing of all of the notes kept during the writing of the U.S. Constitution. I am sure they sold quite a few copies of that title. (I understand it was great for insomniacs that didn't respond to strong drugs.) In those days, the CD-ROM was an answer in search of a question. No one would produce titles because the CD-ROM drives were very expensive (almost $1,000) and therefore there were very few people who had them. As the CD-ROM started to became popular, Corel was one of the early proponents of this medium. More and more titles were released. As more people wanted them, the cost of producing new titles came down. "Multimedia" became a buzzword, and companies began putting video and animation on their CD-ROM disks. Some applications began using the CD-ROM interactively, meaning that the application would play the video, animation, or sound directly from the CD-ROM disk. It wasn't long before a 150K character-per-second transfer rate was considered unacceptable. The video was jerky or would stop at various points in the clip while the CD-ROM drive tried to move data fast enough to keep up.

Along came the double-speed CD-ROM drives, which are still popular today. These spin the CD twice as fast as the older drives. This allows the data transfer rate to be twice as high: 300K characters per second. This is far from perfect and well below the data transfer rates of the newer hard drives, but it is certainly better than the single-speed drives. There are many programs on the market today that not only assume that you have a double-speed drive, but some actually test your CD-ROM drive to see if it is fast enough to run the application.

There is one company that sells a triple-speed drive. It is expensive, and those who have tried it say they don't see that the performance difference justifies the price differential. And now practically everyone has announced a quad-speed drive. They are in the same price range as the more expensive double-speed drives. I have been working with a Plextor (they used to be called Texel) 4Plex CD-ROM drive, and I am impressed. When you must load Photo CDs all day long, the difference in speed is worth the money they are asking. At the time of this printing, the quad-speed drives were in the $500 range. If the manufacturers keep increasing the spindle speed of the CD-ROM drives, they soon may become dangerous. (Can you see it on the evening news? "Tragedy struck a local family today as a CD spun out of control from its 20X CD-ROM drive, crashing through three walls before coming to rest in the family goldfish bowl. Memorial services for the goldfish are pending.")

One of the major headaches of installing a CD-ROM has been getting the system to recognize it. By that, I mean that our old friend DOS does not recognize CD-ROMs. Therefore, a device driver must be installed in the CONFIG.SYS file, and a DOS program called MSCDEX (Microsoft Corporation CD Extensions) must be run before your operating system will recognize your CD-ROM as a logical device (i.e., assign it a drive letter). The good news is that the CD-ROM manufacturers have done an excellent job in the past several years making the installation of the CD-ROM as painless as possible. The price of a basic drive is in the $100-$250 price range. But if you think you want to go out and get one, let's talk about minimum standards so you don't get ripped off and find out that your CD-ROM won't do what you bought it to do.

To run today's CD-ROM products, you don't just need a CD-ROM. You may have seen the symbol "MPC" on boxes and wondered what it meant. It stands for "Multimedia Personal Computer." When CD-ROM drives and sound cards started becoming popular, there was a lot of confusion about what constituted a system that supported multimedia. In other words, there were some unscrupulous people calling products "multimedia ready" that actually could not support one or more elements of true multimedia operation. So a standard was devised by an ad-hoc committee of vendors. Here are the minimum hardware requirements for a computer to be labeled MPC:

- IBM-compatible computer with a 16MHz 80386SX or faster processor.
- Super VGA-capable display, with 640 × 480 dpi in 256 colors.

- Sound card capable of playing MIDI music and digitized sounds
- 80MB hard drive
- CD-ROM with 150K character-per-second transfer rate
- Windows 3.1
- 2MB RAM

At first, software vendors were slow to pick up the use of the MPC logo. Worse, some applications that said they would work on an MPC-standard system actually required a faster, more powerful machine than existed when the original MPC standard was issued. This prompted the MPC group to issue a new standard, called MPC2. The MPC2 standard is a follows:

- IBM-compatible computer with a 25MHz 80486 or faster processor
- Super VGA video, capable of displaying 640 × 480 dpi with 65,000 colors
- Sound card, with ability to play MIDI and digitized sound
- 80MB hard drive
- CD-ROM capable of a 300K character-per-second transfer rate
- Windows 3.1
- 4MB RAM

For some users, the best solution is to buy a complete multimedia kit. This typically comes with a CD-ROM, sound card, and speakers. For the rest of you who already have a good sound card, you may only need a CD-ROM. Make sure it can read Photo-Disc CD-ROMs. If it can, it should meet all of your needs. Beware of older or used CD-ROM drives. They are no bargain and you will end up having to replace it in the very near future. This is especially true of single-speed CD-ROM drives, most of which cannot read PHOTO CDs.

One final thought about CD-ROM drives: There are two general types of transport mechanisms for CD-ROM drives. One requires a special CD caddy. You put the CD-ROM disk in a special caddy and slide it into the drive. You can keep the disk in the caddy, which protects it. This is very convenient. However, these caddies are very expensive; I have seen them as high as $12.00 each. If you are going to have many CD-ROM disks, go for the slide-out transport mechanism, which does not require the caddie.

Video Controllers

Video controllers are a hot area in the PC marketplace. Several years ago, a category of video controller with a specialized graphics-processor chip enabled the users to speed up many of their Windows applications. These are known as Windows or graphics-accelerator boards. These make graphics-intensive applications run much faster. How important is this? First, faster is always better. The early accelerator boards were very expensive, suffered from compatibility problems, and didn't offer much for their very large price tag. Today, there are a large assortment of these cards in the $100-200 dollar price range. There are many strange technical terms that are bandied about in this arena. Companies brag about their Winmarks and their PCI and VL offerings. They talk about true color, 24-bit color, and 65,000. Is it any wonder that people get confused? Let us not get technical on this one; or at least, not too technical. We will be discussing color depth in the chapter on image fundamentals, so for now here are just some basics.

Color depth refers to the number of bits that make up each possible color. If I am using 4-bits to define each possible color in a picture, I can have a maximum of 16 possible colors. If you don't understand binary numbering, just trust me. This means that with 4-bit color, each pixel can be one of 16 possible colors. If we have a color depth of 8-bits (each pixels needs 8 bits to determine its color), then each pixel can be one of 256 colors. If the color depth is 16 bits, then we have 65,000 possible color combinations for each pixel, and thus we say it has a palette of 65,000 colors (abbreviated as 65K colors). The highest possible color depth is 24-bit, also called true color. It has a palette of 16.7 million colors. What is the difference between these color depths and what do you need for the Corel programs?

For Corel PHOTO-PAINT 5, you need to forget 4-bit (16 color). PHOTO-PAINT 5 has an excellent, optimized 256-color capability. And then there is 16-bit (65K) color and 24-bit true color. Visually, 16-bit and 24-bit color are almost indistinguishable from one another. If I see a color photo on my screen in 65K color and another in true color, it is almost impossible to tell the difference between the two because of the limitations of the human eye. Then why use 24-bit color? Good question. If you are doing professional work that requires exact color matches and precise color control between your monitor, scanner, and printer, then you must use 24-bit color. What are the disadvantages of 24-bit color? Performance degradation. The board that is in the system I am using at the moment is one of the newest 64-bit Matrox boards, which can support both 65K and true color, depending on how I set the software drivers. Regardless of the settings, this board really cooks. On another graphics board I have, if I set the board for true color, the speed of the system on redraws will slow down noticeably. Because of the way this second card is designed, it achieves its greatest speed with a color depth of 65K colors. Believe it or not, if I go to 256-color mode, it will actually work slower than if I use 65K color. This is not unusual. The board has been specifically designed to give the best performance at 65K colors.

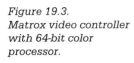

Figure 19.3.
*Matrox video controller
with 64-bit color
processor.*

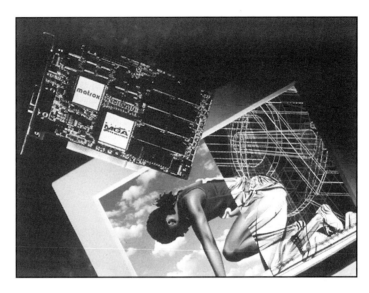

There is always a trade-off between the accuracy of true color and the price of the board. Although pricing is volatile, at this time a good true-color board is in the $400-500 range, while a board that is almost as fast in the 65K color region is in the $250-350 range. Add to this the appearance of 64-bit color processors that are just now appearing on the market. Don't get confused about the number of bits in the color processor; it does not have any relation to color depth.

32-Bit Color, or "The Great Mac Lie"

You may hear about 32-bit color on the Mac. That must be some kind of super color, right? Wrong. It is 24-bit color. The folks at Apple added an 8-bit field called an Alpha channel to the standard 24-bit color. This makes a total of 32 bits. However, the Alpha channel was never specified by Apple. It has been used for video and other application-dependent functions. Now you know the truth about 32-bit color, so don't let the Mac people get away with bragging about having a superior color palette.

VL-Bus Versus PCI

One of the real performance improvements in the area of graphics is not found directly on a video board but rather on the motherboard of your computer. Not long ago, the Video Electronic Standards Association (VESA) decided they needed a way to move large amounts of graphic data to and from the CPU without using the ISA bus. (ISA bus refers to the Industry Standard Association bus. This is the standard bus that is on the PC.) Why would they want to do that? An illustration may help. Many people who commute to work use a freeway to cover a distance from their house to the place where they work. Unfortunately, everyone else uses the same freeway. Therefore, a trip that should take 20 minutes can take an hour. The same is true with the ISA bus. Every bit of data that needs to be processed must travel down the same bus with the same result as in our illustration. The solution? VESA made their own private road to the CPU. It was called the Local Bus. The graphic cards that support the VL-Bus (VESA Local Bus) generally experience a great increase in the overall graphics performance. Next, those clever graphics-board designers put a graphics accelerator on top of the VL-Bus. Of course, it was really fast. Then along came Intel. Intel doesn't like anyone else setting standards, so they made their own version of the VL-Bus, called PCI. The PCI boards (unlike the VL-Bus boards) don't use the ISA bus at all. The acceptance of the PCI bus has been strong, and it appears that both VL-Bus and PCI bus-based graphics accelerators will be around for some time.

Choosing between VL-Bus and PCI is sometimes thought to be an emotional question, but the answer is a little clearer than you may image. If you have a system that uses a Pentium, the PCI bus is the better choice. If you using any of the other x86 CPUs, VL-Bus is a less expensive alternative.

Monitors

There are two primary, measurable factors to consider when choosing a monitor: size and resolution. The screen size (in inches) determines what resolution you can reasonably operate with. It used to be that a good color monitor was one that could display 640 × 480 dots per inch. Now, 1024 × 780 is considered average for programs such as PHOTO-PAINT. Better monitors can work up to 1280 × 1024 or even 1600 × 1200. These kind of numbers are for huge (24-inch) screens performing high-resolution CAD work. A good rule of thumb is that 14- or 15-inch monitors (measured diagonally) should be working at no greater than 800 × 600—or else your friends will start to wonder why you are blinking your eyes all of the time. 17-inch monitors can comfortably work at 1024 × 780 dpi. Don't forget that no matter what resolution your monitor supports, if the video controller can't hack it, you won't have it.

Another consideration is dot size (also called *dot pitch*). This number refers to the size of the actual dot (in millimeters) projected on your screen. In theory, the smaller the dot, the sharper the image. Notice I said "in theory." Certainly there is a difference between a really cheap color monitor that has a .49mm dot pitch and one that has .26mm. But the difference is really only evident when there are extremes between the sizes. There is not a discernible difference between, say, a .28mm and a .30mm dot pitch monitor.

Interface is another consideration, albeit a specious one. When I started using larger monitors, I found that there were monitors that had separate connectors for each color channel and for the control signals. You may have seen them in computer shows, with brightly colored cables coming out of the back of the monitor. It looks so high-end. Well, I did some research with several monitor manufacturers (their engineers, not their salespeople) and found, much to my surprise, that there is essentially no difference between a monitor hooked to a computer via the multicolored cables and via the standard VGA 15-pin adapter. So why do they make them? Because 17-inch monitors are often used for CAD applications, which may or may not be performed an IBM PC with a 15-pin adapter. So by using this method of interface, the manufacturer can address the needs of the entire market rather than making different monitors for everyone. If you are using an IBM-compatible PC, you needn't be concerned.

MPR-2 compliance is also a sensitive issue with some people. The Swedish government has established a set of stringent emission requirements (called MPR-2) to ensure that people sitting in front of monitors do not suffer undue consequences from the electrons bombarding their bodies. If this is important to you, go for it, by all means. However, it isn't one of my concerns. I figure if the radiation doesn't get me, the lack of ozone will. Life is too short to sweat the details.

Input Devices

Digitizer Tablets

Creating a complex mask with a cheap mouse can be a real challenge, so if you are going to use Corel PHOTO-PAINT (or CorelDRAW, for that matter), you may want to have a stylus and a tablet. If you are not familiar with digitizing tablets, here are some basics for you.

Relational or Absolute?

Technically, digitizing tablets (or pads) are absolute positional input devices, while your friendly mouse is a relative positional input device. I'll explain. The mouse is a relative device, meaning the arrow moves when you move the mouse. The information that the mouse imparts to the cursor is relative. That is, I can move the mouse several inches in one direction, lift it up and return the mouse to where I started, and the arrow will not return with it. Why? Because the cursor only "reads" relative motion from the mouse. On the other hand, if I use a digitizer tablet, the cursor receives information about where the stylus is based on its position on the tablet surface. The type of information is called absolute. So, if like in the previous example, we move the stylus several inches in one direction, lift it up and return it to we started, the cursor will return with it.

There are several kinds of tablets out there, but the primary types are pressure-sensitive and non-pressure sensitive. Corel PHOTO-PAINT and CorelDRAW both support the features of a pressure-sensitive stylus. The tip of the stylus is generally set to act like the left-button click of a mouse whenever it is depressed. A pressure-sensitive stylus not only provides a left-click function, but it also passes information to the program that is related to how hard the stylus is being depressed. Some of the styluses have up to 256 levels of pressure sensitivity. What the program does with this pressure information is up to the program. In PHOTO-PAINT, when I have a paint brush selected, depressing the stylus harder produces a darker paint or a wider stroke (depending on the brush selected).

The major players in this market of smaller digitizer pads (6 × 9) are Wacom, Calcomp, and Kurta. All of them have cordless styluses but work on different philosophies. The Wacom is my favorite for reasons of general feel. Unfortunately, because they use the Pen Windows interface method to provide pressure information to the applications, they are not stable with Corel PHOTO-PAINT 5. Chris Dickman reports the same problem with CorelDRAW 5. Several of us have clamored at Wacom about resolving this issue, and by the time you read this, they may have done so. (Check with Corel sales support before you shell out $400-500.) The Wacom stylus is powered by a tiny pickup coil in the stylus itself. This means no batteries to replace, a thinner stylus, and no need to activate the stylus whenever I use it. (Battery-powered cordless styluses have a battery-saving feature that turns off the stylus whenever it is not used for a period of time. To activate it, you must click it on something.)

The CalComp drawing slate has a larger, battery-powered cordless stylus with three-buttons. This enables one of the buttons to function as a double-left click button, which is very handy. This slate can also record sequences and assign them to buttons on the pad.

Kurta has just announced a smaller version of its tablet. The one I worked with had a stylus like a Lincoln Log, and the tablet was a 12 × 12-inch desktop hockey table. I image the new smaller version will work as well as the others.

All of these tablets are in the $400-500 price range. If that makes you gasp, take heart. You can opt for a product called AceCat II, which features a corded stylus and is not pressure sensitive. It sells for around $100. I used one for a season and it was good enough to work with PHOTO-PAINT.

Summary

To successfully operate Corel PHOTO-PAINT 5, consider the following hardware recommendations:

- CPU: 486DX/2 with a VL-Bus or PCI bus motherboard.
- Memory: 8MB of RAM. 16MB is better.
- Hard drive: 200MB SCSI or greater.

- Display: 17-inch monitor. (You can live with a 15-inch, but 17-inch is better if you spend all day in front of the monitor.)
- Video accelerator card: 24-bit is preferred. Use a 16-bit (65K color) card if you can't get a 24-bit card.
- CD-ROM: Double speed. (Quad-speed is better.) MPC compliant. Make sure it can read Photo CDs.

Chapter

20

Bringing the Outside World In

Scanners

Unless you have a digital camera or a video frame grabber, or you are an artist doing all of your original work on the computer, you will have to find some way to get the source images that you need into the computer. The most commonly used device to input photos, line art, or hand-drawn pictures into a computer is a scanner. There are several programs within the CorelDRAW 5 release that support scanners. PHOTO-PAINT is, as its name implies, a program that excels in the editing and manipulation of photographs and images.

You need to use a scanner, be it yours or one at a service bureau, if you are going to bring existing photos and artwork into PHOTO-PAINT.

A scanner is a device that captures an image and converts it into a digital pixel map for computer processing. A scanner is much like a camera and a photo-copier combined and connected to a computer. Like a camera, most scanners capture an image with depth (grayscale or color; see Chapter 22 for a more detailed discussion on pixel depth), whereas a copier records only black-and-white. As with a copier, the object being scanned is usually placed on a glass plate (the copyboard), where it is scanned. The image, however, is not captured on film or reproduced on paper; instead it is stored in a computer file, where it can be opened with Corel PHOTO-PAINT and manipulated to the limits of one's imagination and work schedule.

Because scanners represent a significant investment and very little has been written about them, we are going to spend some time looking at how they work, how to determine what features are necessary, and what tradeoffs can be safely made. To start with, we need to understand how scanners work and how they do what they do.

There are five basic types of scanners in the market today that are of interest to the PHOTO-PAINT user, as follows:

- **Film scanners.** These scanners scan transparencies and negatives. They are like photographic enlargers in reverse. They are usually relatively small (albeit with a big price tag—several thousand dollars) and are limited to working with film. They cannot be used with any other kind of material (e.g., photographs on paper). If you have work that involves a lot of negatives and slides, this is the kind of scanner to have. If you only occasionally need to scan in negatives and slides, go to a service bureau and have them do it.

- **Flatbed scanners.** These units input anything that can be laid flat on top of the glass. They look like your office's photocopy machine. A close cousin of the flatbed scanner is the sheet-fed scanner. The sheet-fed scanner can-not accommodate anything with depth, such as books, three-dimensional objects, etc. Some flatbed scanners can accept thick documents. The flatbed is the scanner of choice for the typical PHOTO-PAINT user. We will spend considerable time exploring this type of scanner.

- **Handheld scanners.** These small scanning devices essentially comprise the recording head of a flatbed. To input the image, you hold the scanner in your hand and move it slowly across the source material. While this device has its place in the desktop-publishing world, it is not what you would use for professional work on a daily basis. While handheld scanners gained popularity a few years ago when flatbeds were very expensive, they have become less popular today due to the significantly lower cost of flatbeds.

- **3-D scanners.** These scanners have been on the market for several years. They can scan objects with depth, height, and width. Usually they are set up on vertical copy stands. 3-D scanners can digitize objects with depth that ranges from a few inches to a few dozen feet. This scanner, like the film scanner, is a specialty item that would only be found in a studio or ad agency. After all, when was the last time you wanted to scan a beach ball?

- **Drum scanners.** This is the ultimate scanner. It can cost more than an expensive car and can be almost as big. These are the scanners that are used when, say, a highly-paid ad agency needs to have an excellent scan of their Nike shoe for a magazine spread in *Sports Illustrated*. They don't use a flatbed scanner, they use a drum scanner. (How much better are the results you see with drum scanner over a top-flight flatbed scanner? Less than you would imagine.)

Scanners allow us to capture an image, be it photograph, drawing, or printed text, and convert it to an "electronic image" that can be placed in Corel PHOTO-PAINT or any other image-editing or layout program. Scanners come in many sizes and shapes. They range in cost from several hundred to over one million dollars (no kidding).

How Scanners Work

Of the five types of scanners discussed, the one of greatest importance to the serious PHOTO-PAINT user is the flatbed color scanner. But even though we will spend much of our time exploring the flatbed, many of the concepts, terminology, and features apply to one or all of the other types of scanners.

A color flatbed scanner needs three things to collect information about an object and transform it into an image file: a light source, a color-separation method, and an imaging head—a Charge-Coupled Device (CCD) array.

> A CCD is an electronic device that measures light intensity and changes it into voltage. The amount of light (the intensity) that strikes the CCD determines how much voltage is produced, much in the same way that your eye sends a greater or lesser signal to the brain as it receives more or less light. The number of elements in a CCD array are part of what determines the resolution of a scanner.

As you watch a flatbed scan an image, you can see a light that moves down the image. What is happening inside the unit is this: After you put the source object on the glass plate (the copyboard), the light source illuminates a thin horizontal strip on the image. This strip is called the raster line. In a moment we will see that the number of raster lines per inch is another component of the scanner resolution. When the light source hits the image on the copyboard, the light reflected off the image is sensed by the imaging head (CCD) and converted into the three primary colors (or one color if it is a three-pass scanner, which I'll explain in a moment). After the raster line has been "read," the scanner mechanism moves the light source/imaging head down the page a very small increment (sometimes less than 1/1200 of an inch), and the process repeats until the entire image has been scanned. That is how it works overall. Now let's explore a few areas in greater detail.

Color scanning uses the three primary colors of light (red, green, and blue, or RGB) to capture the spectrum of colors in an image. The methods used by the scanners are called one-pass and three-pass scanning. Three-pass scanning uses three separate scans to get each of the RGB colors. It gets the different colors either by using different-colored light sources on each of the three passes or by using a single light source with different color filters mechanically placed over the lamp on each pass. The one-pass method actually reads all three colors (RGB) on a single pass. It does so by splitting the reflected light through an optical device (called a trichromatic beam, which sounds like something from *Star Trek*) that separates it into its RGB components. This method is correctly referred to as one-pass, single-exposure scanning. Obviously, three-pass scanning takes longer than the one-pass method. There is a greater chance of color distortion being introduced during the three-scan pass than with the one-pass, because of mechanical variations in the scanner.

Corel *TIP!*

Be advised, there are many three-pass color scanners on the market place. They are generally older models. An exception to this are single-pass scanners that can also do three-pass scans. While the color in a three-pass is acceptable, the time is takes to complete a color scan must be taken into account. The difference in time between an older three-pass scanner and a new one-pass scanner represented over three minutes per scan on some tests I ran on our systems.

Resolution

There are some basic terms you need to understand when looking for a scanner. Resolution is probably the most abused term of them all. The ways and methods used to specify resolution in scanners causes confusion for almost everyone, from the novice end-user to the seasoned professional at your local service bureau. To add to the confusion, some scanner manufacturers play games of "specmanship" to make their product's resolution appear greater than it really is. So then, what is resolution?

Resolution is a measure of the ability to resolve small details. The resolution of a scanner determines the sharpness (clarity) of a scanned image. The term resolution is used by many people to describe the pixels-per-inch (ppi) rating of the scanner. First of all, the resolution of a scanner should be referred to as samples-per-inch (spi) but dpi is generally the accepted term, we will use it in this discussion. If you use resolution as your major criteria to make your scanner selection you may be disappointed with the results. You may also find that your scanner that claimed to have a 1200-dpi resolution actually has far less than you thought. The accurate measure of the resolution of a scanner involves subjects far beyond the scope of this book. Here is what you need to understand about what is called resolution in the scanner market.

There are two measurements (called the x-direction and y-direction sampling rates) that you need to be aware of when looking at scanner data sheets. The number of pixels-per-inch (PPI) that a scanner can detect is determined by its CCD recording head (the x-direction sampling rate) and the mechanical movement of the CCD (imaging head) down the page (the y-direction sampling rate). For example, a scanner that lists its sampling rate as 300 × 600 ppi has a 300-ppi imaging head, and the mechanical scan motor can move that head with an accuracy of 600 ppi. A higher y-sampling rate does not generally increase the scanner resolution.

Corel *TIP!*

A number of scanner manufacturers reverse the order of the x- and y-direction sampling rates on their data sheets. This gives the appearance of the scanner being a higher-resolution device than it really is. After all doesn't a 600 × 300-ppi scanner look better than a 300 × 600? Let the buyer beware.

Considerations in Choosing a Scanner

We are going to explore several of the types of scanners that exist in the marketplace in a little more detail and consider the advantages and disadvantages of the offered features.

I need to clear up some confusion before we can proceed. We will be talking about black-and-white and grayscale scanners. In the good old U.S.A. we refer to older movies and television programs as being "black and white." However, they are not actually black and white—they are grayscale. Please don't try and correct anyone on this misnomer, because you will only confuse them; but trust me on this. When we talk about black and white in this book, we mean there is only black and white in the image. Clip art (also called line art) is black and white or 1-bit; there are no shades of gray. A "black-and-white" photograph, on the other hand, is composed of many shades of gray and is more correctly referred to as a grayscale image.

Handheld Scanners

The handheld scanners are the least expensive (notice I didn't say cheap) of the categories mentioned. Handheld devices require you to take the scanner in your hand and slowly (*very* slowly if the image is color) drag it across the image that is to be captured. While this makes it a good economical choice, it has its limitations.

Handheld scanners are composed of a simple light source and imaging head (CCD) mounted in a plastic housing. Many of them have a little LED (light-emitting diode) near the top of the unit to warn you if you are scanning faster than the scanner can transfer the data to the computer. Handheld scanners are physically limited to an image that is slightly less than the width of their scan head, which is about 4 inches. What if your image is wider than 4 inches? Great question. If the image you want to scan is less than 4 inches in height, you can scan it lengthwise or you can scan it in several overlapping passes. All of the good hand-held scanners come with software that will allow you to rotate the image you had to scan lengthwise or to stitch together multiple overlapping passes into one image. The quality of the scan you get is dependent upon the design of the scanner, the software that comes with it, the steadiness of your hand, and your experience.

Flatbed Scanners

If you haven't been able to figure it out yet, flatbed scanners are the type of scanner that is recommended for PHOTO-PAINT 5 users. Flatbeds scanners can or should be able to accommodate papers or pages up to 8.5" × 14" in size. There are several flatbed scanners that cannot accommodate pages larger than 8.5" × 11", think twice before buying them. Technically, flatbeds cannot scan the pages of a book. My HP Scanjet IICX does books up to 3- or 4-inches thick because the cover is hinged. Since most of the references in this chapter are to flatbed scanners there is little to talk about here. We will be discussing selection criteria for scanners later in the chapter.

Sheet-Fed Scanners

Although sheet-fed scanners are fast disappearing from the scanner market there are still a lot of them out in the world so we should be aware of them.

Sheet-fed scanners are lumped in with the flatbed category by many in the industry, although I can't see how. The difference with sheet-fed scanners is that individual pages must be fed into a thin slot, where they are pulled along by rubber rollers past a stationary CCD. A sheet-fed scanner can accommodate only single sheets of paper as wide as a carriage slot. This can be a real pain if your imaging software has a preview mode (which most do.) The result is that you must load the sheet to be scanned, preview scan it to determine what part of the image on the sheet that you need, then reload the sheet and rescan it, hoping that you put it in close enough to the original position to make the area you selected from the first scan get all that you want. Almost every sheet-fed scanner that I have seen is sold or made by Canon. The Canon IX-12 looks like a fax machine without the buttons; that's because it is essentially a fax machine without the fax electronics. In fairness, I was able to use a sheet-fed scanner for several years before the prices of flatbeds came down out of the $6,000 region (for 300-ppi grayscale). If you have to use a sheet-fed scanner, it will work. However, most of the sheet-fed scanners that I am familiar with are one-bit scanners, not grayscale.

Figure 20.1.
The HP Scanjet IICX. Hewlett-Packard is the scanner company that owns the lion's share of the scanner market. The scanner shown here is a 24-bit color scanner with a street price under $1,000.

Film Scanners

Flatbed, sheet-fed, and handheld scanners have one thing in common: they record reflected light off an image. This is well and good unless you want to scan a film negative or positive (a color slide.) For this you need a film scanner.

A desktop film scanner shines light directly through a negative or positive (also called a transparency) onto a slow-moving slit that contains a CCD. The slit stops, a raster line is read, and the slit moves again. This is far more accurate than a flatbed scanner, but then again, the images are typically 1/60th the size. Desktop film scanners typically offer resolutions from 2000 to 4000 dpi.

*Figure 20.2.
This is the newest
grayscale scanner from
HP. Bundled with OCR
software and a street
price under $500, this
scanner is beginning to
show up on everyone's
desk in the business
marketplace.*

While most desktop film scanners can accommodate film up to 4" × 5", most are designed to work only with 35mm film. And as small as these units typically are, their price is surprisingly high. They are currently ranging in price from $1,200 to $28,000. The good professional units are in the $2,000–4,000 range. So do you need one of these things? Unless you are doing film all of the time, the answer is no. When you need to have film done, go to a service bureau in your own city or use one of the mail-order places that advertises in the back of *Corel Magazine* or *Publish Magazine*. (I have included the information on film scanners and drum scanners in this section just so it will be complete.)

3-D Scanners

All of the scanners considered to this point have been two-dimensional scanners. We should also discuss 3-D scanners. (They are also called array scanners.) The first one of these 3-D scanners I ever saw was at a Spring COMDEX, and it looked like a food warmer for a small pizza. This is a specialty item that is only good for imaging objects like mechanical parts, or objects with depth that cannot fit under the cover of a flatbed scanner. Unless you have to scan in 3-D objects most of the time, I recommend that you have the work done at a service bureau, or else rent (or borrow) a filmless camera and take pictures of the objects in question. I have seen 3-D scanners as low as $900 dollars and as high as $12,000.

Drum Scanners

For years, drum scanners were a mystery to me. I didn't know anyone who owned one, but the professionals always talked about the superiority of the scans they produced. Considering that they sell in a range of $14,000 to $1 million, they must be great. Again, this and the following paragraph are not intended to give you enough information to go out an buy one; they are merely here to satisfy your curiosity regarding these beasts and what makes them so darned expensive.

The first thing that makes drum scanners unique is that they do not use a CCD to record the image. They use a photomutiplier tube or PMT. Now, I have been around electronics since the 60's, and PMTs were old news even back then. So why not use CCDs? Advocates of drum scanners says it is because the PMTs have greater dynamic range. I am willing to accept this argument at face value, but I am also a little suspicious. Most of my work in electronics involved high-end audio. When solid-state amplifiers were introduced into the high-end audio world, they were considered inferior to tube amplifiers. That was the late 60's. Today, tubes are still considered the amplifier of choice by the true "audiophile." Although you can't demonstrate the difference with test equipment, those who insist on tube amps say they "hear" the difference. I think there is a little of that same kind of thinking when it comes to PMTs. Maybe not, but I remain suspicious.

Figure 20.3.
This ScanMate 4000, manufactured by Scan View is considered a mid-range drum scan- ner. It sells for about $35,000 and makes great scans. You prob- ably will never need one, but I thought you might like to see what one looks like. By the way, they do make a less expensive scanner for only $14,000.

The other thing that makes the drum scanner different (other than the fact that it can cost more than a large house) is its glass drum. A print, negative, or trans- parency is fastened with tape on a very high-quality hollow glass drum and then spun at a high rate of speed to scan it. Most drum scanners can accommodate film or images up to 8" × 10" in size. A light is focused on (or through) the image and received by the PMT as it moves in very tiny increments. This is the way the old fax machines used to operate (in a much grosser scale, of course).

A scan made on a drum scanner is more precise and has greater detail than scans made with any other scanner. Drum scanners are less subject to mechani- cal vibrations because of the rate of speed of the drum and the fact that it weighs more than a car.

When do you need a drum scanner? Probably never. When do you need to have an image scanned with a drum scanner? When your client insists, or when you want to see what the very best scan looks like and you are willing to pay for it. (Remember, the service bureau bought that thing to make money, and the first thing they must do is recoup their investment.)

Should You Buy a Scanner?

Ask yourself some questions:

What are you going to use it for?

Are you scanning an occasional piece of clip art into the church bulletin or company newsletter that will be output on your favorite dot-matrix printer? Then your scanning requirements will be minimal. Are you looking to scan in documents that eventually will be sent to a professional printer? Then you must seriously consider a good scanner. There is nothing worse than trying to make images from a bad scanner look good. To help you determine your requirements, read through the following section and see what scanner best fits your needs and your budget.

What kind of images will you be scanning most of the time?

If you are going to be scanning line art that is generally smaller than 4 inches in one dimension or the other (there is a lot of it out there), printed on a dot-matrix or laser printer, a hand-held device or a sheet-fed scanner will suffice. Get (at the very least) a grayscale scanner. I don't personally advise color for hand-held scanners, because it is difficult to get a good color scan with a hand-held device. I will get some nasty remarks from my friends in the handheld scanner companies for saying that, but it is true. Logitech makes a great grayscale handheld scanner called a Scanman 256, and it comes with some excellent Windows software.

Will a handheld scanner meet your needs?

If so, get one and save some cash. Beware of hand-held scanners that are not true grayscale. This is usually the kind sold for an unbelievable price in the slick glossy catalog that arrives at your home every month or so. The difficulty with non-grayscale scanners (technically they are referred to as one-bit, or black-and-white, scanners) is that they simulate grayscale by a technique called "dithering." When you attempt to resize dithered images, you develop moiré patterns in the image. This produces unpredictable printed results. The bottom line is that there are several good hand-held grayscale scanners out there, so there is no longer any need to get a 1-bit or black-and-white scanner.

Do you need a flatbed scanner?

A flatbed scanner is by far the best choice if you can afford it. As I write this book, good flatbed scanners are in the $600–$1,100 range. If that figure causes you to take a deep breath, reread the previous paragraph on handheld scanners. Flatbeds are available in grayscale and color.

Do You Need a Scanner with a TWAIN Interface?

When looking for any scanner, hand-held or flatbed, I strongly recommend you have a TWAIN interface. I'll explain. Not so long ago, it was the responsibility of every company who wrote paint (bitmap) programs to provide the software program necessary to communicate with the scanner. However, every scanner spoke its own language, so to speak, and the result was that unless you owned one of the more popular scanners, you could not access the scanner from within your paint or drawing program. You had to run a separate scanning program (provided with your scanner) to scan your image. After the image was scanned, you could then load it into your favorite paint or OCR program. Some of these scanning programs were so primitive that you could not even see the scanned image after you scanned it until it was loaded into the image-editing program. That may seem like a lot of work, and let me assure you, it was. You had to scan the image in one program, and then import it into another program to work with it and decide if it needed to be re-scanned.

Then one day all of the scanner people got together and said, "Let us all make our scanners speak one language." (Sort of sounds like the story of the Tower of Babel in reverse.) So they came up with an interface specification called TWAIN.

Why is the interface specification called TWAIN? This is one of those mysteries that might puzzle computer historians for decades to come. I have never received a straight answer to the question, but I have received a number of intriguing possibilities. My favorite explanation is credited to Aldus (now part of Adobe) Corporation. They say TWAIN means "Toolkit Without An Interesting Name." My own theory is that while they were battling over what the specification would be (each manufacturer wanted the version that would require the least amount of modification of their own product), it was beginning to confirm the proverb that "East is east and west is west and never the twain shall meet." Logitech, one of the driving forces behind the specification gives a similar answer: "It was a unique interface that brings together two entities, application and input devices, in a meeting of the twain."

The TWAIN interface allows applications such as Corel PHOTO-PAINT to talk to the scanner directly through a common interface. The TWAIN interface allows any program that supports the standard to scan images directly from within the program. More importantly, when I read the Corel Forum almost every single message reporting a problem in scanning does not have a TWAIN interface. That is why you want to make sure you get a scanner with a TWAIN interface.

When you look through the catalogs and talk to the salesman at your local computer retail outlet, you will find that almost all scanners now support TWAIN. It has become such a widely embraced standard that it is very difficult to find a scanner without it. Thus, TWAIN is only an issue if you are buying an older or used scanner.

Company name and reputation

This is an important consideration. Many scanner companies out in the market and the mail-order channel have been manufacturing scanners for other companies and are now beginning to sell direct. While their equipment may be satisfactory, the issue of support becomes important. First, ask yourself, if you are a graphics software developer, which scanners are you going to insure that your software works well with? The answer (in case you didn't know) is the company that has the greatest market share. There is nothing worse than calling technical support to determine why their software cannot communicate with your LUCKY-STAR scanner only to discover they have never heard of it. Stay with the major players. My favorite scanners are made by Hewlett-Packard. There are other good scanners out there but I can't think of any reason, either price or performance, to pick them.

Do you need grayscale or color?

Grayscale scanners should support 256 levels of gray. There are some out there that only support 16, 32, or 64 levels of gray. Do not get a grayscale scanner that supports less than 256 grayscale unless it is a gift or you are using it for OCR (optical character recognition). If it is a gift, immediately place an ad for it in the local paper, sell it, and use the money towards a better scanner.

If you are only doing OCR work, or if you are really watching the old purse strings, then a good grayscale flatbed scanner might be a sensible solution. There are several major companies that are selling their grayscale scanners for a little more than half of what a color scanner costs. If the deciding factor is not money, go for the color. Even if you do not currently have a color output device, I recommend a color scanner. Excellent color output devices are available in the $600 range, and their price continues to get lower each day, so any money spent for the color capability may prove to be a worthwhile investment.

Further Notes on Resolution

The subject of scanner resolution brings out the crazies in many people. It's like this: You are sitting there looking proudly at your brand new laser printer that can print with a resolution of 600 dots per inch. Obviously, you need a scanner that can scan in images at 600 dpi. Right? Wrong! When you begin to scan images, you will discover one of the better kept secrets of the universe: lower resolution is, in many cases, better than high resolution. For now you really only need to be able to determine one thing about the resolution numbers printed on the box: Are they real or magic? Some of the scanner companies advertise that their scanners do 600, 800, and even 2400 dpi (this part of the resolution stratosphere is where the drum scanners live). If you examine their data sheets closely, you may see that the 600-dpi scanner is really a 300-dpi scanner. Are they lying? Not really. They use something called interpolation. Interpolation looks at each line on, say, a 300-dpi scan and then calculates what the dots in-between would look like and inserts them. How well does it work? Well enough for most applications. But you are going to see as we get into our applications that almost everything should be scanned in around 150–200 dpi. There are exceptions to this, but the average PHOTO-PAINT 5 user can get by with a 300 × 600-dpi scanner and do quite well. The main exception is when you know an image is going to be blown up to poster size. That's when you want to haul over to your service bureau and get a high-resolution scan.

How to Avoid Getting Over Your Head in Color Depth

Color depth is becoming the new battleground for scanner manufacturers. I had already told you that a 24-bit color scanner will provide you with 16.7 million colors. A 24-bit color scanner can also capture a greater dynamic range of colors than can be reproduced by the 4-color printing process. The dynamic ranges that will be referenced here are talking about the range of tonal shades from one end of the spectrum to the other. Since it is a very large range it is referenced using a log scale. In other words, all you need to know is that the higher the number the better. Scanners, monitors, and color output devices all have their own dynamic ranges.

Let me give you some numbers that may help you understand: The color output device that has the greatest dynamic range is the color slide. Its dynamic range is expressed as 2.7. Next in line is four-color printing on glossy paper. This is what you'd find in a fancy art book that sits on the coffee table. On a good day, the four-color process can produce a dynamic range (or color range) of 1.9. The bottom of the food chain is newsprint, with a range of 0.9. So what do the scanner manufacturers do? Because they want to convince the people who are currently buying drum scanners to buy their flatbeds, they move away from 24-bit color scanners and begin increasing the number of bits that their scanner can capture. As I write this, several companies have 30-, 32-, and 40-bit scanners, but the final scanner output will still be 24-bit color. The only difference is that they employ software to throw away the noisy color bits and keep the good ones. This raises the question: How do you tell the difference between a noisy color bit and one that is not noisy? I don't mean to make too much light of this subject, because there clearly is a market out there for flatbed scanners that can do almost as well as a drum scanners for a fraction of the cost. But I don't want you to fall prey to the specmanship that goes on in these scanner-hardware ad wars. For 99.9 percent of your jobs, a 24-bit or a 30-bit scanner can produce better results than you need. For the .1 percent of the time that you need a higher resolution or greater dynamic range, go to a service bureau and let them do a drum scan for you.

Scanner Interface Hardware

Your scanner needs to talk to your computer. Capturing and storing images involves the transfer of many megabytes of data from the scanner to the computer in the least amount of time. It is done several ways. One of the more popular ways is to use a SCSI (Small Computer Standard Interface) interface. (Everyone pronounces it *scuzzy*.) It offers high speed and is an increasingly popular, well-supported interface. Another advantage of SCSI is that if you have other SCSI devices (e.g., CD-ROM, tape, Syquest drive, etc.) you can daisy-chain them into the existing SCSI card, saving you slot space in your computer and avoiding installation headaches. Beware, however, of a name game that is played here. The SCSI interface for Apple is a proprietary interface that only works with Macintosh computers. A true SCSI interface can connect directly to a SCSI card, whereas those offering proprietary SCSI interfaces can only plug into their own host adapters (cards).

Other interfaces that are available include IEEE-488, also called GPIB (General Purpose Instrument Bus). The GPIB is unique, and only one scanner house uses it that I am aware of.

Also, printer ports are now being used for more than printers. The advantage of using a printer port as your scanner interface is that it offers high speed with a very standard interface. The disadvantage is that the printer interface was never designed to have multiple devices hanging off it.

Alternatives to Buying a Scanner

"May I Borrow a Cup of Scan?"

There are several alternatives to purchasing a scanner. For instance, if you know someone who owns a scanner, you may want to simply borrow theirs, especially if you have very minimal scanning requirements.

What if you have a PC and your new friend with a scanner has a Mac? No problem. Any Mac that can output to a high-density 3.5" floppy can output in an

IBM-readable format. Corel PHOTO-PAINT can read the Mac PICT files. Watch the filenames, however; they can be quite long in the Mac, so have your friend give you eight-character names with a .PCT extension.

Photo CDs

If your computer can read Photo CDs and you have the original negative of the image you want to use, transferring the image to a photo disc is an excellent solution. Check with some fast-development film houses and you might find that they have a location that does Photo CDs. They don't cost much, and you get a better scan than if you made a photograph and scanned it in yourself.

Service Bureaus

There are more bureaus opening up all the time that don't think it is their job to intimidate you but actually provide you with a service. If you are going to use a bureau, it is best establish a relationship with one place. Then, if they give you a poor scan (it does happen), you can get a replacement without a lot of hassle.

Scanner-Selection Summary

- Handheld and sheet-fed scanners are the most economical but have limitations.
- Flatbeds, overall, are recommended for work that is eventually going to a commercial printer.
- Any scanner you buy should comply with the TWAIN specification.
- Resolution should be in the 300 to 600-dpi range.
- Black-and-white (also called 1-bit) scanners are only suitable for OCR.
- Grayscale (also called 256 grayscale) scanners are good for most desktop-publishing applications. However, if it is 32-shade or 64-shade grayscale, it is only recommended for OCR.
- Color scanners (preferably one-pass color) are the best for all applications.

Importing Images into PHOTO-PAINT

There are many ways to bring images into PHOTO-PAINT, as described in the following sections.

Opening an Image file

The most direct method is to load an image file by opening the file with the File Open command in the File menu.

Dragging and Dropping Image Files

PHOTO-PAINT allows the opening of image files by dragging and dropping them from the File Manager or similar program into the PHOTO-PAINT workspace.

To open a file with drag-and-drop, do as follows:

1. Choose Tile from the Program Manager window menu. (This step may not be required. The object is to have the File manager or a similar program open but not occupying the entire display area.)

2. Open File Manager and click on the desired file. It must be an image file.

3. Click and drag the file into the PHOTO-PAINT window and release the button.

Notes on Dragging and Dropping Files

This feature requires that PHOTO-PAINT be open to operate properly. PAINT can either be open and occupying part of the display screen or it can be reduced to an icon. If it is an icon, drag the file to a point on top of the icon at the bottom of the display.

Dragging and Dropping Graphics from a Graphics Program

It is possible to drag and drop a graphics image from another application (one that supports OLE 2.0) into Corel PHOTO-PAINT.

To drag and drop graphics, do the following:

1. Size the windows of Corel PHOTO-PAINT and the application that created the graphics so that both are visible.

2. Click on the graphic and drag it into Corel PHOTO-PAINT.

Notes on Dragging and Dropping Graphics

There are several things to consider when using the drag-and-drop feature to move graphics into PHOTO PAINT. The item that is grabbed is removed from the original application, so you need to make sure it is saved before you drag it across to PAINT. The graphic is rasterized if it is a vector image (e.g., an image from CorelDRAW). Even though you may have only dragged some text across, it will come into PAINT as a image square (not text) with a rectangular background. One of the best ways to get a graphics image from CorelDRAW into PHOTO-PAINT is to export it as a placeable .EPS file and open it as a normal image file with PHOTO-PAINT.

Acquiring Images with a Scanner

Many times images that are needed in a publication are not in electronic format. There are several ways to convert the images. As mentioned previously, if they are photographic images and you have the negatives, you can have them put on a Photo CD. They can be taken to a service bureau, and for a per-page fee, they will scan them. If you own a scanner, you can scan them directly into Corel PHOTO-PAINT.

There are several advantages to scanning images into PHOTO-PAINT. You can calibrate the scanner you use so that the colors are accurate. (Service-bureau scans will have to be adjusted.) You can also crop, scale, and adjust the images during scanning, saving time and effort later.

Corel PHOTO-PAINT supports any scanner that adheres to the TWAIN interface. Nearly all scanners produced in the last several years support the TWAIN interface. When Corel PHOTO-PAINT was installed on your machine, you had the option of installing a scanner driver at that time. If you chose to install the Corel scanner driver, a line was added to your CONFIG.SYS file that installs a Corel device driver every time the computer is started. If you own a scanner that has its own TWAIN interface driver—for example, Hewlett-Packard comes with a TWAIN interface called DeskScan II—Corel PHOTO-PAINT can use it instead of (or in addition to) the Corel TWAIN interface.

Scanning an image directly into PHOTO-PAINT requires two initial procedures: selecting the source device and acquiring the image.

Selecting the Source Device

The Select Source command allows selection of a TWAIN image input source, such as Corel Image Source or HP's Deskscan II. The sources that appear in the selection box depend on which scanner driver(s) are installed on your computer. If the scanner you want to select does not appear in the Select Source dialog box, then that TWAIN driver has not been installed or the computer does not recognize the scanner due to possible system hardware conflicts.

Check the documentation that came with your scanner to verify proper operation.

To select a source device, do as follows:

1. Choose Select Source from the Acquire Image flyout in the File menu.
2. Select the desired device name from the Select Source dialog box. The default is Corel Image Source (if it was installed).
3. Click Select.

Once a source has been selected, it remains until it is changed. It is not necessary to repeat this step again unless you need to change image sources.

Corel *TIP!*

> I highly recommend that you use the TWAIN driver supplied with your scanner. The driver included with the Corel products was invented by ZSoft Corporation sometime after the American Civil War. It is totally manual and has limited control characteristics. Look at Figures 20.4 and 20.5. Figure 20.4 was scanned using the Corel TWAIN driver without any adjustment. Figure 20.5 was scanned using the Hewlett-Packard Deskscan 2.0 driver that comes with the HP scanners without any adjustment.

Figure 20.4.
This is a scan of a color photo using the Corel TWAIN driver without any adjustments.

Figure 20.5.
This is the same photo from the same scanner, this time using the TWAIN driver that came with the HP IICX scanner without any adjustments. Can you see the difference? If you can't see any difference, I can recommend a good optometrist.

Acquiring an Image

The Acquire command enables you to control the scanner. The dialog box that appears depends on the source device selected. This procedure outlines the for using the Corel Image source driver. While specific items may differ slightly, the overall operation of all the scanner features are the same.

To acquire an image, do as follows:

1. Chose Acquire from the Acquire Image flyout in the File menu. If you selected Corel as the source, the Corel Image Source dialog box opens.

2. Click on Prescan. This performs a preliminary, low-resolution scan on the entire image area.

3. Select the part of the image to be scanned by dragging the corner handles of the marquee in the view area.

4. Click Scan to perform the scan.

The Corel Image Source Dialog Box

This dialog box is displayed when the Corel Image Source is selected in the Acquire Image command. This dialog box may be different if you chose another source in the Select Source dialog box. The dialog box options are detailed in the sections that follow:

Figure 20.6.
This is the dialog box that is used with the HP ScanJet IICX. While it will completely auto-mate the scanning process it allows for precision manual adjustment of scans.

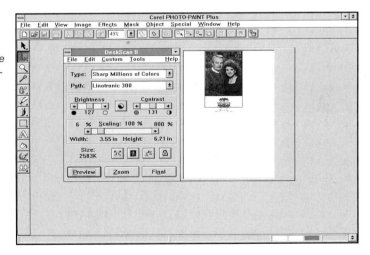

View Area

The view area represents the scanner bed. It includes rulers which display the width and height of the view area. The units of measurement can be changed in the Units box.

Scan Area box

This is a rectangular area with control points at each corner, located inside the View Area. It marks the scanner bed area to be scanned. If your scanner driver allows you to set a custom paper size, you can drag the square control points to resize the Scan Area box. The location boxes are also used to resize the Scan Area box.

Image Information

Image Information displays the image size and available memory in bytes. The image size is estimated on the basis of the size of the Scan Area, the chosen scanning resolution and other parameters as described forthwith.

Scanner list

On the right side, it displays a list of installed scanners for you to select one.

Location selection boxes

The left and top boxes display the distance between the rulers and the top-left corner of the Scan Area box. You can change the location of the scan-area box by changing the values in those boxes. The Width and Height boxes display the size of the Scan Area box. You can change its size by using these boxes.

Resolution box

This allows you to set the resolution to be used to scan the image. The top box is a dropdown list of available resolutions for the selected scanner. If your scanner offers a "custom" resolution, use the second box to precisely set the desired resolution. Note that a higher resolution produces a more accurate and detailed image but requires more time and increases the file size.

Corel *NOTE!*

> Consider your final output device when setting the Resolution value. If you are printing to a standard laser printer (i.e., 300-dpi), you should be using a resolution of no more than 120 dpi. If you have a 600-dpi printer use 150–200 dpi. Resolution higher than the intended output device is a waste of disk space and produces files that are large and sometimes unmanageable.

Units box

This lets you select the units of measurement for the rulers. The current selection appears at the top-left corner of the View Area.

Colors box

This lets you select the maximum number of colors or levels of gray to be used in scanning the image when using a color scanner. The options listed in the box are: 16 million colors, 256 levels of gray, and black and white. To use the Prescan button, grayscale must be the color setting.

Corel *NOTE!*

Consider your final output device when setting the Color value. If you are printing to a standard laser printer you should be using grayscale. If you are printing to a low-to-medium-resolution color printer (e.g., a color ink-jet), try 256 color. Color settings greater than the output device can use are a waste of disk space and can produce files that are large and unmanageable.

Halftones box

This lets you select a halftone pattern for images if you are working in black-and-white mode. The options displayed in the list box are scanner specific and are used to control the dithering produced by scanning in black and white.

Paper Size box

This lets you select a paper size, which is used by the Scanner to determine the maximum size of the scan area. The options displayed in the box are scanner specific. If a "custom" option is listed, use the Scan Area-box control point to set its size.

Settings

This displays the Scanner Setup dialog box, which offers scanner-specific options. Controls that are most often listed here include controls for the brightness and sharpness levels to be applied when scanning the image.

Progress Meter

This provides a visual progress report while the image is being scanned.

Prescan

This displays the document placed on the scanner bed in the View Area. Prescan resets the color setting to grayscale and uses the scanner's lowest resolution. Use this to precisely size and position the Scan Area box.

Scan

This begins the scanning process.

Basics of Digital Image and Color

As I talk with Corel users, I find that there a large number of them who are getting deeply involved with computer graphics with little or no background in the subject. Many books that are on the shelves today assume that you know the terminology and the technical foundation of computer graphics. The result is frustration. This chapter and the other chapters in this section are here to fill in the gaps in your graphics background.

By now you have figured out that Corel PHOTO-PAINT works with bitmapped images. Even if a vector-based (non-bitmap) file is loaded into PHOTO-PAINT, it is converted (rasterized) to a bitmap when it is loaded. To work effectively with bitmap images, it is necessary to understand why they act differently than the object-based images in CorelDRAW. Let us begin by defining our terms.

Basic Computer Graphics Terminology

A word of caution here: There are many terms in the computer industry that are non-standard, colloquial, or just plain dumb. This has lead to one of my theorems regarding computer terminology:

Patently Pointless Theorem #1

The only thing that is universally accepted in the computer industry is that nothing is universally accepted in the computer industry.

I don't expect the Nobel prize for that one, but it goes a long way to explain why there are so many different terms to describe the same thing in the computer industry. I will always try to give you the most commonly used term along with the "correct" term.

My son took the SAT test recently. One of the pre-SAT questions involved the word "peruse." Does peruse mean to study thoroughly or to skim through lightly? I gave him the "skim through" answer—and I found out it was wrong. Even though the correct definition of the word meant to study something thoroughly, I warned him that if he told his teachers that he had perused a book, they would think that he skimmed through it, regardless of the correct definition of the word. Thus, when it comes to communicating ideas, what a term actually means (the correct term) is less important than what others believe it means. In this book, we always try to use the correct term but also include the commonly used term (even if it isn't accurate).

Pixels

Bitmaps are composed of pixels, the individual dots that compose ands image on a computer screen. The term "pixel" is short for PIcture ELement. One way to understand pixels is to think of an image comprising mosaic tiles. When you get close to a mural made of mosaic tiles, it looks like someone had a bad Lego day. This is because you are so close you are looking at individual tiles. But, step away a few feet from the mosaic, the individual tiles begin to lose their definition and they visually begin to merge together. The tiles have not changed their size or number, yet the further back you move, the better the image looks. Pixels in bitmaps work much the same way. As you zoom in on an image, the individual pixels begin to stand out more and the image they produce become less and less evident. There are, of course, major differences between pixels and mosaic tiles. Pixels come in a greater selection of decorator colors (more than 16.7 million, to be exact). And pixels are lighter than tiles. But the way they operate to produce an image is the same.

Size and Resolution

These two terms represent some of the more elusive concepts of digital imaging. An image's *size* describes the physical dimensions of the image. *Resolution* is the number of pixels-per-inch (ppi) that make up an image.

For example, let us say we have an image whose width is 100 pixels and whose height is 100 pixels. The size of the image is described as being 100 x 100 pixels. So how big is this image? Trick question! There is not enough information to know. This is where resolution comes in. If the resolution of this image is 100 pixels per inch, then the image is 1" × 1" inches. If the resolution is 200 ppi, the image would be .5" × .5". If the image has a resolution of 50 ppi, the image would be 2" × 2".

The image size expresses the length (in pixels) of each side. Resolution tells you how many pixels are contained in each inch. If you have been working with PHOTO-PAINT, you may have wondered why an image that is almost 3" wide on your screen is only 1" wide when you print it. That is the difference between screen resolution and printer resolution. If you have always worked in vector-based programs such as CorelDRAW (which is resolution-independent), you never had to know this before. Don't get discouraged—it isn't as difficult to understand as it may first appear.

Screen Resolution

No matter what resolution you are using, Corel PHOTO-PAINT displays each pixel onscreen according to the zoom ratio. For example, if the zoom ratio is 1:1 (which is displayed in PHOTO-PAINT as a percentage of 100 percent), each image pixel takes up a single screen pixel. The display's zoom ratio and printer output are unrelated. If you are a little fuzzy on monitors and pixels, read on. If you know them cold, skip ahead.

When you bought your monitor and/or display card, you may have been bewildered by such measures as 640 × 480, 800 × 600, etc. These numbers refer to the number of screen pixels that the monitor can display horizontally and vertically. For example, let's say you have a plain vanilla VGA monitor. The standard resolution for this monitor is 640 pixels wide by 480 pixels tall (640 × 480). This means that if we have an image that is 600 pixels tall and 400 pixels wide, it will virtually fill the screen. (There are other factors, such as the space taken up by the menu and title bar, etc. We will, for the sake of this example, assume that the workspace area is 600 × 400. If we then go over to our co-worker's system to show her the image on her super high-resolution monitor that has a resolution of 1200×800, the image that filled our VGA screen (at 100 percent, 1:1 zoom level in PHOTO-PAINT) fills only half the screen on her system. If we wanted the image to fill the screen on this system, we would change the zoom ratio on her system to 200 percent. Now each pixel in the image occupies 2 screen pixels on the monitor. Many people have been befuddled when they spent a lot of money to get a high-res (high-resolution) monitor and display card, and instead of their screen images being "ultra-sharp," they only seemed smaller. Now that you know the secret, have your friends buy you lunch and you can explain it to them, too. I have listed some of the standard resolutions that you will encounter on the market today in following table.

Table 22.1. Pixel dimensions of the various monitor types.

Monitor Class	Pixel Screen Width	Pixel Screen Height
Hercules (Monochrome)	720	348
EGA (16 color)	640	350
MCGA (4 color)	640	480
VGA (also XGA)	640	480
SuperVGA	800	600
8514/a	1024	768

With all of the exciting ads for high-resolution displays, it is difficult not to get caught up in the fever to upgrade. If you have a 14" or 15" monitor, you should be using the VGA or SuperVGA resolution setting on your graphics card. If you go for a higher resolution on your display, even if your monitor supports it, your friends may start calling you Blinky, because you will be squinting all of the time to read the screen. Also, be cautious about recommendations from the retail clerk at your super computer discount center. Remember that last week your "computer salesman" might have been bagging groceries at the local supermarket and may know less about computers than you do.

Image Resolution

Let's go back to our 100×100 pixel image area. This image contains 10,000 pixels. ($100 \times 100 = 10,000$. Don't let the math scare you. You have worked this problem before, in high-school math class—except it almost always had to do with how many square feet were in a room. Remember?)

Assuming the number of pixels in the image remains fixed, increasing the size of the image means that we will have fewer pixels per inch and thereby lower resolution. PHOTO-PAINT resamples the image each time it is scaled or resized. (*Resampling* means the number of pixels is increased or decreased proportion-ally to maintain the desired resolution.)

Corel *TIP!*

The terms "resize" and "scale" are sometimes used interchangeably. They don't mean the same thing. Corel PHOTO-PAINT uses the terms correctly. Scaling an image refers to changing the size of an object proportionally. Resizing means that the image size was changed but not necessarily proportionally.

If we double the size of an image in a program that doesn't resample, such as Pagemaker, the resolution is decreased by half. If we reduced the original image size (100 pixels × 100 pixels) by half (to 50 pixels × 50 pixels), the 10,000 pixels would now be crammed into a smaller box. The resolution would double.

Corel *TIP!*

This doubling effect can be helpful at times when you have a low-resolution image. By reducing the size of the image, you increase the resolution. This works against you when the image is already at a high resolution. The image then becomes muddy, because all of the lines become crammed into the smaller image area.

Why is the relationship between size and resolution important to understand? Because when we change the size of objects in the image, we need to be aware of what may result. For example, say we typed in a line of text in PHOTO-PAINT at a small type size, and later we decide to enlarge (scale) the image to twice its original size. Because PHOTO-PAINT resamples any image that is scaled, pixels would be added to make the result look acceptable. If we doubled the image size, we would keep the resolution of the image unchanged by adding pixels. The resulting image could look unacceptable.

Because we understand the relationship between size and resolution, we may wisely choose to remove the image from PHOTO-PAINT, recreate it in CorelDRAW at the correct size, and then bring it back into PHOTO-PAINT.

To repeat: If the file size (number of pixels) remains fixed, as the size of an image increases, the resolution decreases. Conversely, as the image dimensions decrease, and the file size (the number of pixels) remains the same, the resolution increases. This is called an inverse relationship.

You may have noticed that I always added the phrase "if the number of pixels remains fixed." We are going to see in a few pages that there are ways to increase and decrease the number of pixels in an image. When you are working with PHOTO-PAINT, you need to select a resolution based on what you want to do with the image. Are you going to print it? Is it going to be used as a screen image? When you worked with CorelDRAW, these questions were not important. Because it was a vector-based drawing program, it was essentially "resolution independent." The same is not true of bitmap editing programs such as PHOTO-PAINT. When printing an image, a higher resolution translates into a sharper image with greater clarity. If you intend to use the image with a multimedia presentation that will be run from a computer display, the resolution should match the resolution of the monitor that will be used for the presentation. Why is this important? If the resolution of the output device is not considered, there is a possibility that your printed output will experience problems—which leads us to a discussion of printers.

If it were a perfect world, the resolution of the image would exactly match that of the printer (which is measured in dots-per-inch). If we were printing to a 600dpi (dots-per-inch) printer in our perfect world, we would be using a 600ppi-resolution image. Each image pixel would occupy one printer dot. However, it is not a perfect world out there. As a real-world example, let us assume you are printing a 93ppi (VGA) image to a 600dpi (HP LJ4) printer. Each image pixel wants to take up about 6 1/2 dots (6.451612903226 dots, to be exact). Where did this number come from? The printer prints 600 dots in an inch, while our image has only 93 pixels in the same inch. Result? 600/93 = 6.45. Each pixel will thus take almost 6 1/2 printer dots to print. This is where the wicket gets sticky. A printer dot cannot be divided up into little pieces. Printer dots only come in one size. Each pixel dot must be represented by a whole number of printer dots. Our laser printer cannot mathematically reduce each pixel dot to 6 dots. It would distort the image. To maintain an accurate image size, the printer assigns 6 dots to most of the pixels and 7 dots to a few other pixels, as necessary, to keep the image size correct. The result of these occasional fatter-than-they-should-be pixels is something called a Moiré pattern. You may have seen Moiré patterns before and not realized it. I used to be plagued by them when I owned a one-bit scanner that dithered all of my images (i.e., pretend grayscale). When the images were re-scaled, I ended up with these weird, squiggly patterns that ran across my image. These were Moiré patterns, although I didn't know it at the time. Sometimes the Moiré patterns become so bad they develop shapes. I have seen patterns that looked like checkerboards.

(Trivia time: Why is it called Moiré? Because the result looks like the rippled patterns in fabric that are the result of the Moiré process. The difference is, those who apply the Moiré process to fabrics want the effect. We do not.)

So what can we do to get rid of the dreaded Moiré patterns? Set the resolution of your image so that it divides evenly into the printer resolution. Sound like your worst math nightmare? It is simpler than you would imagine. In our previous example, we could have set the resolution of the image to 100. It doesn't take much of a rocket scientist to figure out that 100 goes into 600 six times evenly, i.e., with no remainder. (You shouldn't have to become a math whiz just to operate a bitmap editing program.) My suggestion is to establish some resolutions that work for the output device that you use most often. If you have a 300dpi printer, 75ppi is a reasonable resolution for a low-resolution image, and 150 is excellent for a high-resolution image. A little later in this chapter we will learn how to change (resample) our image so that it looks good on both the output device that we use for proofing and on the high-end image setter down at the service bureau.

Color

Color is everywhere. Even black-and-white is color. (Really.) Color has the greatest and most immediate effect on the viewer of any factor in graphic design. Psychologists confirm that color has an enormous capacity for getting our attention. To use color effectively, we must understand it, both technically and aesthetically. It is a vast undertaking. However, in this chapter we will learn as little as possible to get the job done. (If you need to know more, there is a bibliography in the back of the book.)

Color Depth

Every pixel of a PHOTO-PAINT image has information associated with it that defines its color. The amount of information stored with each pixel is referred to as its color depth, which some call data types. The more information that is stored with each bit, the greater the amount of colors that can be represented. Fortunately, the information can only come in certain sizes, as shown in Table 22.2.

Table 22.2. Color depth for the various image types.

Color Depth	Type of image	Color(s) Available
1 Bit	Black-and-White	2 colors
8-Bit	Grayscale	256 shades of gray
4-Bit	Color	16 colors
8-Bit	Color	256 colors
16-Bit	Color	65,000 colors
24-Bit	Color, also called true color	16.7 million colors
32-Bit	Color, also called CMYK	16.7 million colors

All image-file formats have some restrictions regarding the color depth that each can accommodate, so it becomes necessary to know what color depth you are working with in order to recognize what kinds of colors and other tools you may use with it.

If color depth is new to you, one of the questions you may be thinking is why do we have all of these different color depths? Why not make all of the images 24-bit and be done with it. There are many reasons for the different sizes. One of the major factors that restricts color depth is file size. The greater the number of bits associated with each pixel, the greater the file size. If an image took 20KB as a black-and-white (1-bit) image, it will take more than 480KB as a true-color image. If an 8×10 color photograph is scanned in at 600dpi (don't ever do it!) and at a color depth of 24-bit, the resulting 64MB+ file will probably not even fit in your system. Not to mention that every operation with this image will be measured in hours instead of seconds. There are many other factors that also come into play. Why have a true color image if the output device is a low-end ink-jet printer? The scanner may only support 8-bit color (which is not uncommon). Let's take a closer look at the various color depth types that are being used in the industry today.

Black-and-White Images

This term "black and white" has caused some confusion in the past because old movies and television shows are referred to as being in black and white. They are grayscale, not black-and-white. Don't try and educate anyone on this subject. Just know that the old *Andy Griffith* shows are really in grayscale, not black-and-white.

Real black-and-white images are as simple as they get. One bit of information is used per pixel to define it's color. Because it has only one bit, it can only show one of two states, either black or white. The little pixel is either turned on or it is turned off. It doesn't get any simpler than this.

Black-and-white images are more common than you would imagine. There is a lot that can be done with them. This kind of image is sometimes referred to as line art. It is possible to see black-and-white (1-bit) used for grayscale-looking photographs. I used a scanner for several years that was a one-bit scanner. It approximated the grayscale look by dithering. Such output can be acceptable. The drawback occurs if you must resize it. Then you experience Moiré patterns, which kind of looks like a TV set with bad reception.

Grayscale Images

These are images using eight bits of information for each pixel, producing 256 shades of gray. The shades range from white (0) to black (255). Grayscale is used for many other things besides "black-and-white" photos. PHOTO-PAINT uses grayscale images for Transparency masks, color masks, and color information in several color models.

4-Bit and 8-bit Color

These are also referred to by the term "indexed color." The software creates a reference palette to which all of the colors used in the image are assigned. An 8-bit color image can only have one of a possible 256 combinations of color assigned to each pixel. Now, the software doesn't start in the upper-left corner and take the first 256 colors it runs into as its palette. (You would have some seriously strange images if it did.) Instead, the software looks at the entire color range of the image and selects 256 of the most common colors. Next, it assigns each of the colors in the image to one of those 256 that is the closest to the original color. Images that have a narrow color range look fine in 8-bit color, but color photographs with a wide range of color suffer somewhat by the color reduction.

You won't see many 4-bit (16-color) images anymore. Having said that, almost all of the color wallpapers patterns that come with Windows are 4-bit color images. Today, 8-bit (256-color) images are all over the place. Almost every color image you download from CompuServe is an 8-bit (256-color) image. In fact, the graphic format created by CompuServe, GIF, can only support 8-bit color or grayscale.

16-Bit Color (64K Color)

This color reminds me of EGA. There was a brief time when CGA wasn't enough—there is nothing worse than seeing a graphic computer game in CGA—and so EGA came next. It offered more colors and slightly better resolution than CGA. EGA was then quickly replaced by VGA. In a way, 16-bit color (64K color) is like that. It came when 24-bit color was just too expensive and 8-bit (256 color) wasn't enough. Most of the higher performance cards are now moving towards 24-bit color.

Using 16-bits to define the color depth provides approximately 65,000 colors. This is enough for almost any color image. I have seen the images in 16-bit and 24-bit side-by-side, and it is almost impossible to tell them apart. All things being equal, most of the photo-editing public could work with 64K color from now until the Second Coming and never tell any difference. What are the advantages of 16-bit color? Lower cost graphics card and faster performance, because you are moving one-third fewer bits.

24-Bit (True Color)

True-color images may use up to 16.7 million colors. They are so closely associated with the RGB color model that they are sometimes referred to as RGB 24-bit. (We talk about color models later in this chapter.) RGB stands for Red-Green-Blue. Your monitor makes all of its colors by a combination of these three colors. Your eye perceives color the same way: red, green, blue. The three colors that make up the RGB models each have eight bits assigned to them, allowing for 256 possible shades of each color. Each color gun in the color monitor can display 256 possible shades of its color. The mixing together of three sets of 256 combinations produces a possible 16.7 million color combinations. While true color doesn't display every possible color in all of creation, it gets pretty close. It is the model of choice for the desktop computer artist.

32-Bit Color

Look back at Table 22.2. Do you notice anything unusual about 32-bit color? Although the color depth increased by 25 percent, the amount of color remained the same. Why is that?

There are two answers, because there are two types of color depth that involve 32-bits. The first is more commonly seen on the Mac side of the world. When they say something is 32-bit, they are referring to a 24-bit RGB model with an additional 8-bit channel called an alpha channel. Apple reserved the alpha channel, but it has never specified a purpose for this data. Alpha channel is used by some applications to pass an additional grayscale mask information.

The other 32-bit type of color image expresses a CMYK (Cyan-Magenta-Yellow-blacK) model. (We will discuss the color models in more detail later in this chapter.) In short, human eyes and computer monitors work according to RGB color models. Color output devices (printers) cannot use RGB information to produce accurate color output and must use CMYK information. It still covers a total palette of 16.7 million colors. With the release of PHOTO-PAINT 5, the CMYK 32-bit color model is supported.

Corel *NOTE!*

Most of the graphic processors are advertising that they offer 32-bit and 64-bit graphic processors on their boards. This has nothing to do with color depth. It is a reference to the width of the data path. Theoretically, the wider the data path, the greater the amount of color data that can be moved, therefore the faster the screens are redrawn. Don't get confused by this.

Color Models

I knew I wasn't going to like high-school physics the first day of class. We were asked to calculate the direction we would have to steer a rowboat up a fast-moving river in order to get to a pine tree on the other side. My answer was to row toward the pine tree. I got 1/2 credit. I mention this because, if you were looking for a detailed discussion on color models, you won't find it here. We are going to learn about some of the rules that govern the color models, but it is going to be simple and I think you will find it interesting.

One of the first things they taught me in that physics class I didn't like was that color is made up of components, that, when combined in varying percentages, create other distinct and separate colors. You also learned this in elementary school when the teacher had you take the blue poster paint and mix it with the yellow paint to make green. Mixing pigments on a palette is simple. Mixing colors on a computer is not. The rules that govern the mixing of computer colors change, depending on the color model being used. Color models represent different ways to define color. Let us briefly review some of the color models we have already discussed and introduce a few new ones. Later we will deal with a few of them in more detail.

RGB (Red-Green-Blue) is the color model the relates to transmitted light as the source of color. CMYK (Cyan-Magenta-Yellow-blacK) is a printer's model, based on inks and dyes. Some of the other ones out there are HSB (Hue-Saturation-Brightness) and HSL (Hue-Saturation-Lightness). Hue is unique in the color models in that it ranges across the entire spectrum of available colors. Another color model that is slowly gaining some acceptance is the LAB model (also called CIE), which was designed as an international standard for color. At this point, remember my Theorem #1.

Each color model represents a different viewpoint on the same subject. Each offers advantages and disadvantages. None of them are the whole enchilada. For the casual PHOTO-PAINT user, knowing how to get what you need out of RGB and HSB will more than satisfy your requirements. The individual who must accurately get from the screen to the printed page must get more deeply involved in CMYK.

You can work on the same image in different color models, although you can only have one color model active at any time. Color models are three-dimensional, as you will see when we look at the Color roll-up in PHOTO-PAINT 5. The *color depth* of your image will determine what tools and techniques you will be able to use with them and on them. The *color model* that you are using determines how PHOTO-PAINT will create the color that you will be applying to your image. Both color depth and color models can be changed in PHOTO-PAINT.

RGB Versus CMYK

In our daily conversation, we describe colors inaccurately. If you doubt that, go to the auto parts store and try and get touch-up paint for your car. I did this once with a Chevy I owned. I thought its color was tan. Silly me. It was either golden fawn or hazy dawn, according to the color samples. It wasn't until I retrieved the 8-digit number off of the door panel that I learned my car's exterior color was golden fawn. Was golden fawn an accurate description of the color? No. It was just a name (a silly name) assigned to that specific color. I still referred to my tan-colored Chevy.

Color specificity is commonplace in this business. When you are dealing with high-dollar accounts, the client will often specify what the corporate colors must look like. That is what they want and that is what they will get, without exception. I have personally seen several tens of thousands of dollars spent to correct a color deviation caused by someone missing the correct color number by a single digit in a four-color ad for a national publication. Yet, if I showed you the two ads side-by-side, I doubt that you could find the color that was altered.

So why do colors on the screen look different from the printed output? To understand, we must return to the dreaded high-school physics class.

Color is created by the reflection or absorption of various wavelengths of light. When I look at the blue plastic diskette sitting on my desk, I see the blue because all of the other colors except blue are absorbed by the pigment in the plastic. The blue color was not absorbed but rather reflected, and it found its way into my eye. If I pull out an older 5.25" floppy diskette, it is black. If all of the colors are absorbed and none reflected, then it appears to be black. Moving on, we take a prism and shine sunlight through it. What do we get? A rainbow. Why? Because white light (sunlight, in this case) is made up of all the colors in the universe.

So, all of the colors mixed together should produce black. After all, all of the color pigments will absorb all of the color and reflect nothing, resulting in black. Try it if you like, but it won't work. You will end up with something akin to the swamp creature, but not with black. To understand why, we need to look at the first two theories of color. These are called the **additive theory** and the **subtractive theory**. In spite of their names, these are not mathematical mazes, but they are important to understanding why the color on a computer monitor and the printed page can be quite different.

Additive theory tells us that when Red-Green-Blue are added together, the result is white. The absence of any color is black. This was shown in the example of the prism.

Subtractive theory tells us that when Cyan-Magenta-Yellow are added together, the result is, theoretically, black. The absence of color is white. In reality, CMY together produce only a close approximation of black (the swamp creature), which is why printers use blacK (K) and all good color printing is in the four-color (CMYK) model.

Both theories are correct. Yet the theories contradict. How can both be right? Because the additive theory applies to transmitted light (such as your monitor or TV) and the subtractive theory applies to reflected light (the printed page.)

All of the color images you see on a monitor are controlled by the rules of additive color. When you send the image you have been viewing on your monitor to a color printer, the colors on the page are governed by the rules of subtractive color.

Another example of the two is a color photograph and a color slide. The color slide always looks different than the photograph (I avoided the temptation to say it looks "better.") The color slide displays transmitted light, and the photograph uses reflected light. All of this leads to the following:

Patently Pointless Theorem #2

What you see on the display (transmitted light) **is never what you get** on the page (reflected light).

There are additional obstacles to matching colors. The design and age of a monitor will affect the colors it displays. It will even be slightly different between the time the display is first turned on and a time several hours later, after it has heated up. Two identical displays made by the same manufacturer displaying the same color bars can vary significantly. An image made in an RGB model will not translate perfectly to a CMYK image. Printer's inks do not precisely follow the rules of subtractive color.

What is a person to do? Not so long ago, the only solution was a lot of educated guessing, cursing, and praying for an image to successfully run the gauntlet from the scanner, through the display, and out of the printer. Now things are much better, thanks largely to two separate systems that are included in Corel PHOTO-PAINT 5. They are color-correction systems and color-management systems. While they will be explored in more detail in another chapter, let me briefly summarize the differences between them.

A color-correction system is used to correct the parameters of individual color devices (display, printer, scanner etc.) to compensate for any minor deficiencies in the color response of the unit. I say "minor" because there are limits as to how much correction can be applied.

A color-management system works with the entire system to produce uniform transition between different color devices and color models to produce uniform results.

Both color correction and color management are subjects that are more thoroughly explored later in this book.

Image File Formats

Because there are dozens of file formats, it would be confusing to try to cover them all. Instead we will look at several of the more popular ones and discuss their strengths and limitations. PHOTO-PAINT is aware of the color-depth of your image and changes the drop-down list of the file-format choices accordingly. For example, if you have a 32-bit color image, the drop-down list will be reduced to three file format choices. The order in which the file formats appear in the following sections is the order in which they appear in the PHOTO-PAINT drop-down list.

CPT

This is a native format of Corel PHOTO-PAINT. CPT is the best format to use for keeping your originals. Saving in a CPT format retains all of the associated transparency masks and objects. Saving in any other image format results in the merging of all objects in the image. The only limitation to this format is portability. To my knowledge, there are not any non-Corel Windows applications that can recognize a CPT file.

Windows Bitmap (*.BMP, *.DIB)

BMP (Windows Bitmap) is the native image format for Microsoft Paint, which is included with every copy of Microsoft Windows. It is widely supported by nearly every Windows program. PHOTO-PAINT supports BMP images up to 24-bit color (16.7 million colors). You can also use compression (which is lossless) when you save images as BMP files.

CompuServe GIF (*.GIF)

CompuServe created GIF (Graphics Interchange Format) as a means of compressing images for use over their extensive online network. This has become a very popular format, especially on bulletin boards. As a way to send pictures over phone lines, it can't be beat. It has a major limitation of supporting only 8-bit (256-color) images. PHOTO-PAINT does not offer an option to compress images saved as GIF files.

JPEG/LEAD Compression Formats (*.JPG, *.JFF, *.JTF)

JPEG stands for the Joint Photographic Experts Group, which created the format. JPEG is the most efficient compression format available on the market today. It has quickly become a standard for saving large 24-bit color images by compressing them into very small files. LEAD has attracted a large following as a compression scheme that offers great image compression without the image deterioration of JPEG. Both compression formats cause some image deterioration every time the image file is saved. So, when using one of these formats, save your original in CPT or other lossless formats such as TIFF. Also, with JPEG, use the highest-quality image setting to keep the amount of image deterioration to a minimum.

Corel PHOTO-PAINT offers both compression formats, with many selections possible in each. You can export files in either of the JPEG or LEAD bitmap formats. Images compressed using the JPEG export dialog box can be exchanged between a wide variety of platforms and applications. The JPEG format provides you with superior compression techniques. However, with extra compression comes a loss in file information. The JPEG export dialog box allows you to set options for the export.

JPEG Formats

JPEG Interchange Format (JFF)	Although this is not the pure JPEG format, JFIF is almost identical, and it is the format used most widely for interchanging JPEG images. Note that you should create your JFIF file using the .JFF extension. This format is PC, Macintosh, and UNIX compatible.
TIFF JPEG (JTF)	The TIFF JPEG format will create a TIFF 6.0 file using JPEG compression. This is the only way a TIFF JPEG file can be created. TIFF JPEG files cannot be created from CorelDRAW's usual TIFF export filter, nor can a TIFF JPEG file be imported through anything but the JPEG import filter.
LEAD Format (CMP)	This format will provide you with better compression and better quality than any other JPEG format; however, this is not a standard JPEG format. LEAD CMP files can be read by Corel, Lead applications, and any other application that provides support for this format.

Once you have selected one of the three formats to use, you then have the options of selecting from one of the following JPEG export subformats. (**NOTE:** The LEAD bitmap format does not use a subformat.)

Standard (4:4:4)	This subformat will conform to the standards used by other applications.
Option One (4:1:1)	This subformat will provide additional compression by representing four pixels in the original file with a one pixel approximation. Although the file is approximately 1/4 the size of (4:4:4) files, this subformat will sacrifice quality.
Option Two (4:2:2)	Option Two provides additional compression by representing two pixels in the original file with a one pixel approximation. This too sacrifices quality while the file is approximately 1/2 the size of a (4:4:4) file.

JPEG Quality Factor

You use a slide control to select a quality factor. The minimum value on the slide control is 2, which represents the highest quality file. The maximum value is 255, which provides the highest compression, but at the same time, the lowest quality. Values in between will provide a certain degree of trade off between quality and compressed file size.

LEAD Quality Factor

When exporting in LEAD format, you can enable the Use Lead Quality checkbox and select a preset quality factor from a listbox. These presets can be used in place of numeric quality factors when exporting the LEAD bitmap format. The presets provide the best compromises between image quality and compressed file size. Instead of being numerical settings, the presets are expressed in English. For example: "Quality is much more important than size."

There is no way of knowing which preset LEAD Quality Factor is the best for saving a specific image. Experiment with each option until you find one that suits your needs. The presets explain themselves by their titles, reflecting the compromises they will make between file size and file quality.

Paintbrush (*.PCX)

PCX is one of the original file formats, created by Z-Soft for PC Paintbrush back when Noah was working on the Ark. It is unquestionably one of the most popular image-file formats around, mainly because PC Paintbrush is the oldest painting program for the IBM PC. PHOTO-PAINT supports PCX images up to 24-bit color. The only concern with using PCX images involves importing them into older applications. Because the PCX format has been around so long, there are many versions of PCX import filters around. It is possible, even likely, to find an older application that imports PCX files but cannot read the file exported by PHOTO-PAINT.

TARGA (*.TGA, *.TVA)

This format was originally created for TARGA display boards. If you haven't seen this image format before, it is probably because it is used by a small segment of the professional market that works with high-end color and video. In PHOTO-PAINT, this file format supports up to 24-bit color. Targa does not support 32-bit color (CMYK). Although the Targa format supports 32-bit images, it is 24-bit color with an 8-bit alpha channel, which is not supported by PHOTO-PAINT. Many people believe that the Targa format is technically superior to any other on the marketplace. Others feel it is only good for multimedia support. Because it is a narrow niche format that is not widely used, I can't see any reason to use Targa format when TIFF works as well.

TIFF (Tagged Image File Format, *.TIF)

TIFF is probably the most popular full-color bitmapped format around, supported by every PC and MAC paint program I have ever seen. TIFF is clearly the image format of choice. It is used as a default setting for every scanning program on the marketplace today.

You may have heard that there are many different versions of TIFF, which can conceivably cause some compatibility problems when moving images between programs. To date, the only problems we have experienced with TIFF involved saving images as 24-bit color TIFF files and trying to read them on a application that doesn't offer 24-bit color support.

PHOTO-PAINT supports all color-depth settings in TIFF format, including 32-bit color (CMYK). However, don't save your images in 32-bit color, unless it is specifically requested. Because 32-bit color (CMYK) is very new, you may end up with a TIFF file that many older applications cannot read. Remember that 32-bit (CMYK) TIFF contains the same color information as the 24-bit color TIFF.

Scitex CT Bitmap (*SCT, *.CT)

High-end commercial printers use Scitex computers to generate color separations of images and other documents. PHOTO-PAINT can open images digitized with Scitex scanners and save the edited images to the Scitex CT (Continuous Tone) format. Because there are several restrictions regarding the transfer of images from the PC to a Scitex drive, you will probably want to consult with the person using the Scitex printer before saving to the CT format. It is possible that a TIFF or JPEG format is preferred. Scitex is only available when the image is in 32-bit color (CMYK).

Summary

- Bitmaps are composed of pixels (picture elements).
- Resizing bitmap images causes some deterioration of the image.
- To avoid Moiré patterns on the output, set image resolution so that it divides evenly into the output device's resolution.
- Display resolution is controlled by the Zoom command, regardless of the image resolution.
- The amount of information that is stored with each pixel is referred to as its color depth.
- A color depth of 24 bits and a color depth of 32 bits (CMYK) contain identical color information.
- The term 32-bit color, on a Mac, refers to a 24-bit color model with an 8-bit alpha channel.
- RGB is the color model used by monitors (transmitted light); CMYK is the model used by printers (reflected light).
- Additive theory says that when red, green, and blue are added together, the result is white. The absence of color is black.
- Subtractive theory says that when cyan, magenta, and yellow are added together, the result is black. The absence of color is white.
- Subtractive theory doesn't work precisely in the printing world, so K (black) must be added to CMY to make CMYK models or four-color press.
- Additive theory applies to transmitted light; subtractive theory applies to reflected light.
- Image-file formats determine the type of color information that can be stored.
- CPT is the native format of PHOTO-PAINT and can be used to save mask and object/layer information in addition to the image.
- Every time an image is saved with lousy compression (JPEG or LEAD), the image experiences some degree of deterioration.

22

Third-Party Filters

Given the power of filters, support for the
Adobe Photoshop plug-in standard is a substantial new feature to Corel PHOTO-PAINT.
Plug-in filter sets can add substantial power to
PHOTO-PAINT's already strong feature set.
While the real giants in this arena are Aldus
Gallery Effects and Kai's Power Tools, there
are other players that you may not be aware
of. So let's take a look at a small sample of
what third-party filters can do for you and
what is available.

Installation of Third-Party Filters

Once you've installed the third-party filter set using its installation procedures, loading the filters in Corel PHOTO-PAINT is a breeze. Simply select Preferences (Ctrl+J) from the Special menu and click on the Advanced tab. Click on the Insert button in the Plug-In Directories box and locate the directory where the third-party filter set has been installed. To remove filters from PHOTO-PAINT, select the directory where the filters are located and hit the Delete button. Once you exit the Preferences dialog box by clicking on the OK button, PHOTO-PAINT automatically loads the filters. It takes a moment for PHOTO-PAINT to find the plug-in filters and rebuild the Effects menu. You will have access to your filters without having to exit PHOTO-PAINT and come back in.

Filter files for third-party plug-ins are easily identified by an .8BF file extension. The one exception to this rule are the Aldus Gallery Effects. They have a unique .EFF extension. This is because they were originally designed to work only with Aldus PhotoStyler. By default, PHOTO-PAINT initially looks for its own filters in the \COREL50\PLUGINS subdirectory. All of the filter files provided with PHOTO-PAINT are contained in dynamic link libraries that have a .DLL extension. The reason they do not have a *.8BF extension is two-fold. First, DLLs provide a faster way for PAINT to access the filters. Second, this way you can only use the filters with Corel PHOTO-PAINT. The second point is important in case you have the Plus version of PHOTO-PAINT and were wondering how to load the Xaos tool or one of the other Corel filters into another photo-editing program, such as Photoshop or Picture Publisher. It won't work.

When you install the filters, you may wonder if it is necessary to have them in the subdirectory that was created by their installation program or if it wouldn't be possible to just copy the files into the \COREL50\PLUGINS subdirectory. You can copy all of the filter files in the PLUGINS directory. Make sure that you copy all of the files (including help files) into the PLUGINS directory, and if you have a lot of filters, the initial startup of the filters will occur slightly faster. The exception to moving the filter files is Aldus Gallery Effects. I recommend keeping them in their own unique directory structure.

Corel *TIP!*

> You may find that some of the newer releases of filters give you a choice of installing the filters for Corel PHOTO-PAINT. If the choice is offered, take it. It means the filters will be installed in the \COREL50\PLUGINS subdirectory.

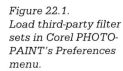

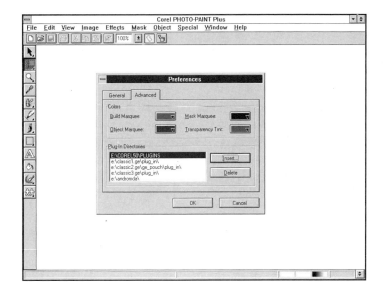

Figure 22.1.
Load third-party filter
sets in Corel PHOTO-
PAINT's Preferences
menu.

A Note on Loading Aldus Gallery Effects

The Aldus Gallery Effects' filter sets are a little unusual. You must locate the plug-in directories for each set, which are buried within several directories. The only explanation I can offer for the unique directory structure with unusual names is that the tiny company which wrote the filters (Aldus—now Adobe—only distributes them) is up in Toronto, Canada. Aldus (now Adobe) has a tradition of referencing central Aldus directories for all of their common programs. See Figure 22.1 for a reference on where the plug-in directories may be located for the Aldus Gallery Effects filters.

Corel *TIP!*

> While it is mostly a matter of personal preference, it can be useful to only load those filters that you need during your PHOTO-PAINT session. Kai's Power Tools, in particular, loads a DLL that takes up system resources when you load it into Corel PHOTO-PAINT. If you won't be using Kai's Power Tools during any particular PHOTO-PAINT session, that's a waste of valuable resources. Since Corel PHOTO-PAINT can load and unload filter sets on-the-fly, you can load and unload filter sets as you need them. When you have a lot of filter sets loaded, it also takes a little longer to load each set initially. Also, remember, that neither Corel PHOTO-PAINT's proprietary filters nor third-party filters load automatically when you open Corel PHOTO-PAINT. Filters are loaded either when you first click on the Effects menu, or when you add filters from the Preferences menu.

A Note on Downloading Free Filters

If you are an avid user of our nation's increasingly large online services, you will find a lot plug-in filters available as freeware or shareware. Before you begin racking up charges downloading all of these wonderful filters, carefully read the filter description. Most of the filters I have found in online services are for the Mac. However, some of the descriptions do not specify that they are only for the Mac. The filter designers are not being deceptive. In most cases they don't know or can't imagine that anyone from the Windows world uses plug-in filters. There are several tell-tale signs that the filter is for a Mac. First, there won't be any mention of Windows in the description. I have found if a filter is available for Windows, the filter designers tend to shout it from the rooftops. Second, look at the file extension of the file to be downloaded. If it has an .SEA extension or any other non-standard IBM compression extension like .ZIP, .ARC, etc., then it is for a Mac.

Kai's Power Tools 2.0

It is not hard to find artwork created with Kai's Power Tools 2.0 (KPT). The KPT filters are as trendy as they are wild. One particular filter, Page Curl, which is new to version 2.0, is already showing up almost everywhere you look. The KPT filter set ranges from very straightforward filters that do not even use dialog boxes to filters that are a universe unto themselves and have dialog boxes that look like they were made for an interactive sci-fi game.

KPT comes with four interfaces (also called "extensions"): Fractal Explorer, Gradient Designer, Gradients On Paths, and Texture Explorer. (The Fractal Explorer interface is shown in Figure 22.2.) The extensions come with hundreds of delightfully named presets, and you can create as many more as you like with Gradient Designer. Furthermore, under the Options button, there are apply modes that act very similarly to Corel PHOTO-PAINT's Merge modes. Each extension has nearly unlimited possibilities as well as the capability to provide very attractive results easily. Although KPT comes with extensive and entertaining help files, some of Kai's explanations are likely to elicit a resounding "Huh?" from most readers. Nevertheless, the help files for Kai's Power Tools are among the most extensive and thorough in the industry.

The difficulty with these filters lies in their sheer magnitude. It is not uncommon to spend hours roaming these universes. Furthermore, these filters often do not easily lend themselves to mainstream business applications (not to mention deadlines). For computer artists, however, not having KPT is almost like a traditional artist not having a paintbrush.

*Figure 22.2.
KPT's Fractal Explorer
dialog box is an
interface into a whole
universe of possi-
bilities.*

Corel *TIP!*

Kai's Power Tools doesn't really like 256-color displays. It will work, but the Explorers will look odd. To get the full effect, you will need to use Full or True Color mode.

*Figure 22.3.
Kai's Power Tools'
extensions are not
crazy about 256-color
display modes.*

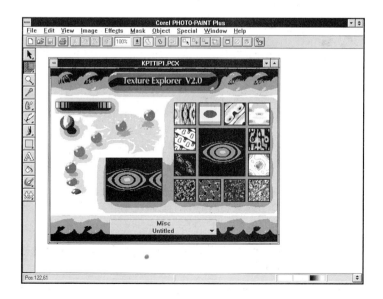

Fractal Explorer

Fractal Explorer is a very powerful and versatile phrasal generator. The fractals can be based on six different sets: Julia, Mandelbrot, M-J Hybrid I, M-J Hybrid II, Julia II, and Julia III. Fractal Explorer uses the blends from the Gradient Designer and "wraps" them around the chosen set. You can access the Gradient Designer extension from Fractal Explorer by hitting Ctrl+G. If you are experienced with creating fractals, you can create them numerically via the Numerical Input option available in the Options menu. Kai doesn't recommend this for inexperienced "fractologists." The fractals generated by Fractal Explorer can take very long to render in high- or even medium-resolution files.

Corel*NOTE!*

If you have Corel PHOTO-PAINT 5 Plus, Fractal Explorer will load in the Special menu alongside the KPT Julia Set Explorer filter that comes with Corel PHOTO-PAINT 5 Plus. They will both have the Julia Set Explorer 2.0 name, but the second one will have all of the phrasal sets from KPT, while the Julia Set Explorer from Corel PHOTO-PAINT 5 Plus only has the Julia set.

Figure 22.4.
This is an example of the kind of images Fractal Explorer can render. The possible variations are staggering. Apply and Opacity settings enable you to merge the phrasal with the original image.

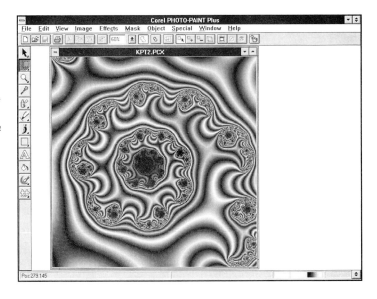

Corel *TIP!*

It can be a little difficult to adjust the Map setting in Fractal Explorer. When you position the mouse cursor over the Map control box, the mouse cursor changes to indicate that clicking on the box brings up the Fractal Sets menu. While you can select the red circle with the normal cursor (if you try hard enough), holding down the Ctrl key will change the mouse cursor to a hand that will make repositioning the circle much easier.

Corel *TIP!*

When using presets, or if you are creating your own phrasal, you may have the gradient render across the top of the image. This strip is for capturing the gradient for inclusion into the Gradient Designer. If you don't want this strip, there is a Draw Gradient Across Option setting in the Options menu that you will need to uncheck. For some reason, many of the presets in Fractal Explorer have the Draw Gradient Across Top option on.

Figure 22.5.
Note the strip at the top of the phrasal. This is rendered along with the phrasal when the Draw Gradient Across Top option is checked in the Options menu.

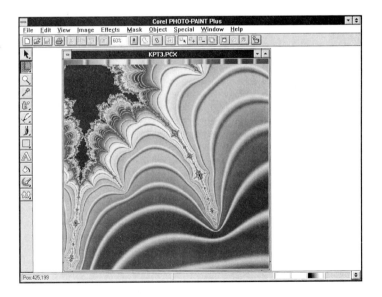

Gradient Designer

Fractal Explorer, Gradients On Paths, and Texture Explorer each use gradients from Gradient Designer as the basis for their color schemes. The help files for Gradient Designer reveal a very large number of useful keyboard shortcuts that can be used in the Gradient Designer extension. Most of the controls in the Gradient Designer extension are fairly straightforward, except for the Gradient Bar.

Depressing and holding the left mouse button on the gradient bar opens up the Pop-Up Color Picker and changes the cursor to an eyedropper tool. The eyedropper tool can pick any color on the screen. The eyedropper selects the color of the area you are over when you release the mouse button. If you don't want to choose any color, click anywhere on the bar separating the Gradient Bar and the Color Bar except on the color-wheel icon or the Spectra button. The bracket above the Gradient Bar is moveable. It allows you to isolate specific areas of a gradient that you want to use.

Figure 22.6.
The Gradient Designer extension is the color basis for the other four extensions.

Gradients On Paths

Gradients On Paths is useful for creating slick borders, lines, and text effects. It's a little tricky to use Gradients On Paths with Corel PHOTO-PAINT 5, but it works great once you know the trick. Let's try it.

1. Open a 3" × 3" image at 150 dpi. Select the Rectangle Mask tool and outline a square or rectangle mask anywhere on the image. Try to make the mask about 2" × 2". Select Create Transparency Mask from the Mask menu and then choose the From Mask option. The Transparency Mask Creation

dialog box will appear. Enter 50 in the Feather option. The Feather option is the critical factor here. The wider the feather, the broader the Gradient Path. The thinner the feather, the thinner the Gradient Path. If you need to keep the mask, uncheck the Remove Mask option. When you click OK, PHOTO-PAINT will use the mask to create a Transparency mask—a process that takes PHOTO-PAINT a long time to implement.

Figure 22.7.
Adjusting the feathering in the Create Transparency Mask dialog box is the key to using the Gradients On Paths extension with Corel PHOTO-PAINT.

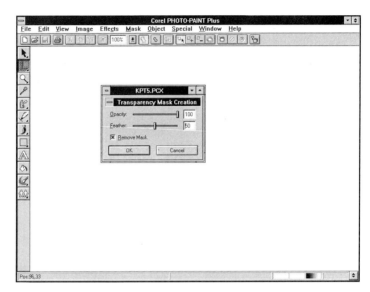

2. Open the Gradients On Paths extension and apply. You will have to remove the Transparency mask if you do not need it any more.

Texture Explorer

Texture Explorer does not work with the original shipped version of Corel PHOTO-PAINT 5. However, Revision B and Corel PHOTO-PAINT 5 Plus do support Texture Explorer. Textures are often very valuable as design elements, and Texture Explorer provides a nearly endless supply of textures that are not from any source image, such as scans of marbles or granites. Clicking on the Mutation Tree (the series of red balls over the tree) mutates the texture. The further up the tree, the more the mutation. Clicking on the Color Mutation Ball (the floating multicolored marble in the upper-left side) mutates the colors of the texture. The band above the Color Mutation Ball has Blend presets. The square texture block surrounded by twelve smaller texture blocks shows the current texture. Clicking on any of the twelve surrounding blocks replaces the texture residing in that block with the one in the center. The Texture presets contain many useful and wild textures.

Texture Explorer uses gradients from the Gradient Designer to build its textures. Press Ctrl+G to open Gradient Designer from within Texture Explorer. Once you've designed the gradient you want in Gradient Designer, select OK to go back to Texture Explorer. You can prevent any texture in the twelve surrounding blocks from changing by clicking on it with the left mouse button while the Alt key is depressed. You can undo a round of Texture Explorer mutations by clicking Crtl+Z.

You can vary the tile size of a texture. The Tile menu is opened by clicking and holding the left mouse button on the center texture. Clicking once on the center texture expands it to cover all of the blocks for better viewing. Simply click on it again to restore it. Texture Explorer also provides the option to add Transparency and to use any of the textures as the basis for a 3D Stereo Noise effect.

Figure 22.8.
Before...

Pressing Crtl+E while in Texture Explorer brings up the Equalizer. The Equalizer gives you control over the coarseness, detail, angles, and diffusion. It has a safe mode that keeps the tiles seamless. When safe mode is off, tiles will not be protected from losing their seamlessness.

Figure 22.9.
...and after, with a
texture from Texture
Explorer added and
with Tie Me Down
selected in the Apply
mode.

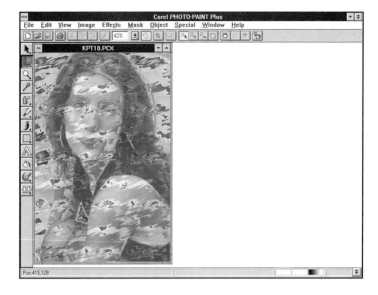

Figure 22.10.
Depressing Crtl+E
opens The Equalizer
control dialog box.

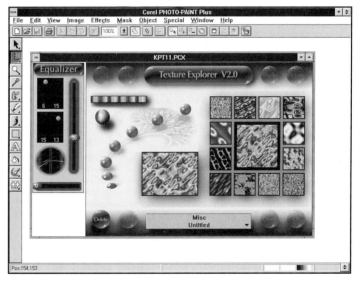

KPT Filters

Along with Kai's Power Tools Extensions, there are 28 additional filters (counting the Seamless Welder). These filters are far more straightforward than the
extensions. Many of the filters can be adjusted by using the keyboard for
various effects. If you apply keyboard adjustments, those settings become the
default until your PHOTO-PAINT session.

3D Stereo Noise

3D Stereo Noise can be used to create those delightful (i.e., annoying) stereo-graphs that you've probably seen in your local mall or doctor's office. The process is simple enough: Take an image (or text in this example) and apply it on a gray background. KPT suggests minimizing contrasts for best effects. Apply a slight amount of blurring with the Gaussian Blur or Soften filters. Then apply the 3D Stereo Noise filter. You can adjust the depth using the keypad. Holding down the 1 key keeps the depth shallow, while holding down the 9 key makes the depth deep. The image included here uses a depth of 3.

Figure 22.11.
Prepare the image by
placing it on a gray
background and
blurring it slightly.

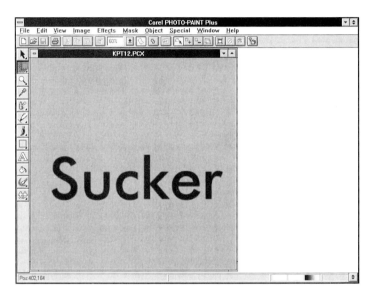

Figure 22.12.
Apply the 3D Stereo
Noise filter.

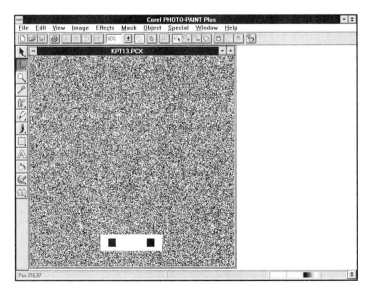

Diffuse More

Diffuse More is like a Diffuse filter on steroids. You can control the intensity of the effect by using the keyboard, with 1 being the least intense and 0 (for 10) being the most.

Figure 22.13.
An example of the
Diffuse More filter with
an intensity of 3.

Fade Contrast

Fade Contrast reduces the contrast to a selected or entire area. This filter can be used to reduce the contrast of a particular area to make text more visible or a graphic element more clear. You can control the intensity of the effect by using the keyboard, with 1 being the least intense and 0 (for 10) being the most.

Find Edges And Invert

The Find Edges And Invert filter does just that. The results can make the image appear to have been sketched in pencil. You can control the intensity of the effect by using the keyboard, with 1 being the least intense and 0 (for 10) being the most.

Find Edges Charcoal

Find Edges Charcoal is a variation of Find Edges And Invert, and depending on the image, the results can be similar. You can control the intensity of the effect by using the keyboard, with 1 being the least intense and 0 (for 10) being the most.

Figure 22.14.
Fade Contrast applied
to a rectangular
masked area with a
setting of 3.

Figure 22.15.
An example of the Find
Edges And Invert filter
with an intensity of 3.

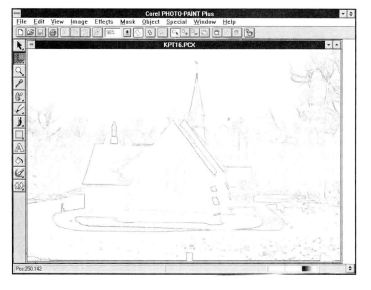

Figure 22.16.
An example of the Find
Edges Charcoal filter
with an intensity of 10
(by holding down the 0
key).

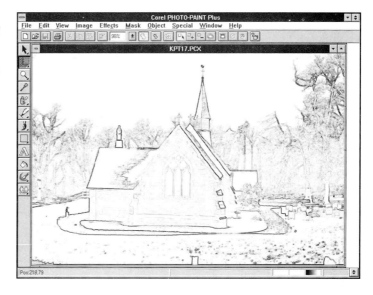

Find Edges Soft

Find Edges Soft is yet another variation of Find Edges And Invert. The effect of
Find Edges Soft is less harsh than that of Find Edges And Invert and Find
Edges Charcoal. The results of this filter appear to be the inverse of the Find
Edges And Invert and Find Edges Charcoal. You can control the intensity of the
effect by using the keyboard, with 1 being the least intense and 0 (for 10) being
the most.

Figure 22.17.
An example of the Find
Edges Soft filter with a
setting of 10.

Glass Lens Bright, Normal, and Soft

Glass Lens Bright, Normal, and Soft, add a spherical 3D ball over the entire image or the selected portion of the image. You can control the position of the light source by using the keyboard. There are 10 positions, from 1 through 0. When the Caps Lock key is depressed, the rest of the image or selection that is not spherized is turned to black, making it easy to select just the spherical area. The Scroll Lock key adds eclipse effects, and the Scroll Lock key with the 5 key simulates a total eclipse.

Figure 22.18.
An example of the
Glass Lens Bright filter
with a position of 7.

Grime Layer

Grime Layer adds a layer of fog or transparent noise to an image. The keyboard can be used to vary the effect of Grime Layer with controls from 1 (faint layer of fog) to 0 (thick black fog). The minus (-) and equal-sign (=) keys add a "snow layer" as well.

Hue Protected Noise Max, Med, and Min

Hue Protected Noise is invaluable for creating mezzotint effects and smoothing out gradients. Hue Protected Noise is different from basic or normal Noise in that it does not add hues when applying the noise effect. Using the keyboard varies the effect of each filter from 1 (60 percent noise) to 0 (100 percent noise). The default for each filter is 80 percent.

Figure 22.19.
An example of the
Grime Layer with a
setting of 3.

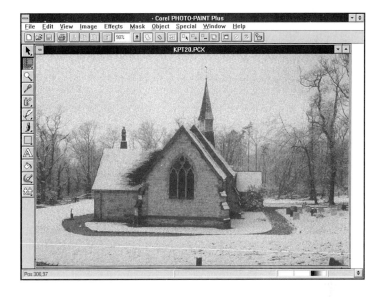

Figure 22.20.
Hue Protected Noise
Med with the default
settings.

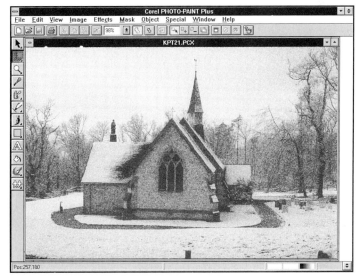

Page Curl

Page Curl adds the effect of a page being turned up at the chosen corner of the image. Ever since this filter was added to Kai's Power Tools in version 2.0, Page Curl has been showing up just about everywhere you look. Pressing the 7 key applies the curl to the upper left, 9 to the upper right, 1 to the lower left, and 3 to the lower right. Holding down the space bar makes the page curl completely opaque. When the Caps Lock key is depressed, the curl orientation is horizontal and when not pressed it is vertical.

Figure 22.21.
Page Curl effect with
the space bar de-
pressed.

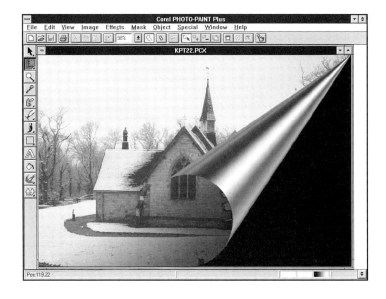

PixelBreeze

PixelBreeze applies a medium diffusion (30 pixels) to the image or selection.
PixelBreeze adds light and fade to the selection with repeated applies. The
amount of diffusion can be controlled with the keyboard, with 1 being the
lowest amount of diffusion and 0 being the highest.

Figure 22.22.
PixelBreeze effect with
default settings.

PixelStorm

PixelStorm applies a strong diffusion (200 pixels) to the image or selection. The amount of diffusion can be controlled with the keyboard, with 1 being the lowest amount of diffusion and 0 being the highest.

Figure 22.23.
PixelStorm effect with
default settings.

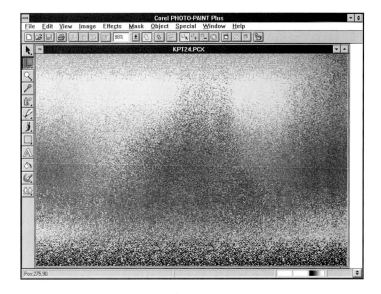

PixelWind

PixelWind applies a medium-strong diffusion (80 pixels) to the image or selection with a Darken Apply mode. The results of PixelWind are substantially different from PixelBreeze and PixelStorm in that PixelWind can actually enhance the image instead of destroying it. The amount of diffusion can be controlled with the keyboard, with 1 being the lowest amount of diffusion and 0 being the highest. A setting of 1 only minimizes the diffusion but enhances the image noticeably.

Scatter Horizontally

Scatter Horizontally diffuses the image on the horizontal axis only. The effect is more visible when applied numerous times. Using the keyboard varies the effect, with 1 being faint and 0 being extreme.

Figure 22.24.
PixelWind effect with
default settings.

Figure 22.25.
Scatter Horizontally
with a setting of 9.

Sharpen Intensity

Sharpen Intensity gives better contrast and bright color images to the image or selection. For quick image contrast, it is a more intuitive filter than Brightness and Contrast, and it is very useful with Photo CD images. The degree of intensity can be varied with the keyboard, with 1 applying faint contrast and 0 applying complete saturation. Repeatedly applying the Sharpen Intensity filter posterizes the image or selection.

Figure 22.26.
Sharpen Intensity
effect with default
settings.

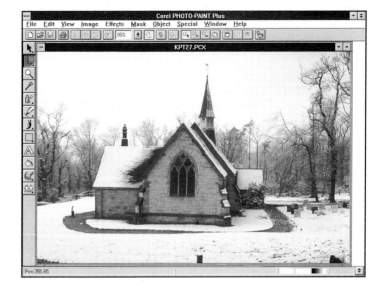

Smudge Left-Darken, Smudge Left-Lighten, Smudge Right-Darken, Smudge Right-Lighten

These Smudge filters blur an image to the right or left while lightening or darkening the image. These filters can create a motion blur effect with repeated applications to a selected area. There are no keyboard controls for these filters.

Figure 22.27.
Smudge Left-Darken
applied three times.

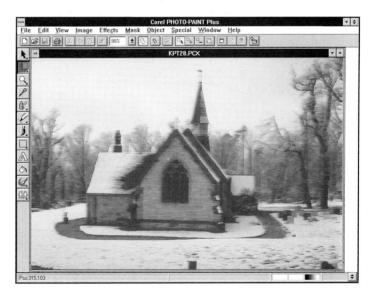

691

Special Blue Noise, Special Green Noise, Special Red Noise

The Special Noise filters add noise with the hues of their respective names. There are no keyboard controls for these filters. The appearance is similar to that produced by a normal noise filter except that the particular color is added. Because the images in this portion of the book are grayscale, there is little point it doing a demo image.

Vortex Tiling

Vortex Tiling seamlessly mirrors the image and then spirals the image around a "vortex," distorting the image heavily in the process. The vortex size can be adjusted with the keyboard, with 1 being a small circle and 0 being a large circle. The default is 5. If you want to go nuts, try the Vortex Tiling filter with multiple applies using different vortex settings.

Figure 22.28.
Vortex Tiling with the
default settings.

Scamless Welder

Seamless Welder takes a square selection and turns it into a seamless tile. In order for Seamless Welder to work, you must choose a square mask with either the Mask or Object tool. You cannot select the entire image, because Seamless Welder needs information from the pixels adjacent to the masked area in order to create the tile. Let's try it.

1. Open any image. (In this example, a portion of the church from the other samples was used.) Select a square area with the Object or Mask Rectangle selection tool by holding down on the Ctrl key while dragging. Make the selection about 1" × 1".

2. Apply Seamless Welder. If the selection is a normal mask, cut the selection, close the image without saving, and select Paste from the Edit menu using the As New Document option. If the selection is an object, drag the image to the PHOTO-PAINT desktop and close the original image. Save the tile in any bitmap format.

3. Open a new file that is three- or four-inches square. Open the Fill roll-up and load the tile as a bitmap (the center button with the checkerboard icon). Click on the blank image with the Fill tool and the tile will fill the image. Remember, the bitmap fill tiles an image when it is larger than the image loaded as a bitmap in the Fill roll-up.

Figure 22.29.
An image created
with Seamless Welder
using a normal mask
selection.

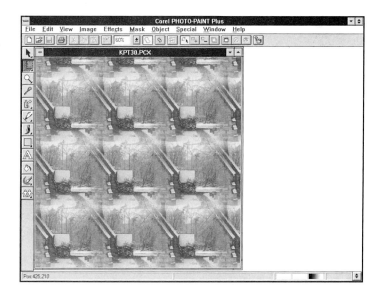

Figure 22.30.
An image created with
Seamless Welder using
an object with the
background layer
turned off.

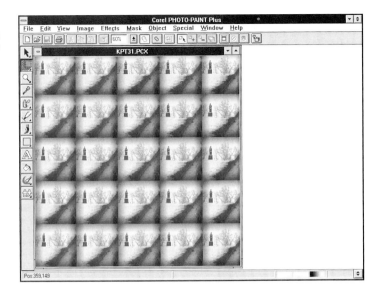

Aldus Gallery Effects

When I first planned this book, it was my intention to talk a little about these filters, show a few screen shots, and move on. However, the more I worked with the Aldus filters, the more I realized two things. One, most of the pictures that you see in sample files in the Aldus manual are not accomplished without some prior application of other filters or some unique (other-than-default) settings. Second, I learned some neat things that could be done with these filters. So, instead of a little section on these filters, we now have a big one.

There are three Aldus Gallery Effects volumes. Each volume has 16 main filters and a sampler for the other volumes. Volume 3 also includes a very valuable Color Balance filter. Aldus' Color Balance filter is significantly more powerful and versatile than Corel PHOTO-PAINT's Hue and Saturation filter for altering color. The real strength of the Aldus Gallery Effects filters is that they accomplish a large number of the standard photo effects that the graphic-design industry tends to look for and need. The Aldus Gallery Effects filters are not as much a world unto themselves as Kai's Power Tools. They arc defined and attractive filters that achieve relatively predictable results quickly and efficiently. When you do not have time to explore the outer reaches of the universe and you need a quick and slick image, Aldus' Gallery Effects are often the best choice.

Corel *NOTE!*

Early copies of Aldus Gallery Effects: Classic Art (Volume 1) are not compatible with Corel PHOTO-PAINT. The first volume was released during the time when Aldus PhotoStyler was the big bitmap-image processing program for the PC. When Photoshop was released for Windows, Aldus released the other volumes and conformed them to the Adobe plug-in standard. Corel PHOTO-PAINT only supports the Adobe plug-in standard, so early copies of Aldus Gallery Effects: Classic Art will not run in Corel PHOTO-PAINT. Aldus has recently re-released Volume One in the Adobe plug-in standard format.

You will find three sample filters from Aldus Gallery Effects on the companion CD of this book. Each is a very good representation of the kinds of filters in the Aldus Gallery Effects volumes. Let's take a quick look at each one.

Sample Filters Included on the Companion Disc

Watercolor

The Watercolor effect paints the image in watercolor style using a medium brush loaded with water and color. The color appears to have dried on smooth paper, leaving dark concentrations of pigment around the edges of the dabs.

To load the filters, simply drag-and-drop them into the \COREL50\PLUGINS directory. You can also load them into any directory that you have inserted in Preferences, if you wish. Watercolor is from the first Gallery Effects volume, Aldus Gallery Effects: Classic Art. Compared to most of the Gallery Effects filters, Watercolor is a little slow.

When you select Watercolor, the Effect Settings dialog box is opened. This dialog box is more or less the same one used for all of the other Gallery Effects, with the actual settings being a little different for each one. You can move the preview box around, but you cannot increase the preview area. The larger the image, the smaller the area you can preview.

One very nice thing about all of the Aldus Gallery Effects filters is that you can save settings. If you spend a lot of time coming up with just the right settings to produce a desired effect, and you need to apply it to 50 other images over the course of the next year, that's no problem. Another handy thing you will notice in the Effects Settings dialog box for the Aldus Gallery Effects filters is a Help button that provides thorough help files for the filters. While the Aldus Gallery Effects filters are fairly straightforward, it helps to read these help files to understand what the filter is supposed to do and what the settings do, so that you can more readily predict results. The images included here show how Watercolor makes an oil painting from Corel's Professional Photo CD-ROM Oil Paintings collection look like it was done in watercolors instead of with the default settings.

Figure 22.31.
Before Watercolor.

Figure 22.32.
After Watercolor.

Corel *TIP!*

Try applying the Emboss effect after applying the Watercolor effect.

Note Paper

Note Paper is from the Aldus Gallery Effects: Classic Art Volume 2. Note Paper does a little embossing and adds grain at the same time. Note Paper's effects show up best in an image that has plenty of areas which contrast between dark and light. This is because Note Paper posterizes dark areas to gray and light areas to white, and then sets up the gray area as a relief from the light area. If your image mostly has light tones, Note Paper will just wash it out, adding a little grain in the process. The images here show Note Paper's effect on an image from Corel's Professional Photo CD Industry & Transportation collection with the default settings.

Figure 22.33.
Before Note Paper.

Figure 22.34.
After Note Paper.

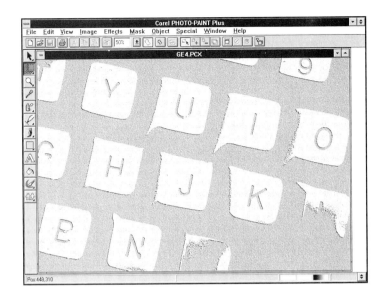

Plastic Wrap

Plastic Wrap is from the Aldus Gallery Effects: Classic Art 3 volume. Plastic Wrap is a very slick filter that makes an image appear to be coated with shiny plastic. The effect is quite invigorating and is especially useful for text effects. The images here show Plastic Wrap's effect on a letter G that has been placed on top of the Flames texture fill with the default settings.

Figure 22.35.
Before Plastic Wrap.

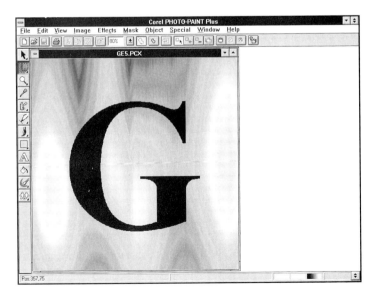

Figure 22.36.
After Plastic Wrap.

While the Aldus Gallery Effects filters were designed to emulate many of the traditional photographic effects accomplished in the darkroom, you don't have to just use Aldus Gallery Effects with photographs. For instance, the texture in each corner of the image that follows was created by adding noise and then applying a different Gallery Effects filter to each corner. Even though the Aldus Gallery Effects filters provide predictable results, that doesn't mean you can't go wild with them. You can really go nuts if you combine Aldus Gallery Effects filters.

Figure 22.37.
The Aldus Gallery
Effects can also be
useful for creating
interesting textures.

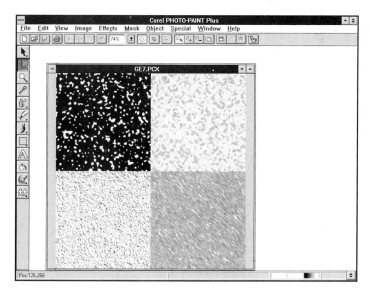

Gallery Effects 1

With all of the hoopla surrounding Kai's Power Tools, people tend to overlook the Aldus Gallery Effects. Yet if I were only allowed to use one set of filters, I would choose Aldus Gallery Effects 1. It offers the greatest range of filter effects. While Effects 2 and Effects 3 each have great things to offer, Effects 1 is still my personal favorite. Scott Hamlin, who wrote part of this chapter, would probably disagree, but I think they are great. Obviously the fine folks at Micrographx who produce Picture Publisher agree. For a long time I thought they had purchased the rights to the filters from Aldus. My reasoning was that their filters have the same names, do the same things, and are even in the same order as those in Gallery Effects 1. Silly me. When asked about it, my man from Aldus mumbled something about reverse-engineering, which my friends at Micrographix denied. (And you thought this sort of thing only happened in politics.)

While Gallery Effects are great, they do carry some minor penalties. Of all of the filters tested by ourselves and the Corel folks, these filters took the longest to load and to operate. If you have a lot of filters and the Effects menu seems to take forever to load the first time you open it, up may want to consider temporarily deselecting the reference to these filters in the Advanced Preferences section.

While we can't tell you how to use all of these filters (for that would be an entire book in itself), I thought it would be helpful to have a brief description of what is available in each volume, beginning with Gallery Effects 1. The filters are referenced in alphabetical order, not by preference or usability.

Chalk & Charcoal

The Chalk & Charcoal effect draws the image onto a solid mid-gray background with coarse diagonal strokes. When you use this effect with Corel PHOTO-PAINT, the charcoal is drawn in the Paint (foreground) color and the chalk in the Paper (background) color. This is a neat effect when you have a photo of someone or something that you want to place as a background. As with many of the filters that change perfectly good images into "natural media" images, make sure your subject is not too subtle. You will notice that after the tiger has had the Chalk & Charcoal filter applied, it still looks like a tiger. Images are like jokes—if you have to explain them, they lose their effect.

Corel *TIP!*

You should adjust the brightness and contrast and color balance of an image prior to applying an effect in order to improve its quality and obtain the best result with the effect.

Figure 22.38a.
This is the original tiger from the Photo CD.

Figure 22.38b.
This is the tiger after the application of the Chalk & Charcoal filter (default settings).

*Figure 22.38c.
This is the same tiger
image treated with the
same filter. The only
difference is a contrast
setting of 50 was
applied to the image
before the application
of the filter.*

Charcoal

The Charcoal effect draws the image onto a surface that resembles rough, textured paper. Major edges are boldly drawn while midtones are sketched using a diagonal stroke. When you use this effect with Corel PHOTO-PAINT, the charcoal is drawn in the Paint (foreground) color and the chalk in the Paper (background) color.

*Figure 22.38d.
Now our tiger is done in
charcoal without the
chalk. Note that
contrast wasn't added
before the filter was
applied, in order to
preserve the subtle
shadings of the image.*

Chrome

The Chrome effect treats the original image as if it were a highly polished, smooth chrome surface.

Image features are represented as hills and valleys in the reflecting surface. I was never able to get much out of this filter, as shown in Figure 22.38e. I tried various combinations of shapes and characters, but so much of the image detail was lost that I recommend this only for abstract backgrounds. If you use this and come up with something awesome, let us know.

Figure 22.38e.
The tiger's face before and after the Chrome filter was applied to it. Afterwards, all of the detail is lost in a sea of reflections. Remember our rule: Don't concentrate on the name of the effect (Chrome), pay attention to what it actually does. Look at the right half of the figure again. Looks like water?

Corel *TIP!*

After applying the Chrome effect to an image, Aldus suggests adding the Brightness and Contrast effect to enhance the reflective nature of the effect. Try increasing both the brightness and contrast.

Craquelure

The Craquelure effect seems to paint the image onto a high-relief plaster surface, producing a fine network of cracks that follow the contours of the image. I love this effect, although the name is a little bit of a mystery.

Figure 22.38f.
Since the Craquelure filter makes the image look like it has been painted on a wall, I thought it would be best if the image itself looked like it was the result of someone painting it. So I cropped the face of the tiger and, using the Smear tool, dragged the white into the image before I applied the Craquelure filter.

Dark Strokes

The Dark Strokes effect paints the image with diagonal black-and-white brush strokes. The lighter areas of the image are pushed towards white and painted with longer strokes that are visible outside of the areas that are not solid white. The darker areas of the image are pushed towards black and are painted with short, tight strokes.

Figure 22.38g.
The Dark Strokes filter.

Corel *TIP!*

After applying the Dark Strokes effect, try sharpening the image using the PHOTO-PAINT Edge Enhance filter to give it a graphic pen appearance.

Dry Brush

This is another filter that makes it appear that you have produced the image using natural media. The Dry Brush effect paints the edges of the image using a dry-brush technique and simplifies the image into areas of common color.

Figure 22.38h.
An image made after using the Smear tool on the edges before applying the Dry Brush filter. The Smear tool in combination with the Dry Brush filter further enhances the painted look.

Corel *TIP!*

After applying the Dry Brush effect, try using the Emboss effect or try sharpening the image with either the Edge Enhance or Sharpen filter in PHOTO-PAINT.

Emboss

If you have been using PHOTO-PAINT for a while, you may think that you already have an Emboss filter and therefore don't need another one. In fact, if you have the Plus version of PAINT, you have *two* Emboss filters. However, this Emboss filter is different from any filter I have every worked with. Instead of changing all of the colors to a solid color with some shading, this filter retains

705

the original colors of the images. It makes the image appear as if it has been raised up from its surface and lit from a specified direction, giving it a three-dimensional appearance.

Figure 22.38i.
A simple application of the Emboss filter to the image on the right.

Corel *TIP!*

For general improvement of the texture of an image, try applying the Emboss effect after applying any other effect.

Figure 22.38j.
Application of a slight emboss to the "stones" in the Rock Concert sign and the wood siding behind the text. Both the stones and the wood siding are seamless tiles from the Plus version of PHOTO-PAINT 5.

Film Grain

The Film Grain effect adds a film-grain texture to the image. An even pattern is added to the darks and midtones of the image. A smoother, more saturated pattern is added to the image's lighter areas.

Figure 22.38k.
The effect of the
default setting of the
Film Grain applied to
our friendly tiger.

Fresco

Yet another of these natural-media wonders. This Fresco effect changes the image so that is looks as if it was rendered in a coarse painting style using short, rounded, hastily applied dabs.

Corel *TIP!*

> When using this filter, be aware that large areas of white or very light colors in the image cause the resulting image to be rendered very dark. I don't know why.

Graphic Pen

The Graphic Pen effect uses fine linear ink strokes to capture details in the original image, making it appear as if the image had been drawn on paper laid against a fine-grained wood surface. The density of the strokes increases in darker areas but is not evident in the lighter areas of the image. When you use this effect from programs that support selectable colors, the ink takes on the foreground color and the paper takes on the background color. Otherwise, the ink is black and the paper white.

*Figure 22.38l.
This Fresco-effect
image was done
several times before
we decided that the
default settings were
the best. This filter
tends to make the
image dark.*

Corel *TIP!*

For better results, try posterizing or increasing the contrast of the image with
PHOTO-PAINT 5 before applying the Graphic Pen effect.

*Figure 22.38m.
Both tigers have had
the same Graphic Pen
filters at the same
settings applied to
them. What is the
difference? The tiger on
the left had high values
of Contrast and
Unsharp filters applied
to it.*

Corel *TIP!*

After applying the effect, blur the image with the Gaussian Blur filter in PHOTO-PAINT 5 to smooth the pen lines.

Mosaic

The Mosaic effect draws the image as if it were composed of small chips or tiles laid down on a flat surface. The "tiles" appear to be lit from the side, enhancing their texture. Tile Size and Grout Width are adjustable and are measured in pixels.

Figure 22.38n.
This is a stained glass image from the Corel Photo-CD collection, treated with the Mosaic filter. (A 12th-century image seemed a good choice to illustrate a technique that was popularized in ancient times.) I didn't use the default setting because it made the tiles too small.

Poster Edges

This filter does not posterize. In fact, a practical use of this filter is a little bit of a mystery to me. The Poster Edges filter reduces the number of color shades in the image and adds dark lines along the edges. Large, broad areas of the image have simple shading, while fine, dark detail is distributed throughout the image.

Corel *TIP!*

Before applying the Poster Edges effect, use PHOTO-PAINT 5 to sharpen the image and adjust the brightness and contrast to achieve greater contrast.

Figure 22.38o.
The Poster Edges effect
was applied with
default setting to the
image on the right.

Ripple

This filter should not be confused with the Ripple filter in PHOTO-PAINT. This filter is great for making some of the Texture Fills in PHOTO-PAINT look like glass. The Aldus definition of the Ripple effect is as follows: "The Ripple effect adds randomly spaced ripples to the image's surface, making the image appear as if it were under water that is being rippled by the wind." I guess you could say it does that. But for another use of the filter, look at Figure 22.38p. The glass in the figure was created with Swirl2 in the Texture Fill roll-up, and then the Ripple was applied.

Figure 22.38p.
The effect of the Ripple
filter in combination
with the Corel PHOTO-
PAINT fills makes
great-looking stained
glass.

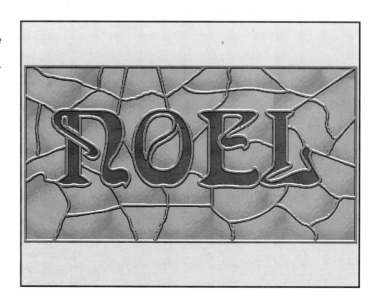

Corel *TIP!*

For images composed of small elements, use the lower settings; for images composed of large elements, use higher settings.

Smudge Stick

The Smudge Stick effect uses short, diagonal strokes to smudge or smear the darker areas of the image. Lighter areas of the image are pushed to a brighter range.

Spatter

The Spatter effect paints the image in a Pointillist style using a spatter airbrush technique.

Figure 22.38q.
The Spatter effect was applied to the image on the left, and the Smudge Stick filter was applied to the image on the right.

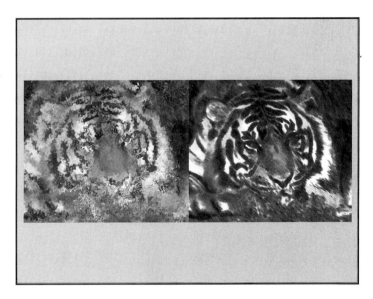

Aldus Gallery Effects 2

Aldus Gallery Effects: Classic Art Volume 2 is a library of painterly effects that can transform scanned photographs and other bitmap images into dramatic artistic works.

Classic Art Volume 2 continues in the artistic lineage of evocative painterly effects established by Classic Art Volume 1. With an emphasis on bold painting and drawing styles, Volume 2 provides a range of effects that can be used alone or in concert with each other.

The 16 effects in Classic Art Volume 2 include Accented Edges, Angled Strokes, Bas Relief, Colored Pencil, Diffuse Glow, Glowing Edges, Grain, Note Paper, Palette Knife, Patchwork, Photocopy, Rough Pastels, Sprayed Strokes, Stamp, Texturizer, and Underpainting. All the effects can be customized for thousands of variations.

Accented Edges

The Accented Edges effect adds edge accents to an image. When the Edge Brightness control is set to a high value, the accents resemble white chalk; when set to a low value, the accents resemble black ink.

Figure 22.39a.
The original to which the Accented Edges was applied in PHOTO-PAINT.

Corel *TIP!*

Try applying this effect before some of the other effects (such as Dry Brush or Watercolor from Volume 1, or the Texturizer effect) to make the final result look even more like natural media, as shown in Figure 22.39c.

Figure 22.39b.
The resulting image.

Figure 22.39c.
Try applying accent
edges before some of
the other effects.

Corel *TIP!*

The Smoothness control in this effect can be used to good advantage in making a photograph look a lot more as if it were painted with a brush.

713

Angled Strokes

The Angled Strokes effect paints an image using diagonal strokes. The lighter areas of the image are painted with strokes going in one direction, while the darker areas are painted with strokes going in the opposite direction.

Figure 22.39d.
An image created using the default setting of the Angled Strokes filter.

Corel *TIP!*

To create an exaggerated version of this effect, scale the image to 50 percent or 25 percent of its original size using PHOTO-PAINT's resample capability, apply the Angled Strokes effect, and then scale it back up to its original size. The result may be sharpened using the PHOTO-PAINT Sharpen filter to make the strokes more apparent. A quicker route to the same effect is to apply the PHOTO-PAINT Edge Enhance filter.

Bas Relief

This filter is very similar to the original Emboss filter in PHOTO-PAINT, but it does a few things that that filter doesn't do. It adds a linear fill to the background. It uses two colors instead of one. The Bas Relief effect transforms an image to appear as though it were carved in low relief and lit to accent the surface modulations. The Bas Relief filter uses PHOTO-PAINT's current Paint (foreground) color and Paper (background) color to render the final result.

Figure 22.39e.
An image created by
applying the Aldus
Angled Strokes filter to
the original and then
applying the PHOTO-
PAINT Edge Enhance
filter.

Corel *TIP!*

To accentuate the effect that the image is sculpted in stone, apply the
Texturizer effect using the Sandstone texture (or others) after the Bas Relief
effect in order to texture the surface.

Figure 22.39f.
To make the exhibit
sign, I used the Shell
object from the PAINT
Plus object collection,
then mirror duplicated
it. Next I applied a Bas
Relief to each shell
individually from
opposite light angles.
With the shells hidden,
the text then had the
default setting of Bas
Relief applied to it. The
finishing touch was to
apply an Unsharp filter
to it.

Corel *TIP!*

To create metallic 3-D text when using PHOTO-PAINT program, do the following: Type the text, then deselect (hide) all but the text using the Layers/Objects roll-up. Then apply the Bas Relief effect. To obtain a different color, set the Paint (foreground) color in PHOTO-PAINT 5 to the desired color.

Corel *TIP!*

To energize low-contrast black-and-white images, apply the Bas Relief effect to them.

Colored Pencil

The Colored Pencil effect draws an image resembling colored pencils on a solid background. Important edges are retained and given a rough crosshatch appearance, while the solid background is allowed to show through the smoother areas of the image.

Figure 22.39g.
An image created from a photograph of a tree that had the Aldus Emboss filter applied to it, followed by the Colored Pencil filter.

To create a Pencil Sketch look, do as follows:

1. Convert the image to grayscale (if it's not already) using the Convert To command in the Edit menu of PHOTO-PAINT.

2. Pick the dominant background color and assign it to the Paper color using the Eyedropper tool.

3. Apply the Colored Pencil effect with the Paper Brightness control at its maximum value.

4. Increase the contrast of the resulting image using the PHOTO-PAINT brightness and contrast controls.

Figure 22.39h.
The same photograph of a tree, converted to a pencil sketch using the technique just described.

Diffuse Glow

The Diffuse Glow effect renders an image as though it were viewed through a soft diffusion filter. Bright areas glow with a diffused light, while other areas are muted with a soft granularity. The Diffuse Glow effect uses PHOTO-PAINT 5's current Paper (background) color for the glow color.

Figure 22.39i.
The top image was our fossil picture that was created with the Bas Relief filter. Now we have applied the Diffuse Glow filter to the image (bottom), which causes a little deliberate graininess and some more shades of lighting, beginning on the left side and gradually disappearing as it moves across to the right. We chose a warm yellow/orange color for this image.

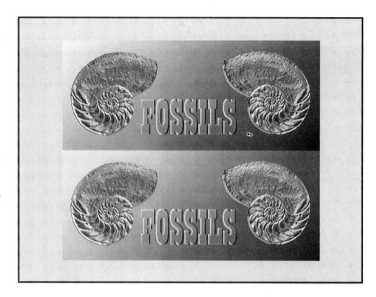

Figure 22.39j.
We have taken the image on top and applied a Diffuse Glow with a very pale yellow, which results in a brightening of the wood background without washing it out.

Corel *TIP!*

To create a hand-colored look, do as follows:

1. Apply the Diffuse Glow effect to a color image.
2. In PHOTO-PAINT 5, duplicate the resulting image into a new object.

3. Remove the color from the duplicate object by applying a -100 percent Saturation filter to it.

4. Center one image directly on top of the other and blend 50 percent Transparency between the effected color and grayscale images.

Glowing Edges

The Glowing Edges effect amplifies the edges of an image in bright, glowing colors. This is a tough one to get a predictive handle on. The one sure thing about this filter is that it inverts the primary background and foreground colors in the image. It seems to need lots of colors in the original image to produce the best effect. As you can see in Figure 22.39k, we have been able to take some multicolored fruit and produce some wonderful neon effects.

Figure 22.39k.
An example of the
Glowing Edges filter
applied to a simple still
life of fruit, producing a
virtual neon festival.

Corel *TIP!*

To enhance the apparent colors in the final image, increase the contrast of the image using the Brightness and Contrast filters in PHOTO-PAINT 5 prior to applying the Glowing Edges effect. Be aware that increasing the contrast can also create new edges.

Grain

This is called Noise in the earlier release of this product. At first it appears to be a Gaussian Noise filter. The Grain effect adds a wide variety of grain types to an image. The Stippled option of this effect uses PHOTO-PAINT's current Paint (foreground) and Paper (background) colors to color the final result. The Sprinkles option uses PHOTO-PAINT's current Paper (background) color to color the added sprinkles.

The grain types available in this effect are good for adding teeth to an image prior to applying other effects. This is especially true with synthetic images that have been created by paint programs, 3-D graphics programs, or with typography. Synthetic images tend to lack the detail of scanned photographs or images from a video source. Adding a small amount of grain will yield better results with most effects. The amount of visible grain in images captured from different sources can be matched by adding grain of the appropriate type.

Figure 22.39l.
This illustrates the effect of adding Grain (noise) to a picture. I chose this photo because it was what we refer to as a "soft" image (low contrast). Notice that by adding noise it appears to have sharper resolution.

Corel *TIP!*

You can simulate the appearance of old photographs by using the various grain types. The effect is enhanced if the image's colors are changed to a sepia tone (yellow/brown tint) using PHOTO-PAINT's Hue/Saturation filters. For a more realistic look, try adding small speckles of paint with a paint tool to simulate bits of dirt. Also, you may want to randomly blur areas of the image using the blur tool of PHOTO-PAINT.

Palette Knife

The Palette Knife effect creates an image rendered in rough applications of color that appear to have been applied with a palette knife. Because the color patches are irregular in size and shape, the result is very obvious and great for making an image stand out on the cover of a brochure.

Corel *TIP!*

For a variety of special effects, posterize your image prior to applying Palette Knife using the Posterize filter in PHOTO-PAINT. Alternately, apply the Accented Edges effect. Also, after applying the Palette Knife effect, use the Texturizer effect to add a texture; for example, use Canvas for an especially realistic depiction of manually applied paint onto a textured surface.

Corel *TIP!*

When the size of the daubs created by the Watercolor effect (from Aldus Gallery Effects: Classic Art Volume 1) are too small (especially when working with large images), first apply the Palette Knife effect with a large Stroke Size setting. Then apply the Watercolor effect for the final Watercolor style.

Figure 22.39m.
A combination of several filters. The original image had Contrast from PHOTO-PAINT applied to it. Then the Palette Knife was applied, followed by the Aldus Emboss filter from Volume 1. Finally, several passes were made with the PHOTO-PAINT Unsharp filter.

Patchwork

Aldus calls this filter Patchwork, but if you are going to keep the image recognizable, you must get the patch size so small that it should be called Needlepoint. The Patchwork effect is supposed to create an image that appears to be stitched using needle and thread. The small squares of color that result are shadowed to depict varying depths. You can isolate or better define features of the final image by first increasing the image's contrast with PHOTO-PAINT's Brightness and Contrast filters, and then applying the Patchwork effect. When the image contrast is increased, large areas of the final image will be flat and not show any of the 3-D surface patches characteristic of the Patchwork effect.

Figure 22.39n.
Here is a fun little thing I quickly threw together. The boot is a floating object from the PHOTO-PAINT 5 Plus collection and, after the Patchwork filter was applied, I applied a Canvas texture using the Texturizer filter from this series.

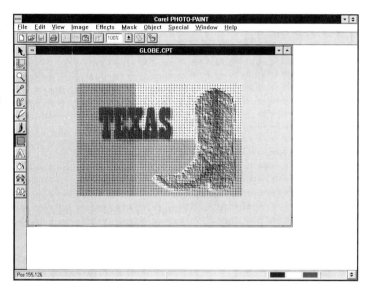

Corel *TIP!*

After applying the Patchwork effect, you can get even more of a needlepoint look by using the Texturizer effect with a fabric texture (for example, Canvas or another scanned cloth texture).

Photocopy

The Photocopy effect shows an image as it would look after being photocopied. Large areas of darkness tend to copy only around their edges, and midtones fall away either to solid black or white, as is characteristic of photocopies. The Photocopy filter uses PHOTO-PAINT's current Paint (foreground) and Paper (background) colors to color (tint) the final result.

Corel *TIP!*

To create a high-contrast, cartoonish, or psychedelic Photocopy effect, do the following:

1. Open the Objects/Layers roll-up.
2. Apply the Photocopy effect to each channel (RGB).
3. Recombine the three channels.

Figure 22.39o.
The default setting for the Photocopy filter applied to our old friend the tiger.

You can simulate the effect of photocopying an image several times, where the quality of the image degrades with each pass. To do so, apply the Photocopy effect on an image twice. The first time, use the default settings. Apply the effect again on the resulting image, but this time decrease the Detail control to the point where amounts of the black areas (created in the first pass) start to dissolve.

To create an excellent pencil-sketch effect, do as follows:

1. Apply the Photocopy effect once or twice, as described previously.
2. Apply the Colored Pencil effect to the result.
3. Using PHOTO-PAINT's Brightness and Contrast filters, increase the brightness and contrast of the resulting image for the desired look.

It's a classic animation technique to photocopy isolated movie film frames and then re-photograph the photocopies on an animation stand. To cut down on the amount of work, frames are chosen that are from one half to one second apart. To create the same look using the Photocopy effect, do as follows:

1. Digitize frames from a video sequence that are either the same number of frames apart (say, 30) or a slightly varying number of frames apart.

2. Apply the Photocopy effect to each frame. For a slightly more variable final animation effect, you can randomly alter the brightness and contrast of each frame before and/or after applying the Photocopy effect, using PHOTO-PAINT's Brightness and Contrast filters.

3. You can optionally add grain to each final image with the Grain effect.

4. You can optionally hand-color areas of each final image with a paint package.

5. Edit out the same number of frames for each final image as there were between each image.

Rough Pastels

The Rough Pastels effect renders an image as if using strokes of colored pastel chalk on a user-selected textured background. In areas of bright color, the chalk is thick with little texture, while in other areas the chalk has been scraped off to reveal the texture.

Figure 22.39p.
A lovely photograph of mountain landscape now looks like a painting after the application of the Rough Pastels filter.

Corel *TIP!*

> To create less of a Rough Pastel effect, set the Relief slider in the Texture Controls to a low value.

Sprayed Strokes

The Sprayed Strokes effect paints an image in disjointed, sprayed strokes of adjustable length and orientation.

Corel *TIP!*

> Try applying this effect before some of the other effects (such as Dry Brush or Watercolor from Aldus Gallery Effects: Classic Art Volume 1, or the Texturizer) to make the final result look even more like it was originally a painting.

To create the appearance of an object being reflected in a wet and shiny surface, do as follows:

1. Duplicate the image object.
2. Apply the Sprayed Strokes effect to the duplicate object.
3. Reflect the top half of the resulting image vertically onto the bottom half.
4. Darken or tint the color in the resulting image to make it look more like a reflection.
5. Combine the reflected image with objects in the original image by selecting the objects and compositing them onto the reflection image background using the available tools in the host program.

The final result will look as if the objects in the image are reflected in rippled water upside down.

Stamp

The Stamp effect renders an image so it appears to be the product of a wood or rubber stamp. The Stamp filter uses PHOTO-PAINT's current foreground and background colors.

Corel *TIP!*

A Texturizer effect can be applied after the Stamp effect to bring some texture (wood, gauze, and others) into the solid areas of color.

To create a stamp-pad look, the Grain effect can be applied after the Stamp effect to break up the large areas of color in the final image.

Figure 22.39q.
Two objects that were
converted to images
resembling a rubber
stamp

If either of these two approaches are used, it is sometimes desirable to increase the brightness and contrast (using PHOTO-PAINT's Brightness and Contrast filters) of the final image to get rid of any minor amounts of texture that are apparent in the lighter areas of the image.

Texturizer

This filter is great. We have already used it several times already, so I won't show any more examples. The Texturizer effect integrates an image with one of many available surface textures. The versatile Texturizer effect allows you to incorporate the texture of your choice into an image (using the Type option of the Texture Controls dialog box). With a scanner, you can digitize fabrics, arborite, wood, screens, or photographs and use them as textures. For maximum texturing, choose a light-source direction perpendicular to the dominant direction of the texture. Textures that are parallel to the light-source direction tend not to show much relief. Note that it is where brightness changes that texture happens. Unless you specify that the texture be inverted, the darker areas of the texture will appear to be lower than the brighter areas. In general, specifying an upper-right light-source position creates the most realistic appearances of relief.

Corel *TIP!*

You can use the provided textures as creative examples. If the automatic tiling of the textures creates a repeat pattern that is too evident, scan in a similar texture large enough for the entire image.

Corel *TIP!*

To make the image appear as if it were painted on a textured surface, try applying the Texturizer effect to images already modified by other effects.

You can use the Texturizer effect to create a random textured pattern. Select the Texturizer effect, set the Texture Relief to 50, and choose Sandstone from the Texture Type list. This random noise pattern can be applied to a white or black background for a fancy appearance. You can also get good results by using it on text.

Underpainting

When I began working with this filter, I thought that Aldus had pulled a fast one and it was Texturizer under a different name. Actually, the two filters act quite differently. The Underpainting effect first roughly paints an image on an underlying, user-selected surface texture, then paints the final image over that. The underlying tones enhance the result. The best way to demonstrate this is to apply the Texturizer to half of one image and Underpainting to the other half.

Corel *TIP!*

Try using other textures, such as wood or paper, to give the impression that the images have been painted on these surfaces.

Figure 22.39r.
The left side of the
image has had the
Texturizer applied
using sandstone with
all other settings at
default. On the right,
the Underpainting filter
was applied with the
same settings. Clearly,
the Underpainting filter
blurs existing images.

Aldus Gallery Effects, Volume 3

This, at the time we are putting the book together, is the most recent volume of the Aldus Gallery Effects. Adobe owns Aldus, and Microsoft owns Imageware (albeit indirectly), so no one knows if we can expect more. If you could only own one set, I would suggest you get the first. There are some neat effects in this third volume, but many are of the once-in-a-blue-moon variety. Several of them will bring your computer to its knees begging for mercy.

Conté Crayon

The Conté Crayon effect (pronounced con-tay) renders an image to appear as though drawn with Conté crayon on a variety of rough, textured backgrounds. This style is characterized by dense darks, highly textured midtones, and pure whites. The Conté Crayon effect uses PHOTO-PAINT's current foreground and background colors to color the final result.

Use a color for the background that is white with a small amount of the foreground color added to it to create a soft, blended look in the final drawing. This color can be created by starting with the foreground color and, in the host program's color picker, increasing the brightness to 100 percent and then decreasing the saturation until a color is created that is light enough for the background but which still retains some of the original foreground color.

*Figure 22.40a.
A photo of a butterfly
where we used the
Conté Crayon effect on
the background and
left the original image
intact.*

Corel *TIP!*

A variety of foreground colors—such as black, sepia, or sanguine—may be chosen to emulate the various common colors of Conté crayon that are available.

Crosshatch

The Crosshatch effect draws an image with the appearance of fine crosshatching throughout. While preserving the details and features of the original image, this effect adds texture and roughens the edges of the colored areas in the image.

Cutout

This filter is one of several filters in Volume 3 that consume considerable system resources. If you are working on an image as large as Standard (Photo-CD), I recommend closing all of your other applications before you use this filter. Consider yourself warned.

The Cutout effect portrays an image as though it were made from roughly cut-out pieces of colored paper. High-contrast images appear as if in silhouette, while colored images are built up from several layers of colored paper. The Cutout effect is also reminiscent of lino-block printmaking techniques, especially when applied to high-contrast original images.

Figure 22.40b.
This is a photo directly out of the Photo-Sampler CD. The Cross-hatch effect is most noticeable in the lighter areas of the image, and in the darker areas it is almost non-existent.

Figure 22.40c.
An original image.

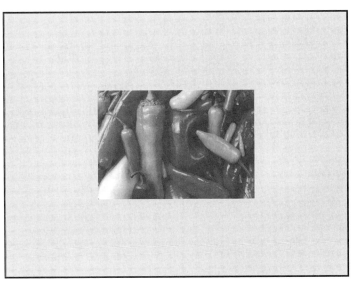

Figure 22.40d.
The Cutout filter has
been applied, but the
color looks washed out.

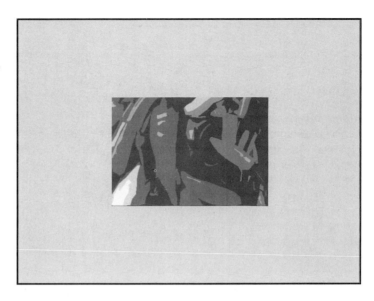

Figure 22.40e
The result of applying a
standard PHOTO-
PAINT Tone Equalize
filter to it and adding a
nice touch of text. The
color of the text is
achieved by using a
Logical XOR setting in
the Object Merge Mode
selector.

Corel *TIP!*

Try applying a small value (less than the default) of the Aldus Emboss effect (from Volume 1) to create an impression of depth and overlap to the layers of the image created with the Cutout effect.

Glass

The Glass effect makes an image appear as if it is being viewed through different types of glass. There are a variety of types of glass available, including Blocks and Frosted. In addition, image files can be specified to act as the refracting glass surface for custom glass effects.

When creating your own custom Glass surface images, remember that any features that are visible in your surface image will show up as areas that will bend and refract the input image. For example, if you have a square in your surface image, the image that is created by the Glass effect using this surface will be unchanged everywhere except around the edges of where the square is located. You can combine the Glass effects to create effects that are not available with a single Glass variation. For example, apply the Glass effect using one surface texture, then apply the Glass effect again using a different surface texture.

If after applying the Glass effect any areas of the image show too fine a level of detail, a single pass of the Blur tool in PHOTO-PAINT will smooth those areas out. A large blur tool or several applications of a smaller blur tool are effective to enhance the appearance of the output of the Frosted glass variation. preprocess the original image with Gaussian Blurs in PHOTO-PAINT or the Diffuse Glow effect (from Aldus Volume 2) prior to applying Glass.

Halftone Screen

This filter produces a fake halftone. The Halftone Screen effect represents an image as if it has been printed using a variety of standard halftone dot screens. The Halftone Screen effect, unlike digital halftone representations, shows the continuous tones of an image in smoothly varying element sizes that blend together like those created by an analog halftone screen. To add a halftone edge to a high-contrast image such as a text image, blur the image in the host program prior to applying the effect to create a soft edge around the objects. Blurring an image prior to applying the Halftone Screen effect can create special variations of the effect.

The Halftone Screen effect uses PHOTO-PAINT's current foreground and background colors to color the final result.

Corel *TIP!*

> Applying the Halftone Screen effect to images that have been posterized in the host program or processed with the Cutout effect will create halftone dots that are the same size in the large flat areas of common color.

Figure 22.40f.
The original image.

Figure 22.40g.
A variation of the
halftone screen.

Figure 22.40h.
After a heavier
application.

I find comfort in knowing that if a client ever needs a fake halftone, Aldus has provided a filter to do the job.

Ink Outlines

The Ink Outlines effect draws an image with fine, narrow lines around the details to create a "corroded" pen-and-ink drawing style. You can change the textures that the Ink Outlines filter creates by processing the image with one of the Paint Daubs variations, or you can add texture by applying the Grain effect filter (from Volume 2) prior to applying Ink Outlines.

If the output of Ink Outlines is too harsh, blur the image with a small blur and then adjust the Brightness and Contrast of the image. Higher-contrast versions of Ink Outlines (made by increasing the Dark Intensity and Light Intensity settings) tend to look more like real pen-and-ink drawings. If these higher-contrast images are blurred successively with a few small blurs in PHOTO-PAINT, they will appear as though drawn with a soft pencil.

For a softened pen-and-ink effect, try applying the Water Paper effect (with a small Fiber Length setting) to your image after applying the Ink Outlines effect.

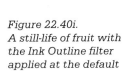

Figure 22.40i.
A still-life of fruit with
the Ink Outline filter
applied at the default
setting.

Neon Glow

This filter saves a lot of work. Everything that it can do can also be accomplished manually though PHOTO-PAINT, but this saves a lot of effort. The Neon Glow effect adds various types of glows to the objects in an image. This effect can be used to create neon lighting effects or to give an object the appearance that it is radiating light and heat. This is an effect that is particularly useful for images consisting of text or simple, high-contrast graphical objects. The Neon Glow effect can produce both "outline" and "inline" glow variations. An outline glow is where the glow appears to be around the outside of the objects in the image, for example, around the outside of a letter. An inline glow is where the glow is on the inside of the letter. Obviously, when the inside areas are small, the Glow Size and Glow Brightness settings would have to be adjusted for the smaller region.

Corel TIP!

> Before applying the Neon Glow to text, apply a Gaussian Blur (setting of 1).

Figure 22.40j.
The text of Glow 1 had
Gaussian Blur applied.
The text of Glow 2 did
not.

Paint Daubs

This is a poor man's Paint Alchemy filter. It works well enough, but if you have PAINT 5 Plus, then you should use that filter instead. The Paint Daubs effect is a suite of effects that render an image in a wide variety of paintbrush styles. A range of brush sizes, from large to small, can be specified to smooth and simplify images or to capture and accentuate fine details. Use the suite of styles in this effect to increase the hand-painted look before applying other effects.

When using large brush sizes, try turning the Sharpness slider all the way to the right. This brings out small color details in the resulting image. These colors can be further accentuated by processing with other variations in the Paint Daubs effect. Most of the styles created by Paint Daubs will benefit from a final application of the Texturizer effect (Volume 2) to enhance the illusion of a painting on a textured background.

*Figure 22.40k.
There are seven
different brush styles in
Paint Daubs. We chose
to show the default,
which is a simple
brush. We took a
perfectly good photo-
graph and made a
painting out of it.*

Plaster

The Plaster effect makes an image appear to be molded from three-dimensional plaster. The dark areas of the image are raised into bumps and plateaus, while white areas are flattened into valleys. This is an effect that is particularly useful for images consisting of text or simple, high-contrast graphical objects.

The Plaster effect uses PHOTO-PAINT's current Paint (foreground) color to replace the dark areas and the Paper (background) color to replace the light areas.

Corel *TIP!*

The Plaster effect will appear most effective when applied on high-contrast images. To change the appearance of the image, apply a negative (invert) image before applying the Plaster effect.

Figure 22.40l.
A photo from the
People Photo CD.

Figure 22.40m.
To highlight the young
lady's face, I inverted
the image using the
Invert filter in the
Fancy group of the
PHOTO-PAINT Effects
menu before I applied
the Plaster filter. After
the Plaster filter, I
applied a 50 percent
Edge Enhance from the
Sharpen group of the
Effects menu.

*Figure 22.40n.
Next I took a copy of
the original photo and
placed it on top of the
plaster at a 20 percent
Opacity setting.*

*Figure 22.40o.
For a final touch, I
added 50 percent noise
to the original photo
and then added a
feather of 80 percent to
the original.*

Plastic Wrap

The Plastic Wrap effect makes an image appear to be wrapped or coated in
shiny plastic, accentuating the surface detail of the image. The parameters of
the effect can also be set to create images that appear to have been made from
Polaroids that have been scratched and textured by hand. In addition to the
surreal shine that the Plastic Wrap effect adds to images, the effect can also be
used to emulate other experimental approaches to photographic image manipulation.

When Polaroids are artistically altered by hand, they are often scratched from the back with a sharp instrument. This leaves a white mark, often along the edges of the image, and sometimes drags the colored pigment along with it. To create an effect reminiscent of this sort of treatment, the Plastic Wrap effect should be applied on the image with a high Highlight Strength setting and a fairly low Smoothness setting. The idea is to have just the right amount of detailed, white lines in the image and to avoid large areas of flat, white reflections.

When the right amount of white lines have been added, apply the Ripple effect (from Aldus Volume 1) to the image at low distortion settings (Ripple Magnitude and Ripple Size) in order to slightly shift and jiggle the white scratch marks and the associated image areas. As Polaroids tend to be highly saturated in color, increasing the Brightness and Contrast of the image in the host program may be beneficial. Slightly blurring the image using the Gaussian Blur filter in PHOTO-PAINT, either before applying Plastic Wrap or as a final step, may also be useful in simulating the altered Polaroid look.

Reticulation

The Reticulation effect simulates the photographic effect of reticulation. Reticulation is created when film emulsion shrinks and distorts in a controlled fashion. This effect renders the darker areas of the image with dense clumps of dark emulsion and the lighter areas with a light stippling of grain. The Reticulation effect uses PHOTO-PAINT's current Paint (foreground) and Paper (background) colors.

To alter the pattern of grain in an image created by the Reticulation effect, you can post-process the image with some of the filters that come with PHOTO-PAINT, such as the Minimum, Median, or Maximum filters. These filters will cause the grain in the images to either swell or close. You can create a range of evocative effects by preprocessing images with the Diffuse Glow effect (from Volume 2) before applying Reticulation. Try adding just a bit of glow with the Diffuse Glow effect.

Corel *TIP!*

Reticulation creates a negative of the image when it is applied. So unless you want the image reversed, use the Invert filter in PHOTO-PAINT before applying the filter.

Figure 22.40p.
An image created by
applying PHOTO-
PAINT's Contrast and
Invert filter to the
image before Reticula-
tion was applied.

Sponge

The Sponge effect creates an image with the appearance of having been painted with a sponge. This filter, when pushed to the extreme settings, can produce some neat effects. The sponge effect is characterized by highly textured areas of contrasting color.

The Sponge effect benefits from a final pass through the Texturizer effect (from Volume 2) to enhance the impression that the image has been painted onto a rough surface. Textures such as sandstone or brick work well, as would textures of rough surfaces that you create yourself .

Figure 22.40q.
The original image.

Figure 22.40r.
If you use the default settings with the Sponge filter, you will end up with a very blurry collection of colored blobs. Brush Size and Smoothness are set to minimum and Definition is set to maximum.

Corel *TIP!*

Try using the Emboss effect (from Volume 1) on the output of the Sponge effect to create an impression of depth. With the right image, the combination of the Sponge effect followed by the Ink Outlines effect can create a strong impression of a fresco.

Stained Glass

When I first saw the description of this filter, I was thrilled. But it soon became apparent that while this is a neat filter, the result doesn't look much like a stained glass. And this filter sucks up memory like you have never seen. If your image is too big, you will start generating error messages telling you that the image was too big. (See Figure 22.40s.) These are not system error messages; they are little notes from the application explaining why it isn't going to finish the filter job you just asked it to do.

The Stained Glass effect is supposed to create an image that appears to be a piece of stained glass, lit from behind as if by the sun. The strength of the light shining through the glass can be varied from an even glow to a focused brilliance. Another problem with this filter is that image detail goes right out the window when you use it. If you apply the Stained Glass effect to a square, you may end up with a circle. There are, however, a few ways to overcome this image destruction.

By using the Object Merge feature of PHOTO-PAINT to blend the enhanced image with the original image, some color and detail information will be brought into the flat areas of color in the Stained Glass image. This technique is most effective if the detail being added to the image does not appear to be on top of the dark lines of the leaded edges in the Stained Glass image.

The Stained Glass effect uses PHOTO-PAINT's current Paint (foreground) color to color the lead borders.

Figure 22.40s.
The memory warning.

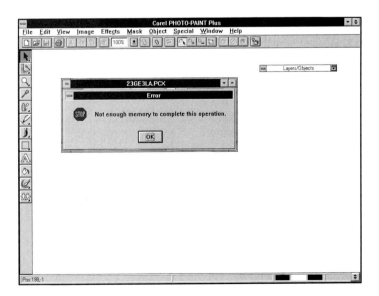

Figure 22.40t.
The original image.

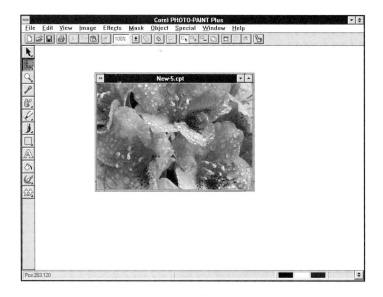

Figure 22.40u.
I would love to tell you that this was a simple application of the Stained Glass filter at the default settings, but it is not. I applied a heavy Contrast, Stained Glass, Aldus Emboss, and Plastic Wrap. Then I applied a mask of the butterfly on top using the Multiply Object Merge. With all of that, it only looks sorta OK.

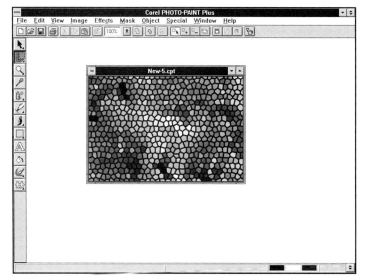

Corel TIP!

By posterizing the original image (the Posterize filter is located in the Special group of the Effects menu) or applying the Aldus Cutout effect before applying the Stained Glass effect, you can create large areas of common color that can enhance the appearance of the Stained Glass effect.

To give the Stained Glass image a slightly "antique" feel, apply the Ripple effect (from Volume 1) to the enhanced image with low distortion (Ripple Magnitude and Ripple Size) settings. You may find that adding a slight amount of grain with the Grain effect (Volume 2) prior to applying Ripple will give the impression of texture that will enhance the antique effect.

Sumi-E

The Sumi-e effect renders an image in the Japanese sumi-e painting style (meaning "ink painting" and pronounced sue-me-ay). The original image is painted as if with a brush and ink on paper. This effect is characterized by rich blacks with soft, blurry edges, suggesting the use of a wet brush loaded with ink on an absorbent paper, such as rice paper.

Figure 22.40v.
The Sumi-e filter was applied to the tiger at near default settings. Next, a Bamboo Blind bitmap fill from the Plus collection was applied as a PHOTO-PAINT canvas.

Torn Edges

The Torn Edges effect renders an image with edges that appear like torn paper. This is an effect that is particularly useful for images consisting of text or simple, high-contrast graphical objects. The Torn Edges effect uses PHOTO-PAINT's current Paint (foreground) and Paper (background) colors.

Corel *TIP!*

Try this effect as a final touch to the output of images processed by the Stamp effect (from Volume 2) or the Photocopy effect (from Volume 2).

Figure 22.40w.
Torn Edges is a great
effect for "roughening
up" type.

Water Paper

The Water Paper effect renders an image with blotchy daubs that appear to have been painted onto damp paper. The painted colors appear to have blurred and run along the fibers of the paper, softening and extending the original outlines of the image.

The Water Paper effect is an excellent choice to apply prior to using other paint-like effects in the Aldus Gallery Effects series, such as Rough Pastels, Paint Daubs, etc. Make sure you experiment with different settings of the Brightness and Contrast sliders, as these greatly affect the appearance of detail in the final image.

The Texturizer effect (from Volume 2) can be used to further enhance the impression that the image created with the Water Paper effect has been painted on damp paper. Any texture such as sandstone, when used with a small Relief value, tends to accentuate the impression that the streaks created with the Water Paper effect were created naturally during the painting process. For a further variation on the his idea, try using the Ripple effect (from Volume 1), at a low setting, to give the impression that the paint has meandered somewhat as it blotched on the damp paper.

Figure 22.40x.
The original image.

Figure 22.40y.
The original image with
Water Paper and then
Texturizer applied to it.

Andromeda

Andromeda Series One is a collection of 10 pseudo-photographic filters. These filters create wild special effects, reminiscent of 60's and 70's imagery. Each filter has a dialog box with a large number of parameters and an ample preview box. The preview boxes all have controls that affect where the filter is applied to the image. While the filters come with a decent manual, there are no help files for the filters.

Designs

The Designs filter is the most elaborate filter in this series. Designs adds patterns or mezzotint effects to the image with various parameters. Designs can add several different textures: Dimensional textures (both 2-D and 3-D), Mezzo Screen texture, and Mezzo Grain texture.

Dimensional Texture contains 96 pre-defined patterns that can be added to the entire or selected portion of a color or grayscale image to provide conventional 2-D texture. Color can be added using the RGB or CMYK sliders in the filter. In addition, the Designs filter can bend, stretch, or warp patterns to create three-dimensional textures.

The Mezzo Screen texture is a texturing option that can only be used on grayscale images using the patterns from the Filters pattern library. In traditional printing, "mezzo line screens" are often used to convert continuous-tone grayscale photos into black-and-white line art. The pattern of the screen breaks up continuous gradation of grayscale tones into correspondingly patterned black-and-white dots that vary in size. The Designs filter emulates this traditional process with several patterns.

The Mezzo Grain texture produces a texture on color and grayscale images that looks like film grain.

Figure 22.41a.
The Designs filter
dialog box.

Figure 22.41b.
The Designs filter
applied with the
parameters shown in
the preceding figure.

Diffraction

Diffraction applies a circular diffraction pattern of spectral rays to an image. The rays consist of the spectral "spokes" as if produced by a diffraction lens placed in front of a camera lens. The effect can be added around bright points of light such as early morning sunrise, bright reflections off shiny objects, or night lights. You can change the length, number, angle, and intensity of the spokes.

Figure 22.41c
The Diffraction filter
dialog box.

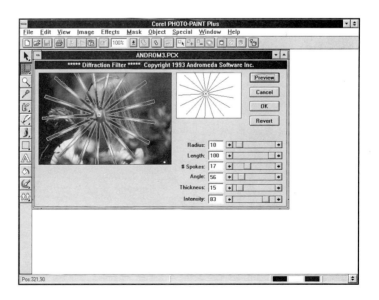

Figure 2.41d.
The Diffraction filter
applied with the
parameters shown in
the preceding figure.

Halo

Halo spreads out and diffuses highlights according to the parameters set in the Halo dialog box. Halos can be in any direction or all directions. Halo shows up best on high-contrast daylight images (the example image is not necessarily a high-contrast image) or nighttime photos with bright spots of light. Bright letters, such as those in a neon sign, or bright points of light will produce a halo that follows the contours of the bright highlight on the darker background. Halo is not like various glow filters discussed in this chapter. For example, Halo does not produce a halo (glow) around a person's head, because the head is probably darker than the background.

Prism

Prism spreads out the spectral colors of a color image. The effect adds a 3-D quality to an image. You can adjust the spread, angle, and intensity of the Prism effect, as well as the area where the effect is applied.

Figure 22.41e.
The Halo filter dialog
box.

Figure 22.41f.
The Halo filter applied
with the parameters
shown in the preceding
figure.

Corel *TIP!*

A watercolor-type effect can be achieved by applying the Halo filter to the
colors created by the Prism filter.

Figure 22.41g.
The Prism filter dialog
box.

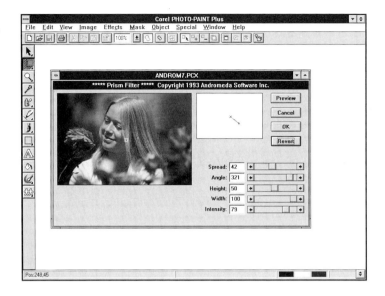

Figure 22.41h.
The Prism filter applied
with the parameters
shown in the preceding
figure.

Rainbow

Rainbow adds a rainbow to the image. You can adjust the angle, radius, fade,
and intensity of the rainbow. The Rainbow filter is additive, and it is visible
against a non-white background. There's even an option to add a Pot of Gold.

Figure 22.41i.
The Rainbow filter
dialog box

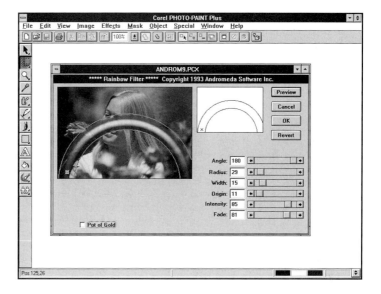

Figure 22.41j.
The Rainbow filter
applied with the
parameters shown in
the preceding figure.

Reflection

The Reflection filter reflects the selected portion of the image. This filter is one of the more substantial and useful filters within Andromeda Series One. You can adjust the area of reflection, the distance between the reflections, and the transition between the reflections. This filter is also great for special effects or for making a reflection on an object such as water or a mirror.

753

Figure 22.41k.
The Reflection filter
dialog box.

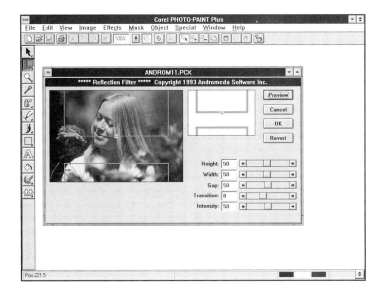

Figure 22.41l.
The Reflection filter
applied with the
parameters shown in
the preceding figure.

Star

The Star filter adds star effects to an image. The stars can be 4, 8, or 16 points. The filter also has settings for adjustable lengths, halos, and suns. You can add multiples stars by clicking on the Add/New button. Interesting variations can be created by setting any one of the Sun, Halo, or Star lengths to 0.

Figure 22.41m.
The Star filter dialog
box.

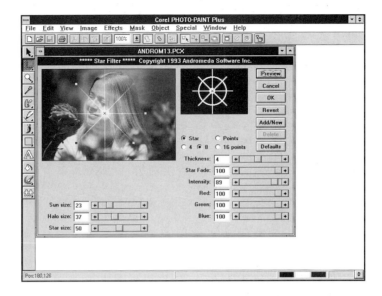

Figure 22.41n.
The Star filter applied
with the parameters
shown in the preceding
figure.

Velocity

Velocity is a very useful and powerful motion-blur filter. You can adjust the area that is blurred, blur the whole image, and apply a one-way or two-way smear. This filter can create interesting special effects with text and is one of the best filters available for creating motion blurs.

Figure 22.41o.
The Velocity filter
dialog box.

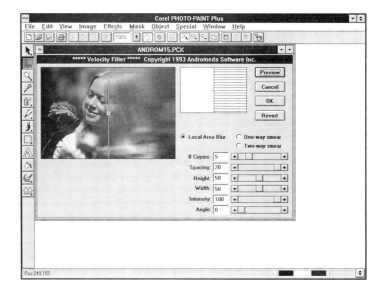

Figure 22.41p.
The Velocity filter
applied with the
parameters shown in
the preceding figure.

Circular Multiple Image

The Circular Multiple Image filter creates multiple images in various circular patterns, for controlled kaleidoscopic effects. Effects can be applied in radial or square patterns with adjustable transitions, areas, radius, width, and intensity.

Corel *TIP!*

Increasing the Transition (feathering) prevents the appearance of sharp edges between adjacent areas.

Figure 22.41q.
The Circular Multiple Image filter dialog box.

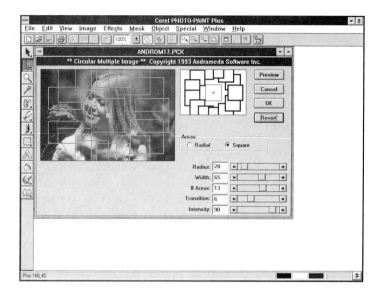

Figure 22.41r.
The Circular Multiple Image filter applied with the parameters shown in the preceding figure.

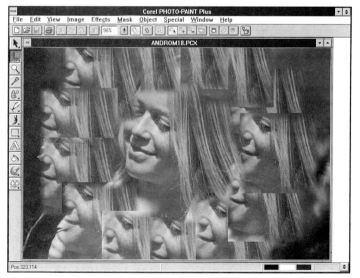

Straight Multiple Image

Straight Multiple Image is a combination of the Reflection filter and the Circular Multiple Image filter. It creates multiple copies of an area of an image according to the parameters set in the Straight Multiple Image dialog box. You can adjust the angle, spacing, number of areas, intensity, and fading of the copies. Copies can be applied in parallel lines or square areas.

Figure 22.41s.
The Straight Multiple
Image filter dialog box.

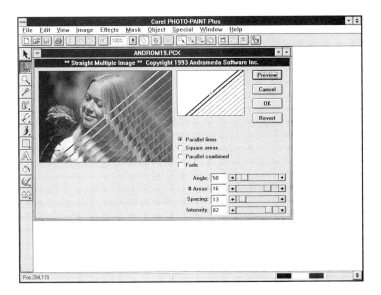

Figure 22.41t.
The Straight Multiple
Image filter applied
with the parameters
shown in the preced-
ing figure.

The Series Two 3-D Filter

The Series Two 3-D filter allows users to create realistic three-dimensional images within PHOTO-PAINT 5. To do this, the filter performs three separate tasks. It creates the scene, illuminates the scene, and then "photographs" the scene.

In screen creation, the filter first allows to select one of a variety of surface or shapes. If you wish, you can "photograph" just the shape for simple dramatic effects. It also allows you to take the active image in PHOTO-PAINT and add it to the scene by wrapping it on the selected surface, even if the surface is not flat. The surface can have any color selected by the user. The background can also be selected, which is necessary to quickly and accurately mask the resulting image with the PHOTO-PAINT Magic Wand tool.

In illuminating the scene, a point light source is provided. The position, intensity, and hot spot of the light source can be can be varied by the user. In addition, ambient or "room" lighting is provided, which can soften the effect or add even more depth. The filter can even create certain lighting effects that are not normally possible.

In "photographing" the scene, the filter allows the virtual camera to be placed almost anywhere with respect to the image. A zoom-lens effect can be employed and controlled as well.

The preview box offers several options. There is a fast view, which gives you a real down-and-dirty look at the expected result. For those willing to wait a moment longer, there is a preview, which gives a very accurate representation of the finished product.

Corel *TIP!*

> Most of the time you will be putting the resulting 3-D image in with another image. The best way to make the 3-D image into an object is to select a background that is very different from the colors in the original image. This way the Magic Wand tool can quickly and accurately mask the image.

The Black Box (Alien Skin Software)

The Black Box began as a collection of six plug-in filters that were created to automate some of the effects that used to be accomplished in Adobe Photoshop through long and complicated procedures. I happened across this company after reading a blurb about them in *Flash* magazine. I called them and was able to talk to the product's creator, Jeff Butterworth.

One of the benefits of working closely with Corel Corporation is that when you find little outfits such as Alien Skin, you sometimes can get their products added to the released version. It is like discovering a star. Nostalgia aside, the result was four of the six filters in The Black Box have been included in the Plus release of PHOTO-PAINT 5. They are Emboss (Called D'Boss), Glass, Swirl and Drop Shadow. The two that didn't make it were HSB Noise and Glow. The four that are included in the Plus Release are discussed in great detail in Chapter 13, "Exploring the Power of the Plus Release." We will limit our discussions to the two remaining filters.

All of Alien Skin's Black Box filters require a Transparency mask to operate. In itself this is no great shakes, but it can be a real pain when doing multiple applications, because the Black Box filters delete the Transparency mask after the filter has been applied. When Corel integrated the four filters into the Plus release, they modified them so they won't delete the mask. This is great for multiple applications of the filter.

Glow

I was surprised when Corel didn't pick this filter up. The Glow filter makes a radiating glow appear around an object, but the ability to add a blurred color behind a selection has many other uses as well, such as in accentuating text.

Figure 22.42.
Text with a 10-percent black fill against a linear fill. The result is the text is difficult to read. By applying a 25-percent black glow filter to the text, the word "glow" becomes much clearer and easier to read.

Corel *TIP!*

> Although a black glow might sound unreal, it can be a useful tool. If there is a low contrast between a light foreground and its background, a black blur will make the text stand out better.

Corel *TIP!*

> You can simulate spray-painted stencils by applying the Invert filter to a selection before applying the Glow filter. the glow will appear inside the original selection as if it were cut out of a stencil

HSB Noise

To me a noise filter is a noise filter, but Jeff Butterworth of Alien Skin is really proud of this one. So, if you are looking for the mother-of-all-noise filters, this is the one to get. Again, HSB stands for Hue-Saturation-Brightness. The HSB Noise filter lets you control how much to vary each of those aspects of the colors in the selection.

Corel *TIP!*

> Leaving the Hue Saturation setting at 0 can simulate Hue-protected noise.

Using
Typestry

CHAPTER 23

Figure 23.1.
Effects created with
Pixar Typestry.

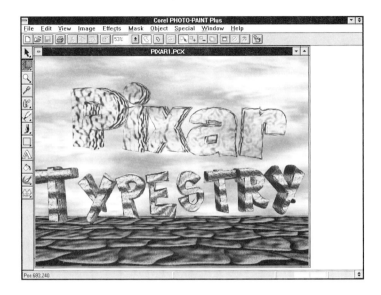

Pixar Typestry

A demo version of Pixar Typestry is included on the companion CD with this book. Typestry is an excellent, though limited, 3-D program that uses Truetype fonts as the basis for three-dimensional imagery. The fact that Typestry has limits is actually a significant asset, since it is not particularly difficult to master Typestry's small feature set. And while Typestry is limited in features, it is not limited in power. The main drawback to Typestry is that you need a fairly strong computer or a lot of patience in order to make Typestry productive.

The product's name is a good indication of what it does. Typestry creates stunning type effects for either still images or animations. Typestry is great for creating lively mastheads, logos, and headlines. (See Figure 23.2.) You can also create new TrueType "fonts" with CorelDRAW to incorporate shapes other than conventional fonts inside of Typestry. Images created in Typestry can be saved in several different file formats that PHOTO-PAINT can import.

Typestry works like other 3-D programs in that you first position the objects, size them, choose lighting, and apply textures (Pixar calls its textures "looks") in wireframe mode, and then you "render" the results. Typestry's wireframe objects are similar to CorelDRAW's shapes, but when the image is rendered it becomes a bitmap. You can render in two ways: to screen (inside of Typestry), or to file (to be manipulated in PHOTO-PAINT). Both ways take an equally long time. If you render inside of Typestry, you have several quality options: Quick 'n' Dirty, Reasonable, and Excellent 'n' Slow. (One refreshing thing about Pixar is that they have a sense of humor and a sense of style.)

Figure 23.2.
Pixar Typestry can be
used to create vibrant
three-dimensional
images that can be
imported into PHOTO-
PAINT for further
manipulation.

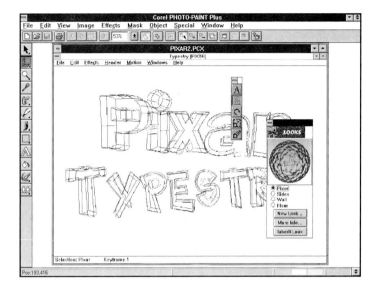

Quick 'n' Dirty just barely gives you a good idea of what the finished product is going to look like. It is useful if you want to make sure everything is in place or all of the options you want have been added. When you begin to get closer to what you want, start using Reasonable, which is slower than Quick 'n' Dirty but faster than Excellent 'n' Slow. Reasonable lets you see the detail better without making you wait overly long. When you are pretty certain you've got it the way you want it, use Excellent 'n' Slow to view the final results. Once you render an image to screen, you can save the file as a BMP file, but only at your screen resolution (usually 96 dpi).

The best way to render a Typestry image for editing in PHOTO-PAINT is to use the Render To File option. You can use the Image Format option located under the Render menu to change the image's size and resolution at any time before you render to file. Pixar files are effectively built in 3-D space before they are rendered. The wireframes for the shapes are for positioning and sizing, so altering the size of the file before rendering is not difficult. If you know you want to have a 4" × 3" image at 300 dpi, you can enter those values before you start. If you later decide you need another inch on the top, simply adjust the Image Format settings. You may have to reposition the wireframe shapes to get the orientation you want, but otherwise resizing is relatively painless.

Corel *TIP!*

The alpha-channel options in Pixar Typestry cannot be used with PHOTO-PAINT. If you stop a file in the middle of rendering or if your computer crashes, you might notice a file called "untitled.?00" (where the ? stands for any letter in the alphabet). These files are temporarily created for shading and are worthless. You can delete them painlessly. Also, if you import a rendered file from Typestry that appears too dark, try adjusting the gamma within Typestry using the Custom Quality Option under the Render menu. If the values for Excellent 'n' Slow look fine on your monitor, load the values from Excellent 'n' Slow.

The toolbar (Figure 23.3) has only five tools, but don't let that fool you. In the case of Typestry, simplicity is power. Since there are so few tools, let's take a look at what each one does and how to use it. As you will see, a little time invested in learning these five tools will enhance your ability to create exciting images easily.

Figure 23.3.
The Pixar Typestry
toolbox.

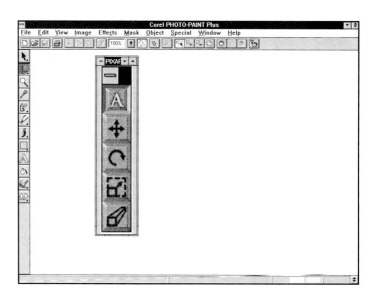

Going from top to bottom on the toolbar, the top button is the Text tool. (See Figure 23.4.) The Text tool creates objects that may have the shape of anything in a TrueType or Type1 font. Typestry dramatically simplifies the shape-making process that is so difficult in many other 3-D programs by building objects using the shapes in TrueType and Type1 fonts. Once a shape is built, though, it is referred to as an object. Whenever you click on the Typestry desktop with the Text tool, the Text Object dialog box is opened, which means that you will only want to use the Text tool when you are trying to build an object. To avoid opening a dialog box every time you click on the Typestry desktop, select one of the other tools, such as the Move tool. (See Figure 23.5.) Whenever you build objects with more than one letter/object, Typestry groups them together. Each object within a group can be ungrouped and treated individually or can be adjusted individually while still grouped by clicking on the individual letter/ object with any of the tools (except the Text tool) twice.

Figure 23.4.
The Text tool.

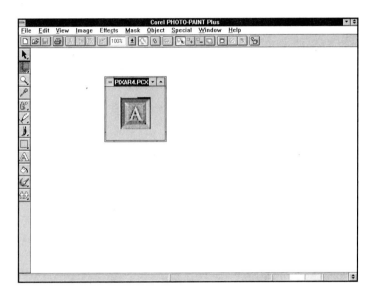

Figure 23.5.
The Move tool.

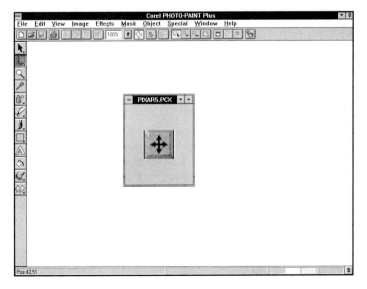

Next is the Move tool, which you can use to reposition the wireframes. Holding down the Shift key while moving an object constrains the movement horizontally or vertically. As with all of the rest of the tools, the Move tool can select individual letters/objects in a group.

Corel *TIP!*

You can use the Move tool or any other tool besides the Text tool to select individual letters/objects within a group to apply looks separately.

Figure 23.6.
The Rotate tool.

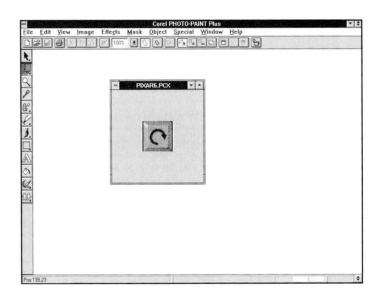

The Rotate tool (Figure 23.6) allows you to rotate text or objects three dimensionally. Right-to-left mouse motion rotates the object around its vertical axis; forward-to-backward mouse motion rotates the object around its horizontal axis. Holding down the Shift key keeps the object from rotating, which gives you an opportunity to reposition your mouse if you need to. Using the Rotate tool can be confusing. If you get lost, you can select Reset Orientation from the Edit menu to start over. If you prefer to enter the rotation degrees numerically, hold down the Control key while you click on the object with the Rotate tool to bring up the Rotate dialog box (Figure 23.7).

Figure 23.7.
Holding down the
Control key while you
click on an object with
the Rotate tool opens
the Rotate dialog box.

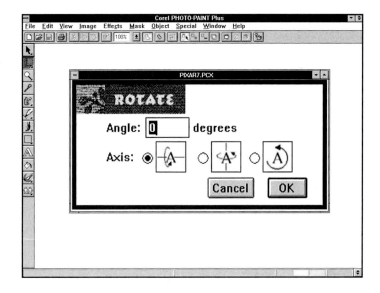

Figure 23.8.
The Scale tool is used
to resize an object's
width, height, and
depth.

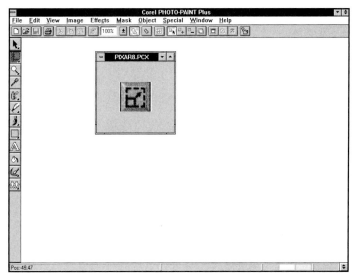

The Scale tool can be used to resize an object's width, height, and depth. (See
Figure 23.8.) Moving the mouse to the right enlarges the selected object, and
moving the mouse to the left shrinks it. Depending on which direction you drag
the mouse first, holding the Shift key constrains the resizing horizontally or

vertically. Holding down the Control and Shift keys allows you to resize the dimensions inversely. (Pixar calls this "volume-preserving" resizing.) If you don't like the results of scaling, you can chose Reset Scale from the Edit menu to restore the object to its original scale. Holding down the Control key while clicking on an object with the Scale tool opens the Scale dialog box (Figure 23.9). The Scale dialog box allows you to numerically enter the Scaling values.

Figure 23.9.
Holding down the
Control key while you
click on an object with
the Scale tool opens the
Scale dialog box.

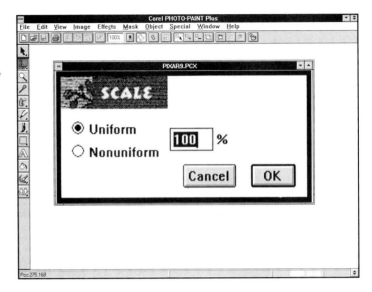

Figure 23.10.
The Extrude tool
controls the amount of
apparent extrusion
(thickness) of an object.

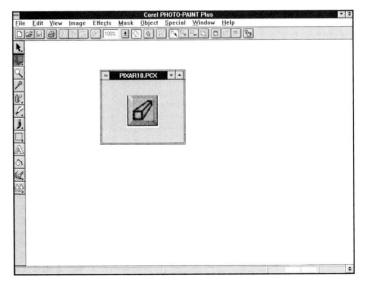

The Extrude tool extrudes or increases the thickness (depth) of an object. (See Figure 23.10.) Dragging the mouse to the right increases the thickness of the object, and dragging the mouse to the left decreases the thickness of the object. Selecting Reset Scale also cancels the action of the Extrude tool. Holding down the Control key while clicking on an object with the Extrude tool opens the Extrude dialog box. The Extrude dialog box allows you to extrude an object numerically. (See Figure 23.11.)

Figure 23.11. Holding down the Control key while you click on an object with the Extrude tool opens the Extrude dialog box.

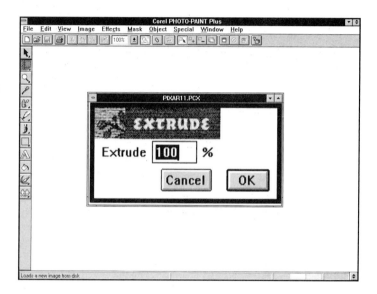

Exercise: Bad Dog Design

Let's go through a simple project to take a look at some of the things that Pixar Typestry can do. We are going to create a logo for a fictitious design shop. This example will use a clip art font from Image Club called Lil' Critters. The point of this exercise is to show that you don't have to use conventional fonts (as in letters or numbers) in Typestry. You can create a font in CorelDRAW from basic shapes or homemade clip art, which you can then use in Typestry.

1. Figure 23.12 shows the results of a Pixar Typestry file with default settings using a dog clip art font from Image Club's Mini Pics Lil' Critters. The image was created by simply clicking anywhere on the Typestry Desktop with the Text tool selected, choosing the Lil' Critters font, typing in the letter for the dog, and clicking on the Build Object button. (See Figure 23.13.)

Figure 23.12.
The dog clip art from
Image Club's Mini Pics
Lil' Critters typeface
with Pixar Typestry's
default lighting and
default Looks settings.

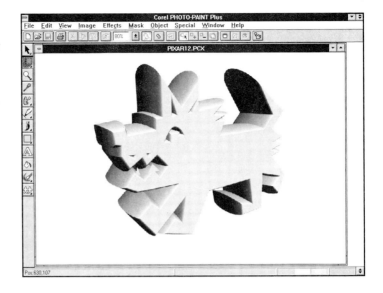

Figure 23.13.
Creating the shapes is
as easy as choosing the
font, typing the
letter(s), and choosing
Build Object.

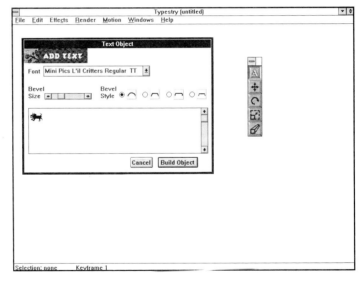

2. Figure 23.14 was created by adding a look to the dog object. Looks are
   texture maps that are created using special algorithms that are computed
   onto the shape. Looks are very powerful, because they can be computed to
   fit any size object without having to worry about resolution. Pixar sells 26

separate looks libraries that include metals, glass, and plastic, as well as many other attractive texture maps. Pixar Typestry 1.1c comes with about 25 looks, ranging from oaks to marble. Pixar also sells a utility called Glimpse that allows you to adjust, manipulate, and even create your own varieties of looks called "instances." If you have an image or texture you want to use from PHOTO-PAINT, you can create an Instance of it with Glimpse. To open the Looks dialog box, you can select Show Looks from the Windows menu or hit F1.

Figure 23.14.
The dog with a look
added from Pixar's
Stucco Looks library.

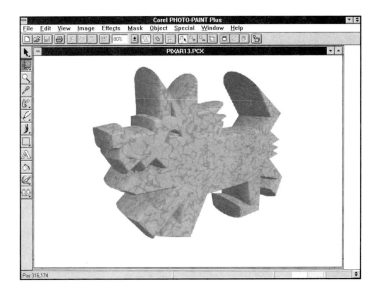

When you select Show Looks or hit F1, the Looks dialog box is opened. (See Figure 23.15.) The Looks dialog box gives you the option of applying looks to the entire object or to its sides. The Wall and Floor option are grayed out because neither a wall or floor has been selected. There are three buttons in the Looks dialog box. The New Look button opens the Looks Browser, the More Info button allows you to modify a look somewhat, and the Inherit Look button lets you use a look from another object.

From the Looks dialog box, the New Look button was selected to open the Looks Browser. The Looks Browser (Figure 23.16) allows you to select looks from the available libraries. The tiny squares along the bottom of the Looks Browser compose the Looks Palette. You can add and remove looks, and variations of looks called instances, from the Looks Palette.

Figure 23.15.
The Looks dialog box.

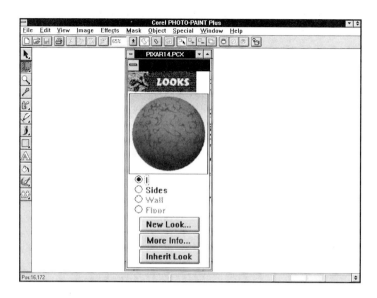

Figure 23.16.
The Looks Browser.

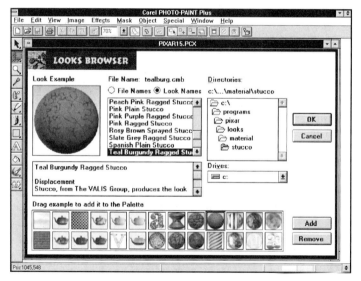

3. If you just want the text or object, than the image at this stage would be fine. You could simply render the file, import it, and use Corel PHOTO-PAINT's masking tools to isolate the text or object to use with any image you like in Corel PHOTO-PAINT. Pixar Typestry, though, gives you the option of creating backgrounds in the form of walls and floors. In the case

of this image, a background was added and an additional look was applied to it. You can add backgrounds by selecting the Backgrounds submenu from the Effects menu.

4. Finally, the dog was resized, the words "Bad Dog Design" were added, and a shadow was added. The Lights roll-up can be accessed in Pixar Typestry by hitting the F2 key. There are several kinds of lights. You can have spot lights, ambient lights, colored lights, and/or lights that cast a shadow. Adding Shadows makes the rendering time take significantly longer. Pixar Typestry gives you 10 different lights to choose from (including ambient light).

Alpha Channels

Pixar Typestry has support for Alpha channels for those programs that support them, such as Adobe Photoshop. Even though PHOTO-PAINT has Transparency masks, you cannot use Pixar's Alpha channel support with Corel PHOTO-PAINT. The format Pixar uses to export Alpha channels is the "TIFF rgba" or "TIFF rgba LZW" formats (the "a" in "rgba" stands for Alpha channel). You can import this file format into Corel PHOTO-PAINT 5.0, but you can't access the Alpha channels.

If you want to place 3-D text or objects over a background in PHOTO-PAINT, you can render the 3-D text or object to file with a white background, open the file in PHOTO-PAINT, and use the Magic Wand to select just the white area. This will work if there is no white in the 3-D text. In this case, an alternative method is to open the Looks Browser within a file that you have rendered 3-D text or objects from, and load the Constant Surface look located in the Looks, Starter, Basic directory. This makes the color of the text solid with no shading.

Then click on the OK button to exit the Looks Browser and go back to the Looks dialog box. Click on the More Info button and change the color to black. Now when you render the file again, you will have a file that is black where the text or object is and white everywhere else. You can load this file as a mask and invert it to isolate easily the 3-D text or object to cut and paste on another background.

Using Images From Corel PHOTO-PAINT in Pixar Typestry

As mentioned previously, Pixar offers a product called Glimpse, which is not included on the companion CD-ROM. Glimpse allows you to create your own instances out of images from Corel PHOTO-PAINT. The thing you have to keep in mind when using your own images as looks is that Typestry's looks are based on mathematical algorithms, whereas your images will be bitmaps. Glimpse uses your bitmap to create instances, but it can't create algorithms out of them, so resolution remains an issue. Also, as you might expect, instances created with bitmap images have larger file sizes than Pixar's looks and instances.

This brief overview of Pixar Typestry has only scratched the surface of the product's capabilities. Pixar Typestry is an excellent complement to Corel PHOTO-PAINT 5. By the time this book hits the shelves, Pixar Typestry 2.0 will be nearing release.

A

Color
Manager

Software-based color management is a new trend in graphics software and hardware. Without color management, artists and designers have to rely on color models such as Pantone and TRUMATCH and/or have to print expensive proofs in order to achieve accurate color. Often proofing is a hit-or-miss proposition that can be especially costly (not to mention time-consuming) if several proofs are required to get the image to look right. It is not uncommon for many designers to just settle for an inferior image because they lack time or funds. Software-based color management was devised in order to deal with this problem.

The color range of a device such as a monitor or a printer is called its *gamut*. The gamut of a monochrome monitor, for instance, is very limited. A monochrome monitor can only display one color, so it thus has a gamut of one color. A monitor that can only display 16 colors has a gamut of 16 colors, and so on. The gamuts of most devices are different. Some high-end drum scanners have a gamut of millions of colors. Most printers have a significantly smaller gamut. You may have a scanner that can scan millions of colors and a monitor that can display all of the colors that your scanner has, but often you will not be able to print all of the colors that your scanner and monitor can scan or display. Color management is all about linking the gamuts of various devices in order to achieve accurate and consistent color through every process from scanning to viewing to printing.

In Corel applications, this is achieved through Color Profiles and System Profiles. A Color Profile is created for each device to provide a link from one device's gamut to any other device's gamut. A Color Profile is created for each device: the monitor, the scanner and the printer. (Note: "Printer," in this context, refers generically to any output device including film recorders and image-setters.) When you have all of the Color Profiles for all of the devices selected, you can create a System Profile. The System Profile is then stored as a CCS file. The System Profile links all of the Color Profiles of each specific device you will be using in order to provide for accurate color throughout the creative process.

Corel *TIP!*

> If you don't have or won't be using a scanner, you can create a System Profile for just your monitor and printer. If you don't have a scanner, the Scanner Color Profile will default to "None." If you do have a scanner, but you don't want it included in your System Profile, simply select "None" for the scanner. All of the other devices require something to be selected, even if it's just "Generic," in order to generate a System Profile.

Once generated, a System Profile will link the gamut of all of the devices specified in the profile and provide for accurate color reproduction. Since most users scan from many different scanners and print to many different printers, you can create as many System Profiles as you need and simply load them as needed.

Corel has attempted to provide a large number of Color Profiles in hopes that you will not need to go beyond the System Color Profile dialog box. If you are lucky, all of the devices you have are on the list. In that case, it is a simple matter of selecting each device and generating a System Profile. Since you can have as many System Profiles as you like, let's generate a bogus System Profile to help demystify the process. The Color Manager is located in the File menu in all Corel applications, including Corel PHOTO-PAINT.

Figure A.1.
The System Color
Profile dialog box.

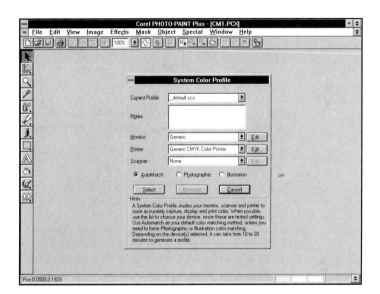

1. Select Color Manager from the File menu. Notice that when you first select Color Manager, the System Color Profile dialog box comes up and has the _default.ccs select and all of the devices are set to Generic and, in the case of the scanner, None. The Generate button is grayed out. Select the NEC MultiSync 3D as the monitor, Agfa SelectSet7000 as the printer, and HP ScanJet IIC as the scanner. Notice that after just one of the devices has been selected, the Generate button becomes active. Select AutoMatch. When AutoMatch is selected when creating a System Profile in Corel PHOTO-PAINT, the System profile is optimized for bitmap images. Conversely, when AutoMatch is selected while creating a System Profile in CorelDRAW, the System Profile is optimized for line art or vector images. The photographic and illustration options are for generating a System

Profile that is optimized for working with spot colors. (Remember, Corel PHOTO-PAINT cannot print spot colors.) Still you may want to use this option if you are using a spot-color specifier such as Pantone to select colors that you are using in Corel PHOTO-PAINT. Enter the name of each device in the Notes section. You can only enter three lines of notes in the Notes section, presumably because you can only have up to three devices for each Profile. If you have a System Profile with the same devices optimized for photographic and for illustration, make a note somewhere in the Notes section so that you can tell the difference. Because you only have eight letters to work with in the System Profile's name, the Notes section is a very handy way to tell them all apart.

Figure A.2.
Create a test System Profile by entering NEC MultiSync 3D for the monitor, Agfa SelectSet7000 for the printer, and HP ScanJet IIC for the scanner.

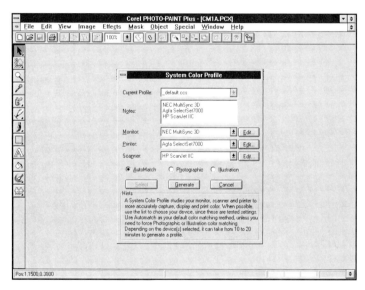

2. Select Generate. In the Generate Profile dialog box, enter a new name for the System Profile, and then select OK. Depending on your system, it will take up to a half an hour to generate the System Profile. When Color Manager is finished generating the System Profile, it stores the CCS file in the Corel50\Color directory. If you ever need to get rid of excess System Profiles (if you get a new monitor, for example), simply delete the CCS file from this directory. Once you have several System Profiles, Color Manager defaults to the last selected or generated System Profile.

Advanced Color Management

If the device you will be using is not listed among the devices that come with Corel PHOTO-PAINT, Color Manager allows you to create your own Color Profiles or to load other Color Profiles. This is accomplished by calibrating your device. Calibration is the process of measuring the output and input values of a particular device and adjusting those values according to a predetermined standard. Color Manager also allows you to Edit existing Color Profiles if they do not suit your needs. This can be accomplished by selecting the specific device in the System Color Profile dialog box and then clicking the Edit button to the right of the list. The available existing color Profiles are almost entirely created by Corel Corporation, but you can distribute Color Profiles you have created to anyone you like. It is much easier to load an existing Color Profile than to create a new one. (Corel plans to make additional Color Profiles available on services such as CompuServe sometime in the near future.)

Figure A.3.
Select Generate and
enter a name for the
System Profile.

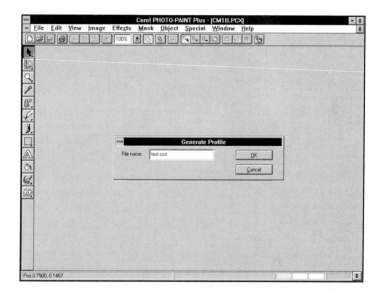

Each of the device lists that are within the System Color Profile dialog box have an "Other" setting. Selecting the "Other" setting for any device sends you into its respective calibration dialog box. Once a Color Profile has been created for a device it is added to the list of devices even if you don't end up creating a System Profile with it.

Advanced Monitor Calibration

Calibrating your monitor can be accomplished interactively or numerically. Unless you have an excellent eye, numerically is usually the better option. Keep in mind that your monitor is subject to several outside factors that contribute to how well it displays the image. Office lighting, how long your monitor has been on, and even the color of the wallpaper in the room can effect how your image displays or how you perceive the image on screen. Monitors generate heat, and the phosphors on the glass change the more you use your monitor, so all monitors display differently as the day progresses. The changes are gradual, so we often do not notice them. Thus, while you can create Monitor Color Profiles interactively, it is a tricky proposition at best. Monitors can be very easy to calibrate numerically if you have the documentation that comes with your monitor or the phone number to the company that manufactures it. If you have to hunt down the monitor's maker, keep in mind that the critical part of the monitor that determines the numbers you are looking for is the monitor's tube. So whoever manufactures the monitor's tube is likely to know the numbers you need.

Interactive Monitor Calibration

If you cannot acquire the manufacturer's settings for the monitor, or if you prefer to calibrate the monitor yourself, you can calibrate your monitor interactively. Again, this is a relatively subjective process. To optimize conditions for calibrating your monitor interactively, take the following steps.

Make sure your monitor has been on for about a half an hour. Next, make sure the lighting in the room is adequate. If the room is very dark or too bright, it will affect how your eyes perceive the colors on the monitor. Make sure the brightness and contrast settings are set properly. (You might have inadvertently bumped up the brightness when you were wiping up that coffee spill the other day.) Finally, maximize the PHOTO-PAINT workspace so that the color of your wallpaper does not influence your color perception. The desktop of PHOTO-PAINT should be set to white or a light grey. If your wallpaper or PHOTO-PAINT desktop is brightly colored, it will affect how you perceive the colors inside of the Interactive Monitor Calibration dialog box. For instance, if your wallpaper is dark blue, all of the blues in the Interactive Monitor Calibration dialog box will appear less blue in comparison.

1. To calibrate your monitor interactively, click on the Interactive button in the Monitor Calibration dialog box. You can use the scanner target photo to help adjust your monitor interactively.

Corel *TIP!*

Do not store your scanner target photo underneath a bright light or on a windowsill in direct sunlight. Light will wash the photo out, rendering it useless for color calibrations.

2. Corel recommends that users avoid adjusting the chromaticity values interactively. Chromaticity values are relatively stable and are usually identical from monitor to monitor. Chromaticity is a measurement of a

color's departure from white light, and it refers to the purity (saturation) and wavelength (hue) of the colors. The default values are almost always correct. If you are highly skilled or adventurous, the chromaticity values can be adjusted by dragging the markers of the Red, Green, and Blue channels to achieve desired results. Note that the x and y values are a measurement of where the color is on each channel's spectrum. Also be advised that the preview is not especially helpful with chromaticity adjustments. If you get hopelessly lost, hit the Reset button to return to the default values.

Figure A.4.
Take care to create the
right environment to
calibrate your monitor
interactively.

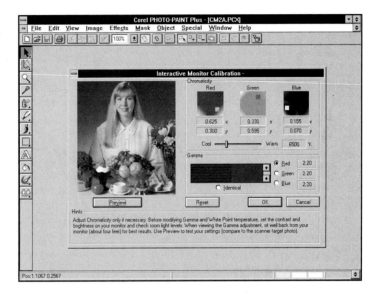

3. Move the slide bar to make the white point cooler or warmer. Moving the slide bar toward Cool makes the white point more bluish. Moving the slide bar toward Warm makes the white point more yellowish. The white point's value, in degrees Kelvin, is displayed to the right of the slider bar. White light is measured in degrees Kelvin. The Kelvin scale ranges in degrees from 0K to infinity. The typical range of most monitors is between 1000K and 20000K.

4. Adjust the gamma for each of the color channels (Red, Green, and Blue). Gamma is the degree of contrast between the darkest and lightest parts of each color. More technically, gamma is a measurement of the relationship between the monitor's input voltage and the resulting luminance. Adjusting gamma affects mostly the midtones. Scrolling up makes the color channel darker, while scrolling down makes the color channel lighter. The gamma settings for each color can be selected between extreme values or .5 on the darker side and 3 on the lightest side. If you wish, you can adjust

the gamma for one color and then apply those settings to all of the channels by enabling Identical after adjusting the color channel.

Numeric Monitor Calibration

Select Other from the Monitor list in the System Color Profile dialog box to open the Monitor Calibration dialog box. Enter a name for the new monitor Color Profile. You are not limited to eight characters, so enter a long descriptive name to help distinguish the Monitor. Enter the monitor's color characteristics into the Monitor Calibration dialog box. The first settings are the red, green, and blue gamma settings. The next set of values are the x and y chromaticity values of red, green, and blue. The last setting is the white point, which is measured in degrees Kelvin. As mentioned previously, these values may be in your monitor's handbook or you can contact the monitor's manufacturer for the values.

Figure A.5.
If you have the manufacturer's settings for your monitor, calibrating your monitor can be easy and painless.

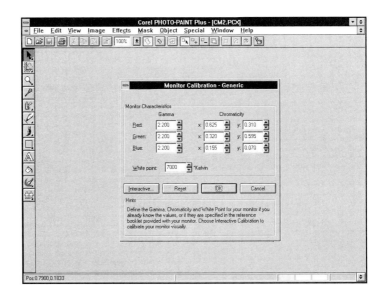

Advanced Printer Calibration

If you acquire a Color Profile for a particular printer from Corel or from someone else, you can load it in the System Color Profile dialog box.

1. Copy the .IM, .RHN, and .GRY files (if it is an RGB printer) into the COREL50\COLOR directory.

2. Follow the directions that follow for calibrating RGB and CMYK printers, bypassing the steps to create the .IM, .RHN, and .GRY files, and simply enter the new .IM, .RHN, and .GRY files instead.

Advanced printer calibration is not for the weak at heart. But if you have the expertise, Corel provides an avenue to calibrate your printer. In order to calibrate your printer, two operations must be performed: calibration and characterization. The calibration process is dependent on whether your printer uses a CMYK or RGB color model. In general, CMYK printers are those used for professional output, such as imagesetters, while RGB printers are mainly the desktop color printers. The printer characterization process is the same for both CMYK and RGB printers. Characterization can be done with either a Color Match file or with the visual method. When characterizing a printer, you can use the supplied files or generate your own. To generate your own .IM, .GRY, and .RNH files, you need a spectrophotometer or a colorimeter. These devices are used to measure the color characteristics of a printer color or colors. They are very expensive devices and are usually only found in high-end imaging houses. If you will be using one of these devices, Corel recommends the following settings:

1. Set the White Base to abs and calibrate it with the manufacturer-supplied white.
2. Set the Illumination Type to D65.
3. Set the Eye Angle to 2 degrees.
4. Set the Filter to None. (Do not use D65 or Pol.)

Calibrating a CMYK Printer

Select Other in the printer list of the System Color Profile dialog box and open the Printer Calibration dialog box.

Figure A.6.
Calibrate your monitor from the Printer Calibration dialog box.

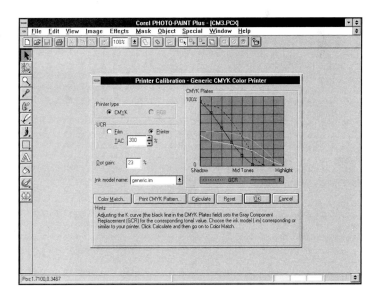

1. Enter a new name for your printer and choose CMYK as the printer type.

2. Under UCR (Undercolor Removal), select Film if you are measuring from imagesetter film, or select Printer if you are measuring from a paper print or imagesetter proof. Imagesetter proofs are the most accurate representation of the device's output because it is created straight from film. Enter a percentage for Total Area Coverage (TAC). The TAC percentage refers to the maximum allowable quantity of ink for the total combined coverage of C, M, Y, and K inks. You can enter TAC values anywhere between 200 and 400 percent.

3. Adjust the K curve within the CMYK Plates box. You can click on Reset to return to the default value if you get lost. As the graph indicates, the K curve measures the percentage of black ink coverage for shadows, midtones, and highlights. Since highlights usually have more white than black, you want little or no black in this area, whereas shadows have more black than white, so you want a lot of blacks in this area. The K curve can only be adjusted at the node points and only vertically along each point in the graph.

4. Enter a dot gain value. The default is appropriate for most jobs, but you can verify it with your printer.

5. Enter a name for the ink model. Ink models have an IM extension. One of the existing ink models may be appropriate. If you don't need to create an ink model, skip steps 6 through 8. For instance, Corel has included a SWOP.IM file. SWOP stands for Standard Web Offset Publication and it is a standard that many printer ink models adhere to.

6. Click Print CMYK Patterns. When the Print dialog box appears, choose your printer and the CMYK320 color pattern is printed.

7. Use a spectrophotometer or colorimeter to measure the CIE XYZ values of each color square in numerical sequence from 1 to 320. Enter the measurements in an ASCII file with three columns: X, Y, Z (with a space separating the columns). If you wish, you can open an existing ink-model file with an ASCII editing utility such as Notepad, enter new values, and then save the file with a new name. Name the file with a name that indicates the particular printer and give it an .IM extension—for instance, Agfass7.IM for a Agfa SelectSct7000. (There is already an IM file for an Agfa SelectSet7000, so don't use that name.) Copy the file into the Corel50\Color subdirectory and return to the Printer Calibration dialog box.

8. Choose the IM model you just created in the Ink Model Name setting within the Printer Calibration dialog box.

9. Select the Calculate button. A gauge will appear while the ink-separation model and dot-gain functions are calculated. The Color Match option becomes available after you select an Ink Model, but you should characterize your printer after you have calculated the ink-separation model and dot-gain functions.

Figure A.7.
This is an example of
what an IM ASCII file
looks like. This is the
ink-model file for the
Agfass7.IM.

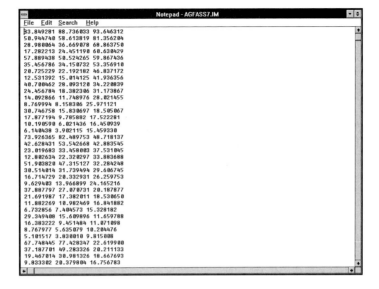

10. Select the Color Match button. After selecting the Color Match button, the Printer Characterization dialog box appears. As mentioned earlier, you can adjust your printer's characterization either by using the visual method or by using a Color Match file. Again, the Color Match method will tend to accomplish more accurate results than the visual method.

The next step is to create a Characterization file. Each printer uses its own set of "device specific" or "device dependent" color as well as its own set of color attributes. To ensure balance throughout the System Profile, Color Manager requires a characterization file for each printer so that each printer's "device independent" color correction data can be referenced. Color Manager uses this file to keep the gamut within the range of the specific printer.

Printer Characterization Using the Visual Method

In order to perform a printer characterization using the visual method, you must first calibrate your monitor. If your monitor is not calibrated, then performing a printer characterization using the visual method is not likely to provide accurate results. (If you have not already calibrated your monitor, click the Calibrate Monitor button and calibrate your monitor using one of the methods described previously.)

1. Select Visual from the Printer Characterization dialog box to open the Visual Printer Characterization dialog box.

2. Click Print Testing Patterns to print the test pattern to the chosen printer.

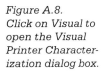

Figure A.8.
Click on Visual to
open the Visual
Printer Character-
ization dialog box.

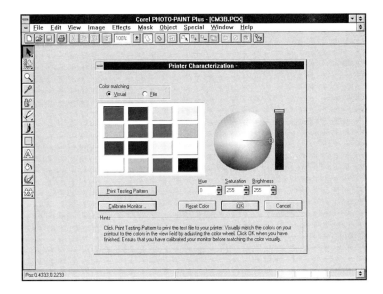

3. With the test pattern next to your monitor, adjust the colors interactively or by entering numeric values so that the test pattern on your monitor matches the printout. The adjustments are standard Hue, Saturation, and Brightness settings. On the color wheel, moving the node around the wheel changes the Hue and moving the node inside of the color wheel adjusts the Saturation. Brightness is controlled by moving the bar to the right of the color wheel up or down. If you need to return any color value to its original setting, select Reset Color.

4. When each color in the Visual Printer Characterization dialog box has been adjusted to match the test printout, select OK.

Printer Characterization with a Color Match File

1. From the Printer Characterization dialog box, choose File.

2. Click on the Print Text Patterns button to print the test pattern to the printer.

3. Use a spectrophotometer or colorimeter to measure the CIE XYZ values of each color square, in numerical sequence from 1 to 80. Enter the measurements in an ASCII file with three columns for the X, Y, and Z values, with a space separating the columns. Name the file with a name that indicates the particular printer and give it an .RHN extension—for example, AGFASS7.RHN for a Agfa SelectSet7000. (There is already an .RHN file for an Agfa SelectSet7000, so don't use that name.) Again, you can open an existing .RHN file from the Corel50\Color directory with a ASCII editor,

enter new values and save the file with a new name. Copy the file into the COREL50\COLOR subdirectory.

4. Return to the Printer Characterization dialog box and select the .RHN file you have just created, then choose OK.

Once you have characterized your printer, simply select OK in the Printer Calibration dialog box and the new Color Profile for your printer appears in the printer list within the System Color Profile dialog box.

Calibrating an RGB Printer

1. Choose RGB in the Printer Calibration dialog box to open another Printer Calibration dialog box.

Figure A.9.
Clicking on the RGB
setting in the Printer
Calibration dialog box
opens this Printer
Calibration dialog box.

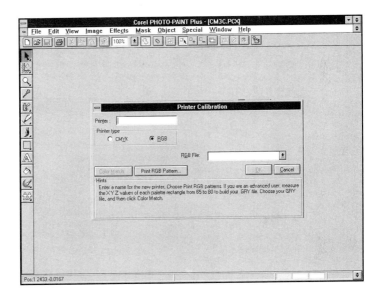

2. Click on the Print RGB Patterns button to print the RGB80 color pattern to the printer.

3. Use a spectrophotometer or colorimeter to measure the CIE XYZ values of the grayscale squares only, in numerical sequence from 65 to 80. Enter the measurements in an ASCII file with columns for the X, Y, and Z values, with a space separating the columns. Name the file with a name that indicates the particular printer and give it an .GRY extension—for example, HP1200.GRY for an HP Deskjet 1200C. (There is already a .GRY file for an HP Deskjet 1200C, so don't use that name.) Note that the HP DeskJet was used as an example instead of the Agfa SelectSet7000. This is because an HPDeskJet is an RGB printer and an Agfa SelectSet7000 is a CMYK printer.

Again, you can open an existing .GRY file from the COREL50\COLOR directory with a ASCII editor, enter new values, and save the file with a new name. Copy the file into the COREL50\COLOR subdirectory.

4. Reenter the second Printer Calibration dialog box by choosing RGB in the Printer Calibration dialog box, and select the .GRY file you just created.

5. Click Color Match and characterize the printer using the visual method or the Color Match file method described previously.

Calibrating a Scanner from an Image

A scanner can be calibrated from an image or from a file. To calibrate a scanner from an image, do as follows:

1. Scan the calibration target provided by Corel, or an IT8 target if you have one. It is very important to scan in raw data. In other words, if your scanner has a calibration option, it needs to be turned off. Again, this is very important; do not use your scanner's calibration options. When you've scanned the calibration target image, save the file as a TIFF file. As noted previously, you need to be sure that the calibration target image has not been altered by exposure to excessive light. If the image is washed out, it will be of no use to you.

2. Open the Scanner Calibration dialog box by selecting Other in the scanner list of the System Color Profile dialog box. Enter a name for the new Scanner. Choose Image with the Scanner Calibration dialog box.

Figure A.10.
Open the Scanner
Calibration dialog box
by selecting Other from
the scanner list of the
System Color Profile
dialog box.

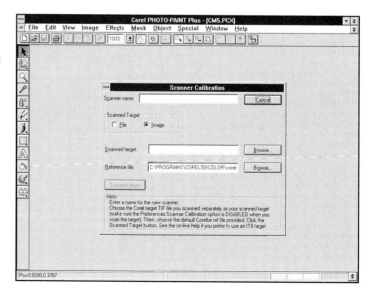

3. Select Browse to the right of the Scanned Target window and locate the scanned target file you just saved.

4. Select a reference file. Corel provides a reference file, but if you are using an IT8 or other proprietary reference file, you can use it here. The file must have an .REF extension.

5. Click on the Scanned Target button to open the Scanned Target dialog box.

6. Drag each of the four corner markers such that they frame the entire color grid. This is not very difficult, since the corners snap to the respective positions when you move them to each corner. The Hints section even helps you by telling you where to snap each point.

7. When you click OK, Color Manager will compare the values of the colors you just framed to the values in the reference file and color-calibrate the scanner according to the reference file.

8. Enter a name and choose OK. A scanner-calibration file will be created with an .SCN extension and will be stored in the COREL50\OLOR directory. If you ever wish to get rid of the .SCN file, simply delete it from that directory.

Calibrating a Scanner from a File

1. Open the Scanner Calibration dialog box by selecting Other in the scanner list of the System Color Profile dialog box. Enter a name for the new Scanner. Choose File with the Scanner Calibration dialog box.

Figure A.11.
Selecting a file from the Scanner Calibration dialog box opens this dialog box, from which you can select a new .SCN file.

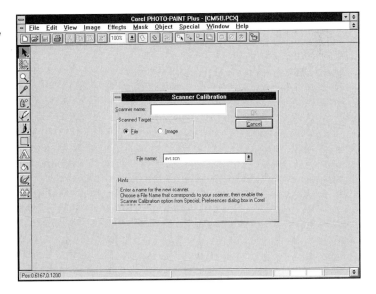

2. Choose a file from the list of available scanner calibration or .SCN files. If you have forgotten to enter a name in the initial Scanner Calibration dialog box, you can enter it here. If you've received the scanner calibration or .SCN file from Corel or from someone else, copy it into the COREL50\COLOR directory.

3. Choose OK.

Summary

While parts of Color Manager can be intimidating to many users, it is the mark of a professional program and it gives users an avenue for accurate color work. If your work requires color accuracy, taking the time to learn how to navigate Color Manager will pay off in faster production, reduced expense in the proofing stage, and increased satisfaction with your output.

B

Photo CD
Sources

This is not intended to be a comprehensive list of Photo CD vendors. Instead I have made a short list of companies I have discovered that offer unusual or exceptional CD products. The list is in no particular order, except that I have divided it into two general categories: Photos and Images and Textures. All collections listed are royalty free. It goes without saying that the major supplier of photos for this book is the Corel Photo CD collection.

Photos and Images

Image Club Graphics, Inc.
729 24th Ave.
Southeast Calgary, Alberta Canada T2G 5K8
(800) 661-9410

These people put out a free monthly catalog that anyone doing graphic design should have. This outfit began life as a clipart/typeface house up in the frozen oil patches of Canada. They were later purchased by Aldus and are therefore now owned by Adobe. In addition to the catalog's ever expanding selection of images from other vendors they feature their own collection of photographic images called Photogear. They have just begun shipping photographs of objects against a white background called Objectgear. The catalog also contains a "tips and tricks mini-magazine" which is an excellent source for ideas.

PhotoDisc
21st Century Media
2013 Fourth Ave., Suite 402
Seattle, WA 98121-9915
(800) 528-3472

This company specializes in digital stock photography. They have a real bargain in their Starter Kit. It has 4095 low-resolution (72 dpi) images on two CD-ROMs and a full-color catalog for $50. The Starter Kit also includes 25 high-resolution images. The images are logically divided into volumes by category: Health and Medicine, Food and Dining, etc. You can also buy volumes containing high-resolution versions of the images. While the volumes cost more than Corel Profession Photos, the images are stunning and worth the money. The images are royalty-free.

NEO Custom Painted Environments, Inc.
2000 W. Fulton St.
Chicago, IL 60612
(312) 226-2426

This outfit makes custom wallpaper. No, not Windows wallpaper. Real, genuine, hand-painted wallpaper. They have a large collection of photos of the wallpaper that they have created over the years. This is what the Photo CD contains. These make excellent backgrounds.

Planet Art
505 S. Beverly Drive, Suite 242
Beverly Hills, CA 90212
(213) 651-3405
(800) 200-3405

If you are looking for truly exceptional images of traditional and classic art then investigate the offerings of Planet Art. While Bill Gates made have paid many millions for some Leonardo DaVinci manuscripts, you can own your own for less than $90. These discs feature the art of Michelangelo, DaVinci, and other famous artists, with 100 images per disc in the Photo-CD format. Planet Art fills a gap that modern creations often miss.

CMCD
600 Townsend St., Penthouse
San Francisco, CA 94103
(800) 664-CMCD (2623)

If you have PHOTO-PAINT 5 Plus you already own 50 of these digital clip-art objects. These clever folks have photographed objects against white backgrounds for easy placement in images, unlike the ones that come with the Corel Plus release have been masked and made into PAINT objects. Each library offers 100 images. These are in categories like Everyday Objects, Just Hands, Just Tools... you get the idea. There are a total of seven libraries at this time. These things are as handy as a pocket in a coat.

Cloud Gallery
Mary & Michael
555 Bryant St., Suite 356
Palo Alto, CA 94301-1700
(415) 326-9567

Here is a wonderful collection of clouds by a charming pair of photographers. They're still trying to find their way around an increasingly crowded marketplace, but they're learning fast. Their first CD-ROM contains 32 stunning skies that will make excellent backdrops for any project. Highly recommended.

Fotosets
4104 24th St.
San Francisco, CA 94114
(415) 621-2061

This is a case of a lighting director/set designer moving her work out into the expanding CD-ROM market place. Robin Ginsberg, the creator, has over 15 years of experience designing and carefully lighting sets for commercial photo shoots. The work in this CD is great. It differs from a lot of the backgrounds that are the result of digital manipulation. The images in this library will provide you with enough backgrounds to impress the even toughest client on your list. Most of the images are also suitable for use as textures.

DiAMAR Interactive Corp.
1107 1st Ave., Suite 1802
Seattle, WA 98104-0902
(800) 685-3547

DiAMAR offers six volumes of photos that are of excellent quality and subject matter. Each volume contains 54 images in multiple resolutions and file formats.

Seattle Support Group
20420 84th Ave. South
Kent, WA 98032
(206) 395-1484

Rumor has it that most of the early Corel Photo CDs came from this stock photography house. They won't say either way. I have only seen one of the discs from their Vintage collection, but it was excellent quality.

Wayzata Technology
2515 E. Highway 2
Grand Rapids, MN 55744
(800) 377-7321

A production house for a large number of CD-ROM products, Wayzata Technology puts out several collections of Photo CDs that are acceptable for use in most publications. Most are very inexpensive.

Textures

Pixar
1001 W. Cutting Blvd.
Richmond, CA 94804
(510) 236-4000

This is the company that makes the copy of Typestry included in the companion CD. They also make two volumes of textures in the form of seamless tiles that can be used with the Bitmap Fill feature of PHOTO-PAINT. I knew I was going to like this company the first time I called them and got a phone mail message that said (after some lengthy routing directions) that if I did not have a touch-tone phone or if my VCR was still blinking 12:00 I should hang on for a human operator. You gotta love a company like that. The two volumes offered are PIXAR One Twenty Eight which contains (you guessed it) 128 seamless tiles, and Classic Textures Volume Two contains 100 seamless tiles. Both volumes cover a wide assortment of textures. I personally have more use for seamless tiles than for stock photography, but then that's me. They offer good images and a nice variety.

Visual Software
21731 Ventura Blvd.
Suite 310
Woodland Hills, CA 91364
(800) 669-7318
(818) 883-7900

If you bought PHOTO-PAINT Plus you received 275 of Visual Software's seamless tiles. Their collection of textures on CD-ROM is called Textures for Professionals. It contains 398 seamless tiles covering a wide variety of surface materials. These include wood, rock, metal, wallpaper, etc. If you only have the basic library of textures that come with Corel PHOTO-PAINT 5, add to it with one of these libraries.

Artbeats
P.O. Box 709
Myrtle Creek, OR 97457
(503) 863-4429

This is the best of the best for textures. It also costs the most. Artbeats does not offer a wide variety of seamless tiles, but rather focuses in on a category and delivers absolutely stunning textures in the form of .TIF files and seamless tiles. Their first offering was Marble & Granite. After that they commissioned artists who are consider the best in their field to produce marbled paper. They photographed the results and produced a collection of marbled paper images. Their latest offering is Wood & Paper. They have spared no expense in getting the best image possible for the .TIF and seamless tiles. The subject matter is professionally photographed in large format. The resulting 4- by 5-inch transparencies are drum-scanned and color corrected to produce the best image possible. Can you tell I'm impressed with their work? Unfortunately, the strength of the product is also its weakness. Whereas the other collections offer a wide variety of textures, Artbeats offers only a narrow range of textures.

The CD-ROM

The CD-ROM included with this book contains a wealth of software that will enhance your use of Corel PHOTO-PAINT. Here's a sample of what you'll find on the CD-ROM:

- Sample plug-in filters
- Sample stock photos
- Sample graphics and clip art
- Corel Mosaic thumbnail files for all bonus graphics included on the *PHOTO-PAINT Plus* CD-ROM
- Demos of commercial programs
- Graphics from the book
- Free CompuServe Information Service membership and software
- Programs and utilities

A CD-ROM can hold so much software that you could get lost just thinking about it. However, we've made it easier for you to navigate through the disc and find what you want. A special Windows menu program allows you to easily explore the included software—you can view photos, install programs, read information about a vendor's product, and more.

Getting Started

Before you can run the software on the CD-ROM, you need to run the setup program on the disc. This program will create a Program Manager group with icons for running the software. It will also copy animation drivers to your hard drive.

Start Windows, if you haven't already done so, and follow these steps:

1. Insert the disc in your CD-ROM drive.
2. Switch to Program Manager or File Manager. Select **F**ile from the menu, then select **R**un.
3. In the Run dialog box, type **D:\CDSETUP.EXE** in the Command Line box and click on OK. If your CD-ROM drive is not drive D, then substitute the correct letter. For instance, if your CD-ROM drive is G, type **G:\CDSETUP.EXE**.
4. The opening screen of the setup program will appear. Click on the **C**ontinue button.
5. The program will create a Program Manager group named *Corel PHOTO-PAINT 5 Unleashed*.

If the setup has completed successfully, you're ready to explore the CD-ROM!

Corel*NOTE!*

The CD-ROM setup program creates icons in Program Manager, even if you're running a different Windows shell, such as PC Tools MultiDesk or Norton Desktop. These icons should also appear within your shell. If they don't, you can run Program Manager and use the icons in it.

To manually run Program Manager, select File+Run from the File Manager menu, type PROGMAN.EXE and click on OK.

Running the Windows Menu Program

When you start the Windows menu program, you'll see an opening screen—click anywhere on the page to begin exploring the disc. Each different screen of the menu program will be referred to as a page. Just think of the program as being like a multimedia book. You can jump directly to sections that interest you, or you can move through the program one page at a time.

Corel*NOTE!*

Your Windows video setup must be capable of displaying at least 256 colors, or the menu program will not display properly. Graphics with lots of colors look pretty ugly on a 16-color display; if you can only display 16 colors, consult your system's manual for information on how to switch to a different video driver with more colors. If you can, set your video system to display 64,000 colors (16-bit color) or 16 million colors (24-bit color).

You can navigate through the disc in several different ways. In the bottom right area of each page, you'll find yellow navigation buttons. To move to the next or previous page, click on one of the left or right arrow buttons.

If you click on the question mark symbol in the lower-right area, a help screen will appear. Pressing the F1 key will also display this help screen. Click anywhere on the help screen to make it disappear.

On some pages, you won't see the arrows that let you move to the next or previous page; you'll see an upward-pointing arrow instead. Each upward-pointing arrow moves back to the previous level of the menu.

To exit from the menu, click the Exit icon in the lower-left area of the screen. You can also press the Alt+F4 key combination to exit the program.

Corel *NOTE!*

If you experience any problems with running the menu program, double-click on the Troubleshooting icon in the Program Manager group. This will open a file with hints and tips for solving your Windows problems.

Sample Commercial Software

Nearly all of the software represented in this section is special versions of commercial programs or samples of commercial collections. In most cases, the programs operate like the full version, with some features (such as saving your work) disabled. The graphics and photo samples are examples of the type of work in each vendor's complete collection.

You'll find detailed information about the software on the disc within the menu program. This information includes a summary of what the software does, contact information for the vendor, special requirements, copyright or usage information, and so on. Read this information before you run a program or view a file. You can also visit your local retailer or contact the software vendor directly for more information on a product.

The software on the disc is copyrighted material. Graphics, clip art and photos must be used under the terms outlined by the vendor of that software.

The following sections are a summary of the commercial software on the CD-ROM. See the menu program for detailed information for each product.

Sample Plug-In Filters

Andromeda series 1 and series 2 Filters
Gallery Effects

Sample Graphics and Clip Art

Pixar 128
KidBAG
Artbeats
MapArt
Mountain High Maps
Clip-Art Connection
MEDSET Medical clip art
ClickArt Incredible Image Pak
AdArt collections

Sample Stock Photos

PhotoDisc
PhotoPro
Cloud Gallery
Corel Professional Photos

Demos of Commercial Programs

Font Chameleon
Font Minder/Font Fiddler
Type Designer
Typestry
DesignWare

Programs and Utilities

ROMCAT
Persimmon PostScript Driver
Paint Shop Pro
WinZip

Software from the Book

Many of the files used by the author in the book are included on this CD-ROM. In addition, you'll find Corel Mosaic thumbnail files for all the bonus graphics on the PHOTO-PAINT Plus CD-ROM. See the menu program for more information on these files.

The files discussed in the book are stored in directories that correspond to the file extension. For example, Photo CD files are in the \PCD directory and .TIF files are in the \TIF directory.

CompuServe Information Service

More than 1 million computer users are a part of CompuServe Information Service, and for good reason. CompuServe has special interest areas for nearly any subject you're interested in, including Corel Corporation products. And you'll find users from across the United States and around the world.

Joining and using CompuServe is now a lot easier, because CompuServe is offering readers of this book a free membership and $15 of free connect time. Plus, a free copy of Windows CompuServe Information Manager (WinCIM) software is included on the CD-ROM. You'll also be able to take a multimedia tour through the worlds of CompuServe.

To register and receive your $15 credit, call (800) 848-8199 and ask for representative number 597. Or, you can write to:

CompuServe Membership Sales
5000 Arlington Center Blvd.
Columbus, OH 43220

Mention the name of this book if you register by mail.

Be sure to visit our forum on CompuServe; we're a part of the Macmillan Computer Publishing forum. "GO SAMS" to reach the forum. You'll find information on our books and valuable software, and you can give us feedback or ask questions about our books.

Index

Add to Your Sams Library Today with the Best Books for Programming, Operating Systems, and New Technologies

The easiest way to order is to pick up the phone and call

1-800-428-5331

between 9:00 a.m. and 5:00 p.m. EST.
For faster service please have your credit card available.

ISBN	Quantity	Description of Item	Unit Cost	Total Cost
0-672-30517-8		CorelDRAW! 5 Unleashed (book/CDs)	$49.99	
0-672-30491-0		Cyberlife! (book/CD)	$39.99	
0-672-30391-4		Virtual Reality Madness! (book/CD)	$39.95	
0-672-30373-6		On the Cutting Edge of Technology	$22.95	
0-672-30301-9		Artificial Life Explorer's Kit (book/disk)	$24.95	
0-672-30320-5		Morphing Magic (book/disk)	$29.95	
0-672-30362-0		Navigating the Internet	$24.95	
0-672-30315-9		The Magic of Image Processing (book/disk)	$39.95	
0-672-30308-6		Tricks of the Graphics Gurus (book/disk)	$49.95	
0-672-30590-9		The Magic of Interactive Entertainment, second edition (book/CD)	$44.95	
0-672-30638-7		Super CD-ROM Madness! (book/CDs) Windows (book/disk)	$39.99	
0-672-30270-5		Garage Virtual Reality (book/disk)	$29.95	
0-672-30413-9		Multimedia Madness!, Deluxe Edition (book/CDs)	$55.00	
0-672-30492-9		3D Madness! (book/CD)	$45.00	
0-672-30570-4		PC Graphics Unleashed (book/CD)	$49.99	
❏ 3 ½" Disk		Shipping and Handling: See information below.		
❏ 5 ¼" Disk		TOTAL		

Shipping and Handling: $4.00 for the first book, and $1.75 for each additional book. Floppy disk: add $1.75 for shipping and handling. If you need to have it NOW, we can ship product to you in 24 hours for an additional charge of approximately $18.00, and you will receive your item overnight or in two days. Overseas shipping and handling adds $2.00 per book and $8.00 for up to three disks. Prices subject to change. Call for availability and pricing information on latest editions.

201 W. 103rd Street, Indianapolis, Indiana 46290

1-800-428-5331 — Orders   1-800-835-3202 — FAX   1-800-858-7674 — Customer Service

Book ISBN 0-672-30516-X

PLUG YOURSELF INTO...

THE MACMILLAN INFORMATION SUPERLIBRARY™

Free information and vast computer resources from the world's leading computer book publisher—online!

FIND THE BOOKS THAT ARE RIGHT FOR YOU!

A complete online catalog, plus sample chapters and tables of contents give you an in-depth look at *all* of our books, including hard-to-find titles. It's the best way to find the books you need!

- **STAY INFORMED** with the latest computer industry news through our online newsletter, press releases, and customized Information SuperLibrary Reports.

- **GET FAST ANSWERS** to your questions about MCP books and software.

- **VISIT** our online bookstore for the latest information and editions!

- **COMMUNICATE** with our expert authors through e-mail and conferences.

- **DOWNLOAD SOFTWARE** from the immense MCP library:
    - Source code and files from MCP books
    - The best shareware, freeware, and demos

- **DISCOVER HOT SPOTS** on other parts of the Internet.

- **WIN BOOKS** in ongoing contests and giveaways!

TO PLUG INTO MCP: → **WORLD WIDE WEB: http://www.mcp.com**

GOPHER: gopher.mcp.com

FTP: ftp.mcp.com

The *Corel PHOTO-PAINT 5 Unleashed*
CD-ROM

The companion CD-ROM includes a special menu program that allows you to easily navigate through the software on the disc. You can view graphics, install or run programs, and much more.

To setup the software, insert the disc into your CD-ROM drive, start Windows and follow these steps:

1. From Windows File Manager or Program Manager, choose **F**ile+**R**un from the menu.
2. In the Run dialog box, type `x:\CDSETUP` and press Enter. `x:` represents your CD-ROM drive letter; for example, if the CD-ROM is in drive D, type `D:\CDSETUP`.
3. The opening screen of the setup program will appear. Click on the **C**ontinue button.
4. The program will create a Program Manager group named *Corel PHOTO-PAINT 5 Unleashed*.

If the setup has completed successfully, you're ready to explore the CD-ROM! See Appendix C for more information about using the software on the disc.

Minimum System Requirements

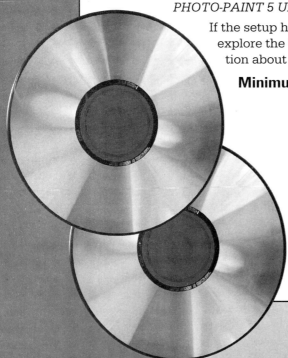

- Corel PHOTO-PAINT 5
- IBM-compatible PC with 386 or better processor
- CD-ROM drive
- SVGA (256-color) graphics display
- 4MB of RAM (8MB is recommended)
- Windows 3.1
- DOS 5.0